Contributing Authors

Rick Brydges (Introduction) has 25 years experience as a manager, leader, trainer, and consultant. His work in Total Quality began in 1985 at the Navy's Personnel Research and Development Center where he did applied research on the application of Total Quality to defense procurement, writing curricula and consulting with program managers and teams. Since then, he has been involved with the planning and implementation of Total Quality in several organizations. He has given numerous presentations and seminars at universities, conferences, professional groups and organizations on the implementation of Total Quality and lessons learned.

Mr. Brydges has a B.S. in Engineering, an M.B.A., and is currently pursuing a Ph.D. His dissertation research focuses on the organizational implementation of Total Quality.

Emanuel R. Baker, Ph.D. (Ch. 1), is president of Software Engineering Consultants, Inc., a consulting firm in Los Angeles, California, which specializes in software engineering services. He has been a consultant in this field since 1984. He has 20 years of technical and managerial experience in the field of software development with specific emphasis on software systems engineering, software configuration management, software quality assurance, software testing, software standards development, and software process assessments. Prior to that he was manager of the Product Assurance Department of Logicon's Strategic and Information Systems Division. In that capacity, along with his duties of managing the department, he also had responsibility for the contract to develop the DOD software quality standard, DOD-STD-2168.

From 1962 to 1980, Dr. Baker was employed with TRW. In 1972 he assumed the position of section head in the Software Systems Engineering Department on the Site Defense Program, a landmark program in the development of standards and procedures for software development, configuration management, and quality assurance practices. Later he transferred into the product assurance area, playing an important role in the continuing development of software configuration management and quality assurance procedures used at TRW.

From 1959 to 1962, Dr. Baker was employed at Aeronutronic as head of the Data Reduction Unit, where he was involved in the conversion of a manual data reduction system to a computerized one. Prior to that, he was an aerodynamics flight test project engineer at Hughes Aircraft. It was there that he had his first exposure to software, learning to program missile failure trajectories on a Burroughs E-102 computer.

Dr. Baker has written and co-authored (with Dr. Matt Fisher) a number of papers and articles on software quality and configuration management. He has conducted seminars in the U.S., Canada, Mexico, Australia, New Zealand, Israel, and Europe on the topic of Software Quality Management. In addition, he has appeared as a panelist at a number of conferences and workshops, speaking on the topic of software quality.

He has a B.S. in Mechanical Engineering from New York University and an M.S. in Mechanical Engineering from the University of Southern California. In addition, he holds an M.S. and a Ph.D. in Education from the University of Southern California.

Lois Zells (Ch. 2), president of Lois Zells & Associates, Scottsdale Arizona, is an internationally recognized author, lecturer, and business consultant, specializing in systems management, project management, and software engineering.

Ms. Zells is founder and principal of the Total Quality Management Systems Group with Joyce Sabel, Bill Stinnett, and Richard Zultner. She is also a member of IEEE, ACM, SIM, and PMI.

Ms. Zells is author of *Managing Software Projects,* a recent book published by QED Information Sciences, Inc. This book is an integral part of Ms. Zells' latest seminar which discusses the application of Japanese TQM techniques to U.S. Software.

Lois Zells graduated Summa Cum Laude in Data Processing Management from the University of Baltimore and received an M.S. in Computer Science from Johns Hopkins University.

Ken Mendis (Ch. 3) is the Department Manager of Quality Assurance at Raytheon, Submarine Signal Division. Mr. Mendis has eighteen years experience in Software QA, Firmware QA, Test Software QA, and Engineering Management of DOD Programs.

Since joining Raytheon in 1977, Mr. Mendis has developed and implemented

SQA programs for fire control, sonar, torpedo, and trainer systems, and for test software and firmware programs. Currently, Mr. Mendis is responsible for Total Quality Management requirements for applications software, test software, and firmware, and for formulating division policy for in-process quality evaluation.

From 1982 to 1986 Mr. Mendis was chairman of the National Security Industrial Association (NSIA), Software Quality Assurance Subcommittee in Washington, D.C. Mr. Mendis was one of the founders of the SQA subcommittee. Since 1978 he has worked closely with the Joint Logistics Commanders to formulate the following DOD SQA policy and standards: DOD-STD-2167 and 2168, MIL-STD-1679, MIL-HDBK-334, and DOD-HDBK-287. He is also chairman of Raytheon's SQA Committee of the Product Assurance Council (PAC).

In 1980 and 1981 Mr. Mendis received the Mission Assurance Award for his significant contribution and in 1986 was selected to represent the Joint Logistics Commanders Joint Policy Coordinating Group on Computer Resource Management at the Fourth Biennial Software Workshop Orlando II.

Mr. Mendis has written several articles and has been the featured speaker on SQA at several national conferences and symposiums.

Mr. Mendis has a B.S. in Electrical Engineering and an M.B.A. in Management.

G. Gordon Schulmeyer (Chs. 4, 16) is manager of software engineering for both commercial and defense programs at Westinghouse Electronic Systems Group (ESG). Mr. Schulmeyer has 30 years experience in software management, software quality assurance, and information processing technology. He is one of the key persons responsible for implementing a software TQM strategy at Westinghouse ESG through the use of Software Quality Improvement Teams (QIT) and Working Groups.

Previously, Mr. Schulmeyer was the manager of SQA at Westinghouse, establishing the SQA Department and formulating the policy and procedures used today.

Mr. Schulmeyer has represented Westinghouse at several conferences and symposiums. He was a panelist for DOD-STD-2168 at the October 1985 IEEE COMPSAC Conference. Mr. Schulmeyer has also written several articles and published numerous books: *Computer Concepts for Managers* (1985), *Handbook of Software Quality Assurance* (1987), *Handbook of Software Quality Assurance* (first revision 1992), *Total Quality Management for Software* (1992) all with Van Nostrand Reinhold and *Zero Defect Software* (1990) with McGraw Hill Book Co.

Mr. Schulmeyer holds a CDP as certified by the Institute for Certification of Computing Professionals (ICCP). He is also a member of the Association for Computing Machinery (ACM) and the American Management Association (AMA).

Mr. Schulmeyer is the 1992 recipient of the prestigious Shingo Prize, the First Prize for Professional Research, administered by the Utah State University College of Business. Mr. Schulmeyer received this award in May of 1992 for his work in Zero Defect Software.

Mr. Schulmeyer has a B.S. in Mathematics from Loyola College, a J.D. Law degree from the University of Baltimore, and an M.B.A. in Management from Loyola College.

Ron S. Kenett, Ph.D. (Ch. 5), is Professor of Operations Management at the School of Management of the State University of New York, Binghamton, New York.

Dr. Kenett holds several honors. He was appointed to the editorial review board of *Quality Progress* in 1987, was elected Fellow of the Institute of Statisticians in 1988, and was elected Fellow of the Royal Statistical Society in 1991. He is listed in *Who's Who in Science and Engineering* and in *American Men and Women of Science.* He received the 1991 GE grant for Continuous Improvement/Total Quality Management. With the help of students and software professionals over a five year period, Dr. Kenett noticeably improved his course "Quantitative Methods in Software Development."

Dr. Kenett has numerous publications in Quality Management, Process Control, Design of Experiments, Software Reliability, Statistical Methods, Biomathematics, and Biostatistics.

Dr. Kenett taught at the University of Wisconsin-Madison, Rutgers University, the Technion, Haifa University and Tel-Aviv University. For two years he worked at Bell Laboratories, New Jersey and was Director of Statistical Methods at Tadiron Corp. for nine years.

Dr. Kenett earned his Ph.D. in Mathematics (1978, Weizmann Institute of Science, Israel) under the supervision of Professor Sam Karlin of Stanford University. He also earned a B.S. in Mathematics (1974) with first class honors from the Imperial College of Science and Technology at London University.

David R. Carey (Ch. 6) is a member of the Aerospace Software Engineering Management staff at Westinghouse, ESG located in Baltimore, Maryland. Mr. Carey is currently the Manager for Electronics Warfare Embedded Software.

Mr. Carey has twenty years experience in real time, mission critical software. For the past nine years he has managed numerous software development projects specializing in Electronic Counter Measures (ECM). Over the last three years Mr. Carey has also emerged as the resident leader promoting Software Metrics throughout Westinghouse, ESG. He is the lead for the Software Metrics Working Group.

Mr. Carey has a B.S. in Electrical Engineering (1967) and an M.S. in Numerical Science (1970), both from the Johns Hopkins University.

Don Freeman (Ch. 6) is a system/software engineering consultant specializing in new business development and acquisition of complex systems. Mr. Freeman retired from IBM in 1988 with 28 years of service. Since then he has worked as an independent consultant for Westinghouse, AT&T and IBM. His experience spans a broad range of complex systems in both government and commercial business areas.

Most recently Mr. Freeman has worked several proposals and provided software engineering support for Navy and Air Force weapons and surveillance systems including the AN/SQQ-89I surface sonar system, AWACS radar upgrade, Advanced Tactical Fighter radar and FDS surveillance sonar system.

Mr. Freeman has promoted process improvement and its implementation since the early 1980s. At IBM Mr. Freeman initiated a process definition team to define the division standard for the system engineering process. Similarly at AT&T he supported development of an improved system engineering process. At Westinghouse he established and is currently promoting the implementation of a plan for updating Westinghouse ESG software development policies, practices and procedures. He is also promoting upgrades to existing configuration management practices which will utilize software metrics.

In a joint effort with Westinghouse, Mr. Freeman is evaluating TQM concepts to implement improvements in software development practices. He has supported software capability and capacity reviews at Westinghouse and was involved in the independent assessment of Westinghouse ESG's software process conducted by the Software Engineering Institute (SEI).

Mr. Freeman recently presented a paper entitled "Standards and Process Definition" at the NSIA Symposium on Software Productivity. He holds five U.S. patents and has published several technical papers.

Mr. Freeman has a B.S. in Electrical Engineering from the University of Florida and an M.S. in Electrical Engineering from George Washington University.

James J. Holden (Ch. 7) is a software manager at Westinghouse ESG. He has 21 years experience in management, systems, and software engineering.

Mr. Holden joined Westinghouse in 1970 on a scholarship program through the Johns Hopkins University. Since 1984 Mr. Holden has managed programs totaling more than 75 million dollars in radar, communications, satellite, and airspace systems. As software engineering manager Mr. Holden is responsible for 250 engineers, staff, and contract personnel.

Mr. Holden is also involved in the Total Quality program at Westinghouse, is a member of the Software Management Quality Improvement Team, sponsor of the Software Planning Quality Improvement Team, a member of the Westinghouse Software Engineering Process Organization and a graduate of the Philip Crosby Total Quality College.

Mr. Holden is also a member of the IEEE and Tau Beta Pi engineering honor society. He has published two papers and has a patent for a fault isolation process for embedded, multiprocessor computer systems.

Mr. Holden graduated from Johns Hopkins University with a B.S. in Electrical Engineering and an M.S. in Computer Science.

Anthony F. Shumskas (Chs. 8, 11) recently retired from the U.S. Air Force as a Lieutenant Colonel. In his last military assignment, Mr. Shumskas was Military Staff Assistant to the Director for Weapon System Assessment (WSA), Deputy Director, Defense Research and Engineering (Test and Evaluation), Office of the Undersecretary of Defense, The Pentagon, Washington D.C.

Mr. Shumskas was WSA staff specialist for 51 major and designated strategic, space, and automated information systems valued in excess $300 billion. He was responsible for assessing the test and evaluation aspects of these programs and for reporting the evaluations to the Defense Acquisition Board and Major Automated Information Systems Review Council Principals. Additionally, Mr. Shumskas was responsible for developing test and evaluation policy for software intensive major systems.

Mr. Shumskas has extensive background in software development for air and space systems. He has written several publications on software management, measurement, quality, test and evaluation and risk management. He is involved in software standardization activities at domestic and international levels. He was a key contributor in developing the DOD Software Master Plan and was a participant in the development of the DOD Software Technology Plan. He helped develop the Software Action Plan for the Director, Defense Research and Engineering. Mr. Shumskas was also a member of the Scientific and Technology Thrust Panel on Acquisition Improvement for the Undersecretary of Defense for Acquisition.

Mr. Shumskas was awarded the Meritorious Service Medal with one oak leaf cluster, the Air Force Commendation Medal with two oak leaf clusters, the Air Force Achievement Medal, Vietnam Service Medal, Republic of Vietnam Campaign Medal, and the Air Force Association's Technical Achievement Award.

Mr. Shumskas has a B.S. in Aerospace Engineering from Penn State University (1969) and an M.S. in Aerospace Engineering from the University of Arizona (1970). He graduated from Squadron Officer School in 1972, Air Command and Staff College in 1978, Defense Systems Management College in 1982, and the National Security Management College in 1985.

Donald J. Reifer (Ch. 9) is an internationally recognized expert in Software Engineering and Management with over twenty years experience in industry and government. As President of Reifer Consultants Inc. (RCI), he has helped several Fortune 500 firms (CAE-Link, Rockwell, Shell, Texas Instruments, Westinghouse, etc.) and government agencies (DOD, NASA, etc.) to effectively manage large software projects, organizations, and technology introduction.

Mr. Reifer has successfully managed major projects, served on source selections, written winning proposals, and led project recovery teams. While affiliated with TRW, he was the Deputy Program Manager for Global Positioning Satellite (GPS) verification and validation projects. As Software Director with the Aerospace Corporation, Mr. Reifer managed over $800 million in software contracts for the Space Transportation System (space shuttle) Directorate. As a Project Leader at Hughes Aircraft, he managed the development of several major weapons systems.

For the past ten years, Mr. Reifer has developed software productivity and quality improvement strategies for firms such as Contel, Honeywell, Texas Instruments, and Westinghouse. He has also helped to create successful product and marketing strategies for other high technology firms (Alcatel, Meridian, Rational, Telesoft, etc.). He has conducted marketing surveys, worked with investment firms (e.g., Paine Webber Development Co.) and served as an advisor to many executives in the computer industry.

Lately, Mr. Reifer has promoted the use of metrics and operational strategies to manage software reuse. He leads the Joint Integrated Avionics Working Group (JIAWG) effort in this area. Mr. Reifer is also developing operational concepts for the OSS and RAASP Reuse Projects.

Mr. Reifer has written more than one-hundred papers and two books on software engineering and management. He is also author of the popular ASSET-R size and SoftCost-Ada cost estimation models. Mr. Reifer is an ACM national lecturer and a member of the Board of Directors of the Ada Software Alliance. His many honors include being listed in *Who's Who in the West,* the NASA Distinguished Service Medal, and the Hughes Aircraft Company Masters Fellowship.

Mr. Reifer has a B.S. in Electrical Engineering from the Newark College of Engineering (NCE), an M.S. in Operations Research from the University of Southern California (USC), and the Certificate in Business Management from the University of California at Los Angeles (UCLA).

James H. Dobbins, CQA (Ch. 10) is an internationally recognized expert in software quality and reliability management, with over 28 years experience in these and related disciplines. Prior to joining the faculty at Defense Systems Management College in October 1990, he was a professor of systems management at the National Defense University. His current responsibilities include that of course director of the Management of Software Acquisition Course and software management instructor in the Program Management Course.

Following his tenure of service as a communications officer in the U.S. Air Force (SAC), he had 21 years of service with IBM Federal Systems Division, participating in the development of numerous DOD and NASA programs. These included the Gemini Program, Apollo Program, Air Force satellite programs, and Navy ASW systems. Following his service with IBM, he joined American Management Systems, Inc. as a principal of the company and Director of Software Quality Engineering.

He is active in numerous professional organizations and has presented many invited papers at conferences throughout the world. Most recently he participated as a featured debater at the International Software Debate in San Diego, and was a featured speaker at the Quality Assurance Institute National Conference on Quality Measurement held in March 1992. As a senior member of the Institute of Electrical and Electronics Engineers (IEEE), he chaired the working group which developed the industry standard for software reliability management, IEEE Std 982.1 and associated Guide 982.2.

In 1985, and again in 1986, he was chosen to participate in the French-American exchange of engineers and scientists program and visited France as a state guest to discuss his work in software reliability with several French companies, interfacing with the French Society for Industrial Quality Control and the French Standardization Society. He was a recipient of the NASA Apollo Achievement Award, and received a special Navy Letter of Commendation for his software test and evaluation effort on the LAMPS Program.

He has served as a consultant to NCR Corporation, UNISYS, RAND Corporation, and Time-Life Books. He authored *Software Quality Assurance and Evaluation,* published by ASQC Quality Press, three chapters of *Handbook of Software Quality Assurance,* Van Nostrand Reinhold (1987 and 1992), and one chapter of *Software Validation,* North Holland Publishing Company (1983). He is author of one chapter of *Total Quality Management for Software* published in 1992 by Van Nostrand Reinhold, and three chapters of *Military Project Management Handbook,* published in 1992 by McGraw-Hill.

His biography has appeared in *Marquis' Who's Who in America, Who's Who in American Education, Who's Who in the South and Southwest, Who's Who in the East, Who's Who in the Computer Graphics Industry, Who's Who in Science and Engineering, Who's Who in American Law, West's Who's Who in U.S Executives,* and *Personalities of the South.*

He holds a B.S. in Physics, an M.S. in Information Systems, and is an attorney-at-law. He received his certification as a Certified Quality Analyst from the Quality Assurance Institute, and has completed the training program conducted by the Software Engineering Institute required to conduct Software Capability Evaluations (SCE).

He is a member of the talent bank of the United States Congress on the subjects of software quality and reliability, a member of ASQC, a Senior Member of IEEE, a member of the IEEE Computer Society, The Boston Computer Society, American Defense Preparedness Association (ADPA), Mathematical Association of America (MAA), MENSA, the Virginia State Bar, the Virginia Trial Lawyers Association, and the Association of Trial Lawyers of America. He is licensed to practice law in Virginia and various federal courts.

He and his wife, Mary Beth, live in Stafford, Virginia, and have a four year old son, Nathan, and a three year old son, Daniel.

Richard Zultner, CQE (Ch. 12), is an internationally recognized consultant, author, educator, and speaker. For the past several years, Mr. Zultner has focused on the importance of implementing software TQM techniques in U.S. industry, specializing in the rapid delivery of high-tech software-intensive systems using daily management methods such as statistical process control (SPC), cross-functional management techniques such as quality function deployment (QFD), and strategic quality management approaches such as Hoshin-Planning. As an avid and long time student of Dr. W. Edwards Deming, Mr. Zultner has promoted these techniques within American industry as the way to compete for world markets.

Mr. Zultner's clients range from Fortune 500 firms to new ventures, and include an array of industries. His firm provides consulting and training in software SPC, software QFD, and software TQM as well as Executive briefings on the "Deming Way to Software Total Quality".

Mr. Zultner is currently writing a book entitled *High Tech QFD: Applying QFD to Software-Intensive Complex Products.*

Mr. Zultner has a Masters degree in Management from the J. L. Kellogg Graduate School of Management at Northwestern University, and has professional certificates in quality, project management, and software engineering.

Herb Krasner, Ph.D. (Ch 13), is the President of Krasner Consulting and specializes in assisting organizations with the evaluation, planning, and implementation of computer software quality and process improvement programs. He is a process management expert consultant for SAIC to the IBM team for the DARPA STARS Program. He is also a consultant to several commercial companies and federal agencies where he is involved with establishing strategic software excellence programs. He is involved with software engineering education and the establishment of an interdisciplinary institute in software technology at the University of Texas. He was a graduate of the first SEI Assessment training class held in June, 1988 and has subsequently served as team leader on over 12 organizational software capability assessments in several companies. He is a member of the Board of Quality Examiners for the Austin Quality Award based on the MBNQA criteria.

His current interests are in applying TQM and process management techniques to the continuous quality and process improvement thrusts in progressive software organizations. He can be reached at Krasner Consulting, 1901 Ringtail Ridge, Austin, TX 78746, phone: 512-328-4264, email: hkrasner@cs.utexas.edu

In 1990-91, he was Manager of the SAIC Software Technology Center where he initiated, managed, and led a new research and development program in advanced software technologies. He was task leader for the DARPA/STARS/IBM Software Process Management System (SPMS) project. He is also the conceptual architect of a set of tools to support the SEI Capability Maturity Model and its application to assessment and evaluation.

In 1988-90 he was a group manager and principal investigator in the Lockheed Research and Development Division—Software Technology Center. He was also the leader of the Lockheed corporate initiative in software process improvement and TQM which established software improvement programs in all of Lockheed's divisions.

Prior to that (in 1983-87) he was the senior technical staff member and leader of the Empirical Studies of Software Development Project in the MCC Software Technology Program (STP). Prior positions held were as: software methodologist and Ada technology specialist at Harris Government Systems; Assistant Professor of Computer Science at Clemson University, Adjunct Professor of Computer Science at University of Florida and independent contract systems analyst.

He has over 20 years of experience in: software engineering research and its management in both industrial and academic settings, method/environment/tool development, practical large system engineering, and university teaching. He is active in professional societies: ACM (19 years) and IEEE Computer Society (17 years), has served as chairman of several international conferences and as the Director of the ACM Scholastic Student Programming Contest. He has served on a number of industry wide task forces on software issues and concerns. He has published and presented his work in many forums. He teaches an ACM sponsored seminar on Continuous Software Improvement. He is a coauthor of a 1992 book entitled *Total Quality Management for Software* published by Van Nostrand Reinhold. He holds the following academic degrees in Computer Science from the University of Missouri at Rolla: BS ('73), MS ('75) and ABD/Phd ('79).

D. Paul Smith, Ph.D. (Ch. 14), is head of the 5ESS® Switch U.S. Customer Interface/Quality Department at AT&T Bell Laboratories in Naperville, Illinois.

He is responsible for quality management of the software development process for the 5ESS® Switching System. He previously worked on the design, development, project management, and quality improvement of 5ESS® system hardware. He joined AT&T Bell Laboratory in 1967.

Dr. Smith received a B.S. in Electrical Engineering from Brigham Young University, an M.S. in Electrical Engineering, and a Ph.D. from Stanford University.

Dennis A. Christenson (Ch. 14) is a Distinguished Member of Technical Staff in the Quality Engineering Group of the 5ESS® Switch U.S. Customer Interface/ Quality Department at AT&T Bell Laboratories in Naperville, Illinois. His current work includes data analysis for software metrics and development of statistical models of software quality and reliability. He joined AT&T Bell Laboratories in 1965.

Mr. Christenson received a B.S. in Electrical Engineering from Iowa State University (1965), an M.S. in Electrical Engineering from the University of Illinois (1966), and an M.B.A. from the University of Chicago (1973).

Alfred J. Lamperez (Ch. 14) is a member of the Technical Staff in the Quality Engineering Group of the 5ESS® Switch U.S. Customer Interface/Quality Department at AT&T Bell Laboratories in Naperville, Illinois. He is also a member of the American Society for Quality Control and the American Statistical Association. Since joining AT&T Bell Laboratories in 1988, Mr. Lamperez has been responsible for applying statistical analysis and modelling as well as quality control techniques to data and metrics from various stages of the software development cycle.

Mr. Lamperez received a B.S. in Statistics from the University of Southwestern Louisiana (1988) and an M.S. in Statistics from Stanford University (1990).

Steel T. Huang, Ph.D. (Ch. 14), is Supervisor of the Quality Engineering Group in the 5ESS® Switch U.S. Customer Interface/Quality Department at AT&T Bell Laboratories in Naperville, IL. He is responsible for the planning, definition, and analysis of software quality and productivity metrics for the 5ESS® Switch U.S. development project. He joined AT&T Bell Laboratories in 1979.

Dr. Huang received a B.S. in Mathematics from the National Taiwan University (1969) and a Ph.D. in Statistics from the University of North Carolina, Chapel Hill (1975). He was also a faculty member at the University of Cincinnati and the University of North Carolina from 1975 to 1979.

Robert G. Mays (Ch. 15) is a Senior Programmer in Market-Driven Quality Process Engineering at the IBM Networking Systems Laboratory in Raleigh, North Carolina. Mr. Mays is currently involved in developing and deploying new software technologies, including improved methods for enhancing existing software products, program understanding, and design reabstraction. His immediate focus is on the development and promotion of a Defect Prevention Process throughout IBM.

Prior to joining IBM in 1981, Mr. Mays developed management systems applications for Eastman Kodak for 12 years.

Mr. Mays was one of the first recipients of IBM's Corporate Quality Award recognizing his contribution toward the development of a Defect Prevention Process.

Mr. Mays received a B.S. degree in Chemistry from the Massachusetts Institute of Technology in 1968.

Barba B. Affourtit (Ch. 17) has been Vice President of Interaction Research Institute, Inc. (IRI) for the past 16 years. IRI is a consulting firm that specializes in training and implementation of the Total Quality Management methodology. Ms. Affourtit worked with W. Edwards Deming in 1981 and 1982 and was the principal instructor for the first follow-up course to apply the Deming methodology.

Ms. Affourtit has provided on location training and consultation to numerous organizations including IBM, USDA, IRS, BLS, the U.S. Navy, the Census Bureau, Allied-Signal, Hospitalization Corporation of America, and New England Medical Center. She is the developer of the STATMAN; a Statistical Management software program that includes all of the process management tools needed for TQM implementation.

Harlan D. Mills, Ph.D. (Ch. 18), retired in 1987 as an IBM Fellow and Professor of Computer Science, University of Maryland. Dr. Mills is currently the President and Chief Technical Officer of Software Engineering Technology, Inc. (SET).

Since founding SET, Dr. Mills has continued to serve on the Air Force Scientific Advisory Board and to teach at local universities. While at IBM, he served on the Corporate Technical Committee and as Director of Software Engineering and Technology for the Federal Systems Division. Dr. Mills was also the principal architect for the curriculum of the IBM Software Engineering Institute, an internal educational facility with a worldwide faculty of over 50. At General Electric Dr. Mills was one of the founders of Mathematica. Dr. Mills has taught at Iowa State, Princeton, New York University, Johns Hopkins University, the University of Maryland, the University of Florida, and the Florida Institute of Technology concurrently with his industrial assignments.

Dr. Mills has made significant contributions to the software engineering field with six books and over 50 papers. He was the first person to recognize that a computer program was a rule for a function and that the power of mathematical rigor could be applied to development and verification of programs. He has spent the last 25 years developing, field testing, and refining these ideas. In writing about Dr. Mills' work, Gerald Weinberg noted ". . . Of course, if the ideas had not been absolutely first rate, the voyage would not have been worth the fare, regardless of Harlan's talents as a writer. But, as you well know, they were first rate ideas—ideas that have had a profound influence on software productivity all over the world."

Dr. Mills has received numerous awards: Honorary Fellow in Mathematics at Wesleyan University, ACPA Fellow, DPMA Distinguished Information Science Award, and the Warnier Award. Dr. Mills received his Ph.D. in Mathematics from Iowa State (1952).

Preface

Total Quality Management (TQM) is more than a motivation program, it is a way of doing business. The successful companies have focused their attention on TQM over the past few years, resulting in products and services that customers want. Startling turnarounds (Ford, KODAK copiers, etc.) have resulted from implementation of TQM.

Total Quality is a business strategy that involves a culture change, and emphasizes continuous improvement in the quality of products, processes, and information within the corporation. There are common elements of the Total Quality movement as reported in *Defense News* Magazine:

1. Management participation and leadership development
2. Establishing goals and measurable objectives
3. Extensive education and training
4. Employee involvement and action teams
5. Customer emphasis
6. Supplier certification and training
7. Recognition.[1]

What about software? How do these concepts of TQM fit in? Do they fit in? Is there a focused effort to apply TQM to software development? Who is doing what, and how? Is there a payoff?

By bringing together, in this volume, the experience of the experts and the quality implications of their work for software, *Total Quality Management for Software* sets the standard for TQM application in software development. Collected here are both the practical implementations of years of experience and the theoretical basis for new, exciting ideas.

Total Quality Management for Software begins with an introduction telling the reader what TQM is so that an understanding of the rest of the book will be clear. There are four parts to *Total Quality Management for Software*. In Part I the stage is set for the quest for software TQM. The application of TQM in mission critical software development is explained. What the Japanese are doing for quality is always interesting. Here the application of TQM to software in Japan is discussed. How software quality assessment through the In-Plant Quality Evaluation of the Defense Logistics Agency can lead a company to Total Quality principles in the software quality arena is discussed. A practical implementation model of how TQM is applied to software development in a United States of America company concludes this part.

Software directions for TQM is the subject of Part II. The software development process is covered with an emphasis on the maturity model. How one measures the development of software to help improve its quality is covered. To achieve total quality, defects in software must be eliminated. There is a chapter to provide an understanding of defects and so help eliminate them. To achieve software TQM one must go into a development project with an adequate understanding of the risks involved. Such risks are highlighted in this part. Reuse is a major aim in all of software development because of the enormous gains it provides in software quality and productivity. This part concludes with a discussion of software reuse and its quality implications.

Part III discusses methods of TQM implementation in software. A seminar is encapsulated in the chapter on TQM methods in software. Testing methods for software quality are covered in this part. Dr. Yoji Akao and Dr. Tadashi Yoshizawa's Quality Function Deployment (QFD) methods as applied to software are shown to achieve satisfactory quality results. The use of statistical controls in software development is relatively new, and Part III covers this application.

Finally, Part IV tells how to achieve TQM in software. At IBM, causal analysis of defects has been instrumental in reducing defects, and therefore in increasing total quality. These concepts are covered in this part. If you want to produce zero defect software, this concept is given credence by the principles in this chapter. SPC (statistical process control) has been very successful in manufacturing, now see its application to software development. Many of the above concepts are tied together in the cleanroom software development methodology of Dr. Harlan Mills which concludes the book.

A brief summary of each chapter highlighting its main thrust is provided for the reader to decide what is of most immediate interest. If information is required from another chapter for complete understanding, adequate cross-references have been supplied within each chapter.

The introduction reviews existing TQM concepts in general. It explains the overall Total Quality Management methods and sets the stage for software implementation.

Chapter 1 covers TQM in mission critical software development. In this introductory chapter TQM methods and quality principles are applied to mission critical (i.e., to the Department of Defense) software development.

Chapter 2 covers software TQM in Japan and reviews the movement of quality concepts in Japan as applied to software. The United States of America has relearned many quality lessons from the Japanese, so there are lessons in the software arena to be learned.

Chapter 3 discusses software quality evaluations to improve a company's software processes. It has become essential to develop attitudes and systems that promote and implement continuous improvement of procedures and processes that help an organization develop quality into its software product.

Chapter 4 discusses company-wide software quality improvement programs. It deals with the rise of total quality in the Untied States of America and how implementation is taking place for software development. An explanation of an existing total quality management program applied to software development is given.

Chapter 5 provides an understanding of the software process. It discusses the need for understanding where a company is in relationship to its software development process. Understanding a company's software development process is critical to being able to apply total quality management to improve it.

Chapter 6 discusses quality measurements in software. The need to measure where you are in order to understand what to improve is a well known principle. To measure total quality management in software means to move toward zero defects.

Chapter 7 covers defect analysis from the unique perspective of a practitioner of the management of software development. He brings his experiences to bear on how to analyze and defeat defects.

Chapter 8 deals with software risk mitigation. Since software development is considered so risky, this chapter considers methods to mitigate that risk in the light of TQM concepts.

Chapter 9 explains the advantages to be gained by effective reuse of software. Quality improves dramatically when software is reused. This chapter relates the methods and benefits of reuse.

Chapter 10 covers TQM methods in software. The chapter will emphasize the software acquisition requirements for TQM.

Chapter 11 explains the correct testing of software for the specific type of software under development. The experience of the author with software tests, tells how testing can, but sometimes does not, produce quality software.

Chapter 12 covers quality function deployment (QFD) applied to software. This chapter covers the QFD concepts of Dr. Yoji Akao and Dr. Tadashi Yoshizawa as applied to software development. These concepts have been successfully applied worldwide.

Chapter 13 discusses continuous improvement which is a focal issue of the TQM movement. In fact, *Kaizan* is Japanese for continuous, incremental improvements, and is being used now to improve software development.

Chapter 14 discusses statistical control of the software development process as it is being applied at the AT&T Labs in Illinois. The unique development method of statistical control is proven in manufacturing and is being proven effective in application to software.

Chapter 15 provides background on defect prevention methods. The defect prevention process has been in use at IBM for over six years. It relies on causal analysis of defects to prevent future defects, but the causal analysis is integrated into the software development process. This concept is important when establishing a TQM position in software development. The application of defect prevention methods to real software development projects provides an excellent introduction to zero defect software covered in Chapter 16.

Chapter 16 provides coverage of zero defect software development. The concepts embodied in the *Zero Defect Software*[2] book will be presented in this chapter. If the achievement of zero defects in software development is accomplishable as the author claims, then 20% of the price of nonconformance in software development could be saved (about $6 billion). The money to be saved by applying the zero defect software method is astounding.

Chapter 17 applies statistical process control (SPC) to software. Statistical process control has been successful in the manufacturing arena. This chapter explores some successes of statistical process control for software.

Chapter 18 provides guidance on a relatively new development method called cleanroom engineering. It is believed that statistical control begins to be achieved with the cleanroom method. Proof of the cleanroom concepts applied to software development has been demonstrated in a number of projects.

Appendix A lists the acronyms used in the book.

The editors thank all of the contributors for their tremendous effort in bringing to *Total Quality Management for Software* an excellent collection of chapters. This collection provides in a single source a wide spectrum of knowledge to assist managers and software developers alike in their quest to establish a TQM program for software development.

The editors also appreciate the patience and help of Dianne Littwin, Senior Editor, and Harvey Satty, Manuscript Editor, Van Nostrand Reinhold, without whose assistance and support *Total Quality Management for Software* could not have been accomplished.

References

1. Moore, W. S., "Singing the Same 'Total Quality' Song," *National Defense.* Copyright 1990 by American Defense Preparedness Association. Reprinted by permission. 1990.
2. Schulmeyer, G. Gordon, *Zero Defect Software.* New York: McGraw-Hill Co., 1990.

G. Gordon Schulmeyer
James I. McManus

Contents

Introduction
The Total Quality Concept

Richard R. Brydges

The purpose of this book is to tie software development to the Total Quality (TQ) movement being implemented throughout United States industry and government. This introduction defines the TQ concept and provides a framework for the following chapters. The framework is based on an article entitled "Singing the Same 'Total Quality' Song" that appeared in the March 1990 issue of the *National Defense* magazine[1]

The article identified and explored the common elements of the TQ movement as experienced by ten corporate implementors. The author identified seven recurring elements in the implementors attempts to employ a business strategy that involves a culture change emphasizing the continuous improvement of the quality of products and services. They are: (1) management participation and leadership development; (2) establishment of goals and measurable objectives; (3) extensive education and training; (4) employee involvement and action teams; (5) customer emphasis; (6) supplier certification and training; and (7) recognition. These elements will be further addressed at the conclusion of this chapter and will be referred to throughout the book.

While these themes represent topical dimensions in implementing a TQ concept, each author uniquely addresses specific methods and applications that help create a TQ environment. The objective in this introduction is to facilitate awareness of the endless stream of possibilities in what has been described as a cultural "paradigm shift."

I will not speculate on the magnitude of change required to create a corporate culture that emphasizes continuous improvement in the quality of products and services because that depends on many situational variables. However, the adoption of such a business strategy in corporate America represents significant change in the way we "think" and "do business," individually and collectively. Without such a shift there are serious concerns that threaten our very industrial existence. The limitations of our quality practices and the need for change are summed up in the Department of Defense *Guide to Implementing TQ.*[2]

> "The Evolution of Causes—In the industrial sector, many industrial leaders became preoccupied with short-term profits and corporate mergers. Unfortunately, in doing so they failed to focus on customer satisfaction, which is not achieved by sales gimmicks, but by quality products as the fundamental basis for a successful business. They failed to set in place a long term vision for their companies, and to communicate that vision to the workforce. They treated quality as an added burden and an added cost, failing to understand that high quality in every process is the key to profitability and increased market-share. Regrettably, they even lost sight of the inherent abilities of their workers to contribute to process improvement. The result has been apathy, loss of self esteem, loss of pride in workmanship, indifference to product quality and absenteeism."
>
> "The Need for Cultural Changes—Our present culture is permeated by an atmosphere of distrust. We devise intricate checks and balances to control every action with a bureaucracy that boggles the mind and causes excessive administrative costs. Meanwhile, we fail to train our managers for leadership, pay little attention to the system that allows counterproductive efforts to go unchallenged, do not properly educate, train or motivate our personnel to be effective and productive, nor do we allow them to contribute to the full extent of their abilities. The fact is that our management style focuses on the failures with elaborate procedures that measure failure and prescribe proper punishment. All this emphasis on detecting failures, almost invites a challenge to try and get away with as much as possible. Rather, we should be putting the desired achievements on the spot light, provide leadership and incentives for success, and measure and reward in accordance with achievements."

Providing the necessary leadership means understanding the very nature of work. That understanding must lead to viable processes, systems, and organizations capable to competing in the global marketplace. With that as the ultimate objective, this chapter and the book will explore possibilities to accomplish that in the field of software development.

However, the ramifications of this undertaking go far beyond creating viable business entities. The capability to develop software will not only determine our ability to compete, but to survive. Whatever the degree of impact, the goal of the software development process should be to produce software that is insensitive to errors regardless of their source.[3] The TQ concept integrates business strategy, process capability and program management in pursuit of that goal, as well as keeping up with the geometric growth of software application. The target and associated possibilities are rapidly moving and it is critical that we create processes and systems that not only stay abreast of requirements, but can actually be employed to identify emergent and future needs.

I.1 WHAT IS TOTAL QUALITY?

From these initial remarks and identification of need, it is important to establish a basic understanding of what the TQ concept is. There are many titles and acronyms used to refer to the concept: Total Quality Management (TQM), Six Sigma, Total Quality Leadership (TQL), etc. This introduction refers generically to the concept as Total Quality (TQ). Other authors refer to the same basic concept using titles that have evolved from their experience and the specifics of that application. What is of primary importance, however, is that the people involved have a common understanding of what the concept means to them, both individually and collectively.

TQ as a pervasive concept can have a range of definitions and meanings based on intent and application. However, it is important that a common understanding be reached to solidify basic quality precepts. Whatever the definition, it will provide a foundation for communication and understanding. Without this basic corner stone, the application becomes fragmented. The concept quickly loses its significance and breaks down into another "program, trend or passing fad." Therefore, it is necessary for a common definition to evolve which is based on the quality precepts discussed throughout the book. But most important of all, that evolving definition must acknowledge input from those involved in establishing a TQ culture and that definition becomes the context for implementation.

TQ definitions range from "doing the right thing at the right time" to more specific language that attempts to embody a number of TQ dimensions. Themes and specific wording may include: customer supplier relationships (both internal and external), meeting the customer needs now and in the future, the combined application of human resources and technology, creating an environment of continuous improvement, involvement and participating management, ongoing education and training.

One example is the Department of Defense definition of Total Quality Management (TQM).[4]

"TQM is both a philosophy and a set of guiding principles that represent the foundation for a continuously improving organization. TQM is the application of quantitative methods and human resources to improve the material and services supplied to an organization, and the degree to which the needs of the customers are met, now and in the future. TQM integrates fundamental management techniques, existing improvement efforts, and technical tools under a disciplined approach focused on continuous improvement."

The ultimate strategy is to provide a comprehensive way to improve quality by examining the way work gets done with a systematic, integrated, consistent, organization-wide perspective.

On the private sector side, the President of Computer Sciences Corporation (CSC), Applied Technology Division summarized in two words the largest single reason behind their TQ initiative—cost and competition. Acknowledging that all their major competitors have embarked on quality improvement initiatives, CSC has set its sights on pursuing the prestigious Malcolm Baldrige National Quality Award. They have defined this effort as follows:

> "Total Quality Management (TQM) is a management technique for continuously improving our performance at every level and in every area of responsibility to ensure customer satisfaction. TQM combines management and statistical techniques with existing improvement efforts under a rigorous, disciplined structure to strive for zero defects in all technical and administrative processes. It demands commitment and requires leadership and training.[5]

This definition and subsequent management principles are derived from the assumption that all work is a process, and that the effectiveness of each process can be measured and improved.

These two examples are representative of both public and private sector initiatives in defining TQ. Whatever choice of emphasis or combination of words, the most important criterion, once again, is that it has relevance and meaning to those involved in the effort. It must provide the focus for achieving "constancy of purpose." It ultimately facilitates continuous improvement through a collective vision of quality. A vision of quality that shifts from defect correction to defect prevention; from quality inspected into the product to quality designed and built into the product; from acceptable levels of defects to continuous process improvement; from approval of waivers to conformance to properly defined requirements; from emphasis on cost and schedule to emphasis on quality, cost, and schedule.

There are those who criticize the TQ movement for not having a more standardized definition or concurrence on what TQ is. While the eclectic nature of the concept lends itself to such variation, it is more important to derive meaning and understanding through the process of definition and implementation. The insights, applications, and experiences cited in this book provide a foundation of understanding from which to develop a definition that uniquely fits your organization and business strategy. It will ultimately provide the basis for practitioners to plan, develop, and implement successful software products using the new quality concepts and principles.

I.2 THE EVOLUTION OF TOTAL QUALITY

The evolution of the TQ concept provides an historical perspective relative to global realities and events. While there have been many notable contributors to the construct including Joseph M. Juran, Kaoru Ishikawa, and Armand V. Feigenbaum, the concept in this country is primarily associated with the work of Dr. W. Edwards Deming.

This man, who was to have an enormous impact upon the development of industry, was born in Sioux City, Iowa, October 14, 1900. Growing up during hard times, he entered the University of Wyoming and received a Bachelor of Science degree in 1921. He received a Masters degree in mathematics and physics from the

University of Colorado at Boulder. His professor of physics, Dr. Lester, suggested that he ought to go to Yale. Having the opportunity to study under notable mathematicians and physicists at that institution, in 1928 he finished his requirements for a PhD. in mathematical physics.

Following his education, Dr. Deming began his career in government as a mathematical physicist in the Fixed Nitrogen Research Laboratory of the U.S. Department of Agriculture (USDA) in 1928, and he remained at that position until 1939. From 1933 through 1953, Dr. Deming was head of the Department of Mathematics and Statistics of the Graduate School of the USDA and made major contributions to the mathematical and statistical education of a whole generation. In 1939 he joined the Census Bureau. After leaving the Bureau in 1946, Dr. Deming opened his office in Washington, D.C. as a consultant in statistical studies, and he embarked upon the crusade which led to the renaissance of industry in Japan, to world prominence and finally to recognition in his own country.[6]

During World War II, Dr. Deming worked with the United States military-industrial complex to build in quality using statistical methods in the mass production of war materials. While that effort was successful, American industry did not continue to expand on those applications in a post war demand oriented market place. With the industrial capacities of Japan and Europe in ruin, everything produced by our intact industrial capacity was consumed on the world market. Suffice it to say that product quality was not emphasized.

While Dr. Deming's quality methodologies and applications had their roots in this country, they failed to realize their potential here. If things had been different, it might have been the U.S. that experienced a quality renaissance. Conditions were right in many ways, but there was a missing essential ingredient, namely management's awareness that there was a growing problem and there was a means to deal with it.

In Japan in 1950 Dr. Deming initiated "a new order of things" as part of their reconstruction efforts. At the request of the Japanese Union of Scientists and Engineers (JUSE), he began teaching Japanese managers, engineers, and scientists how to use statistics to manufacture quality products. Statistics were used to identify process and system capabilities. Once the systems were "in control," they were continuously improved upon by shifting the mean and reducing undesired variation. At the very heart of his teaching is an understanding of the nature of variation.

Dr. Deming was certain he could teach the Japanese how to join the leading industrial nations by improving quality, and as they say, "the rest is history." "I think that I was the only man in 1950," he says, "who believed that Japan could invade the markets of the world within five years."[7]

In gratitude he was awarded Japan's Second Order medal of the Sacred Treasure by the late Emperor Hirohito. The citation indicates that they attribute the rebirth of their industry and its worldwide success to Dr. Deming. The Japanese Union of Scientists and Engineers established the Deming Prize which is awarded to companies annually as their highest award for quality achievements.

As significant as his contributions were, Dr. Deming was comparatively unknown in the United States until June 1980, when he appeared in a network television documentary titled, "If Japan Can, Why Can't We?" This NBC white paper featured, in its final segment, a seventy-nine-year-old American statistician named W. Edwards Deming, who had taught Japanese management and engineers quality as a system, how to pinpoint variation or swings in their processes, enabling them to detect and eliminate defects, thus cutting down on waste and reducing costs while simultaneously increasing productivity. These methods were known as Statistical Process Control (SPC).[8]

More than any other single event, that NBC White Paper set America on a new course toward quality. With a new realization that something had to change for Americans to compete successfully in the global market place, Western management has slowly accepted responsibility to make those changes. Changes which are so significant that they represent a physical and psychological revolution, sometimes described as a cultural paradigm shift. Creative financing, mergers and acquisitions were no longer going to sustain a competitive edge in the market place. Value added activities that translated to product quality and services became the customers' differentiating criteria.

I.3 WHERE DOES IT FIT?

Having generally defined the TQ concept and given a brief overview of its evolution, where does it fit in the American software industry? Designing better software is no different from developing and continuously improving any process. The product is good, reliable quality code that meets the customer's needs and expectations, now and in the future. In hardware it shows in design, fit, and finish. Software quality is not much different.[9]

The advent of TQ presents the American software industry with the challenge of affecting major changes in attitude and direction in achieving "quality first." Attempts to improve software performance, productivity, and quality have attained only limited success. Such attempts include standards development, software technology development, and conducting assessments to establish quantitatively an organization's software development capability.

The management principles of W. Edwards Deming have become the standard for articulating, interpreting, and detailing TQ in sectors that did not previously identify their commonality and congruence with other industries. Detractors note the dissimilarities between manufacturing and software development and maintain that TQ concepts cannot be applied to the software environment. But in reality, TQ is consistent with good software development.[10] The fact is that processes are processes and systems are systems. It is management's challenge to understand them as such and to put methodologies and applications in place to produce the desired level of quality. By understanding this fundamental relationship, which to some may be a "flash of the blinding obvious," designers and managers can use TQ principles and statistical tools to achieve the desired output.

In achieving a TQ environment, I am referring to an organization's culture. Understanding TQ in application and practice requires more than an appreciation of techniques and technology, it requires an understanding of how a culture approaches the deployment of technology. It is the combination of philosophy and technology that uniquely creates a TQ culture. A wholistic combination of the left and right brain approaches, the quantitative and qualitative, and the subjective with the objective that allows management, as well an everyone in the organization, to identify and create a "quality culture."

I.4 DR. DEMING'S TQ CONCEPTS APPLIED TO SOFTWARE DEVELOPMENT

If American management accepts the fact that there needs to be a "paradigm shift," if not a cultural revolution, where do individuals and organizations begin? The good news is that America, and specifically software development, has recognized the necessity for change. Dr. Deming and others have provided the vision and presented possibilities, but that does not create the transformation. We must begin to interpret these ideas in the context of our own reality and create strategies that will use such concepts as Statistical Process Control (SPC), Quality Function Deployment (QFD), Design of Experiment (DOE), and employee involvement among others. The new strategies are summarized in Dr. Deming's Fourteen Obligations of Management and provide a conceptually pervasive foundation from which to begin this journey.

In an article titled "The Deming Approach to Software Quality Engineering,"[11] Richard Zultner interpreted the fourteen points for Management Information System (MIS) managers.

1. Create constancy of purpose for the improvement of development, with the aim to become excellent, satisfy users, and provide jobs. This requires innovation, long-term planning, research, education, and continuous improvement. Everyone must be involved. To achieve constancy of purpose, management must:

   - Establish operational definitions for each step in the systems development process, and define what is meant by "service to customers."
   - Define standards of development, maintenance, and service for the next year and five years ahead.
   - Define the internal and external customer.
   - Develop ways to provide better systems and services in less time, using fewer resources.
   - Invest in tools and techniques for better system development.

2. Adopt the new philosophy. Software engineering has entered a new economic age in which quality is vital to survival. MIS management must awaken to the challenge of producing quality software by learning its responsibilities and leading this change. Mistakes and negativism are no longer acceptable. Most of the quality problems in systems development can be solved only by management. Perhaps the greatest difficulty for management,

once it understands and embraces the Deming approach, is communicating its commitment to the staff. Through its actions and words, management must make it clear that quality comes first and that everyone must join in.

3. Cease dependence on mass inspection (especially testing) to achieve quality. Inspection is not the answer: it is too late and unreliable. It does not produce quality. Quality must be built into the system—or it doesn't exist. Reworking nonconforming specs or code is unnecessary and expensive. Quality comes from improving the system development process, thereby preventing errors.

4. End the practice of awarding business on price tag alone. The price of a product or service has no meaning without an associated measure of quality. Without such measures, business sinks to the lowest bidder, with low quality and high total cost the inevitable result. Instead of cutting costs by getting the lowest bid, management must create long-term relationships of loyalty and trust with single suppliers. That will lower the total cost.

5. Improve constantly and forever the system development process to improve quality and productivity, and thus constantly decrease the time and cost of systems. Improving quality is not a one-time effort. Management must insist that everyone try to constantly improve. This means the system development methodology, standards, and practices must be constantly revised. Whatever the MIS department knows about building systems should be reflected in its formal approach. Policies must be regularly examined to see if they are hindering the quality effort.

6. Institute training on the job. The MIS staff and management must make a commitment to continuous training and education. Quality starts and improves with training. All MIS staff members must understand what their jobs entail and how to do their work. Management must then remove all barriers to using new knowledge—otherwise the training will be wasted.

   An MIS organization must, therefore, establish experts in all areas of system development. Then, it must educate MIS managers and staff to be statistically minded and to understand the nature of variation. Finally, the organization must provide operational definitions of all key steps in developing systems, and train people in their use and improvement.

7. Institute leadership. Management must lead, not punish. It is a manager's job to help people do a better job and make systems more efficient. An organization must look at how its management is supervised as well as at its staff. Project management is a full-time job. Project managers need time to help people, and time to continually prove constancy of purpose. Project managers must be trained in basic and analytical statistical methods so that they can find genuine causes of trouble. This training is as essential as is a solid understanding of the structured tools and techniques is for software engineering. Project managers also need accurate information that indicates when to and when not to take action. Supervision should be focused on those members whose performance is out of statistical control and not on those who performance is merely low. Managers must understand the nature of variation: in any team whose work is in statistical control, half will always be below average.

8. Drive out fear, so that everyone can work effectively. Management should be held responsible for faults in the organization and environment. People must feel secure, or they will not ask questions or request help—even when they do not understand their jobs. MIS staff must not be blamed for problems that only management has the power to remedy. People must feel comfortable to master their jobs and make suggestions for ongoing improvement.

9. Break down barriers between areas. The responsibility of managers must be changed from stressing project schedules to improving quality. They must learn about the problems in different groups, and strive to communicate upstream to the supplier and downstream to the customer. Everyone has a customer.

10. Eliminate slogans, exhortations, and targets that ask for zero defects and new levels of productivity. Slogans do not build quality systems. MIS management should instead post its progress in responding to suggestions and in helping the staff improve quality. There is no substitute for knowledge of software engineering. Only management can change the culture and environment that dominate any individual's performance. Let the people put up their own signs and slogans.

11. Eliminate numerical quotas and goals. Leadership must replace quotas and goals. Quotas and goals (such as schedules) address numbers, not quality methods. MIS professionals, to keep their jobs, might foolishly attempt to meet their current schedule at any cost, without regard to the ensuing damage to users from poor quality. This ensures inefficiency and high cost. A schedule that causes haste and nonconformities instead of quality accomplishes nothing and services no one. Managers should concentrate on helping people do a better job by reducing rework, errors and waste. Everyone must work toward constant improvement, not the achievement of some arbitrary, short-term goal.

12. Remove barriers to pride of workmanship. The responsibility of managers must be changed from stressing project schedules to improving quality. MIS professionals are eager to do a good job—and are troubled when they cannot. Every management system and operating procedure must be examined to determine whether it supports or inhibits ongoing improvement.

13. Institute a vigorous program of education and self-improvement for everyone. Knowledge is a prerequisite for improvement. Both MIS management and staff must be educated in quality and software engineering. Managers should encourage the acquisition of new skills as one way to increase job security. Building better systems requires more knowledgeable system builders and managers. The learning process should never stop.

14. Put everyone to work to accomplish the transformation. The transformation is everyone's job. No one is exempt, especially management. Top MIS management must implement a quality program and carry out the quality mission. Everyone in the organization must understand Deming's 14 points as well as his seven deadly diseases and obstacles.

From these principles or obligations, Deming has recently expanded his thinking into what he describes as "A System of Profound Knowledge."[12] That system consists of four interrelated disciplines: systems theory, statistical theory, theory of knowledge, and theory of psychology. It reflects his interdisciplinary thinking and his own personal growth in recognizing the expanded application of his original concept. The authors in this book explore those applications in terms of software design and development.

I.5 COMMON ELEMENTS AND LESSONS LEARNED

Referring back to the seven recurring elements in ten corporations implementing TQ, W. Savage Moore in her article "Singing the Same 'Total Quality' Song[13] describes the similarities among and the lessons learned by these organizations. Their experience over the past 5 to 10 years has followed similar courses. To benefit from their experience and hopefully minimize "reinventing the wheel," their commonalities are again cited and discussed in the following paragraphs. The corporations included: AT&T Atlanta Works Divisions, Baxter Healthcare, Control Data Corporation Business Management Services, Florida Power and Light, Hewlett Packard, Motorola, United Technologies, Texas Instrument Defense Systems and Electronic Group, Westinghouse Commercial Nuclear Fuel, and Xerox.

1. Management Participation and Leadership Development. The importance of this element is evidenced by the fact that many of the TQ movement titles chosen by the implementors included the words "management" or "leadership." It is recognized that there is an important role for every individual in the corporation, including top executives, middle management, and first level supervisors, as well as each office and factory floor contributor.

    Some TQ implementors cited lack of top management leadership, support, and participation as a major stumbling block. This realization was not new. Top management support has been noted as a major factor in most of the publications that describe the requirements for successful "change implementation." Top management zealots who have leadership ability, vision, and motivational qualities are a boon to the movement. They provide the financial support required and understand and support the need for organizational change.

    Recognizing that all levels of management would experience significant cultural change is important, and the degree to which the corporation is prepared for that change is a factor in success. Middle managers have to be prepared for traditional organizational structures to be dissolved and for responsibility to be shifted to the lowest possible level. They, along with their first level supervisors, are required to develop new leadership and problem-solving skills. In most cases, significant training is required, and often when neglected, creates a stumbling block to the movement.

2. Goals and Measurable Objectives. Most of the TQ implementors placed significant emphasis on the setting of lofty, long-range goals, and the development of measurable objectives at all levels of the corporation. In Motorola, the oldest TQ implementor surveyed, the lofty goal was represented by the title of the movement, "Six Sigma," which translated to a 3.4 parts-per-million defect level. The movement began in 1978; the Six Sigma quality goal was set in 1987 and is expected to be a reality by 1992. Westinghouse has extensive translation of top level corporate strategies to meaningful objectives for business units and managers. Hewlett-Packard uses its internal Quality Maturity System to evaluate how well an organization has driven corrective action to address its deficiencies. Several implementors such as Control Data Corporation have incorporated extensive cost of quality initiatives which provide for measurable goals and shared objectives. The message here is the importance of the whole corporation marching to the same drummer.

3. Education and Training. This element is a major factor for all of the TQ implementors. Most companies felt strongly that they did not do enough up-front training. The reality is that it was impossible to train everyone in everything at the same time, and yet the time-phased approach left many needs untouched for a period of time. The difficult problem to be resolved was determining the critical need for each organization at the appropriate time. At Baxter Healthcare, a Quality Working Group was established at the organizational level with specific responsibility for defining the required educational track for their group's employees.

    Most TQ implementors began with a basic awareness program that introduced TQ and continuous improvement, followed by intensive team training in problem solving and group dynamics. The goal of the educational process was to develop each individual's potential to effect positive change within the corporation on a continual basis. This capability began to evolve through training in problem-solving techniques; however, the educational effort was also focused on developing process understanding. The final crucial step was developing each individual's understanding of approaches and techniques currently available to aid in process improvement. These tools included statistical process control, just-in-time techniques, computer-integrated manufacturing solutions, automation, computer modelling and process analysis techniques.

4. Employee Involvement and Action Teams. This element is the highest priority for almost all of the implementors. Problem-solving teams have been credited as the major source of process improvement ideas and cost reduction activities. Most teams were intra-departmental, capitalizing on the idea that employees have a wealth of untapped knowledge about processes within their work units and have an intense desire to influence their immediate surroundings. Ad hoc teams were also formed that were cross-functional, addressing concerns that cut across organizational boundaries. The teams often resembled quality circles, having their roots in that program. Other

team structures were described as integrally joined to the corporate suggestion program, formed primarily as suggestion evaluation teams.

Employee involvement in its purest form was not necessarily team-oriented. Teams were only one vehicle. The goal was to create an atmosphere where employees were informed enough to make crucial decisions that affected their daily work environment, the long-term future of their departments, and ultimately, the entire corporation. Employee involvement encompassed creating an informed workforce with open communication channels. This was accomplished by some implementors through the use of regularly scheduled information forums and newsletters.

5. Customer Emphasis. "Total Quality" must be defined through the eyes of the customer, and in recognition of this fact, all of the TQ implementors have emphasized their focus on the customer. It began by defining who the customer was, internal and external to the corporation. The second factor was customer feedback, and a relentless dedication to using that feedback to enhance customer satisfaction. Emphasis was placed on personal contact with the customer and obtaining regular feedback on individual and corporate performance. The customer, once defined, determined what the expectations were and where performance could be improved. Customers were also extensively surveyed to determine future corporate directions in some cases.

Customers were invited to visit the supplier facilities and conversely, customer sites were visited by corporate representatives to encourage open communication and mutual education. AT&T Atlanta Works has a dynamic program in place that allows customers to come in house and spend a week in the production areas, learning how the products they use are made. The team of "production specialists" that hosts the customers is then allowed to visit the field for a week to learn how the product is used.

At Motorola all of the top executives take part in formal customer visits. This one-on-one contact enhances personal commitment to excellence and trust on both sides. The overall thrust is toward partner relationships rather than adversarial ones.

6. Supplier Certification and Training. Forging closer supplier relationships is also an element of the TQ movement. This concept was recognized as having a significant impact in successful Japanese corporations. The greatest changes have taken place in TQ implementor's purchasing departments. The new philosophy was to reduce the number of suppliers to a minimum and forge close ties with them, using the leverage of their commitment to mandate excellence in quality of performance by the supplier and continuous process improvement. Xerox, following this philosophy, cut its supplier base from 5,000 to 400 over the seven-year period from 1980 to 1987.

The emphasis on this element included supplier reduction programs, supplier certification programs, supplier training offered by the buyer, supplier visits to the buyer facility, long-term contracting vehicles, and overall investment in supplier development. Purchasing agents assumed new responsibilities as trainers and sellers of the TQ movement. In some cases they were used to audit potential suppliers for quality commitment and dedication to continuous improvement. The purchasing departments, in addition to product design departments, represent one of the few examples of "white collar" originated TQ activity.

Several implementors have developed quality criteria by which they rate, classify, and certify suppliers. Florida Power and Light not only classifies its suppliers to allow for competitive advantages, but they also target, record, and track the cumulative number of quality improvement projects completed by suppliers.

7. Recognition and Incentivizing. Recognition and reward structures provided incentive as well as feedback for a job well done, and in turn proved to be motivating factors. The forms of positive reinforcement used by TQ implementors varied significantly. As a baseline, most corporations had a suggestion program in place where cost reduction ideas were solicited and evaluated, and suggestors received monetary awards. This structure operated quite effectively for some implementors; one division of Control Data Corporation stated a 300 percent increase in suggestion program submittals resulting from TQ emphasis. Several implementors have restructured and renamed their suggestion programs to enhance employee involvement in the evaluation process.

Team rewards generally took the form of a celebration activity, however, beyond that generality, there was a degree of diversity and creativity involved in what shape the activity took. Texas Instruments has a recognition function called the Quality Hall of Fame ceremonies. Awards were used by many implementors to recognize and reward significant contributions.

While many of these recurring elements could be anticipated in any TQ implementation, each situation takes on a unique set of characteristics. It is the journey as well as the ultimate destination that determines success. That success takes time and the results are not always quantifiable. Sometimes it is difficult to put a price tag on long-term customer satisfaction. However, that pursuit must not be deterred in favor of short term profits and quantifiable results. The long-term objective of TQ is to institutionalize the culture and technologies that facilitate continuous improvement in the quality of people, products and services.

I.6 CONCLUSION

The Total Quality concept does not provide instant answers. It is not a panacea, quick fix, passing trend, or new management program of the month. It is a framework through which a desired state can be created. It places an organization in a state of continuous improvement to produce customer-defined quality products. The concept was originally developed for manufacturing, but it can be applied in virtually any conceivable context, inclusive of all products and services provided by either the public or private sectors.

The scenarios for applications range from a single relationship to a complex system involving both internal and external customer-supplier relationships. It is both generalizable and internally consistent to a wide spectrum of organizations as evidenced by the seven recurring elements common to the study previously referenced. Each had uniquely diversified circumstances, but each was able to achieve its objective, the institutionalization of a Total Quality culture. That is, a culture that continuously seeks to improve the quality of its people, products, and services. This book is dedicated to that end.

References

1. Moore, W. S., "Singing the Same 'Total Quality' Song," *National Defense,* (1990). Copyright 1990 by American Defense Preparedness Association. Reprinted by permission.
2. DOD 5000.SIG. Final Draft 15 FEB 1991, "TQM Guide," Vol 1, Key Features of the DOD Implementation, 2.
3. Moseman, L. "Importance of Quality Software to the Air Force," National Debate, Achieving Quality Software, San Diego, CA, 1991.
4. DOD 5000.SIG, *op. cit.*
5. Computer Science Corporation, "Total Quality Management: The Competitive Edge for the 90's," 1990.
6. Mann, W. R., *The Keys to Excellence,* Los Angeles: Prestwick Books, 1987.
7. Dobyns, L. "Ed Deming Wants Big Changes, and He Wants Them Fast," *Smithsonian,* 1990, 74-82.
8. Walton, M., *Deming Management at Work,* (New York: G. P. Putnam's Sons, 1990.)
9. Keene, S. "Software Quality Directions," *Western Decision Sciences Institute,* March 1991.
10. Jensen, R. W., "Applying Quality Management Principles to Software Development," *Computer Science,* 1991.
11. Zultner, R., "The Deming Approach to Software Quality Engineering," *Quality Progress,* November 1988, 58-64. Copyright 1988 by Zultner & Company. Reprinted by permission.
12. Deming, W. E., "A System of Profound Knowledge," February 1989.
13. Moore, W. S., *op. cit.*

TOTAL QUALITY MANAGEMENT FOR SOFTWARE

PART I

Quest for Software TQM

1

TQM in Mission Critical Software Development

Emanuel R. Baker, Ph.D.

Software Engineering Consultants, Inc.

1.1 INTRODUCTION

For years, weapon systems ordered by the Department of Defense (DOD) have been plagued by a set of problems that are well known to everyone: systems are delivered late, over budget, and frequently do not function as required when initially delivered. Often, the cause of the problem is software. Because software is an integral part of virtually every weapon system, it has often meant that the weapon systems costs soar, fall behind schedule, or fail to perform as required because of software problems. The consequences of software failures can have disastrous effects on weapon system effectiveness or on human life. Many of the functional problems have been detected and corrected as part of operational test and evaluation, but, in many cases, these tests fall far short of actual combat conditions. Software operation may not be tested under conditions where serious undetected errors would be exposed. We may not really know how these systems will perform until they are exposed to actual battle conditions.

The DOD long ago recognized that a different approach to the management of software was needed. Even as early as 1970, when the Request for Proposal (RFP) for the Site Defense Program was released, explicit requirements for the control and management of software were specified. These included project-unique standards on Software Quality Assurance and Software Configuration Management. The DOD also recognized that any new approach had to be broadly based—addressing many different aspects of the problems associated with software development. A number of initiatives were begun. Some examples are the development of DOD-STD-2167 (and its successor, DOD-STD-2167A) and DOD-STD-2168, the development of Ada, the establishment of the Software Engineering Institute, the development of the capability maturity model and associated software process assessment, and the Software Technology for Adaptable and Reliable Systems (STARS) Program. This chapter addresses the most recent initiative that has been implemented to zero in on the software quality issue: Total Quality Management (TQM).

As will be demonstrated later on in this chapter, many of the approaches mentioned above are really elements of TQM. Consequently, in some ways, the DOD software community was practicing TQM before it became known as TQM. Accordingly, it wasn't difficult for the DOD software community to adapt to the requirement to implement TQM when efforts began in earnest.

1.2 DOD TQM REQUIREMENTS FOR SOFTWARE DEVELOPMENT

The Evolution of the TQM Requirements

TQM, in the DOD, formally began implementation in earnest on March 30, 1988, with the issuance of a memorandum from the then-Secretary of Defense, Frank Carlucci, stating policy on TQM.[1] In it, he stated 12 principles underpinning the initiative, and directed that the Under Secretary of Defense for Acquisitions take the lead for the TQM thrust by implementing it as an integral part of the acquisition process. On August 19, 1988, the Under Secretary of Defense for Acquisitions issued a memorandum[2] outlining the initial steps to be taken in order to implement TQM in the acquisition process, and appointed the Defense Acquisition Board (DAB) as the steering group for TQM in acquisition. Although both memoranda were directed at DOD organizations, it was clear that defense contractors would have complementary actions to take in the implementation of TQM.

A TQM Master Plan[3] was issued in August of 1988, and a draft Acquisition Strategy[4] was issued in November of the same year. Several implementing documents for use within the individual services have been released (for example, Reference 5), addressing organizational issues related to the implementation of TQM to the acquisition process. Reference 6 is a Navy document addressing the application of TQM to internal logistics processes. Drafts of a DOD policy (policies are promulgated via the mechanism of DOD directives) have been written and put into perspective, but have not been released as of this writing. Nonetheless, the recent updates of DOD Directive (DODD) 5000[137] and its implementing set of instructions, DOD Instruction (DODI) 5000.2,[38] incorporate many of the principles of TQM and apply them to the acquisition process for major systems. No specific mention of TQM is made in these documents, however.

Formal, standardized requirements for TQM for contractors, per se, do not exist. Formal requirements to be imposed on contractors are usually stated in the form of a DOD or Military Standard or Specification, which is then imposed on the development effort via the contract Statement of Work (SOW). Instead, the DOD has specifically adopted the approach of not issuing formal regulations, directives, specifications, or standards. Per the Master Plan[3] and the draft Acquisition Strategy,[4] the main thrust of the DOD effort is to upgrade existing documents to incorporate TQM principles, where appropriate, and to ensure that all implementing documentation, i.e., regulations, directives, specifications, and standards, are all consistent with each other. The recent updates to DODD 5000.1 and DODI 5000.2 are consistent with that approach. A draft guidebook, DOD 5000.51-G,[7] has been circulated within the DOD for review, and although neither the policy nor the guidebook have been officially released, many of the principles are being implemented. Because DOD 5000.51-G is a guidebook, technically, it can only be used for guidance, and cannot be imposed on a contract as a compliance document. Contractors have essentially recognized that their TQM programs more or less have to coincide with the principles contained in it.

The TQM requirements for mission critical software development derive from the TQM requirements imposed on the development of systems, but, here also, no formal requirements exist. Part 6, Section D, of DODI 5000.2[38] incorporates TQM principles for mission critical software, but does not explicitly impose a requirement for a TQM program. Some recent procurements have required that elements of a TQM program be implemented, but these requirements have been imposed through the SOW or other contractual documentation. Because no formal requirements exist, most DOD software contractors have not been implementing TQM for software in any organized manner. Where the requirement for TQM has existed, the various documents cited above (as well as others) have been consulted for guidance.

It is an unfortunate fact of life that in the defense industry, beneficial change often seems to come about mainly in response to DOD actions, and not as a voluntary undertaking. That seems to be the case here, too. Although there are some exceptions, that which has been accomplished appears to have been in response to various DOD programs. We are, however, beginning to see many of the tools associated with TQM, such as statistical process control, Ishikawa diagrams, Pareto analysis, run charts, etc.,[6,7] being implemented by a number of companies.[28,33]

Common Elements of TQM

Every document on TQM issued by the DOD plows virtually the same ground, but states the focus of the effort somewhat differently. The Carlucci memorandum[1] stated the DOD posture on quality; it contained 12 points. A DOD pamphlet on TQM[8] identifies a slightly different basic set of 9 principles. Reference 6 lists Deming's management principles. As identified in the reference, there are 14 principles (16, if sub-groupings are counted) that relate to Total Quality. Volume II

TABLE 1-1   Common Elements of DOD TQM Program

- Quality is everybody's business. There must be a quality awareness throughout the entire organization.
- The focus of the development effort must be on satisfying internal and external customer needs, requirements, and expectations—not just on meeting specifications.
- Quality must be built into the product. It cannot be inspected or tested into it. A greater emphasis is placed on proaction, i.e., the prevention of defects, than on inspection.
- Quality improvement requires management commitment and involvement at all levels. It must be implemented from the top down in every organization. Management must be the leaders in implementing Total Quality.
- The accomplishment of TQM involves training: training in its principles and in the tools and techniques for implementing TQM, as well as training in the fundamentals of how an employee performs his or her job.
- Slogans, exhortations, management by objective, and targets such as zero defects should be eliminated. They create adversarial relationships. Leadership should be substituted, instead.
- The long-term emphasis must be on measurable process and productivity improvement. The entire organization should be dedicated to continuous process and productivity improvement.
- Process improvement begins by understanding the current process first. Process measurements are an essential element for accomplishing this.
- A cross-functional orientation and teamwork (action teams) are essential for continuous improvement in quality. Artificial barriers between functional organizations hamper the team approach.
- Constancy of purpose toward improvement of process, products, and services are essential. They must be recognized and rewarded.
- Suppliers must be indoctrinated in the principles of TQM. Suppliers are members of the team.

of DOD 5000.51-G[7] identifies 11 principles that are part of the Total Quality Management Model for continuous improvement. Moore[9] (also see Introduction to this book) identifies 7 critical elements of Total Quality common among 10 corporations that are leaders in implementing Total Quality in this country. Although each of the documents appears to say somewhat different things, there are common threads that run through the documents. Table 1-1 lists these common elements. These are the themes that are the focus of the DOD effort on Total Quality. These same themes apply to the development of mission critical software.

The accomplishment of the TQM objectives depends on the application of theory and concepts, technology, people, planning, and organization (see Figure 1-1). It also requires management commitment in order to obtain and commit the required resources, and to promote the implementation of the TQM policies. The theory behind TQM and the concepts associated with it, such as prevention and early detection of errors, continuous improvement, focus on the customer, etc., target the effort. Technology, such as statistical analysis, Plan-Do-Check-Act (PDCA), are the tools by which the objectives are accomplished. The company must be organized to accomplish the objectives, from top management on down. People supply the resources necessary to accomplish the objectives. They must be motivated, mobilized, and trained to accomplish its objectives. TQM cannot be accomplished without a plan. The plans must specify the vision and the long-term, medium range, and short-term goals. Clearly, management commitment is a most

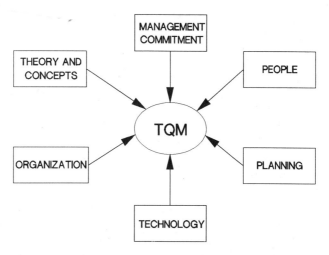

FIGURE 1-1. Resources needed to implement TQM.

vital resource. Without it, attaining the TQM objectives will become a Sisyphean labor. All these elements must be collectively applied to the TQM effort.

It is interesting to note, at this juncture, the work of the International Organization for Standardization (ISO) in their development of ISO Standard 9000-3[41] and the standard for information technology software life cycle processes (as yet unnumbered).[42] ISO Standard 9000-3 is a quality management and software quality assurance standard to be applied to software developed under contract. The other standard defines standardized acquisition, development, operation, and maintenance processes that should be applied to the development of software. In some respects, these are TQM standards. Many of the principles identified in Table 1-1 are contained in the drafts of these standards, such as process and product measurement, process improvement, training, etc. The life cycle processes standard goes one step further and suggests the implementation of a cost of quality program.[7, 43] Cost of quality, a technique utilized by very few companies in the U.S. (IBM and Motorola being notable exceptions), is a means of determining the cost effectiveness of many of the error prevention activities. Through the use of process measures, product quality data, and applying Pareto analyses, those activities which provide the greatest benefit in terms of error occurrence reduction can be identified. It allows organizations to concentrate their efforts on those activities that provide the greatest benefit.

With much of the world utilizing ISO Standards, there has been talk that these standards could eventually replace the DOD standards for software development and software quality. It is conceivable that this could occur, although no official position has been adopted. DOD and other government personnel are participating in the development and/or review of these standards. If nothing else, they are at least attempting to influence the content to ensure that DOD and other federal agency concerns are covered.

1.3 TQM CONCEPTS APPLIED TO MISSION CRITICAL SOFTWARE DEVELOPMENT

In this section, we will look at how these common themes are being implemented by the DOD and by the defense contractors. Each of the themes identified in the previous section must be implemented by weapon systems contractors in the development of mission critical software in order to achieve a viable TQM program.

What the following sections will describe are activities initiated by the DOD related to Total Quality, the response of the defense industry to these initiatives, as well as actions initiated by defense contractors and companies in the commercial sector to achieve Total Quality. Within the DOD, none of these activities are formally subsumed under a Total Quality Management program. They are separate, unintegrated activities that, for the most part, were initiated prior to the Carlucci memorandum. Collectively, however, they add up to a Total Quality approach. By and large, the software industry as a whole has not implemented integrated TQM programs. Exceptions do exist, however. A small number of companies have implemented total programs (see, for example, Chapter 3). Other companies have implemented separate pieces of the concepts described below.

A greater emphasis is needed by companies in the software industry on applying and integrating all the concepts of TQM into an integrated whole. This is true for both the defense industry and the commercial sector, as well.

Quality is Everybody's Business

The theme that quality is everybody's business was at the heart of the development of DOD-STD-2167A and DOD-STD-2168. The effort to develop these standards was kicked off by the Monterey I Software Workshop, which was held in April of 1979 at the Naval Post-Graduate School in Monterey, CA. Recognizing that the standards existing at that time tended to be service-specific, and contained conflicting requirements, the Joint Logistics Commanders (JLC) convened the workshop to address these and related issues. The intent was to investigate the feasibility of creating a single, unambiguous set of standards for software development and quality assurance.

To accomplish these objectives, representatives from both the defense industry and the various affected DOD organizations were invited, demonstrating quite clearly that quality was everybody's concern. The resultant product had to be acceptable to both the DOD and industry.

Of the four panels convened at the workshop, two were dedicated to software quality and acceptance criteria. There was a clear recognition of the failings of traditional inspection-oriented software quality assurance in achieving quality software. Clearly, a "quality assurance" approach that emphasized the evaluation of completed or nearly-completed products yielded very little in the way of dividends. At best, this approach could incompletely detect and correct errors already built into the software (at great cost), but could not reduce or prevent the occurrence of errors. What was needed was a "quality assurance" approach that considered not only conformance to specifications, plans, and procedures, but also considered process quality and fitness for use of the product.

The outcome of the workshop resulted in several different initiatives, culminating in the development of DOD-STD-2167, and the effort which ultimately led to DOD-STD-2168. The philosophy underlying the development of these two standards was elaborated in a number of papers and presentations by Baker and Fisher, Baker and Cooper, and Cooper—some of which are cited in the references.[10, 11, 12, 13, 14] All of these publications clearly stated the need for a structure that was geared toward building quality into the software. All cited the importance of process. All cited the need to evaluate not only the evolving product, but the processes that produced the product, as well.

At the heart of this was the Software Quality Program, which, as originally described in these publications, is different from the Software Quality Program described in DOD-STD-2168.[15] In actuality, no definition of the Software Quality Program exists in DOD-STD-2168, but the objectives of it, as stated in the standard, appear to be more inspection-oriented than process quality-oriented. Evaluations of the products of the development process are required. Process evaluations are also required by DOD-STD-2168, but the purpose of the evaluations seems to be aimed primarily at compliance with plans and procedures, rather than process adequacy. However, when the two standards are applied together (DOD-STD-2167A and DOD-STD-2168), there is a significant improvement over conditions which existed before their advent. At least now there is a recognition of the importance of process for the quality of software, acknowledgement of the importance of documenting what the selected processes are and how they are to be implemented, and a stated need to verify that the processes are implemented as documented.

The original Software Quality Program consisted of three elements:

- The establishment, maintenance, and enforcement of requirements for the development of the software.
- The establishment, implementation, and enforcement of methodologies and processes for the development, operation, and maintenance of the software.
- The establishment and implementation of methodologies, practices, and procedures to evaluate the products of the software development effort and the processes used in the development.

This philosophy was stated in the original version of DOD-STD-2167,[16] released in June of 1985.* It was also stated in more detail in a draft of a guidebook that was circulated with MIL-STD-SQAM, an early draft version of DOD-STD-2168 that came out in October of 1982. The explanatory information in the guidebook, and the references cited elsewhere in this section, all pointed out the multidisciplinary nature of software quality: the fact that the process of building quality in is more critical for achieving a quality product than is inspection. While inspections and tests are important activities, all they will achieve is the identification of errors already built-in. The greatest pay-off is in performing development activities that

---

*For a historical perspective of these standards, see Reference 36.

will prevent errors from occurring, and this involves the cooperative effort of a number of different disciplines.

The present combination of DOD-STD-2167A and DOD-STD-2168 still more or less implement that philosophy, although it is not as explicit as it was in DOD-STD-2167, MIL-STD-SQAM, and associated draft guidebooks.

Throughout the history of the development of DOD-STD-2167, DOD-STD-2167A, and DOD-STD-2168, the defense industry and the DOD cooperated jointly in the review and revision process. Industry was a full partner in the effort to review the drafts of these standards. The initial release of DOD-STD-2167, for example, occurred only after a plan to resolve the issues raised by industry was worked out between the JLC and the participating industry groups. Once again, the concept that "quality is everybody's business" was dramatically demonstrated.

Another factor reflecting the concept that "quality is everybody's business" is the introduction of concurrent engineering and integrated systems design. With these approaches, the requirements definition and system design processes have been expanded to include considerations of not only functionality and performance, but also supportability, maintainability, operation, and manufacturing. As applied to software, this means that the development effort must include consideration of how the software will be maintained, the support facilities and equipment necessary to maintain the software at various levels of support (e.g., depot-level maintenance), as well as any unique requirements for operating the software (if applicable). This is another manifestation of the multidisciplinary approach to software quality, where the concerns of the logisticians, maintainers, and operators of the software are brought to bear on the requirements definition and design processes.

The efficacy of applying concurrent engineering has been unquestionably demonstrated. Table 1-2 lists seven case studies which show dramatic cost and schedule savings, and quality improvements resulting from the application of concurrent engineering.[34]

Prior to the introduction of concurrent engineering and integrated system design, the functional and performance requirements were the main focus of the development effort. Any other considerations were an afterthought or were ignored totally. As a consequence, delivered software was difficult to maintain or operate (or both). When operational or maintenance problems exist in the software, the software is not perceived as quality software. This occurs even if the software has been designed in accordance with functional and performance requirements.[11]

The introduction of concurrent engineering and integrated system design has forced software development organizations to look more carefully at the development effort. It has required early consideration of many concerns. Recent RFPs have required contractors to describe their plans for supportability as part of their proposal response. The Advanced Interdiction Weapon System RFP is a good example of this. Software supportability had to be described not only in the Logistics Support Analysis Plan, but also in the Software Development Plan.

Yet another factor reflecting the concept that "quality is everybody's business" is risk management. Risk reduction is an integral part of the effort to improve the

TABLE 1-2   Concurrent Engineering

Case Study	Cost	Schedule	Quality
McDonnell Douglas	60% Savings on bid for reactor and missile projects	Significant savings (reduction from 45 weeks to 8 hours) in one phase of high-speed vehicle preliminary design; 18 month saving on TAV-8B design	Scrap reduced 58%, rework cost reduced 29%, and non-conformances reduced 38%: weld defects per unit decreased 70% 68% fewer changes on reactor: 68% fewer drawing changes on TAV-8B
Boeing Ballistic Systems Division	Reduced labor rates by $28/hour; cost savings 30% below bid	Part and materials lead-time reduced by 30%: one part of design analysis reduced by over 90%	Floor inspection ratio decreased by over ²⁄₃: material shortages reduced from 12% to 0: 99% defect-free operation
AT&T*	Cost of repair for new circuit pack production cut at least 40%	Total process time reduced to 46% of baseline for 5ESS	Defects reduced by 30% to 87%
Deere & Company	30% actual savings in development cost for construction equipment	60% savings in development time	Number of inspectors reduced by ²⁄₃
Hewlett-Packard Co., Instrument Division	Manufacturing costs reduced 42%	Reduced development cycle time 35%	Product field failure rate reduced 60%: scrap and rework reduced 75%
IBM	Product direct assembly labor hours reduced 45%	Significant reduction in length of PMT design cycle: 40% reduction in electronic design cycle	Fewer engineering changes: guaranteed producibility and testability
Northrop	30% savings on bid on a major project	Part and assembly schedule reduced by 50% on two major subassemblies: span-time reduced by 60%	Number of engineering changes reduced by 45%: defects reduced by 35%

*See Chapter 14 herein.

quality of mission critical software. Risk mitigation is a cooperative effort between the government and the contractor. Risk identification and management involves program office, user, contractor, and support organizations to ensure timely identification of risk drivers, development of effective risk abatement plans, and assessment of risk reduction activities. In some cases, risk sharing between the contractor and the customer is utilized as a means of reducing the risk. Each party will assume some part of the identified risk abatement action. On the government side of the picture, this will usually take the form of a contract-related action, such as use of a cost plus fixed fee form of contract (instead of any other form), or use of multiple award contracts where the technology risk is quite high. Where schedule is an important consideration, the elimination of multiple best and final offers may be selected as the means of sharing the risk in order to start the program faster. Risk management will be discussed further in subsequent sections.

Satisfying Customer Needs

Clear-cut mechanisms for satisfying customer needs do not readily exist yet within the contractual framework established by the DOD. In this framework, organic acquisition commands procure systems for the services, and act as go-betweens between strategic planners (those who conceive the ideas for the new weapon systems), the commands who will be the ultimate users, and the development contractor to develop the system requirements. The acquisition command captures their understanding of the requirements in the form of specifications. Most development efforts are geared toward satisfying the contents of requirements specifications. Implicit in this approach is the concept that the requirements specifications correctly state the needs of the customers. This may not necessarily be true. It all depends on how firm the requirements for the system are when they are established at the beginning of the development effort. It also depends on the requirements analysis skill of the acquisition command personnel assigned to the project.

In developing weapon systems, we are always expanding the envelope of capability. In order for a weapon system to be effective, it must always be at least one step ahead of the enemy's capability. The determination of the enemy's capability is always evolving, since it is highly dependent on intelligence information. Furthermore, we are not dealing with a static offensive or defensive posture on the part of potential enemies. It is not always possible, therefore, to have a precisely specified set of requirements at the start of the development effort. Requirements will always change.

Requirements, to correctly reflect customer needs, have to be developed in conjunction with the customer or user. The goal is to have the customer *influence* the requirements definition process to ensure that the software development process produces software that will meet the true needs of the customer. Methodologies for accomplishing this goal, such as quality function deployment (QFD),[17] have been developed for application to commercial hardware systems. QFD seeks to hear the "voice of the customer." The "voice of the customer" is then deployed throughout the development and manufacturing process. This is accomplished as follows: high level customer needs are defined by customer comments and feedback, and customer surveys. These are refined into lower level, more detailed requirements which are then associated with specific functions in the design and manufacturing processes. Measures which determine if these functions are being properly accomplished are defined. By recording and analyzing these measures, it is possible to determine if the evolving product will meet the customer's needs.

This is not to say that there are hard and fast measures that can be used for all aspects of the quality function deployment. Some measures may be more qualitative than quantitative in nature. Furthermore, measures used to estimate how well an evolving hardware system will satisfy the customer's needs are likely to be more definitive than measures used for software.

Methodologies for applying QFD to software have been proposed by Yoshizawa[18] and Zultner,[19] but are still in their infancy. At the present time, there is not much research into applying methodologies such as QFD to the development of software requirements to better reflect "the voice of the customer"—at least not in the development of requirements for mission critical software. Chapter 12 of this book provides an overview of the application of QFD to software.

Risk management is another important element in the effort to ensure that mission critical software satisfies customer needs. The intent is to identify, control, and reduce the risks associated with the development of weapon systems. Requirements for implementing a risk management program for weapon systems are stated in DODI 5000.2.[38] Specific methods for implementing risk abatement are contained in service-specific regulations and pamphlets. An example of instructions for implementing risk abatement for software is contained in Reference 39, which is an Air Force document. This pamphlet specifies four components of risk: performance, schedule, cost, and support. One intent of the risk abatement process is to ensure that software and operational requirements affected by these risk components are identified and that the development process is geared toward monitoring progress toward abating these risks. All proposed risk abatement solutions must be acceptable to the affected parties.

In closing the discussion contained in this section, it is important to point out that there is an obstacle unique to weapon systems development that makes it difficult to develop requirements cooperatively between customer, user, and contractor. Figure 1-2 illustrates the problem. Budgetary considerations mandate that costs for weapon systems acquisition be well defined prior to their development.

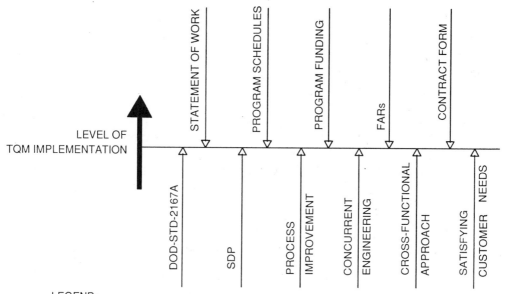

LEGEND:
FAR - FEDERAL ACQUISITION REGULATION
SDP - SOFTWARE DEVELOPMENT PLAN

FIGURE 1-2. Opposing forces affecting ability to cooperatively develop requirements (customer and contractor).

Effectively, this means that hard and fast functional and performance requirements need to exist as a reference point in order for contractors to develop a proposal for the system. These generally appear in the form of a system specification (or a Software Requirements Specification (SRS) in the case of software procurements) and a SOW. Bidders develop their cost estimates based on the content of these documents. Once the contract is awarded, these documents essentially become a baseline for the development of the system, and any changes to the system specification, SRS, or SOW affecting cost or schedule become a contract change. Such an arrangement lends itself to an adversarial relationship between the customer and the contractor. The Government Project Office does not want to pay more money for the system, or allow the contractor to slip schedules, and the contractor does not want to do additional work for no pay and no schedule relief. This holds true even in the case where development of the system begins on the basis of draft specifications. Clearly, in the case where a system's requirements have not been fully defined (which describes the vast majority of weapon system developments), different forms of contract vehicles or contracting relationships will have to exist if "the voice of the user" is to be adequately heard in weapon system procurements.

Some progress along these lines have been made. The process model used by TRW in the development of the Command Center Processing and Display System-Replacement (CCPDS-R) software[20] is one approach for involving the user in the development of the software requirements. While it is not a model that is applicable to all situations, it does reflect a creative approach to the problem.

Quality Must Be Built Into the Product

This is the focus of DOD-STD-2167A and DOD-STD-2168, as discussed above in Quality is Everybody's Business, as well as MIL-STD-1803. These standards emphasize the activities necessary to build quality into the software, and the evaluation activities required for determining if that has been accomplished.

The STARS project also has this an an objective, as well. STARS (which is now under the aegis of the Defense Advanced Research Projects Agency/Information Science and Technology Office (DARPA/ISTO)), through its focus on technology, is seeking the means to assist the developer in building quality into the software. Some of the technology areas which fall under the cognizance of STARS include domain-specific software architectures, common prototyping systems, formal methods, and advanced environments (see Long-term Process and Productivity Improvement, discussed later in this section, for more details). Technology which is developed under the sponsorship of STARS will translate to defense contractors under initiatives sponsored by DARPA.

Management Commitment

Successful implementation of TQM requires management commitment. TQM will not take hold if lip service alone is paid to its implementation. Often, all the trappings will exist to imply management's commitment to one philosophy or another, but the demonstrated enforcement of it is not evident. For example, a software standards and procedures manual may exist in an organization, but there is no expressed mandate from management to follow it. Consequently, it becomes so much window dressing, and the developers do not feel that they are expected to follow it. Management commitment to TQM must be demonstrated by policies that originate at the very top of the organization, and then are implemented at all levels of the organization through management and supervisory direction. During times of "schedule crunch," the policies should not be abandoned. Rather, policies exist to define the contingent conditions, and how the organization will respond under these conditions.

Management commitment within the DOD has been evident from the start. References 1 through 5 are examples of how the requirement to implement TQM has progressed in a top-down fashion. Virtually every agency and major acquisition command within the DOD has a focal point for TQM, and infrastructures for achieving its objectives have been established. Reference 6 is a guidebook for use within the Navy on establishing executive steering committees, quality management boards, and process action teams. It describes their functions and gives examples of tools available to accomplish their roles. Reference 5 identifies areas of activity within the Army Materiel Command where working groups would be established to improve the acquisition process.

Management commitment within the defense industry has also been growing. It has also been growing in the commercial sector of the business world, as well. Reference 9 lists ten leading companies implementing TQM. These include both defense contractors and commercially-oriented enterprises. Interestingly enough, these companies have been involved in the Total Quality movement for 5 to 10 years, indicating an awareness of the necessity for such an approach long before Secretary Carlucci designated TQM as a top-priority objective. More companies are getting on the bandwagon. This results from not only the need to comply with DOD requirements, but also from a growing recognition that foreign competition necessitates a different approach to doing business.

Management commitment is an integral part of the Software Engineering Institute's (SEI) software process assessment methodology (see the section entitled Long-term Process and Productivity Improvement). Software process assessments are conducted for the purpose of establishing the current status of the development process as a means of determining what improvements in the process are necessary. Without the commitment of top management to support the assessment (through commitment of the appropriate personnel, resources, and attendance at selected meetings), the assessment will not be conducted. Top management is also forewarned that conducting the assessment without a commitment to changes commensurate with the findings is a waste of time and money on their part. Considering the number of organizations that have had assessments conducted, this is even further evidence of the fact that management of U.S. defense contractors is getting on the TQM bandwagon.

Training

A great deal of emphasis is being placed on training. Training in Total Quality Management is being offered in the form of in-house training and public seminars and conferences. In-house training is being performed within the DOD, including such programs as those offered by the Defense Logistics Agency (DLA), for the benefit of affected personnel within a given agency or organization. In-house training programs are also being acquired by defense contractors and commercial organizations, as well. Within the public sector, a number of courses and seminars are being offered by professional training organizations, university extension programs, and technical/professional societies. Both hardware and software courses in TQM are being offered. These are courses that discuss TQM as a totality, and look into the history of TQM, its principles, and its methods. However, based on a survey of course offerings from approximately 20 professional training organizations, professional societies, and universities, through the first quarter of 1991, far more public courses on traditional inspection-oriented quality assurance were offered than were offered on TQM. Many courses cover individual topics that compose TQM, but are not part of a TQM instruction program per se.

As the DOD focus on TQM becomes more intensive, this will likely change, and more public courses on TQM will become available.

On the other hand, as the defense budget shrinks in the decade of the 1990s, the availability of funds to support training programs at defense contractor facilities will also shrink. Two outcomes have been observed as companies begin to cut budgets for education and training: (1) at some companies, the number of people going through education and training in various aspects of TQM, or other software engineering disciplines, for that matter, are shrinking in proportion to the shrinkage of the budget, and (2) for other companies, alternative sources for education and training are being sought. In the first instance, no alternative plans for training exist. Training is not considered to be a priority, which is a major obstacle to achieving Total Quality. In the second instance, training is still considered to be of relatively high priority, and instructors from within the organization are utilized in a mixture of working time and after-hours programs to provide the training. What little training funds are available are utilized to acquire training in areas where critical expertise is not available within the company.

Long-term Process and Productivity Improvement

Many people, when they think of TQM, think of it as being synonymous with continuous process improvement. It is an understandable oversimplification. Clearly, it is a very important aspect of TQM. By concentrating on process improvement, it is possible to gain better control of the critical processes in use and reduce the variability of the products which are the outputs of the processes. In this manner, we can begin to improve the quality of the end products.

In the hardware manufacturing world, process improvement is more straightforward than in the software world. To accomplish process improvement for hardware, one starts out with a manufacturing process, measures output and performance, establishes control limits, and attempts to reduce variability by controlling inputs into the process, or by making adjustments to the process itself and its parameters. Models of the process can be established and investigated either on-line or off-line to evaluate current performance or the effects of proposed changes. When the statistical data clearly point out deviations from acceptable expectations, adjustments to the process can be suggested and implemented in the model.

In the software world, the development process, in some ways, can be thought of as a "manufacturing" process. It is, after all, the culmination of the development process that effectively results in the completed software product. The software development process is a highly intellectual, labor-intensive activity. The concept of improving the software engineering process requires more ingenuity. Precise, unambiguous statistical data on development processes are harder to obtain and require more interpretation. The ambiguity of process data, and the need for supporting data for interpretation purposes was pointed very effectively in a paper delivered at the Second Annual Software Quality Workshop by John McGarry of the Naval Underwater Systems Center.[40] McGarry presented data from a specific project which, at face value, indicated that the process of performing walkthroughs resulted in a significant reduction of residual errors, based on errors reported during testing. A more detailed analysis showed that the reduction in errors was an artifact. Budget and schedule constraints forced a curtailment of the test program, meaning that many of the residual errors went undetected.

Another consideration is that the repetitive elements of a manufacturing process (which lends itself to be statistically controlled) do not occur in the development process for a specific software product. The elements occur once in the development process. Lessons learned from applying statistical control to the manufacturing process can be implemented directly into a future production run of that product as a product modification. Lessons learned from applying statistical control to the software development process will generally only reflect themselves in a future product to be developed.

Many of the failures in weapon systems tend to originate as human error, in that their origin is often in deficiencies in establishing requirements, shortcomings in translating the requirements into design, failure to coordinate all aspects of system development, and the like. Whereas automation of the hardware production activity is very highly achievable, automation of the intellectual activities that comprise the software development process is much harder to achieve. It is those human-controlled processes that we are attempting to put under better control in order to reduce the impact of human shortcomings. Accordingly, the need for practices such as prototyping, incremental development, and in-process reviews at the earliest stages of the development process become more important.

It is important to point out that hardware development suffers from some of the same problems as software. Hardware design is also a labor-intensive intellectual undertaking. The ability to measure and control those processes is also limited. The major difference between hardware and software, however, is that after the hardware is designed, a prototype of the system can be built and evaluated before committing to production. Its shortcomings can be corrected before it becomes a finished product. With software, we really do not have that luxury, since the development effort culminates in the completed product. What it does point out, however, is the need to evaluate and establish better processes for software development (such as requirements prototyping or incremental development) to ensure that the requirements are correct before we commit to design, and to ensure that the design is correct before we commit to code.

There needs to be a stronger focus on long-term process and productivity improvement among U.S. defense contractors. In fact, all of U.S. industry could benefit from this approach. With regard to software, a very strong case can be made for this when one considers the enormous success that the Japanese have had from focusing on long-term process and productivity improvement.[23, 31, 33] A concept which is very prevalent in Japanese industry is the concept of Kaizen. Very loosely translated, it means "in for the long haul." The Japanese are not driven by short-term bottom line considerations, and are more concerned with obtaining a greater percentage of the market share for their products. Accordingly, they target for moderate annual gains in productivity and corresponding improvements in quality spread out over a medium range period. For example, Hitachi realized an order of magnitude improvement in software development productivity, and a significant reduction in errors, in approximately a five-year period. The implications of these kinds of improvements on cost, schedule, and quality for mission critical software cannot be ignored.

A number of initiatives to promote process and productivity improvement have been implemented by the DOD. These include the promulgation of DOD-STD-2167A, DOD-STD-2168, and MIL-STD-1803, development of computer-aided software engineering (CASE) tools, supporting environments, Ada, software process assessments, Software Engineering Process Groups (SEPGs), risk management, and benchmarking.

The focus of these efforts has been not only on software development, but on software maintenance, as well. In effect, software maintenance constitutes a miniature software development effort. Whether we are looking at error correction, capability enhancement, or the addition of new capabilities, each one of these activities has a software development cycle associated with it. In the case of simple error correction, this will be a highly abbreviated cycle, whereas the addition of major new capabilities will constitute a full-blown development cycle. When we improve process and productivity, we are reducing life-cycle costs in a number of ways. First, we are shortening development time, thus reducing development cost. By improving process, we are improving the quality of the software and reducing errors, and decreasing maintenance costs. Since the same processes are used for maintenance as are used for development, the improvements in productivity and process reflect themselves in reduced maintenance costs.[35]

Before beginning the discussion of these initiatives, it is important to consider one final item. We must not lose sight of one essential element: people. We can determine what the best possible processes are and implement them, but if the people responsible for implementing them are not properly motivated, well-trained, or competent, it becomes a meaningless exercise. Conversely, if we have the best possible people, but provide them with only mediocre tools for getting the job done, we are not taking proper advantage of their talents. To get the maximum benefit, we need a proper balance between people and process. We need to have the right processes in place, but we also need to have the right people on the job to utilize them.

DOD-STD-2167A, DOD-STD-2168, and MIL-STD-1803

The intent behind developing and promulgating DOD-STD-2167A and DOD-STD-2168 was geared toward process improvement. The concerns which led to the JLC Monterey I Software Workshop centered on the fact that delivered software was usually over budget, behind schedule, of poor quality, and both costly and difficult to maintain. A number of reasons were advanced for this situation. One was that no single set of standards existed within the DOD to govern software acquisition. The standards tended to be service-specific and were sometimes conflicting. Consequently, contractors had to maintain several systems for developing software, which adversely impacted productivity. Another contributing factor was that there were indications that contractors were not using orderly processes to develop software. An American Institute of Aeronautics and Astronautics (AIAA) study conducted in the early 1980s (cited in Reference 14) indicated that, at that time, 27% of defense contractors did not use any development standards at all. From this, one could conclude that these companies did not utilize any codified methodologies for software development. The same study also showed that 30% of the contractors utilized project standards, but did not have company-wide standards. A conclusion that could be drawn from this is that these companies applied organized methodologies on an ad hoc basis. A further conclusion that could be drawn from this is that the quality of the delivered software product varied from project to project.

As pointed out previously, DOD-STD-2167A requires the contractor to implement proven processes in software development. The original, released version of DOD-STD-2167 specifically required the use of top-down structured methodologies. DOD-STD-2167A requires the contractor to "implement a process for managing the development of deliverable software." It further requires the contractor to use systematic and well-documented software development methods for each phase of the development effort. The methodologies that are to be applied to the project are to be documented in the Software Development Plan (SDP), which makes them subject to review and approval by the government project office. The net effect is recognition of the importance of process for software quality.

MIL-STD-1803,[22] "Software Development Integrity Program (SDIP)", is an Air Force Standard which originated at the Aeronautical Systems Division of the Air Force Systems Command. It is not part of the JLC initiatives, but originated, rather, as a consequence of the Aeronautical Systems Division's bad experience with avionics and other airborne software product quality. This standard has been applied to several major aircraft acquisition programs, such as the C-130 gunship and the Advanced Tactical Fighter. MIL-STD-1803 augments DOD-STD-2167A and is to be used in conjunction with it. It goes further than DOD-STD-2167A regarding development processes. For each phase of both the system life cycle and the software development cycle, it indicates the kinds of activities for which the contractor should have codified processes in place, and requires that they be documented in the SDP. For instance, the SDIP does not require prototyping to develop requirements, but strongly suggests that the contractor consider it. It requires that the contractor "identify areas which require prototyping and demonstration to establish software requirements," and then requires the contractor to perform prototyping and demonstration accordingly.

The defense contracting community has received these three standards with mixed reactions. Very few contractors like to have standards imposed on them that, in effect, govern how they do business. Many contractors downright dislike DOD-STD-2167A and DOD-STD-2168. Others, understanding the purpose behind them, accept them with that understanding. Some actually like MIL-STD-1803 and feel that it is a better standard than DOD-STD-2167A. In any event, a major thrust of the JLC effort has been realized with these standards: a greater emphasis has been placed on process by the contractors.

Stars

The original concept behind the STARS Program was to accomplish the following:

- Improve productivity
- Improve quality and reliability
- Promote development and application of reusable software
- Reduce time and cost of developing defense software.

As originally conceived, it was a rather ambitious project, with a number of on-going activities to support these goals. Support was enlisted from both industry and academia from its very beginning to (1) take advantage of their knowledge and expertise, (2) ensure the program's success by enlisting their aid in the planning of the effort, and (3) benefit from new developments in the software engineering disciplines emerging from studies and research being conducted by academia and industry.

Budget cuts have scaled back the program somewhat; however, activity is nonetheless being concentrated in three areas:

1. Understanding the software process
2. Developing software engineering environment (SEE) architectures consisting of a framework of virtual interfaces, populated with tools designed to aid in the design and implementation of Ada software
3. Creating repository mechanisms to store reusable software assets that were readily retrievable for incorporation into new systems.

Much emphasis was placed on developing environments and defining metrics to support process improvement.

The SEI was an element of the STARS Program, as originally implemented. It was conceived as being a joint effort of academia and the DOD, and was established in 1984 at Carnegie Mellon University. One of the better known activities of the SEI is, of course, software process assessments. Another major responsibility assigned to the SEI is transitioning new software technology to industry. The importance of this latter activity for accomplishing the objectives of the DOD TQM effort with regard to defense contractors goes without saying.

In April of 1988, responsibility for the STARS Program was transferred to DARPA. Also in August of that year, contracts were let to Boeing, IBM, and Unisys to begin development of some of the elements of the STARS Program. Efforts during the time period of 1988 through 1990 were primarily exploratory in nature. Starting in April of 1990, emphasis shifted to fostering commercially available solutions to the DOD problems. At the present time, each of the contractors is responsible for the following:

BOEING
1. Continuing the evolution of the specification set for the SEE.
2. Exploring technologies for application to the SEE. Included are Object Management Systems for capturing data and tool integration, X-Windows, and the Andrew File System. Experiments will be conducted on the Engineering Information System to determine its ability to integrate tools in the SEE.
3. Investigating applicability of object manager technology.

IBM
1. SEE domain analysis to develop a Domain Model, which will include a standard vocabulary, taxonomy, generic high level function model, and a preliminary generic architecture.
2. Integrate commercial off-the-shelf (COTS) products and "value added" efforts by the three contractors into an initial set of environment capabilities.
3. Gather, refine, and catalog reusable assets from various sources into a reuse library. Included is development of interchange standards between the library and the SEEs.

UNISYS
1. Integrate into the SEE tools that support formal mathematical verification of Ada software designs.
2. Evolve an open system SEE architecture and develop an environment prototype. Develop virtual interface standards to permit STARS to work with the vendor community to implement these standards for new components.
3. Develop a prototype domain model for Navy C^2 systems as a sample application domain.

Ada
The development of the Ada language involved not only a language, but an environment of tools and utilities to support its use. Here again, a DOD initiative

involved a cooperative effort between academia, industry, and the DOD.[44] Each version of the Ada language requirements specification was reviewed by the widest possible audience of experts not only in the U.S., but in Europe as well, to ensure the adequacy and accuracy of the specification. Competition for the design of the language was opened to the international community. Evaluation of the requirements and design was invited from the North American and European industrial and academic community. Conferences to support the review of the requirements and the design were sponsored by various universities. Four teams were chosen to develop the language, with the intent of narrowing that down to two teams, and then choosing the best product from the remaining two teams. The team that developed the language that was finally adopted was comprised of members from France, West Germany, and the United Kingdom, as well as the U.S.

Much of the language utilization of Ada for all DOD software development efforts was intended to accomplish the following goals:

- Improvement in the quality of delivered software. This would be accomplished by several means. First, use of the language embodied good software engineering principles, such as information hiding and abstraction. Second, the language was designed as an object oriented language, enabling it to better model the problem space (if used correctly). Third, by use of an Ada programming support environment, more uniformity in the development process could be achieved, helping to improve quality. This also had some secondary benefits for maintainability as well, since the code would be more understandable to the software maintainers.
- Improvement in productivity. By its design as an object oriented language, it could enforce a design methodology. Once developers learned object oriented design (OOD) techniques, that would be all that the developers would need, since the language is intended to be used that way.
- Reduction of maintenance costs through the use of a common language throughout all of the DOD. Support for numerous higher order languages and assembly languages at DOD software support facilities would no longer be required, eliminating costs associated with training, compilers, editors, and other support tools for these languages.

A survey taken by Reifer Consultants in 1989[21] reveals that many of the intended objectives associated with the use of Ada are being achieved. The survey showed that, as of that data, 15,000 software engineers had been trained in the use of Ada. Of these, 11,000 had been trained not only in Ada, but in the use of OOD as well, and 5,000 had not only been trained, but had experience in both the use of Ada and OOD. These developers had been employed on a significant number of projects, both commercial and defense-oriented. A substantial body of data existed from which to draw some conclusions about the use of Ada and its effect on quality and productivity.

Figure 1-3 shows the distribution of projects by application area on which Ada had been used for the 70 projects included in the survey. Figure 1-4 shows the

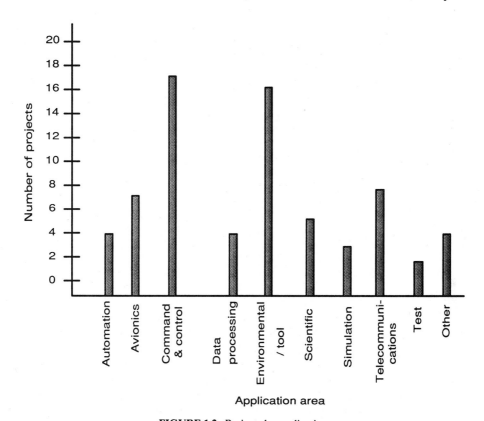

FIGURE 1-3. Projects by application.

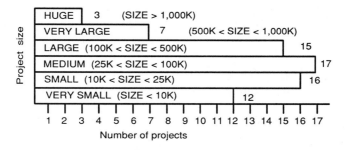

FIGURE 1-4. Projects by size.

project distribution by size. For these projects, productivity rate data was calculated over the entire software development cycle and took into account all activities that occur during it. Error rate data was compared for these projects based on data collected from the beginning of software integration testing to delivery to the customer. Source lines of code were normalized to take into account differences between the programming languages used. The average pro-

TABLE 1-3   Effects on Productivity and Quality

| | PRODUCTIVITY IS IMPROVED | | |
	Average	Range	Avionics
Ada	310 SLOC/PM	$27 \leq \times \leq 1{,}100$	180 SLOC/PM
Other	250 SLOC/PM	$91 \leq \times \leq\ \ 841$	143 SLOC/PM

| | ERROR RATES ARE LOWER | | |
	Average	Range	Avionics
Ada	22 E/K	$8 \leq \times \leq 61$	29 E/K
Other	30 E/K	$3 \leq \times \leq 89$	38 E/K

Where:
   SLOC = Source lines of code
   PM   = Person month
   E/K   = Errors per thousand SLOC

ductivity rate was found to be 310 source lines of code (SLOC) per person-month (PM) for Ada as compared to 250 for other languages. Productivity rates for avionics software projects in Ada were 180 SLOC/PM as compared to 143 for other languages. Error rates also showed improvement. Average error rates for Ada projects were 22 per KSLOC as compared to 30/KSLOC for other languages, For avionics projects, the error rate for Ada projects was 29 per KSLOC as compared to 38/KSLOC for other languages (see Table 1-3).

The study also showed strong correlations between the use of CASE tools and the methodologies associated with Ada (e.g., OOD) relative to productivity improvements. The effect of process improvement on productivity and quality as a result of the use of Ada is evident from the results of this study.

Software Process Assessments

As previously stated, there is compelling evidence of an effective link between software quality and the processes used to develop it.[24] If the processes in use by a software development organization are not well defined or organized, the quality of their software products will not be predictable or repeatable from project to project. Data gleaned from various sources indicate that the Japanese software industry is achieving defect rates two orders of magnitude better than those of the "best in class" U.S. companies.[23] A reason why the Japanese are achieving such low defect rates, based on reviews of the Japanese software industry conducted in 1984 and 1989, is because of their emphasis on understanding and improving the software development process.

The dependency of software quality on process has been characterized by the SEI in a capability maturity model (CMM).[24] The CMM (also referred to as Process Maturity Levels; see Chapter 3 herein) was originally developed by the SEI at the request of the DOD to use as a discriminator for software procurements. The

TABLE 1-4   SEI Capability Maturity Model

Level 1   *INITIAL;* chaotic, ad hoc; not even the most rudimentary procedures exist for project planning or management—neither do any exist for configuration management or quality assurance.

Level 2   *REPEATABLE;* development process is intuitive, rather than codified; procedures for project planning and management, configuration management, and quality assurance exist and are implemented. Success of development projects, however, are very much dependent on key individuals, and not on process.

Level 3   *DEFINED;* procedures and tools for software development exist and are implemented. Processes are codified and followed for all projects. When faced with a crisis, the organization continues to use the defined process.

Level 4   *MANAGED;* minimum basic process measurements have been established. A process data base and the resources to manage it have also been established. Resources to gather and maintain the data have been established.

Level 5   *OPTIMIZING;* process measurements are being taken and entered into the process data base. The process data base is being used to fine tune and optimize the development processes.

DOD felt that companies who did not have in place established and codified software development processes and the tools to facilitate their implementation, could not effectively manage the development of mission critical software, nor ensure the quality of it. Five levels of maturity are described by the CMM. The levels, their names, and the characteristics describing when the organization has reached a given level are identified in Table 1-4.

A methodology, called the software process assessment (SPA), has been developed by the SEI to determine the level at which software development organizations are functioning.[25, 26] Numerous SPAs have been performed by the SEI, and a large number of organizations have been trained to perform self-assessments. The SEI maintains data on the assessments that they perform, as well as the self-assessments. As of June 1989, 167 projects had been assessed. Of those organizations, 86% were found to be functioning at Level 1, and 13% at Level 2.[27] That meant that 99% of the projects assessed did not have well-established, codified software development processes.

Some improvement has been observed since June 1989. As of this writing, no updates to the June 1989 data have been formally released, but anecdotal data is available. At least one organization is now operating at Level 5: IBM's operation at the National Aeronautics and Space Administration (NASA) in Houston. A number of other organizations that were at Level 2 are now operating at Level 3. Nonetheless, far too many contractors are still operating at Level 1 or Level 2. By contrast, many Japanese companies are believed to be operating at Levels 3, 4, and 5,[23] whereas barely 1% of U.S. companies are believed to be operating at Level 3 or above.

Software process assessments are rapidly becoming an integral part of the DOD criteria determining contractor eligibility to compete on new procurements involving software. The DOD TQM Master Plan very specifically states, "source selection strategies will consider continuous process improvement as one element of selection."[3] Several agencies in the DOD are now requiring that contractors demonstrate that they are functioning at Level 2, or in some cases, at Level 3, on the Capability Maturity Model. At the DOD Joint Logistics Commanders Software Workshop held in January, 1991, in San Antonio (San Antonio I), one panel was seriously considering a recommendation to the DOD that Level 3 be made a requirement DOD-wide within one year! The day is fast approaching when such a requirement will exist.

Software Engineering Process Groups

The Software Engineering Process Group (SEPG) is the focal point for process improvement within the organization. Its main function is to serve as the initiator, sustainer, and evaluator of process change. The SEPG can sometimes be the group that defines the process measures to collect in order to determine the adequacy of the development processes being used. Based on the collected process measures, the SEPG determines if the established processes for software development and maintenance are meeting the quality criteria. If it is not, the SEPG researches other available methodologies to determine a suitable replacement. It also evaluates new methodologies as they become available to determine their applicability to the company's products, and their capability to meet quality criteria. If the introduction of a new methodology can effect a material improvement in product quality, the SEPG may recommend its introduction. In making this recommendation, it examines the impact of introducing the new methodology into the environment. It does this to determine if that will create excessive disruption, and significantly degrade the execution of the development or maintenance processes. Project leaders must be consulted regarding the adoption of new methodologies and/or tools to determine if such changes will negatively impact productivity, schedule, and/or cost for their projects.

There is a growing recognition of the importance of the SEPG for software quality, and many companies have begun to adopt the SEPG concept. Many of the companies who have been assessed by the SEI, or who have been trained by the SEI to perform self-assessments, now use SEPGs. In many cases, this has come about as a result of the recommendations made by the assessment team. Some organizations, both defense-oriented and commercial, have established SEPG structures without having an assessment performed. They were established because these organizations recognized that the function performed by such a group is vital for the production of quality software and, consequently, to the success of the organization. Many Management Information Systems (MIS) departments have established Standards Committees which perform many of the same functions performed by an SEPG.

Reference 24 describes strategies for the implementation of SEPGs into the organizational structure and Chapter 3 of this book provides a specific implementation. Organizational size is taken into account in the strategies discussed.

Risk Management

Risk management and process improvement are interrelated. Technical risk is one of the risk factors associated with weapon systems development. One way of mitigating this risk is to employ "tried and true" processes. For a given type of software (for instance, avionics software that allows an aircraft to perform terrain following at low altitude and high speed with very low safety of flight risk), past history may show that utilizing a given set of development processes resulted in software that met their objectives quite well. The probability is good that using the same set of processes for a new development project for similar software will result in a similar quality product. In this case, process improvement is achieved by adapting the development processes to be specific to the types of software products developed. This also results in risk reduction, because a track record exists. Efforts to continuously improve the processes used for each type of software still continue, however, to achieve even more quality improvement, since TQM implies that just being good enough is no longer good enough.

Benchmarking

Benchmarking is not specifically a DOD initiative, but is one of the methodologies for process improvement identified in the "Total Quality Management Guide,"[7] and can be a very effective methodology. It is a method in which the processes in use by an organization are compared against the processes used for the same purposes by organizations who are the recognized leaders. The comparison leads to the establishment of targets and priorities for process improvement. First, processes to benchmark, and their key characteristics, are identified. A determination is then made of what organizations to use for comparison, and the relevant data is collected. Ideally, this should be any company in the industry; however, because of competitive reasons, the likelihood of that happening is low. Different divisions or operating groups of the same company are more likely candidates. Data from competing companies can be collected, however, from journal articles and papers presented at conferences. When a company does something well, they always want the world to know that, and some information becomes available through those means. Having collected the data, a "best in class" target can be established, and a plan put in place to improve the process in question to achieve the benchmarked level of performance.

Reference 45 describes TRW's System Integration Group benchmarking process and its utilization as part of their effort to mitigate the risk from adopting Ada.

Understanding the Current Process

The key to process improvement is gaining an understanding of the current process in place within the software development organization. This understanding includes not only the definition of the processes in use, but also a determination of how well they are working.

To begin process improvement with any kind of effectiveness, an understanding must be ascertained of the processes in use for the various aspects of the software development enterprise. This includes the processes that have been defined and put in place for performing requirements analysis, design, coding, test, etc. Furthermore, different products are likely to require different processes. MIS systems for financial and accounting functions are likely to require different processes than those used to develop and maintain software for guidance and control systems. Additionally, some software may be more critical than others, and will require more rigorous methodologies. Within the category called "mission critical software," some are more critical than others. Software affecting the safety of flight or nuclear safety (for example) are subjected to rigorous safety analyses. This is an additional development process that would not be employed for the development of many kinds of communications equipment included within "mission critical software."

Process improvement results, in effect, from a series of assessments of the current process. An evaluation of the current process takes place against a set of quality criteria (which reflects the kinds of software produced), and, if satisfactory, the process continues to be used as is. If not satisfactory, a change in the process is instituted. In practice, understanding the current process is accomplished in several ways: through process assessments and through process metrics. The SEPG plays a major role in this activity. In some instances, a Process Action Team (PAT) will be convened to obtain the understanding of the current process. See the conclusion of the section entitled Cross-Functional Orientation and Teamwork, for a further discussion of PATs.

A major portion of the SPA process consists of understanding the current process. The questionnaire that is administered to the project leaders (which is based on good engineering software practices), the analysis of the responses, and the discussions with the project leaders and the functional area representatives focus on understanding the current process. The findings summarize that understanding and become the basis for the recommendations for improving the process. An action plan is devised, based on the recommendations, and the SEPG becomes the focal point for its implementation.

As previously indicated, the SEPG is sometimes the organization that specifies process metrics and measures to collect, and does the analysis of the collected data. This is done in order to gain an understanding of the current processes in use, as well as their effectiveness in achieving quality objectives. The collected raw data may come in from various sources in the form of problem reports, or other similar kinds of product quality data. These will generally have some indication as to the phase of the project in which the observable data was collected. The data will then be correlated to some precedent event or activity in order to determine the effectiveness of the process. For example, problem reports recorded during testing could be compared to problem reports recorded during walkthroughs. If the walkthrough process is working correctly, i.e., the bulk of the design and logic errors are being caught prior to test, one would expect to see a significant reduction in problem reports recorded during testing. If a significant number of errors are still occurring during testing, it would indicate, as one possibility, that the walkthrough process needs to be looked at to determine why errors are slipping through.

More emphasis is now being focused on process measurements. Since the quality of the software is greatly dependent on the quality of the process used to develop it, it is important to know how good the processes in use are. It is just as important to know what went right as it is to know about what went wrong. This can only be done by performing process measurements. Heuristically, we know that if a process worked well for a given type of software application, the probability is that it will likewise produce good results for similar types of applications[11] (presuming that the developers have been properly trained in the implementation of the process or methodology, which is another important element of TQM).

More companies are beginning to seriously apply metrics to the development process itself to determine the adequacy of the process (see, for example, Reference 28). The results of this work have become more publicly available through seminars and conferences. Two recent examples are the National Security Industries Association (NSIA) conference held in Williamsburg, VA, in April of 1990, and the Second Annual Quality Workshop, which was held in August of 1990 at the Rochester Institute of Technology, and was sponsored jointly by Rome Laboratories of the USAF (formerly RADC) and the Data and Analysis Center for Software (DACS). Many papers were presented reporting on the experience of various organizations in the use of process measurements.

As pointed out previously, process measures involve product measures. Inspection-oriented quality assurance typically involves evaluations of completed products, for instance, completed drafts of documents. They may also involve error data from tests, such as those conducted during the integration and test phase of the software development cycle (or later). Process measures drive the evaluation activity into taking measures of interim products. For example, some companies will keep track of errors observed during walkthroughs conducted at all levels and may require the developers to keep track of errors observed during unit test. (The use of automated testing tools and integrated tool environments facilitates this kind of record keeping.) Through this kind of record keeping, it is possible to acquire the data to assess the current status of the processes employed.

At the recent San Antonio I JLC Software Workshop, a review of DOD-STD-2168 was performed by one of the panels. One of the deficiencies noted with DOD-STD-2168 is that it is not entirely consistent with TQM initiatives. A specific finding was that there was no requirement for contractors to establish a program for the use of metrics, indicators, or other measures to evaluate the adequacy of products or development processes. The recommendation was made by this panel to update DOD-STD-2168 to include such a requirement.

Cross-Functional Orientation and Teamwork

This is an area where progress has been uneven. Some of the earlier discussions pointed out some notable examples of cross-functional orientation and teamwork. The development of DOD-STD-2167 and DOD-STD-2168 provided some fine examples of teamwork between industry and the DOD regarding the review and improvement of the content of these standards. Academia, industry, and the DOD joined forces to develop Ada. Risk management will sometimes involve risk sharing between the government and the contractor.

Turf battles still tend to dominate, however. As an example, the software engineering organizations in many companies still exclude the Software Quality Assurance (SQA) organization from areas where the software engineers feel that the activity is traditionally software engineering. This is true even in more enlightened organizations where the SQA personnel have been trained as software engineers and are software-knowledgable. In these organizations, SQA is regarded as a checklist activity, and SQA personnel are still regarded as not being literate enough in software to contribute. Persistent outdated attitudes are an obstacle to the accomplishment of this objective of TQM. Chapter 16 discusses how the concept of zero defect software development can transcend the attitude that SQA personnel are only capable of checklist functions.

On the positive side of the ledger, the multidisciplinary PAT concept is beginning to catch hold, even if it does primarily occur in situations where the threat to established turf is minimal. PATs have been proposed for independent verification and validation (IV&V) projects. One proposed application was for the analysis of discrepancy reports. In this case, the PAT was composed of software engineers and technical experts familiar with the technology being implemented by the software. The discrepancy reports were analyzed by the PAT to determine trends, and to determine if the problem was severe enough to refer to a higher authority for resolution. Another application of the concept was in the analysis of the contractor's risk management activities. The intent here was to ensure that the contractor's risk management *process* was effective.

PATs are being implemented within the elements of the DOD, as one would imagine, as a consequence of the TQM initiatives in the DOD. The cross-functional team hierarchy and structure suggested by Reference 6, although a Navy structure, exists throughout the DOD. The names for each level may vary somewhat between agencies and services. At the top level, an executive steering committee exists for each organization or major area of activity. At the next level, there are Quality Management Boards (QMBs), which are cross-functional teams made up of top- and mid-level managers, who are responsible for a specific product or service. PATs are generally composed of staff involved in the process being investigated by the QMB. They generally are responsible for implementing the plans developed by the QMB, and for collecting data on the existing process and the changed process. Reference 29 is an example of how the Air Force applied the cross-functional team concept to problems associated with management of software development.

PATs are also being implemented between the DOD and industry. The Defense Plant Representative Office (DPRO) has instituted an in-plant quality evaluation (IQUE) program (see Chapter 3), as part of the DLA TQM effort. IQUE is concerned with process improvement. There are several instances where the local DPRO in-plant organization has convened a PAT, involving both the local DPRO and contractor personnel. One example is a PAT that was formed at TRW to address the issue of joint surveillance, and focused on issues such as what to perform surveillance on, how to do it, and what the roles of DPRO and the contractor should be in this joint effort. While these PATs have focused primarily on hardware issues, there is no reason why they could not be used to address software.

Suppliers

To properly implement TQM requires that its principles be followed throughout the entire organizational infrastructure, including suppliers and subcontractors. DOD-STD-2167A places the responsibility for product quality on the prime contractor. It stipulates no specific requirements on pass-through of its requirements to subcontractors, however, it does stipulate that the prime contractor "pass down to the subcontractor(s) all contractual requirements necessary to ensure that all software and associated documentation delivered to the contracting agency are developed in accordance with the prime contract requirements." It further requires that nondevelopmental software (which includes COTS) may be incorporated into deliverable software without government approval provided it is fully documented in accordance with the requirements of DOD-STD-2167A, and that the incorporation of nondevelopmental software (NDS) complies with the data rights of the contract.[32]

DOD-STD-2168 augments the requirements on subcontractors and NDS with a set of requirements of its own. In addition to the requirements specified in DOD-STD-2167A, it further requires that "objective evidence exists, prior to [incorporation of NDS into deliverable software], that it performs required functions." With regard to subcontractors, it stipulates additional requirements for assurance that (1) applicable software quality program requirements have been imposed on the subcontractor, and (2) prior to delivery to the government, that subcontractor developed software satisfies prime contract requirements.[15]

As far as hardware is concerned, the practice has been for companies to certify vendors. Hardware components could only be procured from qualified sources. With the advent of the Total Quality movement, even the qualified suppliers have been affected. They, too, must show commitment to the Total Quality movement. Qualified vendor lists have been pared as a consequence to include only such vendors. Reference 9 illustrates this point by citing data that shows that Xerox has cut its supplier base from 5,000 to 400. Other activities undertaken by companies to emphasize this aspect of Total Quality have been supplier certification programs, supplier training offered by the buyer, long-term agreements between buyer and supplier, and investment in supplier development.[9] Such practices are not uncommon in Japan in the software industry.

With the prospect becoming greater for a DOD requirement for all software contractors to be at Level 2 or 3 of the Capability Maturity Model in order to be eligible to compete for a contract, prime contractors will have to become more involved in qualifying suppliers. As a general rule, that is not occurring yet. As each new procurement occurs, teaming arrangements are made based on mutual advantage for the business interests of the partners. This will likely continue until circumstances force a change. If the RFP calls for the prime contractor or the team in general to be at Level 2 or 3, a coalition will be formed of such firms.

As previously stated, 167 projects have had assessments performed as of June 1, 1989. The number of companies involved in these projects was less than 167. (In some cases, only one project per company was evaluated, and in other cases, multiple projects were included in the assessment performed of the company.) Since less than 20% of these projects were at Level 2 or 3, the availability of qualified subcontractors is limited. Admittedly, the number of companies evaluated since June 1989 has increased; however, we are still looking at a total that is believed to be less than 200 companies as of this writing. Indications are that the percentage of companies operating at Level 2 or 3 has not substantially increased. Furthermore, not all of these companies are defense contractors. A number of these organizations are from the commercial sector, and would not be candidates for teaming for defense contracts.

Interest in assessments is increasing. The SEI began a program of vendor-assisted assessments in October of 1990. Nine vendor firms were selected and trained by the SEI to perform assessments. The vendors that were selected were the following:

1. Technology Applications, Inc.
2. Arthur D. Little
3. Software Productivity Consortium
4. Booz, Allen & Hamilton
5. Contel
6. American Management Systems
7. Digital Equipment Corporation
8. Dayton Aerospace Associates
9. pragma Systems Corporation

This program was begun in anticipation of a great increase in demand for assessments, based on a greater probability of a DOD-mandated minimum Maturity Level rating to be eligible to compete for new procurements. Some of that demand is beginning to be visible, but not to the extent expected. Considering that it typically takes 1 to 2 years to progress from Level 1 to Level 2, or 3 to 6 years to progress from Level 1 to Level 3,[30] the urgency is apparent for companies interested in subcontracting for defense work to have an assessment performed. The lead time to progress from level to level is such that companies have to start now to begin the process of achieving higher Maturity Level ratings, if they are not currently functioning at Level 2 or 3.

What is perhaps not as apparent is the necessity for strategic alliances between companies that typically are prime contractors and those that typically do subcontract work. With the limited number of contractors operating at Level 2 or 3, such alliances will be necessary in order to form teams that will meet the minimum Maturity Level requirements. Prime contractors may have to get involved in helping such companies achieve Level 2 or 3 capabilities by means such as sharing tools with them, adapting their own standards and procedures for the subcontractor's environment, training in the use of their development methodologies, etc. Arrangements such as these would necessitate that long term noncompetitive agreements be forged between the members of the team in order to have a consistent capability in place. Such arrangements are common in the Japanese software industry.[23]

1.4 SUMMARY AND CONCLUSIONS

TQM is being adopted by the defense industry, but at a fairly slow pace. Many companies are still in a reactive mode, and are implementing elements of TQM only as a result of RFP requirements or an impending audit. Adoption, in some cases, has come about because RFPs for recent major procurements have stated requirements for a discussion in the proposal of the contractor's approach to implementing TQM. Other contractors do not seem to have an organized approach for implementing a TQM program, and are just implementing bits and pieces as new contracts are awarded. As was pointed out earlier, beneficial change often comes about in the defense industry mainly in response to DOD actions.

Total Quality Management is not a slogan, a buzzword, or today's fad. The requirement—nay, the necessity—to implement it is here now. References 23 and 31 point out that the Japanese are achieving very low defect rates, approximately two orders of magnitude lower than that of the best U.S. companies. Both references cite data showing that Japanese companies develop customized software packages (typical of DOD procurements) in 35% less time than do U.S. companies. Both factors have significance for the quality and cost of mission critical computer software: it *is* possible to produce higher quality software at a cheaper price, in shorter time, which is easier (and cheaper) to maintain. The Japanese have achieved these results using a Total Quality approach. We lag behind in implementing TQM. We need to get behind the Total Quality movement— not only in the defense industry, but in the commercial sector, as well.

The defense industry (and the commercial software industry, as well) needs to focus more on process improvement. With the exception of the companies that have been trained by the SEI to do self assessments of their software development process, relatively few other defense contractors have contracted with the SEI's licensed vendors for SPAs during the first year of the SPA commercialization program. Since the purpose of a SPA is to determine the adequacy of the current process and to determine what improvements are necessary, this low level of response could be interpreted as a manifestation of negligible interest in TQM and process improvement. Interestingly enough, during the first year of commercialization, more interest in having SPAs performed seems to have come from organizations developing commercial software than from those developing defense systems.

There is no "silver bullet." Acquiring bigger and better CASE tools won't achieve better quality in and of itself. In fact, acquiring CASE tools whose capabilities are beyond the organization's capability to use them is counter-productive. Organizations that are operating at Level 1, for example, should be using very simple tools, whereas more sophisticated organizations can effectively use CASE tools with a greater range of capabilities.[30] What is more productive is to determine the organization's level of capability, define what process improvements are necessary, define the measures necessary to assess current and future levels of capability, and acquire only those tools that are compatible with those objectives. Once the organization begins to focus on process improvement in some organized fashion, TQM can begin to take hold.

As we begin to understand how our current processes are working, and where they need improvement, the need for all the elements of TQM—management commitment, training, cross-functional orientation, etc.—begin to become apparent. The only thing that will achieve the kinds of improvement in software quality and development productivity that we need in our defense systems is the application of TQM. It requires hard work and dedication to implement it, but it can be done, and has been done by companies both here and abroad. It must be done if we wish to ensure that our servicemen will receive the best equipment that our shrinking defense budget can afford. It must be done if we are to remain competitive commercially.

References

1. Memorandum, "Department of Defense Posture on Quality," Frank Carlucci, Former Secretary of Defense, 30 March 1988.
2. Memorandum, "Implementation of Total Quality Management in DOD Acquisition," Robert B. Costello, Former Under Secretary of Defense for Acquisition, 19 August 1988.
3. "Total Quality Management Master Plan," Department of Defense, August 1988.
4. "Total Quality Management Acquisition Strategy," Department of Defense, November 1988 (Draft).
5. Memorandum, "Total Quality Management (TQM)," Stanley J. Alster, U.S. Army Materiel Command, 13 February 1989.
6. "A Total Quality Management Process Improvement Model," Navy Personnel Research and Development Center, December 1988.
7. DOD 5000.51-G, "Total Quality Management—A Guide for Implementation," Department of Defense, 15 February 1990 (Final Draft).
8. "Total Quality Management," Department of Defense, Undated and no office of primary responsibility cited.
9. W. Savage Moore, "Singing the Same 'Total Quality' Song," *National Defense,* March 1990.
10. Baker, Emanuel R., and Fisher, Matthew J., "A Software Quality Framework," In *Concepts—The Journal of Defense Systems Acquisition Management,* ed. by Robert Wayne Moore; Vol. 5, No. 4. Fort Belvoir VA: Defense Systems Management College, Autumn 1982.
11. Baker, Emanuel R., and Fisher, Matthew J., "Software Quality Program Organization," In *The Handbook of Software Quality Assurance,* Schulmeyer, G. Gordon and McManus, James I., eds. New York: Van Nostrand Reinhold 1987 (first ed.), 1992 (second ed.).
12. Baker, Emanuel R., and Cooper, V. Lee, "The Case for DOD-STD-SQS," IEEE Computer Software and Applications Conference (COMPSAC), Chicago, IL. November 7-9, 1984.
13. Cooper, V. Lee, "DOD Software Quality Standards," IEEE Computer Software and Applications Conference (COMPSAC), Chicago, IL. October 1985.
14. Cooper, V. Lee, "SQS: DOD-STD-2168," Public Seminar presented by DPMA-EF during 1986 and 1987.
15. DOD-STD-2168, "Defense System Software Quality Program," Department of Defense, 29 April 1988.
16. DOD-STD-2167, "Defense System Software Development," Department of Defense, 4 June 1985.

17. Sullivan, L. P., "Quality Function Deployment," *Quality Progress,* June 1986, pp. 39-50.

18. Yoshizawa, Tadashi, "Quality Function Deployment for Software Development," 2nd International Workshop on Software Quality Improvement, Kyoto, Japan, 22-25 January 1990.

19. Zultner, Richard E., "Software Quality [Function] Deployment," Zultner and Company, Princeton, NJ, 1989.

20. Royce, Walker E., "TRW's Ada Process Model for Incremental Development of Large Software Systems," *Proceedings of the 12th International Conference of Software Engineering,* Nice, France, March 26-30, 1990.

21. RCI-TN-421, "The Economics of Ada," 4 October 1989, Reifer Consultants, Inc., Torrance, CA.

22. MIL-STD-1803 (USAF), "Software Development Integrity Program (SDIP)," 15 December 1988.

23. Yacobellis, Robert H., "A White Paper on U.S. vs. Japan Software Engineering," January 1990.

24. Humphrey, Watts S., "Managing the Software Process," New York: Addison-Wesley, 1989.

25. Humphrey, W. S. and Sweet, W. L., "A Method for Assessing the Software Engineering Capability of Contractors," Technical Report CMU/SEI-87-TR-23. Software Engineering Institute, Carnegie Mellon University, September 1987.

26. Humphrey, W. S. and Kitson, D. H., "Preliminary Report on Conducting SEI-Assisted Assessments of Software Engineering Capability," Technical Report CMU/SEI-87-TR-16. Software Engineering Institute, Carnegie Mellon University, July 1987.

27. Tutorial, "Software Process Assessment," Software Engineering Institute, Carnegie Mellon University, September 1990.

28. Kenett, R. S. and Koenig, S., "A Process Management Approach to SQA," *Quality Progress,* November 1988.

29. "Software Management Initiatives Implementation Plan," Air Force Systems Command Software Action Team, 1 August 1989.

30. "Process Maturity and CASE Technology Transition," *CASE Strategies,* April 1990.

31. Cusomano, M. A., "The Software Factory: A Historical Interpretation," *IEEE Software,* March 1989.

32. DOD-STD-2167A, "Defense System Software Development," Department of Defense, 29 February 1988.

33. Mauro, Paul, "Software Practices in Japan—What We Can Learn," Hughes Aircraft Company, undated.

34. Angiola, P. "The View of Total Quality Management," Presentation of the Office of the Secretary of Defense, 16 November 1989.

35. Shumskas, A. F., "Applying Total Quality Management to the Software Life Cycle," *Program Manager,* March-April 1991.

36. Schulmeyer, G. Gordon, "Standardization of Software Quality Assurance," *The Handbook of Software Quality Assurance,* Schulmeyer, G. and McManus, J. I., eds., New York: Van Nostrand Reinhold, 1987 (first ed.), 1992 (second ed.)

37. DOD Directive (DODD) 5000.1, "Defense Acquisition," 23 February 1991.

38. DOD Instruction (DODI) 5000.2, "Defense Acquisition Management Policies and Procedures," 23 February 1991.

39. Air Force Systems Command and Air Force Logistics Command Pamphlet 800-45, "Acquisition Management and Software Risk Abatement," 30 September 1988.

40. McGarry, John, "Software Acquisition Measures," Second Annual Software Quality Workshop, Rochester, NY, Rochester Institute of Technology, 14-16 August 1990.

41. Draft ISO Standard 9000-3, "Quality Management and Quality Assurance Standards—Part 3: Guidelines for the Application of ISO 9001 to the Development, Supply and Maintenance of Software," 8 March 1990.

42. ISO Project 7.21 Draft Standard, "Information Technology Software Life-Cycle Process," 28 January 1991.

43. Dobbins, James H. and Buck, Robert D., "The Cost of Software Quality," *The Handbook of Software Quality Assurance,* Schulmeyer, G. G. and McManus, J. I., eds., New York: Van Nostrand Reinhold, 1987 (first ed.), 1992 (second ed.)

44. Booch, Grady, "Software Engineering with Ada," Menlo Park, CA: The Benjamin/Cummings Publishing Company, Inc., 1987 (second ed.)

45. Peschel, Alfred H., "Benchmarking and Standardization for Superior Business Performance," Fourth Annual Software Engineering Standards Application Workshop, San Diego, CA, 20-24 May 1991.

2

Learning from Japanese TQM Applications to Software Engineering*

Lois Zells

Lois Zells & Associates, Inc.

2.1 INTRODUCTION

World-class rivals of U.S. companies have created a sudden and widespread outbreak of quality and management reform. Furthermore, the past practices that enabled U.S. organizations to achieve supremacy in international marketplaces are simply not working anymore. To compound matters, the Japanese now plan to develop prominence in the software exporting industry. If we are not careful, American software workers will lose employment to international competition, just as, in recent years, U.S. workers have lost employment in our steel, automotive and electronics industries.

2.2 IMPLICATIONS OF TROUBLE

As long ago as 1987, a major U.S. periodical described — not one, but six — significant software development fiascoes:

- Four of our government's nuclear submarines were launched without their cruise missiles because the missile software was not ready.
- A system defect that blocked a bank's delivery of securities to its customers forced the bank to borrow $24 billion from the Federal Reserve Bank for overnight, a loan that then required a payment of $5 million in interest.
- Computerized radiation therapy equipment went haywire, delivered 80 times more than the prescribed amount of radiation and killed a patient.

- One western-state government almost paid out $4 million in bond interest, interest that was not even due.
- A programmable pacemaker malfunctioned when a patient walked by a department store's anti-theft device.
- A medical infusion pump delivered insulin only at maximum (rather than recommended) doses.

Many U.S. software engineering experts predict that the quality of the software we generate is going to be the issue of the 1990s; *and* that this is an area where we are at a terrible disadvantage. Yet, there is little evidence that many organizations are invoking programs to stave off their risk. Others, also forecast that we will no longer be able to compete internationally—on production costs, on productivity output, and on quality.

In the same vein, the Japanese believe that they will win and we will lose in the competition for dominance of the world marketplace.

2.3 NO SAFE HARBOR IN THE 1990s

The sad fact is that many American executives still do not realize how much their business survival is dependent on being able to govern their corporate information as an organizational asset. And in many cases, if the software that manages that information goes down, the company will soon follow.

Furthermore, survival is just the beginning. The organizations that capture market dominance in the nineties may not be the mere survivors, but may well be those that achieve world-class excellence in their software arena. And there will be no safe harbor for those that do not strive for that excellence.

2.4 COMPONENTS OF TOTAL QUALITY MANAGEMENT

Although they were originally considered applicable in only the manufacturing environment, Japanese quality concepts have caught on in all sectors of the economy. For example, many service organizations like health care and data processing firms are addressing initiatives in total quality management. Our government is especially interested in this approach. To this end, each of our military organizations has major imperatives to implement the quality process.

In reality, a quality discipline embraces several arenas: Total Quality Management (TQM), Quality Function Deployment (QFD), Hoshin Strategic Planning (HSP), Project Management (PM), Statistical Process Control (SPC), Design of Experiments (DOE), Concurrent Engineering (CE), Productivity Gain Sharing (PGS), and Total Employee Involvement (TEI). (Although they are important topics, Project Management and Design of Experiments will not be addressed in this chapter.)

No matter which of these arenas the quality professional is operating in, there are always two fundamental and underlying concepts of TQM. Permeated throughout every level and every position in the organization, there is:

1. A passionate obsession with what it takes to make the customer truly happy, and
2. A relentless focus on continuously improving every one of the processes that contribute to product completion.

Customer satisfaction is ensured by going *directly* to customers to discover just what it is that will make them supremely happy. As an example at Toshiba America, the general managers must spend 20% of their time with their customers; sales managers, 40%; operations managers, 30%; field service management, 20%; marketing, 25%; and engineering management, 5%. At Xerox, a good portion of each employee's performance review is based on a satisfaction rating provided by his or her respective customer(s).

2.5 THE *TOTAL* IN TOTAL QUALITY MANAGEMENT

Total quality management (TQM) means *total,* and, for the U.S., this is one of the most difficult aspects of the entire process. Total means that *all* of the requirements are implemented by *all* of the people *all* of the time. It does not mean that if an organization does not fancy one of the pieces they can simply disregard it and still expect to achieve the desired results. TQM does not mean that participation is inconsistently disseminated, voluntary, or part-time. If every individual in the organization cannot regularly describe his or her current, ongoing quality improvement initiatives, *then TQM is simply not in effect!*

2.6 WHERE ARE THE PAYOFFS?

Declaration of the organization's number one priority issue varies, depending on its unique goals or even the latest theories being touted in the press. Nevertheless, under the obvious and absolute superordinate goal of making a profit, there are three PREMIER organizational goals. They are: increasing quality, reducing costs, and/or reducing schedules.[1] These are the areas that are controllable and in which poor results are reversible! These elements are so closely tied that, if implemented correctly, improvements in any one of them always and automatically causes improvements in the others.[2]

As an example, increasing quality will also cause a decrease in costs and in schedules. In order to decrease schedules, on the other hand, practitioners must look for the jobs (inside of the schedule) that are taking the longest to complete—and shorten them. As part of reducing job durations, practitioners must learn to eliminate all need to repeat any incorrectly completed steps within the job, by ultimately doing each of the steps properly the first time. Of course, this causes corresponding increases in quality and decreases in costs.

In summary, each of the PREMIER goals is simply a different path to the same payoff, increased profits.

2.7 CUSTOMER SATISFACTION, NOT INCREASED PROFITS, IS REALLY NUMBER ONE

Department of Education head David Kearns, until recently the chairman of Baldrige Prize winner Xerox Corporation, has recently announced that during the early years of turning Xerox into a world-class organization, Xerox management made a "huge error." Furthermore, that error wasn't even recognized until three years into the effort. Their PREMIER organizational goals were: (1) improved profits as reflected in Return On Assets (ROA), (2) improved customer satisfaction, and (3) improved market share. Although management consistently stated that the three goals were equal, positioning ROA first in the list implied an order of importance that the employees took very seriously. The quality initiative wasn't making the anticipated progress until customer satisfaction was clearly and consistently designated as number one above the other two.

One Japanese company (that sells a product that contains embedded software) implemented a software quality program in the early 1980s. Having ascertained that software failure was the most important concern of their customers, software quality became number one, above profits. Over a six-year period, they achieved an unprecedented error ratio of no more than 3.5 software failures per one million lines of code (the now famous six-sigma measurement: less than 3.5 flaws per million parts.) Their annual sales increased almost fivefold and their net profits increased four times.

If the bottom line is that improvements in customer satisfaction, quality, costs, and schedules will automatically cause increased profits, why do most organizations still work the problem backwards? Why do so many organizations still believe that across-the-board cost cutting initiatives will increase (and sustain increases in) profits? Why are so many organizations still oblivious to the benefits of making customer satisfaction a number one priority?

2.8 A NEW APPROACH TO SOFTWARE MANAGEMENT

This chapter is about uniting the finest of both American and Japanese quality approaches to bring about improvements in quality and productivity through Software Total Quality Management (S/TQM). It starts with a layman's history of Total Quality Management and then translates these concepts into software management applications.

2.9 A PROPHET IN HIS OWN LAND

W. Edwards Deming, a United States educator and consultant, was invited to Japan in 1947 to help the Japanese government prepare for a census—and he stayed to teach them how to improve the quality of their manufactured goods. Having been badly defeated in World War II, Japan's industrial and financial base was totally in shambles. Japan had no natural resources and limited sources of food for the people. Accordingly, there was an urgent need to completely rebuild the economy. The Japanese needed to be able to develop products that were good enough to export—so that revenues for importing food could be generated. Yet, the Japanese, at that time, had a reputation for producing cheap and shoddy goods. As a consequence, their industrialists were more than willing to listen to any consultant who was sympathetic to helping them. Deming proposed that he could show them how they could not only turn out high quality goods, but also how they could do it faster and cheaper—simply by following his approach. His common sense process was based on creating an engineering workforce that was well-trained in statistical measures for continuous improvement as well as instilling good management techniques throughout the organization. Of course, there was skepticism in some quarters. But many felt that, having lost so much already, they had little else to lose. So, they went ahead with his process. The implementation met with overwhelming success, and in 1960, Deming received the esteemed Second Order of the Sacred Treasure from the Emperor of Japan (the highest award given to foreigners) for his service to the people of Japan. The Japanese now recognize quality achievements in worthy organizations by bestowing the Deming Prize, an award won by many Japanese firms, but only by one U.S. company: Florida Power and Light.

The remarkable reversal of Japan's industrial success has, to a large degree, been attributed to Deming's ideas. His Fourteen Points For Management, Seven Deadly Diseases of Quality, and the Obstacles To Quality have become foundations of the quality process.[3]

By the late 1970s and early 1980s Japan's success started to gain worldwide recognition. The Japanese were achieving unprecedented levels of quality—defects being measured in finite errors per million—and achieving incredible levels of productivity.

Other significant contributors to the development of the quality process are Joseph Juran, Philip Crosby, Armand Feigenbaum, Kaoru Ishikawa, Yoji Akao, and Genichi Taguchi.

2.10 DEMING'S CHAIN REACTION THEORY

Deming's chain reaction theory states that improvements in quality always and automatically result in reductions in schedules and cost, increases in productivity, increases in market share, and consequently increases in profits.[3] It is important to understand that choosing quality does not trade-off against profits. It is a fundamental tenet of this approach that the two areas are not mutually exclusive. If comparable improvements are not realized in both areas, then the organization did not understand the concept of quality or it did not work on the right processes.

Managing to any of the PREMIER organizational goals will ultimately require (or cause) the quality of a process to be improved. It is a premise of this chapter that using the PREMIER goals (to drive the selection of the key processes for a quality initiative) is simply a variation on the Deming chain reaction theory.

2.11 GRAPHICS: A CENTRAL THEME

One picture, it is said, is worth a thousand words. And when the picture is wrong, it's glaringly wrong. Used across the quality disciplines, there are several exciting and powerful management and statistical techniques that are supported by graphic tools, some recently developed and some tried and true. These techniques and tools help to create breakthroughs into new thinking, to capture and analyze data, to isolate problem areas, to prioritize issues, and to verify strategies. The techniques and their graphic tools fall into two categories: (1) the Seven Management (7M) techniques and tools, and (2) the Quality Seven (Q7) techniques and tools. (See Figures 2-1 and 2-2.)[4] Depending on the text describing either of the two categories, the list of the seven techniques and tools that comprise each group varies. The 7M tools are selected from affinity diagrams, relationship diagrams, tree diagrams, process decision program charts, project management networks, prioritization matrices, multidimensional matrices, and matrix data analysis charts. The Q7 list contains histograms, Ishikawa (cause and effect) diagrams, Pareto charts, scatter plots, control charts, flow charts, run charts, graphs for trend analysis, and check sheets.

2.12 CONTINUOUS IMPROVEMENT

Total Quality Management is not a program and it is not a method of manufacturing. It is a management process for achieving continuous improvements in quality, schedule reductions, higher productivity, and lower costs.

The old adage "if it's not broke, don't fix it" is abandoned. Since improvements do not remain static once a goal is achieved, the new emphasis stresses that—even if something appears to be working—it can always be made to work better. Continuous improvement means fervently, passionately, and forever challenging and upgrading the status quo.

In Japan, the word for continuous improvement is *Kaizen*.[5] For many workers, Kaizen is taken so seriously, it is almost like a second religion. Furthermore, every day in every way Kaizen drives the business decisions. This daily emphasis is another major difference between the U.S. and Japanese quality management styles. The daily focus is always on solving the challenge of how to make each process better and better. Furthermore, when the Japanese work on improvement initiatives, they are always calm and unemotional. No one is the least bit interested in blaming a producer for doing a poor job. Because deviations are viewed as

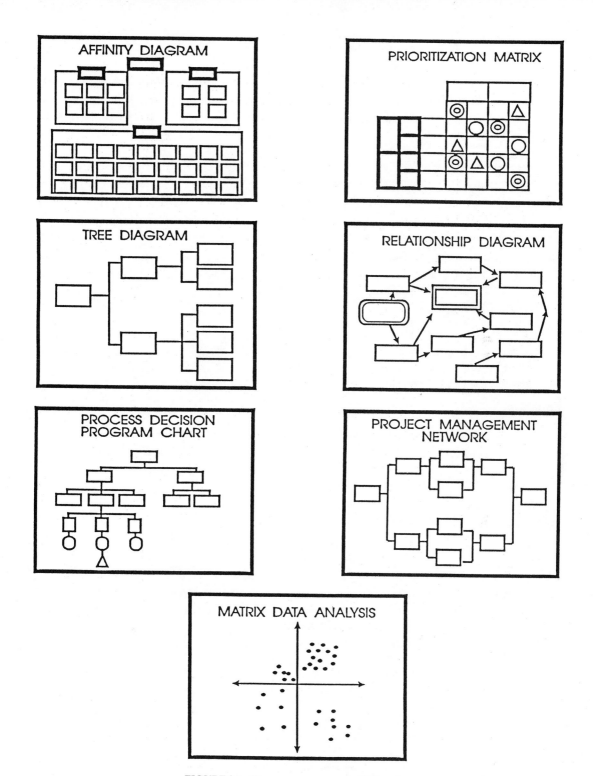

FIGURE 2-1. The seven management (7M) tools.

43

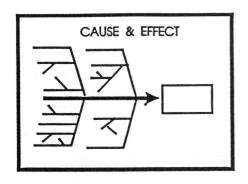

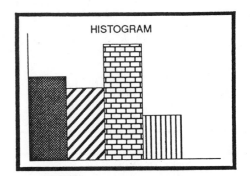

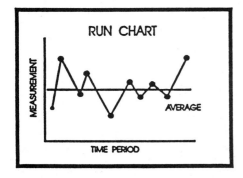

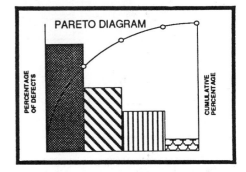

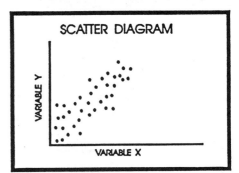

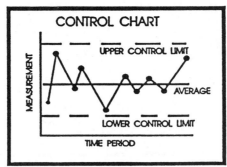

FIGURE 2-2. The quality seven (Q7) tools.

opportunities to reflect and learn, people continuously concentrate on finding out what's still not perfect and how to fix it.

2.13 CONTINUOUS IMPROVEMENT AND LOCKING IN THE GAINS

Making small changes at a time (continuous incremental improvements) and learning how to lock in and hold the gains are the basic tenets of a Total Quality Management continuous improvement process.

Many U.S. companies are still very good at thinking up new ways to improve their business results. These good ideas may even be instituted; and improvements in productivity may be realized. However, the sad fact is that most of these companies don't know how to stabilize, lock in, and sustain their gains. Once their innovations have been implemented, it appears that these organizations then become distracted by other crises. In this fire-fighting mode, another wheel that squeaks the loudest gets the attention, any improvements that have been made to the first process start to degrade, and it isn't until the first process becomes a problem again that it gets any additional consideration. By that time, the early improvements have all but disappeared. (See Figure 2-3.) What is needed is a way

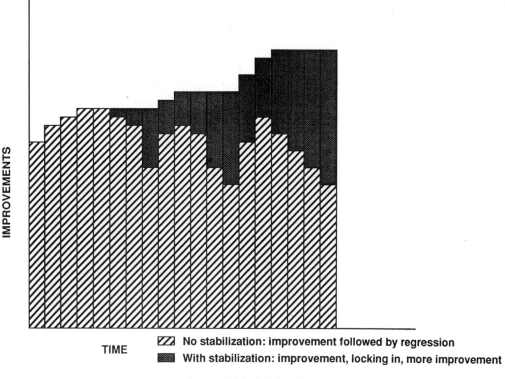

No stabilization: improvement followed by regression
With stabilization: improvement, locking in, more improvement

FIGURE 2-3. Stabilization.

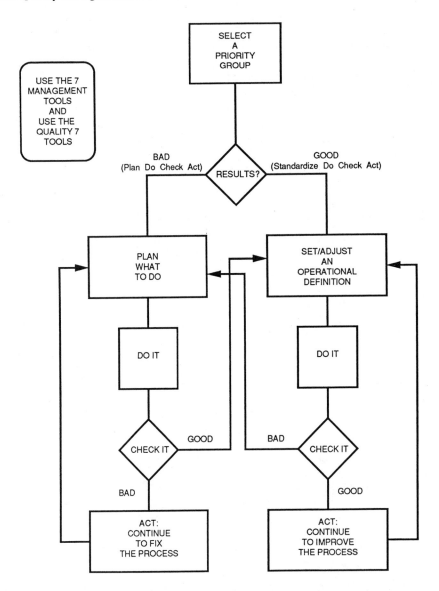

All steps of PDCA and SDCA done on a daily and monthly basis: During planning, standardizing, and both act steps, use the 7M and Q7 to innovate. During both check steps, measure and analyze using the 7M and the Q7

FIGURE 2-4. Plan; Do; Check; Act (PDCA); Standardize; Do; Check; Act (SDCA).

to stabilize the gains, so additional improvements may subsequently be heaped upon the originals. Little-by-little, the small incremental improvements ultimately add up to major accomplishments.

The goal is achieved by changing the organizational culture and by breaking out of existing traditional mindsets. To a large degree, this is accomplished by systematically using the 7M and Q7 tools and techniques described in TQM literature. The rest of the formula for success must be filled in by the vision and commitment of the leaders of the organization. (See the discussion on strategic planning later in this chapter.)

One way to break out of the traditional mindset is to implement the Shewhart/ Deming cycle for continuous improvement.[6] (See Figure 2-4.) The 7M tools and the Q7 tools are used to prioritize and select improvement opportunities as well as to evaluate the results of any efforts. On a daily basis, the steps of the cycle are invoked: the Plan, Do, Check, Act (PDCA) cycle is used to fix problems; the Standardize, Do, Check, Act (SDCA) cycle is used to maintain the gains.

2.14 CONTINUOUS IMPROVEMENT AND SOFTWARE TOTAL QUALITY MANAGEMENT

From a software management perspective, continuous improvement initiatives concentrate on the Kernel of the Model for Software Total Quality Management. (See Figure 2-5.[7]) The remainder of the model will be addressed later in this chapter.

Circle 1   VISIBLE, DEMONSTRABLE, SUSTAINED MANAGEMENT SUPPORT
Circle 2   STRATEGIC PLANNING FOR INFORMATION ASSET MANAGEMENT
Circle 3   A PROCESS FOR SOFTWARE TOTAL QUALITY MANAGEMENT
Circle 4   TOTAL EMPLOYEE INVOLVEMENT / PRODUCTIVITY GAIN SHARING

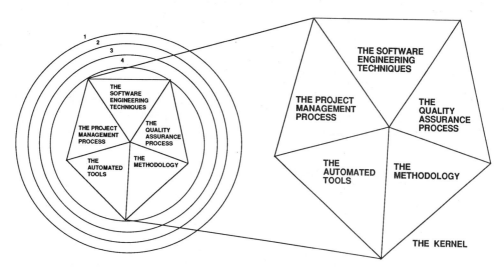

FIGURE 2-5. A model for software total quality management (S/TQM).

THE SOFTWARE ENGINEERING TECHNIQUES

Effective software development and maintenance requires expertise in the software engineering techniques that must be applied in order to produce quality systems: structured analysis, design, and programming; real-time analysis, design, and programming; information engineering; and/or object-oriented analysis, design, and programming.

THE PROJECT MANAGEMENT PROCESS

Project management expertise requires superior performance in a management process that is defined to include: strategic systems planning; project planning (partitioning, estimating, scheduling); and project management (resource management, status reporting, managing to plans.)

THE QUALITY ASSURANCE PROCESS

The implementation of software engineering process improvement addresses: verification and validation; requirements traceability; walkthroughs; inspections; phase reviews; independent testing; configuration management (versions of source code and corresponding test cases, versions of documentation, change management, release management); quality and risk assessments; the measurement process; the process improvement approach; and consulting assistance.

THE METHODOLOGY

It is essential to have written procedures: job aids; technical papers; roadmaps for development alternatives (large projects, small projects, rapid development, prototyping, software selection, etc.); the identification of phase deliverables, phase completion and success criteria; task steps and operational definitions; checklists; and template project plans—for the techniques, skills, and tools that support the project management process, the software engineering process, and the quality assurance process.

THE AUTOMATED TOOLS

The kernel of the model for S/TQM is completed by providing automated tools for doing analysis, design, data base management, programming, application generation, estimating, project scheduling, and project management.

2.15 THE IMPORTANCE OF THE KERNEL

Careful consideration shows that each of these five components are very closely intertwined. Furthermore, the S/TQM process demands that the organization focus on continuously improving and achieving excellence in every step of all of the components of this entire kernel. Yet, many companies fall prey to the misguided belief that, if they can develop expertise in one area, it will negate the need to attend to the others. Unfortunately, this is a fallacy. As a case in point, automated tools are productivity aids; they do not replace the need for expertise in the software development techniques. For example:

- Providing analysts with the latest state-of-the-art CASE tool will not do very much good if the analyst does not know how to do analysis.
- Providing planners with project scheduling software does very little to improve the group's ability to meet its target dates, if the planners do not know what jobs to enter into the software system.

The Japanese have stated that if employees are not motivated to deliver high quality in their work and if they are not well-trained (in the first four parts of the kernel), then giving them automated tools will simply serve to lead them to disaster all the sooner.

To develop excellence in each step in all of the components of the kernel of the model for S/TQM is no small feat. Since attainment of the goals of S/TQM is a multiyear effort, the process requires an appreciation of the rewards for quality and a total commitment to a long-term plan for implementation.

2.16 DEFECT-FREE SPECIFICATIONS

To the surprise and chagrin of those who look for their productivity solutions in fourth-generation languages and in code generators, the greatest improvements come not from the coding process, but from robust analysis and design specifications. Experts in software systems management point out that 40 to 65% of the delivered software failures arise from poor analysis and design. Consequently, it is essential that each analysis and design step must become immune to the error-producing conditions that surround the development process. This is accomplished by applying TQM to create a software engineering environment in which each analysis and design step will produce a defect-free specification.

2.17 QUALITY IS BUILT IN—NOT TESTED IN

In the past, this philosophy has received more lip service than actual implementation. There are still many software managers who believe that longer, richer, more rigorous testing education will improve the quality of their systems. Consequently, they merely buy more testing classes and more testing consulting.

Fortunately, there are organizations that are finally realizing what is meant by the words "quality is built in," and which realize that quality really cannot be tested into the system. Since the fastest, cheapest, highest quality way to build software is never to make any mistakes during development and never to do any job more than once, it is a good idea to learn how to do the right things right—the first time, every time. Thus, good system development techniques are the essential requirements for improved quality, and they may not be ignored.

2.18 THE COST OF QUALITY

The cost of poor quality represents any and all costs that the organization incurs from having to repeat a process more than once in order to complete the work correctly. TQM carefully considers the costs of invoking the quality process in relationship to the costs of poor quality. These quality costs are classified into four groups:[8]

THE COST OF PREVENTION

This represents the total costs of efforts that result in the highest quality products that are delivered at the lowest cost. Learning how to do the right work right the first time comes about as a result of creating a software engineering environment most conducive to success and providing practitioners with all of the education, methods, standards, tools and consulting support required to enable them to reach their quality goals. The long-term strategy of the continuous improvement process is consequently expanded to include the implementation of a method of prevention for each step in the kernel of the model for S/TQM. (Figure 2-5) Since the elimination of rework goes hand-in-hand with increases in quality, and decreases in schedule and cost, this is the fastest, cheapest, and highest quality approach to building software.

THE COST OF APPRAISAL

As surprising as it may seem, once people learn how to complete each development step correctly the first time, they may cease total reliance on reviews and inspections as a means of identifying and eliminating errors and defects.[9] However, the goals of prevention for each step in the kernel of the model for S/TQM are realized only over the long term. In the interim, until the group achieves their desired prevention levels, the members will need to invoke appraisal techniques such as verification and validation, reviews and inspections, and quality and risk assessments. These techniques will contribute to increases in quality at a moderate cost to the company. Furthermore, considering the savings realized from early detection and elimination of errors and defects, it may be easy to prove that there are actually no bottom-line costs associated with the appraisal process.

THE COST OF INTERNAL FAILURES

The costs of eliminating errors discovered during testing (and prior to implementation) are considered internal costs. If practitioners have the skills to develop a complete and comprehensive set of test cases and if they can then measure the time and effort involved in executing those test cases one time, those one-time measurements represent the cost of testing. Every minute spent after the first execution of those test cases represents the costs of internal failures. Examples of costs attributed to internal failures are specification reexamination and correction, redesign, recoding, retesting, and so on. These costs increase dramatically in relationship to the first two categories while quality is, at the same time, correspondingly reduced.

As an example, analysis errors discovered during testing may cost 15 to 75 times more to fix than those that are discovered and fixed during the analysis phase.[10] This confirms that practitioners are doing the analysis work during the testing phase, at the wrong time, and at a much higher cost—in terms of quality, completion dates, and money. (The same case may be made for design.) Viewed from this perspective, it becomes apparent why a quality initiative that is aimed solely at testing education is likely to yield unsatisfactory results.

THE COST OF EXTERNAL FAILURES

These are the costs associated with putting the system right during its maintenance period. Studies suggest that about half the maintenance effort is spent putting in features that were intended to be there in the first place, but didn't make it. This causes the poorest quality at the highest cost to the company, about 30 to 100 times more, according to Boehm.[11] Furthermore, Boehm's figures do not include the costs of operational losses that result from poor system performance.

In many organizations, there seems to be a disconnect between an inordinate push to meet a project completion date and the subsequent costs of maintenance. Obviously, this is a serious conflict and needs to be resolved before any quality improvement efforts are inititated.

2.19 PREVENTION: THE CRITICAL COMPONENT

The long-term objective of a quality process is to implement a method of prevention for each step in the kernel of the model for S/TQM, thereby achieving the goal of doing the right things right the first time, every time.

Immediate opportunities for improvement in the short-term will be realized if the organization invokes the appraisal process. Furthermore, organizations must resist the temptation to urge teams to go forward into design before the analysis work has been entirely and correctly completed or to go forward into coding before the design work has been entirely and correctly completed. For example, analysis will be done completely and it will be done correctly. It's just a question of when the organization does it and how much they're willing to pay for it. (If not done during analysis, will it be completed during design or during testing or during maintenance?) Simply stated, this means front-loading the effort into analysis and design—perhaps spending as much as 40 to 65% of the project before writing a single line of code. Of course spending more time up front while doing analysis and design incorrectly buys no gain at all. Therefore, an essential ingredient of success is the implementation of the prevention process described above.

2.20 METRICS

How is it possible to determine if each step has truly become immune to the error-producing conditions and is thus producing a defect-free specification? It is because quality improvement is measurable. The British physicist Lord William

Kelvin said that "when you cannot measure it, ... your knowledge is of a meager and unsatisfactory kind." Tom DeMarco further supports this premise by proposing that "you can't control what you can't measure."[12] And if you can't control something, you will be hard pressed to improve upon it. Thus, careful accumulation and interpretation of measurement data is an essential component of TQM.

2.21 STATISTICAL PROCESS CONTROL

TQM requires that managers begin to apply statistical thinking; therefore, the mathematical discipline of Statistical Process Control (SPC) is a key element of the quality process. SPC is a scientific measurement and decision-making approach, where decisions and plans are formulated on the basis of actual collection and evaluation of the correct measurement data—rather than on only intuition or past experience.

Every development effort consists of a series of steps that must be completed in order to ultimately implement the system. For example, each of the components of the kernel of the model for S/TQM may be partitioned into its many operable steps. Each of these steps is then regarded as a process that has its corresponding inputs and outputs.

The quality of each output is primarily determined by the rules that govern the execution of the step (process) that created it. However, a fundamental aspect of reality is that the outputs of all processes vary over time. These differences are the result of either natural causes of variation or abnormal causes of variation. In particular, abnormal causes represent forces outside the process (human error, unforeseen events, freak occurrences, etc.), acting on the process with an adverse affect. If there are any number of abnormal causes acting on the process, then it will be out of control and unstable. Therefore, no one can predict its performance with any degree of confidence or justification. Without performance predictions, quality goals may not be set, measured, or evaluated.

The goal of the model for S/TQM is a complete set of stable kernel processes that deliver consistent, predictable performance. Trying to continuously improve an unstable process in the model is an exercise in futility. It is not even possible to accurately determine if the process has been improved—or not. However, a software management effort that is under statistical control will produce the expected results within the desired ranges of quality, time, resources, and costs. The mathematical SPC techniques used in conjunction with the 7M tools and Q7 tools help practitioners to use measurements to tell if each process is in control or out of control.

It is important to stress that the goal of realizing a complete set of stable kernel processes must be a long-term objective, given that there may be hundreds of processes. The secret lies in using the direction set by the organization's PRE-MIER goals to select the critical, few key processes on which to work. For example, if schedule reduction is the PREMIER goal, iteratively applying statistical process control techniques to perfect the key processes that take the longest in the project plan will ultimately lead to the desired compression of cycle time. If quality improvement is the PREMIER goal, iteratively applying statistical process control techniques to perfect the key processes that have the highest error and defect rates will ultimately lead to the desired quality levels. And, of course, achieving any one of the PREMIER goals naturally satisfies the others as well.

Organizations should take heart; their goals are achievable, albeit over many years. On the other hand, if groups become discouraged and never start, they may not ever realize even a modicum of improvement.

2.22 THE CONCEPT OF OPERATIONAL DEFINITION

Being in control by itself doesn't always mean that the output of the process will necessarily satisfy the producer's needs. It only means that consistency has been achieved, even if the output is consistently disappointing. Another requirement for continuous improvement is the concept of operational definition. (Figure 2-4) This is a simple, but also very demanding and rigorous method. An operational definition is a rich and concise description of how to do every operable step in the kernel of the model for S/TQM, a definition that enables practitioners to tell if the output of the step is good or if it's bad. Therefore, for every key step, three good examples of output (form and content) and three bad examples of output (form and content) are to be provided. Usually, practitioners have little trouble finding enough bad examples; it's finding the good examples that presents the real challenge.

Operational definitions are essential for the quality process. They are required in order to be able to collect meaningful data, and are necessary even just to be able to communicate effectively. If it is not possible to operationally define a process, then how will practitioners know what they are talking about and how to judge success?

The operational definition also provides a narrative on how to complete the step; what is to be tested or measured; how it is to be tested or measured; and the criteria for judging completion and success of the step. Operational definitions become essential components of the methodology. (Figure 2-5)

2.23 QUALITY FUNCTION DEPLOYMENT (HOUSE OF QUALITY)

One of the uniquely Japanese creations, the *house of quality* concept is a collection of many of the best ideas that they have come up with in the more than twenty years they have been practicing TQM. The house of quality is the basic communication tool of the value analysis approach known as Quality Function Deployment

(QFD) and was developed in the late 1960s by Shigeru Mizuno and Yoji Akao.[13] (See chapter 12.)

Over the years, several approaches to QFD have emerged, the house of quality being one of these. (See Figure 2-6.) There is nothing impenetrable about understanding this figure which maps one part of the system against another; but it will require some energy to become accustomed to its unique forms and their usages. The "walls" and "ceilings" of the house are defined (albeit not built) first, e.g., the customer requirements and design requirements, respectively. Next, the importance of the "walls" to the "ceilings" of the house are interrelated and correlated, using predetermined formulas that are part of the process. Finally, the results are crystallized into numeric values called targets. As an example, the final derived targets could represent the prioritization of design requirements when mapped against the priorities of customer requirements. In this manner, unlike traditional houses, it appears as though the foundation in the house is the last thing to be defined. The house of quality has been popularized in the United States by Hauser and Clausing of the American Supplier Institute.[14] It is important to note that there is no single commonly accepted QFD system. QFD is implemented differ-

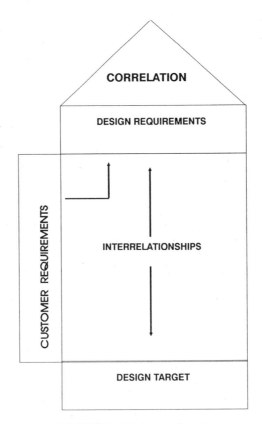

FIGURE 2-6. The house of quality.

ently wherever it is practiced. Another very prevalent QFD approach has been introduced in the U.S. by King at GOAL/QPC.[15]

QFD uses a variety of the Seven Management (7M) hierarchical diagrams, decision-making techniques, and multidimensional matrices as the communication tools for identifying, interrelating, and correlating functionality, features, potential causes of failure, proposed new technologies, costs, optimal resource/skills deployment, and other customer needs. It is a series of actions for escorting developers through a pre-analysis process—while ensuring that they've covered all of the bases.

The bedrock of QFD is the conviction that products should be designed to reflect the voice of the customer; that is, the customer's needs, desires, and tastes. QFD goes beyond the process control that SPC provides. It is a powerful set of prioritizing routines and graphical communication techniques that are used to capture that voice of the customer from three perspectives: what customers can verbally express, what they silently take for granted they will get, and what the developers can anticipate will truly excite customers.[16] What QFD does is bring that perspective into the process. Furthermore, the techniques of QFD are excellent candidates for translation into software engineering practices. Many of the current software specification techniques are weak from the perspective of not being able to capture and address the issues of who the customer really is, what is most important to the customer, and which customers should receive the highest priority. Lack of a clear definition of these elements is a significant contributor to the creeping commitment that often destroys any success potential a project may have.

Even if one were able to assume that most practitioners are currently capable of completing a correct analysis phase (not always a safe assumption,) what is still missing is the pre-analysis specification. During this pre-analysis phase, customers are identified; their high-level wants, needs, and tastes are captured and prioritized; and the customers are prioritized with respect to who should drive feature and functionality decisions. Customer requirements are initially prioritized by customer area (called customer segments, in keeping with market segments.) A very important aspect of this process is the resolution of conflicts in customer priorities. This is very effectively resolved by completing the pairwise comparisons in an analytical hierarchy process evaluation.[17] (See Figure 2-7.)

In an analytical hierarchy process evaluation, customers (in this case, four internal users A, B, C, and D) are mapped on rows and columns and compared, one to another. The value "1" is placed wherever like intersects with like, e.g., "A" to "A." Moving on in this example, "A" has a very strong preference over "B." Therefore, "7" is placed in the intersection where they meet. Since this automatically implies that the opposite will be true when comparing "B" to "A," the reciprocal of "0.14" is placed in that intersection. At the conclusion of the comparisons, the columns are totaled and then, in a second matrix, normalized. Last, the rows of the second matrix are totaled and averaged. These averages represent the final prioritization of the users, where "A" gets 51% of the say, "C" gets 24% and so on.

OPINION	HIGHEST PREFERENCE	VERY STRONG PREFERENCE	STRONG PREFERENCE	MODERATE PREFERENCE	EQUAL PREFERENCE
VALUE	9	7	5	3	1
RECIPROCAL	1/9	1/7	1/5	1/3	1
DECIMAL	0.11	0.14	0.20	0.33	1.00

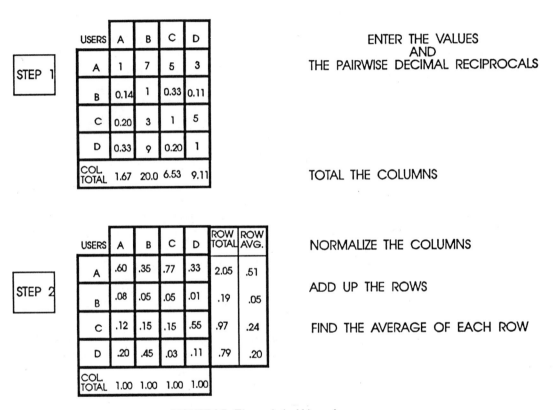

STEP 1

ENTER THE VALUES
AND
THE PAIRWISE DECIMAL RECIPROCALS

TOTAL THE COLUMNS

STEP 2

NORMALIZE THE COLUMNS

ADD UP THE ROWS

FIND THE AVERAGE OF EACH ROW

FIGURE 2-7. The analytical hierarchy process.

In another vein, QFD is designed to minimize the chance of moving from step to step with incomplete, conflicting, or erroneous specifications. (See Figure 2-8.) The users are mapped against the high-level user requirements. These prioritized user requirements are worked against feature requirements. These prioritized feature requirements, in turn, drive the prioritization of the analysis specification requirements and so on. Each step results in a new matrix; and the process ensures that no errors, omissions, ambiguities, conflicts and contradictions are introduced from matrix to matrix. Similarly, no requirements will accidentally be dropped from matrix to matrix.

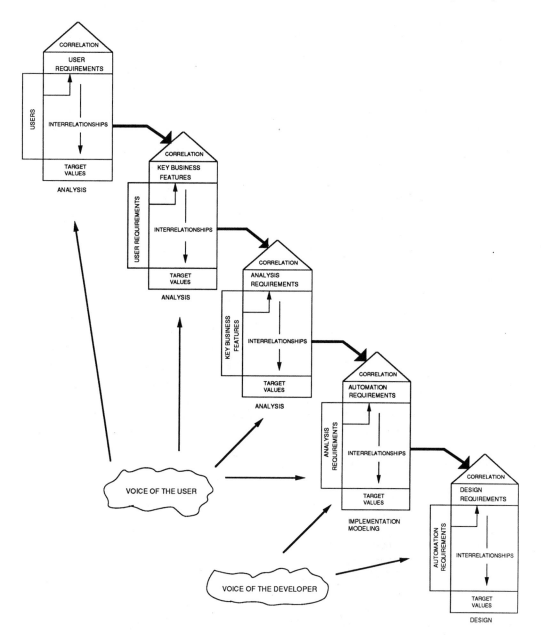

FIGURE 2-8. Software quality function deployment.

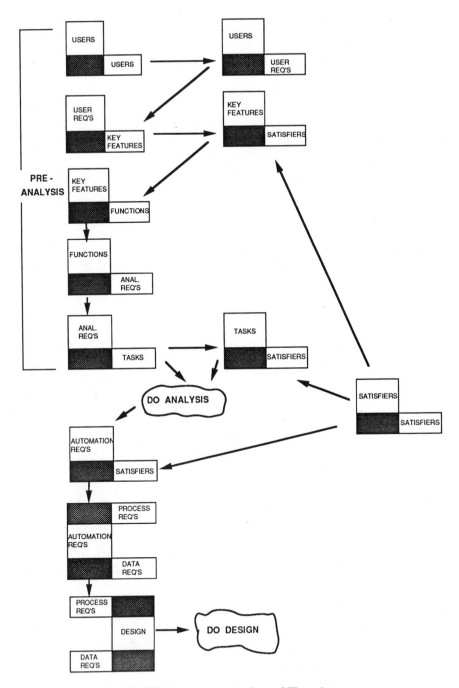

FIGURE 2-9. A proposed software QFD roadmap.

In reality, purist practitioners of Akao's technique may easily wind up with over 100 matrices. U.S. manufacturers often invoke two-to-three dozen matrices. Still in its infancy, the number and type of matrices in QFD for software are continuously being improved by the several organizations in the U.S. that are now using it in their software development efforts. (See Figure 2-9.) Satisfiers represent the critical success factors that have been prioritized using the analytical hierarchy process evaluation. A user requirement may be to transmit documents; it may be implemented through an online facsimile feature; the functions of the facsimile feature may be speed and clarity.

The QFD process helps to identify and resolve problems before the analysis and design stages and then to identify the operational features and procedures necessary to alleviate the issues and complete the work. At the conclusion of the pre-analysis effort, practitioners know who's in, who's out of the product/project effort and what's in, what's out of the product/project effort.

As an interesting aside, Dr. Akao noted that using QFD cuts the problems experienced in the early phases by one-half and has correspondingly reduced the development time from one-half to one-third. This may be translated in software terms to mean that front-loading the analysis and design and doing these processes correctly pays off, with the greatest savings, naturally coming from not having to rework the deliverables during system testing.

Richard Zultner pioneered the concept of Software Quality Deployment (SQD), using the King approach to significantly strengthen the existing approaches for completing analysis and design.[18] His techniques effectively deploy the current and future customer requirements throughout the system life cycle.

2.24 CROSS FUNCTIONAL TEAMS

Cross-functional teams are defined as consisting of anyone and everyone (in or out of the organization) who can in any way impact the end date of the project or the quality of the product. Cross-functional work teams are composed of skilled representatives (internal customers, analysts, designers, outside suppliers, etc.) from every avenue that can affect the successful outcome of the project.

2.25 THE CUSTOMER PROVIDER CHAIN

Adding the requirement of everyone in or out of the organization often requires the creation and sustenance of a customer-provider chain. (See Figure 2-10.) Each link in the chain assumes a dual role. That is, each link is a provider of services to one other link; but is also a customer to a different link.

In the illustration, the vendor engineering department is the provider of services to the vendor marketing department. The vendor marketing department is the customer of the vendor engineering department and is the provider of services to the corporation's software engineering department. The corporate software engineering department is the customer of the vendor marketing department and the provider of services to the corporate marketing department. And so on.

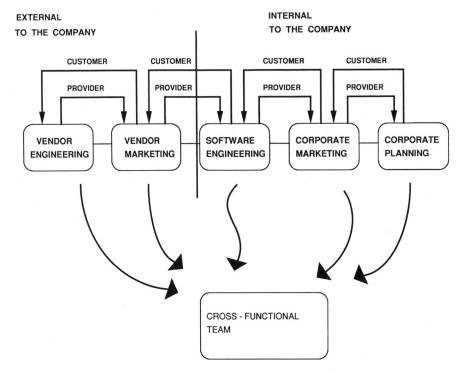

FIGURE 2-10. The customer-provider chain.

Finally, representatives from each of the groups may be selected to make up a cross-functional team.

2.26 CONCURRENT ENGINEERING

Concurrent Engineering is another quality concept that can be adapted to software management. It is the systematic management and simultaneous execution of the many steps (in the analysis, design and development of a product) that must be completed by all of the cross-functional areas. Consequently, concurrent engineering also requires a fully-dedicated cross-functional work team. This approach is intended to cause all product developers, from the outset, to consider all elements of the software life (from system conception to system termination,) including the PREMIER goals of customer satisfaction, quality improvement, cost reduction, and schedule compression.

Concurrent Engineering cross-functional teams work in a structured, proactive forum whose charter it is to ensure that all of the S/TQM philosophies are integrated into the development process. Each member of the team must also be helped—through training and consulting assistance—to achieve proficiency in the software engineering techniques. Additionally, organizational studies have shown that the probability of two people talking in an office falls off quite sharply when a

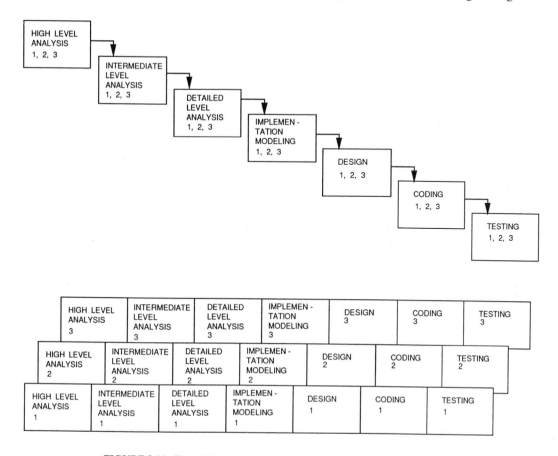

FIGURE 2-11. Phased development compared to simultaneous development.

distance of only ten to twenty yards separates them. After 30 yards, it's as if the two people are on separate coasts. In a concurrent engineering environment, work teams assemble in a "family room" setting. Segregated from the general population, this is a separate office with no internal partitions, with designated meeting pods, and with all of the cross-functional project members in attendance.

Finally, the members are also taught skills in breakthroughs and innovation, project planning, team building, problem solving, brainstorming, issue clarification, and decision making.

Once the skills are honed, the typical waterfall approach of development may be replaced by overlapping and simultaneous development. (See Figure 2-11.) A variation on concurrent engineering, development may be partitioned and simultaneously executed; and the phases may eventually even be overlapped. Practitioners are advised to use caution here. Simultaneous and/or overlapping development is not a short-term solution. It takes increased knowledge levels to implement this practice and several years to achieve a degree of proficiency that is high enough to offset any risks that may be associated with this type of concurrency.

2.27 EMPOWERMENT

Employee empowerment is also a characteristic of TQM. Each member of the organization has the documented authority and accountability to make success happen—no matter what it takes. If an organization is really serious about TQM and these qualities are not present, complete, comprehensive, and consistently applied, then that organization is probably wasting its time.

Unfortunately, the definition of employee empowerment has frequently been misunderstood. Empowerment does not mean that workers are given free rein to do (or not do) whatever they please. However, it does mean that managers must yield more of the decision-making power than they have formerly held. It does mean that—within the constraints of organizational objectives and the constraints of the role individuals play within the organization—workers can invoke their own solutions to problems without getting permission first.

Authority must go hand-in-hand with accountability. A good example of how not to effectively use empowerment is to designate a project manager in a matrix structure who has no authority over the workers on the project and then to hold him or her accountable for the outcome of the project.

2.28 JAPANESE STRATEGIC PLANNING

When U.S. researchers went to Japan to learn about TQM, they found that the one thing that all world-class Japanese organizations had in common was their approach to, what in the West is called, strategic planning. (See Figure 2-12.)[19] The Japanese supplement their strategic planning process with Hoshin Kanri, a term that has been loosely translated in the U.S. to mean policy deployment, the intent being to distribute the corporate vision to everyone in the company.[20] The vision permeates downward and the realities of implementing that vision are rolled upward and integrated into the plan.

Hoshin Kanri is an established planning process for identifying and executing strategic organizational breakthroughs and for confirming a clear corporate direction. The process enables the organization to focus on a finite number of issues, ensuring that goals are achievable and realistic. Everyone in the company is riveted on these issues, concentrating their efforts; and unlike most traditional American strategic planning efforts, the results are outstanding. Also unlike U.S. planning, this is a daily and dynamic planning process, one that allows organizations to accommodate changing business conditions, accurately and consistently hitting moving targets.

Like QFD, there is no single cookbook approach. Nevertheless, Hoshin Kanri is always process-driven, not results-oriented. As in all tenets of TQM, customer satisfaction is a key prerequisite; and all requirements that are necessary to satisfy the customer are woven into the corporate plan. Similarly, quality is considered supreme. Of course, the ultimate goal of every organization is to make a profit— that is self-evident; but this planning process is not directly linked to profits nor is it in any way linked to performance reviews that are based on numerical quotas. By

Circle 1   VISIBLE, DEMONSTRABLE, SUSTAINED MANAGEMENT SUPPORT
Circle 2   STRATEGIC PLANNING FOR INFORMATION ASSET MANAGEMENT
Circle 3   A PROCESS FOR SOFTWARE TOTAL QUALITY MANAGEMENT
Circle 4   TOTAL EMPLOYEE INVOLVEMENT / PRODUCTIVITY GAIN SHARING

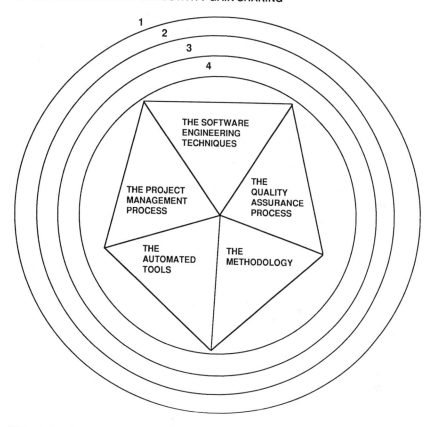

FIGURE 2-12. A model for software total quality management (S/TQM).

choosing to drive the planning process with the organization's PREMIER goals, Hoshin planning carries the implementation of Deming's chain reaction theory upward to the highest levels of the organization.

Starting at the top of the organization, the vision is translated in a few achievable goals, the corporate goals. In turn, each level of the organization breaks these goals into their own goals. This process continues until everyone in the organization understands the role that they, as individuals, play in achieving organizational objectives. Everyone in the organization manages their jobs as though they personally own the company; and every activity performed every day is related to how it affects the goals.

A high level of senior management commitment must demonstrate an uncompromising desire for success. The senior managers must be day-to-day participants, providing support, time, and resources. Furthermore, the process must be so important to them that their participation is never delegated. Deming found this to be the single, most important step in the quality process.[21] The effort should not even be considered without this commitment, and it should be cancelled if it disappears after the effort has been initiated.

Since continuous improvement is again a key component of the process, plans are continuously reviewed and improved, throughout the implementation process. This is another of the areas in which there is a significant difference between U.S. strategic planning and Hoshin Kanri. Continuous improvement here means that plans are reviewed and improved upon on a **daily** basis. There is continuous feeding into the current as well as into the next year's plan.

Hoshin Kanri requires distribution and coordination of all plans across all departments and all functions: up and down, back and forth. This is done in order to ensure that reality is integrated into the planning process—as well as to prevent cross-functional/departmental conflict and counterproductive and misdirected individual activities across projects and functional departments.

There is also a strong link between Hoshin planning and the data that pinpoints the organization's performance strengths and weaknesses. This performance data is generated through **daily** control, using SPC and the PDCA/SDCA cycle (Figure 2-4). Every person uses PDCA/SDCA every day on their every output that is in process—not after the fact. It is this day-to-day process by which incremental improvement happens. Used to identify detailed and/or broad system problems in which breakthrough is required, PDCA/SDCA becomes a way of life.

Down through the entire organization, there are cascading goals and action plans. They are woven into declarations that become leveled manifestos in which each management level articulates their goal. These manifestos are reviewed on a daily basis and subject to PDCA/SDCA. The manifesto is owned, shared, and modified by all of the members of that management level. Each final document provides a target, an ideal toward which all activity in the unit is directed. It serves as a powerful reminder of "where we're bound," especially during troubled times.

As in most strategic business planning exercised, the group creates a vision, a 3- to 5-year roadmap, and a set of 12-month objectives. Now, a 6-month detailed tactical implementation plan is also created.

The vision results from an in-depth understanding of the outside world, e.g., environmental analysis (social, regulatory), economic analysis, new venture opportunities, and how the organization fits into the vision in the long-term. Always driven by the focus on customer satisfaction, the process of developing the vision is initiated through outside information gathering from investigation and integration of the external perspective of customers and competitors, independent market research, mini-innovation searches from other sites, literature, consultants. The findings are assessed from an unbiased long-range perspective external to the organization and then from how to retrofit the organization into the conclusions.

The vision is synthesized and the findings are mapped into a clear and succinct mission statement. The mission statement should have three or four measurable definitions of success so that members will have clear goals to work towards.

Furthermore, they must be specific enough so that participants will know that they have succeeded and will be entitled to their reward.

The vision and the mission must be clearly communicated to everyone in the organization and at all levels. Similarly, the development of the vision and mission is likely to result in the evolution of an entirely new vocabulary that must be introduced to the organization. Finally, management's commitment should be publicized (Figure 2-12).

The 3- to 5-year corporate roadmap includes the broad areas that need improvement or they will block attainment of the vision. It sets performance improvement opportunities, goals, and priorities.

The 12-month corporate objectives are driven by the 3 to 5 year corporate roadmap, refining the broad areas into a few key objectives that must be achieved in the coming year, identifying the truly broken systems and the real opportunities for improvement.

Before moving on to finalizing the strategic plan, the planning group begins to deploy the plan downward and across the organization. This is accomplished by taking a draft of the vision, roadmap, and objectives to selected levels within organization, checking for reality and support. Within the constraints of organizational objectives and the constraints of the role individuals play within the organization, everyone and anyone may make modifications to the plan. These changes are automatically rolled upward to the highest level. (This is another area where U.S. strategic planning falls short.)

In the detailed 6-month tactical implementation plan, each manager sets monthly targets and makes weekly assignments, subsequently using this detail to track and manage the effort. These detailed plans also state what activities have to be done and the roles and responsibilities of the change sponsor, change agents, facilitators, work teams, and so on. Five months into the first 6-month plan, the 12-month objectives are reviewed and revised to reflect the next 12-month objectives and strategic targets; and a new tactical implementation plan for the next 6 months is created. As a consequence, two 12-month plans and two 6-month plans are prepared per year, fostering rolling objectives that are continuously fed into the planning process.

Because the world is changing so fast that companies have to be able to change rapidly, they have to work harder to figure out what to do. Having two 6-month deadlines each year demands a more concise focus, leaves less room for procrastination, and causes a greater sense of urgency to hit the target. Also, given that the detail is prepared every 6 months, the plan doesn't take as long to prepare. Some organizations prepare two plans: one with a desired set of goals and objectives and one with a conservative set of goals and objectives, along with recovery strategies.

While it is possible to invoke a Hoshin-type planning process only at the software management level, to the degree that the plan may not truly reflect organization direction, its usefulness may be limited.

Regardless of having been implemented at the corporate level or the software management level, this is not a trivial exercise or one that is completed in a weekend. One of the reasons that the strategic planning process has been largely unsuccessful in the U.S. in the past, is that it has been a rushed episode and implicitly viewed as a onetime exercise, to be shelved at its completion. Furthermore, the full benefits of Hoshin Kanri are not realized unless the total process has been implemented. And, because the total Hoshin Kanri process requires skill in a few potent actions that will take several **years** to master and institutionalize, many U.S. organizations will lose patience and abandon the effort.

2.29 TOTAL EMPLOYEE INVOLVEMENT

Total Employee Involvement (TEI) has provided breakthroughs in productivity, the quality of products, and the quality of work life—often surpassing even the highest expectations of the participants (Figure 2-12).

TEI starts with the assumption that every employee comes to work every day wanting to do a good job. This is certainly true in the software engineering world—where most participants are highly motivated self-starters who take a great deal of pride in producing quality products. Furthermore, most software engineering professionals become very demoralized when they are forced to produce poor quality work.

Bill Stinnett, a member of The TQM Systems Group, describes TEI as "an ongoing, multifaceted approach that systematically involves all employees from all levels and functions within the organization in a process of continuous improvement. Decisions are made by the people with the expertise and not necessarily the people with the power."[22] With TEI, project bottlenecks are easier to identify and, through systematic analysis, eliminate.

TEI deploys the responsibility for quality throughout the organization by coordinating the skills to design and build products. Using the cross-functional team-building process, all of the people within (and without) the organization who can directly affect the product's outcome collaborate from the product's inception (Figure 2-10).

Michael Brassard[23] holds that:

- The person doing the job is most knowledgeable about that job
- People want to be involved and do their jobs well
- Every person wants to feel like a valued contributor
- More can be accomplished in groups than individually, and
- Every organization has undiscovered "gems" just waiting to be developed.

Once more, the operative term is "total." The organization must execute all parts of the process, not just the ones that are most appealing.

TEI is clearly and concisely linked to the business objectives of the organization; therefore, it is not a program whose intent is merely to enhance employee motivation. It is based on cross-functional product-group focus instead of the traditional vertical functional organization. The cross-functional product groups may be called work centers, and are composed of ten or fewer people whose output contributes to a finished product. Employee empowerment is an essential characteristic of TEI and work centers. These work centers are self-regulating groups that:

1. Identify a problem of special interest to their work area, learn problem solving and conflict resolution techniques, and apply those methods to solving the problem, and
2. Continually identify and document all conceivable answers to the questions "How can we be more productive?", "What can we do to increase the corporate bottom line?", and "How can we make this a better place to work?"

There is a group sponsor for each work center: the person who ensures that the center's work is linked to the critical business processes and who keeps the efforts moving toward the corporate vision. However, the center is led by one of the center members. He or she plans and manages the meetings, tracks the action items, and ensures participation by all members. Only individuals who have been taught the necessary group facilitation skills may be work center leaders.

All solutions are rolled back up into the organization's master plan and coordinated for fit. It is not unusual for center members to identify different issues from what management perceives them to be—yet, the issues still support the organizational vision. When this occurs, it is advisable that management let the centers change the issues—as long as the new issues still support the corporate goals and do not attempt to change corporate direction.

There are also appointed bridge decision-makers: managers who are designated to handle the problems that can't be resolved by the centers. The bridge group is a formal group of managers, board of directors, divisional vice-president(s), and/or other top managers. When the decisions can be made by center members, they act immediately. If not, they elevate the issue(s) to the bridge decision-makers. The resulting decision may then be (1) yes—we'll do it right away; (2) yes—but we'll do it later and here is the date and plan; or (3) no—and here is why not. There is always an immediate response to workers, with the Number 3 response requiring face-to-face communication. Problem registers may be used to record both the problem and its decision.

In another vein, the work center members may feed their ideas for improvement into a suggestion system. Masaaki Imai[24] says that the Toyota workers send in approximately 1.5 million suggestions a year and that Toyota implements about 95% of them. They really take TEI seriously.

Finally, people need to be taught and led in this endeavor. It does not happen by legislation. Other types of training that are necessary include team leadership, group facilitation, active listening, nondestructive confrontation, negotiation and persuasion, project planning, brainstorming, issue clarification, and decision making. Frequently, cross-functional training also plays an important part in the process.

As a result of TEI, the level of trust builds between management and workers; people believe that success is attainable; and a lot of problems get solved. However, participative and collaborative management won't work if only some members of the organization are involved. Everyone from all levels of the organization must be involved, even the skeptics. If there are skeptics, they should be encouraged to participate anyway. For example, a deal may be struck with a recalcitrant employee: "try it; give it your all; at the end of the trial period, say 6 months, tell us honestly what you think is still wrong; if you still want out, you can leave, with no fear of reprisal. But during that time, you are expected to do your best; and management promises to do everything they can possibly do to work to insure success."

2.30 PRODUCTIVITY GAIN SHARING

Many organizations haven't yet learned how to energize their people. They aren't any closer to solving this riddle than before turn-of-the-century U.S. engineer Frederick Taylor inaugurated his now-famous management methods.

In the search for motivational techniques, the concept of Productivity Gain Sharing (PGS) is not new (Figure 2-12). PGS plans have been on the American scene since the late 1930s, early 1940s. They began as attempts to save companies from imminent disaster. However, by the 1950s, many plans reflected a broader philosophy—specifically a commitment to cooperation and improved use of human resources. During the 1960s, interest in PGS waned; but it has resurfaced in the last 15 years.

PGS is used to increase employee identification with, and thus commitment to, the organization by providing opportunities, both to participate in decision making and to share in financial gains. Since Productivity Gain Sharing is a performance measurement and reward system that is in line with the PREMIER goals of the quality initiative, the success and acceptance criteria are concisely defined at the outset. For example, if the goals are high quality and reductions in cycle time, then those should be key among the strategies, measurements, and reward structures known at the beginning of the initiative. Organizations will need help in this area, because they must be careful of what they measure. If they measure the wrong things, they will get the wrong results. As an example, the performance evaluation systems of most organizations are currently in direct conflict with TQM concepts and will need major revamping before the improvement process is initiated.[25] It is also imperative to let people know what they will be measured on (perhaps to even encourage them to participate in selecting the measurements and rewards), and also to let them know that they will be rewarded for doing the job, and for doing it right.

Often, employees view opportunities for involvement to be just as important as an actual cash bonus. This is because some members of the work force will not be motivated by financial gain. For example, older employees who have fulfilled the bottom levels of Maslow's actualization hierarchy may not be good candidates for financial reward incentives. They may more willingly respond to quality of work life incentives. On the other hand, many companies have found that financial rewards can be an effective inducement to changing long-standing attitudes and behavior, thus revitalizing older and more mature facilities.

Still other firms have found that PGS has been an excellent way to relate compensation to organizational performance. In these firms, annual pay increases are modest, but healthy bonuses are in order when related to organizational performance. Similarly, demonstrable increases in productivity, reductions in cost, and increases in quality are rewarded with bonuses to the participants. Some organizations tie PGS to group performance rather than individual performance. Finally, many PGS incentives are tied to the level of participation in and results from the suggestion system.

2.31 IMPLEMENTATION OF SOFTWARE TOTAL QUALITY MANAGEMENT

Organizations that are looking for the quick fix should not consider embracing this process. People are often surprised at how hard this type of effort actually is and they are astonished at its scope. For example, the cultural transition from traditional management practices to quality management concepts alone is very difficult. Many have also not been prepared for the surprise at how hard it is to then pass from quality concepts to TEI.

Perseverance, organizational commitment, personal commitment, vision, and courage are required as each new challenge arises. Most importantly, successful institutionalization of a quality process requires top management leadership. Ultimately accountable for the effective implementation of any quality process, they must provide visible, demonstrable, and sustained support of the program.

Failure by management to understand the fundamental nature of the change process, the implications of the change, and the scope of its impact will surely undermine the success of an otherwise well-intentioned project. Similarly, if the organizational leaders are unable or unwilling to take the necessary actions to secure resources, or cannot fulfill their role requirements, they must be reeducated or replaced. Otherwise, the quality initiative is likely to fail to meet its stated objectives. Thus, all levels of management must demonstrate an uncompromising desire for success. They share in the training, and become day-to-day participants in the process. Drop-in membership is not deemed appropriate.

Additionally, nothing is likely to happen until the organization gets enough champions—intense advocates of the faith. These believers are the ones that start breaking down the barriers to success. In the same vein, it is improbable that workers will be willing to change if it is not clear that the new behaviors will be valued and rewarded by their managers. For example, management must agree not to send out paradoxical messages that only serve to confuse and frustrate their employees. As an illustration, a directorate memo followed by noticeable absence from the program, or by behaviors that send contradictory and conflicting messages, will simply degrade the introduction into a meaningless exercise, leaving participants feeling frustrated and hopeless. The bottom line is that management commitment must be both real in substance and perceived as real by the employees.

2.32 THE INTRODUCTION

In keeping with the spirit of continuous improvement and small changes at a time, it is advisable to invoke a process that is evolutionary rather than revolutionary.

This means that the S/TQM process will be institutionalized in phases, where the first phase is an introductory phase.

A complete phase one introduction may take a year to a year-and-a-half. It is advised that, before an organization launches a full scale implementation, they should initiate the development of their vision. They first review the TQM process concepts, crystallize their TQM philosophy and then assess and define how it fits within their current cultural environment. This is accomplished through professional presentations and consulting, focus-meetings, brainstorming sessions, innovation searches, surveys, and group planning sessions.

Since the implementation of TQM requires the confirmation of a serious commitment on the part of any organization, the group will want to assess their current culture—the opinions and positions of the various levels there. Therefore, some of the introduction steps will include evaluating sponsorship commitment, assessing the organization's value system, using a change readiness scale to evaluate if the organization is positioned to improve, and completing an employee attitude survey to determine a baseline of the employees perception of the total workplace. At this point, the group should pause to determine if they are truly positioned to succeed. If they are not, it may be advisable to cancel the project. If the organization decides to go forward, the group will also need to define the roles, responsibilities and accountabilities of the change sponsors and change agents who will implement the new philosophies.

In an evolutionary process, 20 to 40% of the top and middle managers should be fully trained in the first year. Additionally, small segments of the entire organization should be piloted—for example, segments of the software engineering department and one or two corresponding customer areas. There should be no more than 50 to 75 people per pilot phase. This strategy supports a lower risk factor, but it also requires a longer investment of time and resources until organizational maturity is achieved.

The success of the S/TQM mission is directly related to how well the plans are linked to the overall business objectives. Therefore, no effort should proceed without:

- A declaration of direction (vision and mission statements)
- High-level strategic, tactical, and operational plans, and
- A project plan for addressing immediate opportunities for improvement, for supporting transition strategies, for pilot implementation, and for institutionalization.

Well-staffed and well-financed programs will succeed if implemented wisely. On the other hand, cheap programs will likely fail—no matter how hard the group may try. If cost becomes an issue, the organization should reduce the scope of the project rather than compromise on the selection of the implementation approach or the number or quality of resources.

The absolute minimum elapsed time before even a modicum of any meaningful, long-lasting changes are seen is 9 to 12 months. Then, if implemented properly, it will take—at the very least—two years to develop a respectable level of internal expertise in statistical process control, quality function deployment, concurrent engineering, total employee involvement, and so on. A corporate-wide implementation of the TQM process will take most organizations anywhere from 5 to 10 years.

2.33 EAST MEETS WEST

The Japanese approach is process-oriented, effort-driven, long-term, gradual, practically painless, emphasizes the importance of an organization's people, and works best when companies can accommodate slow-growth strategies. On the other hand, U.S. industry is usually results-oriented, performance-drive, short-term, innovative with great-leaps-forward, abrupt and often volatile, emphasizes the importance of an organization's technological/procedural capabilities, and operates under fast-growth expectations. It's going to take the West a long time to reconcile these differences and to select a decent subset of TQM processes that each organization will want to integrate into its culture.

2.34 THE VALUE OF TQM

Bob King says that it is possible that even if the U.S. makes great strides towards improvement, the Japanese will continue to find new breakthroughs and maintain their competitive position, and it's also possible that Americans will lose interest and shift to next year's "instant pudding."[26] Nevertheless, if an organization:

- Does the right things (determined by strategic planning)
- On time (developed through effective project management)
- With enough skilled resources (aided by training, consulting, and resource management), and
- Does things right (through quality engineering and software engineering),

they will increase productivity, reduce delivery cycles, reduce the costs of providing systems and services, and reduce chronic waste. They will bring about significant increases in customer satisfaction, speed of execution, the quality of systems and services, and employee motivation. Their customers will get the products that are best qualified, most useful, and most economical. Their workers will become the best performers. The polarization between customers and developers will dissipate. The organization will become the best place to work. And the company will often gain the competitive advantage and anticipated increased profits and growth.

2.35 ACKNOWLEDGMENTS

I am indebted to many people for sending these ideas into the universe, chief among them are W. Edwards Deming, Yoji Akao, Michael Brassard, and Bob King. Were it not for Richard Zultner, I would never have stepped on this path at all. Thanks to Bill Stinnett and Joyce Sabel for enhancing my journey. I would also like to thank my clients for the chance to use and refine these ideas over the last few years, from them I have really learned about Applying Total Quality Management in U.S. Software Engineering. My special thanks to Ken Pratt for his help in ensuring that this chapter is understandable, especially in the segment on QFD and for the examples used to clarify the illustration in Figure 2-9. Finally, I would like to thank the hundreds of students who have attended my quality seminars and who have also shared their invaluable experiences with me.

References

1. Imai, Masaaki, *Kaizen: The Key to Japan's Competitive Success.* New York: McGraw Hill, 1986.
2. Deming, W. Edwards, *Out of the Crisis.* Cambridge: MIT Center for Advanced Engineering, 1986.
3. *Ibid.*
4. For an excellent description of the 7M and the Q7, see Brassard, M., *The Memory Jogger Plus.* Massachusetts: GOAL/QPC, 1989.
5. Imai, Masaaki, *op. cit.*
6. Deming, W. Edwards, *op. cit.*
7. Zells, Lois, Adapted from *Managing Software Projects.* Massachusetts: QED Information Sciences, Inc., 1990.
8. Crosby, Philip B., *Quality is Free: The Art of Making Quality Certain.* New York: McGraw Hill, 1979.
9. Deming, W. Edwards, *op. cit.*
10. Boehm, Barry W., *Software Engineering Economics,* Englewood Cliffs: Prentice Hall, 1981.
11. *Ibid.*
12. DeMarco, Tom, *Controlling Software Projects.* New York: Yourdon Press, 1982.
13. Akao, Y., Editor, Translated by G. Mazur, *Quality Function Deployment: Integrating Customer Requirements Into Product Design.* Massachusetts: Productivity Press, 1990.
    Akao, Y. and Mizuno, S., "Quality Function Deployment—An Approach to CWQC," Union of Japanese Scientists and Engineers, Tokyo.
14. Hauser, J. R. and Clausing, D., "The House of Quality," *Harvard Business Review,* May-June, 1988.
15. King, B., *Better Designs in Half the Time.* Massachusetts: GOAL/QPC, 1989.
16. Kano, N., Seraku, N., Takahashi, F., and Tsuji, S., "Attractive and Normal Quality," *Quality* 14(2) Japan Society for Quality Control, Tokyo.
17. Saaty, T. L. *Decision Making for Leaders,* Pittsburgh: University of Pittsburgh Press, 1988.
18. Zultner, Richard, "Software Quality [Function] Deployment: Applying QFD to Software," *Proceedings of 13th Rocky Mountain Quality Conference,* 1989.
19. Zells, Lois, *op. cit.*
20. King, B. *Hoshin Planning.* Massachusetts: GOAL/QPC, 1989.
21. Deming, W. Edwards, *op. cit.*
22. Stinnett, W. D. and Hanson, R. G., *Corporate Madness.* Phoenix: Leadership Press, 1990.
23. Brassard, M., *op. cit.*
24. Imai, Masaaki, *op. cit.*
25. Deming, W. Edwards, *op. cit.*
26. King, B. *Hoshin Planning, op. cit.*

3

Software Quality Evaluation

Kenneth S. Mendis

Raytheon Submarine Signal Division

3.1 INTRODUCTION

Government and industry have come to understand that previously acceptable quality norms for software development are no longer acceptable. Customer satisfaction, reliability, productivity, cost, and for industry, market share, profitability, and even survival are directly affected by the quality of an organization's products and services. It has become essential, therefore, to develop attitudes and systems at all levels of an organization that promote and implement continuous improvement of procedures and processes that will help an organization develop quality into its software product. Developing these Total Quality Management (TQM) attitudes into improving the software development process is the key to meeting the software IQUE (In-Plant Quality Evaluation) quality challenge.

The Defense Logistics Agency (DLA) has developed and is implementing a new quality approach known as IQUE or In-Plant Quality Evaluation. This procedure replaces the current Contractor Quality Assurance Program (CQAP). First, it is important to understand that the term In-Plant Quality Evaluation implies continuous process improvement techniques being applied by a contractor to processes being used to produce goods and services. The concept of continuous improvement methodology is an integral part of the TQM methods and is explored in some detail in Chapter 13. However, it is new to software developers, who frequently work in an environment that puts forward the belief that software development is never completed until delivery or until the last software problem report has been written. Given this belief, the goal of most software developers is to minimize the number of errors and limit them to those that have the least impact on a mission. IQUE drives a stake right through the heart of this belief.

The concept of IQUE includes management commitment, people development, quality excellence, and user satisfaction, which, one may recall from the introduction to this book, are basic tenets crossing all TQM implementations. When this concept is implemented, it embraces techniques that use process and product quality to evaluate the quality of an organization's software products. It is of interest to note that IQUE, like TQM, is based on the teachings of Deming, Juran, Taguchi, Crosby, and others.

IQUE focuses on working with the software developer, working with the software user, and working with contracting agencies to develop a product that meets the customer's needs. It means working as a team to measure and continuously improve the processes. It is proposed that IQUE, when applied properly, will result in software product quality.

The goals of IQUE are to achieve customer satisfaction, improve product quality, and reduce life cycle costs for software. IBM refers to this as "Market-Driven Quality." Its objective is to deploy throughout the organization people who know what their responsibilities are—a team of experts working together at cutting defects to zero, i.e., defect free software. At Raytheon it is referred to as "Quality starts with fundamentals." Raytheon's plan for achieving defect free software is to get back to basics—basics in development, basics in customer satisfaction, basics in pride in work, basics in teamwork, i.e., a team of experts working together to keep costs down and produce quality products. If this challenge were accepted, we would abandon developing software in a vacuum as independent artisans. Rather, we would establish a discipline that strives to improve the process itself, and that process starts with knowing the fundamentals and developing an attitude to improving the process.

3.2 WHAT IS IQUE?

As viewed by the government, "IQUE is an initiative designed to examine the adequacy of a contractor's process to consistently produce conforming products and to identify opportunities for process improvements through analysis of process measurement data" (DLAM 8200.5).[2] IQUE mandates that the government work with contractors to develop a plan capable of achieving continuous process improvements. IQUE also mandates a need for comprehensive knowledge by the government's quality assurance representative (QAR) of the product and process associated with the design and development of a software product. In interpreting this requirement, DLA has suggested that IQUE will encompass process and product proofing algorithms, that when applied to a software development process will help assure the outcome, i.e., the software product performs to meet its intended requirements.

To help put this plan into effect, DLA in DLAM 8200.5 has suggested that IQUE should involve the following:

- Contract review
- Process measurement planning
- Process proofing
- Data collection and analysis
- Product audits
- Corrective action[3]

CONTRACT REVIEW

The QAR is required to identify and understand the requirements in the contract as they relate to the prime contract, purchase orders, and subcontractors. Deficiencies and ambiguities noted are reported to the contracting officer via the contract administration office, on the appropriate government form. In addition, the QAR will discuss software quality assurance (SQA) requirements with the contractor personnel and document the intention of the government to monitor the software development through attendance at design reviews, process measurements, and product audits; proofing the adequacy of the process, data collection, and analysis. What this means for contractor divisions doing government contracts with the IQUE requirements is that QARs are now being asked to review contract documentation to assure that they meet governing standards and contract requirements. To avoid difficulties later in the development process, it becomes critical for contracting officers on both sides to ensure that software standards such as DOD-STD-2167A[4] and DOD-STD-2168[5] are properly tailored. All agreements are in writing and are not allowed to be some verbal understanding between technocrats.

PROCESS MEASUREMENT PLANNING

Identifying the process sequence of each operation to the next and previous operation, and verifying the contractor's development flow against actual development flow is what process measurement is all about. DLA suggests that the way to accomplish this is by reviewing and evaluating the various software related plans: Software Development Plan, Software Quality Program Plan, and Software Configuration Management Plan. Once this is accomplished, the QAR is then asked to verify the requirements in the contractual software development standard(s) and specification(s) to see if they are addressed in the plan. In Section 3.6 more detail is given concerning the use of measurement tools as a means of process measurement planning.

PROCESS PROOFING

Process proofing requires the use of data flow diagrams to assist in determining the adequacy of the software development process. Outputs of the process will be identified and subjected to product audits. An example of such process proofing includes proof for flowing contractual and contractor imposed requirements into working level documents. Another example of process proofing includes proof of support processes having a direct impact on product quality of software sub-contractors. Or one may be asked to demonstrate how the output of the Software Requirements Specification was reviewed for adequacy against contract requirements. Process proofing puts the burden of proof on the developing organization.

DATA COLLECTION AND ANALYSIS

The surveillance framework for data collection and analysis consists of three parallel paths; software development engineering, software quality evaluation, and software configuration management. In order to meet the intent of this surveillance framework the IQUE requires the QARs to:

a. Identify the risk management assessment plan employed by the contractor and to monitor those risks throughout the contract period of performance.
b. Use quality metrics to monitor complexity, ratio of tests passed to tests run, number of defects in the software, completeness and traceability of the requirements, number of test failures unresolved, number of known defects, and percentage of software not tested.
c. Measure complexity by using the McCabe's cyclomatic complexity and Halstead's difficulty metrics.
d. Monitor process improvement in software development using Pareto analysis, trend charts, and cause and effect diagrams.
e. Perform product audits.
f. Review deliverable documentation.
g. Assure conformance in the code itself to program design language (PDL) constructs, header identification standards, and lines of code per module standards at the time of the Physical Configuration Audit.
h. Witness formal testing.

PRODUCT AUDITS

Product audits are examinations or tests of process outcomes performed on a continuing basis subsequent to contractor examination. Product audits are used to gain assurance of consistent conformance to contract requirements and serve as the primary element for product acceptance. There are three areas in SQA considered candidates for product audits. They are documentation, code, and test. The QAR is now expected to perform a review or inspection of deliverable documentation and its related source material. The QAR is expected to perform conformance verification to PDL constructs, to header identification standards, and to line of code module standards.

CORRECTIVE ACTION

Corrective actions under IQUE are targeted to nonconformances to contract requirements. Generally, they are related to defects that are found as a result of examination or test, process proofing, or customer complaints. Emphasis is placed on verbal communication and solving problems at the lowest level. However, in instances where requests for corrective actions go unresolved, written notification and escalation of actions will be accomplished.

3.3 IQUE—A SELF ASSESSMENT

Originating in Washington, DC, the Defense Logistics Agency's Process Action Team (PAT) (the PAT concept is covered in some detail in Chapter 4) for assessing IQUE implementation status at facilities developed a procedure for assessing the status of IQUE methods being employed within cognizant government facilities. The PAT defined and developed five IQUE program maturity levels. The framework used roughly parallels the quality maturity structure developed by Crosby[6, 7] and characterized by Watts Humphrey[8] in *Managing the Software Process.* The PAT defined the IQUE program maturity as levels 1 through 5. The maturity structure is intended for use with an assessment methodology that is presented to the QAR in terms of a series of questions with YES NO answers. The assessment questions are based on the assumptions that the IQUE development and implementation is a process that can be managed, measured, and progressively improved.

3.4 HOW WILL IQUE IMPROVE SOFTWARE PRODUCTS?

Applied to software development, software IQUE represents a change from CQAP procedures. CQAP required government QARs to spend most of their time reviewing and reverifying a contractor's operations and processes that may have been performed *some time ago.* For example, the QAR may review the design review activity and corrective action system that occurred during the design phase of a product that is presently in the system integration phase. The process may have been delinquent, but there is very little that can be done at this stage of the development to correct the deficiency. The best any one can expect is that the delinquent process has had minimal effect on product quality.

Software IQUE Represents a Change

Because software development is a phase dependent activity, IQUE makes use of continuous improvement tools and problem solving techniques to assure that a contractor phase-related activity is being adhered to. QARs are now able to tailor an SQA program to a particular product and facility by implementing continuous process improvement techniques during the performance of the particular activity of that phase. Software IQUE institutes a surveillance framework for software development, software quality, and software configuration management.

What Can We Expect from IQUE?

"Software IQUE is evolving at my plant," said Mike Polly, SQA Section Manager. "Presently, I inform my DPRO (Defense Plant Representative Office) representative of all software milestone activity. DPRO has requested that they be kept informed as to software review activity, and I do that. I provide them with my progress reports and generally keep them up to date." David Larson, SQA Manager at another facility, had this to say, "IQUE at my facility is concentrated around our automated corrective action system. Our delinquent list is given to DPRO. At present, DPRO is in the process of developing measurement points to monitor continuous improvement." Paul Savickas, SQA Manager at yet another facility, had this to say about software IQUE: "At a recent review of our IQUE maturity level we were rated a strong level 2. At maturity level 3 the QAR is required to make measurement of our process and to evaluate it for improvements. We are beginning to see that." Savickas reports that IQUE initiatives have taken the QAR corrective action system directly to software development personnel. In the past QAR evaluations concentrated on software quality assurance personnel and records. IQUE has given DPRO an avenue to audit project-related software development files and folders directly, and that means going directly to the developers and holding them accountable.

3.5 WHAT DOES SOFTWARE ENGINEERING NEED TO DO TO MEET THE CHALLENGE?

Software engineering must establish and implement continuous process improvement measurement points and metrics that provide top management with visibility into continuous process improvement methodologies. A tool currently in use and being applied to a number of software developers is the Software Engineering Institute (SEI) method for assessing the software engineering capability of a contractor. The assessment methodology used by the SEI is based on the principle that prior experience is a good predictor of future performance. Therefore, the assessment guide was designed to assist software organizations with the ability to identify areas where they should make improvements in their own capability. SEI establishes five process maturity levels and two technology advancement levels. Evaluators are given a series of questions and asked to evaluate an organization's maturity to develop software. Process maturity 1 is the lowest maturity, while process maturity 5 is the most advanced. Further explanation of this assessment methodology is given in Chapter 1 (See Table 1-4 therein).

Education is another tool that will help bring about this attitude revolution. Since IQUE is intended to bring change, what is being done to bring about this cultural revolution? One SQA manager reported that he had written a newsletter article and had it published in order to introduce the idea at his plant. In addition, he said that his top management had been briefed. Within the government, QARs have been sent to IQUE school. QARs are being trained how to measure their progress in implementing the IQUE concept.

3.6 WHAT DOES SQA NEED TO DO?

SQA needs to develop a measurement policy to help define practical and acceptable measuring techniques and measurement points. Structured problem solving methodologies can help identify opportunities for improvement. Every work activity has inputs and outputs. Critical points in the process should be selected, and measurements should be taken at the input, at the output and within the process. These measurements will provide the feedback, if continuous improvements are being accomplished, and help identify the most serious problems to be resolved. Tools such as histograms, Pareto diagrams, exit criteria reports, and cost of quality analysis help to determine the most likely cause of problems. This subsequently helps to achieve continuous improvement.

PARETO CHARTS
Pareto charts are bar graphs arranged in descending order representing the relative contribution of each element of the total problem. The technique is based on the Pareto principle, which states that a few of the problems often account for most of the effect, sometimes called the 80-20 rule. Joseph M. Juran referred to this as the "vital few and the trivial many." The Pareto principle focuses our attention on the vital few, not the distracting, trivial many. To apply the Pareto principle to software, first define software quality. A good starting point is the identification of the quality factors (metrics). Next, select a subset of the factors. Finally, establish a hurdle rate up front that must be met. Once this has been established, apply it to the software modules. The result is a Pareto analysis that helps to identify the critical components. For a detailed explanation of the Pareto principle applied to software see the *Handbook of Software Quality Assurance.*[9]

STATISTICAL PROCESS CONTROL (SPC)
SPC is a method of determining the cause of variation based on a statistical analysis of the problem. SPC uses probability theory to control and improve processes. It has proven to be an effective tool for improving performance of any process. It helps identify problems quickly and accurately. It also provides quantifiable data for analysis, provides a reference baseline, and promotes participation and decision making by the people doing the job, that is, empowerment. Chapter 17 provides the details of SPC applied to software development.

HISTOGRAMS
A histogram is a graph that displays frequency of data in columnar form. A histogram helps identify changes or shifts in process as changes are made. It shows how variable measurements of a process or product can be made, and it helps in the establishment of standards. Once standards have been set measurement can be compared to these standards with a histogram.

CHECK SHEETS
A check sheet is a list of check off items that permit data to be collected quickly and easily in a simple, standardized format that lends itself to quantitative analysis.

Check sheets facilitate data collection by providing a standardized format for recording information.

EXIT CRITERIA REPORTING

Exit criteria reporting is a systematic method for identifying interdependency problems by defining objectives and listing inputs and outputs for major tasks, functions, or activities. By firmly identifying exit criteria for a software development phase it becomes clear to all concerned parties when the task (phase) is completed. It clarifies roles and responsibilities, resolves conflicts, eliminates duplications, and opens lines of communication.

COST OF QUALITY ANALYSIS

Cost of quality analysis is a system that provides managers with cost details often hidden from them. Cost of quality consists of all costs associated with maintaining acceptable quality, plus costs incurred as a result of failures to achieve this quality. Cost of quality categories include costs associated with cost of conformance: prevention, appraisal costs, cost of nonconformance, internal failures, and external failures. "The Cost of Software Quality" by James H. Dobbins and Robert D. Buck in the *Handbook of Software Quality Assurance*[10] provides additional details.

WORK FLOW ANALYSIS (WFA)

A structured system to improve a work process by eliminating unnecessary tasks and streamlining the work flow is called work flow analysis. WFA identifies and eliminates unnecessary process steps by analyzing functions, activities, and tasks. A good example of WFA applied to software development is the software development process chart in G. Gordon Schulmeyer's book *Zero Defect Software.*[11]

BENCHMARKING

A method of measuring processes against those of recognized leaders is called benchmarking. Benchmarking helps establish priorities and targets leading to process improvements. An example of benchmarking is the use of the SEI guidelines and procedures for assessing how to develop software in accordance with modern software engineering methods.

3.7 WHAT THE EXPERTS SAY ABOUT SOFTWARE QUALITY EVALUATION

The rules to achieving a successful software quality evaluation program can be best stated in terms of W. Edwards Deming's famous steps to quality. Deming's message is simple, yet powerful. "If I had to reduce my message for management to just a few words, I'd say it had to do with reducing variation."[12] By reducing variation you have established the foundation of a philosophy of continuous improvement. Of course, this means that everyone must participate, which, in turn, requires leadership. This statement is a summary of Deming's "14 points," which calls for fundamental changes in the way software is developed.

Kaoru Ishikawa[13] has been a leader in Japan's quality effort from its inception. For Ishikawa, "Japanese quality is a thought revolution in managing. It is an approach representing a new way of thinking about management." Ishikawa coined the phrase "the next process is your customer." Forty years later, the "internal customer" is still a rather foreign idea to United States software developers. Unfortunately, throwing it over the wall to the next process is still the norm rather than the exception.

Joseph Juran, an author of many quality and management related books, has this to say, "Any idea that a single department, such as quality, is responsible for quality, is simply ludicrous." According to Juran, the primary responsibility of upper management in the quality arena is to produce breakthroughs.[14]

3.8 RECOMMENDATIONS

To achieve continuous process improvements, IQUE should be portable across developments. It may need adjustments to meet specific development techniques; however, it should not be reinvented each time. The challenge is to look for ways to remove nonvalue added cost from the software development process and to measure the improvements being made as nonvalue added costs are reduced. Nonvalue added costs occur because someone did not do his or her job correctly the first time.

Today, SQA programs for Department of Defense software related projects cost approximately 6% of the software development cost. It has been my experience that 1% of that budget is nonvalue added, and that software engineering's nonvalue added contribution is approximately 10% of the budget. This can amount to an 11% savings to the corporation if things are done correctly the first time in software development.

The challenge for software developers is to learn to develop software products correctly the first time—a basic tenet of TQM. Your customer, the person to whom you turn over your product, is adding nonvalue added cost to the product if he or she is required to verify what you have done. Faced with today's shrinking defense budget, organizations that minimize their nonvalue added costs and continue to produce a quality software product are the ones that will be successful software developers in the future.

References

1. Schulmeyer, G. Gordon, *Zero Defect Software*. New York: McGraw Hill Book Company, 1990.
2. Defense Logistics Agency Manual 8200.5. *In-Plant Quality Evaluation*. Alexandria, VA: DLA, Oct. 1990.
3. *Ibid.*
4. U.S. Joint Logistics Command, DOD-STD-2167A. *Military Standard—Defense System Software Development*. Washington, DC: NAVMAT 09Y, 1988.
5. U.S. Joint Logistics Command, DOD-STD-2168. *Military Standard—Defense System Software Quality Program*. Washington, DC: NAVMAT 09Y, 1988.

6. Crosby, Philip B., *Quality is Free: The Art of Making Quality Certain.* New York: McGraw Hill Book Company, 1979.
7. Crosby, Philip B., *Running Things: The Art of Making Things Happen.* New York: McGraw Hill Book Company, 1986.
8. Humphrey, Watts S., *Managing the Software Process.* Reading: Addison-Wesley, 1989.
9. McCabe, Thomas J. and Schulmeyer, G. Gordon, "The Pareto Principle Applied to Software Quality Assurance," In the *Handbook of Software Quality Assurance.* New York: Van Nostrand Reinhold Company, 1987 (first ed.), 1992 (second ed.).
10. Dobbins, James H. and Buck, Robert D., "The Cost of Software Quality," In the *Handbook of Software Quality Assurance.* New York: Van Nostrand Reinhold Company, 1987 (first ed.), 1992 (second ed.).
11. Schulmeyer, *op. cit.*
12. Deming, W. Edwards, *Out of the Crisis.* Massachusetts Institute of Technology, Center for advanced Engineering Study, 1986.
13. Ishikawa, Kaoru, *What is Total Quality Control?, The Japanese Way.* Englewood Cliffs: Prentice Hall, 1985.
14. Juran, Joseph M., *Management of Quality,* 4th edition. New York: Juran Institute, 1981.

General References

Mendis, Kenneth S., A Software Quality Assurance Program for the 80s. *ASQC Technical Conference Transactions.* 1980.
Mendis, Kenneth S., "Personnel Requirements to Make Software Quality Assurance Work," In the *Handbook of Software Quality Assurance.* New York: Van Nostrand Reinhold Company, 1987.

4

Company-Wide Software Quality Improvement Programs

G. Gordon Schulmeyer, CDP
Westinghouse Electronic Systems Group

4.1 INTRODUCTION

This chapter provides a framework of how to arrive at a software Total Quality Management (TQM) program. To accomplish the objective a number of steps are taken to arrive at the framework.

Introductory remarks include a discussion of the evolution of TQM and the current position of quality versus some traditional (archaic) views. The concept of the cost of quality is introduced. Some introductory remarks relevant to TQM, from Robert B. Costello are given to set the stage. The introduction finally gives the Sikorsky Aircraft TQM model based on the Deming cycle.

Definitions are nontrivial in the TQM arena because it is a "way of life," not a discrete event. So, an attempt is made to define TQM from several perspectives. Also, elements that make up TQM are defined. The elements highlighted are continuous improvement, empowerment, and quality function deployment.

Because TQM has various implementations, it is instructive to see how others have implemented TQM to show how it can best be done in one's own environment. How to break down barriers to TQM implementation is covered. The steps and stages of TQM implementation are given to help the TQM process along. Implementations discussed include those of Philip Crosby, the Deming/Juran model, and the Westinghouse Electric Corporation "conditions of excellence."

Working Group Teams (WGTs) or other incarnations of the same concept are crucial to successful implementation of TQM. So, a philosophy of WGTs, the responsibilities of WGTs, and steps for a successful WGT are given.

The next section focuses on the software development process and its maturity stages. The software process maturity levels are described in some detail. There is a comparison with the maturity stages of a TQM implementation. A successful implementation for maturing the software development process at Westinghouse Electronic Systems Group (ESG) is covered with detailed descriptions of each element.

In the software TQM section, how the software development process is being combined with the TQM concepts at Westinghouse ESG is described. The benefits of bringing TQM methods and concepts to software development process maturity methods are given. This is an actual description of a company-wide software quality improvement program. Another software TQM method primarily concerned with measurement for correction comes from Dr. Victor Basili. It is called the quality improvement paradigm and is described in the software TQM section.

Evolution of TQM

In Table 4-1 the evolution of the Total Quality Management movement is highlighted. Clearly, the United States of America had the expertise and leaders first. However,

TABLE 4-1   Evolution of TQM[17, p. 2, 3]

Walter Shewhart Bell Labs 1920s	Statistical control to reduce variability
W. Edwards Deming Japan 1950s	Organization wide quality control
Joseph M. Juran Japan 1954	Total quality control

Kaoru Ishikawa
  Japan   1960s
	Quality is individual responsibility; top
	  management provides quality leadership

Philip Crosby USA 1980s	Standard of performance is "zero defects"

TABLE 4-2   Cost of Quality[36, p. CH-60]

Industry	QC/Sales	Source
Service	>25%	Philip Crosby
Manufacturing companies	>20%	Philip Crosby
Various organizations	From 4-5% to 35-40%	Douglas Montgomery
Manufacturing companies	15-20%	Quality Progress
Manufacturing companies	10-20%	Detroit Diesel Allison
Typical factories	30%	Business Week
Manufacturers	25-30%	RCA
Various companies	20-40%	Dr. H. James Harrington, Poor Quality Costs

in the 1950s and 1960s the U.S. exported that knowledge to Japan where it took hold. Now, the U.S. is preparing to bring that TQM expertise back.

Quality Cost

A survey conducted by TASC (The Analytical Sciences Corporation) of existing reports and studies on the cost of quality did not produce surprising results. The generally accepted level of the cost of quality turned out to be 20 to 30% of sales. This cost of quality by industry is illustrated in Table 4-2. QC/SALES represents the cost of quality as a percent of sales.

The classical way of measuring quality costs are limited to scrap, rework, and warranty costs. TQM sets new standards in quality costs measurement because it goes below the surface, beyond traditional methods. TQM recognizes the old way as merely the tip of the iceberg, of equal importance are the elements below the surface. The elements above the surface of the iceberg (old way) are: documented rework, scrap, and warranty. (It is of some interest that in 1987 Dr. Barry Boehm said, "There is a 30% to 50% productivity leverage factor available by eliminating rework during software development."[5, p. 51]) Those below the surface of the iceberg (the new way) are: customer dissatisfaction, high inventory, late charges, overtime, redesign, late parts, hazardous waste, rush delivery, hidden rework, lost business, past due receivables, missed schedules, failure analysis, low morale, confusion, high overhead, excess floor space, duplication of effort, and shortage meetings.[38, p. 3]

Defense Department Comments

Two leaders in the Defense Department kicked off massive TQM programs and attempted to improve understanding of TQM by the following comments. Robert B. Costello, when he was Under Secretary of Defense for Acquisition, said,

"Total Quality Management is not a finite program with a beginning and an ending. It must be woven into the fabric of management style. It must be built into the way we do our day to day business. As you well know, many governmental and industrial organizations throughout the world are moving in the total quality management direction. I may point out they are not doing it for altruistic reasons. Many companies have been bitten by high scrap and rework costs, recalls, inefficiencies in all departments, and by customer complaints that threaten both profits and market share."[9, p. 5]

He further said,

"Total Quality Management is not a vague concept, nor a program. It's a managed, disciplined process for improving quality, increasing productivity, and eliminating

TABLE 4-3   Two Views of Quality[33, p. 1]

Traditional View	Current Posture
• Productivity and quality are conflicting goals	• Productivity gains are achieved through quality improvements
• Quality defined as conformance to specifications or standards	• Quality is correctly defined requirements satisfying user needs
• Quality measured by degree of nonconformance	• Quality is measured by continuous process/product improvement and user satisfaction
• Quality is achieved through intensive product inspection	• Quality is determined by product design and is achieved by effective process controls
• Some defects are allowed if product meets minimum quality standards	• Defects are prevented through processes control techniques
• Quality is a separate function and focused on evaluating production	• Quality is a part of every function in all phases of the product life cycle
• Workers are blamed for poor quality	• Management is responsible for quality
• Supplier relationships are short term and cost oriented	• Supplier relationships are long term and quality oriented

nonvalue added activity. From a conceptual viewpoint, total quality management makes the top manager squarely responsible for the quality of the organization."[9, p. 4]

Jack Strickland, when he was director of industrial productivity and quality for the Office of Assistant Secretary of Defense for Production and Quality, highlighted two views of quality—the traditional view and the current posture. Table 4-3 provides the list of these changing views.

The Department of Defense (DOD) *Total Quality Management Master Plan* points out that a consistent, regular process improvement cycle provides the means for translating goals, such as those given above by Robert B. Costello, into practice. The first step is to identify and define the processes by which work is accomplished. Once the processes are defined, relevant measurement points may be identified. Opportunities for improvement are identified and prioritized. The most promising solutions are implemented, and their effectiveness monitored. If ineffective, new solutions are tried. The process improvement cycle continues identifying opportunities for improvement, implementing solutions, and monitoring their effectiveness.[13, p. 2]

To be successful, TQM requires a disciplined approach for action such as the process improvement cycle extracted from the DOD *Total Quality Management Master Plan*. At Sikorsky Aircraft they have developed a structured method for improving processes. The model (Figure 4-1) is based upon the Deming cycle and is founded upon data and statistical analysis.

Everyone from the Chief Executive Officer (CEO) to the hourly employee follows this structured method of process improvement at Sikorsky Aircraft. With it, one is able to identify the processes that are producing a problem, flowchart and analyze the operations in a process, collect and analyze data to determine root causes, make changes, and monitor whether the changes result in improvement.[38, p. 3]

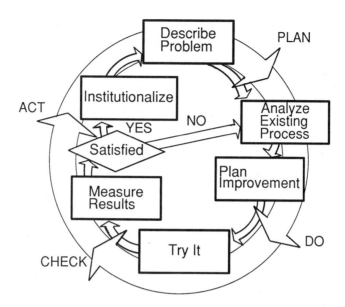

FIGURE 4-1. Sikorsky improvement model.[38, p. 3]

4.2 DEFINITIONS OF TQM

Total Quality Management is the term generally adopted by the United States government for the continuous improvement of processes and systems using an integrated managed system, teamwork, and quantitative methods to achieve customer satisfaction.[39, p. 4]

In an effort to define what is common in most of the TQM programs the following critical elements are identified:

1. Management participation and leadership development
2. Goals and measurable objectives
3. Education and training
4. Employee involvement and action teams
5. Customer emphasis
6. Supplier certification and training
7. Recognition and creation of incentives[27, pp. 30-32]

Such common principles being applied in excellent companies are: (1) recognition of the entire work force as thinking people, not just management; but everyone; (2) encouragement of workers to identify errors, propose solutions and solve problems in the work place (in other words follow Dr. Deming's advice and "drive out fear"); (3) promotion of teamwork by eliminating the "we vs. they" attitude (in a typical organization, management and the employees are divided into two camps—stop that); (4) the making of everyone a shareholder in the future of the company; (5) establishment of pride in workmanship and products; (6) concentration on prevention.[18, pp. 1465-1466]

Another view of the elements of TQM as seen by the chairman and CEO of Martin Marietta Corporation, Norman R. Augustine, is provided: first, and most important, TQM is worker empowerment; second, TQM is goal-setting (the ultimate goal of TQM is perfection; third, TQM is quantification, measurement, and feedback; fourth, and finally, TQM is teamwork (teamwork means workers and managers working together as a team).[2, p. 2]

John Marous, former chairman and CEO of Westinghouse Electric Corporation says, "Total Quality is a process . . . our most powerful strategy for winning in the world marketplace. It results in value creation for our shareholders, personal pride and satisfaction for our employees, and quality performance for our customers."[25, p. 20]

Quality Function Deployment

TQM has a significant focus on customer emphasis and Quality Function Deployment (QFD) provides a roadmap for how to improve a company's response to the customer. Quality Function Deployment is the "voice of the customer." It is a technique developed by the Japanese for integrating the customer into the company's systems engineering team. The starting point for QFD is a positive statement of what the customer wants and needs. This technique converts customer requirements into specific design and production requirements. QFD implementation involves creating a team which includes all functions of the company.[1, p. 15]

For QFD deployment a company should ask itself these questions:

- What do customers want (attributes)?
- Are all preferences equally important?
- Will delivering perceived needs yield a competitive advantage?
- What are the engineering characteristics that match the customers' attributes?
- How does each engineering characteristic affect each customer attribute?
- How does one engineering change affect other characteristics?[12, p. 54]

QFD is a conceptual map that provides the means for cross-functional planning and communications. A method for transforming customer wants and needs into quantitative, engineering terms.

Products should be designed to meet customer wants and needs so that customers will buy products and services, and continue to buy them. Marketing people, design engineers, manufacturing engineers, and procurement specialists work closely together, from the time a product/service is first conceived, to be able to meet customer requirements. QFD provides the framework (Figure 4-2 portrays the "House of Quality" framework) within which the cross-functional teams work.[12, p. 54]

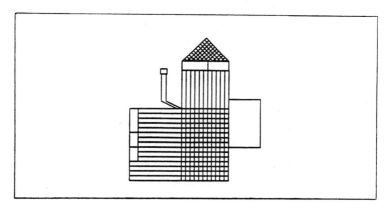

FIGURE 4-2. Quality function deployment.[12, p. 54]

4.3 IMPLEMENTATIONS OF TQM

Since resistance may exist at all levels for a quality program implementation, the following rules would prove helpful to break down the barriers and move the quality program forward:

- The quality group should answer directly to and receive full support from the highest manager. This would allow the quality group not to be influenced or distracted and would heighten the priority of the program.
- The program should be developed and implemented with an attitude of try it first and buy-in second. A proof-of-the-need would be given by organizations in disagreement. The program could be modified later by its own improvement program.
- The staff necessary to develop and support the program should be limited to two or three professionals. Clear communications and the building of a strong technical base, to share information and experiences, is essential.
- Routine control of products and improvements in process should still be the responsibility of each product center.
- Each product center should be measured and controlled on their ability to accept and successfully use the program.
- The quality program itself should be measured and controlled on its ability to improve product and service quality.

The role of this newly-formed quality group should include:

- Establishing fundamentals to be used for quality control.
- Establishing fundamentals to be used for quality improvement.

- Supplying measurements (including metrics and reports) for both control and improvement.
- Developing training programs in statistical quality control and improvement techniques.[26, pp. 4C-10, 4C-11]

TQM Implementation Factors

Having broken down the existing barriers, one needs to move forward with a TQM implementation strategy. The factors for successful implementation of a TQM program are:

1. Leadership—displays support, establishes legitimacy, and commits resources.
2. Ownership—involve the people who will be affected by the movement to TQM.
3. Norms for diversity—encourage *new* attempts to resolve problems and issues.
4. Continuous development—support attitudes of employees which attempt to improve operations of the organization.
5. Consistency—understand the way a product or service is processed and the end-product (outcome). This focuses on the employee having the "big picture."[24, pp. 3-4]

Since the implementation of TQM is a complex organizational challenge, other major factors for that implementation of TQM are: awareness of need, organizing and planning, developing of human resources, and continuous improvement. Do we need this TQM methodology?, we should ask ourselves. When we concur we are ready to proceed. To proceed it is necessary to plan and organize for success. This is not a quick fix, but an overall method for improvement. The improvement comes from the development of human resources. This really means training at every level for satisfactory understanding for implementation. The last dimension is constant improvement. This instills the idea of continually improving quality and productivity, and thus constantly decreasing cost.[17, pp. 14-15]

TQM Steps

Once the factors for TQM implementation are understood, steps need to be taken for TQM implementation. Table 4-4 from an IRS (Internal Revenue Service) training program summarizes the steps and stages of the quality improvement process. These represent Joseph M. Juran's "Project by Project" 8 steps to quality improvement. (Dr. Juran makes the point that all improvements are made on a project by project basis.[40, p. 44])

The quality improvement process is composed of a five part cycle that takes a company from start to short term results to long term dedication and continuous improvement. This is represented by the Sikorsky Aircraft method covered above. (1) Frame working orients the effort right from the beginning. This entails understanding the problems. (2) Planning helps define where to apply effort. (3) Testing the problems and creating controls comes next. This means gathering data and designing experiments. (4) Executing the quality program solves problems and cements company-wide involvement. (5) Finally, the quality effort is promulgated and

TABLE 4-4   Steps of the Quality Improvement Process[21, p. 16]

Steps	Questions	Stages
1. Identify problems	*WHAT?* What is wrong? What needs to be improved?	Identify
2. Select problems	*WHO?* How many people affected? *WHEN?* How often?	Create Priorities
(Problem statement)	*WHERE?* Location? *HOW?* Under what conditions? *WHAT?* What does it cost?	
3. Analyze root causes	*WHY?* What causes this?	Analyze
4. Identify solutions	*WHAT?*	
5. Select solutions	What can be done to change/improve this?	Resolve
6. Test solutions		
7. Implement solutions		
8. Tract effectiveness		

TABLE 4-5   TQM Methodologies Comparisons

Deming/Juran	Crosby	Westinghouse
Deming's 14 Points; Quality Function Deployment (QFD); Breakthroughs	Four Absolutes of Quality	12 Conditions of Excellence
Executive Steering Committee (ESC)		
Quality Management Board (QMB)	Quality Council	Quality Management Council (QMC)
Process Action Team (PAT)	Quality Improvement Team (QIT)	Quality Improvement Team (QIT)
Working Group Team (WGT)	Corrective Action Team (CAT)	Process Quality Improvement Team (PQIT)

expanded to leverage short term successes to long term behavior.[22, p. 36] (Reprinted by permission of the publisher, from *Management Review*, January, 1988, Copyright ©1988. American Management Association, New York. All Rights Reserved.)

TQM Methodologies

Table 4-5 contains a comparison chart of the main points of various TQM methodologies.

Deming/Juran Method

The Deming/Juran method includes the 14 points of Deming, the House of Quality method employed in Quality Function Deployment, and Dr. Juran's breakthrough concept. This approach contains "empowerment" (participation) and continuous incremental improvement.

A summary of Dr. Deming's message is:

1. Top management must become involved, provide leadership
2. Work on the system, not the workers
3. Use statistics (e.g., problem analysis, control charts)
4. Help the people; provide tools
5. Focus on a single (or a few) vendors; establish a long-term relationship
6. Continuous improvement[16, p. 5]

Taking that summary to its specific elements are Dr. Deming's Fourteen Points:

1. Create constancy of purpose
2. Adopt the new philosophy
3. Cease dependence on inspection to achieve quality
4. End the awarding of business on the basis of price tag
5. Improve constantly and forever
6. Institute training on the job
7. Institute leadership
8. Drive out fear
9. Break down barriers between departments
10. Eliminate slogans, exhortations, and targets
11. Eliminate work standards (quotas)
12. Remove barriers that rob workers of pride
13. Institute a program of education
14. Put everybody in the company to work[40, p. 22]

A grouping of those Fourteen Points of Dr. Deming are suggested as follows:

- New philosophy of management—1, 2, 8, 10
- Breaking organizational barriers—7, 8, 9, 11, 14
- Quality improvement—3, 4, 5
- Developing human resources—6, 8, 12, 13[40, p. 29]

Good management used to be thought of as getting the ideas out of the boss's head into the hands of the workers. Today good management means empowerment. We must make quality improvement integral to every job, rather than incidental to the job. There is a large difference between managers who are quality cheerleaders and managers who participate in developing hands-on, quality how-to.[6, p. 5] (Reprinted by permission of publisher, from *Management Review*, January, 1991, Copyright © 1991. American Management Association, New York. All Rights Reserved.)

In general, participative management involves workers in the planning and control of their own work activities. Four major varieties of participation can be identified: (1) in goal setting; (2) in making decisions; (3) in solving problems; and (4) in implementing change. Participation in goal setting has workers and management set the performance standard with respect to output. Participation in decision making is the evaluation and examination of alternatives that have already been developed by management and by the workers. Participation in problem solving involves subordinates who have the thinking capacity to analyze information and to develop new ideas on the basis of that information. Participation in change is the most difficult and complex because it requires managers and employees to participate in generating, analyzing, and interpreting organizational data in order to develop specific innovative change solutions to organizational problems.[29, p. 16, 17]

To be successful in TQM with Process Action Teams (PATs) and Working Group Teams (WGTs) it is necessary to give the workers the power to do what is necessary to correct what is wrong. Empowerment means giving people the authority and resources to make more decisions. When your company focuses on TQM, it must empower subordinates to solve more problems, which is a stronger form of participative management just elaborated upon. The savings and benefits of this empowerment has been documented to be the right thing to do.[8, p. 199, 200]

Other portions of the Deming/Juran method of TQM are the QFD method and Dr. Juran's breakthrough concept. QFD, remember, is the methodology to focus on customer satisfaction. Joseph M. Juran has defined breakthrough to mean change, a dynamic decisive movement to new, higher levels of performance.[23, p. 2]

TQM advocates continuous process improvement through employee involvement in every facet of the business. The heart and soul of TQM is leadership by participation, not just through words but by senior management involvement. Employees are treated as thinking people, restoring pride in workmanship and pride in being part of a winning team.[18, p. 1463]

The implementation of the Deming/Juran method of TQM involves the use of the Executive Steering Committee, the Quality Management Board, the Process Action Team, and the Working Group Team. Each is now described. The Executive Steering Committee (ESC) has the top managers of the organization as its members. Its functions include developing TQM philosophy, policy, and plan; identifying major customer concerns and requirements; providing resources for process improvement; and determining the effectiveness of process changes.

The Quality Management Board (QMB) has the midlevel managers of the organization as its members. Its functions include identifying significant processes; defining specific output goals; establishing process action teams; designing process improvements; process evaluation; and providing recommendations for system changes.

The middle manager plays a criticial role in tying together the implementation of TQM. That manager is the linking pin (Figure 4-3) between executive management and the workers. The support given the workers by the middle manager is the feature that really makes TQM work, because that middle manager is the one responsible for implementation of executive direction.

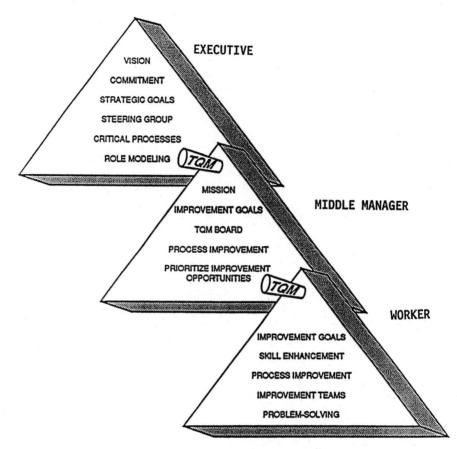

FIGURE 4-3. Middle manager as TQM link.[12, p. 26]

The Process Action Team (PAT) is composed of the managers and workers who work most directly with the processes being investigated. Its functions include developing specific process flowcharts; analyzing process performance; identifying critical factors for process improvement; and elevating issues to higher level TQM organizations for implementation and resolution.[40, p. 39-41]

The Working Group Team (WGT) is composed of workers, foremen and/or supervisors working on the process which needs improvement. They are the present implementors of the process, know it the best, and are in the best position to understand how to improve it. By detailing the process models developed by the PAT, the WGT can understand how best to improve. The WGT recommends and implements the means to measure where the process is now. As the WGT recommended corrective actions are implemented, the measurements continue to ensure improvement. The WGT makes it happen.

Crosby Method

Philip Crosby's four absolutes of quality management are:

Definition—Conformance to requirements
System—Prevention
Performance standard—Zero defects
Measurement—Cost of quality

Philip B. Crosby has explained that there is no real difference between "quality management" and "total quality management." Managing quality is a matter of establishing a clear policy on quality, ensuring that everyone involved has a common practical education on the vocabulary and tools of the subject, and ensuring that the management of the organization insists that the organization is going to do what they said they were going to do. TQM means that, but so does plain old "quality management."

In many cases raising a distinction between quality management and TQM delays having to take action, or being specific about policy. In TQM the performance standard is zero defects. Many do not care for the goal of zero defects or defect free software. That is a tough standard, even though it is nothing more than exactly what we have promised our customers. However there has always been pressure to do less.

"Continuous improvement" if you run across the term, Kaizan is Japanese for continuous, incremental improvements,[12, p. 7] for instance, as a program can be utilized to avoid heading for defect-free performance. As we get better each day our comfort zone is entered and we can be satisfied. Surely and eventually we are going to hit zero defects, right? If we move 10% nearer the target each week we will never get there.[10, p. 38]

Crosby's implementation approach focuses on providing a balance of training and consulting. Philip Crosby Associates, Inc. (PCA) encourages organizations to get everyone involved. However, empowering people without appropriate education is a formula for disappointment. PCA advocates a "phased approach" to educate the entire organization starting with top management. The prototype team is trained while helping them implement TQM in their processes. More training is given as more TQM tools are needed. It is recommended that each team's training be spread over several months with practical applications and implementations interspersed.[39, p. 7]

PCA advocates the use of teams because no single person has the knowledge, insight, creativity, and drive to cause quality improvement throughout the organization. To avoid the establishment of an entrenched bureaucracy, PCA finds that a team orientation to quality improvement moves things along very nicely. Some examples of the types of teams might be:

- Steering Committee—of top management to provide strategic direction.
- Quality Councils—of appropriate personnel to share information about quality, and to evaluate the progress of the organization's efforts.

- Quality improvement team (QIT)—of operating management to steward the specific actions.
- Corrective Action Team (CAT)—of appropriate personnel to deal with specific problems and opportunities.

There is a basic parallel with the Deming/Juran teams, so that Quality Council = QMB, QIT = PAT, and CAT = WGT as shown in Table 4-5.

Westinghouse Method

The Westinghouse Electric Corporation's TQM concepts are discussed here for two reasons. First, because they are representative of many industrial implementations; and second, the author is more familiar with the Westinghouse implementation than with others. Westinghouse Electric Corporation's implementation of quality management has as its cornerstone the 12 Conditions of Excellence shown in Figure 4-4.

Although every operation will have its own unique way of implementing TQM, there are four imperatives which must always be addressed. They are customer orientation, human resource excellence, product/process leadership, and management leadership.

The customer orientation imperative says that everything starts with the customer and the customer's perception of value. Customer satisfaction requires a company to provide a value-to-price ratio which is equal to or superior to world-class competition. Setting world-class requirements, as dictated by the customer's needs and perceptions, is at the heart of "doing the right things."

The human resource imperative says that the most important resource for TQM is people. And the key ingredients are motivation, training, and educa-

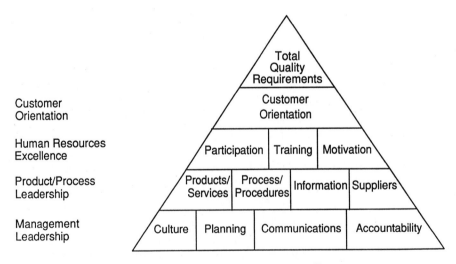

FIGURE 4-4. Conditions of excellence.[37]

tion. Dedication to TQM requires a significant effort for directed knowledge and skills acquisition.

The product/process leadership imperative tells us that products are all the things supplied to the customer, including services. Processes include everything done to supply the customer with these products and services. Overall, achieving TQM is a systems problem. One must effectively integrate the three elements included in providing any product or service: work flow, people structure, and information systems.

The management leadership imperative requires special emphasis on: training, objectives, communications, incentives, measurement, and feedback.[37, p. 3]

The teams for the Westinghouse method again are similar to the Deming/Juran method. These teams include a Quality Council or Quality Management Council = QMC, Quality Improvement Team (QIT) = PAT, and Process Quality Improvement Team (PQIT) = WGT. These comparisons are shown in Table 4-5.

4.4 WORKING GROUP TEAMS OF TQM

In the TQM methodologies chart (Table 4-5) the workers implement TQM through the Working Group Team (WGT); synonyms are corrective action team and process quality improvement team. Because WGTs are the way to empowerment, the WGTs process needs to be understood. All must take responsibility for success of TQM and that responsibility runs through these characteristics of WGTs:

1. Recognize that you own the process.
2. Acknowledge that you are responsible for quality improvement.
3. Arrive at a consensus definition of this quality improvement process.
4. Quantify aspects of the process with statistical process control.
5. Prioritize aspects requiring quality improvement.
6. Specify actions to achieve quality improvement.
7. Document the plan of action.
8. Record progress and report success.[28, p. 8]

To achieve item 6, actions to achieve quality improvement, a formal corrective action system must be formulated. It should start with the first line supervisor and quality engineer and culminate with the chief executive and his/her staff. Problems that cannot be solved must be quickly passed up with no recriminations.[31, p. Q12]

WGT Responsibilities and Steps

Project teams aim to achieve an overall higher standard of quality in the areas selected by proposing solutions which solve problems correctly the first time instead of fixing only the symptoms of significant underlying problems. The WGTs employ an exhaustive diagnostic problem-solving process and then recommend permanent solutions. The work of the WGTs must be viewed as a "journey," and not as a quick fix.

To travel this "journey," WGTs have responsibilities that include:

a. Team members use prescribed diagnostic problem-solving tools.
b. Meetings are held weekly.
c. All members participate in all meetings.
d. Meetings follow a written agenda. Assignments for the next meeting will be given out at the conclusion of the meeting.
e. Team members complete assignments in a timely manner.
f. Team leaders review meetings for effectiveness.[14, pp. 4-5]

When the responsibilities are understood, it is necessary to take the basic steps for operation of a WGT, which are:

1. Identify key areas for process improvement.
2. Specify customers and their requirements.
3. Identify and quantify cause and effect relationships.
4. Verify cause and effect relationships.
5. Optimize the process to achieve the most efficient balance between speed, cost, and quality, and confirm the results.
6. Define operating requirements of the acceptable process.
7. Institute control procedures for problem prevention.[28, p. 8]

In summary, Working Group Teams (WGTs) are small teams of people who represent all elements of a process. These teams are composed not only of workers, but of supervisors, schedulers, engineers, suppliers, and anyone else who contributes to the process from beginning to end.[16, p. 1531]

4.5 SOFTWARE ENGINEERING PROCESS ORGANIZATION (SEPO)

The quality payoff is maximized when considered during early phases of developing a product or service. It is then that many problems can be prevented. Thereafter, the leverage of prevention (Figure 4-5) is reduced as correction of problems—a more costly procedure—becomes the dominant mode. A key aspect of this concept is designing products and services that can be produced with high-yield within the capability of the manufacturing or service process. Designs that are immune to manufacturing and operational use variability are said to be robust. A manager who fails to provide resources and time for prevention activities is practicing false economy.

Software Maturity Assessment

The Software Engineering Institute (SEI)[20] has provided guidelines and procedures for assessing the ability to develop software in accordance with modern software engineering methods. This includes specific questions and a method for

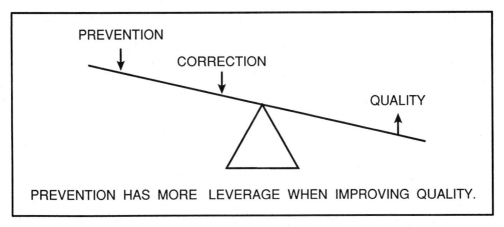

FIGURE 4-5. The leverage of prevention.[12, p. 5]

evaluating the results. Because an understanding of proper software engineering practice is only now developing, standard, well-accepted measures do not yet exist.

The SEI assessment methodology to perform software engineering has been divided into three areas:

1. Organization and resource management
2. Software engineering process and its management
3. Tools and technology.

The qualities assessed are different for each of these areas. Also included is an understanding of the experience level of the software development personnel.

Assessment methodology is based on the principle that prior experience is a good predictor of future performance. Since there are exceptions to this principle, consideration must be given to both current capabilities and future plans for software process improvement.

The assessment process is focused on defining and clarifying the positive attributes of good software engineering practices. It is further recognized that the state-of-the-practice of software engineering is steadily advancing and that additional criteria and a higher level of experience will be appropriate for judging software engineering capability in the future.

As stated in the SEI Technical Report,[20] assessment questions are based on the following premises:

- The quality of a software product stems, in large part, from the quality of the process used to create it.
- Software engineering is a process that can be managed, measured, and progressively improved.
- The quality of a software process is affected by the technology used to support it.[41]

MATURITY LEVEL / KEY CHALLENGES

LEVEL	CHARACTERISTIC	KEY CHALLENGES	RESULT
5 OPTIMIZING	IMPROVEMENT FED BACK INTO PROCESS	STILL HUMAN INTENSIVE PROCESS MAINTAIN ORGANIZATION AT OPTIMIZING LEVEL	PRODUCTIVITY & QUALITY
4 MANAGED	(QUANTITATIVE) MEASURED PROCESS	CHANGING TECHNOLOGY PROBLEM ANALYSIS PROBLEM PREVENTION	
3 DEFINED	(QUALITATIVE) PROCESS DEFINED AND INSTITUTIONALIZED	PROCESS MEASUREMENT PROCESS ANALYSIS QUANTITATIVE QUALITY PLANS	
2 REPEATABLE	(INTUITIVE) PROCESS DEPENDENT ON INDIVIDUALS	TRAINING TECHNICAL PRACTICES - REVIEWS, TESTING PROCESS FOCUS - STANDARDS, PROCESS GROUPS	
1 INITIAL	(AD HOC)	PROJECT MANAGEMENT PROJECT PLANNING CONFIGURATION MANAGEMENT SOFTWARE QUALITY ASSURANCE	RISK

FIGURE 4-6. Software process maturity levels.[20, p. 23]

Also, of concern to TQM are:

- The level of technology used in software engineering should be appropriate to the maturity of the process.
- Software products developed for DOD are acquired under contracts invoking DOD-STD-2167A, *Defense System Software Development.*[41]

To provide a structure for assessment, five levels of process maturity (Figure 4-6) have been postulated.

Process Maturity Levels

1. Initial. The initial environment has ill-defined procedures and controls. The organization does not consistently apply software engineering management to the process, nor does it use modern tools and technology. Level 1 organizations may have serious cost and schedule problems.
2. Repeatable. At level 2, the organization has generally learned to manage costs and schedules, and the process is now repeatable. The organization uses standard methods and practices for managing software development activities such as cost estimating, scheduling, requirements changes, code changes, and status reviews.
3. Defined. In level 3, the process is well characterized and reasonably well understood. The organization defines its process in terms of software

engineering standards and methods, and it has made a series of organizational and methodological improvements. These specifically include design and code reviews, training programs for programmers and review leaders, and increased organizational focus on software engineering. A major improvement in this phase is the establishment and staffing of a software engineering process group that focuses on the software engineering process and the adequacy with which it is implemented.

4. Managed. In level 4, the process is not only understood but it is quantified, measured, and reasonably well controlled. The organization typically bases its operating decisions on quantitative process data, and conducts extensive analyses of the data gathered during software engineering reviews and tests. Tools are used increasingly to control and manage the design process as well as to support data gathering and analysis. The organization is learning to project expected errors with reasonable accuracy.

5. Optimizing. At level 5, organizations have not only achieved a high degree of control over their process, they have a major focus on improving and optimizing its operation. This includes more sophisticated analyses of the error and cost data gathered during the process as well as the introduction of comprehensive error cause analysis and prevention studies. The data on the process are used iteratively to improve the process and achieve optimum performance.[20, pp. 1-6]

There is a guide (Table 4-6) to assess the status of TQM implementation. That table is laid out in a fashion similar to the software process maturity levels chart (Figure 4-6), and so is a thread to help tie TQM implementation maturity with software process implementation maturity. Also see Chapter 1 for Capability Maturity Model.

Westinghouse Software Process Organization

In response to an SEI assessment Westinghouse Electronic Systems Group (ESG) software organizations defined the Software Engineering Process Organization (SEPO). A description of the Westinghouse ESG SEPO is given here because this is a critical element in the company-wide environment to achieve total quality management for software engineering. The organization is matrixed, the programs are diversified, and the groups are multi-divisional and geographically distributed. Within this framework, the Westinghouse ESG SEPO model is pictured in Figure 4-7 and reflects the constraints and composition of the organization.

Westinghouse ESG's SEPO is composed of three components: (1) the software management steering committee (SMSC); (2) various technology groups; and (3) an administrative group.

The model is configured to address the needs of Westinghouse ESG by having representation from each software group. Each component of the model serves a specific role in defining, documenting, and improving the software engineering process. Furthermore, each component interacts to ensure uniformity and consis-

TABLE 4-6   TQM Implementation Status Guide[12, p.11]

TQM Category	Top Management Commitment	Obsession with Excellence	Organization Is Customer-Driven	Customer Satisfaction
5	Continuous improvement is a natural behavior even during routine tasks	Constant, relative improvement in quality, cost, and productivity	Customer satisfaction is the primary goal	More customers state intention to maintain long-term business relationship
4	Focus is on improving the system	Use of cross-functional improvement teams	Customer feedback used in decision making	Striving to improve value to customers is a routine behavior
3	Adequate money and time allocated to continuous improvement and training	TQM support system setup and in use	Tools used to include wants and needs in design	Positive customer feedback; complaints used to improve
2	Balance of long term goals with short term objectives	Executive steering committee set up	Customer needs and wants are known	Customer rating of company is known
1	Traditional approach to quality control • Inspection is primary tool (control of defects, not prevention) • Better quality = higher cost • Significant scrap and rework activity • Quality control found only in manufacturing departments Management by objectives improperly used for all departments			

tency of software process issues. It is the SMSC which acts as the unifying and central component for software process improvement across the organization. The technology groups, which are composed primarily of senior level practitioners, are the primary vehicle for the definition, evaluation, and insertion of new technology within the organization. The administrative group documents the process and performs periodic assessments of the organization. Each component is discussed in further detail in the sections which follow.

Software Management Steering Committee

The SMSC is composed of managers from each software group and software quality within Westinghouse ESG. The SMSC is currently chaired by one of these software managers, and it serves as the focal point for software process improvement within Westinghouse ESG. Both the technology groups and the administrative group receive their direction and leadership from the SMSC. Its major functions are to:

1. Establish software engineering policies for ESG.
2. Ensure the compatibility of software policies with system policies.
3. Ensure the compatibility of software policies with customer requirements.

TABLE 4-6   Continued

TQM Category	Training	Employee Involvement	Use of Incentives	Use of Tools
5	Training in TQM tools common among all employees	People involvement; self-directing work groups	Gainsharing (cross-functional teams)	Statistics is a common language among all employees
4	Top management understands and applies TQM philosophy	Manager defines limits; asks group to make decision	More team than individual incentives and rewards	Design and other departments use SPC techniques
3	On going training programs	Manager presents problem, gets suggestions, makes decision	Quality related employee selections and promotion criteria	SPC* used for variation reduction
2	Training plan developed	Manager presents ideas and invites questions, makes decision	Effective employee suggestion program used	SPC used in manufacturing
1	Traditional approach to quality control • Inspection is primary tool (control of defects, not prevention) • Better quality = higher cost • Significant scrap and rework activity • Quality control found only in manufacturing departments Management by objectives improperly used for all departments			

*SPC used as an example

4. Specify technical/management activities to support software process improvement and technology insertion.
5. Establish and then evaluate the performance of the technology groups.
6. Analyze the software process data and software metrics collected by the administrative group, and
7. Make recommendations to resolve software policy issues.

Technology Groups

The technology groups are staffed from all the software groups of ESG. Members are practitioners who dedicate some time to software process improvement through technology group membership. This practice has proved to be very effective over the past six years. The membership of these groups overlap, thus supporting the sharing of information and technologies among all groups. Each technology group is chaired by a software engineer and receives its direction from the SMSC. The major common functions of the technology groups are to:

1. Develop software process definition
2. Develop appropriate standards and procedures for software
3. Develop software process databases

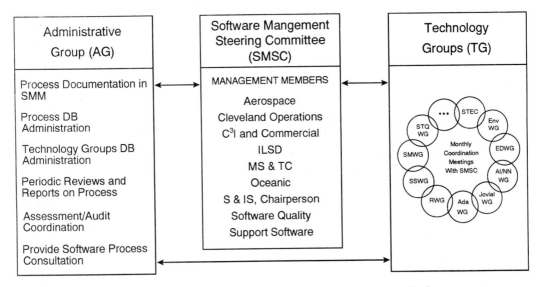

Administrative Group (AG)	Software Mangement Steering Committee (SMSC)	Technology Groups (TG)
Process Documentation in SMM Process DB Administration Technology Groups DB Administration Periodic Reviews and Reports on Process Assessment/Audit Coordination Provide Software Process Consultation	MANAGEMENT MEMBERS Aerospace Cleveland Operations C^3I and Commercial ILSD MS & TC Oceanic S & IS, Chairperson Software Quality Support Software	

FIGURE 4-7. Software engineering process organization (SEPO).[32, p. 7]

4. Identify, screen, and evaluate technologies
5. Establish plans for transferring and inserting new technologies into the organization
6. Develop plans for training/education.

Administrative Group

The administrative group is staffed with a software engineering support staff of managers and engineers. Its major functions are to:

1. Document the software process definition in the Software Management Manual
2. Maintain a centralized repository of software process data
3. Maintain a centralized repository of data (or data directory) for the technology groups
4. Provide periodic reviews and reports on the status of ESG's software process
5. Coordinate/conduct periodic audits/assessments for ESG software.

The collective activities of all three components comprise the Westinghouse SEPO.[32, pp. 6-8]

Since all parts of SEPO must be chartered, it became necessary to standardize a charter format for each element and every technology group of SEPO. That format follows:

NAME—SHORT TITLE
Charter
Date
Name
Purpose
Functions
Management
Membership
Authorization[32, pp. A-1, A-2]

4.6 SOFTWARE TQM

Throughout industry, most software middle management has not been willing to try quality techniques which originated from the manufacturing of hardware. Many believed that their individual quality programs were sufficient even though the quality results indicated otherwise.[26, p. 4C-9]

Traditionally, software engineering efforts have concentrated on essentially minimizing user dissatisfaction from the software development process. The focus was on detecting defects (by inspection, testing, or logging complaints), looking upstream to analyze the causes of the defects, and then working to eliminate those causes from the software engineering process. This approach seeks to minimize user's complaints (negative quality).

Today, software engineering should concentrate more on maximizing user satisfaction from the software engineering process. The focus is on preventing the causes of defects by a deeper understanding of the user's true requirements. One should work downstream to design quality into the system, and continuously work to improve the software engineering process with innovation. This approach seeks to maximize the user's compliments (positive quality).[43, p. 7]

Westinghouse Software Implementation

To improve the software engineering process with innovation at Westinghouse ESG we are combining the SEPO elements with the Westinghouse TQM methods. Figure 4-8 is a portrayal of the interface of the elements between TQM methods and the heart of the SEPO, i.e., the working groups.

The working groups are listed in the figure and it may be seen that they are the major technical drivers in software development. The working groups are composed of representatives from various divisions and multiple projects as already described. The working groups focus on cycle reductions. These cycle reductions regularly produce higher quality and productivity.

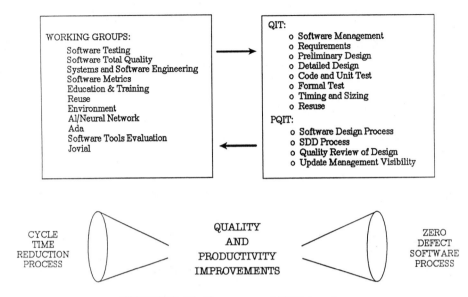

FIGURE 4-8. Working groups and QIT interaction.

For software management, the TQM implementation is the Westinghouse methodology. So, there are QITs to model the software development process and PQITs to uncover and correct process deficiencies. The process implementation modeled is based on the zero software defects method described in the author's book.[30]

The working groups are directed on improvement to the product through project implementations (which follow Juran's idea). The QITs and PQITs are directed on improvement to the process through software development process charting and decomposition. The software development process chart is shown in the appendix to Chapter 16.

Each process is decomposed in the standard Process Model (Figure 4-9). The numbers on the model need a description. Number 1 describes the process. In the case of software development it is the expansion of a higher level software development process chart. Number 2 tells what outputs come from the process. Number 3 lists the inputs to the process. Number 4 tells who the customer is for this process. Remember this is more often than not an internal customer. What that customer requires of you (of your process) is number 5. The suppliers to the process are number 6. Number 7 is the requirements for the process placed on the suppliers. Finally, number 8 provides various controlling elements for this process, including procedures/policies, training/education, equipment/facilities, and quality standards.

With the software development process modeled the process improvements achieved by the PQITs are transferrable to the SEPO working groups as illustrated in Figure 4-10. This provides the working groups with a process that interconnects to product improvements.

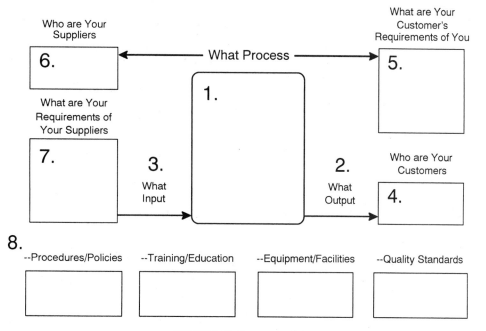

FIGURE 4-9. Process model.

A Defense System Management College[4, p. 6] course ties software TQM together in a similar conceptual manner. Software TQM consists of two parts: process control and production methods, and product quality control and assessment.

TQM–SEPO Bridge

Figure 4-11 provides a flow diagram of the bridge between the TQM activities and the SEPO organization. The question of how to institutionalize and promulgate the recommendations of the software PQITs has been asked often in the software TQM environment.

The Software Total Quality Working Group (STQWG) functions as this bridge to SEPO. The STQWG, taking account of the PQITs and acting on recommendations for corrective action, uses the SEPO technology working groups expertise for review. Of crucial importance is the SEPO Systems/Software Working Group (SSWG) (also refer to Figure 4-10) because it is specifically responsible for the software process.

Remember Dr. Deming's exhortation number 9, given in Section 4.3, to "break down barriers between departments." From a TQM perspective, the figurative "BRIDGE" presented in Figure 4-11 is representative of the Westinghouse ESG commitment to breaking down these barriers. The bridge is also a real connection at Westinghouse ESG between TQM and software process improvement.

When the STQWG deems it is appropriate, the PQIT corrective action recom-

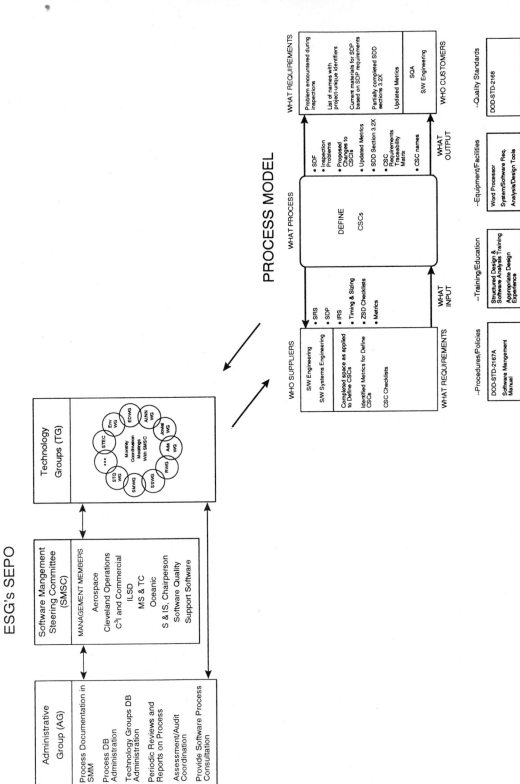

FIGURE 4-10. Process model and SEPO interaction.

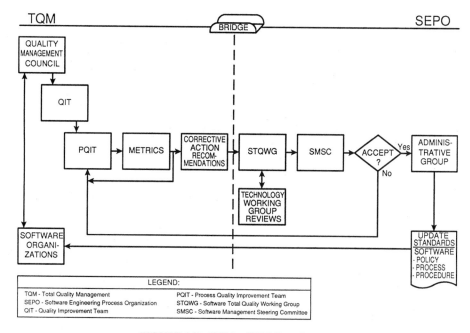

TQM   BRIDGE   SEPO

FIGURE 4-11. TQM—SEPO flow diagram.

mendation is flowed to the Software Management Steering Committee (SMSC). The approval authority for recommendation implementation rests with the SMSC.

Once approved, the corrective action is handed off to the SEPO Administrative Group which incorporates the recommendation into the software standards. When promulgated, the standard returns to the process owners, the software organizations, for implementation.

TQM for Unprecedented Systems

At Westinghouse ESG much of the software development is done for unprecedented systems. In May 1990 Dr. Richard Sylvester of the MITRE Corporation asked, "Can you use TQM for unprecedented systems?"[35] Some description of unprecedented systems is now given, and a response is provided.

A precedented system consists of three fundamental factors: a requirements factor, an architecture factor, and a team factor. Regarding the requirements factor, a precedented system is one in which the system requirements, and hence the software requirements, are very well defined and understood by the team responsible for implementing those requirements. Regarding the architectural factor, a precedented system has a proven hardware and software architecture. For a system to be precedented in its development requires that it have an experienced development team consisting of systems engineers, and designers and developers of hardware and software who have worked together before on a similar project, so that their process of working together is well-established. A precedented system, then, is one in which the development deals with requirements and architectural performance that are both understood, and which has a team that "has been there before." An unprecedented system is one in which not all of these elements are available to the development.[34, pp. 3, 6]

Because the best description of an unprecedented system involves a requirements factor, an architecture factor, and a team factor, each factor needs to be addressed in relation to TQM. First, the team factor would, in fact, be helped by TQM implementation because a major factor and strength of TQM is team focus and building. The architecture factor is not as clearly helped by the TQM methodology. But, by building a PQIT/working group to accomplish software architectural understanding, TQM can provide help. The PQIT/working group should be composed of the developers and the customer for understanding the user needs. Finally, most difficult to benefit from TQM is the requirements factor. Dr. Deming's message says, "help the people, provide tools." This simple shibboleth of TQM will help the requirements factor of unprecedented systems. Even though these are new requirements, the tools for requirements decomposition and tracing will help software developers handle the uniqueness better. These tools, of course, are also used for requirements of precedented systems.

Quality Improvement Paradigm

Dr. Victor Basili, with the Computer Science Department of the University of Maryland, has provided a quality improvement paradigm[3] for software development. This paradigm for quality improvement of software has the following main points. Characterize the current project and its environment. Set the quantifiable goals for successful project performance and improvement. Choose the appropriate process model and supporting methods and tools for this project. Execute the processes, construct the products, collect and validate the prescribed data, and analyze it to provide real time feedback for corrective action. Analyze the data to evaluate the current practices, determine problems, record findings, and make recommendations for improvement for future project improvements. Package the experience in the form of updated and refined models and other forms of structured knowledge gained from this and prior knowledge so that it is available for future projects. The steps of this paradigm are:

1. Develop a set of corporate, division, and project goals for productivity and quality, e.g., customer satisfaction, on time delivery, improved quality.
2. Based upon these goals, define operational definitions (in the form of questions) that characterize, evaluate, predict, and motivate quality and productivity.
3. Specify the measures needed to be collected to answer those questions and to track process and product conformance to the goals.
4. Develop mechanisms for data collection.
5. Collect, validate, and analyze the data in real time to provide feedback to projects for corrective action.
6. Analyze the data in a post mortem fashion to assess conformance and make recommendations for future improvements.

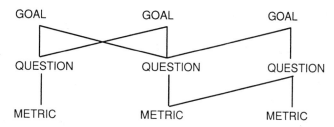

FIGURE 4-12. The GQM model.[3, p. 3]

This Goal, Question, Metric (GQM) model is shown in Figure 4-12. A goal links two models:

- A model of the object of interest, and
- A model of the quality perspective,

and develops an integrated model. For example: Goal: characterize the final product with respect to defect classes; Question: what is the error distribution by phase of entry?; Metric: requirements errors.

A process goal example is used to analyze the system test process for the purpose of evaluation with respect to defect slippage from the point of view of the corporation.

The System Test Process Model follows these steps:

Goal: Generate a set of tests consistent with the complexity and importance of each requirement.

Procedure: 1. Enumerate the requirements, 2. Rate importance by marketing, 3. Rate complexity by system tester, 4 . . .

The Defect Slippage Model follows these steps:

Let F_c = the ratio of faults found in the system test to the faults found after the system test on this project.

Let F_s = the ratio of faults found in the system test to the faults found after the system test in the set of projects used as a basis for comparison.

Let $QF = F_c/F_s$ = the relationship of the system test on this project to faults as compared to the average on the appropriate basis set.

A simple interpretation of the Defect Slippage Model is:

if $QF > 1$ then

        method better than history
        check process conformance
        if process conformance poor
          improve process or process conformance
        check domain conformance
        if domain conformance poor
          improve object or domain training

```
if QF = 1 then

        method equivalent to history
        if cost lower than normal
            method cost effective
            check process conformance

        . . .

if QF < 1 then

        check process conformance
        if process conformance good
            check domain conformance
            if domain conformance good
                method poor for this class of project
```

Based upon the goals, we interpret the data that has been collected. We can use this data to characterize and understand what project characteristics affect the choice of processes, methods, and techniques, and which phase is typically the greatest source of errors. We can use the data to evaluate and analyze what the statement coverage of the acceptance test plan is, and how well the Cleanroom process (Chapter 18) reduces the rework effort. We can use the data to predict and control, e.g., given a set of project characteristics, what the expected cost and reliability are, based upon our history. We can use the data, again, to motivate and improve. For example, we can determine for what class of errors a particular technique is most effective.

Again, software TQM consists of two parts: process control and production methods, and product quality control and assessment.[4, p. 6] Improving the software process and product requires the continual accumulation of evaluated experiences (learning) in a form that can be effectively understood and modified (experience models) into a repository of integrated experience models (experience base) that can be accessed and modified to meet the needs of the current project (reuse). Systematic learning requires support for recording experience, off-line generalizing and tailoring of experience, and formalizing of experience. Packaging useful experience requires a variety of models and formal notations that are tailorable, extendible, understandable, flexible, and accessible.[3]

4.7 CONCLUSIONS

No improvement can be categorized as a complete success unless control is established at a new level of performance. To control the improvement at its new level and prevent reversal of the improvement, measurements must be established and specific individuals assigned the responsibility to monitor the new processes.[19, p. 4C-21]

In his book, *Software Quality: Concepts and Plans,* Robert Dunn says of software: "Perhaps we should view a quality improvement program not simply as an agent for change, but as an agent for change in the direction pointed to by measurement."[15, p. 191]

There is a way to measure TQM implementation improvements. A total quality fitness review is a process for reviewing total quality programs and practices of an operation. It provides a confidential snapshot of the operation's strengths and weaknesses from a total quality viewpoint. It also gives recommendations for improvement areas.[42, p. 4]

The Defense Science Board Task Force dealing with problems in federal government computer software development and regulation spoke for all government managers when it reported that the software problem was "that we cannot get enough of it, soon enough, reliable enough, and cheap enough." A proposed solution, not universally accepted, would be to apply to software development the same statistical quality control methods advocated by W. Edwards Deming and used with remarkable success in Japanese industry, in essence, the application of TQM methods to software.[7, p. 10]

Finally, with regard to software development in the United States of America we must begin and continue to follow the vision of W. Edwards Deming who said, "We have to make a nationwide commitment to quality. There are no shortcuts. The Japanese made a commitment to quality nearly 30 years ago and they are still learning and moving ahead faster and faster."[11, p. Q31]

References

1. Angiola, Peter, *The View of Total Quality Management,* Presentation material from Directorate for Industrial Productivity and Quality of the Department of Defense, 16 November 1989.
2. Augustine, Norman R., "TQM is the Key to Being a Winner," *Martin Marietta TODAY,* No. 1, 1990.
3. Basili, Victor, "Improving the Software Process and Product in a Measurable Way," Presentation at Monroeville, Pennsylvania on 13-14 December 1990.
4. Bergstrom, Deane F., *Software Total Quality Management Presentation to Defense Systems Management College,* Rome Air Development Center, 15 February 1990.
5. Boehm, Barry W., "Improving Software Productivity," *IEEE Computer,* Copyright © 1987 IEEE, New York, September, 1987, Reprinted with permission of IEEE.
6. Brown, Donna, "10 Ways to Boost Quality," *Management Review* 80(1), Copyright © January 1991 by American Management Assn., Inc., Reprinted by permission.
7. *Bugs in the Program—Problems in Federal Government Computer Software Development and Regulation* Washington, D.C.: U.S. Government Printing Office, 1990.
8. Cannie, Joan Koob with Donald Caplin, *Keeping Customers for Life* New York: AMACOM, 1991, Copyright © 1991 by American Management Assn., Inc., Reprinted by permission.
9. Costello, Robert B., Presentation at the Air Force Scientific Advisory Board, The National Defense University, 20 October 1988.
10. Crosby, Philip B., Editorial on "What Does TQM Mean?," *Quality Update* Nov.-Dec. 1989.
11. Deming, W. Edwards, "Product Quality—It Does Work," *Quality* 1980.
12. Department of Defense, *Total Quality Management—A Guide for Implementation (Draft) DOD 5000.51-G* 23 March 1989.
13. Department of Defense, *Total Quality Management Master Plan* August 1988.

14. Department of the Treasury, Internal Revenue Service, *Service Center Director Memorandum SC-O 12-47 Rev. 1* 29 January 1988.

15. Dunn, Robert M., *Software Quality: Concepts and Plans,* Englewood Cliffs: Prentice-Hall Inc., 1990.

16. Glovka, Robert M., "The Changing Role of the Quality Professional in Support of Total Quality Management," *NAECOM Conference Proceedings,* 23-27 May 1989.

17. Greebler, Carol, *Total Quality Management Course Material,* Developed for Defense System Management College by Navy Personnel Research and Development Center, 1988.

18. Hansen, Richard L., "An Overview to the Application of Total Quality Management," Aeronautical System's Division, U.S. Air Force, 1990.

19. Horvath, Jeffrey P. and Katherine B. Dalmia, "Using Quality Improvement Methodologies As a Tool for Improving Management Processes," *Juran Institute Conference Proceedings,* Atlanta, Copyright © 1989 by Juran Institute, Inc.

20. Humphrey, Watts S. and W. L. Sweet, *A Method for Assessing the Software Engineering Capability of Contractors Technical Report CMU/SEI-87-TR-23* September 1987.

21. Internal Revenue Service, *Ogden Service Center Quality Improvement Process Training Charts* 17 June 1988.

22. Johansson, Hank and Dan McArthur, "Rediscovering the Fundamentals of Quality," *Management Review,* January 1988, Copyright © 1988 by American Management Assn., Inc., Reprinted by permission.

23. Juran, Joseph M., *Managerial Breakthrough,* New York: McGraw-Hill Book Co., 1964.

24. Landau, Samuel, *Total Quality Management as an Organizational Change Effort: Implementation Requirements,* Navy Personnel Research and Development Center, 1988.

25. *Leading with Total Quality,* Brochure from Westinghouse Electronic Systems Group, April 1990.

26. Malik, Roy G. and Richard A. Snell, "Planning, Developing, and Implementing a Quality Program Across Multiple Product and Service Organizations," *Juran Institute Conference Proceedings,* Atlanta, Copyright © 1989 by Juran Institute, Inc.

27. Moore, W. Savage, "Singing the Same 'Total Quality' Song," *National Defense,* March 1990.

28. Ogden Air Logistics Center, *OO–ALC/MM Quality Improvement Implementation Plan–QP4* 17 June 1988.

29. Sashkin, Marshall, *A Manager's Guide to Participative Management,* New York: AMA, 1982, Copyright © 1982 American Management Assn., Reprinted by permission.

30. Schulmeyer, G. Gordon, *Zero Defect Software,* New York: McGraw-Hill Book Co., 1990.

31. Sikovy, Loel J., "Product Quality–The Organization," *Quality* 1980.

32. *Software Process Assessment Action Plan,* Westinghouse Electronic Systems Group, 31 January 1989, Copyright © 1989 Westinghouse Electronic Systems Group.

33. Strickland, Jack, "Total Quality Management," *Army Research, Development & Acquisition Bulletin,* March-April 1988.

34. Sylvester, Richard J. and Albert C. Vosburg, "Software Engineering Risks in Unprecedented Systems (draft–Not Yet Published)," The MITRE Corporation, September, 1990.

35. Sylvester, Richard J., private conversation held on 16 May 1990.

36. TASC, *Total Quality Management–The Path to Cultural Change TR-5308-8-4,* October 1988.

37. *Total Quality—A Westinghouse Imperative,* Management Overview, May 1986.
38. *Total Quality Management at Sikorsky Aircraft,* Brochure, 1990.
39. *Total Quality Management Training and Implementation Services Price List Catalog,* Office of Personnel Management, Supplied by IIT Research Institute, Rome, NY 12440, 1 September 1990.
40. Total Quality Management (TQM) Awareness Training, DCASR Philadelphia, 1988.
41. U.S. Joint Logistics Command, DOD-STD-2167A, *Military Standard—Defense System Software Development,* Washington, D.C.: NAVMAT 09Y, 29 Feb. 1988.
42. Westinghouse Productivity & Quality Center, "Total Quality—A Westinghouse Imperative," May 1986.
43. Zultner, Richard E., CQE, "Software Quality [Function] Deployment—Adapting QFD to Software," Copyright © June 1989 by Richard Zultner, Reprinted by permission.

PART II

Software Directions
to TQM

5

Understanding
the Software Process

Ron S. Kenett

School of Management
State University of New York

5.1 INTRODUCTION

This chapter is about understanding the software process so that it can be improved. Such improvements are necessary in order to gain (or retain) competitive advantage. The basic premise of Total Quality Management (TQM) for software is that improved software development processes, including maintenance of operational software, lead to reductions in rework activities, shorter development cycles and increased customer satisfaction. The objective is to produce better software at a faster pace, thereby reducing costs and providing more value to the final customer.

This is in direct contrast to an approach relying solely on inspections and reviews to assure compliance of the finished product with customers needs and expectations. Deming[1] quotes an extreme case of overinspection where the contractual acceptance criterion for a certain circuit board required four different inspectors to indicate approval by signature for each of the 1100 components on the board—a total of 4400 signatures per circuit board. Software modules provide another example where the typical production of error free units relies heavily on inspections and tests. Deming has a clear message to management: "Cease dependence on inspection to achieve quality. Eliminate the need for mass inspection by building quality into the product in the first place—Do it right the first time."

The basic concepts and tools used in this chapter are borrowed from the areas of Process and Quality Management. The main concepts are introduced in the

119

next section using, initially, examples from manufacturing and service industries. These concepts are then applied to the software development environment. The contrast between software development, manufacturing and services, provides a perspective for viewing TQM in the software development framework. The third section covers what many organizations consider to be a standard kit of tools for process improvement. These tools, the "Magnificent Seven," are presented in the context of software development using real life examples. Section 5.4 discusses methods for assessing an organization's software engineering capability. In conclusion, a section on strategic planning for software quality improvement deploys a generic strategic plan for organizations which plan to improve their competitive position in the software development area.

5.2 BASICS OF PROCESS MANAGEMENT

Processes are easily recognized in environments with repetitive operations. For instance, a bank teller handles customer requests using a procedure that is designed to provide customers with a uniform level of service. In order to achieve this uniformity banks typically provide employees with training programs and written material describing policies and procedures. As a second example consider a machine operator who automatically inserts electronic components into printed circuit boards, has a set of specifications listing requirements for the inserted components, an operator's manual to follow, a maintenance schedule to comply with and a troubleshooting handbook to help overcome unexpected problems.

Both the bank teller and the machine operator are in charge of processes where "inputs" are transformed into "outputs." The teller satisfies a customer request using a form completed by the customer, a terminal, a printer, verbal instructions from his supervisor and what he has learned in the bank's training program. All these are inputs to the process. The teller transforms these inputs into an output or "product" that has an impact on the customer. This transformation is called a "process." The rendered service is the output. The inputs are provided by "suppliers," some internal to the bank and some external.

A key factor in improving processes is feedback. One prime source of feedback on the performance of a process is derived from simply asking the customer. This is typically done using written surveys and customer interviews. An important characteristic of processes in the service industries is that their products cannot be stored and that there is no possible inventory build-up. On the other hand the machine operator can produce batches of circuit boards that can wait on carts or conveyor belts for the next manufacturing step to begin.

The insertion of components' process transforms bare circuit boards into assembled boards, ready to be soldered and tested. The feedback on the components' insertion process comes from several sources: internal feedback from the operator's self-inspection procedure using the specifications for the inserted components and external feedback coming from the soldering and testing processes. These sources of feedback provide information on the degree to which the automatic insertion process meets specified requirements and internal customers' needs. Specifically the testing group can be perceived as an internal customer of the automatic insertion group.

A high percentage of error free assembled boards, when first tested, is a basic requirement of the test group. High failure rates result in "waste" consisting of high work-in-process inventory, retesting, rework activities and long production cycle times. Again, as in the bank's teller case, the process, its internal customers and its internal suppliers are relatively easy to identify. Feedback loops can be naturally created and activated.

How do these concepts apply to software development? Looking at a glossary of software engineering terminology[2] one finds that a *Process* is defined as "A sequence of steps performed for a given purpose; for example, the software development process." Under the term *Quality* one finds "(1) The degree to which a system, component, or process meets specified requirements. (2) The degree to which a system, component, or process meets customer or user needs or expectations." These definitions apply globally to the software development process.

Understanding the software development process takes one more step. *These definitions are equally applicable to the subprocesses that make up the software development process.* The basic strategy behind a Software Quality Improvement Plan consists of:

1. Identifying the subprocesses, their inputs and outputs, their internal suppliers and internal customers.
2. Constructing relevant feedback loops and organizational structures to induce improvements of the various software development subprocesses.

IEEE and Military Standards

This discussion is based on IEEE[3] and military[4] standards for software development. The IEEE 730.1-1989 standard stipulates that, as a minimum, eight types of reviews are to be conducted:

1. Software Requirements Review (SRR)
2. Preliminary Design Review (PDR)
3. Critical Design Review (CDR)
4. Software Verification Review
5. Functional Audit
6. Physical Audit
7. In-Process Audit
8. Managerial Reviews.

These audits and reviews implicitly delineate several subprocesses and their expected "outputs." A separate section of the IEEE standard deals with "Problem Reporting and Corrective Action" indicating how feedback is provided to resolve problems and improve these subprocesses.

The DOD-STD-2167A standard states: "The software development process shall include the following major activities, which may overlap and may be applied iteratively or recursively:

a. System Requirements Analysis/Design
b. Software Requirements Analysis
c. Preliminary Design
d. Detailed Design
e. Coding and Computer Software Unit Testing
f. Computer Software Component Integration and Testing
g. Computer Software Configuration Item Testing
h. System Integration and Testing."

Moreover, "During the software development process, the contractor shall conduct or support formal reviews and audits as required by the contract." Again, several subprocesses are identified and compliance with the standard requires a formal mechanism for reviewing the outputs of these subprocesses.

Both standards focus mainly on specific contracts or projects, not on the development processes. They emphasizes reviews and inspections as the means to assure compliance with customer needs and expectations. Limits on the number of allowable errors are sometimes even specified. In the early MIL-STD-1679 (Navy)[5] document (now obsolete) one finds the specification that no errors which cause a program to stop or degrade performance without alternative work-around solutions are allowed. However, one error per 70,000 machine instruction words, which degrades performance with a reasonable alternative work-around solution, is allowed; and one error causing inconvenience and annoyance is allowed for every 35,000 machine instruction words.

Processes and Internal Customers

The software development life cycle, as described in the IEEE and military standards (and in most of the software engineering literature) can be broken down, generically, into seven main phases as shown in Figure 5-1.

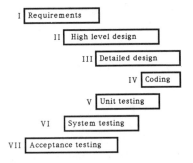

FIGURE 5-1. Software development life cycle.

Each phase is a subprocess with a defined "product," "internal customers," and "internal suppliers." The standards indicate how a given software product completes each one of these phases. The focus of Total Quality Management for software is on controlling and improving the subprocesses represented by the various software development phases. Entering the next phase is equivalent to delivering a product to a customer. An important customer is the development group responsible for carrying out the next phase.

This approach is in sharp contrast to a culture characterized by "tossing the software over the fence." Internal customers have needs and requirements that are either made explicit in a formal statement or left to be implicitly determined. In both cases these requirements can be misunderstood, incomplete, not realizable, or not mutually agreed upon. Moreover it might be impossible to determine and measure whether a "product" actually conforms to customer requirements.

Juran[6] provides three major methods for discovering customer requirements and needs:

- Being a customer
- Communicating with customers
- Simulating customers' needs.

Since a process can have a multitude of customers, Juran advocates the use of flow charts and Pareto analysis to classify customers as belonging to the "vital few" or the "useful many" (note: in recent years Juran changed his terminology of the "trivial many" to the "useful many").

One might argue that there are no "processes" in software development since each requirement document, software module or software version is unique. However the steps involved in their development are repetitive.

Work-in-Process Inventory

Recognizing the existence of development processes is a necessary first step towards process improvement. Like in the electronic assembly plant, inventory can pile up between subprocesses such as carts with printed circuit boards waiting to be soldered or tested. In software development the work-in-process inventory takes the form of software modules waiting to be integrated or features that have to go through detailed design or coding. Processes that "do it right the first time" typically carry no work-in-process inventory. The corollary being that work in the process levels are indicators of poor performance.

Feedback Loops

Figure 5-2 is a sketch of supplier-customer relationships and feedback loops superimposed on the seven main development subprocesses. The sketch does not indicate additional feedback provided from audits and reviews.

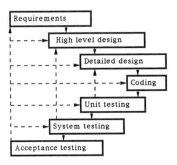

FIGURE 5-2. Feedback in the software development life cycle.

As an example, consider the System Integration and Testing process. The output of this process is a software version released to users. The users performing acceptance tests are clearly the major customers. The suppliers to the process are software developers who supply software modules after completion of unit testing. Other suppliers include requirements engineers who supply requirements documents specifying what the user expects to get in the released software version. A major source of feedback to the "owners" of the System Integration and Testing process consists of defects and misunderstandings reported by the users.

Process Improvements

Improvement of this process requires an ability to answer questions such as: Why wasn't the defect detected? What type of testing could have found the defect? What kind of changes could be made to System Integration Testing to detect such a defect? Improvements can be achieved by changes in procedures, training of personnel, addition of tools such as test coverage probes, increased automation, simulated faults insertion, etc. Sometimes just formalizing a process by preparing its flow chart, identifying its internal customers and researching their needs produces improvements.

Kenett and Koenig[7] describe an automated software development framework integrating disparate software engineering methods and tools that cover the activities of Preliminary Design, Detailed Design, Coding, Unit Testing and System Integration and Testing phases. Under such an environment, the goal of each software development phase is the production of a product milestone. Each product milestone is defined in terms of specific "chapters" and "templates" of a software development library. Such an integrated environment is partially guaranteeing, by design, compliance to internal customers' requirements.

Reviews are merged in the automated software development methodology in order to detect errors in the product milestones. Reviews are necessary for assessing compliance of requirements that could not be fully addressed by the automated software development environment. In the case of computerized software engineering tools it is up to the developers of automated environments to meet internal customers needs and expectations. In general, improvements of the software development process span three major areas:

- Increased error prevention
- Earlier error detection
- Decreased error correction costs.

Typical questions that help determine what changes should be made to improve a software development process are:

- When in the software life cycle do errors occur?
- When and how are errors detected?
- What could have been done to detect the errors earlier?
- When are the errors corrected and at what cost?
- What causes, and what could have prevented, the errors that do occur?

In order to answer these questions effectively, and proceed to make necessary changes in the software development process, two issues have to be addressed simultaneously. One issue deals with effective communication of existing problems in meeting internal customers needs and in answers to questions such as those listed above. The other issue deals with organizational structures that have to be established in order to make practical use of the available information.

The basic process improvement tools described in the next section are field-tested graphical tools that are used as a "communication medium." They enable an organization to work effectively, using teamwork, towards the identification and resolution of defects, problems, and errors. The major organizational structures required to carry out process improvement using these basic tools include a top management steering committee or quality council, quality improvement teams, training programs, and a recognition and reward system. We will not elaborate on these organizational issues, but refer the reader to Chapter 4.

5.3 THE "MAGNIFICENT SEVEN" APPLIED TO SOFTWARE DEVELOPMENT

The preface to the English edition of the famous text by Kaoru Ishikawa on Quality Control[8] states: "The book was written to introduce quality control practices in Japan which contributed tremendously to the country's economic and industrial development."

The Japanese work force did indeed master an elementary set of tools that helped them improve processes at a faster rate than was true in the West. These tools were introduced to Japan in the 1950s by W. Edwards Deming and Joseph M. Juran. The West woke up in the 1980s to discover that there is a "new economic age" where only those excelling in product and process quality survive. One outcome of this awakening is the recent widespread use, in the West, of these elementary problem solving tools. Seven of the tools were nicknamed the "magnificent seven" and they are:

- The Pareto Chart
- The Histogram
- The Run Chart
- Flow Charts
- Cause and Effect Diagrams
- The Scatter Diagram
- Check Sheets

Examples showing applications of some of these tools in the software development context are presented next. More details can be found in the texts by Ishikawa[8] and Juran.[6]

The Pareto Chart

The Pareto Chart displays, using bar graphs sorted in descending order, the relative importance of problems by category. Pareto charts are used to choose the starting point for problem solving, to monitor changes, or to identify the basic cause of a problem. Unsorted error distributions have been applied to software problems for several years[9] and are even part of an IEEE standard.[10]

Two Pareto charts are presented in Figures 5-3 and 5-4. They are based on an analysis of errors in two subsequent versions of software in a PBX electronic switch. Errors reported in version 4 and version 5 were labeled according to the software unit where they occurred. For example the "EKT" category makes up 2.3% of the errors in version 4. In version 5 that category made up 7.8% of the errors. This difference can be attributed to an assignable cause. Why such a difference? Possible answers are different testing methods, changes in requirements,

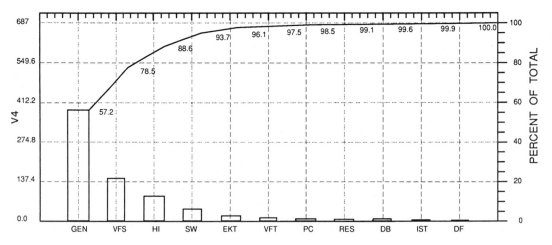

FIGURE 5-3. Pareto chart of software errors in version 4.

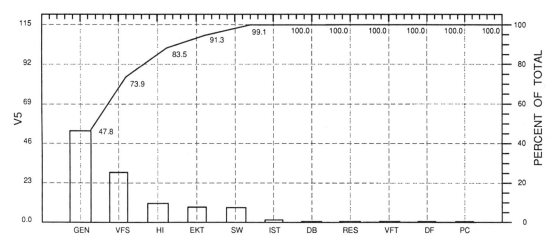

FIGURE 5-4. Pareto chart of software errors in version 5.

new personnel, etc. What can we learn from this about the process? In both versions the "GEN," "VHS," and "HI" categories account for over 80% of the errors. These appear to be the chronic problems on which major improvements efforts should concentrate. (For more on statistical methods used to compare Pareto Charts see Kenett.[11])

The Histogram

In an effort to develop meaningful decision criteria for for exiting the System Integration and Testing process, Kenett and Pollak[12] analyzed data collected on a real operational software system by John Musa of AT&T. The data consists of CPU seconds of software operations between failures. A histogram graphically displays the distribution of CPU seconds and enables us to characterize the level and variability in these numbers. Figure 5-5 presents a histogram of the CPU seconds. The distribution is skewed to the right. In eight cases the system operated for over 2000 CPU seconds before failing. The gap between 1500 and 1800 seconds indicates that improvements tend to occur in "jumps." Most runs lasted between 100 and 400 CPU seconds. The average value of this distribution is 580 CPU seconds; a very partial and misleading summary of the data.

The Run Chart

Spreading these numbers over time, in the order they occurred, enables us to construct the run chart displayed in Figure 5-6. The increase, over time, of CPU seconds between failures is apparent. We can see that over 25% of the total system operating time accumulated in testing occurred between the last 10 failures (out of 136). In contrast, the first 25% of total operations saw over 80 failures. When should we stop testing the software? Using a sequential procedure, Kenett and

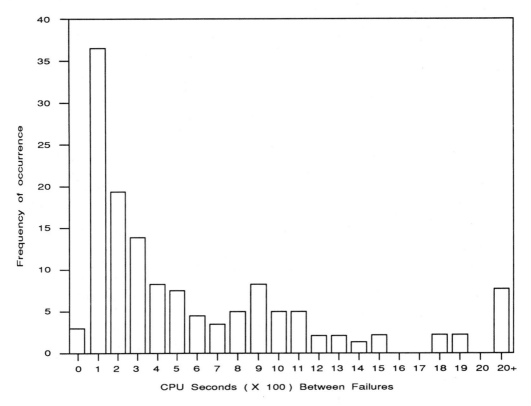

FIGURE 5-5. Histogram of CPU seconds until failure.

Pollak[12] determined that the software system under testing met a Mean Time To Failure requirement (MTTF) of 1000 CPU seconds after the 107th failure. At that point the software could have been released. Other required MTTF levels would obviously lead to other conclusions.

In another example Knuth[13] kept track of all changes made in the development of TeX, a software system for typesetting, during a period of ten years. His log book contained, in 1988, 850 items classified into 15 categories. Quoting Knuth: "The history of the TeX project can teach valuable lessons about the preparation of highly portable software and the maintenance of programs that aspire to high standards of reliability."

The fifteen classes are:

A—Algorithm	F—Forgotten	P—Portability
B—Blunder	G—Generalization	Q—Quality
C—Cleanup	I—Interaction	R—Robustness
D—Data	L—Language	S—Surprise
E—Efficiency	M—Mismatch	T—Typo

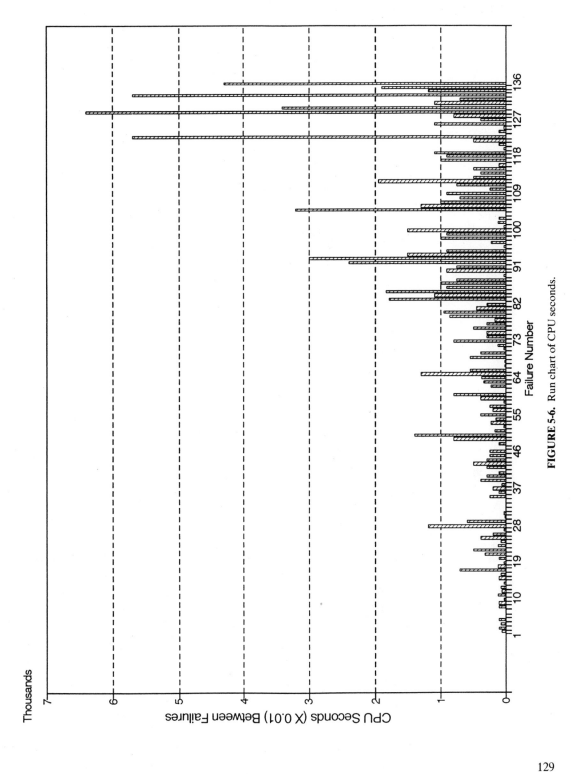

Thousands

CPU Seconds (X 0.01) Between Failures

Failure Number

FIGURE 5-6. Run chart of CPU seconds.

129

The A, B, C, D, F, L, M, R, S, T classifications represent development errors. The C, E, G, I, P, Q classifications represent "enhancements" consisting of unanticipated features that had to be added in late development phases. These enhancements indicate a lack of understanding of customer requirements and, as such, can be considered failures of the requirements analysis process. Figure 5-7 shows a run chart of the accumulated number of failures of each type in TeX78, with errors at

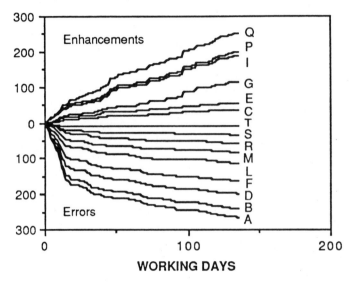

FIGURE 5-7. Accumulated failures of TeX78.

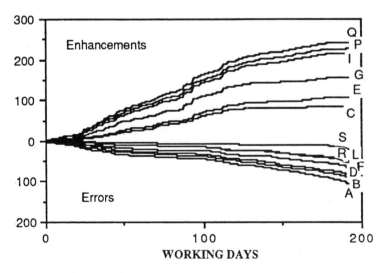

FIGURE 5-8. Accumulated failures of TeX82.

the bottom and enhancements at the top. Initially the log entries are mostly errors with occasional enhancements of type I; at the end, however, enhancements C, G, and Q predominate. Figure 5-8 depicts data for TeX82. Here most failures are enhancements with no errors of type M or T. However Knuth makes a sad confession: "That's because the debugging phase of TeX82 does not appear in the log, not because I learned how to make fewer mistakes."[13]

Flow Charts

An audience of software developers requires no introduction to flow charts. They are presented here as a problem solving tool. In that capacity flow charts can be used to describe a process being studied or to describe a desired sequence and order of a new, improved system. Often preparing a flow chart is the first step taken by a team looking for ways to improve a process. The differences between how a process could work and how it actually does work exposes redundancies, misunderstandings, and general inefficiencies. As an example consider drawing a flow chart of a process, such as coding, in an environment familiar to you. Coding a module should involve, in most cases, only three steps:

1. Studying the relevant segment of the detailed design document
2. Coding
3. Compiling and linking.

All other activities are indicators of problems in the coding process. A flow chart of how things are actually done in your familiar environment would be a first step towards process improvement.

Cause and Effect Diagrams

Cause and Effect diagrams (also called fishbone charts) are used to identify, explore, and display all the possible causes of a problem or event. The diagram is usually completed in a meeting of individuals who are knowledgeable, from first hand, with the problem being investigated. For demonstration purposes, Figure 5-9 shows a Cause and Effect diagram listing causes for an unsuccessful design review. The diagram represents "minutes" of the meeting and points to directions for possible improvements. It is standard practice to weight the causes by impact on the problem investigated and then to initiate projects to reduce the harmful effects of the main causes.

The Scatter Diagram

A Scatter Diagram is used to display what happens to one variable, when another variable changes, in order to test a theory or make forecasts. For example one

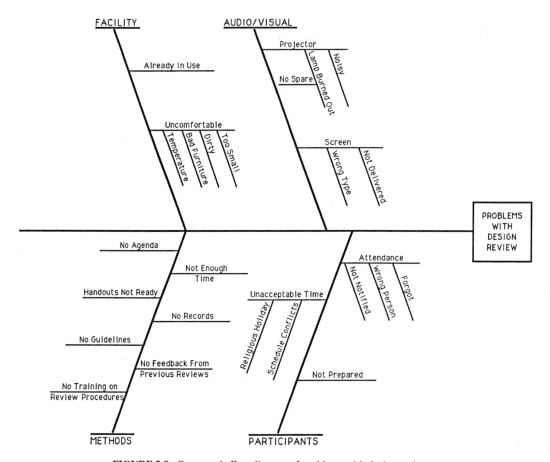

FIGURE 5-9. Cause and effect diagram of problems with design reviews.

might want to verify the theory that the relative number of errors found in inspections declines with increasing unit sizes. Another relationship worth investigating is the amount of code inspection preparation time versus unit size. Scatter diagrams can help us to understand what controllable variables are related to the number of errors found during inspections or to provide a method for flagging troublesome modules during inspections.

Check Sheets

Finally, Check Sheets are basic data collection mechanisms. Configuration Control systems typically provide a readily available source of information where data analysis can provide insights on process improvement opportunities.

5.4 ASSESSING THE SOFTWARE DEVELOPMENT ENVIRONMENT MATURITY LEVEL

A recent article reports that, out of several hundred U.S. software development projects evaluated by the Software Engineering Institute (SEI), 75 to 85% experience unplanned and chaotic activities.[14] SEI has set guidelines and procedures for assessing the ability of potential Department of Defense contractors, or any other interested organization, to develop software in accordance with modern software engineering methods.[15]

As previously noted in this book (Chapters 1 and 4), the SEI assessment methodology is broken down into three areas:

1. Organization and resource management
2. Software engineering process and its management
3. Tools and technology.

The first area deals with functional responsibilities, personnel, and other resource facilities. The intent is to ascertain whether these functional responsibilities are clearly delineated and assigned. In terms of the concepts introduced in Section 5.2 it deals with issues of process ownership and identification of internal customers and suppliers. The second area is concerned with the scope, depth, and completeness of the software engineering process and how the process is measured, managed, and improved. The existence of feedback loops, the use of basic improvement tools and the organizational structures discussed above are of direct consequence to this area. The third area covers software development tools and technologies used in the software engineering process. The integrated software development framework mentioned earlier is an example where an extensive automated development environment is in operation.

Using a detailed scoring method, software engineering organizations are ranked according to a five level "maturity scale," previously discussed in this book. The article quoted at the beginning of this section[14] claims that 15 to 20% of the projects assessed by SEI are at level two, and very few are operating at any higher level.

Malcolm Baldrige National Quality Award

Another set of guidelines that can be adapted to assess a software development environment maturity level is provided by the criteria of the Malcolm Baldrige National Quality Award.[16] The award was created by public law in 1987. The actual awards are presented, every year, by the president of the United States at special ceremonies in Washington. Robert Mosbacher, the current secretary of commerce, has described the award recipients: "The winners of this award have made quality improvement a way of life. Quality is their bottom line, and that kind of can-do attitude makes for world-class products and services."[15]

The award examination is built upon a number of key concepts:

- Quality is defined by the customer.
- The senior leadership of businesses needs to create clear quality values and build the values into the way the company operates.
- Quality excellence derives from well-designed and well-executed systems and processes.
- Continuous improvement must be part of the management of all systems and processes.
- Companies need to develop goals, as well as strategic and operational plans to achieve quality leadership.
- Shortening the response time of all operations and processes of the company needs to be part of the quality improvement effort.
- Operations and decisions of the company need to be based upon facts and data.
- All employees must be suitably trained and developed and involved in quality activities.
- Design quality and defect and error prevention should be major elements in quality activities.
- Companies need to communicate quality requirements to suppliers and work to elevate supplier quality performance.

The examination process covers seven categories that represent the major components of a quality management system. Each category is rated separately up to a maximal number of points. This limit is a reflection of the weight carried by the various categories. The categories and their maximum limits in the 1991 guidelines are:

1. Leadership	100 points
2. Information and Analysis	70 points
3. Strategic Quality Planning	60 points
4. Human Resource Utilization	150 points
5. Quality Assurance of Products and Services	140 points
6. Quality Results	180 points
7. Customer Satisfaction	300 points

"So far few software development organizations can compete seriously for the award, and even fewer made the effort. Mentor Graphics Corp. is one of the exceptions . . . Mentor went through a major overhaul of its development methods three years ago and has since integrated the Baldrige criteria into its current development processes. For instance, Mentor uses "cross teams" including software engineers, customer-support and marketing staffers, and key customers in the development of its software. Involving customers in the process helps shorten product-development cycles and clarify customer requirements. Software developers are motivated to produce high-quality products for the same reasons that hardware manufacturers are: competitive advantage."[14]

For more information on the SEI assessment methodology and the Malcolm Baldrige National Quality Award criteria see the material in References 15 and 16.

5.5 STRATEGIC PLANNING FOR SOFTWARE QUALITY IMPROVEMENT

This concluding section discusses the strategic planning process for software quality improvement. The emphasis is on quality improvements. The processes of quality planning and quality control are only briefly covered. Quality improvement is the organized creation of beneficial changes in process performance levels. Quality planning, on the other hand, is the activity of determining customer needs and the development of products and processes required to meet those needs. Finally, quality control is defined as the managerial process during which actual process performance is evaluated and actions are taken on unusual performance. (For more details on topics of quality management see Juran.[17])

Godfrey[18] lists seven milestones that delineate a road map for the top management of organizations planning their journey towards quality improvement. With some modifications, these milestones are:

- AWARENESS   of the competitive challenges and your own competitive position.
- UNDERSTANDING   of the new definition of quality and of the role of quality in the success of your company.
- VISION   of how good your company can really be.
- PLAN   for action. Clearly define the steps you need to take to achieve your vision.
- TRAIN   your people to provide the knowledge, skills, and tools they need to make your plan happen.
- SUPPORT   actions taken to ensure changes are made, problem causes are eliminated and gains are held.
- REWARD AND RECOGNIZE   attempts and achievements to make sure that quality improvements spread throughout the company and become part of the business plan.

Quoting Juran:[16] "For most companies and managers, annual quality improvement is not only a new responsibility; it is also a radical change in style of management—a change in culture . . . All improvement takes place project by project and in no other way." The message is clear: (1) management has to lead the quality improvement effort and (2) any improvement plan should consist of stepwise increments, building on experience gained in initial pilot projects, before expanding horizontally to cover all subprocesses.

Strategic Planning

A generic plan for driving a software development organization towards continuous process improvement and a case study implementation of the plan is presented in Kenett and Koenig[7] and Kenett.[19] An expanded adaptation of this plan consists of the following five steps:

1. Define an integrated software development process.
2. Support this framework with an automated development environment.
3. Identify key areas for process improvements.
4. Within these areas: assign ownership, determine metrics, create feedback loops, provide training, and establish pilot projects.
5. Support and fortify the continuous improvement efforts.

The first three steps are to be carried out by an interdisciplinary team of experts from the various software development phases. The last three steps have to involve management and working groups centered around the main development subprocesses. Step three sees the phasing-out of the experts team and the phasing-in of improvement projects and middle management direct involvement. The whole effort requires a dedicated "facilitator" and management's commitment and leadership. The global objective is to include every member of the software development organization, its suppliers and customers, in the continuous process improvement effort.

Continuous improvement is not a new concept. The challenge is in the implementation. Piet Hein[20] wrote:

"The road to wisdom? Well, it's plain
and simple to express:
　　Err
　　and err
　　and err again
　　but less
　　and less
　　and less."

Understanding the software process and implementing a continuous process improvement strategy is only the beginning of a never ending journey. Survival and competitive advantage are forcing modern organizations to take this journey.

References

1. Deming, W. Edwards, *Quality, Productivity, and Competitive Position,* Boston, MA: MIT Center for Advanced Engineering Study, 1982.
2. ANSI/IEEE Std 610.12-1990, *Glossary of Software Engineering Terminology,* IEEE Standards Office, P.O. Box 1331, Piscataway, NJ 08855-1331.
3. ANSI/IEEE Std 730.1-1989, *Standard for Software Quality Assurance Plans,* IEEE Standards Office, P.O. Box 1331, Piscataway, NJ 08855-1331.

4. DOD-STD-2167A, 29 February 1988, *Military Standard Defense System Software Development,* Department of Defense, Washington, D.C. 20301.

5. MIL-STD-1679(Navy), 1 December 1978, *Military Standard Weapon System Software Development,* Department of Defense, Washington, D.C. 20360.

6. *Juran's Quality Control Handbook,* J. M. Juran editor-in-chief, fourth edition, McGraw-Hill Book Company, 1988.

7. Kenett, R. S. and Koenig, S., "A Process Management Approach to SQA," *Quality Progress,* pp. 66–70, November 1988.

8. Reprinted from *Guide to Quality Control* by Dr. Kaoru Ishikawa with permission of the Asian Productivity Organization. Distributed in the U.S., Canada, and Western Europe by Quality Resources, White Plains, New York.

9. Schulmeyer, G. G. and McManus, J. I., *Handbook of Software Quality Assurance* (second edition), New York: Van Nostrand Reinhold, 1992.

10. ANSI/IEEE Std 982.1-1988, *Dictionary of Measures to Produce Reliable Software,* IEEE Standards Office, P.O. Box 1331, Piscataway, NJ 08855-1331.

11. Kenett, R. S., "Two Methods for Comparing Pareto Charts," *Journal of Quality Technology,* 23, January 1991.

12. Kenett, R. S. and Pollak, M., "A Semi-Parametric Approach to Testing for Reliability Growth, with Application to Software Systems," *IEEE Transactions on Reliability,* Vol. R-35, 3, 1986.

13. Knuth, D. E., "The Errors of TeX," Report No. STAN-CS-88-1223, Department of Computer Science, Stanford University, Stanford, CA 94305.

14. Davis, D. B., "Software Companies Bugged by Lack of Quality Control," *Electronic Business,* October 15, 1990.

15. Humphrey, W. S. and Sweet, W. L., "A Method for Assessing the Software Engineering Capability of Contractors," Technical Report CMU/SEI-87-TR-23, SEI Carnegie Mellon University, Pittsburgh, Pennsylvania 15213.

16. 1991 Application Guidelines—Malcolm Baldrige National Quality Award, National Institute of Standards and Technology, Gaithersburg, MD 20899.

17. From *JURAN ON LEADERSHIP FOR QUALITY: An Executive Handbook* by Joseph M. Juran. Copyright © 1989 by Juran Institute, Inc. Reprinted by permission of The Free Press, a Division of Macmillan, Inc.

18. Godfrey, A. B., "Buried Treasures and Other Benefits of Quality," *The Juran Report,* 9, Summer 1988.

19. Kenett, R. S., "Managing a Continuous Improvement of the Software Development Process," *Proceedings of the Annual Conference on Quality Improvement,* IMPRO 89. Juran Institute, Inc., 1989.

20. Hein, Piet, *Grooks,* MIT Press, 1966.

6

Quality Measurements in Software

Dave Carey

Westinghouse Electronic Systems Group

Don Freeman

Consultant

6.1 INTRODUCTION

This chapter describes how Total Quality Management (TQM) concepts relate to establishing and operating a software metric program on a development project that has significant software content.

There are many obstacles to successfully setting up and running a metric program. These obstacles are formidable enough to cause most software metric programs to be viewed as a failure by the development communities that use them. Attempts to overcome these obstacles have met with mixed results because the problems are far from trivial. One reason is that we are dealing with both cultural and technical problems that are often difficult to pin down.

The underlying concepts of TQM offer an opportunity to overcome many of these obstacles. TQM concepts can provide a roadmap through the maze that stands between us and a successful metric program. This, however, is only half of the story. There is an interesting synergism between TQM and software metric. First, TQM concepts can be used to properly set up a metric program; then, the metric program becomes a key part of the total quality improvement effort for the project under measurement.

This chapter explores the synergistic relationship between TQM and software metrics. It illustrates the use of TQM concepts to define measurement principles that can be used to set up a successful metric program. The chapter also illustrates how the metric program then supports the TQM goals and objectives of the development project.

The intent is to provide practical guidelines for implementing a metric program for a development project. To do this, a systematic framework is needed to organize the work required to set up and run a metric program. Figure 6-1 illustrates this framework. It divides the effort into five major tasks. The emphasis in this chapter is on the three preparation tasks define the development process; design the measurement system; and plan the implementation. These tasks are an essential prerequisite to a successful metric program. Unfortunately there is a tendency to skip these tasks and immediately start collecting measurement data. This is analogous to starting code development without requirement definition, system design, or implementation planning.

One important TQM concept pervades all five tasks and therefore will be discussed here. This TQM concept has to do with the importance of identifying all of the users; treating them like customers; and satisfying their needs. The concept goes a step further. It asserts that quality should be defined in terms of customer satisfaction. In other words, the product is high quality when the customer says it is.

There are a number of potential customers for the metric data. The most influential customers include:

1. Customer acquisition offices
2. Customer program offices
3. Contractor program management
4. Contractor process improvement groups.

Of these four groups, contractor program management has the most impact on the success or failure of an individual metric program. Without its enthusiastic support, the metric program is doomed from the start. Program management will expect the metric to provide benefits that outweigh the cost and inconvenience of implementing a metric program. Therefore, a clear statement of the cost and

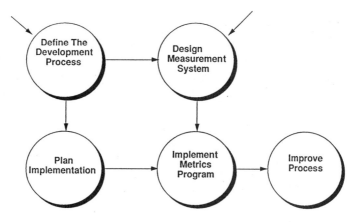

FIGURE 6-1. Total quality metric program.

benefits is usually a prerequisite for getting program management support. This cost/benefit business case should cover both general benefits and benefits of specific value to the program managers.

Perhaps the most important benefit of metric to program managers has to do with their ability to make informed decisions. Being forced to make uninformed decisions because the data isn't available is a common problem. Metrics data provided by the various disciplines is one of the primary mechanisms that program managers use to make informed decisions. Software metric are often more critical than metric from the other disciplines because most program managers do not have the software experience to fall back on. This benefit alone should be enough to convince program management of the value of software metric.

For example, consider a program manager who must decide whether to implement a customer requested change in hardware or software. He asks the hardware and software managers to provide the data needed to make an informed decision. The hardware manager presents detailed metric data that shows a high cost of rework if the change is implemented in hardware. The software manager presents general data but is unable to quantify the cost of rework. It is no surprise to anyone that the program manager chooses to make the change in software. To make matters worse, he may significantly underestimate the cost of making the software change.

It is hard to put the blame for this on program management, particularly if the business case for software metric has never been prepared and presented. The hardware development process was well defined and well measured while the software development process was not. In this situation it is only human nature to view the hardware development process as rigid like a stick and to view the software development process as compressible like a spring.

The rest of the chapter uses Figure 6-1 as an outline. A section is devoted to each task. The focus is on providing guidelines for the software engineers responsible for establishing a metric program on their development projects. No attempt is made to provide "cut and dried" cookbook solutions for the problems of setting up and maintaining a program. Cookbook solutions just do not exist.

6.2 DEFINE THE DEVELOPMENT PROCESS

Defining the development process (Figure 6-2) is the first step in developing a successful metric program. It is more than just an important step; it is an absolute prerequisite to success. Understanding the relationships between: (1) metric, (2) the development process and (3) Total Quality Management (TQM) will help explain why process definition is so important to the overall success of any metric program.

This section defines the role of metric in TQM. It shows how metric help improve the development process in ways that result in improved quality. In doing this, it illustrates the key role that process definition plays in linking a metric program to quality improvements.

This section also provides some guidance on how to define the software development process. Process definition is a complex subject that is far beyond the

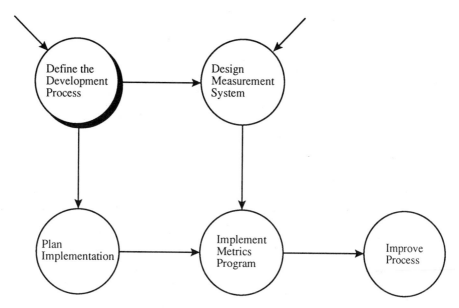

FIGURE 6-2. Development process definition.

scope of this chapter. As a result, this discussion is limited to those aspects of process definition that relate to the gathering and analysis of metric data.

The Role of Metrics in Total Quality Management

The ultimate reason for having a metric program is to improve total quality. This extends to all aspects of software development. Metrics are linked to total quality improvement by the following three notions:

1. Total quality improvement results from process improvement.
2. A controlled process can be improved.
3. Metrics are a mechanism for process control.

In other words, metrics are used for control of the software development process so that it can be improved in ways that increase total quality. Understanding this relationship will improve our chances of designing and implementing a successful metric program. The software development process is the link between metric and total quality. The ability of a metric program to contribute to total quality is directly related to how well the software development process is defined. A poorly defined process essentially breaks the link between a metric program and its primary objective of improving total quality. Also, experience has shown that in many cases defining the process is the most difficult part of the metric program. This is the reason that so much emphasis is placed here on process definition. The following paragraphs provide an elaboration of these three notions.

TOTAL QUALITY IMPROVEMENT RESULTS
FROM PROCESS IMPROVEMENT

One of the fundamental tenets of TQM is that quality and process are tightly linked together. Process improvement is a center piece of the TQM philosophy. A process problem is almost always the root cause of a quality problem. The process problem could be a missing or incorrectly defined activity. The problem could be unrealistic schedules or inadequate resources. Whatever the problem, process improvement is a primary road to increased quality.

Increased quality is not the only benefit of process improvement. Process improvement also increases productivity, resulting in lower cost and a shorter development time. It is useful to tie quality, cost, and schedule together under the umbrella name of "total quality." This broader definition of the term total quality makes sense because quality, cost, and schedule are so closely interdependent. It is pure folly to try to improve one of them while ignoring the other two. The result is usually to improve one at the expense of the other two. For example, attempts to reduce product cost will invariably reduce quality if it is not being continuously measured.

A CONTROLLED PROCESS CAN BE IMPROVED

The key to process improvement is control. The software development process is like most processes—it is inherently unstable. In fact, any human intensive process, if left to its own device, will deteriorate with time. It takes constant effort just to keep the process from getting worse, let alone better. This constant effort, when implemented in a systematic manner, takes the form of a control mechanism. This control mechanism operates on the process to stabilize and then improve it.

METRICS ARE A MECHANISM
FOR PROCESS CONTROL

A useful way to think of metrics is illustrated in Figure 6-3. The software development process is a system whose primary input is requirements. Its primary output is the software system. The metric program can be thought of as a control system that takes measurements on the development process, analyzes these measurements,

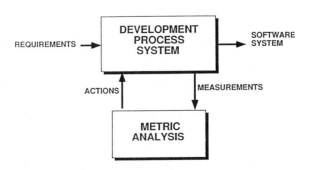

FIGURE 6-3. Metrics feedback paradigm.

and feeds back corrections for problems with the process. The metric program inserts probes into the development process. These probes are carefully placed to collect data that can be analyzed to detect and in some cases predict process failures.

There is an interesting analogy with an electrical circuit, such as an audio amplifier. All amplifiers have feedback circuits to help stabilize the output. Disconnect this feedback path and the amplifier becomes unstable and may go into oscillation. The circuit can actually destroy itself. Most people can relate to the idea of the process getting out of control and self destructing.

Treating metrics as a feedback mechanism is useful because it encourages us to keep the focus on the process. It emphasizes the central role that the process plays in defining the metric. In a sense, we use metrics to fine tune the development process. Everything done to define, collect and analyze metrics must be explicitly tied to the process being measured, corrected, and improved. If we lose sight of the process at any step along the way, the metric program is in serious trouble.

Development Process Definition

So far, this section has provided background and justification for the need to define the development process before defining the metric. Given this, it is necessary to define the development process in enough detail to intelligently use metrics. This is a difficult and arduous task. You may be fortunate enough to be on a project that has already defined the process. Unfortunately, it is more likely that the process is not defined in enough detail. In this case, you will probably have to complete this definition yourself. The result of Section 6.2 is intended to help you in this endeavor. Prepare for the possibility that defining the process may be the most difficult part of the metric program. A useful head start in this may be found in G. Gordon Schulmeyer's *Zero Defect Software*.[1]

As noted previously, a metric program is no better than our understanding of the process that it is measuring. Measuring a poorly defined process is of little value. If the process is not well understood, then there is no baseline to measure against. The last thing we should do is try to measure it. It is hard to imagine a more risky course of action than to experiment with the process at the same time it is being used to develop a deliverable system. Guiding principles on any subject should be:

Do not use metrics to discover how the process *should* work;
Use metrics to discover how the process *is* working.

The following paragraphs provide guidance to help ensure that the development process has been defined in enough detail to meet the needs of the metric program. It is not a comprehensive discussion of how to define the software development process, which is beyond the scope of this chapter. The focus here is on determining if the process has been adequately defined.

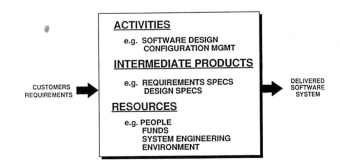

FIGURE 6-4. Software development process is a system for building systems.

DEVELOPMENT PROCESS AS A SYSTEM FOR BUILDING SYSTEMS

Process definition is simplified by recognizing that the development process is a system; a system for building systems. From a metric point of view, it is one of two systems that we need to measure. The other one is the deliverable system. It is important to keep these two systems separated while defining the process. This will greatly simplify the task.

The software development process is a system made up of activities, products, and resources as illustrated in Figure 6-4. To adequately control the process, it will be necessary to measure key attributes of the input, output, and internal operation of the process.

Defining the process is not an easy task. It is, in fact, a formidable task to define the objects (i.e., activities, products, resources) that are the building blocks from which the development process is constructed. It is an even more formidable task to define the complex functional, temporal, organizational, and financial relationships among these objects.

Even though it is a difficult and time consuming task, members of the metric organization must play an active role in defining the development process. They are the only ones who can ensure that the development process is defined in sufficient detail to meet the needs of the metric program. This translates into the following specific objective:

> Ensure that the process objects (i.e., input requirements, output software, activities, products, and resources) that need to be measured are clearly identified and characterized.

The following three step approach will help meet this objective.

DEFINE MAJOR ACTIVITIES

The first step involves identifying the major activities of the development process.

The best approach is to start with a general purpose paradigm that systematically identifies the major activities. There are a number of paradigms in use today. Extensive literature is available on the pros and cons of these paradigms. The best choice will depend on a number of factors that are unique to the specific develop-

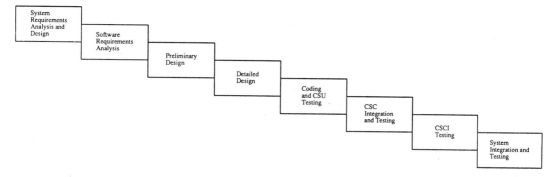

FIGURE 6-5. The waterfall software development model from DOD-STD-2167A.

ment problem. The important thing is to have a paradigm that forces a top down structure on the process definition task.

The simplest choice is the traditional waterfall paradigm illustrated in Figure 6-5. It is extensively used and it does provide a good example. It defines an orderly set of activities that are performed in sequence. It has been in use since the early 1970s and was probably derived from hardware development methods. There are several versions of the model. The one included here is from "Defense System Software Development" (DOD-STD-2167A).[2]

The waterfall paradigm allows us to point out a misconception that is common to all general purpose paradigms. The misconception is that they can be directly used on a project. Experience has shown that this is never the case. In practice, general purpose paradigms usually require modification to meet the specific project needs. This is illustrated in Figure 6-6. Most projects require incremental software and hardware development. The general purpose waterfall paradigm ignores this problem. Figure 6-6 shows a modified waterfall paradigm that reflects incremental software and hardware builds that are integrated into incremental system builds.

This is typically the first of many customizing steps needed to get from the general purpose paradigm to a process model that is executable on a specific project. It is important to start with a good paradigm.

As a word of caution one should recognize that most general purpose paradigms address only the development activities. Management activities (e.g., risk management, quality assurance, and configuration management) are not addressed. These activities need to be added to provide a complete definition of the software development process.

DEFINE SUBACTIVITIES

The second step is to decompose some, if not all, of the major activities at least one level down. From a metric point of view this will be driven by the need to identify subactivities that have unique measurement needs.

For example, consider the major activity called detailed design. Perhaps the best way to measure the progress and quality of this activity is to define and measure a single subactivity called design inspections.

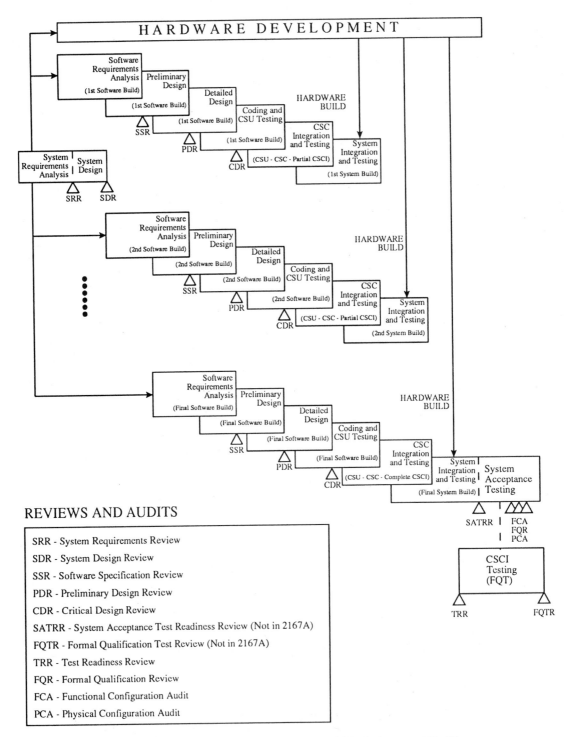

FIGURE 6-6. Example of phased development activities for incremental builds.

The number of levels of subactivities will depend in part on what needs to be measured. In other words, the granularity of the process definition depends on where we need to insert measurement probes. This in turn depends on where the process is expected to fail. The point is that the metric organization should focus on defining those subactivities that are most likely to be incorrectly implemented.

The third step is to correct the common problem of the lack of adequate documentation. A development process that is poorly documented almost always fails. Communications and training are difficult even when the process is well documented. For all practical purposes, the following rule applies:

Any part of the development process that is not clearly documented does not exist.

A final word of caution about taking too narrow a view of the software development process. Neither the software development process nor the metric should be thought of in isolation; they are both part of a larger system. There is a tendency to become a "software isolationist." In today's world of embedded systems created by integrated development teams, it is becoming increasingly difficult to separate the software process from the total system process. This makes it more difficult to separate software metric from total system metric. We must look well beyond the software process and include any activities that impact the ability of the software organization to get its job done. The software organization often does not control its own destiny. Many so-called software problems are caused by process failures that are, in reality, outside the software development process.

6.3 DESIGN THE MEASUREMENT SYSTEM

One big problem with establishing a metric program is knowing what to measure (Figure 6-7). There is a lot of confusion about what to measure and how to use the results. Engineers have always relied heavily on metric to get quantitative assessments of the quality and cost of the products and services they provide. Most engineering disciplines have very mature metric selection techniques. Some have been collecting metric data since the last century.

Compared with this, software engineering is a young discipline. In its short history, software started out as an art, then became a science and only recently has been viewed as engineering. Since metric is an engineering discipline, this has further delayed its introduction in the field of software. As a result, most software developers have relatively limited experience with metrics. Because of this limited experience, selecting software metrics is still complex.

One approach is to treat metric selection as a design task. Treating it as a design task encourages us to use systematic top-down techniques to accomplish the task. Consider the following top-down steps:

1. Define goals for collecting the metric data.
2. Establish measurement objectives that support the goals.
3. Select metrics based on the development process support objectives.

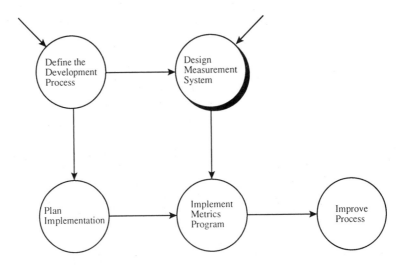

FIGURE 6-7. Measurement system design.

The actual metric selection is the third step. Starting with step 3 is a bottom-up approach to a problem that needs a top-down solution. The following paragraphs describe these steps.

Define Goals for Collecting Metric Data

Defining the goals for collection of the metric data is the first step in this top down process. Knowing why the data is being collected will have a significant impact on what data is gathered. Figure 6-8 identifies the four most common goals for collecting and analyzing metric data.

DISCOVER THE PROCESS
This is typically the goal of a research organization. It assumes that we treat the process or some part of the process as a black box. The metric data is used to try to infer attributes of the process that will help us define it. This goal is included here for completeness even though it is not the focus of this chapter.

EVALUATE THE PROCESS
This is also typically a research goal. However, it assumes that a part of the process has been defined so that it can be evaluated. This is typically done using prototyping. The problem is finding a project on which to run the prototype. Very limited prototyping of the software development process should be allowed on active projects. The experiment should be carefully controlled to ensure it does not do more harm than good.

CONTROL THE PROCESS
UNDER MEASUREMENT
This is typically the goal of software management of an active project. This is also the most common goal for a metric program. Unfortunately, this goal is plagued by

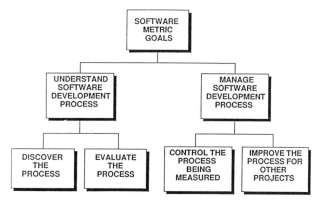

FIGURE 6-8. Metrics program goals.

a number of nontechnical problems. These problems largely derive from a common source. Just about everyone on the project from the program manager to the entry level programmer finds metrics to be personally threatening.

IMPROVE THE PROCESS
FOR OTHER PROJECTS
This is typically the goal of a process improvement organization. Data is gathered on active projects rather than being used to control the project that gathered it. It is used to improve the development process on future projects.

This chapter focuses on the last two software metric goals.

Establish Measurement Objectives that Support Goals

Common sense tells us that we need to know the objectives of the metric program. They establish the top level requirements that govern everything that follows. The problem comes when we try to put this idea into practice. There is a tendency to define the objectives in very high level terms. At the highest level, the objective of any metric program should be:

Produce the highest quality software at the lowest cost on the shortest schedule.

This is true, but it does not help much. There is too big a gap between this objective and the selection of specific metrics. The objectives should be stated so that they are "executable." They need to be specific enough to allow us to select specific metrics. They must be quantifiable to permit measurement.

Translating the typical high level objectives into objectives that can be used to select metrics is a nontrivial task. The best way to select objectives is to tie them to potential problem areas with the development process. Focus on areas where process problems are anticipated. Measuring everything in the process that moves, will inundate us with costly data that is of limited value and that consumes the time of our most valuable people. Measuring and analyzing data is both time consuming and expensive. Focusing on potential problem areas is the only way to have a cost effective metric program.

It is important to know what kinds of process problems may occur. This helps ensure that we measure things directed towards the diagnosis of specific process problems. Without this focus measurements are little more than shots in the dark.

Select Metrics Based on the Development Process

Selecting metrics takes a great deal of judgement and common sense. Unfortunately, common sense is not very common. There are numerous papers that propose a confusing array of metrics. It helps to have a top down organizing structure for sorting through the information that these publications provide. Figure 6-9 provides such a useful organizing structure that views all software metrics in two general categories. One category includes metrics that measure the development process system. The other category includes metrics that measure the software system produced by the development process. Within each general category, we have found it useful to have at least one additional level of partitioning. This organizing structure serves two important purposes. First, it encourages the process focus presented earlier in this chapter. Second, it focuses on determining whether the proposed metrics are a complete set (i.e., do they cover the complete process?).

An example is included here to illustrate these notions. Two important metric publications (particularly for DOD Air Force projects) are *Software Management Indicators* (AFSCP 800-43)[3] and *Software Quality Indicators* (AFSCP 800-14).[4] The goals of these publications are to "provide management visibility into the software development process and promote the development of quality software products . . ."

Figure 6-10 provides an analysis of the metrics defined in AFSCP 800-43 and 14, using the development process defined by DOD-STD-2167A. As illustrated, 800-43/14 do a fairly good job of providing both progress and quality metrics for each major activity in the development process. One noticeable weak area is quality indicators for the preliminary design activity.

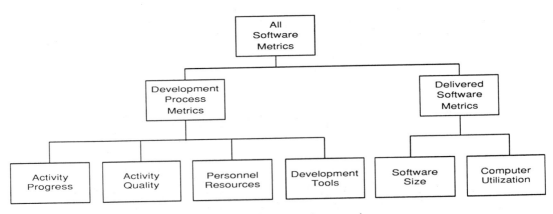

FIGURE 6-9. Software metrics categories.

AFSCP 800-43 Software Management Indicators

Indicator	Software Requirements Analysis Progress	Quality	Preliminary Design Progress	Quality	Detailed Design Progress	Quality	Code and Unit Test Progress	Quality	CSC Integration and Test Progress	Quality	System Integration and Test Progress	Quality	Formal Qualification Test Progress	Quality	Process Resources People	Tools	Software System Size	Utilization
Requirements and Design Progress																		
CSCI SRS/SDD	X		X															
CSCI IRS/IDD	X		X															
Software Development Progress																		
CSCI Design Progress					X													
CSCI Code & Unit Test Progress							X											
CSCI Integration & Test Progress									X		X		X					
CSCI FQT Progress													X					
Incremental Release Content																		
Requirements and Design Stability																		
CSCI Requirements Stability		X	X															
CSCI Design Stability			X	X														
CSCI SPRs					X		X		X		X		X					
CSCI Software Action Items					X		X		X		X		X					
Software Development Personnel															X			
Software Development Tools																X		
Software Engineering Environment																X		
Software Test Environment																		
Software Size																	X	
Software Resource Utilization																		
CPU Utilization																		X
Memory Utilization																		X
I/O Utilization																		X

AFSCP 800-14 Software Quality Indicators

Indicator	Software Requirements Analysis Progress	Quality	Preliminary Design Progress	Quality	Detailed Design Progress	Quality	Code and Unit Test Progress	Quality	CSC Integration and Test Progress	Quality	System Integration and Test Progress	Quality	Formal Qualification Test Progress	Quality	Process Resources People	Tools	Software System Size	Utilization
Completeness Quality Indicator		X																
Design Structure Quality Indicator						X												
Defect Density Quality Indicator						X				X		X		X				
Fault Density Quality Indicator								X		X		X		X				
Test Coverage Quality Indicator										X		X						
Test Sufficiency Quality Indicator												X						
Documentation Quality Indicator						X												

FIGURE 6-10. Air Force systems command software metrics publications.

151

6.4 PLAN THE IMPLEMENTATION

The next step in developing a successful metric program is to plan the implementation process. We will describe this activity as the third step in our TQM metric process. Figure 6-11 illustrates this step in the overall process but in reality can be accomplished in parallel with the "Design the Metric Set" step. This activity is not necessarily complex but it does require basic understanding of how the metric program activities will function within the scope of overall program activities. In this section we discuss four steps necessary in the metric implementation process. The steps are:

1. Establish an independent metric organization to implement the metric program.
2. Establish relationships between the metric organization and all relevant engineering disciplines and program organizations.
3. Establish the project metric program and identify all process, products and project relationships.
4. Identify the data collection activities to be implemented for the project.

Although the four step approach is not necessarily new or unique, we hope that the following discussion of each of the steps should give a potential metric practitioner enough foundation to ensure a successful metric program. What we seek is meaningful information about our processes to promote continuous process improvement, a TQM technique.

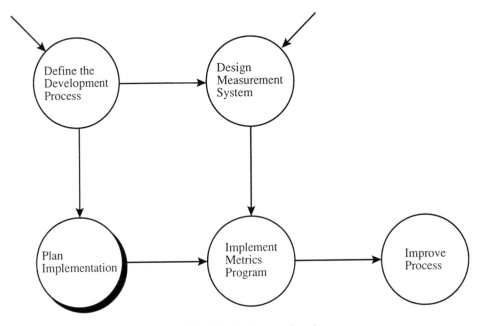

FIGURE 6-11. Implementation plan.

Metric Organization

Now that a metric program is ready for implementation, one of the first questions that needs to be answered is, "Who is going to collect, maintain and interpret the metric data?" Some people feel that a successfully implemented metric program should be an integral part of the software development process and as a consequence a separate or independent metric organization is not desirable. We strongly agree that the metric program should be an integral part of the software process but strongly disagree that the metric organization not be separate. In this section we will justify the need for a metric organization. We will also show an organizational structure that will ensure the consistent application of policies, methods, procedures, definitions, and level of detail for all aspects of a Total Quality metric process.

First of all, we firmly state "that metric program activities should be incorporated as a natural part of any program software development process." This is not to say that the care and feeding of metrics should be in the hands of software developers. One of the principle reasons for establishing an independent metric organization is to remove subjectivity that would potentially bias or corrupt their program's metric data. For the same reason the program management organization also should not be allowed to collect metric data. They have their own agenda and biases that could corrupt the metric data.

The establishment of an independent organization helps to create an engineering discipline of metric experts. This is especially true in the area of metric data analysis. Often untrained personnel will choose some particular perspective to interpret metric data in a totally erroneous way. Perhaps an example would be useful to illustrate this problem. We have observed people using the metric "error density" to measure the quality of developed software. Let us use five errors per thousand lines of developed code in this metric example. One program group's conclusion was that "because the error density was low this measure was a clear indication of inadequate testing of the delivered software." Another group might use this same metric to conclude that "because the error density was low they had a software development process that introduced very few errors into the delivered software." The truth is that the use of the "error density" metric by itself is worthless. Anyone assuming a measure of software quality using that metric will most likely come to an erroneous conclusion. Perspective is a sinister metric characteristic that needs understanding and should be dealt with accordingly by personnel trained in the interpretation of metric data results, i.e., metric experts.

The independent metric organization will ensure that the collection, analysis and reporting of metric data along with the information feedback and corrective action process is successfully executed. The independence of this metric organization will allow the software development organization to pursue its normal course in parallel.

A typical software metric organization, illustrated in Figure 6-12, encompasses the four major metric activities. The following paragraphs describe the basic elements of each activity to facilitate understanding of the metric organization's activities.

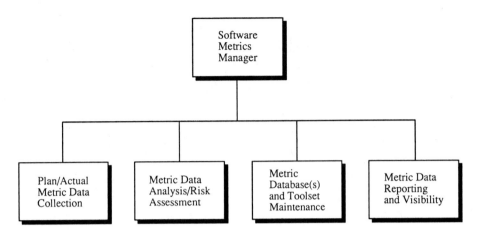

FIGURE 6-12. Software metric organization.

The *Planning/Actual Metric Data Collection* group is responsible for the generation and insertion of all program planning and actual metric data into the program metric database. This group ensures the consistency, appropriateness, responsiveness, and level of detail of data for the entire program. This element of the metric organization is primarily responsible for all of the following activities:

1. Identify all metric data to be collected.
2. Identify all metric reports that will be generated from collected metric data. This also includes working with the Analysis group to ascertain their report requirements.
3. Identify all program interfaces necessary to obtain metric data and to communicate, status, issues, and corrective action information.
4. Classify all metric data collection activities into the categories of: Original Plan Data; Change Plan Data; and, Actual Program Data.
5. Collect all metric data by the categories described in the previous step.

The *Metric Data Analysis/Risk Assessment* group is responsible for the analysis of all collected metric data. Methods used to accomplish metric analysis include: Pareto Analysis; cause and effect; statistical sampling; extrapolation projections; and, regression and trend analysis. These methods are given further coverage in Chapter 2. Many of the metrics collected can be analyzed using the "direct or primary" method. Primary measurements are those that have a one to one relationship, e.g., plan milestone data versus collected actual milestone data.

The more difficult type of analysis of metric data can be categorized as "indirect or secondary." This type of analysis requires metric expertise in all areas of the software development process and often requires the use of common sense. A heavy emphasis in the first two sections of this chapter has been based on the use of common sense for this reason.

Secondary analysis is concerned with using methods to solve problems discovered or anticipated by the "primary" analysis process. This process often must look at metrics that are not directly associated with a specific problem. An example of this type of activity is the analysis of program requirement volatility metrics and how they affect the problem of a schedule variance discovered by the "primary" analysis. We could look at the requirements data with respect to the number of rework hours being expended to process software requirement changes. From this type of data, we may discover that our development schedule is being severely impacted. This "secondary" type of analysis can become quite complex in its search for knowledge of the program processes that require corrective action.

In the above example, the changes to requirements could have had a very adverse effect on the progress being made on the program. Analysis of metric data would have identified the problem and possible solution. The analysis activity needs metric experts and is essential in the feedback portion of any process or program TQM effort.

This activity also works closely with any program risk activities to establish risk elements, define their associated risk limits, and generate responsive alarms when limits are exceeded. In the early planning stages of any program, this group is closely integrated with the metric data collection activity. This group's emphasis during the planning phase is to ensure that the program and all of its associated plan data provide for a balanced program process.

This activity should be primarily focused on the consistent definition and relationship of all program plan data and should include all aspects of task allocations costs, personnel, schedule, and products. Once the metric baseline has been established, this group will constantly be analyzing the actual collected metric data with respect to the baseline plan. Assessments will be made with results and corrective action recommendations forwarded to all affected activities and program disciplines.

The *Metric Database(s) and Toolset Maintenance* group ensures the configuration and integrity of the metric data base. This group maintains the identity of all personnel and their access privileges to program metric data. For those organizations that have an automated metric toolset, which we highly recommend, this section is also responsible for the maintenance of the tools and the associated metric data generated by the utilization of the toolset. This group from time to time will also be requested to provide different or unanticipated retrieval access to the metric database.

The *Metric Data Reporting and Visibility* group of our metric organization is responsible for the accurate and responsive reporting of all metric data. All reports should be provided on a timely basis to software management, program management, and support operations. The reporting group must know what standard reports to generate, and their content and level of detail. Also this group must be able to support nonstandard or unique reporting activities.

A metric program organization requires a complete staff of personnel for full implementation. Although the size of the organization may vary with program size and complexity, the organization should, at a minimum, be staffed with professionals with bachelor degrees. Also recognize that the big payoff from this organization will occur when they have been sufficiently trained and have acquired enough experience to benefit the productivity and quality of the software development process and its generated products.

Metric Organization Relationships

An important task to be accomplished before a metric program can commence is to identify and establish all of the necessary communication interfaces that exist between the software development and software metric processes. If the metric organization is to implement a successful TQM program, it must interface with the following program engineering disciplines, as illustrated in Figure 6-13: Program Management; Software Engineering; Software Configuration Management; and, Software Quality Engineering. These interfaces should be somewhat informal to facilitate the flow of information between the various program activities.

The software metric organization interfaces with the program management organization in two major areas. The first area is involved with the acquisition of all startup program resource information and the second area is involved with measuring actuals against the planned resources. This activity is also closely coordinated with the software development organization. The primary types of resource data to be collected are schedule, cost, and personnel.

The first type of program resource data to be obtained is the master program schedule information. Program schedule data may vary in level of detail from program to program. Some may identify individual configuration item activity, phases of development, build activity, and major reviews, however, there are some that do not. The most important schedule data to obtain or calculate is the overall amount of calendar time that the program has allocated to the software effort. The second type of schedule data to obtain are the major milestone dates that establish intermediate or development completion mile posts. The metric program will use this initial schedule data to establish a Standard Software Schedule (SSS). This is especially true for DOD-STD-2167A development processes and will be discussed further later in this section.

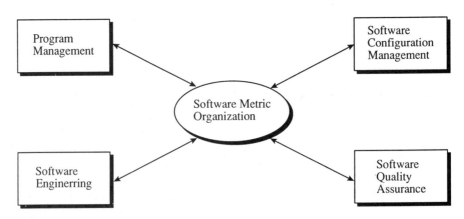

FIGURE 6-13. Software metric relationships.

Program Management defines the Contract Work Breakdown Structure (CWBS). It is from this cost breakdown that all software cost allocations are grouped. One of the first activities for the metric group is to roll up or translate all software work packages to the CWBS. Often during the planning phases of the program, the metric group will work closely with program management in the creation of the CWBS (elaborated upon later in this section). This is an important activity because to collect meaningful metrics it is advantageous to establish a Standard Software WBS (SSWBS).

The second aspect of cost data obtained from program management is the actual amount of money or labor hours allocated to the software effort. This data is needed along with the schedule information to establish the original program resource baseline for software development. The most important activity that the metric group can do during the planning stages of any program is to calculate the amount of cost and schedule risk that program management has accepted. With only product size and schedule information, the program's schedule position relative to the "region of impossibility" can be calculated.

The last type of program resource data to obtain is the personnel data. The staffing plan is generated once product, cost, and schedule data are made available. One important piece of information to be retained for the personnel database is skill level. We will see later that the ability to apply the correct skills to the software development activities can have a considerable affect on the progress of any program. Using the cost and schedule data will lead to personnel staffing curves that will illustrate possible planning problems. Also, with only product size and schedule information, we can easily calculate the program's schedule position relative to the "region of impossibility." This type of calculation along with the staffing profile curves provide some of the earliest information that can be communicated to the program and software development organizations to achieve better program planning. Therefore, once we have acquired the initial program resource data, our focus for metric is to determine if the program's software development process is balanced.

All of the discussion so far has been about the establishment of the original program baseline. Once the baseline is generated, program management will be very interested in how well the software development effort is performing with respect to the established plan. Therefore, throughout the software development life cycle the metric group will be communicating progress assessment metric data back to program management.

The next metric organization relationship to discuss is the one with software engineering. Before we discuss the interface activities with this group, let us address the topic of "threat." If detailed metrics are to be collected on any program, the software organization will probably be the most sensitive to the potential use of metrics to measure individual performance. There is one thing about metrics that reminds us of the Star Wars trilogy and its religious concept of the "force." Like "the force" the proper use of metrics can provide a wonderful benefit to a program. However, there is a "dark side" of metrics when applied improperly. If metrics are used as a club to threaten developers, the potential benefits received by the program through the use of metrics will be lost. In addition, there is a risk of severely destroying the trust that existed between management and the software developers. Therefore, it is imperative for all levels of management to keep in mind that if metric data is used as a club to threaten developers, then like a throwaway container, the metric can be used only once. Remember, we seek knowledge and information about our software processes and that requires the input and enthusiastic cooperation from all members of the development team.

The interface with the software organization should be handled in a cooperative, threatless manner—professionally. It is from this group that detailed milestone data, both planned and actual, performance data, sizing, timing, and development status is obtained. Most of this activity is rather simple and straightforward. However, there is one piece of information that this group provides which is important in the assessment of program progress. This information that always seems to get lost, or as some would say "willfully abandoned," or is not recognized, is called "program configuration" data. If you recall from the previous discussion with respect to the interface or relationship to program management, it was stated that one of the first things to establish is the "program baseline." Once created, this includes cost and schedule plans, most programs will insist upon holding on to those plans even after the plans have become invalid. At this time the program begins its "muddling phase," which seems to be interminable. As a consequence of all the undocumented changes that creep into a program and due to the fact that we never seem to notice or do not really care what they are, we ultimately end up without a planned program. Trying to maintain the configuration of the program, its associated plans and organization is possibly the most important activity the metric organization can do in achieving a TQM process.

The third organization to interface with metrics is the software configuration management group. The metric group is interested in obtaining error data for the developed software product. This usually is a class of data that is owned by the configuration management group. Metrics is very interested in this data from three perspectives. The first type of data is concerned with error models and prediction of the error activity during software development. During the very early stages of development, models that will predict error find and fix rates are generated. Once created, the metric program desires to analyze the actual rates as they occur.

The second type of data to be analyzed are the characteristics of the type and severity of the error data, which is covered extensively in Chapter 7. Error type helps us understand where errors are being introduced into the software process, and severity provides knowledge of the quality of the product. For those who must use error density, remember that by itself it is useless, however, the ratio of error density during development against error density during deployment does give information relative to the quality of the software developments test process.

The third type of error data that metrics are interested in is the cost to fix errors. Calculating the "price of nonconformance" (PONC) is one of the major goals of any TQM program. After all it is this cost, or waste, that the TQM process desires to minimize or eliminate. One of the biggest benefits that can be obtained by any program is the correct information that leads to the reduction in PONC.

The last major organizational group that metrics interfaces with is the software quality organization. Metrics desires to analyze software process oriented data that is collected by this group. This data normally exists in the form of checklists and often provides valuable information relative to how well the software team is following their defined software development process.

Another type of data that the quality group captures is "milepost" data. This data provides progress assessment information that is often necessary relative to proving conformance to required contract and process procedures.

Process, Product, Program Relationships

The relationships of program metric data is discussed in this section. In particular, attention is given to the four aspects of metric data: cost, personnel, schedule, and product. Their relationships to each other is graphically depicted in Figure 6-14. The first thing to recognize in this figure is that the three metric aspects of cost, personnel, and schedule belong to the program resource group. It is from this group that a program obtains all of the resources necessary to carry out the software development activities that eventually give value to the products of the project. All of these program metrics are closely related to each other and any change or perturbation to any one will always have some effect on at least one of the others.

Cost data long with milestones, schedule data, is almost always used to monitor the progress of program development activities. Please notice, and this is very important, it was not stated that cost data was used to control program activities. During the planning phase of any program, a Work Breakdown Structure (WBS) is

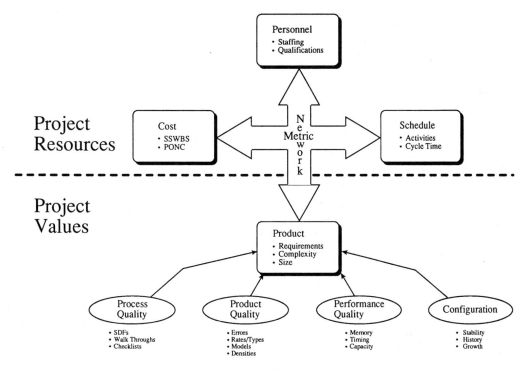

FIGURE 6-14. Metric relationships.

generated. It is this structure that identifies the various program activities and the associated collection of funds for each. For anyone who desires to achieve a total quality process he or she must consider the notion of a standard WBS. For software, we will call this WBS a Standard Software WBS (SSWBS). An example of a SSWBS is shown in Figure 6-15. This example is partitioned hierarchically along the "waterfall" model and closely associates itself to DOD-STD-2167A.

Creating an SSWBS provides for three major program advantages. The first benefit of a SSWBS is that development activities and their level of detail are defined early in the program. This gives a scope or framework for cost monitoring throughout the program development life cycle. The second advantage of the SSWBS is to provide the actual cost of rework. Depending on the level of detail allocated to capture this data, the SSWBS can provide information as to the sources, the extent, and cost of all software rework activities. One of our major objectives in any TQM process is to develop methods to reduce the Price of Nonconformance (PONC). The third benefit of the SSWBS is that it provides a method for collecting cost data from other programs that use the same standard so that common activity cost can be accumulated.

This metric data is invaluable in the elimination of program rework and the fine tuning of the overall software development process. Once allocated to the SSWBS, cost metrics are related directly to all schedule activities. This is obvious when one considers the simple equation, activity labor cost equals activity time (schedule) multiplied by engineering activity (personnel). The cost relationship to product is achieved for individual products such as a Computer Software Configuration Item (CSCI), or an accumulated set of products such as a Computer Software Component (CSC).

Personnel metric data accounts for all staffing plan data and is related to cost

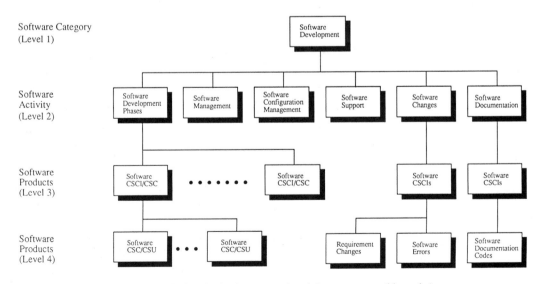

FIGURE 6-15. Standard software cost breakdown structure (hierarchy).

and schedule metric data as described in the previous paragraph. Like the close relationship that exists between cost and schedule, personnel metric data is closely related to product metric data. Recognize that personnel data is an essential component to cost and schedule analysis activities, but given fixed schedule resources, staffing profiles will most often be adversely affected by changes to the product metric data. This relationship is particularly sensitive with respect to changes in the product requirements or errors in product size estimates.

Although not directly measurable against the other metric data, personnel data does contain an attribute that affects how well planned cost and schedule predictions are successfully achieved. This attribute of the personnel data is called staff qualifications. Often original cost and schedule estimates are made with a selected mix of qualified personnel. It is important to maintain this perspective of personnel mix because without it, staffing head count can be maintained and yet the efficiency or productivity of the various software activities may not match up with the other resource metric data.

The third aspect of resource metric data is schedule information. The benefits of having a SSWBS to formalize cost data collection was described earlier. In a completely similar manner, all schedule metric data should be collected using a Standard Software Schedule (SSS). An example of a DOD-STD-2167A schedule is shown in Figure 6-16. This example identifies a standard set of activities to be scheduled for each of the software development phases required in DOD-STD-2167A.

Software Development Phases	Software Schedule Activities			
System Requirements Analysis/Design	Develop Preliminary SRS	Develop Preliminary IRS		System (PDR)
Software Requirements Analysis	Develop Software Requirements Specification	Develop Interface Requirements Specification		Software Specification Review (SSR)
Software Preliminary Design	Define CSCs	Develop Preliminary Software Design	Develop Preliminary Interface Design	Preliminary Design Review (PDR)
Software Detailed Design	Define CSUs	Develop Detailed Software Design	Develop FQT Design	Develop Detailed Interface Design	Critical Design Review (CDR)
Software Code and CSU Testing	Generate CSU Test Procedures	Generate CSU Code	Test CSUs	Develop CSC Test Procedures
CSC Integration and Testing	Run CSC Test Procedures	Generate Final STD FQT Procedures	Conduct Test Readiness Review (TRR)	Run CSC Test Completeness FQT
CSCI Testing	Update STD with FQT Procedures	Conduct Test Readiness Review (TRR)	Run CSCI Test Completeness FQT	Generate SPS and VDD
System Build Integration and Test	Create Local Build	Perform Local Build Test	Create System I&T Baseline	Perform System Build Completeness Test	Generate VDD
Formal Qualification Test	Conduct Test Readiness Review (TRR)	Run Required FQT Tests	Conduct FCA/PCA	

*See Figure 6-6 for a list of acronyms.

FIGURE 6-16. Standard software schedule.

One of the major benefits of setting up an SSS is that like the SSWBS all planned activities and their associated sequence of operation are identified early in the planning process. Another benefit occurs because cost can be directly related to the various scheduled activities. Over time, analysis of activities and their associated cost allow weights to be allocated to the detailed schedule activities. This type of information provides subsequent programs an opportunity to better layout and estimate the resources necessary for their program.

Once generated, the relationship between the SSS and the SSWBS becomes very strong. This strong bond between cost and schedule has a major benefit in that changes incurred by the program will clearly show their affects upon both cost and schedule. One of TQM's major goals is to reduce cycle time. First of all, any process changes aimed at cycle time reduction require that process schedule time has to be measured to determine if success is being achieved. Detailed analysis of the schedule and cost data not only provides for direct feedback, it also identifies those processes where maximum "bang for the buck" can be achieved.

The last aspect of metric data that is closely related to all of the resource group is the product metric data. There are five attributes of the product metric data that not only relate to each other but also to the resources identified previously in Figure 6-14. The product group is made up of product, process, quality, performance, and configuration attributes. The product attribute is closely related to cost, schedule, and personnel because this attribute identifies all products, their groupings and respective size. The second attribute of the product metric data is associated with the process being used to generate the product. This data usually manifests itself in the form of inspections and checklists and as such should be directly related to schedule resource data. Product quality data is primarily concerned with the collection of product error data. This data not only identifies errors to products but also accounts for the rates at which errors are being discovered and resolved, the types of errors being discovered and where in the process the errors are being introduced. This type of product data is very closely related to cost resource data and is essential in our analysis of the reduction of the PONC. Although not directly related to the resource data group, the product performance data often provides predictive information relative to our ability to successfully complete all program activities. Historically, when performance data such as memory, timing, and throughput are not acting as anticipated, one can expect that associated cost and schedule resources will be affected, sometimes in a catastrophic manner. The last attribute of the product is its configuration, both product and process. More than any of the other product attributes, the configuration, stability, history, and growth of the product have a direct relationship with the resources provided. It is the failure to maintain or recognize this data that leads to the typical, "over cost" and "late schedule" conditions that often are discovered late in the program. More than anything else, it is this failure that leads to the classic, 90% reported complete when in reality the software product is only 50% complete. Unfortunately, at the 90% reported completion point, usually 90% of the program's resources have been consumed.

Therefore, in summary of this section, picture the four metric attributes, cost, schedule, personnel, and product to act like the surface of a balloon. Alter, change, perturb, etc. any one of the attributes will cause a change in one or more of the other three. Determining the cause and the extent of the change is what program metric analysis is all about.

Metric Data Collection

The various metric data collection activities necessary to implement a metric program are discussed in this section. Although we will repeat some of the material discussed in the previous sections, the focus of this section is aimed at the actual metric data collection activities. Before any metric data can be collected, we need to identify what data to collect. This identification should be closely related to satisfying the program goals and objectives described earlier. Normally, for programs this data can be grouped as follows:

Milestone data—schedules, SSS
Cost data—allocations, SSWBS
Personnel data—staffing, qualifications
Quality data—error; models, predictions, categories, etc.
Performance data—size, memory, timing

Once the desired metric data is identified, the next step is to lay out or establish the program baseline. This requires that the cost, schedule, staffing, and product metric data be generated and analyzed to make sure that the entire process is balanced. Predictive error models should match up with the established planning resource and product data. One thing to remember when generating the plan baseline is that not all product and schedule plan data can be defined in the beginning. Although the high level baseline, CSCI level, can be initially generated, the lower level product and schedule information cannot be defined until the proper development phase has been encountered in the program. However, even at these later stages, care should be exercised to ensure that no lower level metric data is inconsistent with its higher level counterpart.

Once the metric plan baseline has been established and coordinated with the software development effort, start collecting actual data. The first stage of the collection activity will be relatively easy and straight forward, simply collect the actuals, make the desired measurements and report the results. The second stage of data collection becomes more difficult because the development team will want to change the metric baseline. These changes will initially show up as missed schedule milestones. Once this stage begins, all of the other baseline data is going to be affected. Upon entering stage two, always remember the following four things:

1. There is a problem with the program plan.
2. Primary metric analysis will identify the result of the problem.
3. Secondary metric analysis will identify the cause of the problem.
4. Corrective action will always contain the requirement that the metric plan baseline be reestablished.

In the previous section, we discussed metric relationships and identified that any change to schedule, cost, personnel, or product will cause changes to the entire set. Remember, a successful metric program must always keep the process balanced. We cannot overstate this condition. It is imperative that a metric implementation maintain the configuration of the software development process. Capture all changes and make sure the program impacts resulting from these changes are identified and reported to all affected program personnel.

Stage three of the metric data collection process occurs when the program refuses to make necessary changes to bring the metric baseline back into a balanced state or a work around process has been implemented to balance the baseline at some time later in the program. During this stage, data collection activities are like stage two except that all measurements and results must be made against two baselines, the current one and the projected one. Extreme care must be exercised during this stage because measurement against the existing metric baseline will often create crazy or ridiculous results and it is here that most metric programs fail or are abandoned.

Regardless of the stage that the metric data collection activity is involved with, ensure that all metric reports are generated in a timely manner. Keep the reports simple and provide the reports to associated organizations that have a vested interest in the reported data.

6.5 IMPLEMENT THE METRIC PROGRAM

Now that we have gone through the steps to understand our software metric development process:

Establish our metric goals and objectives,
Recognize the need for an independent metric organization, and
Understand all of the relationships that exist within the metric program,

we are ready to implement the metric program as shown in Figure 6-17. In this section we will discuss some practical data collection processes that will provide for maximum project benefit. Before we continue, let us reflect on the previous sections. "The planning for the metric program is everything," and the implementation part is like the Nike commercial "just do it."

Remember the eight basic steps necessary to implement the metric program:

1. Setup a metric organization.
2. Generate the metric plan baseline.
3. Make sure the process is balanced.
4. Collect actuals, this includes all changes.
5. Make the measurements.
6. Analyze the measurements.
7. Generate reports and make available to all interested or affected parties.
8. Feedback all problem data and work around plans.

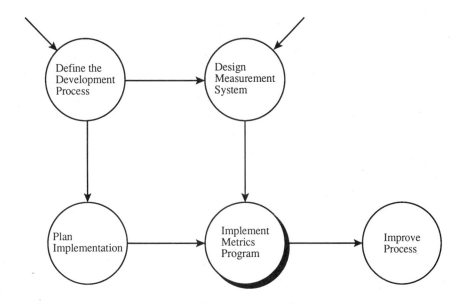

FIGURE 6-17. Metrics program implementation.

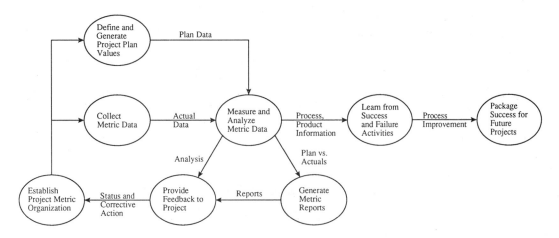

FIGURE 6-18. Software metric process.

In carrying out these eight steps, see Figure 6-18, do not fall into the trap of becoming a data collection activity. Maintain focus on providing meaningful, pertinent information for the program and its developers. Keep the activity, its measurements and reports as simple as possible. For those programs that will do all metric activities manually, there are a few basic guidelines to keep in mind. First of all, the most obvious limitation to a manually implemented program is in the amount or degree of metric detail that can be acquired. This is particularly true when the program is undergoing frequent or drastic changes. Trying to manually keep the metric baseline, the metric actuals and changes up-to-date can be murderous. Therefore, if at all possible and regardless of the detailed level of the recorded data, it is highly recommended that the implementation of the metric activity be automated as much as possible. However, if a manual implementation is used, remember to keep it simple.

Most automated metric programs are implemented around a central database and provide for access, data security, and ease of operation. Any automated implementation of the metric database should account for the highly dependent relationships that exist among all of the attributes of the metric data. This is especially true among the cost, schedule, personnel, and product metric data.

After the data has been collected, measured, and analyzed, the results must be reported to all required, interested, and affected parties. Regardless of the method, manual or automatic, used to generate the metric reports, keep them simple, meaningful, and informative. Often these reports identify an alarm region about the metric plan data. This is used as a variance buffer between the plan and actual metric data. Once an alarm threshold has been crossed, the event must be reported. Usually, when this condition occurs, risk mitigation or work around procedures are implemented, and close attention will remain on the variance until the problem is successfully resolved.

6.6 PROCESS IMPROVEMENT

From our knowledge of the process/capability maturity model (Chapters 1 and 4), we know that once our process has been defined and we can successfully measure it, the opportunity to optimize the process is achievable. In this section, shown in Figure 6-19,

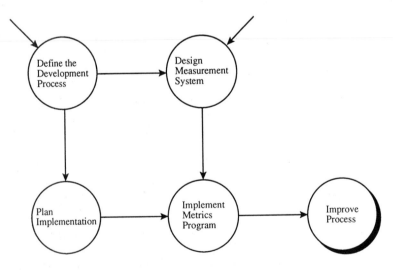

FIGURE 6-19. Process improvement.

we will discuss a cyclic activity that will provide for a continuous optimization of our process. Once our process is defined, the process improvement cycle consists of:

1. Defining our goals and objectives,
2. Defining and collecting data that provides information relative to our goals and objectives,
3. Making quantitative assessments,
4. Learning from our successes and failures,
5. Packaging our successes for future use, and
6. Providing information for the next cycle.

The first three steps of the process optimization cycle have already been discussed. However, for the sake of continuity, a brief overview of those steps are given. The first step requires that our goal and objectives need to be established. From our metric activities, issues should be identified, ranked, and prioritized. After this activity is complete, risk identification and assessment of those issues should be formulated with insight objectives being established for those risks. Necessary measurements are made for data definition and collection phase. During this phase, the source(s) of data are identified, collected, organized, and saved for quantitative assessment. During the assessment process, measurements versus identified risks are analyzed, performance indicators are reviewed with process improvement results being documented and reported. Relative to lessons learned, the following three activities are necessary for continuous process improvement:

1. Document the measurement experiences,
2. Determine if the identified issues are satisfied, and
3. Determine if new issues for process improvement are needed.

Once lessons learned activities are completed, successes for process improvement need to be packaged and reported for future optimization opportunities. During this process, improvement recommendations are identified and documented for use by subsequent program usage. Finally, a report of the recommendations should be made and presented to top management.

References

1. Schulmeyer, G. Gordon, *Zero Defect Software,* New York: McGraw-Hill Book Co., 1990.
2. U.S. Joint Logistics Command, DOD-STD-2167A, *Military Standard—Defense System Software Development,* Washington, D.C.: NAVMAT 09Y, 1988.
3. U.S. Air Force, AFSC Pamphlet 800-43, *Software Management Indicators,* Andrews Air Force Base, Washington, D.C., Headquarters AFSC, 1990.
4. U.S. Air Force, AFSC Pamphlet 800-14, *Software Quality Indicators,* Andrews Air Force Base, Washington, D.C., Headquarters AFSC, 1987.

7

Defect Analysis and TQM

James J. Holden III
Westinghouse Electronic Systems Group

7.1 PURPOSE

Defect analysis and its role in the Total Quality Management (TQM) process represents perhaps the single most important aspect of software development process improvement activities. Total Quality demands that defects be eliminated from not only all products delivered to internal and external customers, but also from the processes that create the products. In this chapter, a discussion of the historical view of defects and their removal will be revisited. This historical view deals with the means of eliminating defects by inspection techniques, proofs, and testing. The sources of errors are identified and emphasis placed on improving the technique for earlier identification and removal. This practice of inspecting a product for defects is referred to in this chapter as the product domain.

More recent practices in defect analysis have begun searching for the process flaw that permitted the error to be introduced in the first place, in other words, how can the defect be prevented from occurring? This concept is not new or even recent, but the practice within U.S. industry is recent, unfortunately. Most metrics and analysis until very recently have dealt with the product domain.

In this chapter, the analysis of process defects, failure of the process to generate correct results, is addressed. This aspect of defects is referred to as the process domain.

Noteworthy is the seemingly indiscriminate use of terms such as bug, error, defect, fault, and failure. Perhaps more literature exists on definitions of terms such as these than on the actual actions required to eliminate these anomalies in the software products and processes. Although not intended to be dissertation on the subject, some time will be spent on the terms and their true relevance to the defect analysis process and TQM.

The primary reason for writing this chapter is to review the present methods of defect analysis, the merits of these approaches, and to look at some "real world" methods that are not only effective but also efficient. Cleanroom techniques[4] (also see Chapter 18 herein), zero defect software,[3] statistical process control, inspection techniques, and software testing will be surveyed for their role in the defect analysis process.

7.2 HISTORICAL VIEW OF DEFECT ANALYSIS

What is a Defect?

At the risk of adding this document to the long list of reference materials on definitions of terms for software defects, a quick look at the definition of a defect is necessary as a reference point for this chapter. The more classic definition of a defect evolves from "lower" level anomalies such as errors, bugs, and faults. This classic definition can be encapsulated as shown.

Error: A conceptual, syntactic, or clerical discrepancy which results in one or more faults in the software.[20]

Fault: A specific manifestation of an error. A discrepancy in the software which can impair its ability to function as intended.[20]

Failure: A software failure occurs when a fault in the computer program is evoked by some data, resulting in the computer program not correctly computing the required function in an exact manner.[2, p. 489]

Defect: A defect is either a fault or a discrepancy between code and documentation that compromises testing, or produces adverse effects in installation, modification, maintenance, or testing.[1, p. 6]

Bug: A cute term for a defect. Banned by increasing numbers of software professionals as making defects tolerable to the programmer.

Having gone through this short summary, another definition has entered the stage recently. This definition does not attempt to categorize the inability of a system to perform correctly by use of multiple definitions but rather when in the life cycle the anomaly is detected. In *Zero Defect Software,*[3] G. Gordon Schulmeyer defines the terms error and defect as:

Error: An error is an unwanted condition or occurrence which arises during a software development process and deviates from its specified requirement. It may be detected immediately or go undetected until some corrective action process finds it, but it is always eliminated prior to the delivery to the customer.[3, p. 33]

Defect: A defect . . . is that specific kind of unwanted condition or occurrence which has defied all attempts . . . to be eliminated during development and, in essence, is delivered to the customer.[3, p. 33]

So enough of this, let's make the world a less complicated place to live in.

A defect is any deficiency in any product/process that fails to meet the requirements of the customer, internal or external.

Forget the rest, TQM directions dictate that all defects, by this book's definition, are to be eliminated in such a fashion as to reduce the cost of defects, improve customer satisfaction, and produce quality products. If a product/process is ineffectual, find the root cause of the problem and eliminate it.

How Are Product Defects Detected and Removed?

Earlier in this section, a list of techniques and approaches were itemized that all strive to identify defects and remove them from the product. The evolution of these techniques has been rapid and has been a natural lead-in to the TQM process improvement strategies of late within U.S. industry.

Inspection techniques have long been the method for defect detection and removal. Michael E. Fagan introduced the design and code inspections[5] to initiate a process by which defects could be detected early in the development process. These inspections improved the cost, schedule, and quality of the software products. One important aspect of these inspections early in the process was that for the first time, defect data on the point of entry of defects was clarified. Although the granularity of the information was not sufficient to clearly specify the exact process error that introduced the error, the region of search was reduced significantly.

In the Japanese environment, inspections are part of an overall Poka-yoke (mistake proofing) technique. The Japanese inspections are "inspections in which specified characteristics of each unit are examined or tested to determine conformance with requirements."[7] The concept of source or self inspections and successive inspections at each "handover" in the development process once again reduces the propagation of defects but does not necessarily fix the process.

Inspection techniques improve product quality, reduce cost and schedule, and add responsibility to the process at the individual employee level. They are essential in the gathering of defect data for evaluation. How the information is used is the critical aspect.

Statistical Quality Control (SQC) provides a formal process for the evaluation of products. SQC is the application of statistical measures along the process key points in the development of the product. It has been applied in manufacturing processes for many years with great success. The application of SQC in software development is relatively new (see Chapter 17). C. K. Cho addresses SQC in terms of sampling the software product such that the software is acceptable if the number of defects in the sample set is less than the acceptable number of defects in the sampling plan.[8]

The Cleanroom software development methodology (see Chapter 18) focuses on error prevention rather than error removal.[4, p. 111] Formal SQC methods use input probability distributions and random sampling to form the basis for software reliability prediction.[9, p. 2] This technique introduces the formal verification of the design satisfying all of the structural testing goals. The process provides early feedback into the process so that specifications can be tightened, and verification rigor improved.

The zero defect software (ZDS) concept[3] embraces the Japanese concept of source inspection and successive inspection to reduce the creation and propagation of errors (see Chapter 16). The fundamental concept is that at each hand-off of a product within the software development process, the source (software engineer) inspects the product against the standards and requirements. The product is "certified" as correct by the source and passed on to the next user, where another inspection is performed by this user to verify that what expected is what was received. Identical checklists are used so that the criteria for success is well understood by all participants.

One key aspect of the ZDS approach is that not only is there an inspection at the end of each step in the process, but the originator of the product is provided a clear and definitive statement of the expectation via the checklist. Checklists are provided at the start of the activity and used as a task statement for the software engineer defining the job. Understanding of job requirements has long plagued software developers as a critical reason for defective products.

Finally, testing has long been the method for defect identification and removal. Unit tesing, functional string testing, integration testing, system testing, acceptance testing, and independent verification and validation (IV&V) testing are classic approaches to testing. The amount of testing to be performed and the amount of time consumed is a function of the initial product quality. Most existing information on software defects is the result of testing. Testing is essential in verifying that the product performs as required. Since testing is well understood by nearly all software professionals, no more will be said.

The above techniques and many more provide the capability to detect defects in the software products. Assuming that some methods for detecting errors are in place, what does one do next? What data should be gathered? What mechanisms for data collection should be implemented? How should the data be used? How does the process affect the data gathered and vice versa.

7.3 DEFECT ANALYSIS IN THE PRODUCT DOMAIN

Data Gathering

As Robert Dunn writes in *Software Defect Removal,* "System analysts and programmers are seldom given to contemplating their errors. Faults, once found and corrected, are forgotten as attention is redirected to forward progress."[1, p. 253] The methods of error prevention above provide the groundwork for defect analysis and process improvement. Collecting data in the development process is not an easy task. The culture places more emphasis on product than on process and any task that impedes or is perceived to impede progress towards the ultimate goal—

delivery of the product—is viewed as unnecessary and therefore usually unsup-ported by management as well as by engineering staff. This mentality is the single biggest threat to a successful TQM program and process improvement.

In the true spirit of TQM, defect data collection has to:

1. Have clearly defined objectives and goals understood by all,
2. Have a well defined data gathering process,
3. Have a defined process for evaluation that leads to an improvement method for the product development,
4. Be inherent in the product/process being measured, and
5. Be as invisable and unobtrusive as possible in the product/process being measured.

Goals and Objectives of Defect Gathering and Analysis

First, let us consider the goals and objectives of a defect data gathering and analysis process. The obvious objective of the process is defect prevention, defect detection, and defect removal. Right? Of course, but not from a TQM process improvement viewpoint.

Phillip Crosby's approach to quality management looks at the cost of quality.[19] The cost of quality (COQ) is composed of the sum of two elements:

1. The Price of NonConformance (PONC), and
2. The Price of Conformance (POC).

This view of quality breaks down one of the cultural barriers in dealing with product costs—it relates the quality issue in terms of dollars and cents. The PONC of a given product is the cost and schedule impacts incurred because a defect existed in a product. For software, the optimists believe that the PONC is about 30%; the realists put the figure at 50%. Putting this information into perspective, the U.S. industries including the U.S. government spend $30 billion per year on software. If the PONC is 30%, then $9 billion per year is "wasted"; if the PONC is 50%, then $15 billion per year is "wasted" in rework. This number is staggering.

Now consider the POC. All of the inspections, all of the testing not directly related to requirements verification, all of the tooling for defect detection, all of the software quality assurance personnel, etc., are part of the POC. It is estimated that 20% of the software development costs are involved in POC, and the author believes that this number is conservative.

Using the Crosby equation for the COQ and applying it to the $30 billion per year investment.

$$COQ = PONC \{30\%\} + POC \{20\%\}$$

$$COQ = \$9 \text{ billion} + \$6 \text{ billion} = \$15 \text{ billion per annum}$$

Going back to the originally stated objective: defect prevention, defect detection, and defect removal; perhaps it is reasonable to restate the objective as minimization of the cost of quality. The difference is that now a critical aspect of TQM is addressed: cost. Fagan inspections[5] have often been bypassed under the premise that they are too expensive and schedule consuming. Statistical methods often are subject to the same criticism. Therefore, in determining the objective of data collection and defect analysis, cost and schedule must be considered. This is not a "non-TQM" thought as purists sometimes maintain, but rather a "total" TQM thought since the objective of TQM is to provide quality products that meet requirements including cost and schedule constraints in a competitive environment.

At the risk of supporting Acceptable Quality Level (AQL) versus TQM, Figure 7-1 illustrates the trade-off in cost of quality. Burrill and Ellsworth describe the PONC as the cost of failure and the POC as the cost of prevention plus appraisal.[10] The goal of TQM is to move the minimum cost point towards the 0,0 point on the plot. Can we ever get to 0,0? Unfortunately, the answer is probably no, but the closer the better, and that is what TQM is all about.

Based on the above considerations, the objective statement for data collection and analysis is to gather data that provides for a clear identification of:

1. The defect type/category,
2. The point within the process where the defect was introduced,
3. The point within the process where the defect was detected,
4. The cost/schedule impact to the product development (PONC),
5. The cost/schedule impact to detect the defect (POC), and
6. The method used for defect detection,

so that a process improvement can be initiated, if justified, through defect analysis.

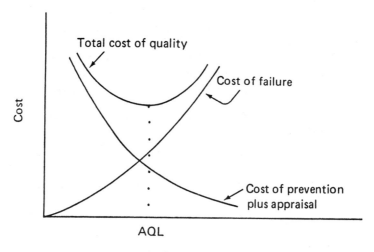

FIGURE 7-1. Traditional view of cost of quality.[10]

7.4 DEFECT GATHERING AND ANALYSIS PROCESS DEFINITION

The definition of a defect gathering and analysis process is not dependent on the software development methodology being utilized nor on the defect identification technique implemented. The rules for an improvement process, i.e., the steps and actions required to gather and record defect data, using Fagan inspections is the same as for a ZDS implementation. The crux of the issue is to document a procedure that is in and of itself a TQM process.

Every defect technique, no matter how primitive or advanced, has inherent information that, if properly gathered and categorized, leads to process improvement. Going back to the stated objectives for data gathering, each element needs to be clarified in terms of procedure and required of the organization can be adapted to the TQM process or whether the process needs to be adapted to the culture (hopefully one day to be redirected at changing the culture). Realistically, the latter condition exists for most organizations today.

Changing the organizational culture requires changes in attitudes of both management and the professional. The professional needs to recognize that the software development activity has two objectives: develop a quality product for delivery to the customer, and record historical information so that the next program can be improved such that the first objective is more easily achieved. Management has the tougher job in this case. They must be willing to accept that the short term gain on a program may compromise the long term future of the company and accept that some overhead costs are necessary. Further, management must be convinced that the return on investment has near term opportunities. As one manager put it, "In the long term, we're all dead." A compromise is clearly necessary to balance the long and short term aspects of the TQM process. A reasonable compromise is described later in this chapter.

Centralized Data Base of Defect Information

Regardless of the decision to either change the culture or adapt the TQM process, it is absolutely necessary to set up a method for creating a central data base of historical project defect information. At Westinghouse Electric Corporation Electronic Systems Group, a Software Engineering Process Organization was formed to provide a focal point for software process control and information exchange.[12] Victor Basili at the University of Maryland had developed the Experience Factory to provide for centralized collection and analysis of project data in pseudo-real-time. Hewlett-Packard has been evolving a process improvement program that is now called the Software 10X Goal utilizing a corporate wide initiative to achieve a tenfold improvement in design process and the ability to solve problems.[13]

If the organization is ready for a culture change and is properly trained to accomplish the task, then the procedure for the recording and analysis of defect information is the responsibility of the organization developing the product. The maturity of the organization is critical to this decision. Accepting the responsibility for, first and foremost, admitting that a defect has been introduced and, second, that it is necessary to do causal analysis in process is not a natural tendency. Periodic reviews of the defect information must be intrinsic in the process and the actual development personnel assess the data for project specific insight into the processes in use.

Historical data bases are used to provide lessons learned early in the development when compared to the project performance to date. The analysis of the data is fed back into the process in real time. Clearly, advisory personnel are imported into the defect evaluation process to provide objectivity and additional insight. The key is that the information is evaluated internally with outside assistance. The benefit of this approach is that the personnel involved in the project are involved in the improvement and understand the basis for the improvements and the yield to be gained. Often this is missing in an exported evaluation.

If the organizational culture is not ready for the change to a TQM approach or the change would seriously undermine the success of the company in the short term, then adapting the process of data gathering and analysis is necessary. This adaptation basically is to export the data for evaluation. The evaluation organization must investigate the data collected and insert the level of detail required for process evaluation and improvement. This is very difficult and requires an extraordinary group of evaluators. It is easy to say that the data should be self-supporting but the assumption is that the organizational culture did not support the discipline to do this.

One type of proven method for exported data analysis is the Experience Factory approach.[11] Victor Basili has been working with this concept and has applied the principle to projects at the University of Maryland and at NASA. The fundamental operation of the Experience Factory is that there is an organization outside the project organization that has the data, knowledge, and training to evaluate the data collected from a given project and provide knowledge based recommendations and insight into how the project can best be accomplished. Figure 7-2 depicts the flow of information both to and from the Experience Factory. This process is continuous throughout the development from reviewing the contract requirements and software development methods proposed for the project to evaluating defect data. In this environment, the project organization must gather data but the analysis and feedback is the function of the Experience Factory. If you will, the Experience Factory is a human expert system for software evaluation.

The Westinghouse ESG approach to software process improvement integrates the projects and processes through the Software Engineering Process Organization (SEPO). The SEPO coordinates the administrative functions of the software process (procedures, manuals, etc.) with the technology aspects (languages, tools, etc.). This centralization crosses product lines and locations and permits all ESG software development departments access to the data base. Results of the productivity and defect data are presented to the president of ESG quarterly. The TQM process improvement is integrated into the SEPO as discussed previously in Chapter 3. All statistics and data are gathered and centralized within the SEPO and then disseminated for evaluation in Quality Improvement Teams (QITs) and

PROJECT ORGANIZATION   **EXPERIENCE FACTORY**

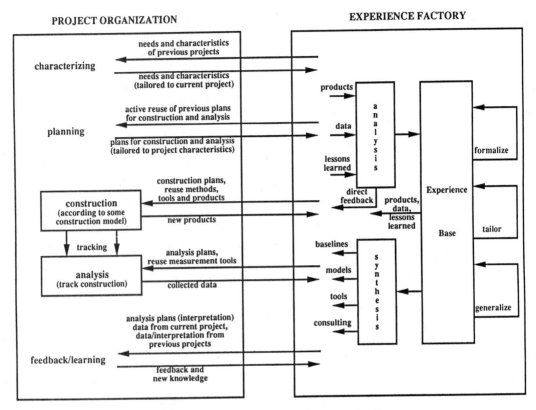

FIGURE 7-2. Experience factory data flow.[11, p. 477]

Process QITs. This approach is similar to the Experience Factory but does not provide real time feedback to the projects. Results to date show that a 15% annual reduction in defects has been achieved with a new goal of 35% per year set for 1991.[14]

Definition of Data Collection Points

Data collection points in the development process should occur at all reviews, inspections, tests, and deliveries. Data collection should be formalized and understood as an objective of the process. Further, data collection should not only include the information from the engineering disciplines but information gathered from independent testing, software quality assurance, and customer reviews. Data collection points should be scheduled just as deliveries and activities are scheduled. Results (summarizations of the data collection milestone) should be presented at project reviews and forwarded to the centralized data base.

One problem introduced by self inspections is that the occurrence is unscheduled in the general sense. These inspections are nearly continuous during certain phases of the software development process. Therefore, it is necessary to schedule reviews of self inspection data at regular but logical intervals. If we consider an example or two, the collection points become more obvious.

During the development process, documentation deliveries are required. As part of a self inspection, the conformance of the document to standards is verified. Defects are noted and corrected before submission to the user (SQA, customer, et al). A logical data collection point is with the submission of the document. The results of the collection should be presented as part of the document submittal and forwarded to the centralized data base.

During the unit test phase, results of unit tests are recorded as part of the process. However, individual unit performance is not necessarily significant. Waiting for all unit tests to be completed would be close to being suicidal if a process defect existed. Therefore, monthly or biweekly collection of data would be appropriate for this phase of the development. This information should be presented at these regular intervals to the software program management and forwarded to the centralized data base.

Figure 7-3 illustrates how the data collection process should be integrated into the scheduling process. The milestones for data collection and presentation should not be treated as second class events. In the big picture, these events may be more important to the success (cost, schedule, and performance) of the program than the completion of coding or delivery of a document. A recent program found this to be the case for document submittals. By evaluating the defect data and the process that generated the documents, the critical aspect that

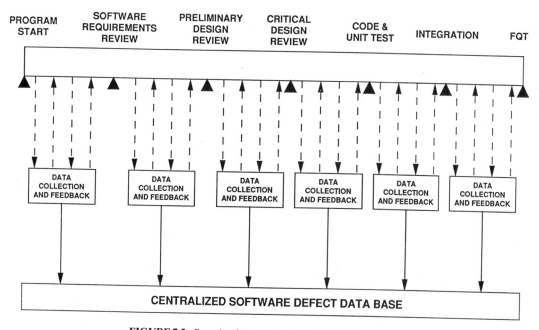

FIGURE 7-3. Sample of data collection schedule integration.

led to the customer's poor reception of the document was interpretation of the requirements, a familiar problem to many. By changing the method of generation and review, the cost of the document was reduced by 50%, a significant amount for an 800 page document. And since this book is addressing TQM techniques, the change in approach required customer participation which, in turn, required changes in the customer's review process. Both the supplier and customer adapted the process to reduce the defects and improve the performance. Incidentally, the level of effort for the customer was reduced as well as for the supplier.

Definition of Data Collection

Once the data collection points are determined, the person responsible for the data collection procedure needs to determine what data is to be collected based on the data available and the level of analysis desired. For most modern development practices, a great deal of data is readily available at the time the defect is detected. Considering the six stated elements of the data gathering objective:

1. The defect type/category
2. The point within the process where the defect was introduced
3. The point within the process where the defect was detected
4. The cost/schedule impact to the product development (PONC)
5. The cost/schedule impact to detect the defect (POC)
6. The method used for defect detection.

Items 1, 3, and 6 are immediately available. Items 2, 4, and 5 may require additional effort. Item 2 can be immediately available if the point of data gathering is the point of introduction.

7.5 DEFECT CATEGORIES AND TYPES

Defect Categories

The recording of defect type and category has been covered by numerous authors for many years. Traditional categories are: (1) requirements definition defects, (2) design defects, and (3) implementation defects. However, in Barry Boehm's *Software Engineering Economics,* documentation defects contributed 25% of the software product defects.[15] Therefore, add documentation defects to the fundamental categories.

At this juncture, most processes add the "other" category. This category "covers a multiple of sins" and makes the defect analysis process very difficult. This author sees the "other" category as a "non-TQM" process. Definition of categories must be clear and readily usable by the data collection activity. In the spirit of TQM, only start the process with 4 categories. Form a team of software professionals to draw upon their experiences and identify any categories not covered by the basic four. Add these categories to the process and move forward. If more categories are required later, then add them as part of the data collection improvement process (remember that the process of defect collection and analysis had to be in and of itself a TQM process).

Also recommended is the category of test. Procedural errors in testing often cause undue losses in productivity and suggest defects that are not present in the software but rather in the process by which the software is verified. Procedural problems with the testing process can amount to as much as 50% of the testing time required to accomplish the task. Therefore, for data collection categories, we have:

1. Requirements definition defects
2. Design defects
3. Implementation defects
4. Documentation defects
5. Testing defects.

Defect Types

Beneath the defect category is the defect type. Defect types allow the functional area of software that contained the defect to be isolated. In *Quality Assurance for Computer Software,* Robert Dunn and Richard Ullman defined the types of defects as: computational, logic, input/output, data handling, interface, data definition, database, and the infamous "other."[16] This definition of defect types is acceptable when put in the context of category. Once again, the idea of "other" is rejected as undesirable in a TQM process.

For the requirements definition category, interface defects, data definition defects, and functional statement of required processing defects are appropriate defect types. For the design category, interface defects, data definition defects, database definition defects, logic defects, and human factors defects are reasonable defect types. For the implementation category, all of the Dunn and Ullman types are appropriate. For the documentation category, new types are required. Based on experiences on projects dealing with the extensive documentation, typos, form and format, and content defect types are fundamental elements. For the testing category, procedural defects may be typed as inadequate detail, incorrect steps, incorrect definition of input, incorrect definition of required output, incorrect definition of success criteria, and human factors. For every defect category, customer dissatisfaction and quality review rejection are added to the defect type.

For each defect type, a definition of the term is necessary and provided as follows:

Interface: Defects of this type encompass hardware to software, software to software, and man to machine (also referred to as user system) interface requirements.
Data definition: Defects of this type encompass improper definition of data base size and structure, critical parameters, and limitations on data.

Functional statement: Defects of this type cover inaccurate statement of the requirement, incorrect interpretation of the requirements, failure to state a requirement, and omission of special processing limitations.

Database definition: This type covers the incorrect design of the database structure including access technique (semaphore, queue, stack, etc.), availability (information hiding), field definition, and allocation of memory.

Logic: Errors in design logic such as incorrect decision types, incorrect implementation of the requirements, and incorrect branching or looping are encompassed by this type.

Human factors: This type of defect covers failure to conform to human factors requirements for ease of use, terminology and representation, and operator actions as well as readability and understandability of the user interface.

Computational: Incorrect implementation of equations, truncation and round-off, and incorrect data typing are covered.

Input/ouput: This type is similar to the software to software interface. The delineation is that defects of this type are incorrect implementations of interfaces such as parameter list in incorrect order, accessing the wrong files and records, overloading the input/output devices, incorrect formatting of data.

Data handling: This type includes improper use of indices, failure to initialize data, mixed mode arithmetic, and loss of data.

Typos: Self explanatory but requires investigation as to why the spell checker did not correct.

Form and format: Incorrect or inconsistent paragraph titling, indentation, list identifiers, type style, writing style, and location of information are among the form and format defects covered by this type.

Content: This type is the first type in which the conformance crosses over into the subjective realm. Obvious omissions of information are entered. However, less obvious is the lack of sufficient detail to make the document understandable and usable. This type is a common defect type for which the solution is not simple.

Inadequate detail: Inadequate detail in a test procedure causes the tester to make an error of omission in the execution such that the specified success criteria is not achieved although the software may have performed as required, designed, and implemented.

Incorrect steps: Incorrect steps in a test procedure cause the tester to make an error in the execution of the procedure such that the specified success criteria is not achieved although the software may have performed as required, designed, and implemented.

Incorrect definition of input: This defect type covers the incorrect specification of the input parameters to the procedure such that the specified success criteria is not achieved although the software may have performed as required, designed, and implemented.

Incorrect definition of required output: This type covers the incorrect specification of the output data to be gathered and analyzed so that the success of the test can be ascertained. Also covered is the failure to identify all outputs such that the software may appear to meet requirements but actually does not in all cases.

Incorrect definition of success criteria: If a procedure incorrectly states the success criteria either by specifying an incorrect "pass" value or by failing to identify all cases for success, then this defect type is used.

Human factors: Although the test procedure may correctly identify the steps, input, output and success criteria, the procedure may fail to be executable by human beings. Classic examples of these types of defects are time critical data entry requirements where human error is extremely likely. Also covered in this type are procedural steps that are not understandable or sequenced such that operator error is likely.

Customer dissatisfaction: Often overlooked in most defect history data bases, the number of negative customer comments is critical in understanding the necessary process and product changes required. Customer dissatisfaction requires subtyping in these areas.

Quality review rejection: Similar to customer dissatisfaction, independent quality review rejections should be recorded and subtyped for later analysis.

Defect Detection Point

Now that the categories and types of defect data are defined, the remaining data required for defect analysis must be gathered. The point within the process where the defect was detected should be captured. The entry may be the functional point within the process model where the inspection, review, or delivery took place or the data collection point on the schedule when the defect was identified. It is recommended that the functional point in the process model be used if one exists. If one doesn't exist, then the first step in the TQM process for software development for your organization should be to create one. A good starting point is DOD-STD-2167 A[17] or Appendix A of Gordon Schulmeyer's *Zero Defect Software.*[3, Chapter 17, Appendix A] The method used for detection of the defect is dependent on the approach but usually can be identified as inspection (self, successive, independent), review, or test.

Defect Introduction Point

The point in the process where the defect was introduced can be simple or very difficult to ascertain dependent on the proximity of the introduction of the defect to its discovery. In the optimal case, the defect is detected in the phase where it was introduced, i.e., there was no propagation of the defect in the process. Unfortunately, this is not always the case even in the most disciplined TQM processes. Also unfortunate is that, although the point of introduction of the defect may be the single most important data item gathered in the TQM process when process improvement is considered, it is often the aspect thought most unimportant by the developers and defect recorders in the current environment. The culture requires a change. For organizations that are relative novices in the TQM process and defect data collection, determination of the phase where the defect was introduced is a good starting point. Although crude in its ability to highlight areas for improvement, it does limit the area of search. For more mature organizations, the process within the activity should be identified if possible.

Within Westinghouse ESG, the software process model has been decomposed several times with each decomposition adding a refinement in the definition of the specific processes that generate the software. The first decomposition yielded an 18 page process flow and the second decomposition yielded an activity list of processes totaling more than 800 distinct actions in the software development process. In parallel with the generation of the activity list was the identification of suppliers and customers, inputs and outputs, and the governing standards and practices. From this data, Westinghouse ESG is now poised to address the root cause of the defect at a level where real, measurable improvement is possible.

Regardless of the level of detail, the recording of the defect introduction point is critical to process improvement. Whether the analysis is intrinsic in the mature organization or a separate organization performs the analysis of the defect data, the time invested in identifying the point of introduction of the defect is time well spent.

Defect Cost Data—PONC/POC

Now the going gets tougher. The cost/schedule impact to the product development (PONC), and the cost/schedule impact to detect the defect (POC) are not readily available in most organizations. For companies dealing with U.S. government developments, particularly the Department of Defense, accountability is required for costing information. Most of these companies have charging structures that permit allocation of funds and charges against those funds to be recorded. For commercial companies, the structure for tracking the expenses against tasks is not as commonplace. It may be necessary to generate a simplistic charging structure to accommodate the data gathering. The critical aspect is to permit the recording of cost and schedule information against nonconformances.

Again, Westinghouse ESG through its SEPO has identified a standardized method for tracking the PONC and POC. A standardized software Work Breakdown Structure (WBS) (see Chapter 6), a method of identifying all of the tasks to be performed and associating an account to track the costs, has been established. Each task has an account for the initial cost of generation of the product within the process: documentation, code, review material, etc. For each of these tasks, a rework account also exists that tracks the effort to correct the defects. The granularity of the task identification is quite coarse, as it should be, for the objective is to gather the PONC and not identify the point of defect entry. Perhaps not surprising is that the process of accounting requires improvement. Engineering discipline and well defined procedures and task definition statements are critical in order for the staff to correctly record the data.

In the commercial environment where sophisticated accounting structures are not inherent, a simple structure would be:

1. Identify the tasks and associate an initial and rework account
2. Employees enter hours worked against each task in a data base
3. At the conclusion of the development, the data base is used to establish the PONC.

Finally, the cost of detecting the defect must be gathered. In many organizations, a separate quality organization exists whose primary function is to inspect/evaluate the quality of the products. These costs are readily captured as discussed above for the development and the PONC. The cost of inspections inherent in the software development process is less readily captured. As was the case with the PONC, a discipline is required to capture the data. Employees must be cognizant of the tasks and well educated on the need to capture the data accurately. Earlier the objective to drive the COQ to the 0,0 point was noted. Nearly every organization in the software industry today is faced with a PONC that is 1.5 to 2.5 times the POC. Therefore, most companies are emphasizing the PONC as the number to drive down. However, the POC must also be driven down by efficient processes for defect detection and correction and eventually prevention.

7.6 DEFECT DATA GATHERING PROCEDURE

Now that the fundamental data to be gathered has been established, a procedure for gathering the data must be defined. The Westinghouse SEPO is an excellent example of how the procedure can be implemented to establish corporate practices. Through the leverage of a corporate sponsored program, every software development activity can be standardized in terms of fundamental development process and data collection for defect analysis and process improvement. To assist the reader in establishing a procedure for data collection, the following checklist is provided.

1. Has a software development process model been defined?
   a. Have data collection points been identified for the model?
   b. Has responsibility for the data collection and analysis been assigned?
2. Has a procedure been written for the recording of the data?
   a. Has the procedure been reviewed and understood by all developers/reviewers?
   b. Has a data base system been established for data analysis?
3. Has a review/feedback process been established for the data collected?
   a. Have program review points been scheduled on a regular basis?

b. Has a feedback mechanism been identified either into the current program or for future programs?

4. Has a corporate level commitment been established to gather, analyze, and disseminate the analysis of the data to all programs including a process improvement program?

7.7 DEFECTS IN THE PROCESS DOMAIN

To this point, all of the attention has been focused on the product domain and justifiably so. The product domain is where the defects are visible for most of the development activities. In commercial applications, the product domain is all that is visible to the end user. Development cost overruns and schedule delays are not typically seen outside the corporation. Under TQM concepts, these aspects of development are also defects but in the process domain. In other words, a "perfect" product that does not meet schedules or cost objectives may have consequences as bad or worse than a defective product that is on time or over cost. Remember that TQM is performance, cost and schedule. Stated slightly differently, TQM is meeting all customer requirements.

The process domain defect is defined by the author as any variance from planned cost and schedule objectives including underruns and early deliveries. At this point I am sure that there are some managers screaming "heresy!" and about to dismiss this discussion as the ravings of a lunatic purist. How can an underrun or early delivery be a defect? Planning is a part of the product development process. If a process is well defined and repeatable, then the planning should reflect that process accurately. If a significant underrun or early delivery indicates that the process has a variance that is not predictable, the reason for the event should be analyzed as if it were a defect so that the process can be better understood and the method captured for later project posterity.

What happens if the "defect" is perversely treated by having a party over the overwhelming success of the program? Without understanding the why, the next job may revert to the original process performance. Unfortunate for the next program manager, the estimate for completion was based on the latest improved productivity and cycle time. When the program cost and schedule begins to erode, the program manager is faulted for poor management. Since the process was not necessarily repeatable, the pressure to find out why performance is down comes too late. In many cases where processes are dependent on the individuals involved and not the definition and formality of the process, wild fluctuations in performance are noted. This is precisely what the Software Engineering Institute has indicated in low level processes. Firing he manager may or may not help. The bottom line is that after record profits come record losses and the environment is stressful. Compounding the problem is the typical reaction to cut some corners and now the product is defective, late, and over cost. Not a pleasant business picture.

So restating the author's original definition, a process defect is *any* variance from planned cost and schedule objectives including underruns and early deliveries.

Given this definition, defect measurement is necessary and treated in a similar fashion to the product defect.

Defect Categories

Following the same logic as with the product defect, there are categories of defects:

1. Cost
2. Schedule.

Defect Types

There are types of defects for each category:

Initial generation overrun: cost of generating the original product exceeded planned cost for the product or phase excluding rework.
Generation overrun with rework: Cost of generating the original product met planned cost but rework caused overall cost overrun.
Initial generation underrun: Cost of original product generation less than the planned cost without rework.
Generation underrun with rework: Cost of generating the original product plus cost of rework resulted in overall cost underrun.
Initial schedule slippage: Time required for generation of the original product exceeded planned excluding rework.
Schedule slippage with rework: Original product generation met planned schedule but rework caused schedule slippage.
Initial early schedule completion: Time required for generation of the original product significantly less than planned excluding rework.
Early schedule completion with rework: Original product generation plus time required for rework significantly less than planned schedule.
Cost variance from external influence: Cost of product generation varied from planned due to external influence not controlled by process owner. Examples are change in requirements, late availability of computer resources, etc.
Schedule variance from external influence: Time to complete product generation varied from planned due to external influence not controlled by process owner. Examples are change in requirements, late availability of computer resources, etc.

Defect Data Collection in the Process Domain

Most managers who have ever developed any product have performed process domain data collection, i.e., they have tracked cost and schedule progress. The question is whether or not the data tracked was timely, accurate, definitive, and comparable to standards. Although many organizations collect the data at the end of the program as a post-mortem, the author believes that regardless of the maturity of the organization in TQM or process definition, it is imperative to initiate a TQM process in-line to the project development. Survival is at stake.

Data collection points for the process defect gathering should be at regular intervals scaled to the cost and schedule of the development. For instance, if the program is a 5 year activity, monthly collection points are appropriate as the upper bound. If a program is funded at $1 million then data collection at intervals where $50 thousand of expenditure is planned is a reasonable expectation.

Most of the problems with the present tracking of cost and schedule in the industry today centers around the word "definitive." How many times has a program been 90% complete for 50% of the job? The reason for this phenomenon is lack of definitive milestone, i.e., a binary system of milestones; either it is done or it is not. Lois Zells (Chapter 2), recognized process and TQM expert, stated at an ACM symposium at the University of Maryland that milestones should be activities requiring 4 to 40 hours of effort and no more.[18] The author insists that objective evidence of completion is essential to the establishment of milestones and cost/schedule performance measurement. Cost and schedule information must be definitive.

Another view is the concept of "entry" and "exit" criteria. For each phase of the software development, a well defined set of criteria must be met to pass through the next phase. By defining these criteria, two objectives are achieved. First, the software development team has a set of clearly defined objectives against which the products of their labor will be compared. The establishment of these criteria in and of themselves provides a clarity that is often missing in many development processes. Second, the definitization of entry criteria provides a concrete standard by which the next "customer" can assess the quality of the product being received and provide objective evidence when the product is defective.

7.8 DEFECT DATA ANALYSIS

Robert Dunn addresses the defect analysis in great detail in Software Defect Removal and touches upon process quality control and defect prevention via process (methods, procedures, or tools).[1, pp. 274-280] This chapter concentrates on the defect analysis as it relates to process improvement and TQM. The defect data analysis process is a three step process that, once the detailed process definition and data collection process are in place, is simplistic.

Step one is to identify the areas requiring improvement that will be addressed. This is typically accomplished by a Pareto analysis. Westinghouse ESG uses the PONC as the discriminating parameter, i.e., the process that causes the highest cost impact is the one to be addressed first. An ancillary discriminator is cycle time since "time is money." Other discriminators can be number of product/process defects, rework cost per defect, and total test time as a percentage of product development time.

Step two is to perform causal analysis to identify the root cause of the defect. This analysis requires that the process step identified by the data collection activity by further decomposed and analyzed for process defect. Suppliers, customers, standards, training, tools, and other aspects of the process should be microscopically viewed for the specific activity that introduced the defect. Root causes generally fall into the categories of:

1. Incomplete definition of requirements
2. Incomplete definition of the process
3. Poor communication of requirements/process
4. Inadequate training
5. Inadequate process
6. Inadequate tools
7. Incorrect process
8. Human error.

The list of categories is in order of historically most likely cause of the defect. Note that although humans (the workers) are usually blamed for all the problems, they are the least likely source of the defects as pointed out previously by Dr. W. Edwards Deming. Further, if human error were the only source of problems in the current software quality dilemma, the industry would be in excellent condition.

Step three is to identify the corrective action to the process so that the defect is eliminated by eliminating the cause. Mature, in-line TQM processes correct the problems during the development cycle. Processes are so well defined that immediate analysis and feedback are inherent in the process and the development team. Less mature cultures and organizations deal with process improvement via a "lessons learned" process that eliminates the defect on future programs. The critical aspect of step three is to capture an improvement and institutionalize it. The continuous improvement of the process will lead to ever improving product quality, improved productivity, and increased profits.

A special case was noted earlier in the process domain. The cost and schedule defects, particularly overruns and slippages, require in-line correction no matter how mature the culture. Often, even if the visibility into the variance is timely and definitive, the corrective action does not address the root cause but rather the symptom. Additional personnel, more inspections, adding another item to a checklist, working longer hours are typical responses. The root cause identification always provides the proper solution to alleviate the problem in the most expeditious fashion, lowest cost and highest yield. Chapter 15 on defect prevention elaborates on a methodology for accomplishing this.

An example of this occurred on a program the author is familiar with that was developed in the mid-1980s. Schedules had eroded; costs were exceeding plan. The solution chosen was to go to three shifts, seven days per week. The result of the action was further erosion of the schedule (productivity decreased on a per week basis) and costs continued to grow. The root cause was poor definition of interfaces and interrelationships of functions. The appropriate TQM solution was to stop spending effort on integration until the interfaces were properly identified. This was not the chosen solution since the prospect of stopping the work was unacceptable to the program. Fortunately, a middle ground solution was proposed, at some risk to the software manager. Shifts were reduced and teams work schedules adjusted to permit interfacing on a verbal basis. Productivity improved. Shifts were further reduced and more interfacing of teams initiated. Productivity improved again. Communications were improved addressing the root cause of the problem and success finally achieved.

In the process domain (cost and schedule) early detection of defects is critical. More important is to analyze the data, identify the root cause, and apply the corrective actions. In-line process improvement is essential. Beware, there is a risk associated with in-line TQM. Short term losses are often required for long term gains. It is often difficult to prove to a disbeliever, before the fact, that TQM is the most effective approach.

7.9 SUMMARY

To summarize the critical aspects of defect analysis.

1. Defect analysis begins with a well-defined development process and data collection procedure.
2. TQM requires a commitment to institutionalize the defect detection and analysis process and provide feedback for process improvement.
3. Defects are present in two domains: the product domain and the process domain.
4. The cost of quality is the price of nonconformance and the price of conformance and a balance is required to drive the cost of quality to the 0,0 point.
5. Process domain defects include cost and schedule variances even in the positive direction since the process must be repeatable to be TQ.

References

1. Dunn, R., *Software Defect Removal,* New York: McGraw-Hill Book Co., 1984.
2. Lloyd, D. K. and Lipow, M., *Reliability: Management, Methods, and Mathematics,* 2nd edition, published by authors, Redondo Beach, California, 1977.
3. Schulmeyer, G. Gordon, *Zero Defect Software,* New York: McGraw-Hill Book Co., 1990.
4. Dyer, M., "A Formal Approach to Software Error Removal," *The Journal of Systems and Software* 7, Elsevier Science Publishing Co., 1987, pp. 109-114.
5. Fagan, M. E., "Design and Code Inspections and Process Control in the Development of Programs," IBM-TR-00.73, June, 1976, p. 125.
6. Zultner, R., "The Deming Approach to Software Quality Engineering," *Quality Progress,* vol. XXI, no. 11, November 1988, Copyright 1988, American Society for Quality Control, Inc., Milwaukee, Wisconsin, p. 60, reprinted by permission.
7. Shingo, S., *Zero Quality Control: Source Inspection and the Poka-yoke System,* Andrew P. Dillon, trans., Cambridge, Massachusetts: Productivity Press, 1986, pp. 18-21, reprinted by permission.

8. Cho, Chin-Kuei, *Quality Programming: Developing and Testing Software with Statistical Quality Control,* New York: John Wiley and Sons, Inc., 1987.

9. Dyer, M., "The Cleanroom Software Development Process," in Kitchenham, B. and Littlewood, B., *Measurement for Software Control and Assurance,* London: Elsevier Appl. Sci. Publishers, 1989.

10. Burrill, C. W. and Ellsworth, L. W., *Quality Data Processing,* Tenafly, New Jersey: Burrill-Ellsworth Associates, Inc., 1982, p. 50.

11. Basili, V. R., "Software Development: A Paradigm for the Future," *Proceedings IEEE Computer Society International Computer Software and Applications Conference,* IEEE Service Center, Piscataway, New Jersey, Copyright 1989, pp. 475-476.

12. Westinghouse Electric Corporation ESG, SEPO.

13. Ward, T. M., "Software Measures and Goals at Hewlett-Packard," Presentation at Juran Institute Conference, Copyright 1989, Juran Institute, Inc.

14. Schulmeyer, G. G., Presentation on TQM at Westinghouse ESG SEPO Symposium, May, 1991.

15. Boehm, B. W., *Software Engineering Economics,* Englewood Cliffs: Prentice Hall Inc., Copyright 1981, p. 383, reprinted by permission.

16. Dunn, R. and Ullman, R., *Quality Assurance for Computer Software,* New York: McGraw-Hill Book Company, 1982, p. 243.

17. U.S. Department of Defense, DOD-STD-2167A (USAF), *Military Standard—Software Development Methodology.*

18. Zells, Lois, "Applying Japanese Total Quality Management to U.S. Software Engineering," ACM Conference at University of Maryland, April 29, 1991.

19. Crosby, Phillip, *Quality Is Free,* New York: McGraw-Hill Book Company, 1979, pp. 119-126.

20. Dunn, R., *op. cit.,* p. 6.

8

Software Risk Mitigation

Anthony F. Shumskas

8.1 INTRODUCTION

Risk is the traditional way of expressing uncertainty in a system's life cycle. Often the degree of risk is expressed in the form of subjective assessments of high, medium, and low. In the mathematical sense, risk is the probability at a given point in the system's life cycle that predicted goals cannot be achieved within available resources. The risk assessment form, i.e., subjective, mathematical, or a combination of both, is affected by the various risk components' complexity and the compounding uncertainty associated with assumptions concerning risk sources. Risk is normally not treated with mathematical rigor during the early life cycle phases. As the system progresses through the life cycle and assumption uncertainty diminishes, the degree of mathematical precision increases.

Successful management and fielding of systems depends upon the effective use of risk identification, assessment, reduction, and control techniques. Traditionally, there are three kinds of risk associated with system development: technical, cost, and schedule risks. Risk mitigation (control) techniques used in system development have as their primary purpose the reduction of the operational and support risks associated with decision risk.

Software often presents a significant source of risk in all these areas. Assessing, controlling, and reducing software risk through effective and interactive development, quality, test, and support programs are often key factors in the reduction of system risk. Many are familiar with the classical cost, schedule, and technical risks associated with hardware development, but are unfamiliar with assessing software related risks in these areas or how to combine hardware and software risk assessments to obtain an integrated software-sensitive system risk perspective.

To ensure terminology consistency, the following definitions are used in this chapter:

Risk management: The practice of applying discipline to the development and/or acquisition process. It is composed of three fundamental elements: risk assessment, risk analysis, and risk handling.

Risk mitigation: Total quality management (TQM) requires management's commitment to effectively use quality programs, techniques and procedures to continually improve the process and resultant products. Similarly, risk mitigation is management's commitment to and application of risk management to gain visibility into the process, control and improve the process and products, and include risk management into the TQM tool suite.

Risk assessment: The process of examining a program and identifying areas of potential risk.

Risk analysis: Examining the change of outcomes with modification of risk input variables. It is more involved than risk assessment and should identify the most critical variables, with insights about desired options for risk handling.

Risk handling: The identification and application of options available to reduce or manage selected risk areas. The typical options available include: risk avoidance, risk control, risk assumption, and risk transfer.

Risk control: The process of achieving the desired outcomes by methods of continual application of management techniques to the risk items or areas.

Acquisition risk: The degree of uncertainty associated with system acquisition due to a combination of cost, schedule, and technical risk.

Cost risk: The degree of uncertainty associated with system acquisition life cycle budgets that may negatively impact the program.

Schedule risk: The degree of uncertainty associated with the ability of the program to achieve desired milestones (outcomes) within the planned time.

Technical risk: The degree of uncertainty in the development engineering process that may keep the program from meeting its technical specifications or may adversely affect overall system quality and performance.

Decision risk: The degree of uncertainty associated with the deployment of a developed system due to a combination of operational and support risk.

Operational risk: The degree of uncertainty that system deployment will result in the fielding of a system unsuitable for its intended use, including the residual of technical risk from the development process.

Support risk: The degree of uncertainty associated with the ability of the system to be maintained and/or enhanced after fielding within the planned support concept and resources.

System risk: The composite degree of uncertainty from acquisition risk and decision risk resulting in the acquisition, development, and deployment of all hardware and software elements that compose the total system.

While application of software risk analysis is a difficult task with few well-defined approaches, it is possible to define a framework for software risk assessment, management, and mitigation which is compatible with the various risk techniques applicable to hardware risk. Risk management is an iterative process that requires managers to establish objectives and regularly assess their programs for impediments to achieving these objectives. It can be used to place in perspective the magnitude of the cause and effects of changes, to develop options, and to make decisions that control the outcome. To perform these functions, managers need visibility into the software aspects of their programs.

Techniques for obtaining visibility into a system's software development, quality, test, and support aspects are being applied on an ever increasing basis. Currently, these techniques take the form of relative trend data, or indicators, software quality factors, and software metrics. As these visibility techniques mature and become more quantitative, software risk mitigation techniques will also shift from the subjective to the quantitative.

A template showing the general flow for establishing risk control is presented in Figure 8-1. This template operates in a building-block fashion. Risk assessment is

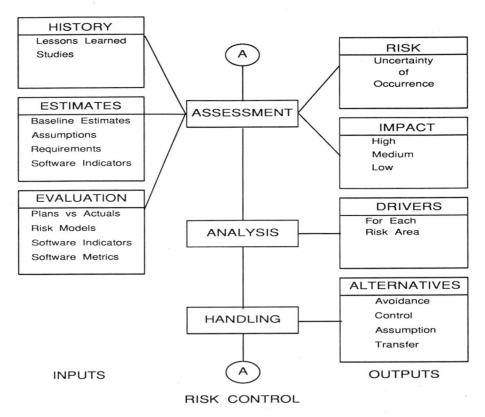

FIGURE 8-1. Software risk management template.

the first step in developing a software risk mitigation approach. Data sources for assessing software risk include history, estimates and evaluations. Historical lessons learned and previous study reports on similar programs are useful in framing the approach. Baseline estimates, assumptions, requirement documents, and software measurement data are important for setting necessary constraints on the risk mitigation approach. Program evaluations, risk models, and assessment of planned versus achieved objectives provide essential control for assuring that a risk mitigation approach works.

Risk assessment requires a broad, high-level understanding of executive management perspectives of strategy and overall executability. Assessment in each risk area can be, and should be, performed by the various technical disciplines, including software quality, assigned or matrixed to the program. This task's expected outcome should be the actual risk assessments and associated system impacts.

Risk analysis is conducted to determine: where and when the consequence of risk is likely to occur; magnitude of exposure; and risk impact; drivers; and areas of greatest concern. Once risk has been identified and evaluated, risk handling is performed.

Risk handling is the determination and evaluation of alternatives to reduce or mitigate risk exposure. Risk handling alternatives typically fall into four categories: avoidance; control or prevention; assumption; and transfer. The alternative selected depends on where the program is in the development process, and the options available.

Risk control is a full-time, iterative process throughout the software's life-cycle. It is a means by which management identifies and manages vulnerability and concern areas. Continuous use of risk control provides the needed discipline for making informed decisions.

8.2 TECHNICAL RISK

Technical risk is the cornerstone of risk control. From it, all of the other risk areas derive inherent probabilities of occurrence. Uncertainties and risks inherent in the technical aspects of software development can have major impact on the likelihood of obtaining system objectives. Software development success can significantly impact the likelihood (probability) of cost and schedule overruns, achievement of required operational capabilities, and the ability to correct errors and implement enhancements in the post deployment software support (PDSS) environment.

One way to address software technical risk (Figure 8-2) is to first identify the risk drivers. By identifying the drivers, one can identify the history, estimation, and evaluation requirements necessary to effectively manage software technical risk. Software technical risk drivers typically include requirements, both stated and derived, constraints, available technology, and developmental approach.

Software requirements can be broken down into a series of key elements that provide the greatest amount of uncertainty in achieving technical objectives. Typically, these elements are: complexity of system requirements implemented by

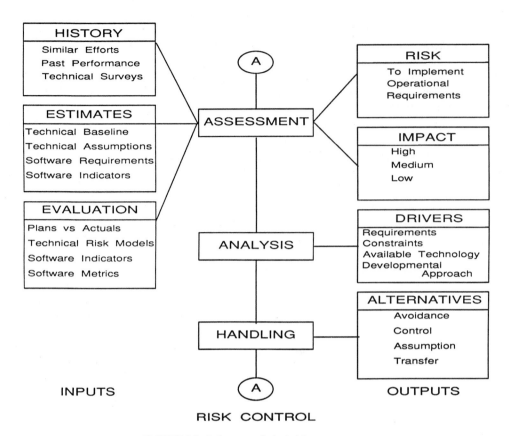

FIGURE 8-2. Software technical risk management.

software; size or magnitude of the software to be developed; requirements stability; impact of support requirements on software design; and ability to decompose and allocate system-level maintainability, quality, and reliability requirements to the various software components.

Resource constraints often take the form of limitations imposed by the physical characteristics of the computer hardware, availability of experienced personnel, and secondary limitations due to cost and schedule. Other constraints that can contribute to uncertainty include the application of standards, especially if the standards have been improperly tailored, mandatory use of furnished equipment and software engineering products; and environmental aspects of the system that affect computer hardware selection or design.

Available technology affects normally arise from choice of language(s) used to implement the software design, especially implementation language and environment maturity; maturity and availability of hardware technology necessary for system and software implementation; availability and maturity of the software tool environment necessary to assess, develop, test, and accept operational software; impact of data rights on the ability to implement and support new technology; and the developer's experience in applying new technology.

Developmental approach impacts software risk through use or absence of prototypes and reusable software; adequate documentation availability to support prototype transition and reuse of existing software; availability of tools and resources (facilities, terminals, access time, etc.) for development environment; application of sufficient management control to provide discipline, structure, visibility, and continuous improvement to the development process; complexity of interfaces internal to the developing agency and other external agencies; and the contribution to uncertainty attributed to software integration at system, configuration item, and component levels.

Following technical risk driver determination, the next step is to identify the necessary inputs for effective risk handling.

HISTORY

Review of similar development efforts and the developing agency's past performance for this type of application software aids in identifying technical uncertainty. Assessing the capability/capacity to develop the required software is useful in identifying work place changes that could reduce technical risk. Surveys of technical literature and related laboratory efforts contribute to assessing technical risk, especially in the areas of prototyping, software reuse, language utilization, and technology insertion.

ESTIMATES

Comparing the proposed technical baseline with technical baselines from similar development efforts provides insight into the degree of uncertainty (risk) being introduced into the development effort. Insight gained by comparing pre- and post-development baselines aids in assessing the new development's proposed technical baseline. Critical analysis of technical assumptions, especially functional allocations between hardware and software, should be accomplished as early as possible, but no later than system and software requirements analysis. During requirements analysis, the software requirements' scope and nature are clarified, with further refinements as the development effort matures. Technical baselines can be used to identify which indicators are useful during development and form the planned portion of the computer resource utilization, software requirements definition and stability, and software development tool indicators.

EVALUATION

For risk handling, periodic evaluations should be performed to ensure that technical risk has not increased to unacceptable levels. Evaluation frequency should be based upon the degree of risk exposure management is willing to accept. During development, primarily during full scale development and earlier, when software prototypes may transition into final software products, a comparison of actual and planned technical baselines should be initiated. Deviations from planned baselines should be considered as sources of change in technical risk. Management indicators provide a useful tool for visual representation of these deviations. Quality indicators can be used to gain insight into the quality and maturity of the developed software products. Appropriate choice and use of software quality factors and supporting quality metrics also contributes to the evaluation process (Table 8-1). Evaluation results can be tailored for use in existing risk models.

Risk handling begins with a detailed assessment based on the inputs described above. The probability that the desired outcome will not occur, and the impact magnitude if the desired outcome is not achieved are then determined for the potential technical risks. Total technical risk can then be assessed by evaluating the resultant product of probability and impact magnitude. Table 8-2 presents a sample set of rules of thumb that can aid in determining that desired outcomes will not occur and relates rules to possible risk impact assessments.

After evaluating technical risk, composite risk factors can be ranked to determine those needing immediate attention and those with the most potential for risk reduction. Analysis is then performed to ensure that the correct technical risk

TABLE 8-1   Examples of Technical Characteristics and Related Software Quality Factors

Technical Characteristics	Software Quality Factors
Human lives affected	Integrity Reliability Correctness Testability
Long life cycle	Maintainability Portability Flexibility
Experimental system or high rate of change	Flexibility
Experimental technology in hardware design	Portability
Many changes over the system life cycle	Flexibility Reusability
Real-time application	Efficiency Reliability Correctness
On-board computer application	Efficiency Reliability Correctness
Processing of classified information	Integrity
Interrelated systems	Interoperability

TABLE 8-2   Quantification of Probability and Impact of Technical Failure

| Technical Drivers | Magnitude | | |
	Low (0.0-0.3)	Medium (0.4-0.5)	High (0.6-1.0)
Requirements			
Complexity	Simple or easily allocatable	Moderate, can be allocated	Significant or difficult to allocate
Size	Small or easily broken down into work units	Medium, or can be broken down into work units	Large, cannot be broken down into work units
Stability	Little or no change to established baseline	Some change in baseline expected	Rapidly changing or no baseline
PDSS	Agreed to support concept	Roles and missions issues unresolved	No support concept or major unresolved issues
R & M	Allocatable to hardware and software components	Requirements can be defined	Can only be addressed at the total system level
Constraints			
Computer resources	Mature, growth capacity with design, flexible	Available, some growth capacity	New development, no growth capacity, inflexible
Personnel	Available, in place, experienced, stable	Available, but not in place, some experience	High turnover, little or no experience, not available
Standards	Appropriately tailored for application	Some tailoring, all not reviewed for applicability	No tailoring, none applied to the contract
GFE/GFP	Meets requirements, available	May meet requirements, uncertain availability	Incompatible with system requirements, unavailable
Environment	Little or no impact on design	Some impact on design	Major impact on design
Technology			
Language	Mature, approved HOL used	Approved or non-approved HOL	Significant use of assembly language
Hardware	Mature, available	Some development or available	Total new development
Tools	Documented, validated, in place	Available, validated, some development	Unvalidated, proprietary, major development
Data rights	Fully compatible with support and follow-on	Minor incompatibilities with support and follow-on	Incompatible with support and follow-on
Experience	Greater than 3 to 5 years	Less than 3 to 5 years	Little or none
Development Approach			
Prototypes and reuse	Used, documented sufficiently for use	Some use and documentation	No use or no documentation
Documentation	Correct and available	Some deficiencies, available	Nonexistent
Environment	In place, validated, experience with use	Minor modifications, tools available	Major development effort
Management approach	Existing product and process controls	Product & process controls need enhancement	Weak or nonexistent
Integration	Internal and external controls in place	Internal or external controls not in place	Weak or nonexistent
Impact	Minimal to small reduction in technical performance	Some reduction in technical performance	Significant degradation to nonachievement of technical performance

drivers for a particular application have been identified. For risk handling, possible courses of action are:

Avoidance. This can involve descoping technical objectives to a more achievable level, changing the developmental approach, or using a preplanned product improvement (P3I) or evolutionary development strategy to achieving desired technical objectives through successive enhancements to more technically achievable baselines. Avoidance techniques are viable primarily during the early stages of development. Late application often takes the form of risk transfer.

Control. One could apply parallel development efforts, intense management reviews, rapid prototyping, or conduct additional trade-off studies.

Assumption. Management can accept the technical risk, manage the software development effort appropriately, and remain aware of decreased probability of success.

Transfer. Software requirements could be realigned through the requirements analysis process, and, in some cases, be implemented by hardware instead of software. Another possibility, in some integrated systems, is to reassign the requirement to other system elements. Under no circumstances should software technical risk be transferred to operations and support phases of the system life-cycle.

8.3 COST RISK

Cost estimates, normally deterministic, are fundamental to program management. Costs for individual program elements are usually expressed as a single value representing the "best" available estimate. Software cost estimates are usually determined by using one or more cost estimating techniques, such as analogies, bottom-up, and available cost models, including COCOMO, SLIM, and PRICE-S. History from prior development efforts form the foundation for most software cost estimation models. Most models do *not* have sufficient empirical data from software efforts structured as we have been discussing. Some of the models have been modified to present a "best" guess at software development cost under a structured environment.

Software cost estimating techniques, unfortunately, are also based on a sizing estimate, total lines of code (expressed in thousands of source lines of code (KSLOC)), and incorporate the required effort associated with quality as a percentage of the KSLOC effort. The problem is that most KSLOC estimates, especially the early ones, are inaccurate by 1 to 10 orders of magnitude. Some promising new models that use a combination of software functional analysis and KSLOC have produced sizing accuracies approaching −20% (the minus sign means lower than actual).

Software cost estimates are affected by competing drivers (Figure 8-3) and the approaches used to manage and control technical and schedule risks. Cost drivers

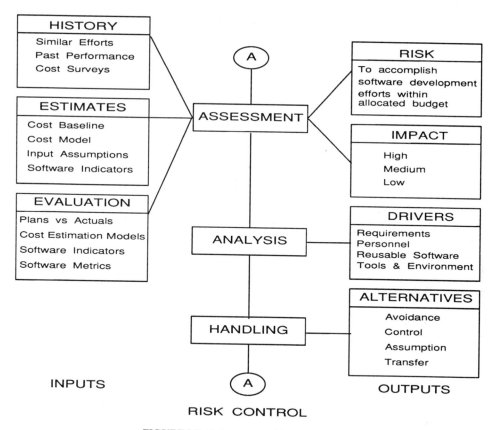

FIGURE 8-3. Software cost risk management.

normally fall into four areas: requirements complexity, personnel, reusable software, and tools and environment.

Requirements complexity directly affects any cost estimate. Critical cost model complexity inputs include software size (magnitude of development effort); identification of computer resource constraints that can affect design approach and may limit implementation of required functions; type of application (real-time, embedded, criticality to system function, etc.); security requirements; and technology availability. These inputs directly impact costs associated with design and implementation. Requirements instability provides a link which indicates a high degree of uncertainty on all other requirements related inputs.

Software development is labor intensive. Personnel factors contribute significantly in controlling software cost risk. Factors such as availability of personnel to meet proposed staffing profiles, proper discipline mix (systems and software engineering, configuration and documentation management, quality, test, etc.) involved in software development, appropriate experience base in the disciplines familiar with the particular application, use of automation to increase productivity, and environment used to manage and resolve personnel issues should be included in the cost risk management approach.

Reusable software is often presented as a means of reducing cost risk. There are several areas associated with reuse that should be investigated to verify the claim, including: availability of software for reuse; extent of modifications to meet the "new" application; evaluation of specific software language requirements prior to reuse; access to sufficient software data rights and documentation to meet support concept requirements and any planned recompetitive support contracts; and certification that provides documented evidence that reusable software meets requirements of the "new" application and can be integrated with system hardware and software.

Another area to consider is software tools and environment. Software development facilities and tools (host computer hardware, terminals, access time, software development, quality and test tools, simulators, etc.) should be evaluated to assess their availability, applicability to the development effort, availability and cost of data rights that must be obtained for any deliverable computer resources and support software, costs associated with configuration management, and the developer's familiarity, or experience, with these facilities and tools.

After cost risk drivers have been identified, the appropriate inputs necessary to support management's cost risk handling approach need to be determined.

HISTORY
Reviewing similar development efforts and past cost performance for this type of application software development contributes to the identification of budget uncertainty. This review also aids in determining the type(s) of software cost estimation model(s) best suited for a specific development effort. Comparing historical projections with the actuals for the previous efforts is beneficial in calibrating cost estimates and models.

ESTIMATES
Proper selection of software cost estimation models is crucial in controlling cost risk. Selection of the wrong model can cause development to be underfunded. Input assumptions validation for the selected model(s) need to be accomplished by a combination of management, technical, and cost personnel. Once accomplished, the cost estimate should be baselined. Since personnel levels are one of the primary cost drivers, staffing profiles should be baselined in conjunction with the cost estimate. These baselines can then be used to form the planned portion of software development staffing and cost/schedule deviation management indicators.

EVALUATION
Programs can suffer from both scarcity of financial resources and misapplication of those resources. The net effect, in either case, can significantly delay program completion and add to the development effort's total cost. An effective software cost risk handling function can help ensure that costs do not increase to unacceptable levels. Monitoring planned versus actual expenditure rates through use of

**TABLE 8-3   Examples of Cost Characteristics and Related
Software Quality Factors**

Cost Characteristics	Software Quality Factors
High system cost	Reliability Flexibility
Many changes over life cycle	Flexibility Resuability
Ease of correction and change	Maintainability Flexibility
Ease of Reuse	Portability Flexibility Reusability
Performance verification	Testability Correctness

cost/schedule control system (C/SCS) and similar techniques can be applied to software developments, just as they are to hardware developments. As cost model input assumptions are refined, cost models can be rerun to obtain better cost estimates at completion. Management indicators can be used as a tool for visually tracking deviations from cost and staffing baselines. Completeness, defect density, fault density, test coverage and documentation quality indicators can also help identify the potential for cost overruns due to poor quality software products. Appropriate choice and use of software quality factors and metrics. (Table 8-3) can also contribute to the cost evaluation process.

Following a detailed assessment of these inputs, the probability that the desired outcome will not occur and the impact magnitude if the desired outcome is not achieved are then determined for the potential cost risks. Total cost risk can then be assessed by evaluating the resultant product of probability and impact magnitude. Table 8-4 contains a sample set of rules of thumb that can aid in the evaluation process.

After evaluating cost risk, composite risk factors should be ranked to identify those factors with the most potential for risk reduction and management attention. Cost risk drivers should be reviewed to ensure that the correct drivers have been identified for a specific software development effort.

Cost risk handling should always be accomplished on a total system life-cycle cost analysis basis. Possible courses of action for cost risk handling include:

AVOIDANCE

Software cost avoidance is normally achieved by reducing the software development effort's scope, obtaining additional resources, "streamlined" acquisition practices, and P3I or evolutionary software development strategies. Extreme caution must be exercised in applying cost avoidance techniques to ensure that necessary documentation, nature and scope of test required to adequately demonstrate objective achievement, and software quality requirements are not eliminated.

TABLE 8-4   Quantification of Probability and Impact of Cost Failure

Cost Drivers	Magnitude		
	Low (0.0-0.3)	Medium (0.4-0.5)	High (0.6-1.0)
Requirements			
Size	Small, noncomplex, or easily decomposed	Medium, moderate complexity, decomposable	Large, highly complex, or not decomposable
Resource constraints	Little or no hardware-imposed constraints	Some hardware-imposed constraints	Significant hardware-imposed constraints
Application	Non real-time, little system interdependency	Embedded, some system interdependency	Real-time, embedded, strong interdependency
Technology	Mature, existent, in-house experience	Existent, some in-house experience	New or new application, little experience
Requirements stability	Little or no change to established baseline	Some change in baseline expected	Rapidly changing or no baseline
Personnel			
Availability	In place, little turnover expected	Available, some turnover expected	High turnover, not available
Mix	Good mix of software disciplines	Some disciplines inappropriately represented	Some disciplines not represented
Experience	High experience ratio	Average experience ratio	Low experience ratio
Management environment	Strong personnel management approach	Good personnel management approach	Weak personnel management approach
Reusable Software			
Availability	Compatible with need dates	Delivery dates in question	Incompatible with need dates
Modifications	Little or no change	Some change	Extensive changes
Language	Compatible with system & PDSS requirements	Partial compatibility with requirements	Incompatible with system or PDSS requirements
Rights	Compatible with PDSS & competition requirements	Partial compatibility with PDSS, some competition	Incompatible with PDSS concept, noncompetitive
Certification	Verified performance, application compatible	Some application compatible test data available	Unverified, little test data available
Tools and Environment			
Facilities	Little or no modifications	Some modifications, existent	Major modifications, non-existent
Availability	In place, meets need dates	Some compatibility with need dates	Nonexistent, does not meet need dates
Rights	Compatible with PDSS & development plans	Partial compatibility with PDSS & development plans	Incompatible with PDSS & development plans
Configuration management	Fully controlled	Some controls	No controls
Impact	Sufficient financial resources	Some shortage of financial resources, possible overrun	Significant financial shortages, budget overrun likely

CONTROL

Cost control can be achieved through stringent management reviews, continuous updating of cost estimates based upon real-time inputs of technical and schedule accomplishments, and conducting additional cost trade-off studies. Appropriate tailoring and application of customer mandated standards, and early user involvement in operational requirements analysis also contribute to controlling cost risk.

ASSUMPTION

Management can accept the cost risk, structure the software development accordingly, and remain cognizant of the probability of successful program accomplishment within available financial resources.

TRANSFER

Software functions that have high cost risk could be transferred to related programs that have the resources to successfully implement these functions. Under no circumstances should cost risk be transferred to the system life-cycle's operational and support phases. Transferring cost risk to these phases is counterproductive to reducing life-cycle costs.

8.4 SCHEDULE RISK

Schedule estimation has a direct linkage with cost estimation. Like cost estimates, schedule estimates are also deterministic. Both can be broken down into the components that make up the system's overall cost or schedule. In schedules, this breakdown includes critical paths, networks, interim milestones, review points, etc. Schedule risk control includes determination of the range of times covering the span between earliest and latest dates for program completion, with detailed schedules and risks. Schedules are not realistic unless resources to complete individual activities are available when needed. Schedule risk control should combine uncertainties of the various activities, range between shortest and longest time frames, "most likely" or "best" schedule, and the risk of not meeting the desired initial operating capability (IOC) or marketing date.

Schedule estimates are impacted by several competing drivers, some of which are not controllable by management. Approaches used to manage and control cost and technical risks can also impact schedule risk. Typical software schedule risk drivers include resources, need dates, dependencies, and requirements (Figure 8-4).

The primary resources that can affect schedule include personnel, facilities, and financial factors. Personnel resources impact software development in a slightly different manner than the way in which they impact hardware development. Too few software personnel can negatively impact schedule risk in the same way that too many can. Facilities and financial resources impact software schedules in the same way they impact hardware schedules.

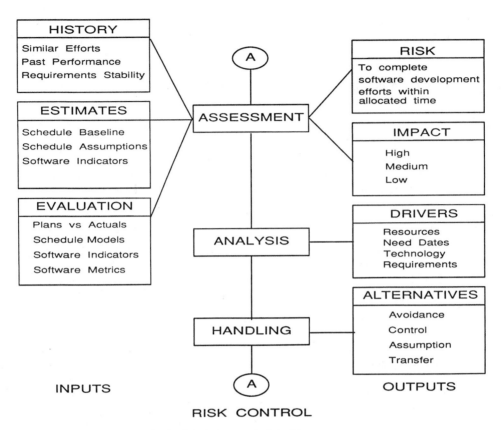

FIGURE 8-4. Software schedule risk management.

Need dates are usually determined by factors which management can and cannot control. Among the aspects outside management's control are market or customer need date changes that can encourage schedule compression (increased risk); economic factors such as changes in funds availability, and "political" changes that influence IOC, financial commitments, and technical content. Need dates which management can control to some degree include internal interim milestones, acquisition dates of development, quality, and test tools, and delivery dates of items furnished to subcontractor(s).

Technology can also directly influence schedule. New technology insertion may not be compatible with an externally imposed IOC due to technology immaturity, availability (need dates that are incompatible with when the technology can move from the laboratory to the applications environment), and the experience the developer has using the new technology.

Another driver that can have a direct bearing on schedule is requirements. If requirements, especially derived or inferred requirements, are not known, defined, and consistent with desired outcomes, schedule risk can be adversely affected.

Just as in technical and cost risk, requirements complexity and stability also influence schedule risk.

When appropriate software schedule risk drivers have been determined, it is then necessary to identify the inputs necessary for schedule risk control.

HISTORY

Reviewing similar development efforts and past performance can significantly help identify areas of schedule uncertainty. Particular attention should be paid to the impact that requirements instability has had on other program schedules. Comparison of planned and actual schedules for historical developments, along with an understanding of the reasons for the differences, also helps in determining ways to control risk.

ESTIMATES

By comparing pre- and post-schedule baselines of related historical development efforts, the proposed development schedule's validity can be assessed. Critical analysis of development schedule baseline assumptions should also be made. Schedule baselines can form the planned portion of the software progress (development and test) indicator.

EVALUATION

In performing the risk control function, periodic evaluations should be performed to ensure that schedule risk has not significantly increased. This evaluation should attempt to balance development effort realities with any imposed artificial or political constraints. Evaluation frequency should be based on the degree of risk exposure that management is willing to accept. In comparing schedule baselines with actuals, deviations should be considered to determine the source of the change as well as their impact on risk assessment. The software progress indicator can be a useful tool to visually portray these deviations throughout the development effort. Correctness, fault density, test coverage, and documentation quality indicators can aid in determining if product quality could have a schedule impact.

What is often overlooked in developing a schedule is the impact of product and process quality on the schedule. What good does it do to have a task completed on time, only to find that it was done wrong and additional time is required to correct the errors. Appropriate choice and use of selected quality factors can help ensure that the system works correctly and is developed on a timely basis. A combination of system requirements and Table 8-5 can help you select and prioritize the key software quality factors and related metrics.

Schedule risk handling begins with an in-depth assessment of these inputs. This is followed by a determination of the probability that the desired schedule will not be achieved, and the magnitude of the impact. By evaluating the combination of probability and magnitude, total schedule risk can be assessed. A set of rules of thumb (Table 8-6) can assist in determining these.

When schedule risk has been evaluated, composite risk factors can be ranked to identify those needing the most attention and those with a high potential for risk

TABLE 8-5   **Examples of Schedule Characteristics and Related Quality Factors**

Schedule Characteristics	Software Quality Factors
Requirements conformance	Correctness Reliability Maintainability Integrity Interoperability
Resource utilization	Efficiency
Ease of reuse	Portability Reusability
Performance verification	Testability Correctness Reliability Usability
Ease of correction or modification	Maintainability Flexibility

TABLE 8-6   **Quantification of Probability and Impact of Schedule Failure**

Schedule Drivers	Magnitude		
	Low (0.0–0.3)	Medium (0.4–0.5)	High (0.6–1.0)
Resources			
Personnel	Good discipline mix in place	Some disciplines not available	Questionable mix or availability
Facilities	Existent, little or no modification	Existent, some modification	Nonexistent, extensive changes
Financial	Sufficient budget allocated	Some questionable allocations	Budget allocation in doubt
Need Dates			
Threat	Verified projections	Some unstable aspects	Rapidly changing
Economic	Stable commitments	Some uncertain commitments	Unstable, fluctuating commitments
Political	Little projected sensitivity	Some limited sensitivity	Extreme sensitivity
GFE/GFP	Available, certified	Certification or delivery questions	Unavailable or uncertified
Tools	In place, available	Some deliveries in question	Uncertain delivery dates
Technology			
Availability	In place	Some aspects still in development	Totally still in development
Maturity	Application verified	Some applications verified	No application evidence
Experience	Extensive application	Some application	Little or none
Requirements			
Definition	Known, baselined	Baselined, some unknowns	Unknown, no baseline
Stability	Little or no change projected	Controllable change projected	Rapid or uncontrolled change
Complexity	Compatible with existing technology	Some dependency on new technology	Incompatible with existing technology
Impact	Realistic, achievable schedule	Possible slippage in IOC	Unachievable IOC

reduction. Analysis is then conducted to ensure that the correct risk drivers have been identified. Following evaluation and assessment completion, management's course of action for risk handling can be established. Possible courses of action are:

AVOIDANCE
This might include descoping the program's technical objectives to a more achievable level within available schedule and IOC needs. Another approach may be to combine descoping with a P3I or evolutionary development strategy (avoiding "grand designs") to provide an initial capability and growth to the desired IOC through successive enhancement programs. Obtaining additional resources, if the software requirements structure promotes parallel, independent development, may also contribute to avoiding schedule risk.

CONTROL
Management could institute frequent informal or internal reviews to attempt to control the schedule. Other possibilities include: continuous updating of the schedule based on real-time inputs of interim milestone completions, but not a "floating" schedule baseline; conducting additional system trade-off studies; streamlining the acquisition process; and applying total quality management to improve the process' performance.

ASSUMPTION
While remaining aware of the probability of schedule accomplishment, management could accept the inherent schedule risk and manage the development effort appropriately.

TRANSFER
Realignment of some software requirements to a hardware implementation or other system elements may be possible. Schedule risk must not be transferred to either the operational or support phases of the program. This often causes severe political and public customer criticism that could cause program cancellation.

8.5 OPERATIONAL RISK

The primary objective of applying risk control techniques during the development process is to reduce the risk that an "immature" or improper system will be placed into the customer's operational environment. Nothing is worse than having a dissatisfied customer. While operational risk is primarily composed of the residual technical risk expected at IOC, cost and, particularly, schedule risk can also contribute. Using a range of estimates, identifying the most likely outcome, and assessing the risk of having a system that does not meet requirements in the customer's operational environment are all components of operational risk control.

Software operational risk estimates can be influenced by both competing risk drivers and the approaches used to control technical, cost and schedule risks. Typically, operational risk drivers fall into three categories: user perspective, perceived technical performance, and the performance envelope (Figure 8-5).

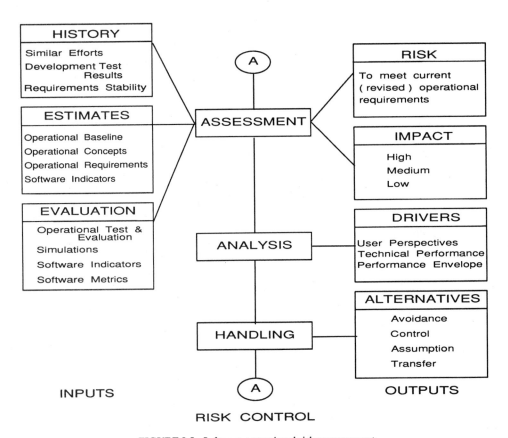

FIGURE 8-5. Software operational risk management.

Customer (user) perspectives often directly influence any software operational risk assessment. Their perspectives range from the subjective to the objective (quantifiable). Perspectives are also based on what the customers thought they were going to get, which may not necessarily be consistent with original system requirements. Perceptions are also subject to change as the evaluators, customer(s), and time changes. The degree that your development and operational test environment replicates the customer's environment can also influence perceptions of the software, system, and system interfaces.

Technical performance, although subjective to some degree, is generally more objective. Aspects such as man-machine-software interfaces, whether the software consistently performs its required functions, how easily the software is able to adapt to changes in operational use, the effort and time required to correct deficiencies or incorporate other changes, and the degree of software resistance to outside tampering are often included in technical performance assessments.

Software performance envelope's adequacy, as it contributes to the system envelope, in meeting operational requirements also influences operational risk.

TABLE 8-7   Examples of Operational Characteristics and Related Software Quality Factors

Operational Characteristics	Software Quality Factors
Security	Integrity
Performance verification	Testability Correctness Reliability
Supportability (Enhancement, modification, or correction)	Maintainability Flexibility Reliability
Resource utilization	Efficiency
Ease of use	Usability
Operational recovery	Maintainability Reliability Usability Interoperability Correctness Integrity

The ease of modifying the software envelope to meet changes or to incorporate new capabilities, such as P3I or evolutionary development incorporation, can also play a role in assessing and controlling software operational risk.

This emphasizes the need for having a firm understanding of the customer's requirements and an agreed upon means of conveying objective, versus subjective, data between the developer and the customer as the primary communication medium. Subjective data will continue to play a role, but we can move toward the stage of science. Table 8-7 can serve as a departure point for customer-developer discussions to determine the key "ilities" needed in the operational environment. This will also help to refine the "ilities" you choose for the other risk areas.

After software operational risk drivers have been identified, management can then determine what inputs are necessary for its risk control approach.

HISTORY

Previous experience gained from the user on similar systems provides insight into how the users can and do perceive systems that are shifting from development to operational use. Development test and evaluation results and any combined development/operational test and evaluation results can aid in identifying specific operational risk concerns, especially if these tests results have been included in the technical risk assessments during development. Management's approach to dealing with requirements instability also plays a critical role in identifying and controlling operational risk. The software progress management indicator, especially the indicator's test progress portion, and the fault density, test coverage, and test sufficiency quality indicators can assist in establishing historical trends directly related to a specific program.

ESTIMATES

By comparing the user's proposed operational baseline, operations concepts, and current operational requirements with development requirements, differences that could affect the use of the developed software product can be identified. Particular attention should be paid to those user requirements that were not included in the initial software delivery, but are planned for incorporation by P3I or evolutionary development efforts. Software management and quality indicators, especially the software requirements definition and stability indicator, can assist in recognizing user requirements not in the initial software delivery. These indicators provide time-phased identification of how and when development requirements were either incorporated as new or revised user requirements or were baselined as part of the system for P3I or evolutionary development. These indicators could also be of value in estimating software capabilities that will be implemented and available at IOC.

EVALUATION

Test results, especially operational test results, form the core of the system evaluations that can be used in controlling operational risk. These results can be complemented through use of simulation techniques, especially in those cases where test of system-level capabilities in an exposed environment could compromise those capabilities. Continued application of software management and quality indicators mentioned previously during the operational test, can be useful in obtaining visual representations of the software's maturity and readiness for use in the customer's operational environment. Software quality factors (Table 8-7) can be of value throughout the software's operational life. All of these inputs can be used to refine and update assumptions used in the technical risk model. This model can then be rerun to obtain better estimates of the technical capabilities achievable at IOC. Deviations from the agreed-to operational baseline should be considered as the prime sources of change in the operational risk assessment.

Operational risk control should begin during development, normally prior to the system requirements review, and no later than completion of the preliminary design review, and continue throughout the system's life-cycle. Beginning with the types of inputs previously described and frequent consultation with the customer (user), a successful risk control program can be implemented. Potential operational risks should be assigned a probability that desired outcomes will not occur and a magnitude of impact if the desired outcomes are not achieved. Total operational risk can be assessed by evaluating the resultant product of probability and impact. A sample set of rules of thumb that can assist in determining probability and impact are presented in Table 8-8.

Once operational risk has been evaluated, composite risk factors can then be ranked to determine those needing the most management attention and those with the most potential for risk reduction. Further analysis should also be performed to ensure that the correct operational risk drivers for a particular software application have been identified.

TABLE 8-8   Quantification of Probability and Impact of Operational Failure

Operational Drivers	Magnitude		
	Low (0.0-0.3)	Medium (0.4-0.5)	High (0.6-1.0)
User Perspective			
Requirements	Compatible with the user environment	Some incompatibilities	Major incompatibilities with "ops" concepts
Stability	Little or no change	Some controlled change	Uncontrolled change
Test environment	Representative of the user environment	Some aspects are not representative	Major disconnects with user environment
OT & E results	Test errors/failures are correctable	Some errors/failures are not correctable before IOC	Major corrections necessary
Quantification	Primarily objective	Some subjectivity	Primarily subjective
Technical Performance			
Usability	User-friendly	Mildly unfriendly	User-unfriendly
Reliability	Predictable performance	Some aspects unpredictable	Unpredictable
Flexibility	Adaptable with threat	Some aspects are not adaptable	Critical functions not adaptable
Supportability	Responsive to updates	Response times inconsistent with need	Unresponsive
Integrity	Secure	Hidden linkages, controlled access	Insecure
Performance Envelope			
Adequacy	Full compatibility	Some limitations	Inadequate
Expandability	Easily expanded	Can be expanded	No expansion
Enhancements	Timely incorporation	Some lag	Major delays
Threat	Responsive to change	Cannot respond to some changes	Unresponsive
Impact	Full mission capability	Some limitations on mission performance	Severe performance limitations

When an understanding of the risk factor, associated drivers, assessments, and evaluations are obtained, a risk handling course of action can then be established. Possible courses of action are:

AVOIDANCE
Management could solicit user and supporter involvement to ensure that developers fully understand operational and support requirements. Another possible way to avoid software operational risk is by baselining a system to meet some, but not all, of the operational requirements, and using P3I or evolutionary development to implement the full requirements set. A variation of this approach can also be used if requirements are unstable: baseline the current system, then use P3I or evolutionary development for the requirement changes. Either of these approaches

could also be used in the event that new technology is not available when needed to meet IOC. In some cases, avoidance may not be an option due to political, market, or customer sensitivities associated with the program.

CONTROL
Just as in technical risk, management could apply parallel development efforts, rapid prototyping, or conduct additional trade-off studies. This can also include implementation of frequent management reviews with both the developer and user to control operational risk.

ASSUMPTION
In some cases, political, market, and/or customer sensitivities with the program or its IOC data can force risk assumption as the only option open to management. In this event, management accepts the inherent operational risk, manages the development effort accordingly, remains aware of the probability of not meeting the operational objectives, and ensures that higher management is aware of and accepts the increased risks involved.

TRANSFER
Software requirements could possibly be realigned by the requirements analysis process to other systems, including hardware components, to reduce risk. Another possibility, in some integrated systems, is to implement the requirements in other elements of the integrated system where they may be a lower operational risk.

8.6 SUPPORT RISK

As systems become increasingly sophisticated, with more emphasis on the need for computers and software to implement critical functions, software is rapidly becoming the key element in overall system effectiveness. Post deployment (delivery) software support (PDSS) costs and associated concerns play a major role in the overall system supportability. There are several issues which complicate the control of risk in the PDSS environment. Among these issues are: determination of what facilities, personnel, and procedures are necessary for PDSS; PDSS customer requirements; and what resources are available for PDSS.

Software support risk control has several important aspects. First, it should be applied throughout the system's life cycle. Who wants to buy a system and not be able to have it fixed or have to have it replaced with a new system tomorrow? Second, in order to control risk, an estimate of the PDSS activities (personnel, procedures, number of change requests, number of fixes, etc.) should be obtained. Can you afford unhappy customers because your PDSS system can't respond quickly enough to meet their needs? Third, the computed risk is a measure of the inability of PDSS resources to meet predicted (both yours and the customer's) software support requirements. How would you feel if you bought a brand new car and couldn't get it fixed because the dealer didn't have any mechanics?

PDSS estimates are often influenced by several competing drivers (Figure 8-6)

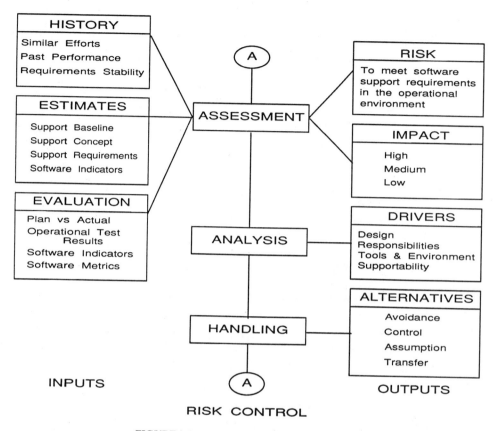

FIGURE 8-6. Software support risk management.

and the approaches used to manage and control all of the other risk areas. Typically, software support drivers fall into four categories: design responsibilities, tools and environment, and supportability.

Software design characteristics are probably the most controllable PDSS risk driver. Characteristics affecting software supportability include aspects such as software design complexity, including related attributes of software size, structure, and interrelationships; deliverable documentation adequacy to support PDSS; software development effort completeness; extent and implementation of configuration management practices for both operational and support software; and stability of the design itself.

The responsibilities allocation process should address: who is responsible for PDSS management and at what software products levels; who is responsible, and at what level, for configuration management of both system and software products; who is responsible for the software's technical management; and who is responsible for software change implementation, and the nature of the modifications they can implement, as well as their relation to the configuration managers? This process must address PDSS support for changes originating during operational use, as well as those resulting from P3I or evolutionary development and fielding.

Availability of software tools and facilities necessary for PDSS is another significant driver. Whether PDSS facilities already exist or must be built, how many, their locations, and compatibility with the "expected" support workload can have a major impact. Adequacy of existing software support tools and the tools that are to be delivered as part of the development effort also contribute to support risk. Compatibility of support computer hardware, both host and target computers, with facilities and software support tools can have a major influence on the ability to meet PDSS requirements. Another element that can affect both support and operational risk is the distribution system that will be used to physically implement the system's software changes.

Software supportability can be driven by the anticipated change's magnitude, type, complexity, and priority. The degree that software modifications affect operational interfaces, both internal to a given system and external to other systems, can greatly influence the timeliness of change implementation and the degree of testing required prior to incorporating the modification into the operational configuration. Supportability can also be affected by the experience, discipline mix, and personnel available to fulfill the PDSS function. Compatibility of planned release cycles for software updates with operational needs and changes in user requirements can significantly impact support risk. Procedures used by multiple PDSS activities can have a major influence if they are incompatible with each other, and do not contribute to the net quality improvement of the operational software.

After identifying the appropriate software support risk drivers, management can then identify the inputs necessary to support their risk control program.

HISTORY
Historical PDSS activity profiles, the degree to which PDSS concerns and requirements influenced previous software development requirements, and the delivered software products' quality gathered on similar systems can aid in estimating the amount of PDSS change activity. This PDSS change activity helps assess the compatibility of the planned PDSS concept with projected change frequency, number of changes, and magnitude of the changes. Information gathered on development processes, schedules, and initial quality of delivered software products can be useful in determining the amount of software development that must be completed during PDSS. Responsiveness of the corrective action system during development, especially during the dedicated test, can be an indicator of the software design's responsiveness to change and the adequacy of available documentation and support tools. Requirements stability during full scale development can also be an indicator of how operational and support expectations have changed since development began. During the latter development stages and the operational and support life-cycle phases, software progress, fault density, test coverage, test sufficiency, and documentation indicators can contribute to the historical data base for a specific program.

ESTIMATES

A key support risk element is recognition that supportability is important to both the software user and supporter. Therefore, any risk assessment methodology that ignores the interests of one of these parties may result in a risk that is unacceptable to the other. One way to avoid this is through use of a user/supporter software support baseline. This baseline should include an agreed-to understanding of the PDSS software release cycle; projected change activity level; and the projected personnel, tools, and resources needed for PDSS. This baseline can be used to refine the PDSS concept and associated support requirements. A combination of PDSS baseline, support concept, and requirements can be used to refine and influence software development requirements and to produce software with increased supportability at a lower life-cycle cost. The software development tools indicator can be helpful in identifying necessary PDSS support tools. Continued use of the mentioned indicators during PDSS can contribute to refining PDSS estimates.

EVALUATION

Tracing PDSS baseline changes and attributes, such as timeliness, completeness, product adequacy, etc., of completed PDSS-specific objectives can play a major role in evaluating software support risk. A combination of test results with responsiveness of the corrective action system can provide valuable insight into the relative ease of incorporating changes of various categories, complexities, and priorities, as well as refining the evaluation of operational software development completeness and maturity prior to PDSS. All of the software management and quality indicators can contribute to evaluating support risk. Using Table 8-9 to refine, and in some cases define, the PDSS requirements with your customer, you can then select appropriate quality factors and metrics. The software indicators, quality factors, and metrics used during development can be applied with equal effectiveness during PDSS, which is really software development under a different guise.

TABLE 8-9   Examples of Support Characteristics and Related Software Quality Factors

Support Characteristics	Software Quality Factors
Requirements conformance	Correctness Testability Reliability
Supportability (Enhancement, modification, or correction)	Maintainability Flexibility Reliability
Resource utilization	Efficiency
Processing of classified information	Integrity Correctness Reliability

TABLE 8-10   Quantification of Probability and Impact of Support Failure

Support Drivers	Magnitude		
	Low (0.0–0.3)	Medium (0.4–0.5)	High (0.6–1.0)
Design			
Complexity	Structurally maintainable	Certain aspects difficult	Extremely difficult to maintain
Documentation	Adequate	Some deficiencies	Inadequate
Completeness	Little additional for PDSS incorporation	Some PDSS incorporation	Extensive PDSS incorporation
Configuration management	Sufficient, in place	Some shortfalls	Insufficient
Stability	Little or no change	Moderate controlled, change	Rapid or uncontrolled change
Responsibilities			
Management	Defined, assigned responsibilities	Some roles and missions issues	Undefined or unassigned
Configuration management	Single point control	Defined control points	Multiple control points
Technical management	Consistent with operational needs	Some inconsistencies	Major inconsistencies
Change implementation	Responsive to user needs	Acceptable delays	Nonresponsive to user needs
Tools & Environment			
Facilities	In place, little change	In place, some modification	Nonexistent or extensive change
Software tools	Delivered, certified, sufficient	Some resolvable concerns	Not delivered, certified, or sufficient
Computer hardware	Compatible with "ops" system	Minor incompatibilities	Major incompatibilities
Production	Sufficient for fielded units	Some capacity questions	Insufficient
Distribution	Controlled, responsive	Minor response concerns	Uncontrolled or nonresponsive
Supportability			
Changes	Within projections	Slight deviations	Major deviations
Operational interfaces	Defined, controlled	Some "hidden" linkages	Extensive linkages
Personnel	In place sufficient, experienced	Minor discipline mix concerns	Significant concerns
Release cycle	Responsive to user requirements	Minor incompatibilities	Nonresponsive to user needs
Procedures	In place, adequate	Some concerns	Nonexistent or inadequate
Impact	Responsive software support	Minor delays in software modifications	Nonresponsive or unsupportable software

As in other risk areas, following in-depth assessments of types of inputs just mentioned, potential support risks should be assigned a probability of failure and impact magnitude to address and evaluate total software support risk. A sample set of rules of thumb that can assist in the evaluation process are contained in Table 8-10.

Following evaluation of support risk, composite risk factors should be ranked to identify those factors with the most potential for risk reduction and management attention. Support risk drivers should also be reviewed to ensure that correct drivers have been identified. Participation by software users and supporters should be encouraged for evaluating and reviewing support risk drivers.

An understanding of risk factors, drivers, assessments, and evaluations enables implementation of a risk handling program. Possible courses of action include:

AVOIDANCE
Support risk avoidance should be accomplished prior to the software's transition to the operational and PDSS environments. Some generic development process flaws that can be controlled to avoid support risk are overly ambitious development schedules; extensive and frequent functional expectation changes from those when development began; poor planning or low priority given to PDSS requirements; and inadequate configuration management plans, procedures, implemented practices, and automated tools support.

CONTROL
Management should actively solicit user and supporter involvement to ensure that developers understand the nature of support and operational environments, and that support requirements are adequately balanced with other system requirements. Additionally, management can attempt to balance developmental risks with total life-cycle risk and, in particular, support risk.

ASSUMPTION
Support risk assumption is not solely within the developer's management purview. The user and supporter are the ultimate agencies responsible for assumption of support risk. Development, political and market sensitivities can be major contributors in "forcing" support risk onto using and supporting activities.

TRANSFER
In some cases, it may be possible to implement some software requirements, including support requirements, in other system elements, where there may be lower support risk. Realignment during the requirements analysis process to other integrated system components may also be a possibility. When a system has been placed in the operational and PDSS environment, there is very limited opportunity for support risk transfer.

8.7 RISK AREA TRADE-OFFS

Significant benefits can result from the ability to measure software risk, compare risk with historical data, pinpoint risk drivers, and project alternative risk reduction choices. There are many factors that can have a negative impact on software risk. Among these are interrelationships among the various risk areas and the negative impact in one or more risk areas that a positive change in another risk area can have. Figure 8-7 contains a sample of the relationships that can exist among software risk areas.

This figure is only representative of risk area relationships. It should not be interpreted as the "norm" or typical way one risk area affects another. The following assumptions pertain to the portrayed relationships:

Prototyping and pre-planned product improvements (P3I) and/or evolutionary development are used to reduce technical risk. Relationships are for the initial software delivery.

Cost risk reduction is attempted by descoping the original requirements and using P3I and/or evolutionary development to achieve full requirement compliance. Again, relationships shown are for the initial delivery.

Schedule risk reduction is approached by obtaining additional resources, using prototypes, and strict baselining of requirements.

Operational risk reduction is attempted by responding to all user (customer) requirements changes throughout the development process.

Baselining operational requirements and not descoping the development effort by eliminating or reducing software documentation, test or quality are used to reduce support risk.

The relationship between risk areas can also be affected by the relationships among the software quality factors ("ilities"). Figure 8-8 presents typical interrelationships among the factors. Management needs to be aware of these relationships in the selection, use, and analysis of software quality factors and associated metrics.

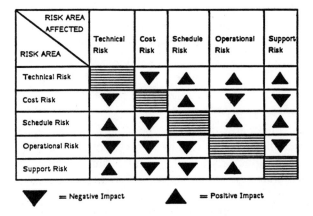

FIGURE 8-7. Sample software risk area interrelationships.

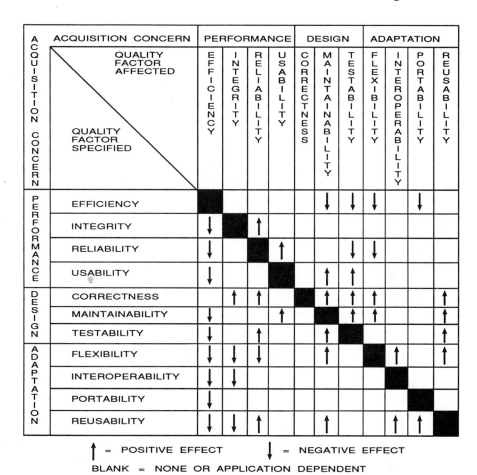

Acquisition Concern		Performance				Design			Adaptation			
	Quality Factor Affected → / Quality Factor Specified ↓	Efficiency	Integrity	Reliability	Usability	Correctness	Maintainability	Testability	Flexibility	Interoperability	Portability	Reusability
Performance	EFFICIENCY	■					↓	↓	↓		↓	
	INTEGRITY	↓	■	↑								
	RELIABILITY	↓		■	↑			↓	↓			
	USABILITY	↓			■		↑	↑				
Design	CORRECTNESS		↑	↑		■	↑	↑	↑			↑
	MAINTAINABILITY	↓			↑		■	↑	↑			↑
	TESTABILITY	↓		↑			↑	■				↑
Adaptation	FLEXIBILITY	↓	↓	↓			↑		■	↑		↑
	INTEROPERABILITY	↓	↓							■		
	PORTABILITY	↓									■	
	REUSABILITY	↓	↓	↑			↑		↑	↑		■

↑ = POSITIVE EFFECT   ↓ = NEGATIVE EFFECT
BLANK = NONE OR APPLICATION DEPENDENT

FIGURE 8-8. Software quality factor relationships.

General References

The following documents are the primary sources of existing policy, standards, definitions, and procedures used in developing the risk mitigation approach for software-intensive systems.

DOD Instruction 5000.2, "Defense Acquisition Management Policies and Procedures," February 23, 1991.

DOD 5000.2-M, "Defense Acquisition Management Documentation and Reports," February 23, 1991.

MIL-STD-1521B, "Technical Reviews and Audits for Systems, Equipments, and Computer Software," June 4, 1985.

DOD-STD-2167A, "Defense System Software Development," February 29, 1988.

DOD-STD-2168, "Defense System Software Quality Program," April 29, 1988.

RTCA/DO-178A, "Software Considerations in Airborne Systems and Equipment Certification," Radio Technical Commission for Aeronautics, March 22, 1985.

CMU/SEI-87-TR-23, "A Method for Assessing the Software Engineering Capability of Contractors," Software Engineering Institute, September 1987.

AMC-P 70-13, "Software Management Indicators," January 31, 1987.

AMC-P 70-14, "Software Management Indicators," April 30, 1987.

AFSCP 800-14, "Software Quality Indicators," January 1987.

AFSCP 800-43, "Software Management Indicators," August 31, 1990.

AFSC/AFLC Pamphlet 800-45, "Acquisition Management Software Risk Abatement," September 30, 1988.

B. W. Boehm, "Software Risk Management: Tutorial," IEEE Computer Society Press, 1989.

IEEE Std 1044, "A Standard Classification for Software Errors, Faults, and Failures," March 1987.

IEEE Std 982-1989, "Guide For The Use of Standard Dictionary of Measures To Produce Reliable Software," March 1989.

9

Software Reuse for TQM

Donald J. Reifer, President

Reifer Consultants, Inc.

9.1 INTRODUCTION

Software reuse is "hot." Everywhere you look, someone is writing about the topic.[1] Articles appear in all of the right journals and a number of interesting textbooks have appeared on the market.[2, 3] In these articles, the benefits of reuse (higher productivity, competitive advantage, etc.) have been extolled along with its virtues (faster time to market, higher quality, etc.). The hype is reminiscent of the "structured revolution" that occurred just over a decade ago. You are probably asking by now: "Have we really entered another revolution? Why has the topic suddenly received so much attention? Is reuse all smoke and mirrors or is there substance behind the blitz? Is software reuse the magical silver bullet[4] that the industry has been trying to find?" These and other questions should come to mind, especially those pertinent to the topic of reuse's impact on TQM.

Being in the midst of both a "fiscal" and "software crises," most firms are currently aggressively searching for ways to increase their productivity, reduce their costs and improve their quality. Reuse represents a natural means to achieve these goals. It seemingly permits firms to leverage their large and often diverse inventory of existing software to quickly meet their user's demands, reduce their effort, meet their schedules and improve their customer satisfaction. The motivation is good and the quest for continuous improvement righteous. Why then, haven't we taken advantage of software reuse in the past? Has some technological breakthrough occurred that has prompted the community to focus so much attention on the topic? Are there new paradigms, methods, and tools available that allow us to take better advantage of the technology? How does reuse contribute to Total Quality Management? What are the barriers to reuse and how are they to be overcome? What can and what can't be done to improve my own situation?

This chapter was written to address these questions. It does this first by introducing the reader to the topic and challenge of reuse and its relationship to Total Quality Management (TQM). This discussion emphasizes that systematic reuse has been able to and can improve the quality of the deployed processes, products delivered, and service levels achieved. Next, we present an understanding of the state-of-the-art versus the current state-of-the-practice of reuse. We do this by surveying the industry and the research establishments. Finally, we conclude by discussing the hopes, promises, and future directions of reuse, especially as they impact TQM strategies.

9.2 REUSE HOPES AND PROMISES

As we have seen in earlier chapters of this book, most firms are trying to improve their software productivity, reduce their costs, and improve their quality. They are doing this because systems we are developing are getting bigger, more complex, and more dependent upon computers for their usability, functionality, and performance. Requirements for systems are getting tougher. Users are expecting more as systems become more distributed and intelligent. Managers are demanding that we focus on delivering quality products on-time and within budget. Everyone is demanding that we do a better job.

Software is providing system designers with the intelligence they need to meet these challenges and meet the ever increasing customer demand for added adaptability, portability, and interoperability. In addition, software is finally being recognized as both a product and a strategic asset needed to successfully make, manufacture, and market computer-based products.[5]

As the software workload increases, so does the demand for new ways of doing business. Reuse, as a strategy, takes direct aim at the desire for increased efficiencies. By reusing software assets, we reduce the amount of effort required to develop the desired functionality. As equivalent effort decreases, productivity rises as it is measured using the following economic formula:

$$\text{PRODUCTIVITY} = \text{OUTPUT GENERATED/INPUT USED TO GENERATE THEM}$$

A Chinese friend of mine once explained the duality of productivity using a story. In China, when you want to improve the productivity of workforces building a tunnel through a mountain, you use the following strategy. You start two teams drilling the tunnel at either end of the mountain. If these teams meet in the middle, productivity improves because less input is needed to produce a standard output (one tunnel). If they don't meet in the middle, productivity also improves because more output (two tunnels) are generated with a standard input. In other words, you are in a "win-win" position using a strategy that capitalizes on the dual nature of productivity.

Both of these strategies are in use in the software industry today. The increased output strategy relies on mechanization (i.e., arming people with the methods, tools and equipment they need to make them more effective) to improve the overall effectiveness of software engineers. In contrast, the input reduction strategy relies on reuse to reduce the amount of work that needs to be done to build a standard product. Pursuing either strategy yields results. Pursuing both strategies at the same time yields more because of the synergy that exists as both approaches are being pursued in parallel.

The progress we as an industry are making in the areas of ergonomics, methods, tools, and environments is just part of the success formula. While these advances will help increase productivity, evidence yields the understanding that they alone will not generate the orders of magnitude improvements in productivity and quality needed to cope with the increases in size and complexity characteristic of the systems we are building. We need to complement our output-based strategy with one that systematically permits us to reuse our software legacy (input-based). Although it will help, improving staff effectiveness through mechanization (i.e., arming people with the tools they need to do their jobs) alone will not generate the results most firms are searching for. Reuse will thereby enable us to reduce our workload as we tunnel through the software mountain. It is like beginning drilling in a cave that already takes us halfway towards our destination.

9.3 REUSE AND TQM

The focus of this book is Total Quality Management (TQM) for software. Therefore, let us look at how reuse impacts TQM, its goals and recurring elements. These can be enumerated as follows:

1. Reuse enables firms to take advantage of their past experience and use it to enable continuous improvement of the products, processes, and information used within the corporation.
2. Reuse should represent a corporate goal. To make reuse happen in practice, the following seven recurring elements of TQM must be implemented:
    a. Management participation and leadership development
    b. Establishment of measurable goals and objectives
    c. Extensive education and training
    d. Employee involvement and action teams
    e. Customer emphasis
    f. Supplier certification and training
    g. Recognition.
3. Reuse involves a culture change which requires both new technical and managerial approaches to be organizationally inserted as needed improvements are being realized by the firm.
4. The benefits of reuse do not come free. Considerable turmoil will occur as reuse is introduced into the firm. Making software objects (designs, algorithms, tests, code, etc.) reusable, costs money. Someone will have to pay for it. In addition, making these software objects accessible also takes effort.

Investments are needed along with an infrastructure that provides a framework that enables us to manage reuse. The infrastructure must be flexible enough to accommodate the advances that are being made in the state-of-the-art and in the practices that we use to manage it. All of those affected by the infrastructure should be asked to participate in its evolution. Incentives should be provided along with education. Measurement must be an integral part of the framework. Cost/benefits must be understood and quantified. Customers must be enlightened and suppliers need to be certified.

In other words, reuse and TQM go hand in hand. As firms develop their software reuse strategies, the participatory, goal-oriented principles of TQM should be applied. A buyer-seller model[6] for reuse should be implemented and a consumer orientation should be maintained. Education and incentives should be provided. Then, as these strategies are implemented, firms should measure the results and respond to the findings. Feedback should be used to implement the philosophy of continuous improvement as a part of TQM. Technology should be inserted and channeled so that the products that evolve are high quality. Champions are needed to tackle the many technical, managerial, and political challenges related to the culture change. Reuse for reuse sake should be avoided. Reuse must make good business sense. When it does, it will happen.

9.4 SYSTEMATIC VERSUS AD HOC REUSE

You are probably asking the questions by now: "If reuse is so good, why have we not done it before? Why all the interest and the hype? What have been others' experiences and what are the upsides and downsides associated with them? Is it really possible? And, if so, how do I do it?"

While we have been attempting to reuse software components for years, current practice has been for the most part ad hoc and limited to source code. There are many reasons for this phenomenon:

1. The software technology to make anything but code reusable was not well established, and this technology was not codified. In other words, reuse was left to the individual programmer.
2. The software processes related to the systematic reuse of reusable objects were not well defined, and standards and guidelines for institutionalizing reuse were not even contemplated.
3. Design methods and languages used by industry did not facilitate building reusable objects.
4. The tooling needed to make reusable objects readily accessible to consumers was not available.
5. The incentives needed to motivate firms to spend money on reuse were not available.
6. The management infrastructure (i.e., policies, practices, and protocols) needed to manage reuse was not defined.

Fortunately, advances in all six of these areas have been made within the last few years by the software engineering community. Software technology has matured to the point where new methods, languages, and tools are beginning to become available that make building reusable objects (the term objects is chosen instead of components within this chapter to convey the idea that more than code can be developed to be reusable) technically and economically feasible. For example, object-oriented techniques and languages (Ada, C^{++}, Smalltalk, etc.) which facilitate the design and development of reusable objects are now the rage of the industry. As another example, several reuse libraries (i.e., collections of objects) and library systems (i.e., software that makes these collections accessible) are being sold commercially.

Advances in the reuse process and management areas have also been made. For example, several reuse process models exist, as do operational scenarios for managing the staffs and organizations using them. And major projects like the Strategic Defense Initiative (SDI) and Advanced Tactical Fighter (ATF) are committed to using these models and infrastructures. In addition, standards for categorizing reusable objects and for sharing them across reuse library systems are also being developed under the auspices of these projects. In other words, we have made a lot of progress in the field of software reuse. In addition, we have advanced to the point where we can build design and tests to be reusable.

Please note that the terms reuse and reusable have different meanings within the context of this chapter. Reuse refers to the activities associated with using an object more than once within and/or across development projects (i.e., identifying candidates, adapting them to customer requirements, and integrating them into an applications system). Reusable implies that the object developed was generated with reuse in mind (i.e., some extra effort was expanded to make the object more general-purpose). Let's now look at these reuse processes and products more closely and discuss their TQM impacts.

9.5 REUSE PROCESSES, PRODUCTS, AND QUALITY RELATIONSHIPS

Figure 9-1 illustrates what we will call the three parallel paradigm life cycle.[7] Domain engineering and asset management activities are undertaken in parallel as applications are engineered by traditional software groups using conventional life cycle processes. Each of these processes, their activities, data flows, and artifacts generated are defined more specifically as follows:

1. Domain Engineering. The process of identifying, designing, and developing reusable objects by using domain knowledge to home in on the candidate objects which have a high reuse capacity. The processes involved in domain engineering are illustrated in the data flow diagrams which appear as Figure 9-2. Table 9-1 provides a data dictionary for these diagrams and Table 9-2 lists the artifacts that are generated as their products. The goal of this activity is to populate a reuse library with an inventory of Reusable Software Objects (RSOs) that have a high reuse potential.

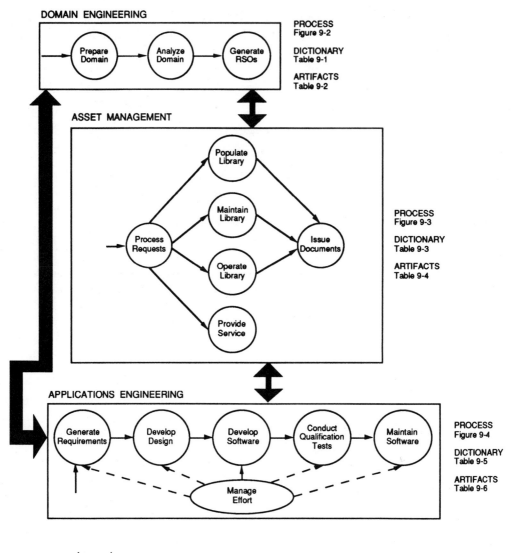

FIGURE 9-1. Software reuse process flows.

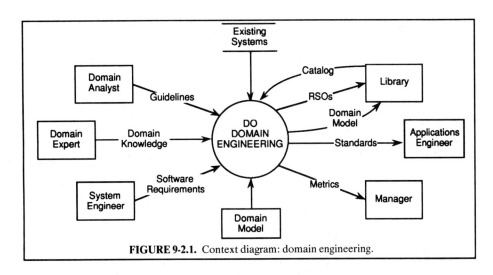

FIGURE 9-2.1. Context diagram: domain engineering.

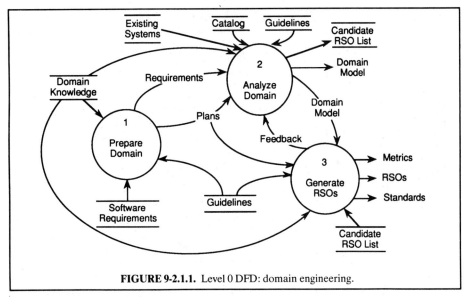

FIGURE 9-2.1.1. Level 0 DFD: domain engineering.

Legend

RSO = Certified RSO $\overline{\text{RSO}}$ = Uncertified RSO

FIGURE 9-2. Domain engineering process.

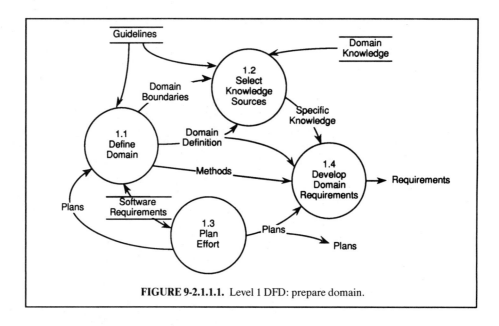

FIGURE 9-2.1.1.1. Level 1 DFD: prepare domain.

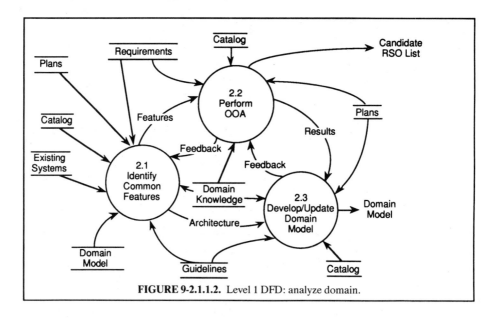

FIGURE 9-2.1.1.2. Level 1 DFD: analyze domain.

Legend

RSO = Certified RSO $\overline{\text{RSO}}$ = Uncertified RSO

FIGURE 9-2. Domain engineering process. *(Continued)*

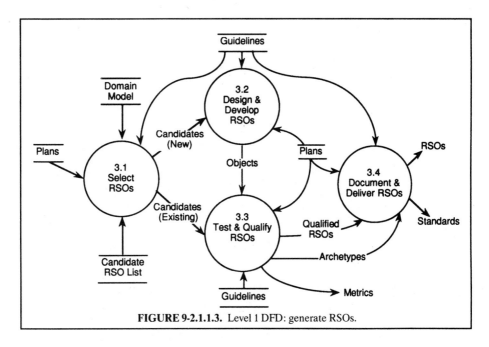

FIGURE 9-2.1.1.3. Level 1 DFD: generate RSOs.

Legend

RSO = Certified RSO $\overline{RSO}$ = Uncertified RSO

FIGURE 9-2. Domain engineering process. *(Continued)*

2. Asset Management. The process of identifying, categorizing, cataloging, and making proven software objects (or information about them) available to potential users in a timely and efficient manner. Objects are called assets in the hope that they will be treated as such in the future (i.e., software will be capitalized instead of expensed on the ledgers). The processes involved in asset management are illustrated in the data flow diagrams which appear as Figure 9-3. Table 9-3 provides a data dictionary for these diagrams and Table 9-4 lists the artifacts that are generated as the product of the activities. The goal of this activity is to make high quality RSOs readily accessible to those who can use them.

3. Applications Engineering. The process of analyzing, specifying, designing, implementing, integrating, testing, and maintaining software based upon the existence of reuse-based methodology, domain knowledge, and recoverable assets. The processes involved in applications engineering are illustrated in the data flow diagrams which appear as Figure 9-4. Table 9-5 provides a data dictionary for these diagrams and Table 9-6 lists the artifacts that are generated as their products. The goal of this activity is to reuse as many RSOs as possible as software is built to satisfy user requirements.

TABLE 9-1   Domain Engineering Data Dictionary

The following definitions are offered for the data elements which flow between activities in Figure 9-2:

Archetype	A Reusable Software Object (RSO) that is used to model or prototype another object.
Architecture	The structure or relationship between components of a design developed with reuse specifically in mind.
Candidates (Existing)	Those existing RSOs identified as candidates for acquisition.
Candidates (New)	Those new RSOs identified as candidates for the application.
Candidate RSO List	A list of candidate RSOs that fulfill the user's requirements.
Catalog	Possibly a centralized source of information about the RSOs which populate the Library.
Domain Boundaries	The limits or extent of an application area or domain.
Domain Definition	The definition of the abstractions which describe a domain.
Domain Engineering	The process of identifying a candidate domain from a cost performance analysis, selecting domain analysis, design and implementation methods, doing domain analysis, domain design and domain implementation activities, and creating domain assets to support applications engineering.
Domain Knowledge	An essential part of the knowledge base which characterizes the domain.
Domain Model	A representation of the domain's contents, structure and internal relationships.
Existing Systems	The skills, knowledge and abilities that the organization gains from past experience (both written and verbal) on past developments.
Features	The composition and form of the items which characterize the requirements.
Feedback	The return to origin of evaluative or corrective data about an action.
Guidelines	A set of practices which are developed to direct implementation of domain engineering activities (guidelines are less rigid than standards).
Library	An element of the software engineering environment used to locate and acquire RSOs that are potentially reusable within and across projects.
Methods	A set of steps, representations, rules and examples developed to guide the solution of a problem.
Metrics	Standards set for measurement.
Objects	An element of the software work breakdown structure for a system derived according to the criteria of information hiding and abstraction.
Plan	A roadmap which describes how domain engineering activities will be conducted. The plan typically describes the work to be done, who will do it, the resources required, the methods to be used, the controls to be invoked, the schedules to be met and a variety of other relevant information.
Qualified RSOs	Those Reusable Software Objects (RSOs) which have been qualified to meet customer standards.

TABLE 9-1   Continued

Results	Outcomes of Object-Oriented Analysis (OOA) which include class and object abstractions and their relationships.
Requirements	A list of generalized needs stated for the domain.
RSOs (Reusable Software Objects)	Life cycle products that are created during the software development process that are needed to operate, maintain and upgrade deliverable software during its lifetime and that have the potential for reuse (design, code, tests/test cases, etc.).
Software Requirements	A set of functional, performance, interface and/or design expectations for the software.
Specific Knowledge	That set of knowledge pertinent to the domain under study.
Standards	A set of procedures established by general consent as a model or example of how to develop RSOs.

Whenever possible, the JIAWG Reusable Software Program Operational Concept Document[24] and the IEEE Standard Glossary of Software Engineering Terminology[25] were used as the sources for definition.

TABLE 9-2   Domain Engineering Artifacts

The following primary RSOs result from activities illustrated in Figure 9-2:

Artifact	Generated By:	Contains Information on:
Domain Model	Domain Analyst	Domain scope Domain boundaries Domain organization Domain structure Potential RSOs
Methods	Domain Analyst	Solution steps Representations Rules Examples
Metrics	Domain Analyst	Development progress Domain size and complexity Productivity and cost
Plans	Manager	Budgets Management controls Schedules Staffing profiles
Requirements	System Engineer	Generalized requirements for an application domain • Functions • Performance
Standards	Software Engineer	Documentation guidelines Configuration management approaches Quality expections
Guidelines	Software Engineer	Style guidelines

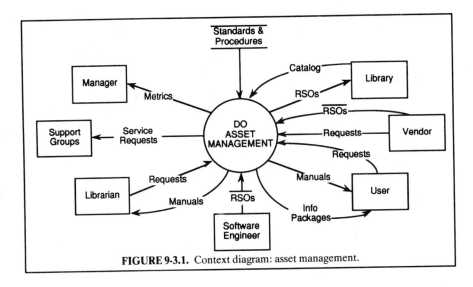

FIGURE 9-3.1. Context diagram: asset management.

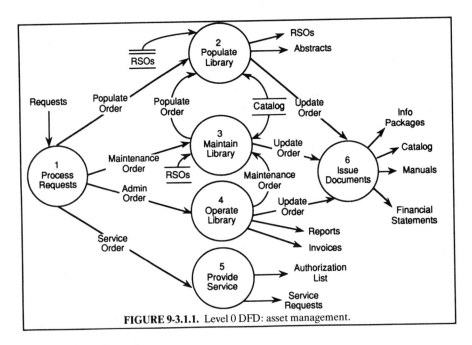

FIGURE 9-3.1.1. Level 0 DFD: asset management.

Legend

RSO = Certified RSO $\overline{RSO}$ = Uncertified RSO

FIGURE 9-3. Asset management process.

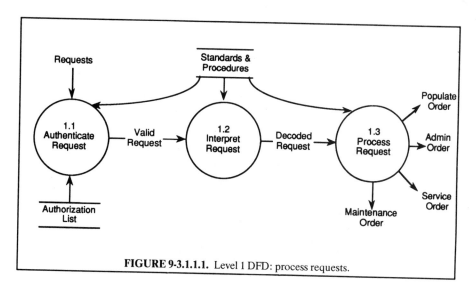

FIGURE 9-3.1.1.1. Level 1 DFD: process requests.

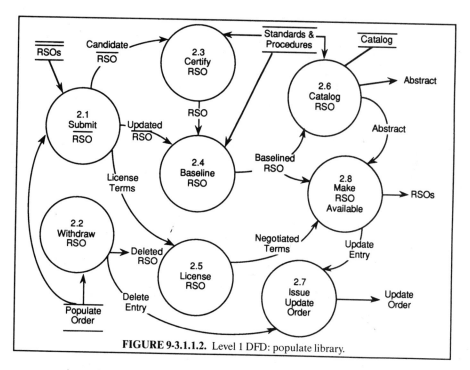

FIGURE 9-3.1.1.2. Level 1 DFD: populate library.

Legend

RSO = Certified RSO   R̄S̄Ō = Uncertified RSO

FIGURE 9-3. Asset management process. *(Continued)*

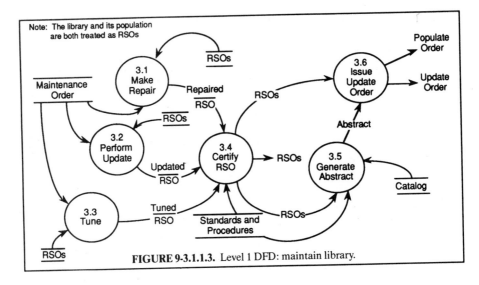

FIGURE 9-3.1.1.3. Level 1 DFD: maintain library.

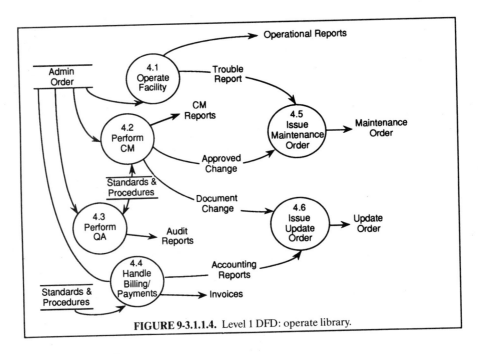

FIGURE 9-3.1.1.4. Level 1 DFD: operate library.

Legend

RSO = Certified RSO $\overline{RSO}$ = Uncertified RSO

FIGURE 9-3. Asset management process. *(Continued)*

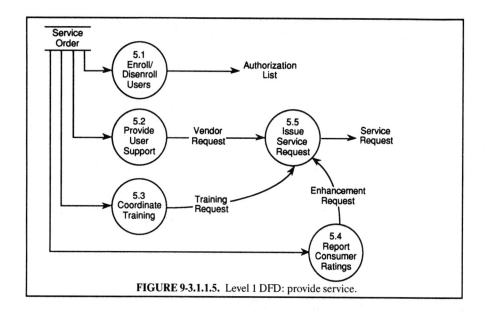

FIGURE 9-3.1.1.5. Level 1 DFD: provide service.

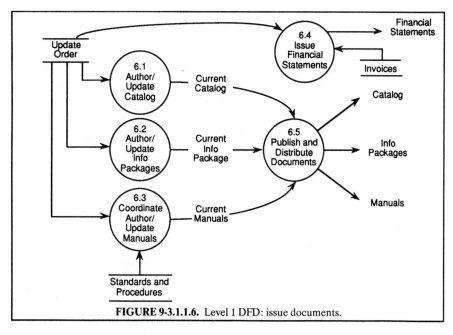

FIGURE 9-3.1.1.6. Level 1 DFD: issue documents.

Legend

RSO = Certified RSO $\overline{RSO}$ = Uncertified RSO

FIGURE 9-3. Asset management process. *(Continued)*

TABLE 9-3   Asset Management Data Dictionary

The following definitions are offered for the data elements which flow between activities in Figure 9-3:

Abstract	A summary which categorizes and describes the features and capabilities of a RSO.
Accounting Reports	Periodic reports which summarize the status of all billings, charges and payments for asset management services.
Admin Order	An asset management work order which authorizes the Librarian to issue a document or perform some library management service.
Approved Change	A change that has been approved by the appropriate Change Control Board (CCB).
Audit Reports	Reports issued by Quality Assurance reporting results of process and product audits.
Authorization List	A list of all those persons authorized to request asset management services.
Baselined RSO	A Reusable Software Object (RSO) whose configuration has been placed under change control.
Candidate RSO	The RSOs chosen to potentially populate the Library.
Catalog	Possibly a centralized source of information about the RSOs which populate the Library.
Change Logs	The status accounting logs which provide the version and update history of all RSOs in the Library.
CM Reports	Configuration Management (CM) status accounting reports issued to status problem reports, change requests and version progress.
Current Catalog	The current version of the Catalog.
Current Manuals	The current version of the User's and Librarian Manuals.
Current Info Package	The current version of the Info Package.
Decoded Request	A validated petition which identifies the authorized services to be performed.
Deleted RSO	A RSO which has been withdrawn from the current Library population.
Delete Entry	A notice which identifies a deleted RSO.
Document Change	A notice which describes an approved document change.
Enhancement Request	A user petition to either improve services or the capabilities of a RSO.
Financial Statements	Statements issued periodically to report billings/payments by user organization.
Info Package	The collection of information sent to prospective users which describes the capabilities and services offered by the Asset Management Organization.

TABLE 9-3   Continued

Invoices	Billings for use of asset management services.
Library	An element of the Software Engineering Environment used to locate and acquire RSOs that are potentially reusable within and across projects.
License Terms	The standard terms established to license a RSO for use within the Library.
Maintenance Order	An asset management work order which authorizes the software development organization to repair, update and/or tune the Library and its population of RSOs.
Manuals	Refers to the User's and Librarian's Manuals devised for the Library.
Metrics	Standards set for measurement.
Negotiated Terms	The negotiated terms and conditions for use of a RSO which is provided commercially or with limited rights.
New RSO	A RSO that has just been made available to Library users.
Populate Order	An asset management work order which authorizes the Librarian to add/delete a RSO to/from the current library population.
Repaired RSO	A RSO which has been repaired, but whose capabilities have not yet been recertified.
Reports	The collection of CM, QA, financial and operational reports issued periodically to provide status information about asset management services.
Requests	Petitions made for asset management services by authorized users.
RSOs (Reusable Software Objects)	Life cycle products that are created during the software development process that are needed to operate, maintain and upgrade deliverable software during its lifetime and that have the potential for reuse (designs, code, tests/test cases, etc.).
Service Order	An asset management work order which authorizes the asset management support group to enroll/disenroll users and/or provide user support for training.
Service Requests	A petition for service from some organization outside of the asset management group.
Standards and Procedures	That set of software standards and procedures adopted for use by the asset management group.
Training Requests	A petition to a training organization for service (i.e., a standard course or some form of computer-based instructional product).
Trouble Report	A document which describes a problem with the Library or RSO in enough detail that a maintenance order can be issued to fit it.

TABLE 9-3   Continued

Tuned RSO	A RSO whose performance has been perfected to meet approved requirements.
Update Entry	A Notice which identifies a new or updated RSO.
Updated Order	An asset management work order which authorizes the Librarian to make needed changes to the Catalog, Info Packages and/or Manuals.
Updated RSO	A RSO which has been updated to fulfill an approved set of new user requirements.
Valid Request	A petition for service which has been validated.
Vendor Request	A request to some commercial vendor to provide user support.

Whenever possible, the JIAWG Reusable Software Program Operational Concept Document[24] and the IEEE Standard Glossary of Software Engineering Terminology[25] were used as the sources for definition.

TABLE 9-4   Asset Management Artifacts

The following primary RSOs result from activities illustrated in Figure 9-3:

Artifact	Generated By:	Contains Information on:
Catalog	Librarian	Library contents RSO capabilities/status Licensing terms and conditions
Info Packages	Librarian	Enrollment procedures Library services Library fees
Invoices	Librarian	Billings for services
Manuals	Software Engineer and Librarian	Library administration Library usage
Metrics	Software Engineer	Development progress Library cost-benefits Library efficiency and effectiveness RSO size and quality
Plans	Manager	Budgets Management controls Schedules Staffing profiles
Requests	Various people	Needed services Required actions, budgets and timelines
Requirements Designs Code Tests/test cases Documentation	Software Engineer	Legacy for reuse within and across projects

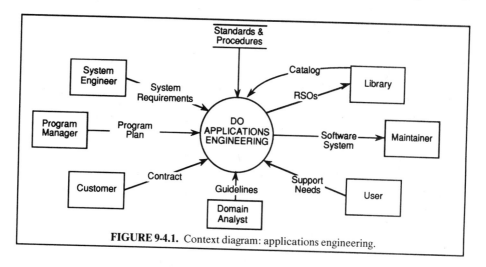

FIGURE 9-4.1. Context diagram: applications engineering.

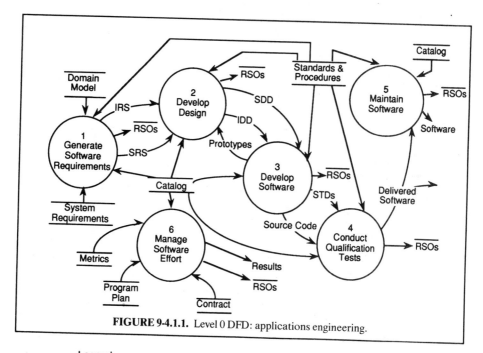

FIGURE 9-4.1.1. Level 0 DFD: applications engineering.

<u>Legend</u>

RSO = Certified RSO $\overline{RSO}$ = Uncertified RSO

FIGURE 9-4. Applications engineering process.

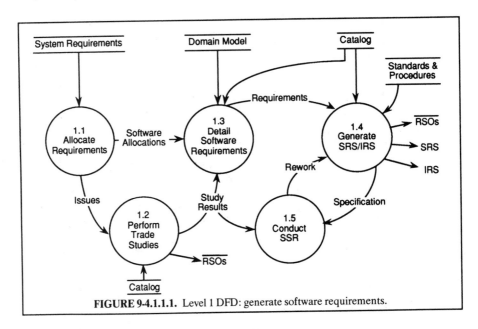

FIGURE 9-4.1.1.1. Level 1 DFD: generate software requirements.

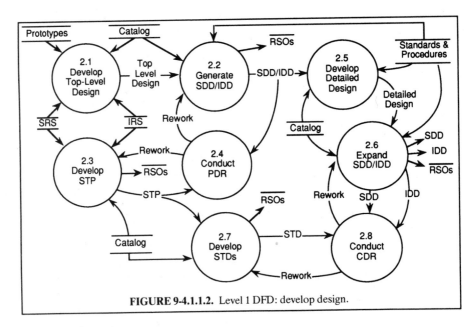

FIGURE 9-4.1.1.2. Level 1 DFD: develop design.

Legend

RSO = Certified RSO $\overline{RSO}$ = Uncertified RSO

FIGURE 9-4. Applications engineering process. *(Continued)*

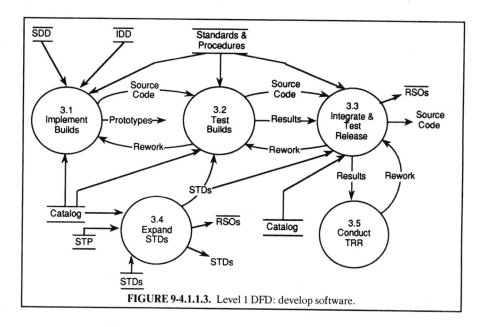

FIGURE 9-4.1.1.3. Level 1 DFD: develop software.

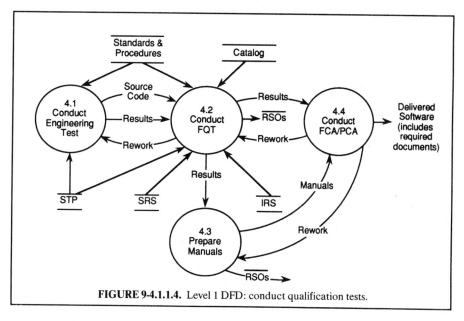

FIGURE 9-4.1.1.4. Level 1 DFD: conduct qualification tests.

Legend

RSO = Certified RSO $\overline{\text{RSO}}$ = Uncertified RSO

FIGURE 9-4. Applications engineering process. *(Continued)*

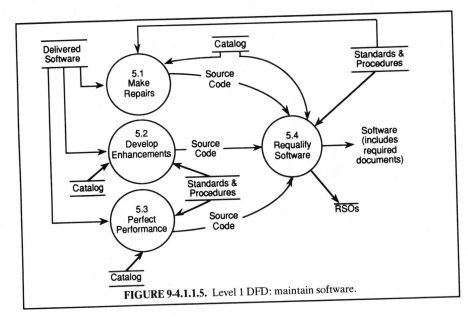

FIGURE 9-4.1.1.5. Level 1 DFD: maintain software.

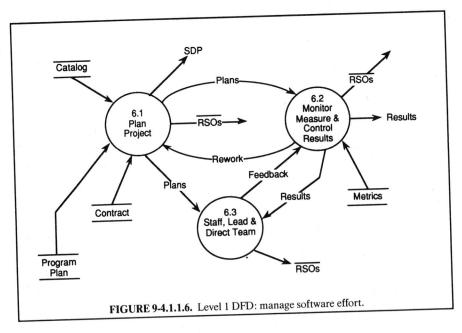

FIGURE 9-4.1.1.6. Level 1 DFD: manage software effort.

Legend

RSO = Certified RSO $\overline{\text{RSO}}$ = Uncertified RSO

FIGURE 9-4. Applications engineering process. *(Continued)*

TABLE 9-5   Applications Engineering Data Dictionary

The following definitions are offered for the data elements which flow between activities in Figure 9-4:

Catalog	Possibly a centralized source of information about the RSOs which populate the Library.
Contract	An agreement for breach of which there are legal remedies.
Delivered Software	The as-built and as-tested version of the software which passed the FCA/PCA (Functional Configuration Audit/ Physical Configuration Audit) and all related required documentation.
Domain Model	A representation of the domain's contents, structure and internal relationships.
Detailed Design	The activity of refining and expanding the top level design to specify in detail the descriptions of the sequencing and control logic, data structures and data definitions to the extent that the design is sufficient to begin implementation.
IDD (Interface Design Document)	A document which describes the design of the data and control interfaces between software components within a CSCI (Computer Software Configuration Item).
IRS (Interface Requirements Specification)	A document which describes the software-to-software and hardware-to-software interface requirements for a Computer Software Configuration Item (CSCI) or group of CSCI's.
Issues	Those matters that are in dispute. Issues can be managerial, technical and/or political.
Metrics	Standards set for measurement.
Plan	A roadmap which describes how application engineering activities will be conducted. The plan typically describes the work to be done, who will do it, the resources required, the methods to be used, the controls to be invoked, the schedules to be met and a variety of other relevant information.
Program Plan	A document which describes the approach that will be taken to manage a project or group of projects. A Program Plan describes the work, schedules, resource, requirements and management approaches that will be used to develop, integrate, test and operate all elements of system including hardware and software.
Prototypes	An original model against which something (designs, algorithms, code, etc.) is patterned. Prototypes are typically built "quick-and-dirty" and thrown away after they have served their purpose.
Requirements	Conditions or capabilities needed by the user to solve a problem or achieve an operational objective.
Results	Consequences that occur due to actions.
Rework	To process or redo to meet the original goals or requirements.
RSOs (Reusable Software Objects)	Life cycle products that are created during the software development process that are needed to operate, maintain and upgrade deliverable software during its lifetime and that have the potential for reuse (designs, code, tests/test cases, etc.).

TABLE 9-5   Continued

SDD (Software Design Document)	A document which is refined in parallel with design activity and used to capture the top level and detailed designs (see activity definitions).
Software	Computer programs, procedures, rules and possibly associated documentation and data pertaining to the operation of a computer system.
Software Allocations	Those system level requirements allocated to be performed by the software element of the system (as opposed to the hardware or people parts).
Software System	The integrated collection of computer programs, data bases and descriptive documentation that performs all of the functions on the target hardware that the user specified.
Source Code	The computer program expressed in a source language (i.e., a high order language like Ada or assembly language). Typically, source code is assembled, compiled or interpreted to produce the codes that are loaded into the computer (object code).
Specifications	Documents which describe, in a complete, precise verifiable manner, the requirements, behavior, design, and/or other characteristics of a system or a system component.
SRS (Software Requirements Specification)	A document which describes in detail the functional, performance and design requirements established for a CSCI (Computer Software Configuration Item).
Standards and Procedures	A document which describes the standards and procedures to be used for design, development, test, documentation, configuration management and quality assurance of the applications software. These standards and procedures should address reuse.
STDs (Software Test Descriptions)	A document which defines the tests, describes the test cases, identifies test expectations and provides step-by-step test procedures.
STP (Software Test Plan)	A document which prescribes the approach to be taken for test activities. The plan typically identifies the items to be tested, the testing to be performed, test processes, test schedules, personnel needs, reporting requirements, evaluation criteria and any risks requiring contingency planning.
Study Results	The outcomes of studies.
Support Needs	Those needs identified by the user and maintainer of the system of which the software is part.
System Requirements	The requirements established for the collection of people, equipment and methods which accomplish the set of functions which the user specifies along with any performance expectations.
Top Level Design	The activity of analyzing design alternatives and defining the design typically includes definition and structuring of both processing and data components, definition of interfaces and preparation of timing and sizing estimates.

Whenever possible, the JIAWG Reusable Software Program Operational Concept Document[24] and the IEEE Standard Glossary of Software Engineering Terminology[25] were used as the sources for definitions.

TABLE 9-6   Applications Engineering Artifacts

The following primary RSOs result from activities illustrated in Figure 9-4:

Artifact	Generated By:	Contains Information on:
IDD/SDD	Software Engineer	Top level detailed design for the software • Software architecture • Software Program Design Language (PDL) • Software interface design
IRS/SRS	Software Engineer	Functional, performance, interface and design requirements for the software • Requirements model (functional or object oriented form) • Hardware-to-software interface requirements • Human interface needs
Metrics	Software Engineer	Development progress Productivity and cost Product size and quality
Plans	Manager	Budgets Management controls Schedules Staffing profiles
RSOs	Software Engineer	Legacy for reuse within and across projects
Software System	Software Engineer	Source and object code Descriptive documentation
STD/STP	Software Engineer	Test plans, descriptions, cases, expectations and procedures Test results (either in appendixes or reports)

As the data flow diagrams indicate, more is involved in a reuse program than first meets the eye. The data flow diagrams also illustrate quite a number of artifacts which could be built to be reusable. Of course, it may not be desirable to make these objects RSOs. The four factors which influence this decision are illustrated in Figure 9-5 and elaborated as follows:

1. Cost. The costs of acquiring reusable objects and making them available to potential users can be quite high because make/buy, operations, maintenance, and infrastructure expenditures must be factored into the formula. As a consequence, the cost/benefits associated with reuse of RSOs must be carefully evaluated. In addition, the costs of quality must be factored into the decision as the cost/benefits are assessed using techniques which take into account present worth and cost of money.[8]
2. Quality. The quality of the objects and services offered also needs to be assessed. The Goal-Question-Metric approach advanced by Bob Grady in his book[9] serves as a useful model. The key to achieving a desired level of quality is to trade off the desired quality level against functionality, performance, and cost. This means that several levels of quality may need to be provided as RSOs are acquired and placed in a reuse library. Probably one of the biggest

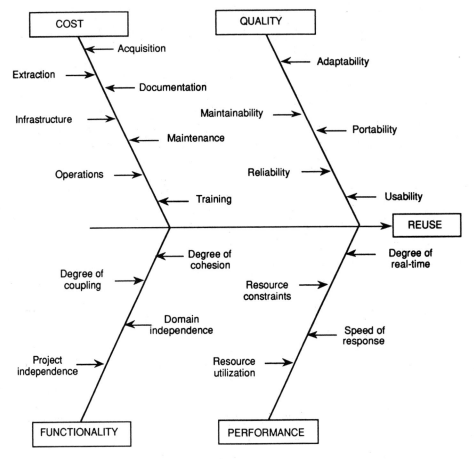

FIGURE 9-5. Reuse influence factors.

barriers to reuse is the lack of confidence users have relative to RSO quality. Therefore, care must be taken to ensure that specified levels of product and service quality are provided.

3. Functionality. The functionality furnished and its independence from both a domain specific and project point of view can also greatly influence the degree of reuse that is being achieved. In order to address this factor, domain engineering activities need to be performed in parallel with the applications engineering tasks. Domain engineering provides developers with a proper understanding of what features and functions the RSOs must have in order to be reused within and across projects.

4. Performance. Realization of an acceptable common solution to a domain specific application is often driven by performance issues. Although not normally considered as part of the quality triangle, performance is such an important issue in reuse that we believe it needs to become part of the trade

offs conducted. Even if an object has the desired functionality, our experience indicates that users will be unhappy with it no matter what its cost and quality if it does not perform as expected.

As noted above, the establishment of a systematic framework for reuse embodies the principles of TQM. The framework needs to be established in a participatory manner so that everybody understands the expectations. Goals need to be set and results need to be measured so that improvements will become apparent. Rewards need to be established and organizational barriers broken as team approaches replace the efforts of individuals. A cross functional orientation needs to be maintained as a process oriented way of thinking is inserted into the organization in a Kaizen[10] manner (a large number of improvements represents a large improvement).

9.6 STATE-OF-THE-ART VERSUS STATE-OF-THE-PRACTICE ASSESSMENT

As we have already shown, the software community has made great progress over the past five years in addressing the technical challenges posed by reuse. New paradigms, methods, and tools have been developed as researchers have focused primarily on defining reuse packaging and process guidelines.[11] The emphasis seems to have been placed on devising domain specific processes, object-oriented analysis methods, and library systems which are an integral part of the programmers' toolset arsenal. For example, the Software Productivity Consortium (SPC)[12] has devised a synthesis process which helps software engineers build their designs, code, and tests to be reusable. As another example, SofTech as built a reuse library system for the U.S. Army called RAPID[13] that acts as a repository which stores and makes reusable parts available to users. The aim of these and other efforts is to develop the technology base so that systematic and not ad hoc software reuse can be practiced as the norm within American industry.

While some limited successes have been reported by practitioners, it appears that systematic software reuse has not become as widespread as hoped for within the software community.[14] The reasons for this are few, and simple. First, it is hard to identify software objects with a high reuse potential. It is also hard to justify the added costs needed to build reusable objects. Unfortunately, while everyone talks about reuse, few provide the financial incentives needed to make it work in practice. Second, a workable management infrastructure for reuse has not been developed, proven, or operationally inserted by its champions. The policies, standards, practices, and incentives needed to insert reuse into practice are just now beginning to be devised within industry.[15] Third, and most importantly, the business case issues related to software reuse have not been thoroughly explored. If it costs more to build software objects to be reusable, who is going to pay the tab? How will these costs, and those related to inserting and operating the reuse infrastructure, be recouped? What investments are needed and how can they be minimized? What is the return-on-investment, return-on-capital, and period? These and a host of other questions need to be answered before reuse catches the attention of the executive. Work on this important topic is just now starting to appear in the literature.[16, 17] Considerably more effort is needed before industry will be convinced to spend money on reuse.

The following summary, which is based on a survey[18] we conducted some years ago, identifies six findings that we recently reported in *American Programmer*[19] relative to how the state-of-the-practice of reuse compares with the state-of-the-art:

1. Many research efforts are aimed at systematic reuse. With the advent of domain engineering paradigms, object-oriented analysis methods, and languages like Ada and C^{++}, technology exists to package software for systematic reuse. Many on-going efforts are aimed at exploiting these advances. For example, the Department of Defense is sponsoring the CAMP,[20] RAPID, and STARS[21] efforts as technology demonstration efforts. In addition, most large corporate research centers, the Software Engineering Institute (SEI) and the Software Productivity Consortium (SPC) have very active reuse programs. Although many researchers are working on the technology base, few have devoted sufficient attention to technology transfer and management issues associated with reuse. Scaling up still looms as the issue as solutions that work in the small are tried in the large. Pilot projects and experimentation are needed to determine what works and what doesn't in practice.

2. Much software exists that can be reused. A great deal of off-the-shelf, public domain, and commercial software exists that could be reused if potential consumers knew what was available, from whom, in what condition, and how to acquire it. In addition, large bodies of existing software sit ready to be mined within firms, government depositories (NASA's COSMIC, etc.), and computer vendor user's groups (IBM's SHARE, etc.). The term mining was deliberately chosen to infer that a deliberate decision was made to recover the object. Unfortunately, most of what is available from these sources is code and documentation examples. Few, if any, designs and tests are available for generalized reuse. Designs represent objects with extremely high reuse potential especially when source code can be generated directly from them.

3. Quality of available software is often an issue. In addition to not knowing what exists, most potential consumers don't trust what is available. The quality of public domain, commercial, or mined software is always an issue. Because of the potential risks, it is often easier to build software anew. Of course, software engineers would reuse software if the quality of it were certified and made self-evident prior to its being placed in a reuse library. As noted previously, multiple levels of quality need to be provided so that users can archetype (i.e., use RSOs as prototypes) as well as reuse what is in their libraries.

4. Reuse methods are relatively immature. Object-oriented methods are appealing because they allow software engineers to package software objects (designs, code, tests, etc.) with reuse in mind. While Object-Oriented Design

(OOD) methods can be used effectively to build reusable software objects, the risks associated with using Object-Oriented Analysis (OOA) methods for domain analysis and synthesis tasks seem to have limited their potential.[22] Most OOA methods seem too mature to use in a production environment. The reasons for this are many and include: evolving definitions, lack of robustness and consistency, lack of defined rules and real-world examples, lack of behavioral modeling capability, lack of tool support, lack of experience, lack of trained personnel, and development constraints (tight budgets and schedules).

5. Reuse requires more tools than just a library. The requirements noted above force the reuse toolset to be much more than just a software library with relational database capabilities. Browsers are needed to scan catalogs, abstracts, or listings and identify objects of interest. Faceting schemes need to be married to query languages. A variety of metrics and performance analysis tools are needed to instrument and analyze the cost-effectiveness of the library and the quality of the components contained within it. Traceability tools are needed to relate software objects to requirements of interest. Object managers are needed to control the information that flows between libraries and other tools. Report generators and configuration management tools are needed to provide status accounting and status information. In essence, the design of a reuse toolset impacts the design of every aspect of the environment in which it is to be accommodated. Reuse will probably continue to be practiced ad hoc until such tooling is provided as an integral part of our production environment.

6. Reuse management and infrastructure issues need considerable attention. I do not believe that reuse is a technical problem. The technology currently exists to increase the levels of reuse achieved in practice by an order of magnitude. The ingredients that seem to be missing are the organizational and management structure needed to transfer promising software reuse technology from the research center into practice in an industrial setting. Operational concepts for using this structure need to be developed along with the metrics and economical models that prove reuse to be a workable and sound idea. While some work has been done on infrastructure and incentives by the JIAWG and others,[23, 24] little of this has filtered out to industry.

9.7 REUSE HOPES, PROMISES, AND FUTURE DIRECTIONS

As you probably have inferred from my remarks, I believe that much more work needs to be done, primarily in the management area, before we will be ready to take advantage of the software reuse technology base. While the potential benefits are available, the infrastructure needed to capitalize on them is not. The good news is that a lot of very talented people are working the challenge. I have no doubt that sound, managerial solutions will be proposed soon. Progress will be made as pilot projects and experiments indicate which of these solutions work and which do not. I am very upbeat and optimistic about the future.

From a quality perspective, reuse presents the means to make relatively large improvements quickly. After all, the more we use an object, the less error-prone it becomes, especially when its capabilities are known, its quality is maintained, and it is placed under strict configuration management. But, "if" is a very large word especially when software is involved. And, the quality of RSOs will suffer "if" we take the same type of shortcut with RSOs that we take when we maintain applications systems. As a result, I believe that organizational initiatives are needed as part of the changeover to reuse. The reasons for this are simple. Although quality is everybody's business, someone needs to be held accountable for the quality of the reuse products, processes, and service levels.

Organizing for reuse is a political issue. Everybody is for reuse, but nobody wants to be held responsible for it. As a result, I anticipate that centralized reuse organizations will become common within the industry in the next five years. These organizations will be the advocates for reuse. They will be given the task of facilitating the insertion of reuse into the production shops. They will be given staffs, budgets, and resources, and will suffer all of the problems all of the other centralized shops suffer as they try to do their job. The primary challenge the reuse organization will face will be one of acceptance. Imagination will be needed to convince project leaders that reuse is something that they and not their counterparts on other projects should do, even though there may be some risk involved. Rewards may have to be provided as bonuses and promotions become tied to the achievement of reuse goals. The insights we have derived from past technology introductions (CASE, Unix, etc.) tell us that inserting a good thing like reuse will take time, talent, and perseverance. Hopefully, the early adopters will provide the evidence needed to convince the nay-sayers of the merits of changeover.

Of course, I am banking on reuse catching on in the future. I have dedicated my time and energy to devising economic models and measures to demonstrate the cost-effectiveness of reuse in the future. For example, I recently developed a reuse version of the COCOMO software cost estimating model[27] so that I could perform reuse cost-benefit tradeoffs. I am also developing reuse metrics and measures as part of my work on the Reusable Ada Avionics Support Packages (RAASP) contract.[28]

In summary, software reuse is a technology that is coming of age. The technology permits us to systematically reuse our legacy to improve software productivity and quality. Exploitation of this technology in the future will be difficult because a culture change is needed. Management, not technical challenges, will dominate as the changeover occurs. Success will come to those who innovate and bring about the culture change quickly using TQM principles.

ACKNOWLEDGEMENTS

The author acknowledges that much of the work reported in this chapter was developed under contract to the Naval Weapons Center and CTA Incorporated under the apt leadership of Mr. Jay Crawford and Mr. Dan Kielty. He also acknowledges the many inputs from the members of the Joint Integrated Avionics Working Group (JIAWG) reuse working group.

References

1. Baldo, James, Jr., *Reuse in Practice Workshop,* for Defense Analysis Document D-754, Apr. 1990.
2. Caldiera, Gianluigi and Basili, Victor R., "Identifying and Qualifying Reusable Software Components," *Computer,* IEEE Computer Society, Feb. 1991, pp. 61-70.
3. Biggerstaff, Ted J. and Perlis, Alan J., *Software Reliability* (Volumes I and II), ACM Press, 1989.
4. Brooks, Frederick P., Jr., "No Silver Bullet: Essence and Accidents in Software Engineering," *Computer,* Apr. 1987, pp. 10-19.
5. "Can the U.S. Stay Ahead in Software?" *Business Week Magazine,* Mar. 1991, pp. 98-105.
6. Marciniak, John J. and Reifer, Donald J., *Software Acquisition Management,* New York: John Wiley and Sons, 1990.
7. Reifer, Donald J., *Joint Integrated Avionics Working Group Software Reuse Handbook, Volume 1, Fundamental Concepts* (Draft), RCI-TN-455, Dec. 1990.
8. Reifer, Donald J., Joint Integrated Avionics Working Group Reuse Metrics and Measurement Concept Paper, RCI-TN-456C, Nov. 1990.
9. Grady, Robert B. and Caswell, Deborah L., *Software Metrics: Establishing a Company-Wide Program,* Englewood Cliffs: Prentice-Hall, 1987.
10. Imai, Masaaki, *Kaizen,* New York: McGraw-Hill, 1986.
11. Gautier, Robert J. and Wallis, Peter J. L., *Software Reuse with Ada,* New York: Peter Pereginus Ltd., Publishers, IEEE Computing Series, 1990.
12. Software Productivity Consortium, "A Domain Analysis Process," Jan. 1990.
13. Ruegsegger, Theodore B. and Guerrieri, Ernesto, "The RAPID Center Library as a CASE Tool," Proceedings CASExpo, Spring 1989, *Softech Report TP289,* May 1989.
14. Reifer, Donald J., *Final Report: Findings of Reuse Survey Task,* RCI-TN-410A, Aug. 1989.
15. U.S. Army, *Software Reuse Guidelines,* AIRMICS Report ASQB-GI-90-015, Apr. 1990.
16. Barnes, Bruce H. and Bollinger, Terry B., "Making Reuse Cost-Effective Software," IEEE Computer Society, Jan. 1991, pp. 13-24.
17. Reifer, Donald J., *The Economics of Software Reuse,* RCI-TN-488, Mar. 1991.
18. Reifer, Donald J., "Managing Software Reuse," ACM Tutorial, Nov. 1990.
19. Reifer, Donald J., "Software Reuse: Myth or Reality," *American Programmer,* Mar. 1991, pp. 18-23.
20. McDonnell Douglas Missile Systems Co., "Developing and Using Ada Parts in Real-Time Applications," CDRL No. A008, Contract No. F08635-88-C-0002, Apr. 1990.
21. STARS Technology Center, *STARS Newsletter,* Aug. 1990.
22. Reifer, Donald J., "White Paper on the use of Object-Oriented Techniques," RCI-TN-433, Jan. 1990.
23. Fairley, Richard, Pfleeger, S. L., Bollinger, Terry B., Davis, Alan, Incorvaia, A. J., and Springsteen, B., *Final Report: Incentives for Reuse of Ada Components (Volumes 1 to 5),* George Mason University, 1989.

24. Tracz, Will, "Tutorial: Software Reuse Emerging Technology," IEEE Computer Society, 1986.

25. Reifer, Donald J., *Joint Integrated Avionics Working Group Reusable Software Program Operational Concept Document (OCD),* RCI-TR-075D, Sep. 1990.

26. IEEE, *Software Engineering Standards* (Third Printing), May 1987.

27. Reifer, Donald J., *Multiple Instance Reuse Modeling,* RCI-TN-472, Feb. 1991.

28. Reifer, Donald J., *RAASP Metrics and Measurement Plan,* RCI-TN-469A, Dec. 1990.

PART III

Methods for TQM in Software

10

TQM Methods in Software

James H. Dobbins,* CQA

Professor of Systems Acquisition Management
Defense Systems Management College

10.1 INTRODUCTION

Applying TQM methods to software implies that a number of cross-dependent elements are present. To achieve the objectives of TQM requires the participation of managers, developers, users, and support personnel. One of the most pervasive misconceptions regarding TQM, and one which often gets in the way of implementing effective TQM methods in software, is the idea of a TQM program. TQM very definitely involves a total cultural change, and requires leadership. But TQM is not:

A program
A motivational campaign
A set of tools and techniques
Easy
A six-month mentality.

TQM involves the implementation and application of some very fundamental concepts to the development of software. These are: (1) conformance to requirements, proposed by Crosby, (2) fitness for use, proposed by Juran, and (3) never

---

*The ideas expressed in this article are those of the author, and are not to be interpreted as the official position of the United States Government, Department of Defense, or the Defense Systems Management College.

ending improvement, proposed by Deming. It involves every one in the organization, each doing their current best, and each taking the personal leadership to do what they can to continuously improve. TQM is necessary for corporate survival because a company can assume that if it does not achieve the TQM cultural change, its competition will. TQM depends on the results of models and measures, but it also enhances, it does not replace, judgment and experience. A company does not have a TQM mentality just because it employs a new tool or method. It is the difference between the management of quality and the quality of management. It is necessarily a cultural change. In some organizations it is a cultural evolution. In others, it is a cultural revolution. It depends on the starting point. But it does not matter whether TQM is a revolution or an evolution. What does matter is that the cultural change happens, and permeates the thinking process of each and every employee in terms of how they view themselves in the organization, how they view their job, and how they accept the concept of process ownership. It is putting our focus on problem prevention, not problem detection.

We must also ask what the alternative might be. There is no such thing as an injection of TQM vaccine to prevent quality defects. It takes time to change a culture. It may not be a motivational campaign, but it is a form of motivation. It is motivation of the work force through process change, and through a new way of thinking and doing. It is eliminating bad processes and improving good processes. It is focusing on why something works and how we can make it work better, not focusing on why it failed.

From a systems acquisition viewpoint, this involves a wide array of participants from different organizations, with differing perspectives, and with varying understandings of TQM commitment, each operating from different baselines, and working toward a commonly recognized goal. This is not a trivial condition to manage.

10.2 CONFORMANCE TO REQUIREMENTS

Correctness

For any system, but especially for large systems, leadership must be evident in the requirements generation process, both individual leadership as well as project leadership. TQM requires fundamental individual leadership throughout an organization. TQM can be achieved much more successfully by leading the way than by pushing others towards a goal. It is like the difference between pulling a rope and pushing a rope.

Conformance to requirements involves first of all a reasonable, complete, correct, and consistent set of requirements against which conformance can be evaluated. Requirements are developed in response to some particular need. In the commercial world, the need is driven by commercial competition, which is in turn a reflection of a perceived current or future customer need or desire. In the defense industry, the need is driven by the knowledge and understanding of a particular known or evolving threat against which some form of defense or countermeasure must be developed.

In both instances there are users. In the commercial world, the ultimate users are those who will use, or be subjected to the use of, the product. For example, the product may be an automobile or an X-ray machine. The ultimate user may be an automobile buyer or a patient in a hospital. In the case of the X-ray machine, the patient is the end recipient of the product in use, whereas the X-ray machine operator is the functional end user of the machine. In the other case, the automobile, the users are the buyer-drivers who can tell you what they do or do not like about current automobiles, but can usually tell you nothing about engineering requirements. In the case of the X-ray machine, the patient has virtually no input. The determiners of the requirements for X-ray machines are the radiologists and machine operators.

In both commercial cases the manufacturers are producing a system. The automobile is a system involving both hardware and software. Approximately 5% of the cost of a new automobile is for the software in that automobile. In the X-ray machine, software is controlling the operation, including the dosage level, in response to operator command. The requirements for either system must be defined in ways which take into account the functionality, reliability, safety, human factors, ergonomics, technical feasibility, and cost of the target system.

Since the historical track record for software indicates that approximately 40% of the software life cycle defects are traceable to problems in the software functional requirements, conformance to requirements involves two fundamental issues: correctness of the requirements, and then conformance to the correct requirements. It makes no sense to put significant effort into assuring conformance with an incorrect set of requirements.

User Involvement

User involvement for software principally addresses the degree to which the users assist in establishing the requirements for the software. In the commercial world, it is not always easy to identify who the users are who ought to be consulted. We cannot ask automobile buyers, or hospital patients, what the requirements ought to be for the software going into the product lines, even though it is ultimately their safety and comfort which has to be kept in mind. The determination of the requirements has to be spread among various technical and market experts, and the input from these experts must be coordinated through a systems engineering discipline.

In the United States Department of Defense (DOD), the user involvement is much more clearly understood, since the users of a military system can and should provide input to the requirements. It is the users themselves who will fly the aircraft, man the radar, or fire the weapon being built.

User involvement, once sufficiently achieved, requires that the processes of software requirements definition be established in such a way that the resultant final requirements are self-consistent, comprehensive, include no To Be Determined (TBDs, also referred to as holes in the spec) elements, and are both technically feasible and manageable. They must also embody a form of translation from the operational language of the user to a form of expression which is meaningful to, and can be understood and implemented by, the software engineers.

Evaluation and Measurement

The consistency and correctness of software requirements does not just happen, and the continuous improvement of requirements cannot happen except through a cultural change and a process improvement. It is much easier to improve the tools and environments with which software engineers work than it is to improve people. As long as organizations insist on writing software requirements in prose form, requirements will be a source of significant software errors. To evolve the requirements generation process away from prose specification generation toward a method which is more conducive to the production of correct and consistent specifications will necessarily require change. Change in work methods, change in the way specifications look, change in the process by which specifications are produced, and a change in the way specifications are evaluated. The need for individual involvement is clear, and the need for leadership is equally clear. Any cultural change requires commitment and support from the top, and implementation acceptance at every level of involvement. With regard to requirements, this means the acquisition and use of one or more of the emerging specification generation techniques, and in most instances will require the use of Computer Aided Software Engineering (CASE) tools. Many such tools have been developed, each of which has its own strengths and weaknesses. Some are language restricted, some are hardware environment restricted, some work well for small systems but fall if used for large, complex systems, some look at the requirements as a state machine system, and others exhibit different views of the system. There is no one method which is THE METHOD, or THE BEST method for everyone. One or another may be best, for one organization on one or more projects. Regardless of which products are considered, the software engineers should select one which is characterized by ease of use, but most importantly by the ability to perform comprehensive real-time analysis and evaluation of the requirements product as it is being developed. The generation of correct requirements is a total quality process involving a combination of technically competent people being able to do good thinking and making the personal commitment to continuously improve the way they work and what they produce, supported by technology which prevents, or immediately identifies the results of, typical human error. The process should also provide for continuous and accurate documentation of the current state of the requirements.

The requirements development process should have built-in methods for iteration. As the requirements undergo development, those producing the requirements will analyze and evaluate conditions or problems not previously considered. The producers must build into the process a continuous requirement for iteration to validate the correctness of what has been done before. Each requirement which has been identified is based on a given state of knowledge, and a set of assumptions. It is necessary to iterate regularly to ascertain whether newly acquired knowledge is merely additive or if it impacts any of the prior knowledge or challenges any of the underlying assumptions. Each requirement of the system will have to be validated, and therefore must be measurable. A requirement which cannot be measured and validated is not really a requirement.

Conformance

Conformance to correct requirements involves employee commitment, communication, education, and measurement. Every requirement must be measurable at some point in the development process. There must be a progressive form of measurement from one level of the system to the next. This progression begins with the evaluation of individual modules or objects, and ends with either a final acceptance test or a user evaluation. A requirement which cannot be measured is not a requirement. There is no way to determine if the requirement has been incorporated, or incorporated correctly. The requirement must include the performance necessary, and the criteria for acceptability. It is the criteria against which the test case results will be judged. This means that the requirements themselves must be specified in such a way that they can be evaluated and measured.

In DOD systems acquisition, the issue of conformance to requirements is a multilayered set of conditions which must be managed. The government program manager has a prime contractor selected for development. The prime contractor may have one or more subcontractors. The program manager also has a user community to satisfy, higher headquarters to satisfy, as well as Congress to keep informed. To the program manager, conformance to requirements means conformance to system requirements. A team attitude must therefore permeate the effort if the system development is to succeed. Just having one part of the system, the software or the hardware, working correctly will not do any good if the system itself is nonfunctional. To have the best chance for success, the team members must each have adopted a TQM culture. They must each have a defined, measurable, and repeatable process of development. This is as true for software as it is for hardware.

Self-Assessment

In software development, the defined allocated requirements must be consistent with and supportive of the overall system requirements. If the contractor developing the software is to have a TQM mentality, and have a well defined way of ascertaining whether the requirements are being implemented correctly, then the contractor must have some way of baselining itself quantitatively. The contractor must have some way of both measuring itself, and defining its process of development and control of the software. It is virtually impossible to improve continuously, or even at all, if you cannot determine where you are to begin with, and that cannot be done unless the process is at least defined and repeatable. If a company cannot tell where it is, it cannot possibly tell if it has improved and to what degree. No track runner or competitive swimmer can ever say they have improved their time just because they think they have. The stopwatch tells the story. Either they have or have not improved.

When the Software Engineering Institute (SEI) at Carnegie-Mellon first performed their contractor assessment,[1] over 86% of the companies assessed were at level 1 on a scale of 1 to 5. Level 1 meant they did not have a measurable, definable, repeatable process for software engineering, and little or no quality consciousness. Level 1 means the company operates by purely reactive management. At level 2, a company has repeatability. That is, some previously mastered tasks can be repeated. Several companies at level 2 seem to slip back to a level 1 in response to schedule pressure or changes in management. At level 3, the company knows the difference between directions and a map. Directions show you how to get to a specific place from a specific starting point, by following one set of instructions. If any detours or other unexpected roadblocks appear, the odds of getting to the destination are severely diminished. At level 3, it is like having a map which allows you to get to any other point from any starting place, and being able to respond to unexpected roadblocks as they appear. A level 3 company has a well defined process which is characterized and well understood. At level 4, the company is process managed, and the processes are measured and well controlled. At level 5, the company is optimizing on process improvements. This does not mean there is an optimum. It means that the company is continually striving to make whatever process they now have as good as it can be, and is likewise looking for better and more efficient ways to effect those processes.

In the SEI assessment, only one company reached level 3. A few were at level 2. Since that time, one facility of one company, the IBM office in Houston producing the space shuttle software, was evaluated by the Jet Propulsion Laboratory (JPL) and achieved a level 5. At the present time (1991), SEI has identified only three projects at level 5, two in the United States and one in Japan.

To rely on a company to produce software, particularly large and complex software projects, without knowing what their assessment rating is, and expect that company to produce high quality software, is an extreme program risk. This risk has apparently been present, and to a significant degree, for quite a long time without the community in general, or the government, being aware of the magnitude and extent of the risk. This risk is compounded when the software developer is also producing the software functional requirements as a deliverable item.

It is therefore incumbent on software development companies to be assessed, to determine whether they have a defined, controlled, and repeatable process of software development, and to begin across the board improvements. When initiating the improvements, a measurement base must be set up so that the results of the improvements can be measured and evaluated on a regular basis.

Domain Knowledge

As important as the assessments are, the company must also have a way of determining the domain knowledge of their project team. Domain knowledge is that body of knowledge contained within the members of the project team (not just within the company at large) which is specifically relevant to the project to be undertaken. This includes knowledge of the current technology and experience in the application of these skills on prior projects.

Measures

The question always arises as to what measures should be selected, and how they should be computed. In selecting measures, a company can turn to many of the already available sources, such as DOD regulations, standards, and directives. There is also the series of IEEE software standards. Some of these standards such as IEEE STD 982.1 and Guide 982.2, assist the company in putting into place a life cycle measurement process.

IEEE STD and Guide 982.1/982.2 assist a company in establishing a process to manage software reliability, establish evaluation of both the products and the processes, and provide the complete set of input data (primitives) required for the measures as well as the computational methods. Therefore, when establishing a data base for a software engineering measurement methodology, a company should focus on the primitives upon which the measures are based. The primitives are those items which are directly measurable or observable. They become the component part of derived measures. For example, the radius of a circle can be considered a primitive. The area of a circle is a derived measure. Often, derived measures are based on already identified primitives. If the data base is established for primitives, then the history data is captured. If a different measure, which is based on some subset of these same primitives, is desired at a later date, then the measure can be computed with a historical trend perspective instead of having to look only forward. If the data base has only the resultant values of derived measures, this capability is lost.

Once a potential contractor decides to determine their SEI assessment level, they can obtain help from several sources. To date, nine contractors have been authorized by the SEI to assist companies in their self-assessments. In addition to the SEI itself, several members of the faculty at the Defense Systems Management College (DSMC) at Ft. Belvoir have been certified by the SEI to conduct assessments. A number of companies have received the self-assessment training from SEI and are already performing self-assessments.

Regardless of how a company is assessed, if its leadership has not provided a TQM mentality, the assessment will be of little use. Regardless of how often the assessment is conducted, it is only a starting point. Each time an assessment is performed, it identifies the current level of capability, but more importantly it determines the point from which to begin the next capability improvement. It is not the final goal, but only one mark in the sands of time. Those who achieved level 5 have said that they got there, and stay there, because of a quality attitude which permeates every part of the organization. They are constantly looking for ways to improve. They also have developed an extensive set of measurements which are evaluated continuously.

Failure Model Analysis

The focus of any such evaluation must be on the process. Most measurements will describe the present quality condition of products. But the important concept is process improvement. Once the defects have been determined, they must be evaluated as to type and category. A failure model analysis must then be established to determine the root cause and net impact of each defect type and category. Once this is determined, then the development process must be changed to attack the defects at their root cause. This may require training and education, a new technology, a change in management philosophy, or any number of other things or combination of things. Whatever actions are established, they must be focused on process quality improvement, and must be measurable in some way.

Government Expectations

When the government begins an acquisition process, especially in the climate prevalent today, it is these kinds of contractor TQM processes and activities which are examined when reviewing proposals. This is becoming more a reality every day as the program managers go through the training courses at DSMC which have been mandated by Congress. Several of the professors at DSMC now serve on source selection committees or assist in reviewing proposals. Government program managers are expected to implement TQM within their own program office organization, and expect it of the contractor team. This means they expect it of the prime contractor, and expect the prime contractor to demand it of any subcontractors.

10.3 FITNESS FOR USE

We are continuously bombarded by stories of the $600 hammer, the $500 toilet seat, and other tales which make good press and generate a lot of attention in Congress. We also see a large number of contractors doing good work under conditions which prevent them from proving their systems under actual operational conditions. Although as American citizens we expect every product used by consumers to be fully tested, the government recognizes that not every weapon system purchased can be fully tested under operational conditions. It is a tribute to industry that so many systems do work, and work so well, as seen most recently in the Persian Gulf conflict.

It is easy to see whether a hammer or a toilet seat serves its intended purpose, and whether it is over-engineered or over-specified. It is not that easy with software. Software fitness for use is often equated with conformance to requirements. However, this is not always the case, especially when the requirements are faulty or where the user community did not have sufficient input to the requirements. A software system can be in perfect conformance to the requirements, and still not be fit for use.

Risk Factors

The program manager must be conscious of two different software management concerns, (1) degree of difficulty and (2) software size. There are separate risk factors for each, and the measurement and evaluation process is different for each. The degree of difficulty assessment is one in which the user community can assist. The estimation of software size, particularly for a new development, usually rests with the developer. With regard to degree of difficulty, the user and the developer, provided they are allowed to interact, can work together to bound and describe the elements of difficulty and the attendant risks. They should work together so that the functional concepts of the user can be converted to software engineering language that the developer can understand and implement, and therefore can assess. Working together, effective communication is crucial to success.

Prototyping

When the degree of difficulty is considered high, the program manager has a number of methods from which to choose to mitigate risk and enhance the overall system quality. One method suggested is the effective use of software prototypes. This is not the quick and dirty, deliver it to the government without documentation, kind of prototype. It is part of incremental development, or evolutionary acquisition. It is using a prototype to validate and solidify the requirements as defined by the user. It is proving concept feasibility. It is developing, quickly, a working example of the to-be-developed system. It is not a mockup, but rather a functioning element of the intended system. It is a means for giving the users and the developers very early feedback on the user interface, including the "look and feel" of the system, as well as the system functionality. The prototype is not the product which should be the final deliverable article, nor should it be delivered at all. It is usually thrown away. This upsets some government program managers. After all, they paid for it. It was built with government resources. Why should they not receive it? In effect, they do. In the final software product, they receive all the knowledge gained by the development and evaluation of the prototype. For software, it is that domain knowledge, incorporated into the properly built software system, which is of real value. In the final product, the knowledge gained is retained and incorporated, and the benefits of the formal development processes are added. Software is not hardware. It is not tangible, or fabricated by machines. Software is the recordation, and incorporation into the system, of the results of the thought process, analysis, and applied domain knowledge and expertise of the developers. The prototype is merely one more step in the attainment of the requisite knowledge and experience. The benefit, all the benefit, is received by the government in the final product. The documentation is also complete, making field support easier, or even possible.

The prototype method has other useful purposes. It is used to establish logical relationships among operating functional elements of the intended system that are not amenable to formal analysis. It is further useful for validating requirements which are provable by testing or by operational demonstration.

Given this, it must be understood that the typical waterfall model as described in DOD-STD-2167A may not be a suitable software development paradigm for development strategies which are based on prototyping, which are high-risk, which are dependent on a significant volume of reusable components (see Chapter 9), which are based on object-oriented design, and which are developed in Ada. Program managers need to understand this, acquisition professionals need to understand this, and all need to be able to evaluate the risks and alternatives and make good decisions. This is extremely difficult without a pervasive TQM mentality.

User Involvement During Test

One other method for ascertaining software fitness for use is to provide for user involvement during system tests or immediately following the final system test. It is necessary for the developer to make the user aware of and understand what it is, from a software engineering point of view, the users want, and why. The users must be made to understand if the desired goal is even possible, or how much time and money it will require.

On one series of Anti-Submarine Warfare (ASW) systems, the contractor developed the system, conducted the planned tests, went through the final acceptance test, and then provided for a few hundred hours of customer user testing. The contractor essentially turned the test facility over to the users for testing prior to delivery to the field. The users themselves, using their own test data, satisfied themselves as to the fitness for use of the system before the system ever left the contractor facility.

There is no way this sort of user involvement can be accomplished effectively without a TQM mentality permeating the contractor facility. The software developers must begin the initial development task with the idea of continuous quality assessment and improvement being a part of their process. This kind of fitness for use evaluation means that the software is assessed, and, if necessary, corrected, at every step of the total development process. To do so requires some form of immediate in-process assessment and feedback.

Inspections

TQM in software development begins at the beginning, with every person involved doing what they can to assure that the product is the best it can be at that time. It means that the functional requirements are written and evaluated, and possibly prototyped, before final design begins. if the requirements are, for whatever reason, written in prose, then they must be evaluated. The technique of design and code inspections, developed by Michael Fagan,[2] has been used quite effectively for document inspections, including requirements documents. At one company, when the inspection process was applied to the requirements documents, there was a 33% drop in defect density during design and code phases. The important thing to remember is that it is an inspection process. It is not a tool or device. Inspections are done by people, to and for each other. Everyone involved has a stake in the outcome of the entire system. It is the system which must work. The process is applied by people, and is only as effective as the people are willing to make it. If a TQM mentality is not present, the likelihood of the process working effectively is small. If a TQM mentality is present, the inspections will be conducted properly using trained teams, the results will be captured and analyzed, and the data evaluated to see how the software engineering process itself can be improved. It is one process being used to positively benefit another process. That is TQM at work. It is process driven and it is the processes which are improved in order to see a resultant quality improvement in the products.

Effect of Inspections on Tests

By doing formal inspections, at least 70% of the life cycle defects in the software can be removed before the first unit test. This has a considerable effect on how the test process itself is used. In an environment where TQM is not prevalent, traditional testing is seen as the primary place to find and fix software defects. In a TQM environment, testing is the life cycle phase where the correctness of what has been done before is validated, and error detection is not the primary purpose. In a TQM environment, software development involves iteration on the requirements, iteration on the decisions and assumptions behind software, design, evaluation, correction, and validation at each phase, and the code itself is the final recording of the results of these multilayered processes.

In a TQM environment, unit test is done using formal methods of structured analysis and the tests are designed to check every independent path through the module.[3] There is a variety of software tools on the market which can be used to analyze each module, to validate the results of the unit test, and to validate that every independent path through a module has been tested. Some of these tools are restricted to one language, and some are multilanguage capable. Some can operate in a microcomputer environment, while others require workstations, or even mainframes. Regardless of the project under development, the management team should make sure that these kinds of validation and assessment tools are available to the software development team. There is no net cost since the benefits of the tools in terms of manhours saved means that these tools pay for themselves in a very short time. Some even provide capabilities which would be impossible to do by hand.

Productivity

In a TQM environment, the contractor management team makes available to the developers the tools and technologies which will increase their productivity. Productivity in this context does not mean volume produced. It means volume produced correctly. This includes the requirements, design, code, and the documentation for all these. Managers have to understand that productivity is diminished every time an error found during test must be corrected. Every line of code that has to be modified during test because of an error, is a reduction in productivity of at least two lines of code. The line of code originally produced is lost, and a replacement line must be written to take its place. If the replacement code is more than one line, the productivity is diminished even further. On top of that, the industry average is that at least 14.7%, and as many as 50% of the fixes made to software are bad fixes. This further compounds the impact on productivity, not to mention product quality. Therefore, it should be crystal clear to any manager that doing the job correctly the first time, even if the time for the start of code development is delayed, is much more productive than rushing into code only to have to change it later because of inadequate requirements analysis or design effort. Rushing into code buys the project nothing but problems and increased cost.

Visibility

Building in sufficient time for the contractor to do effective requirements and design analysis, including formal inspections, does not mean that the effort is done blindly. The program manager must establish the right level of visibility, on a frequency that is reasonable, so that management of the effort during requirements and design can be accomplished. This requires that the program manager have visibility into the progress, direction, and results of the requirements and design analysis, without unnecessarily impeding the progress being made.

Relying on the Preliminary Design Review (PDR) and Critical Design Review (CDR) process is not sufficient. The program manager should establish a Computer Resources Working Group (CRWG) to perform continuous assessment and evaluation of the progress and the process, and make appropriate recommendations. The program manager must also have built into the contract the means and requirements for establishment of the CRWG, as well as both access to and cooperation from the development contractor. The visibility should focus on the process, and the measurements should flow from analysis of that process and evaluation of the products produced to date. The intent of the visibility is awareness, management control, and the need for access to the level and kind of information needed to make the best decisions possible at the time they need to be made. Since the developer and the program manager should have the same ultimate objective, the development of a system which performs in accordance with correct requirements and is fit for its intended use, a degree of openness and cooperation should be established. Too many developers seem to feel that the buyer should be kept in the dark as much as possible. This may be a valid approach if the buyer is a potential or actual competitor, but not if the buyer is the government. If the government is buying the labor, and the fruits of that labor, then it should have access to and visibility into the effort being expended.

There is a corresponding responsibility on the part of the program manager to refrain from interfering with the development or behaving in an obstructive and abusive manner. There should be a clear understanding, and it is an inherent requirement of a TQM mentality, that the visibility is proper and for the purpose of assuring that the effort is as correct as it can be, and that the entire buyer-supplier team is working together to achieve the ultimate program objectives. The visibility, in the absence of actual fraud, waste and abuse, should never be used as any sort of club against individuals. Neither the developer nor the program manager should ever seek to inflict punishment for making mistakes. They should work together to affect the process so that the mistakes are not repeated. If this is accomplished, everyone benefits.

The visibility is achievable in a number of ways. The developer can make available to the program manager the results of regular software quality evaluation reports. The developer can provide the program manager with the results of the software engineering analyses and configuration management information. The program manager can also build into the contract the requirement to periodically deliver products in their in-process condition. This may make sense if the government has access to various analysis tools which can be run against the products. The results of the analysis can be made available to the developer for its information. For example, if the program manager has a source code analyzer, and the developer is at the stage of code generation, the developer, assuming it does not have such a tool, could deliver a set of source code to the program manager to be analyzed. Alternatively, the program manager could make the analysis tool available to the developer as Government Furnished Information (GFI), to be used by the developer on behalf of the government on this project, and the results periodically provided to the program manager. A third alternative is to assign this evaluation task to an IV&V (Independent Verification and Validation) agent who has access to such a source code analyzer.

In any instance, both the program manager and the developer management must establish a measurement based management information system geared to the critical success factors of the program.[4] The measurements included are those which are common to programs of the type under development, as well as those which may be specific to this particular program. The factors for which measurements are required are those which address the typical issues of cost, schedule, performance and support, as well as visibility into the management and technical issues which mean the difference between program success and failure. Some of the general issues requiring measurement and continuous management attention include risk management, the stability of a qualified industrial base, effective communications, effectiveness of quality control, change management, user involvement and support, and the management of political influencing agents.

In considering fitness for use, the interrelationships among the user involvement in requirements identification, user contact with the developer, the analysis of requirements, design and code, the management insight and resultant decisions, the effectiveness of software quality and configuration management organizations, and the test activity planned for the system must be viewed with the same system level view as any part of the technical system. These interrelationships and their effectiveness are a significant element of the TQM culture in software development. The level of cross-organization cooperation and the degree to which a teamwork attitude is prevalent is a direct indicator of the extent to which TQM is a positive factor in systems development. The likelihood of success of the software effort is directly related to this cooperation.

Formal Reviews

Going even further, there are many who advocate that if TQM is prevalent in software development, there should be a change in the method of reviews for software. In MIL-STD-1521B, the various reviews and audits are described, and these provisions are incorporated into DOD-STD-2167A and its Data Item Descriptions (DIDs). They argue, and this author agrees, that the CDR was inherited from the hardware development process, but has no place in software. It was originally required to evaluate the final design before the machine tooling was initiated to build the hardware, because tooling is a process of considerable cost. An error at this point could set the program back many months. For software, the CDR has no such counterpart. There is no tooling. There will probably be software defects. Some will be found and others will not be found during development and test. Every error found has the potential of impacting the design or the requirements, as well as the code. There is nothing magical about the point in time when a CDR is done, and in fact the CDR should not be done on the software. Instead, there should be continuous review and evaluation of the software design, making one CDR, or any CDR, as a formal mechanism, rendered useless except as a formal way for the program manager to issue a stop work order if that should be necessary. From a cost and productivity point of view, this is important. The developer may easily spend as many as 30 to 60 days, and untold numbers of manhours, working and reworking the thousand and one slides to be presented at a CDR, and during this time real productivity on the program slows to a grinding pace, or even a halt.

In a TQM environment, with continuous visibility and evaluation, and sharing of the information between developer and the program manager, the CDR becomes superfluous. Everything which needs to be known to make a decision has already been provided and verified on a continuing basis. The cost to the government is saved, the developer productivity is enhanced, and the program risks are mitigated. The fitness for use is continuously evaluated due to the user involvement and the continuous software engineering assessments.

The alternative is a formal CDR. Typically attended by hordes of people, and the most productive activity is often drinking gallons of coffee and squeezing donuts. It is antithetical to the concept of TQM that the information needed by the program manager for the decisions which need to be made is not presented until a formal CDR. Unfortunately, in many cases this is exactly the situation. To change this, methods have to be interjected into the contracting and performance evaluation process to provide for the regular and continuous flow of pertinent information. Since much of the information the program manager requires is the same information the contractor requires to exercise proper management of itself and the subcontractors, there should be little or no need for the contractor to generate significant amounts of extraneous information just for the government program manager. There must also be a willingness to manage in a cooperative environment, and, assuming the domain knowledge is present in the project team, to develop the kinds of software development process control which will lead the contractor to achieve a rating of at least level 3 on the SEI assessment. That takes management and technical commitment, as well as understanding and ability, to manage the project Critical Success Factors.

10.4 CONTINUOUS PROCESS IMPROVEMENT

Continuous process improvement (also see Chapter 13) implies that there is some definable and measurable process to improve. In software engineering, it is necessary that there be processes at each phase of the development life cycle which can be improved. There are also ancillary processes such as configuration management, software quality, and test and integration, each of which supports software development and each of which can also be improved.

For any process which is to be improved, there must be a baseline. This baseline is the measured starting point for that next phase of improvement. The developer must therefore become sufficiently organized (see Chapter 3) to have definable and measurable processes which are measured, analyzed, and evaluated. As part of the evaluation, the developer must determine what has been measured, what needs to be measured, and what the goal should be for improvement.

Reusability

Software reusability is often cited as an example of TQM in action. To achieve effective reusability in software, especially in embedded systems, is not as easy as one might suspect (see Chapter 9). Given the attention focused on Ada, what are the reusability issues?

One issue is identifying the software to be reused. That requires an extensive domain analysis, and there are no tools yet developed that provide that sort of analysis. It is an expensive, manual, time consuming process. It has been said that the highest area of reuse in software is in proposals.

Another question is deciding at what state the product is to be reused. If the requirements and design are done, and if the code is produced by an automated code generator, such as those already on the market, does one focus reuse on the requirements and design, and not worry about source code reuse?

Given the rapid pace of hardware advances, a method of identification of software tied to particular hardware environments will be a necessity. For example, was the source code written to be optimal in an 8-bit, 16-bit or 32-bit machine? Was the hardware, like the Rational Computer, designed to run only Ada, or was it a more general purpose machine?

Reuse is considered a significant step in achieving productivity increases. It also has the potential for lowering cost. But will there be a price to pay in performance? If software is designed to be reusable (flexible design) will that mean slower performance?

The contract issues involved in software reuse also need to be resolved. If the contractor wants to reuse its own work on multiple contracts, the buyer may lose some control over what is included. If the software is developed using capital funds, can the government demand a right to the source code? Conversely, can a contractor profit from the development of a suite of software developed on a variety of different government contracts? Once the government pays for the software, is it public domain software, and, if so, can the developing contractor charge other taxpayers for that same software?

If the government wants to give software to a contractor to incorporate, who is liable for failures in that software? What about a private company incorporating reusable software received from another company into its own product? How can the risk of failure in reused software be mitigated? How does a contractor provide a warranty when part of the product contains reused software from another source?

These and many other issues are still to be decided when software reuse is contemplated. That there are questions and issues should not deter entrepreneurial spirits from pursuing effective approaches to reusable software. Arriving at an effective how-to will provide the impetus to resolve the many ancillary issues and questions.

Critical Success Factors

Determining what should be improved can be determined in part by identifying the Critical Success Factors (CSF) of software engineering management for the company or the project. The CSF identification process was first brought to public attention by John Rockart,[5] and elaborated further by Bullen and Rockart.[6] CSF are identified as "the limited number of areas in which results, if they are satisfactory, will ensure successful competitive performance for the organization. They are the few key areas where things must go right for the business to flourish. If results in these areas are not adequate, the organization's efforts for the period will be less than desired."[7] If these activities are not done well, the project will not succeed except by accident. Clearly, the CSFs are "areas of activity that should receive constant and careful attention from management."[8] Executives can identify their CSF, the assumptions on which each CSF is based, and the measures associated with each.[9] Once identified, the CSF serve as the basis for the development of the information system each project manager requires to be successful. The software development contractor management can determine their CSF, establish their information system requirements, determine the data and measures needed as input to the information system, and in the process can establish their initial baseline. It is just common sense that the places to begin, and continue, improvement are those areas which are critical to success, and not on those areas which have no impact on success. Without identifying the CSF, it is uncertain whether the areas selected for improvement are selected because of their importance, or because of their ease and convenience. It therefore appears evident that one method for bringing TQM into focus is to use the CSF identification process as the basis for selecting the areas for continuous improvement. If the managers of a company continuously focus on improving those areas most critical to their success, and do not waste resources trying to improve those areas which have no impact on success, then TQM will have real meaning, both now and in the future.

To successfully use CSF to drive the TQM activity, it is necessary to identify the CSF, and to develop a CSF based information system. It is also necessary to identify the assumptions on which each CSF is based, and to continuously evaluate the validity of the assumptions. If the assumptions become invalid, chances are the CSF will change, and the identification and measurement process has to be updated. This has happened repeatedly both within the software community and in other fields. How often have we wondered if the latest topic of conversation is a real breakthrough or just a passing fad? There have been numerous examples of changes which have brought about real improvements in software engineering, and have set, or may now be setting, the criteria against which all new software is or will be measured. Some of these have been the development of High Order Languages, Structured Programming, Data Flow Diagrams, Software Inspections, Program Design Languages (PDL) and, more recently, Object-Oriented Programming, Neural Networks, and Artificial Intelligence.

Sometimes the impact of these methods is not evident until considerable time has passed. Sometimes the changes occur slowly over time, and sometimes they happen overnight. Consider what happened in the automobile industry. In the 1950s, automobiles were advertised according to style, amount of chrome, and how fast they could go from zero to sixty. Now, there is much more concern for environmental protection, fuel economy, and passenger safety. The same kinds of transitions happen in software development, but they are not always as obvious, especially to those in higher management who do not have an extensive software background. By using the CSF identification methods, and being conscious of the assumptions underlying the CSF, and when those assumptions may no longer be valid, the risk is reduced, and continuous process improvement has the greatest chance for success.

The point being made here is that once a process is selected for improvement, and real progress is being made, it is hard to turn loose. But if the data provided by the manager's information system, assuming it is a reliable information system, shows that the software engineering process being improved has become obsolete due to an advance in software technology, the management team has to recognize that change in state and have the courage to turn the process loose in favor of an improved method.

When looking at CSF methods for software, it helps if one understands the different ways in which CSF identification has previously been used. Some of these results are:

1. The use of CSFs as a means for MIS planning.[10] An important outcome of this research was the recommendation that CSF identification not be driven by current information production capability within the organization, but rather by the actual information needs of management.

2. Variation of CSFs over stages in the project life cycle.[11] In this research the authors hypothesized a set of CSFs, and then conducted a validation study based on empirical evidence. The objective was to identify a set of CSFs, for each life cycle phase, that were general rather than company or industry specific, and to determine the relative importance of the CSFs across life cycle phases.

3. Using CSFs as a basis for evaluating the reliability of information systems.[12] In this research the author developed reliability of an information system as a measure of the system's success based on CSFs. This research addressed the problem of the difference between behavioral and perceived measures of Information Systems (IS) effectiveness due to (1) a lack of conceptual foundation to guide proper measurement development, and (2) the absence of a rigorous program of measurement validation. This research identified the need to define CSFs and to identify how they are interconnected.

4. Use of CSFs as a key step in overall planning of strategic information systems.[13] In this research the author defines a nine step process for IS planning, incorporating CSF identification and use as a major step in that process. Important in this research is the idea of cross-responsibility for CSF achievement, i.e., since all CSFs are critical to success, the executive management should organize in such a way that everyone has an interest in and a dependency on the success of the others.

5. Developing a dual look at CSFs.[14] In this research the authors stress the importance of using the CSF identification process to identify major causes of project failure and then rank these major causes by relative value. This is in addition to identifying the major requirements for project success.

6. Using CSFs to evaluate effectiveness of existing information systems.[15] This research investigates the use of CSFs to evaluate the effectiveness of existing IS systems based on the degree to which critical items of information needed for success are provided by the system management reports.

7. Comparative analysis of the differences between CSF management approaches and process management approaches, and the advantages of the CSF approach.[16] The author's view is that if the inquirer wants to know what management is, then the process view should be studied. However, if one wants to know why selected organizations are successful in highly competitive environments, then one must study the three critical success factors of (1) corporate strategies, (2) human resources, and (3) operational systems. His conclusion is that the truly successful companies deal with these three CSFs differently from the way they are dealt with in other companies.

It is logical to conclude that success in software development is a function of the effective management of technology and people; no big surprise. To incorporate the CSF identification process, and use the information to better manage the risks and determine the direction for continuous improvement, all within the context of overall project and company success, is an approach designed for maximizing potential success where the benefit of TQM is supported by a formal

CSF identification methodology. The beauty is that the CSF/TQM methodology can be applied to software engineering processes just as easily as any other management and development process. It can be applied to the software development processes, as well as to support processes such as Configuration Management, Software Test, and Quality Evaluation.

10.5 CONCLUSION

Software TQM methods are diverse, ever changing, and as dependent on a given software engineering environment as anything else. But achieving software TQM is not just the application of a set of tools, methods, or motivational campaigns. It is hard work. It is instituting a cultural change. It is changing the way people think and work. It is effecting a change from which there is no turning back. We have all seen our shares of fiascos. A tragedy occurs when we haven't learned from the fiasco.[17] One of the most evident signs of a lack of TQM is when the program office of either the government or the contractor begins to grow. It signals an out of control condition. It means no management, and no management control.

There are a variety of methods available, today, to achieve software TQM. A few have been noted here. Others are being introduced daily by the more progressive companies. Find out who the leaders are, and then emulate, do not just follow.

References

1. Humphrey, Watts S. and Sweet, W. L., "A Method for Assessing the Software Engineering Capability of Contractors," *Technical Report CMU/SEI-87-TR-23, ESD-TR-87-186,* Carnegie-Mellon University, Software Engineering Institute, Pittsburgh, Pa., Sept. 1987.
2. Fagan, M. E., "Design and Code Inspections to Reduce Errors in Software," *IBM Systems Journal,* Jul. 1976.
3. McCabe, T. J., "Structured Testing: A Software Testing Methodology Using the Cyclomatic Complexity Metric," U.S. Department of Commerce, National Bureau of Standards (now the National Institute of Science and Technology), Department of Computer Science and Technology, *NBS Special Publication 500-99,* Dec. 1982.
4. Dobbins, J. H., "Critical Success Fctors in Government Program Management," Defense Systems Management College, *Research Report DSMC-SET-01-91-0001,* DSMC, DRI, Ft. Belvoir, Va. 22660, Jan. 1991.
5. Rockart, J. F., "Chief Executives Define Their Own Data Needs," *Harvard Business Review,* Mar.-Apr. 1979, Vol. 57, No. 2, p. 81.
6. Bullen, Christine V. and Rockart, J. F., "A Primer On Critical Success Factors," MIT Sloan School of Management, *CISR WP No. 69,* Sloan WP No. 1220-81, Jun. 1981.
7. Rockart, J. F., *op. cit.,* pp. 81-93.
8. *Ibid,* p. 85.
9. Dobbins, J. H., *op. cit.*
10. Shank, M. E., Boynton, A. C., and Zmud, R. W., "Critical Success Factor Analysis as a Methodology for MIS Planning," *MIS Quarterly,* Jun. 1985, pp. 121-129.
11. Pinto, J. K. and Prescott, J. E., "Variations in Critical Success Factors Over the Stages in the Project Life Cycle," *Journal of Management,* Vol. 14, No. 1, 1988, pp. 5-18.

12. Zahedi, F., "Reliability of Information Systems Based on the Critical Success Factors—Formulation," *MIS Quarterly,* Jun. 1987, pp. 187-203.
13. Jenster, P. V., "Using Critical Success Factors in Planning," *Long Range Planning,* Vol. 20, Aug. 1987, pp. 102-109.
14. Walsh, J. J. and Kanter, J., "Toward More Successful Project Management," *Journal of Systems Management,* Jan. 1988, pp. 16-21.
15. Bergeron, F. and Begin, C., "The Use of Critical Success Factors in Evaluation of Information Systems: A Case Study," *Journal of Management Information Systems,* Spring 1989, Vol. 5, No. 4, pp. 111-124.
16. Chung, K. H., *Management: Critical Success Factors,* Newton, MA: Allyn and Bacon, Inc., 1987.
17. Humphrey, Watts S., *Managing the Software Process,* Reading, MA: Addison-Wesley, 1989.

11

Software Testing Methods for TQM

Anthony F. Shumskas

11.1 INTRODUCTION

In today's rapidly changing environment, and faced with increasing fiscal constraints, it is imperative that Total Quality Management (TQM) principles be used to improve the performance of the acquisition process and the resultant product quality. Further, as systems become increasingly complex and dependent on computer and software technologies to fulfill customer requirements, it is essential that TQM principles be applied to improve software test and evaluation (T&E). Correspondingly, it is essential that software T&E provide appropriate information to support continuous acquisition process and product improvements. With this software dependence increase, fundamental issues arise which impact the T&E strategy for software-intensive systems:

1. What is production-representative or production software?
2. What are the software impacts on dedicated system test readiness?
3. How should software impacts be considered in the certification process for dedicated tests?
4. What are the retest/recertification requirements associated with software changes/modifications?

To answer these questions, software T&E must be considered within the overall TQM and system T&E framework. As software-intensive systems continue to dominate modern commercial and defense system applications, software T&E will play an ever expanding role in overall system T&E planning and execution. Accordingly, it is imperative that the T&E community have an understanding of how software T&E and total quality management impact the following areas:

1. Software T&E planning and execution. Specifically, the T&E program must be structured to be efficient and cost-effective, while providing the: necessary quantitative evidence of software maturity and readiness for use (measurement); feedback necessary for process and product improvement; and evaluation that supports management's decisions.
2. The certification of system readiness for dedicated test and evaluation. In particular, definitions for production-representative or production software-intensive systems must be considered, as well as their relationship to certification of readiness for and conduct of dedicated T&E.
3. The T&E community's role for frequently modified software. This includes modifications during the development process and the subsequent software upgrades that many systems undergo during production and fielding, sometimes annually.

11.2 SOFTWARE T&E AND TQM RELATIONSHIPS

The T&E community has preached for years that quality software-intensive systems result from: (1) expressing realistic requirements for both the contractor and customer (operational user); (2) a cost effective, relevant, timely, and balanced test process that quantitatively demonstrates the achievement of performance requirements; and (3) a valid evaluation and assessment process that provides the basis for current performance and a predictive basis for system success or failure. The point being that T&E offers the TQM community precisely the quality-first, customer driven, people-oriented approach required to meet today's unprecedented process and product challenges.

Inherent in TQM is the notion that all acquisition functions can profit from a total commitment to continuous process improvement. Certainly, software T&E has room for improvement. To do so, requires adapting TQM principles to the acquisition process and to software T&E's role within that process.

As TQM becomes increasingly institutionalized within commercial and defense development and/or acquisition processes, it is important to recognize that the TQM philosophy is equally applicable to the system's hardware and software elements. However, it must be understood that TQM leverage areas are different for hardware and software, thereby influencing T&E planning and execution. While the TQM philosophy is the same for all system elements, applying TQM to software-intensive systems requires a different perspective in order to instill and maintain management's commitment to continuous improvement.

Total quality management takes a total life-cycle view of system development and production (Figure 11-1). Material, labor, and overhead dominate life-cycle

Percent of Influence

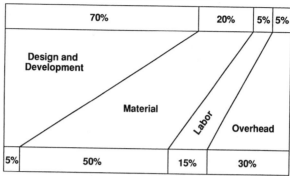

Percent of Product Cost

FIGURE 11-1. TQM leverage areas.

costs for production programs. However, design and development influences life-cycle costs the most, while only accounting for the smallest percentage of life-cycle product cost. Many of today's Total Quality Management practitioners, across the full product/process spectrum, while not ignoring design and development, concentrate on improvement in the material (production), labor (also production related), and overhead aspects. This, in part, may be due to the background of many of today's senior managers and their familiarity with hardware manufacturing.

While this perspective is valid for the hardware elements of the finished product, it must be noted that it is not applicable for the system's software elements. For example, software production costs are basically negligible when compared to hardware production costs. In fact, the major element of software production costs is the cost associated with the hardware, i.e., electronic media (disks, read-only-memory, etc.) used to deliver software to the user.

While software is different, it does not mean that software is not manageable. A product's software can benefit from total quality management when software versus hardware differences are recognized and understood, and when management makes a conscious decision to pro-actively manage and improve all process and product elements associated with providing quality products to their customers. This positive management action will improve their competitive advantage within either the commercial or defense sectors.

Applying Total Quality Management's total life-cycle perspective to the system's software elements, while recognizing the differences associated with the software life-cycle, presents a different set of considerations and process areas for exploitation in achieving continuous improvement (Figure 11-2). For example, there is a direct correlation between effort expended and product costs, with no significant impact on the relative percentages. However, effort expended directly acknowledges the labor intensive activities associated with software development, operations, and maintenance.

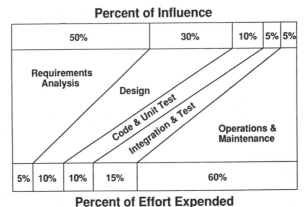

FIGURE 11-2. Software TQM leverage areas.

It is easily recognized that four of the leverage areas, requirements analysis, design, code and unit test, and integration and test, are directly associated with the software development process. Therefore, one could say that while operations and maintenance clearly dominate software's total life-cycle effort, development is the predominant influence on life-cycle effort.

An understanding of activities taking place during software operations and maintenance can further clarify the "true" software leverage areas. During operations and maintenance, the typical functions performed are: (1) identification and correction of previously existent errors, faults, or failures which were undetected during either initial development and test or maintenance and test; (2) modifications to improve system performance without adding new performance capabilities, e.g., changes to account for system hardware enhancements or shortfalls, or to improve user interfaces; and (3) enhancements to add new performance capabilities. All these are just different forms of software development activities.

Recognizing that software operations and maintenance is just another form of software development, it is possible to improve software's total-life cycle costs and product quality by concentrating on improving software development activities and applying development process improvements to the operations and maintenance phase. This has three benefits: (1) improving the software development process should result in higher quality software that meets the user's needs in the operational environment; (2) higher quality software should require less maintenance to correct previously existent errors, faults, and failures; and (3) improving the software maintenance (development) process should also produce higher quality software that meets the user's needs with reduced errors, faults, and failures.

Applying total quality management techniques to the software development phase identifies a further refined set of process activities for analysis and improvement (Figure 11-3). As used here, "definition" includes requirements analysis; "design" is the application of software engineering discipline to translate the requirements into a detailed "blueprint" that meets the requirements; "develop-

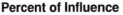

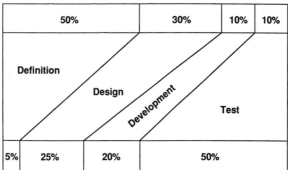

FIGURE 11-3. Software development TQM leverage areas.

ment" is the code ("manufacture") and integration of the software components into a functional, quality software product; "test" is the full gamut of activities associated with evaluating the software's quality and performance levels from the unit level to the integrated, final product; and "pre-production" costs could be from either initial development or specific software maintenance (development) activities. Again, there is a dichotomy, for while definition has the largest influence on software cost, test, apparently, is the single largest opportunity for cost reduction.

The adequacy in defining software requirements, the degree of software engineering discipline applied to the design during development, and the quality of the development process all directly influence the extent and nature of software test planning, execution, and evaluation. These interrelationships are important, especially in developing and maintaining today's software-intensive systems, where there is an up-front emphasis on designing-in quality, instead of testing quality into the product just prior to customer delivery.

The commitment to TQM seeks to satisfy cross-functional goals of quality, cost, schedule, customer need and suitability. It concentrates on three types of evaluation measures: process, product, and behavioral change measurements. Process measurements track process performance with respect to the customer's requirements, both internal and external, and to manage and evaluate products and services. Project measurements provide insight into the overall improvement process. Behavioral change measurements provide observable, consistent evidence that TQM is being supported and is working. Software T&E must effectively use similar measures to improve the software T&E process and provide credible information for improving the system acquisition process and products.

To acquire these measures, TQM invokes a set of generic tools (Figure 11-4) that excludes T&E. So the dilemma presented is—Should T&E embrace TQM or vice versa? Actually, the answer is both. This is especially true when dealing with today's software-intensive systems.

To examine the roles of TQM and software T&E, it is necessary to incorporate

- BENCHMARKING
- CONCURRENT ENGINEERING
- DESIGN OF EXPERIMENTS
- TEAM BUILDING
- QUALITY FUNCTION DEPLOYMENT
- TIME MANAGEMENT

- CAUSE AND EFFECT DIAGRAMS
- COST OF QUALITY
- INPUT/OUTPUT ANALYSIS
- NOMINAL GROUP TECHNIQUE
- STATISTICAL PROCESS CONTROL
- WORK FLOW ANALYSIS

FIGURE 11-4. Typical TQM performance tools. (Note the absence of test and evaluation.)

both of these into a system perspective for acquisition systems. This requires examination of: software T&E's role in system T&E; the role of T&E in TQM, from both software and system perspectives, to support continuous process and product improvement; and the application of TQM techniques to improve the effectiveness and efficiency of software T&E.

11.3 SOFTWARE T&E'S ROLE IN SYSTEM T&E

System T&E is not an end unto itself. Rather, it is a crucial, synergistic, and pivotal element that must maintain a balance between changing customer expectations and documenting credible, trustworthy results to support acquisition decisions. This balanced strategy provides the basis for real "value added" to the acquisition process. Tests should not be conducted to define quality, but rather as a modus operandi for verifying the achievement of required quality levels. Continuous evaluation, beginning early in the development cycle, should be used to analyze interim test results to ensure that the products are on a maturity path that will achieve the end goal: quality systems that meet user requirements.

T&E is a continuum of activities interwoven within the acquisition process. Software T&E activities do not fit into rigid or discrete compartments; they range from component or subsystem level concerns to broad, system-level concerns. Those engaged in system acquisition need to understand the relationship of software T&E interests that are vitally needed to support the acquisition process. The software T&E's role in determining when to model and when to simulate must be better understood. Additionally, software T&E plays a key role in assuring that models and simulations are operationally verifiable and analytically flexible. In short, software T&E's purpose is to articulate, from a software engineering perspective, an accurate and trustworthy performance evaluation of a system's ability to satisfy a customer's need.

Software engineering institutionalizes active incorporation of engineering discipline into the software development process. Current software engineering environments provide for the addition of an "object-oriented" to the traditional "top-down" approach for requirements definition and implementation. This enhances the T&E process by producing quantitative, objective requirements and performance levels that can be measured and verified through test, analysis and evaluation.

Government, professional, international, and industry software standards define a management structure, not a technical structure, for software acquisition and support. These standards produced a foundation for implementing viable evaluation techniques. Capitalizing on existing policy and standards, the T&E community can incorporate software reliability, test, and evaluation into system T&E planning. This, in turn, causes the system's development agency and customer to begin identifying specific software related performance objectives in a system's context and the measures of merit that are to be used to verify achievement of these objectives. This is a direct application of TQM principles by the software T&E community to encourage process improvements in requirements definition, analysis, and allocation through a combination of feedback and T&E process improvements.

11.4 APPLYING T&E TO TQM

To examine the role of T&E in the overall TQM approach, consider what T&E provides to TQM. T&E provides the management foundation for obtaining and assessing the truth about a systems performance in support of the decision making process. It promotes objectivity in the evaluation process by balancing point estimates and growth assessments to obtain evidence of system maturity. Through a series of checks and balances, it adds documented, verifiable discipline to the acquisition process. Lastly, the T&E process supports the acquisition process by providing a sufficient amount of information to support procurement decisions.

Effective software T&E requires three basic elements: (1) discipline and knowledge of the process and products; (2) requirements definition and understanding; and (3) attributes that can be measured throughout the system's life cycle to verify requirement's satisfaction.

Software T&E has a pivotal role in the development process. Under or over testing, and similar incomplete or exhaustive assessments, hamper T&E's utility and effectiveness in making timely management decisions. Test results and (product and process) evaluations must be fed back to the development community for process and/or product quality improvement, as well as, to identify ways to more effectively use resources.

The first step is to determine where you are and where you are trying to go. This is accomplished by analyzing the system's test results and product evaluations for feedback to the development community for process and/or product quality improvement. It also involves a frank assessment of the current T&E process to identify more effective ways to use test assets.

This is followed by T&E participating in the system engineering process. T&E's goal is to assist in refining the development process, particularly with respect to changes that drive modifications to testable attributes and performance characteristics. Additionally, for T&E to remain viable, it must focus its endeavors on quality efforts that produce a balanced approach to test and evaluation. An approach that recognizes the need to improve test resource utilization in light of current limitations, but continues to provide realistic and trustworthy test results to support decision makers.

Finally, a balance between expectations and resource limitations must be achieved. This requires the T&E community to develop a culture that fosters an attitude of testing smarter and not necessarily testing more. Most importantly, this balance must continue to provide trustworthy and customer relevant results, be they factual or predictive. The T&E community will have failed if it evades methodical verification of technical and operational performance only to have the customer use test data to reach a conclusion of less-than-adequate system performance.

T&E planning's key challenge is to be the Monday-morning quarterback on Saturday morning. Being able to predict tomorrow's areas of technical, development or test risk requires much attention. This is particularly important when many system requirements reflect mature "end-point" performance levels, whereas evolutionary acquisitions with interim system configurations and performance thresholds can provide a road map to system maturity. To be effective, a balanced T&E program must permit engineers to extrapolate from current technical performance (conceptual quality) levels the likelihood of achieving mature operational performance (fieldable quality).

The ability of the software T&E community to predict success or failure is directly related to another fundamental TQM element, the ability to define and use measures. Software measurement initiatives directly impact our ability to test and evaluate software. While domestic software measurement has not reached a mature state of practice, the Japanese have committed themselves to software measurement with some very interesting positive results. These include the reduction of test by up to 35%, with a corresponding increase in test effectiveness.[1]

Software measurement approaches range from relational trend indicators to specific metrics. Indicators, though not absolute, use a combination of planning goals and trend data to enhance the evaluation process and provide status assessment tools. Indicators provide the development community with management tools for immediate use and also produced data for metric calibration by the research community. The Institute of Electrical and Electronics Engineers (IEEE) adopted this approach in their *Guide For The Use of Standard Dictionary of Measures to Produce Reliable Software.*

These activities contributed to improving the software requirements process by providing mechanisms for defining quantitative software technical and operational characteristics and thresholds for incorporation into the system characteristics and thresholds. Software T&E advocates use this foundation to implement measurement and evaluation techniques to meet management requirements. This enhances the ability to define test requirements and resources at both the system and software levels and leads to the development of quantitative techniques for measuring success. These initiatives are contributing to the establishment of quantifiable measures that permit confidence building and traceability throughout the software life cycle.

Through the synergistic effects of these initiatives, it is now possible to significantly improve the reliability of software intensive systems, while reducing the amount (cost) of testing and improving test efficiency. This is achieved by effectively applying the concepts of TQM to the software development, test, and evaluation processes to obtain the full benefits of T&E.

Software T&E is serious business, particularly since it is difficult to find threads of operational realism in results derived from myriad laboratory, subsystem, or component research driven test environments. By itself, improving the quality of testing is a challenge, but along with credible evaluation results it can become increasingly difficult to achieve. This same challenge is also experienced in trying to obtain effective, efficient T&E planning and execution. T&E program quality is an intrinsic issue with serious resource implications for the development process. A T&E program that exhibits high quality is likely to possess credible results useful to the senior decision-makers.

11.5 SOFTWARE T&E PLANNING AND EXECUTION

What is required to provide a level of understanding sufficient to meet today's complex software T&E challenges? The answer was provided almost a hundred years ago by the British physicist Lord Kelvin. In 1891, he stated, "When you measure what you are speaking about and express it in numbers, you know something about it. But, when you cannot measure it, when you cannot express it in numbers, your knowledge is a meager and unsatisfactory kind. It may be the beginning of knowledge, but you have scarcely, in your thoughts, advanced to the stage of science." Software measures obtained through test are insufficient to resolve the software crisis. Test must be accompanied by application and effective use of (1) evaluation techniques to provide realism and meaning to the measurements and (2) management awareness and commitment to balance affordability and executability decisions with evaluation results. This strategy promotes development and fielding of software that will meet system requirements.

Software test, appropriately used, can lead to increased responsiveness and reliability of software-intensive systems. An evolutionary software development strategy that instills confidence in software products can be successfully realized through a phased implementation of existing test methodologies. This approach utilizes a combination of measurement, statistical process control, evaluation techniques, test methodologies and management principles throughout the acquisition process to enhance software productivity and reliability.

The approach is consistent with Total Quality Management (TQM) concepts and should significantly contribute to improving our competitive advantage in the software arena. By capitalizing on the TQM approach, i.e, by designing and building quality into software, test can contribute to reducing the introduction of errors into the software. Test also provides the foundation for using software evaluation techniques to prevent and/or reduce error introduction and to enhance the early identification and resolution of errors. In turn, an increase in overall software development efficiency is promoted by reducing the number of formal tests. Formal tests can be reduced through increased evaluation effectiveness fostered by better understanding of the development environment and system requirements, i.e., by testing smarter, not more, and by using quantifiable measures to support the evaluation process. The approach also contributes to the reduction in both acquisition and support costs by advocating a total life cycle approach to software development, including modification efforts after the system is fielded.

The road map to system maturity is based upon the concept of an "event driven" acquisition process, where decisions are supported by events and demonstrated or confirmed through T&E. When executed effectively, T&E can provide quantitative evidence of readiness to proceed forward and to successfully achieve the acquisition milestones. The interrelationship between system maturity and the acquisition decision process is one of the primary aspects of test planning. When complete, the test plan can be utilized as a control mechanism to evaluate the program's progress through the acquisition process (Figure 11-5). The test plan is a means to provide for discipline as well as management insight into the acquisition process, and totally supports TQM principles.

Effective software test planning and execution (Figure 11-6) focuses on four fundamental issues directly associated with TQM, expressed as follows:

1. Where are you now? Define the known system technical and performance baselines, and current status in the development process towards the next set of objectives and milestones.
2. Where are you trying to go? Define the technical and operational performance objectives of the development effort. State how these will be verified and define the criteria for "success."
3. How are you going to get there? Define the test and evaluation program content that will support risk control and fielding of viable software-intensive systems. Ensure that the T&E program provides quantitative information as evidence of system viability and for use in controlling risk.
4. How do you know when you're there? Define the measures of merit that will be used to validate achievement of performance and technical objectives.

Software T&E Planning

From a process perspective, the test plan identifies the management structure and strategy used for acquisition. From a product and process perspective, the test plan clearly defines the customer's requirements, translates them into measurable performance characteristics, or quality attributes, and specifies what type of data

THE TEST PLAN IS THE IDEAL APPROVAL DOCUMENT TO:
 • IDENTIFY MANAGEMENT CONTROL STRUCTURE
 • DEFINE CUSTOMER AND SYSTEM PERFORMANCE REQUIREMENTS
 • DELINEATE OPERATIONAL AND TECHNICAL PERFORMANCE CHARACTERISTICS
   (QUALITY ATTRIBUTES)
 • INTEGRATE DATA AVAILABILITY WITH THE SCHEDULE FOR:
   • MANAGEMENT DECISIONS
   • COST, SCHEDULE AND PERFORMANCE ASSESSMENTS
 • PROVIDE TREND DATA FOR SYSTEM MATURITY (QUALITY) ASSESSMENT

FIGURE 11-5. How the test plan supports TQM implementation.

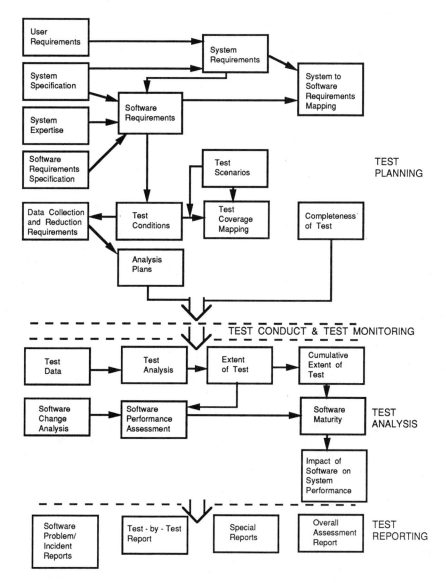

FIGURE 11-6. Software test and evaluation activities.

will be available to the decision making process and cost, schedule, and performance assessments.

From a product perspective, the test plan provides the trend data and assessment mechanisms necessary to evaluate system maturity (quality) as the process and product progress through the acquisition life cycle.

Testing alone will not satisfy our needs. The accompanying process of evaluating test results and determining the degree of achievement and satisfaction of both developmental and operational requirements is the final prerequisite for balanced, quality T&E to support continuous improvement in the acquisition process. The combined T&E program must also be structured and executed in a manner that is consistent with the acquisition strategy and the information needs of the decision makers throughout the acquisition process. This requires a systematic T&E program that is responsive, valid, and predictive.

Strategic software T&E planning identifies target areas for improvement. These targets may, for example, be in major test facility capabilities, test asset utilization, or in test strategy and policy. Whatever the target, the overall goal must be to improve test efficiency, effectiveness, and usefulness.

Among the dominant causes for high error rates are incomplete, or misunderstood, knowledge of requirements (especially derived requirements) and improper implementation of the requirements, i.e., requirements and design errors. Requirements errors can be reduced through a requirements analysis process that combines human verification and statistical evaluation, e.g., requirements definition, stability, completeness, to refine/define system objectives (requirements, including derived requirements) to a level of understanding compatible with the functional criticality of the software.

Process evaluation techniques, e.g., resource utilization rates, development and test status, and cost/schedule deviations, can be used to identify early critical software design features and/or functions that require a combination of increased management attention to prevent error introduction and/or increased test emphasis to ensure critical error detection. Product evaluation techniques, e.g., error or failure rates, ratio of correct outputs to total outputs, test coverage, test sufficiency, and documentation indexes, can be similarly used during T&E activities, beginning during requirements analysis, to ensure that any existing critical errors are detected. This also provides management insight into the degree of success associated with the error/failure prevention techniques being employed. The combination of error prevention and early detection (identification) also supports the identification and development of required test scenarios that exercise the software in ways that are truly representative of the user's environment.

A key ingredient in obtaining highly reliable software is discipline. Commitment to using TQM methods to improve both process and products is but one aspect of the required discipline. Another, often overlooked, aspect is effective management control of stated and derived requirements creep during the development effort. Requirements baselining to obtain a verified, reliable software product is essential to reducing the risks of inserting additional requirements. This is the essence of evolutionary software acquisition, i.e., to build upon existing capabilities to add enhanced capabilities.

Given that requirements are properly defined through the requirements analysis process, test and evaluation personnel can adequately define a "stress" test scenario to ensure that software products are tested and evaluated in a user representative environment. This, in turn, will result in increased software reliability, but not error free software.

Test techniques applied to the proposed user environment, combined with defined requirements and system criticality, can be used to determine which software components need T&E emphasis throughout the development process. By combining statistical techniques with engineering discipline techniques, software error introduction, during requirements analysis, design, and coding activities, can be reduced. For example, by applying mathematical proofs of correctness for software algorithms and verification and validation techniques, the industry average of 50 to 60 errors per thousand lines of code has been reduced to less than 10 errors per thousand lines of code, the current average for delivered software.[2]

Early and increased use of test techniques to improve requirements analysis, definition, and implementation does not come without additional up-front costs. The additional costs typically range between 5 to 12% above the traditional costs of these activities. While the additional cost can be considered relatively small, the reduction in total development cost can be substantial. Studies by Murine[3] have shown that the following benefits are achievable as a direct result of increased application of test techniques: (1) 33 to 35% reduction in development costs; (2) approximately 50% reduction in test cost; and (3) a 50% reduction in the documentation needed to define the specifications, with a corresponding increase in specification readability and understandability.

In conjunction with requirements definition and analysis difficulties lies the perplexities of defining test attributes that provide measures of requirement achievement. This dilemma often results in the use of test, not to verify the achievement of performance levels, but rather to define "acceptable" performance levels. The early and continued use of balanced T&E methodologies can result in identifying specific measures of merit, attributes, and associated performance thresholds to be achieved during the software development process.

Effective and productive test attributes must meet three criteria: (1) be consistent and quantifiable, preferably objective, measures; (2) be usable for articulation of requirements and subsequent evaluation of actual capabilities; and (3) provide traceability, or audit of maturity, throughout the life-cycle.

Candidate attributes are also found in DOD-STDs 2167A and 2168, the various service software indicator pamphlets, and IEEE standards and guides. These candidates meet the prerequisite criteria for effective and productive attributes. They are, however, by no means complete, nor should a given T&E program use all of them. To be effective, management must make conscious decisions to identify, implement, and use attributes that contribute to the primary objective of developing a software-intensive system that meets defined performance and customer requirements. Blind use of all available attributes only devotes too many resources to data collection and analysis without a commensurate return on investment.

No matter what the fidelity or extent of T&E envisioned, poor planning and execution and incomplete or useless test data will diminish the perceived contribution of T&E to the acquisition process. Throughout the T&E period of performance, the basic thrust ought to be checking the hypothetical against the actual. Emphasis needs to be placed on checking the essential realism, veracity, and value of the test, not just its plausibility (Figure 11-7).

WHAT IS QUALITY TEST AND EVALUATION?

AN EFFECTIVE, EFFICIENT BALANCE OF:

- COMPLEMENTARY TESTING
  - COMPONENT
  - SUBSYSTEM
- GROWTH TESTING
  - MODELS & SIMULATIONS
  - ENVIRONMENT
- COMPLIANCE TESTING
  - STRESS TESTS
  - OPERATIONAL TEST

WITH THE GOAL OF PROVIDING:

- SUBSTANTIATED EVALUATIONS
- UNBIASED ASSESSMENTS

FIGURE 11-7. Quality software T&E components and goals.

Software T&E Execution

Test execution is composed of three basic elements: test conduct and test monitoring; test analysis, or evaluation; and test reporting, or feedback to the development process. For successful TQM, test activities must have and effectively use: evaluation tools for improving the ability to assess development status and product quality; measurement and test tools throughout the development process to promote the early identification of errors; and the early and continual application of test and evaluation practices to compliment error prevention methodologies. This combination of practices and viable implementation procedures augments the TQM process by providing quantifiable measures that permit confidence building and traceability throughout the system's life cycle and forms the basis for an evolutionary software development, acquisition, and T&E strategy. Software test execution must be consistent with TQM concepts to contribute to improving the developer's competitive advantage.

T&E is conducted throughout the various phases of the development process to ensure acquisition and fielding of an effective and supportable system by providing feedback to the engineering process to verify compliance with requirements. This includes compliance with technical performance specifications, supportability, suitability, and operational effectiveness objectives. Feedback is essential not only to the development community, but is key in promoting customer acceptance. This is particularly evident in the "high tech" arena where technology solutions are procured before customer requirements have been solidified.

There is an old saying that those who fail to learn from the past are doomed to repeat it. As systems become increasingly complex, with the continued increase in competition for scarce national resources, the T&E challenge is to ensure that the execution of planned tests will adequately "test and stress" the sought-after system. This will provide sufficient, quality results necessary to equip evaluators engaged in the decision making process. As we approach the twenty-first century, it is likely that testing will evolve into computer based assessments of projected performance. Consequently, software T&E must be able to validate the simulators so that test results and evaluations can be truly representative and predictive of system performance, not just that of the simulator. This anticipated growth in the use of models and simulations, which we are just starting to see today, is a prime example of the continuing need for feedback and improvement.

When failures occur, test result analysis plays a key role in turning "failure" into "success." It is a success only if analysis identifies what went wrong, helps in the correction process, and verifies that the fix cures the problem. Remember, when there is a test failure, it's not the test that failed, but the system under test. The test was a "success" in that it caught a previously undetected discrepancy.

11.6 CERTIFICATION AND DEDICATED TEST & EVALUATION

Test environment fidelity influences test thoroughness and product quality determinations. Sufficient tests must be conducted in an adequately representative target system environment to demonstrate the correct implementation of software specifications and requirements. Further, it is essential that the test demonstrate the intended functional performance in the operational configuration at the system level. Software certification and dedicated test and evaluation involves:

a. Demonstrating compliance with system requirements under real user conditions. This can be accomplished by using either simulated, actual, or a combination of simulated and actual environmental and/or performance characteristics.
b. Demonstrating the system's ability to function in the presence of external disturbances and selected failure conditions.

Certification Requirements

The development activity should, as an integral part of their software process formally determine, i.e., certify, when a software-intensive system is ready for dedicated assessment by the T&E community. Additionally, the development activity should determine whether the system is production-representative, i.e., functionally equivalent to the production system, with on-going development effort to finalize the production configuration, or the production article. As part of the development activity's certification process, the development activity should certify that the system's software components:

1. For certification of a production-representative system:
   a. Have completed and passed Functional Qualification Test (FQT). FQT provides quantitative evidence that the system meets its functional requirements, and should be the final developing activity controlled test

event prior to dedicated T&E community conducted testing. Since additional errors, faults and failures may have been encountered during FQT, the T&E community should require that no FQT actions remain open and that all software changes required to correct system and/or software errors, faults, and failures have been implemented and appropriately retested.

b. Contain no software patches. A limited number of patches, the software equivalent of a hardware "white-wire," may be required due to preproduction hardware configurations that impact, but do not functionally limit system performance. While the T&E community recognizes this, they should strongly encourage the certified system to possess completely compiled software code.

c. Contain no customer requirement-unique software. The T&E community, in order to ensure test result and evaluation integrity, should not accept "different" software versions during dedicated testing. This inhibits the developing activity from "tailoring" software versions to specific test events. Accordingly, the certified system and its associated software components should be ready for test across the total operational requirements spectrum, with no software changes/updates required.

d. Have no open multisystem compatibility issues. Networked or system-of-systems interoperability and interdependence issues pose unique T&E challenges. Therefore, the T&E community should insist that system/system, system/platform, and total system integration be completed prior to initiating dedicated operational system test, with no software changes/updates required to address "unique" compatibility issues.

e. Are supportable. Part of the dedicated test should assess system supportability by typical system "maintainers." Without appropriate system documentation and training, the validity of any test and evaluation of system supportability would be suspect. Before beginning any supportability testing, required user and maintainer documentation should be correct and available. Training for operators and maintainers should be complete and should address issues in support of evolutionary systems.

f. Is compatible with existing fielded configurations for evolutionary systems. "Grand Designs" of software-intensive systems are widely recognized as a major contributor to the failure to provide quality software-intensive systems on time, within cost and schedule, and responsive to user requirements. To account for this, many development efforts are taking an "evolutionary" approach to fielding systems by building a "limited capability" system, with planned growth capabilities and related development activities, to capitalize on customer feedback, and to mature the system's performance over time. This requires the T&E community to consider upward and downward compatibility impacts with already deployed systems and, when required, to consider the customer's ability to independently and successfully incorporate new releases into their current system. The T&E community should require the developing activity to address the impact of new software releases on fielded configurations and their logistics support, including provisions for field/deployed upgrade and maintenance.

2. For certification of production systems, in addition to the above, the software-intensive system should have successfully passed all Production Qualification Test (PQT) requirements. The T&E community must insist, prior to initiating dedicated test and evaluation, that no open or additional software changes are required, and that all system failures, faults, or errors requiring software changes have been implemented and appropriately retested to insure the validity of previous test results.

Dedicated Test & Evaluation

Only those systems that are formally certified by the development activity as ready for dedicated test and evaluation will be tested. If, during the conduct of dedicated test and evaluation, it is determined by the T&E community that any of the appropriate (production-representative or production) certification requirements have not been met, dedicated test and evaluation should be immediately stopped. Dedicated test and evaluation should not be resumed until the development activity corrects the shortfalls and recertifies the system's readiness for dedicated test.

11.7 TEST REQUIREMENTS FOR SOFTWARE CHANGES AND UPDATES

System functional capability enhancements or discovery of additional failures, faults, or errors during test or operational service will often necessitate post-certification software changes. Such changes can lead to "secondary" software failures, faults, or errors, i.e., they were either not present or not detected, when the system was first certified or subjected to dedicated test and evaluation. Since testing detects the presence of errors, not their absence, careful consideration must be given to the verification/validation of the software changes and their impact on previous system certification and test and evaluation results. The primary focus must be to maintain the integrity of the system's performance evaluations.

In-depth analysis of the change(s) should be conducted to determine the scope of retest and any criticality level modifications. This effort should ensure the same level of confidence in the software after the change(s) as was achieved during the original certification and dedicated test and evaluation program. The analysis should, at a minimum, consider:

1. Software criticality level, including changes in level due to the change(s). If the change(s) increases the modified software's criticality to the achievement of required operational performance requirements or demands satisfaction of more stringent performance requirements, a more extensive retest/recertification effort may be required than was otherwise anticipated. High order language

(HOL) revisions to criticality levels 1, 2, and 3 software should require, at a minimum (analysis may dictate additional regression test requirements) retest of affected: (1) Computer Software Units (CSUs), (2) CSU interfaces, (3) Software interfaces at both Computer Software Component (CSC) and Computer Software Configuration Item (CSCI) levels, (4) Hardware/software interfaces, and (5) Portions of the total software system and related weapon system components affected by the change. Revisions to level 4 software may be implemented on the basis of analysis and/or retest provided the change(s) does not affect the criticality level.

2. Regardless of criticality level, all software changes involving assembly language(s), patches, or conditional compilations should require retest of all test cases and procedures used during initial certification and dedicated test and evaluation. While this may be an overly conservative approach, these types of software modifications have an increased likelihood of secondary failure, fault, or error introduction that necessitates additional retest rigor. Recognizing that these type of software modifications are often used to "react" during emergency situations, the T&E community, in conjunction with the development activity, should, at a minimum, determine the appropriate scope of regression testing to ensure that critical operational performance characteristics are maintained, prior to implementing the emergency software modification.

3. Software development and change implementation methodologies, to include:

    a. Technology maturity, including maturity of development and test tools, e.g., compilers, assemblers, linkers and link/loaders, debuggers, code analyzers, operating systems, and automated test and evaluation tools, including models and simulations.

    b. Development approach and history, to include:

        1. The degree of software engineering and language experience demonstrated by the development/change agent in designing and implementing software, including software changes, for the operational system. Lack of experience will normally increase the probability of the introduction and detection of additional software errors, thereby increasing the retest/recertification effort.

        2. Extent of a Computer Software Unit (CSU), Computer Software Component (CSC) and Computer Software Configuration Item (CSCI) independence. A high degree of interdependence, at any software level, may drive an increase in the requirements for retest/recertification.

        3. The developer/change agent's process level and maturity, as determined through the independent application of the Software Engineering Institute's methodology,* or similar methodology, for assessing the software engineering capability[4] of the development/change agent.

---

*Refer to Chapter 1 for a description of the Software Engineering Institute's Process Capability (sometimes referred to as Maturity) Model.

Changes implemented by a development/change agent with a process maturity level less than level 3 (as defined by the Software Engineering Institute's methodology) may require a more extensive retest/recertification effort than for a process level 3, or higher, development/change agent.

4. Software test and evaluation methodologies and history, to include: (1) Requirements testability, (2) Test completeness, (3) Test coverage, (4) Adequacy of test case(s) and procedure(s), and (5) Retest completeness.

c. Capacity and maturity of delivery and physical update processes. Retest/recertification effort may be adversely impacted if the software's delivery and physical update process is immature, i.e., on the beginning phases of the learning curve, or does not have the capacity to handle rapid or large changes. If this is the case, additional retest/recertification may be required following change implementation in the operational system. To ensure integrity of test and evaluation results, the following guidelines can be used to define test article configuration identification(s):

1. A software change not affecting the certification and/or operational test and evaluation basis or the software's functional interchangeability may be identified by a software status change on the outside of the unit and by a subpart number and/or stored software identification change of the memory device(s) affected.

2. A software change causing a change in the certification and/or operational test and evaluation basis or the software's functional noninterchangeability with previously deployed systems will require a new software part number and/or new stored software identification of the memory device(s) affected and also a new part number of the unit itself.

11.8 SUMMARY

Test is a crucial total quality management leverage area for continuous improvement of software-intensive systems. While it is inappropriate to test quality into systems, especially as the production decision approaches, establishing and enforcing prerequisites for test and evaluation can be a key motivator in ensuring application of engineering discipline to design and build quality software-intensive systems that are responsive to the customer's needs.

Quality software T&E is an effective, efficient balance of: complementary testing, at the component and subsystem levels; growth testing, model utilization, appropriate simulations and environment tests; and compliance stress and operational testing (Figure 11-8). Quality T&E's goal is to provide substantiated evaluations and unbiased assessments. Software development will have truly embraced TQM when *quality test and evaluation becomes synonymous with quality systems.*

Meanwhile, T&E must be an integral element of any effective TQM strategy. They are not mutually exclusive events. T&E must bring realism to the affordability, executability, and system performance/effectiveness assessments vital to acquisi-

- T&E IS AN INTEGRAL ELEMENT OF AN EFFECTIVE TQM STRATEGY
- TQM AND T&E ARE NOT ENDS ONTO THEMSELVES
- T&E MUST BE BALANCED AMONG REALISM, AFFORDABILITY AND EXECUTABILITY
- CREDIBLE SYSTEM PERFORMANCE/EFFECTIVENESS ASSESSMENTS ARE VITAL TO ACQUISITION AND DEVELOPMENT DECISIONS
- THERE ARE STILL TEST CHALLENGES TO BE ADDRESSED
  - MODEL/SIMULATION UTILIZATION AND PROLIFERATION
  - COUNTER MEASURES/THREAT REALISM

FIGURE 11-8. Software T&E success conditions.

tion decisions. Stated in another fashion, a quality-oriented strategy is predicated, at least in part, on the T&E community's ability to provide sufficient, substantive information to decision makers that promotes an affordable balance of the system's quality and cost.

Achieving balance between test and evaluation requires the application of management commitment. Any additional early expenditures will be more than offset by: (1) improved requirements definition and implementation; (2) error prevention and early detection/correction; and (3) a test program focused on verifying requirements achievement instead of establishing requirement specifications.

Test alone, is insufficient to resolve the software crisis. It must be accompanied by application and effective use of (1) evaluation techniques to provide realism and meaning to the measurements and (2) management awareness and commitment to balance affordability and executability decisions with evaluation results. This strategy promotes development and fielding of software that will meet system requirements.

DEFINITIONS

The following definitions are used in this chapter.

1. *Adequacy of test cases, test procedures (test inputs, expected results, evaluation criteria):* Test cases and test procedures should specify exactly what inputs to provide, what steps to follow, what outputs to expect, and what criteria to use in evaluating the outputs. If any of these elements are not specified, the test case or test procedure is inadequate. (Source: DOD-STD-2167A)[5]
2. *Adequate test coverage of requirements:* This criterion means that: (1) every specified requirement is addressed by at least one test, (2) test cases have been selected for both "average" and "boundary" situations, such as minimum and maximum values, (3) "stress" cases have been selected, such as excursion and out-of-bounds values, and (4) test cases that exercise combinations of different functions are included. (Source: DOD-STD-2167A)
3. *Certification:* For certification of readiness for operational test and evaluation, the DOD Component's developing agency shall formally certify that the system is ready for the dedicated phase of operational test and

evaluation to be conducted by the DOD Component operational test activity. (Source: DODI 5000.2)[6]

4. *Completeness of retesting:* Retesting consists of repeating a subset of the test cases and test procedures after software corrections have been made to correct problems found in previous testing. Retesting is considered complete if: (1) all test cases and test procedures that revealed problems in the previous testing have been repeated, their results recorded, and the results have met acceptance criteria, and (2) all test cases and test procedures that revealed no problems during the previous testing, but whose test functions are affected by the corrections, have been repeated, their results recorded, and the results have met acceptance criteria. (Source: DOD-STD-2167A)

5. *Completeness of testing:* Testing is complete if all test cases and all test procedures have been performed, all results have been recorded, and all acceptance criteria have been met. (Source: DOD-STD-2167A)

6. *Computer Software Component (CSC):* A distinct part of a computer software configuration item (CSCI). CSCs may be further decomposed into other CSCs and Computer Software Units (CSUs). (Source: DOD-STD-2167A)

7. *Computer Software Configuration Item (CSCI):* A configuration item for computer software. (Source: DOD-STD-2167A)

8. *Computer Software Unit (CSU):* An element specified in the design of a Computer Software Component (CSC) that is separately testable. (Source: DOD-STD-2167A)

9. *Formal Qualification Testing (FQT):* A process that allows the contracting agency to determine whether a configuration item complies with the allocated requirements for that item. (Source: DOD-STD-2167A)

10. *Level 1—Critical:* Functions for which the occurrrence of any failure condition or design error would: (1) prevent the accomplishment of an operational or mission essential capability specified in baselined requirements; (2) prevent the operator's accomplishment of an operational or mission essential capability; or (3) jeopardize personnel safety. (Sources: DOD-STD-2167A and DO-178A)[7]

11. *Level 2—Crucial:* Functions for which the occurence of any failure condition or design error, for which *no* alternative work-around solution is known, would adversely affect: (1) the accomplishment of an operational or mission essential capability specified by baselined requirements so as to degrade performance; or (2) the operator's accomplishment of an operational or mission essential capability specified by baselined requirements so as to degrade performance. (Sources: DOD-STD-2167A and DO-178A)

12. *Level 3—Essential:* Functions for which the occurrence of any failure condition or design error, for which *an* alternative work-around solution is known, would adversely affect: (1) the accomplishment of an operational or mission essential capability specified by baselined requirements so as to degrade performance; or (2) the operator's accomplishment of an operational or mission essential capability specified by baselined requirements so as to degrade performance. (Sources: DOD-STD-2167A and DO-178A)

13. *Level 4—Non-essential:* Functions for which failures or design errors could not effect required operational or mission essential capability and are an inconvenience to the operator. (Sources: DOD-STD-2167A and DO-178A)
14. *Testability of requirements:* A requirement is considered to be testable if an objective and feasible test can be designed to determine whether the requirement is met by the software. (Source: DOD-STD-2167A)

References

1. Sunazuka, T., Azuma, M., and Yamagishi, N., "Software Quality Assessment Technology," *Proceedings, International Conference on Software Engineering,* London, England, Aug. 1985.
2. Bush, M. W., "Software Product Assurance Section Activities," Jet Propulsion Laboratory, Mar. 1989.
3. Murine, G., "Role of Software Quality Metrics in DOD-STD-2167A," *Proceedings ASQC Western Regional Conference,* Feb. 1988.
4. CMU/SEI-87-TR-23, "A Method for Assessing the Software Engineering Capability of Contractors," Software Engineering Institute, Sep. 1987.
5. DOD-STD-2167A, *Defense System Software Development,* Feb. 29, 1988.
6. DOD Instruction DOD Instruction 5000.2, *Defense Acquisition Management Policies and Procedures,* Feb. 23, 1991.
7. RTCA/DO-178A, "Software Considerations in Airborne Systems and Equipment Certification," Radio Technical Commission for Aeronautics, Mar. 22, 1985.

General References

MIL-STD-480B, *Configuration Control—Engineering Changes, Deviations, and Waivers,* Jul. 15, 1988.

MIL-STD-483A, *Configuration Management Practices for Systems, Equipment, Munitions, and Computer Programs,* Jun. 4, 1985.

MIL-STD-1521B, *Technical Reviews and Audits for Systems, Equipments, and Computer Software,* Jun. 4, 1985.

DOD-STD-2168, *Defense System Software Quality Program,* Apr. 29, 1988.

IEEE Std 1044-1987, *A Standard Classification for Software Errors, Faults, and Failures,* Mar. 1987.

IEEE Std 982-1989, *Guide For The Use of Standard Dictionary of Measures To Produce Reliable Software,* Mar. 1989.

12

Quality Function Deployment (QFD) for Software: Structured Requirements Exploration*

Richard E. Zultner, CQE

*Zultner & Company**

12.1 INTRODUCTION

Quality Function Deployment (QFD) was developed over 20 years ago in Japan as an advanced quality system made up of an integrated set of quality tools and techniques to provide customer-driven products and services. In order to improve customer satisfaction by developing products and services that deliver more value, it was necessary to listen to the "voice of the customer" throughout the product development process. The tools and techniques of quality function deployment were developed and organized into a powerful framework by Dr. Yoji Akao, and other top Japanese quality experts. In recent years a number of leading North American firms have discovered this approach and are using it to improve their products, and their product development process.[1, 2, 3, 4]

Since 1982, leading Japanese organizations have been applying QFD to their software development efforts with impressive results.[5] Dr. Tadashi Yoshizawa was a pioneer in the application of QFD to software in Japan.[6] NEC IC Microcomputer Systems, which received a Deming Prize in 1987 for its world-class software quality efforts, is a world leader in applying QFD to software.[7] In 1989, a two-volume 360 page report was released by the Information Processing Promotion Industry Association to further the development of high quality software by Japanese firms through the use of QFD.[8] Since 1988, North American software organizations have begun to apply QFD to software.[9] Good results have been reported by leading firms such as AT&T Bell Laboratories.[10] DEC,[11, 12] Hewlett-Packard,[13, 14] IBM,[15]

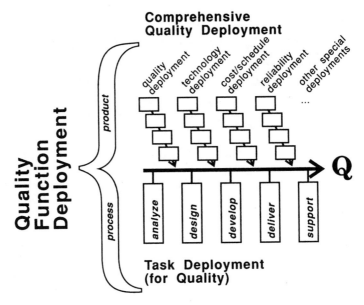

FIGURE 12-1. Comprehensive quality deployment.

Texas Instruments,[16] and others. QFD is fast becoming an essential part of Total Quality Management (TQM) for world-class software organizations.

QFD Structure

QFD, as developed in Japan, has a sophisticated structure with many specialized deployments (see Figure 12-1). QFD applies its tools and techniques to improving the product, and to the process of product development,[17] services,[18] and software.[19] The traditional starting place for QFD is the determination of customer requirements—quality deployment.

Quality Deployment

The Quality Deployment (QD) component of QFD has tools and techniques for the exploration and specification of customer requirements or "demanded quality." Once captured, the customer requirements are translated and deployed into technical requirements or "quality characteristics" in the A-1 or "House of Quality" matrix. This can be done at various levels of sophistication, ranging from four matrices,[20] to a dozen.[21] Products with multiple customers require a different starting point—a decision about who the customers are.

Customer Deployment

The Customer Deployment (CD) component of QFD is particularly important for software, as one software product must satisfy many types of customers. This

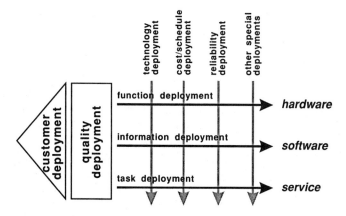

FIGURE 12-2. QFD deployments.

involves the determination of which types of customers the organization is trying to provide a product/service for. It precedes the determination of requirements in Quality Deployment (see Figure 12-2). You must first decide who your customers are before you can listen to their voices.

Complex Products

A special challenge exists for complex products/services—those involving a combination of hardware, software, and service, or those where nontrivial design decisions must be made at the system, subsystem, and component levels. Complex products/services require more than a handful of QFD matrices—and the matrices must be used with sophistication. Both "horizontal" and "vertical" deployments are required to handle this complexity (see Figure 12-2).[22]

Horizontal Deployments

There are three basic horizontal deployments that follow from the development of customer and technical requirements in Quality Deployment. Function Deployment (FD) drives the design of the hardware aspects of complex products/services. Often this involves determining the functions, mechanisms, and components for a hardware product, such as medical equipment. This is where value analysis enters into the QFD process. For hardware products, the technical capabilities must be deployed into functions. The functions are in turn deployed into mechanisms, components, and materials.[23] Information Deployment (ID) handles the information (or data-and-processing) aspects of a complex product/service. These aspects are not necessarily automated—but can be automated with software, such as patient records. For software intensive products and services, the technical capabilities must be deployed into data-and-processing—which is all that software does. Or in more modern software engineering language, *objects* with encapsulated data and methods. Task Deployment (TD) addresses the activities required to satisfy the customers, such as professional patient care. The task deployment component of QFD includes value analysis techniques (such as the quality systems diagram, and the quality activities table) to identify and make visible the key activities of the product development process for software and hardware applications. It also is central to the application of QFD to service businesses.

A combined example would be a training class—the training room environment and physical course materials would be developed via function deployment. The course content would be developed via information deployment. And the delivery approach would be developed with task deployment. Each deployment utilizes a particular set of analysis techniques and matrices.

Any and all of these deployments may be required for a complex product. This is where design occurs, and where the *hows*—precisely how the design will work, and how specific technologies will be applied—are decided. Design concept selection, reliability engineering, breakthrough engineering, and other approaches can be fruitfully employed here.

Vertical Deployments

The horizontal deployments may require addressing special concerns of the project or organization during design and development. Specialized "vertical" deployments exist to visibly deploy defined concerns across potentially all three horizontal deployments. Technology Deployment (TD) seeks to routinely deploy new technology or technical competencies in developing products/services. High-tech product/service organizations are keenly interested in leveraging their research and development strengths into new products and services. Cost/Schedule Deployment (CD/SD) sets cost/schedule targets and seeks the necessary reduction in cost/schedule to meet those targets. Cost reduction is often applied to hardware, where the costs of materials and manufacture dominate. For software and services, costs derive primarily from the labor hours expended, so schedule reduction is more appropriate. Reliability Deployment (RD) looks at failure modes and how to prevent or ameliorate the effects of failure.

The Seven New Tools

A special set of seven "new" tools (the 7 MP tools; also discussed in Chapter 2, Figure 2-1) for management and planning were developed for use with QFD and Hoshin Planning (see Figure 12-3).[24] Unlike the seven quality control tools (7 QC tools), these new tools work on language data and relationships.[25] The tools are: matrix data analysis charts (or prioritization matrices), affinity diagrams, relations diagrams (also known as interrelationship digraphs), hierarchy diagrams (also known as tree diagrams, or systematic diagrams), matrices (including tables), precedence diagrams (or arrow diagrams), and process decision program diagrams. These tools were developed to be used by improvement teams outside manufacturing.[26]

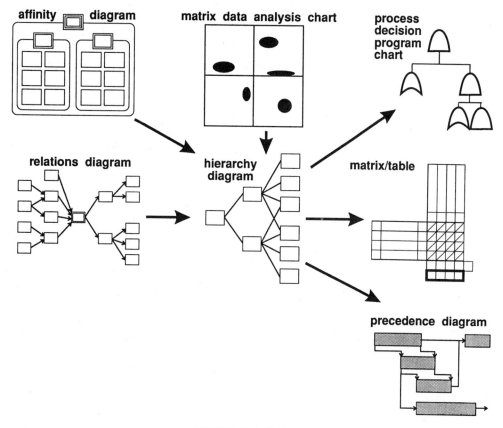

FIGURE 12-3. 7MP tools.

Application

In addition to managing the project, project resources must be focused on the high-value software elements (from the customer's perspective), in two ways: by improving the product, and by improving the process.[27]

Improve the Product

QFD contains tools and techniques aimed at improving the software product. Comprehensive quality deployment includes quality deployment, technology deployment, cost deployment, and reliability deployment.[28] It also can accommodate any special concern you face with a corresponding deployment—such as usability, reuse, or security, etc. QFD provides forward and backward traceability of value in the life cycle, and value is why customers want software. Leading software firms in Japan, including NEC IC Micon, began applying quality deployment to their software efforts a decade ago.

Improve the Development Process

QFD contains tools and techniques that apply to the process of software engineering—the "service" side of software. Task deployment is used to build quality activities into the software life cycle.[29] If your methodology is weak from a quality perspective, it could be strengthened and streamlined with this part of QFD. This half of QFD can be applied to a software development methodology in order to put QFD into the methodology—in effect, bootstrapping QFD into a software organization. In this way the methodology developers, having applied QFD to their product, the methodology, are only asking the developers to do what they ordinarily do. Many methodologies suggest the use of various quality tools and techniques—but these tools were not used by the methodologists in developing the methodology.

Improve the Strategy and Execution

The general approach of QFD, and the tools and techniques of QFD, can be applied to the strategic issues of software. Such an approach would concern itself not with the horizontal integration across functions (like QFD), but with the vertical alignment of organizational units with the strategic vision. This becomes a different quality system from QFD. Such a system for hoshin kanri ("strategic quality deployment," or, "quality policy deployment") has been developed in Japan and is known in North America as Hoshin Planning, or policy deployment. Such a system builds on a foundation similar to software value analysis[30] and information engineering,[31] but adds a very strong deployment (visible execution of strategic intent) capability for superb execution of strategy while avoiding the problems of traditional Management-by-Objective-type systems.[32, 33]

Many in Japan consider QFD to be the most powerful single system for quality. It is a mature, complex system, but offers great benefits once it is mastered. The learning curve for QFD is comparable to that of Structured Analysis or Information Engineering. The gains are equal if not greater than these traditional software engineering approaches.

12.2 COHERENT SOFTWARE DEVELOPMENT

QFD applied to software requires that we reexamine some fundamental concerns with respect to software development.

Traditional Development is Incoherent

Traditional development is unfocused with respect to quality. The best analyzed requirements are not the best designed. The best designed elements are not the best coded. The best code is not the best documented. It is only by chance that the best efforts of one phase receive the best efforts of a subsequent phase. Traditional development does not focus best efforts any more than an incandescent light bulb focuses it's rays—it is incoherent (see Figure 12-4). Incoherent processes are

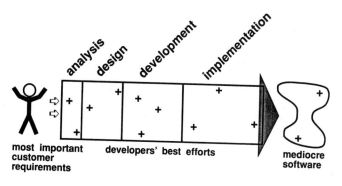

FIGURE 12-4. Incoherent development process.

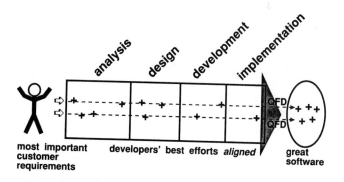

FIGURE 12-5. Coherent development process.

inefficient and expensive ways to satisfy customers, often forcing trade-offs of quality for schedule or resources.

A Coherent Approach with QFD

In order to satisfy the customer within the schedule and resource constraints that all projects face, it is necessary to concentrate our best efforts on those things of greatest importance to the customer. It is necessary for each activity of the development process to be in step, or coherent. Light waves from a laser are in step so they reinforce each other to produce a narrow beam of intense, high energy light. The efforts of all developers on a project must reinforce each other to deliver superb software. To do this requires that during analysis we obtain the customer's priorities for their requirements and pass this on to the next phase in a visible way. Each subsequent phase must direct the developer's best efforts to the high-priority items, and continue to pass the priority information on to the next phase (see Figure 12-5).

12.3 ZERO DEFECTS ISN'T GOOD ENOUGH

Traditional Quality Systems

An organized approach to quality with tools, techniques, and a set of methods is a quality system. QFD is quite different from traditional quality systems, such as Statistical Process Control (SPC), which aims at the minimizing of negative quality. With these systems the best you can get is zero defects, which is not good enough. In addition to minimizing defects, we must also maximize positive quality (see Figure 12-6). Just because there is nothing wrong with the software does not mean there is anything right with it from the customer's perspective.

Statistical Process Control (SPC)

A process in statistical control is stable and delivers consistent (predictable) performance, and can be improved by analyzing and then changing the process. A process that is not in control exhibits no consistent performance. The resulting variation may be so wide that no one could tell if a change improved the process or not. Therefore, first get the process in control (stable with consistent performance), then improve the capability of the process, i.e., the level of performance. In any team whose work is in (statistical) control, half will always be below average. It is those outside the control limits that management must attend to. Basic training in analytic statistics is as essential for quality, as a solid understanding of the structured tools and techniques is for software engineering. Three important areas for thinking statistically are testing, purchasing, and improving software development.

It is essential for software organizations to collect, properly interpret, and improve via metrics.[34] It is necessary, but not sufficient for the software development process to be in a state of statistical process control. That only means it is stable, predictable, and capable of improvement. It does not necessarily mean we can satisfy the customer with it. We must have, as an integral part of the development process, a quality system to assure customer satisfaction. In addition to statistical process control, which helps us to avoid dissatisfying the customer, we must use quality function deployment, which helps us to satisfy and delight the

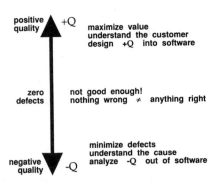

FIGURE 12-6. Quality continuum.

customer. We must understand what is valuable to the customer, and deploy that understanding of value throughout the entire software development life cycle. Such value deployment is at the heart of QFD and it allows us to hear the "voice of the customer" more clearly.

Modern Quality Systems

In the past, most software engineering efforts have concentrated on minimizing customer dissatisfaction from systems development. The focus was on detecting and correcting defects by walkthroughs and testing.[35] With the addition of error cause removal, traditional quality approaches have sought to prevent defects by process improvement. These approaches seek to minimize customers' complaints (negative quality). It is necessary, but not sufficient to prevent, detect, and correct defects. That's not enough, because the absence of negatives (defects) only makes a system less bad (i.e., not dissatisfying), not good.[36]

Quality Function Deployment (QFD)

Customer-centered software development concentrates on maximizing customer satisfaction from the software engineering process. The focus is on preventing dissatisfaction by a deeper understanding of the customer's wants and needs. And then deploying these expectations downstream in order to design value into the system, while continuously working to stabilize, improve, and innovate the software engineering products and processes. This approach strives to maximize the customers' compliments (positive quality). Only strong positives can make a system so good customers boast about it—the true test of delighting customers.

As customers typically cannot provide us with all the exciting and expected requirements, it is the responsibility of the analyst to ask *why* until we have understood at a fundamental level the problems and opportunities of the customer. We must know *why* they do what they do, *why* do they have the problems they do, and *why not* for their opportunities. Only by getting close to the customer, and understanding why they are asking for what they are asking for can a complete set of requirements be confidently prepared. Perhaps the fact the few customers find their software excitingly satisfying suggests that there is room for improvement in many analysis techniques and methodologies.[37]

12.4 EXPLORING REQUIREMENTS FOR CUSTOMER DELIGHT

There are a number of pioneering software engineering efforts to explore customer requirements[38] and quantify customer needs.[39] These advances can be best harnessed in a complete quality system that deploys the *voice of the customer*— what they value, their objectives—throughout the software life cycle.

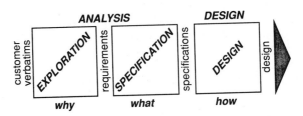

FIGURE 12-7. Understand the customer.

Specification

The first phase of a system development project must be to understand not only what the customers want and need but why (see Figure 12-7). Traditionally software projects have begun with a "concept" phase where the developers decide the type of system they will build. Or they just begin with "specifications" and seek to simply record what the customer wants. This approach assumes that the customer has previously analyzed their problems and opportunities and can articulate them clearly to analysis.

To satisfy customers, we must understand their objectives. Objectives define *what must change* for tomorrow and *why.* Stimulus-response/behavior modeling approaches using events or objects define well *what will be the same* as today—which objectives do not handle well. Events and objects also offer an additional perspective to ask about problems, opportunities, and strategic direction—the source of objectives—and refine the answers into objectives. But events and objects do not focus on the business future, merely on what is essential. We must understand what the business should be—not just what it is now, or simply what it can be. Objects and events do not deal directly with the *purpose* of the business area to be supported. Mere examination of the current system does not yield all the data and processes necessary to seize new business opportunities with the proposed system.[40] It is objectives that define the "new" events and "new" objects the proposed system supports—and *why.* Objects and events are necessary, but not enough. They must be complimented by objectives. The value of a new or enhanced system to a customer depends on what additional objectives it can help them achieve. That is what customers consider great software.

Exploration

What is required to build great software is an exploration phase. A phase of exploring with the customers on a cross-functional team what the problems are—and why the problems exist. Of understanding what the opportunities are—and why the opportunities exist. The purpose of the exploration phase is to gain an understanding of the customer's stated wants and needs, and to uncover additional unstated wants and needs based on an analysis of context. The nature and magnitude of the problems and opportunities must be understood in order to establish the priorities. With this knowledge, a specification phase can then analyze and detail the requirements. Without this knowledge, a purpose-less and value-less specification results.

12.5 THE SOFTWARE "HOUSE OF QUALITY"

There are two ways to identify types of customers. Matrix data analysis charts, employing multivariate techniques such as factor analysis, cluster analysis, or conjoint analysis provide a quantitative way to identify customer segments if the required amounts of data are available. A simple matrix identifying characteristics of customers can provide a simpler, alternative approach that works well even with small amounts of data.

QFD for simple products and services may start with "customer requirements," or "demanded quality." For complex products and services, the customer requirements of users, buyers, and other stakeholders must be considered. As complex products and services often must serve many types of customers, it is necessary to clearly understand exactly who the customers are, what requirements they have, and to what extent. Types of customers must be identified, and the requirements of each type determined and prioritized, *before* beginning work on the A-1/House of Quality matrix.

Listening to the Voice of the Customer

What QFD does is to provide a system to convey requirements from raw customer expressions to the proposed logical data and process models, and beyond, so that nothing is lost. From the most tentative expression of a want or need by a customer, to a delivered feature in an installed system, the customer's voice must be heard and deployed. This deployment—a rigorous, clear communication of requirements—defines and preserves the value the customer has for proposed system capabilities. To define objectives involves four distinct steps.[41]

1. Capture: To be able to deliver a satisfying system to customers, we must start with the capture of raw customer expressions. What are their problems, their opportunities, their strategic directions? Whatever the customer wants or needs to do about these concerns, becomes an objective. This requires listening very carefully and rigorously to the "voice of the customer."[42] What is required is to maximize the "native" listening in order to get true requirements undistorted by preconceptions.
2. Translation. These raw customer expressions are carefully translated into clear, concise, and concrete objective-items. Each item—in the general form of verb-qualifier-object—is supported with a thorough narrative (one-half to three pages) that captures the source, details, calculations, and priorities for each item. The customer must agree with the final translated item and supporting narrative.
3. Organization. Once translated, the items must be arranged in a hierarchy that is meaningful to the customer. Affinity diagrams and relations diagrams (a.k.a.

"mind maps," or interrelationship digraphs) may be used to create the hierarchy.[43] The preliminary hierarchy is then represented in a tree-like diagram—the Hierarchy Diagram. Each customer requirement item (or objective) is supported by narrative. This is a diagram that some CASE tools now support.

4. Prioritization. The customer requirements can be prioritized with a simple 1–5 scale, as was originally done in Japan. Recent Japanese advances on the mathematical foundations of QFD show a trend toward the use of the Analytic Hierarchy Process (AHP) in QFD.[44] The AHP requires slightly more effort, but provides superior accuracy of results along with consistency checking and sensitivity analysis.[45] This method employs pairwise comparisons on hierarchicly organized elements to produce a very accurate set of priorities. Developed over 20 years ago in North America, AHP as been used in a wide variety of settings to establish priorities and improve the accuracy of decision making.[46, 47] Further, the calculations required can be carried out by a spreadsheet, or through the use of available. AHP software.

In working through these definition steps, it is necessary to recognize and define each type of requirement as it is encountered.

Customer Requirements

Sources of Requirements
There are direct, indirect, and historical sources of customer requirements. Direct sources are interviewing and observation. Indirect sources are mail and phone surveys. Historical sources are complaints and compliments on prior products and services.

Types of Requirements
To satisfy customers, we must understand how meeting their requirements affects satisfaction. There are three types of requirements to attend (see Figure 12-8).[48]

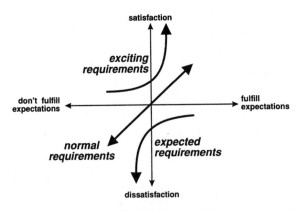

FIGURE 12-8. Kano model.

Normal Requirements

One difficulty with some analysis approaches is that they only ask customers what they want. The easiest requirements to uncover in this way are the normal requirements. These requirements satisfy (or dissatisfy) in proportion to their presence (or absence) in the delivered system. Swiftness of operation is an example for some customers. The faster (or slower) the software is, the better they like (or dislike) it. Only for these wants is satisfaction linear and bi-directional.

Expected Requirements

In order to avoid disappointing customers, we must deliver on expectations so basic they might not be stated. Many customers find it difficult to think of (or articulate) these expected requirements. Their presence in the system meets expectations, but does not satisfy customers. Their absence, however, is very dissatisfying. On-line help is an example for some customers. Since customers assume it, they may not think to mention it. They may even be unaware a system could possibly be delivered without it. Meeting expected requirements goes unnoticed by most customers. Not meeting them is disastrous for customer satisfaction. Expected requirements are *musts* that must be met.

Exciting Requirements

The most difficult requirements to uncover are those that are unexpected—or beyond the customer's expectations—yet are highly satisfying when delivered. The absence of these exciting requirements does not dissatisfy because they are not expected. The presence of "wow, it even does this . . ." features can succeed in satisfying customers so well they boast about their software. Customers have a hard enough time articulating just their expectations (normal requirements), much less anything beyond that (exciting requirements). A fully-integrated multimedia windowing environment is exciting (at least for some customers). A truly successful system delivers at least a few wows.

Voiced Requirements

The 7MP tools of QFD handle language data and allow it to be organized and refined (see Figure 12-3). Customer requirements are organized using the "KJ method" to produce an affinity diagram. This is to surface the "deep structure" that the customer has for the requirements.

Unvoiced Requirements

Unstated requirements may be uncovered by "going to the gemba"—the place where your product/service adds value for the customer—and observing with your own five senses the context of product/service use. These observations can be organized in a customer context table. Such static context analysis techniques are an extension of existing problem analysis approaches. Additional unvoiced requirements may be uncovered by dynamic context analysis using any of the four types of relations diagrams, also known as interrelationship digraphs.[49] This tool allows for the discovery of significant requirements which no customer may have mentioned. Exciting and expected requirements are frequently found this way.

Combined Requirements

The final result is a hierarchy diagram (also known as a tree diagram) with all significant customer requirements. A three-level hierarchy works well even for very complex products/services. The tertiary level requirements may be defined as the whys—why the customer would value our product/service.

Customer Requirements/
Technical Requirements Matrix

The software characteristics and capabilities necessary to support the customer requirements must be determined. These technical requirements must be identified and organized into a hierarchy. They are then carefully related to the customer requirements they support. The customer requirements/technical requirements matrix (also known as the A-1b matrix) supports this (see Figure 12-9). In Figure 12-10, an ideal distribution is filled in as an example. The following six steps would guide one through each element to be filled in for the sample A-1b House of Quality matrix.

1. Enter customer requirements and priorities. The customer requirements and priorities are determined and entered. The priorities may be determined in a prior matrix, or directly at this point with the Analytic Hierarchy Process (AHP). For each selected customer requirement, the verbatim expressions of customer problems, opportunities, aesthetic, and lifestyle concerns are gathered by interviews, surveys, team analysis sessions, focus groups, trouble reports, problem logs, suggestions, and compliments for existing products/services. These expressions are sorted and refined into clear, concise statements of customer expectations on a customer voice table. This preliminary sorting drastically reduces the tendency to go into an A-1/House of Quality with items which are not true customer requirements.

2. Identify technical requirements. The technical requirements are generated for each customer requirement.

3. Determine contributions. The degree to which each technical requirement contributes toward the satisfaction of each customer requirement is entered in the cells. The upper left hand (unshaded) triangles hold this (unweighted) contribution value.

4. Calculate coverage. Before simply accepting the technical requirements as listed, it is wise to examine the "coverage" of the technical requirements against the customer requirements. The upper left hand (unshaded) triangle values are summed by rows, and normalized for a simple measure of requirements coverage. The high priority customer requirements should receive coverage proportional to their priority. If this is not the case, it may be wise to seek additional technical requirements for the most important customer requirements.

5. Calculate (unweighted) results. In order to see if the customer requirement priorities have been accurately deployed, it is necessary to compare the unweighted technical requirement weights with the weighted results. The

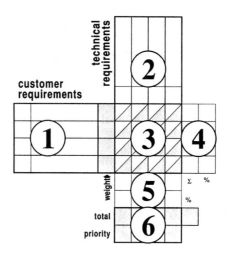

FIGURE 12-9. Customer requirements/technical requirements (A-1b) matrix.

House of Quality/A-1b: ideal (benchmark) distribution

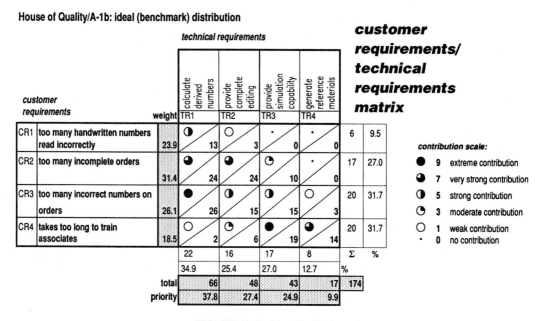

FIGURE 12-10. Idea distribution.

upper left hand (unshaded) triangle values are summed on the left side by rows and normalized to get the weights of the requirements without the effect of the customer segment priorities. The flap may be removed after checking.

6. Calculate final (weighted) results. The lower right hand (shaded) triangle values are summed on the far right side by rows to get the weights of the requirements with the effect of the customer segment priorities. The effect of

the customer segment priorities should be reflected in the difference between the weighted and unweighted figures. Due to a consistent use of ratio scales, the requirement weights will already be normalized—and therefore the intervals and ratios between the results are accurate indications of relative importance.

Symbols

In filling in the degree of contribution, the use of traditional Japanese symbols is widespread. But these symbols have no intuitive meaning for most nonJapanese. It is desirable for an international symbol set to be used that offers greater intuitive understanding and a more accurate visual perception of importance (see Figure 12-11).

Other desirable characteristics for the QFD symbols are to provide an accurate "visual response surface" on the matrix. That is, the visual symbol density should correspond to the weight of the symbol. With the traditional Japanese symbols, the triangle is visually heavier than the open circle—the opposite of their mathematical meaning. In addition, the symbol set should be reasonably extensible. The traditional scale of 1,3,9 limits accuracy at the point of input. At least the practitioner should have the option of finer distinctions if they feel they can make judgements that precisely. The international symbols can even be extended to the intermediate even numbers.

Distribution

The customer requirement priority is then multiplied by the cell value divided by the scale maximum (which is 9 in North America), and this weighted contribution value entered in the lower right hand (shaded) triangles. The use of ideal distribution, instead of the traditional independent distribution, provides easier to interpret weighted contribution values, and identical final priorities. The weighted cell values are also now scale independent, and would be the same in North America or Japan. The weighted cell values (or global priorities) are benchmarked against the scale maximum.

Japan	U.S.	Int'l	Value	Meaning
	◎	●	9	extreme contribution
		◕	7	very strong contribution
◎		◐	5	strong contribution
○	○	◔	3	moderate contribution
△	△	○	1	weak contribution

FIGURE 12-11. QFD matrix symbols.

Technical Requirements

The technical requirements are implementation-free statements of what must be provided in the product/service to satisfy the customer requirements. They are best described as *the whats*—what the product/service must do to satisfy the customer requirements. Their target values indicate the level of performance required when the technical requirements are implemented.

Technical Characteristics

There are two types of technical requirements. Technical characteristics are attributes of the product, and are not deployable into functions, information, or tasks. These technical characteristics are used later by the designer in selecting design concepts for the product/service.

Technical Capabilities

The second type of technical requirements are technical capabilities. These capabilities are deployable into functions, information, or tasks. Their target values indicate the level of performance required by any design implementing the functions, information, or tasks.

As the technical requirements are free of any assumed or presumed implementation technology, it is not appropriate in analysis to look for conflict using a roof (as is common in hardware QFD) until much later (in design). During design, the designers may construct a hardware QFD-like roof on the House of Quality. It is perhaps more important that they understand not only that a conflict exists, but the *cause* of the conflict—which is what any design must actually address.

The central role of the A-1b/House of Quality matrix is that it is the point of connection between the *whys* of the customer—stated in their terms, describing their problems and opportunities—and the *whats* of the software engineer—stated in technical terms, but free of implementation details. This provides us with a clear understanding of what we must do to satisfy the customer, without prejudging how to do it (which will be decided by the designer in the design phase).

12.6 QUALITY DEPLOYMENT FOR SOFTWARE

To deploy the voice of the customer throughout the software development process, it is necessary to employ a chain of matrices (see Figure 12-12).

Customer Segments/Customer Requirements Matrix

Once the customer segments, or types of customers have been defined, the requirements must be gathered from each type of customer. The requirements are then used in the customer segments/customer requirements matrix (also known as the Z-1 matrix) to understand precisely which segments value which require-

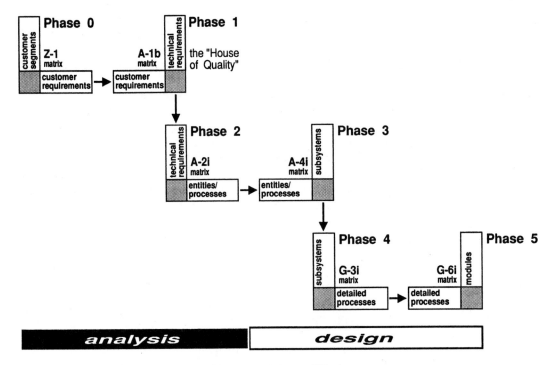

FIGURE 12-12. Software QFD phases.

ments, and to what extent. This final weight is then deployed to the A-1/House of Quality matrix.

Customer Requirements/Technical Requirements Matrix

The product/service characteristics and capabilities necessary to support the customer requirements must be determined. These technical requirements must be identified and organized into a hierarchy. They are then carefully related to the customer requirements they support. The customer requirements/technical requirements matrix (also known as the A-1b matrix) supports this.

Technical Requirements/ Entities-and-Processes Matrix

Once the technical requirements have been defined, the requirements must be gathered from each type of customer. The requirements are then used in the customer segments/customer requirements matrix (also known as the A-2 matrix) to understand precisely which entities and processes support provide which technical requirements, and to what extent. This final weight is then deployed to the A-1/House of Quality matrix. The usual sequence is as follows:

- Entities-and-Processes/Subsystems Matrix. The product/service characteristics and and capabilities necessary to support the customer requirements must be determined. These technical requirements must be identified and organized into a hierarchy. They are then carefully related to the customer requirements they support. The entities-and-processes/subsystems matrix (also known as the A-4 matrix) supports this.
- Subsystems/Detailed Processes Matrix. Once the customer segments have been defined, the requirements must be gathered from each type of customer. The requirements are then used in the subsystems/detailed processes matrix (also known as the G-3 matrix) to understand precisely which segments value which requirements, and to what extent.
- Detailed Processes/Modules Matrix. The product/service characteristics and capabilities necessary to support the customer requirements must be determined. These technical requirements must be identified and organized into a hierarchy. They are then carefully related to the customer requirements they support. The detailed processes/modules matrix (also known as the G-6 matrix) supports this.

12.7 THE VALUE CHAIN

This chapter has secondarily touched on some recent developments in North American QFD research and applications. Among them are:

- Standardized Format. A benefit of standardization for the QFD process is reuse of a standard format for all QFD matrices and tables. Using the figures in this chapter as an example, there are only four components needed to assemble any QFD matrix or table: (1) the hierarchy or list of tertiary items, (2) the priority and targeted values, (3) the cells, and optionally (4) the matrix "flaps" to check coverage and unweighted vs. weighted results. In addition to handling all matrices and tables in all deployments, new and customized matrices and tables can easily be assembled with these four simple components.
- Fundamental Structure. Beyond the basics presented here, there is Comprehensive QFD (see Figure 12-1). In CQFD there is a pattern of matrix-table-matrix for customer and quality deployment. This pattern can continue through all QFD deployments. The mini-matrix method used in this chapter works with a series of streamlined, smaller-than-traditional matrices, each focused on a single purpose. For the newcomer to QFD, this offers an easier set of smaller steps to achieve initial QFD benefits more rapidly. For the experienced practitioner, it offers the power to construct an efficient set of relevant matrices custom-fitted to their project.
- Weight Deployment. There are several "paths" through the sophisticated structure of QFD as it has evolved over two decades in Japan. The primary

path is that which deploys *value* from one aspect of QFD, such as customer requirements, to another, such as technical requirements. This value deployment, or "weight deployment" in Japanese terms, is central to the delivery of value to the customer in order to delight them. And it is this unique contribution of QFD to the development of products and services that yields major benefits. The precise sequence of the additional matrices (and table) that go beyond the basic sequence presented here depends on the nature of the software development process and the concern of the software organization. Each horizontal and vertical deployment (see Figure 12-2) may have its own chain of matrices, interlocking with the basic sequence presented here.

- Defined Entries. A key element to the successful use of QFD is the need for each entry in each matrix to be understood in the same way by all team members. This requires definitions for each customer segment, each customer requirement, and so on. These definitions can be placed in a data dictionary, or repository, just like similar supporting definitions for structured analysis and information engineering.

- Target Values. The setting of target values quantifies the capabilities required to satisfy the customer. This gives designers a clear target to shoot for. If the target values can be satisfied, the customer should be satisfied. This is where designed experiments and Taguchi methods enter the QFD process.[50]

- Target Value Deployment. Just as the matrices transfer (or deploy) value from one QFD dimension to the next, there are tables in the QFD process that visibly define and deploy the target values for customer segments, customer requirements, technical requirements. and so on, throughout the software development process. These tables allow an organization to address any number of special concerns in an integrated way for a particular project. A full treatment of these tables is beyond the scope of this chapter.

12.8 CONCLUSION

A basic introduction was presented for applying Quality Function Deployment (QFD) to complex products and services with multiple types of customers—software. This approach has been tested on several project teams tackling high-tech software-intensive products. Although results to date are very promising, further refinement is still occurring. The author encourages anyone with insights, questions, or critiques to contact him, and assist in the continuous improvement of QFD in theory and practice.

ACKNOWLEDGEMENTS

I would like to thank my clients and their project teams for the chance to test and refine the ideas presented in this chapter. I would like to thank my *senseis:* Dr. Yoji Akao, Tadashi Ofuji, Satoshi Nakui, Bob King, Kurt Hofmeister, and many others. And I would especially like to thank my consulting colleagues in Europe, North America, and Japan for their penetrating questions and systematic insights.

References

1. Sullivan, Lawrence P., 1986, "Quality Function Deployment," *Quality Progress* 19(6)(June):39-50.
2. Hauser, John R., and Clausing, Don, 1988, "The House of Quality," *Harvard Business Review* 66(3)(May-June):63-73.
3. King, Bob, 1989, *Better Designs in Half the Time: Implementing QFD Quality Function Deployment in America,* 3rd ed., Methuen, MA:GOAL/QPC.
4. Bossert, James L., 1991, *Quality Function Deployment: A Practitioner's Approach,* Milwaukee, WI: ASQS Quality Press.
5. Aizawa, S., et. al., 1982, "General Purpose Wave Form Analysis Program Development," (In Japanese) *Quality Control 33,* special issue (November):360-366. Tokyo: Japan Union of Scientists and Engineers.
6. Yoshizawa, Tadashi, et. al., 1985, "Software Quality Deployment and Supporting Systems," (In Japanese) In *27th Research Conference Transactions,* 1-9. Tokyo: Japan Society for Quality Control.
7. *NEC IC Micon Deming Prize Application* (In Japanese). Kawasaki City, Japan: NEC IC Microcomputer Systems Company, 1987.
8. *High Quality Software Production through Quality Function Deployment* (In Japanese). Tokyo, Japan: Information Processing Promotion Industry Association. ISBN 4-87566-084-7, 1989.
9. Zultner, Richard E. "Software Quality Deployment," In *GOAL/QPC 5th Annual Conference Proceedings.* Boston, MA: GOAL/QPC, 1988.
10. Thompson, Diane M. M., and Fallah, M. Hosein, 1989, "A Systematic Approach to Product Definition," In *A Symposium on QFD Transactions,* 279-285. Novi, MI: ASI, ASQC, and GOAL/QPC.
11. Cohen, Louis, 1988, "Quality Function Deployment," *National Productivity Review* 36(2)(Summer):197-208.
12. Thackeray, Ray J., and Van Treeck, George, "QFD for Embedded Systems and Software Product Development," In *GOAL/QPC 6th Annual Conference Proceedings.* Boston, MA: GOAL/QPC, 1989.
13. Shaikh, Khushroobanu I., "Thrill Your Customer, Be a Winner," In *A Symposium on QFD Transactions,* 289-303. Novi, MI: ASI, ASQC, and GOAL/QPC, 1989.
14. Betts, MaryAnn, "QFD Integrated with Software Engineering," In *2nd Symposium on QFD Transactions,* 442-459. Novi, MI: ASI, ASQC, and GOAL/QPC, 1990.
15. Sharkey, Allen I., "Generalized Approach for Adapting QFD for Software," In *3rd Symposium on QFD Transactions,* 380-416. Novi, MI: ASI and GOAL/QPC, 1991.
16. Moseley, Jan, and Worley, Jim, "Using QFD to Gather Customer Requirements for Products that Support Software Engineering Improvement," In *3rd Symposium on QFD Transactions,* 244-251. Novi, MI: ASI and GOAL/QPC, 1991.
17. Akao, Yoji, ed., *Quality Function Deployment: Integrating Customer Requirements into Product Design.* Translated by Glenn Mazur. Cambridge, MA: Productivity Press, 1990.
18. Akao, Yoji, "Recent Aspects of QFD on Service Industry in Japan," In *ICQC 89 Conference Proceedings,* pp. 18-26. Buenos Aires: Argentine Institute for Quality Control, 1989.
19. Zultner, Richard E., "Software Quality Deployment: Applying QFD to Software," In *2nd Symposium on QFD Transactions,* pp. 132-149. Novi, MI: ASI, ASQC, and GOAL/QPC, 1990.

20. Sullivan, Lawrence P., 1986, "Quality Function Deployment," *Quality Progress* 19(6)(June):39-50.

21. King, Bob, *Better Designs in Half the Time: Implementing QFD Quality Function Deployment in America.* 3rd ed. Methuen, MA: GOAL/QPC, 1989.

22. Zultner, Richard E., "Before the House: The Voices of the Customers in QFD," In *3rd Symposium on QFD Transactions,* pp. 450-464. Novi, MI: ASI and GOAL/QPC, 1991.

23. Snodgrass,Thomas J., and Kasi, Muthiah, *Function Analysis: Stepping Stones to Good Value.* Madison, WI: University of Wisconsin, Madison, 1986.

24. Mizuno, Shigeru, ed., *Management for Quality Improvement: The 7 New QC Tools.* Cambridge, MA: Productivity Press, 1988.

25. Brassard, Michael. *The Memory Jogger Plus.*™ Methuen, MA: GOAL/QPC, 1989.

26. Ozeki, Kazuo, and Asaka, Tetsuichi, *Handbook of Quality Tools: The Japanese Approach.* Cambridge, MA: Productivity Press, 1990.

27. Akao, Yoji, ed., *Quality Function Deployment: Integrating Customer Requirements into Product Design.* Translated by Glenn Mazur. Cambridge, MA: Productivity Press, 1990.

28. Zultner, Richard E., "Before the House: The Voices of the Customers in QFD," In *3rd Symposium on QFD Transactions,* pp. 450-464. Novi, MI: ASI and GOAL/QPC, 1991.

29. Akao, Yoji, "Recent Aspects of QFD on Service Industry in Japan," In *ICQC 89 Conference Proceedings,* pp. 18-26. Buenos Aires: Argentine Institute for Quality Control, 1989.

30. Curtice, Robert M., *Strategic Value Analysis.* Englewood Cliffs: Prentice-Hall, 1987.

31. Martin, James, *Information Engineering, Book II: Planning & Analysis.* Englewood Cliffs, NJ: Prentice Hall, 1990.

32. Deming, W. Edwards, *Out of the Crisis.* Cambridge, MA: MIT Center for Advanced Engineering Study, 1986.

33. Zultner, Richard E., 1991. "The Analytic Hierarchy Process in Total Quality Management," Presentation at the *2nd International Symposium on the Analytic Hierarchy Process.* Pittsburgh, PA: Joseph M. Katz Graduate School of Business, University of Pittsburgh.

34. Fenton, Norman E., *Software Metrics: A Rigorous Approach.* London: Chapman & Hall, 1991.

35. Yourdon, Edward, *Structured Walkthroughs.* 4th ed. Englewood Cliffs: Prentice-Hall, 1989.

36. Akao, Yoji, ed., *Quality Function Deployment: Integrating Customer Requirements into Product Design.* Translated by Glenn Mazur. Cambridge, MA: Productivity Press, 1990.

37. Zultner, Richard E., "Software Quality Deployment," In *GOAL/QPC 5th Annual Conference Proceedings.* Boston, MA: GOAL/QPC, 1988.

38. Gause, Donald C., and Weinberg, Gerald M., *Exploring Requirements: Quality Before Design.* New York: Dorset House, 1989.

39. Gilb, Tom, *Principles of Software Engineering Management.* Wokingham, England: Addison-Wesley, 1988.

40. Gane, Chris, and Sarson, Trish, *Structured Systems Analysis: Tools and Techniques.* New York: Improved System Technologies, 1977.

41. Zultner, Richard E., "Before the House: The Voices of the Customers in QFD," In *3rd Symposium on QFD Transactions,* pp. 450-464. Novi, MI: ASI and GOAL/QPC, 1991.

42. Hauser, John R., and Clausing, Don, 1988. "The House of Quality," *Harvard Business Review* 66(3)(May-June):63-73.

43. Brassard, Michael, *The Memory Jogger Plus.*™ Methuen, MA: GOAL/QPC, 1989.

44. Tone, Kaoru, and Manabe, Ryutaro, 1990. *Analytic Hierarchy Process Applications,* (In Japanese). Tokyo: Japan Union of Scientists and Engineers.
45. Zultner, Richard E., "The Analytic Hierarchy Process in Total Quality Management," Presentation at the *2nd International Symposium on the Analytic Hierarchy Process.* Pittsburgh, PA: Joseph M. Katz Graduate School of Business, University of Pittsburgh, 1991.
46. Saaty, Thomas L., *Decision Making For Leaders: The Analytic Hierarchy Process For Decisions in a Complex World,* rev. 2nd ed. Pittsburgh: RWS Publications, 1990.
47. Saaty, Thomas L., *The Analytic Hierarchy Process: Planning, Priority Setting, Resource Allocation,* rev. 2nd ed. Pittsburgh: RWS Publications, 1990.
48. Kano, Noriaki, Seraku, Nobuhiko, Takahashi, Fumio, and Tsuji, Shinichi, "Attractive and Normal Quality," (In Japanese) *Quality* 14(2)(February):39-48. Tokyo: Japan Society for Quality Control, 1984.
49. Mizuno, Shigeru, ed., *Management for Quality Improvement: The 7 New QC Tools.* Cambridge, MA: Productivity Press, 1988.
50. Ryan, Nancy E., ed., *Taguchi Methods and QFD: Hows and Whys for Management.* Dearborn, MI: American Supplier Institute, ASI Press (313) 336-8877, 1988.

13

Continuous Software Process Improvement*

Herb Krasner

President, Krasner Consulting

Continuous process improvement is the operative mechanism for change within a TQM Framework.

This chapter on the subject of continuous software process improvement is organized into six major sections that: (1) introduce and motivate the subject matter, (2) present an empirical basis of software process phenomena, (3) present the definitional process framework, (4) present the typical goal models for organizational software improvement programs, (5) introduce and describe the ASPIRE model of iterative improvement realization, (6) describe the emerging technology base and (7) conclude with observations on the future of such initiatives in the software industry.

13.1 INTRODUCTION

"If it ain't broke, don't fix it" is a popular U.S. management maxim used to refer to a lack of commitment to process improvement. In direct contrast to that belief is the notion of continuous process improvement, recently popularized as the Kaizen style of management. Many U.S. and International software companies are taking up the Kaizen banner because they believe that it is necessary in order to survive in the first changing world of high technology-based software business and to keep up with their competition.

Kaizen[14] is best defined as that cultural philosophy which actively empowers the employees of a company (individually and collectively) to make incremental and revolutionary changes to their processes that improves (in some definable way) the company's products and services and that ultimately contribute to

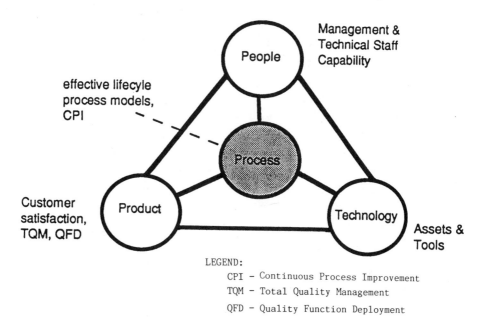

LEGEND:
CPI – Continuous Process Improvement
TQM – Total Quality Management
QFD – Quality Function Deployment

FIGURE 13-1. The process centric view of software development.

customer satisfaction. Management creates this culture by allowing active participation to occur. It is an inherently process-oriented (as opposed to strictly results-oriented) way of thinking about how people can do their jobs better. The Kaizen philosophy assumes that constant improvement is both desirable and necessary. In addition to overall results, a Kaizen manager will be interested in: disciplined methods, time management, development of worker skills, participation and involvement in decision making, morale, and effective communication.

In this chapter we take a process centered view of the software engineering enterprise. As seen in Figure 13-1, we recognize that this process centered view must capture the important aspects of the: people involved, the products produced, and the technologies used. The process view always emphasizes the how of such matters (e.g., how people interact, how products are delivered, and how are certain tools used) which exists within the context of organizational and project objectives and constraints.

From a systematic point of view, a process (in general) is concerned with the transformation of inputs into outputs so as to add value in line with the process objectives, and at the same time minimize entropy. The inputs are modified to put the product in a form that is fit for customer use and is available when and where needed. Behind every product development is a total set of processes which at that level comprise a larger process. Thus, total productivity is the sum of the productivity of each process. Because the process is the basic unit of productivity and quality, improvements are made at the process level.

As seen later in this chapter a process can be very broad or very narrow in scope. Our definition of process applies equally to large complex systems with many sub processes, such as a large information system development, as well as to the specific tasks in a development method.

The Relationship of Process Quality to Product Quality

Figure 13-2 pictorially describes the relationship between the quality of a resultant product and the process that produces that product. The term *product* describes both goods and services which are the result of one or more processes. Goods would include software, documentation, and other associated materials, while services include value-added activities such as maintenance, testing and evaluation, engineering analysis, secretarial support, information management, procurement, financial services, and customer support. Two potential improvement strategies are shown, one which focuses on improving the product by inspection and defect reporting techniques, and the other which focuses on improving the process that produced the flawed product. The latter is prevention oriented because it attacks the fundamental causes and mechanisms that introduce quality problems. In other disciplines, it has been shown that the process focused approach to improvement is less costly than the other approach.

Over the years, management strategies for quality control in the U.S. became very product focused. As a result, companies put in place elaborate and costly quality-control systems to ensure that the output met customer expectations. More recently, they began to realize that if the process that produces a product is good, the resulting product will, in turn, also be good. Watts Humphrey of the SEI asserts that "the quality of a software system is governed by the quality of the process used to develop and maintain it." An immature process is thus considered to be high risk and would likely have cost, schedule, and quality problems, whereas a mature process would have reasonably consistent results across projects with cost, schedule, and quality under control.

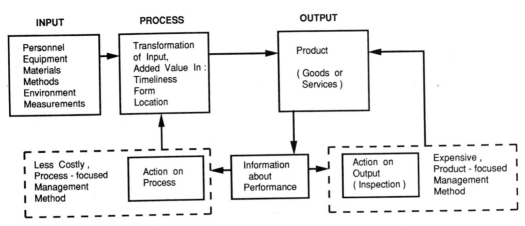

FIGURE 13-2. Good process leads to good product.

For example, if proper design contributes to the characteristics of a good reusable software component, we can, by monitoring and controlling this "design for reuse" process, obtain a good part. Conversely, if we fail to monitor and control this process, we will have to later inspect the component to the best of our ability and technology, and if the quality requirements are not met then initiate significant rework.

13.2 AN EMPIRICAL BASIS FOR PROCESS IMPROVEMENT

Previous studies[2] have demonstrated the substantial impact of behavioral (i.e., human and organizational) factors on software productivity and quality. To dramatically improve project outcomes, Weinberg (1971),[21] Curtis, Krasner, Shen and Iscoe (1987),[7] and DeMarco and Lister (1987)[9] argue that we must understand how human and organizational factors affect the execution of software development tasks. Software tools and practices conceived to aid individual activities have been disappointing because they have not provided benefits that scale up on large projects to overcome the impact of team and organizational factors that affect the design process.

In 1985-1987, the empirical studies team (Herb Krasner, Bill Curtis, Diane Walz, Neil Iscoe, Vincent Shen, Jeff Conklin, Raymonde Guindon and Nancy Pennington) of MCC's Design Process Group conducted three studies to gather process data on professionals' designing software systems in a range of situations. The first study used thinking aloud protocols in a controlled laboratory setting to study the cognitive processes of individual designers. The second study involved the observation, videotaping, and data collection of a design team of a medium-sized development project (8 to 10 persons) over several months in order to study team dynamics. The third study involved a field study of 17 large development projects in the MCC shareholder companies in order to study how the process of development is affected by organizational and project factors.

- Individual software engineers. In our study of individual, experienced software engineers working on the standard elevator control problem, we observed: the differences in design strategies and solutions, the ways in which many levels of abstraction and detail are worked at the same time, the ways in which designers understand and elaborate requirements through explorations of their mental model of the problem environment, and the discovery-oriented nature of their problem solving. Furthermore we identified seven sources of process breakdown.[11] Implications for the design of software technology to better support individual professional designers were generated.
- High performance team. In our longitudinal design team study[19,20] we observed the processes of group divergence and convergence about goals, processes, plans, issues, and system design. We saw that problems can arise in the accomplishment of a group task when individual team members hold conflicting assumptions, goals, beliefs, etc., which are not discussed and/or resolved. These conflicts can cause conflicting or incompatible system

components. Team members attempting to integrate various individual efforts may find difficulties/incompatibilities due to the differences in these underlying beliefs. The process of design by a team is an information pooling task and therefore difficulties in communication can be expected. The identification and characterization of design "inflection points" can lead to more effective management of the problem solving process in team design. Implications for software environments to support a high performance design team were developed.

- Large organizational projects. An extensive field study of 17 large software development projects (in 9 companies) attempted to describe the processes and mechanisms through which productivity and quality factors operate. These descriptions supported our need to understand how different tools, methods, practices, etc., actually affect the processes controlling software productivity and quality. We identified the key problem areas spanning the boundaries between project, organization, and external settings.[15] We identified problems in: the acquisition and dissemination of sufficient application knowledge, the effect of requirements change and uncertainty, the artificial barriers to software technology transfer, the dynamics of design evolution, and the special problems of government contract developments. We also identified and described project level phenomena related to multigroup communication breakdowns. Implications for software environment coordination technology to support large projects of remotely distributed teams were developed.

- Level to level observations. Across these three studies we observed how some process breakdowns occur, how some get solved, some get amplified, and how some new types occur as you go from individual to team to large projects and organizations. The mechanisms underlying the breakdowns at the individual level were the lack of knowledge about some important aspect of the design or limitations in human information processing and memory capacity. At the team and organizational levels these were still important precursors of many of the breakdowns observed, however, they were augmented by interpersonal and organizational processes to create the breakdowns in a multiperson, multigroup design effort. We have identified interpersonal mechanisms providing synthesis and integration that allow teams to compensate for individual limitations, e.g., boundary spanners. These are the communication mechanisms that provide for the coordination of mental models of the design and its process across a project staff. The processes of design integration and synthesis cannot be effectively translated into a software system unless coordination processes are effective.

One of our overall conclusions was that, since large software systems are still generated by humans rather than by machines, their creation must be analyzed and modeled as a collection of behavioral processes represented at several behavioral levels. As a result we created and defined the layered behavioral model presented in Figure 13-3.[6] This model emphasizes factors that affect psychological, social, and organizational processes, in an attempt to understand how they subsequently affect process effectiveness, productivity, and quality.

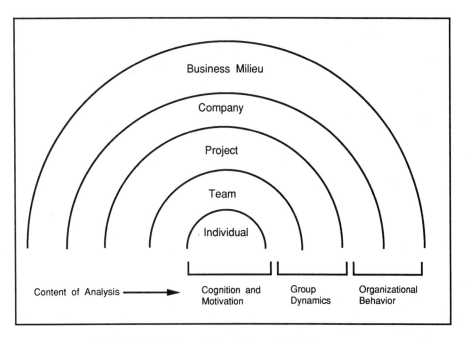

FIGURE 13-3. The layered behavioral model of software processes.

The layered behavioral model focuses on the behavior of those creating the artifact, rather than on the evolutionary behavior of the artifact through its development stages. At the individual level, software development is viewed as an intellectual task subject to the effects of cognitive and motivational processes. When the development task exceeds the capacity of a single software engineer, a team is convened, and social processes interact with cognitive and motivational processes in performing technical work. In larger projects, several teams must integrate their work on different parts of the system, and interteam group dynamics are added on top of intrateam group dynamics. Projects must be aligned with company goals and are affected by corporate politics, culture, and procedures, Thus, a project's behavior must be interpreted in the context of its corporate environment. Interaction with other corporations either as co-contractors or as customers introduces external influences from the broader business marketplace. The cumulative effects on software development can be represented in the layered behavioral model. The size and structure of the specific project determines how much influence each layer has on the development process.

The layered behavioral model encourages thinking about a software project as a system with multiple levels of process involved. This is orthogonal to traditional process models by presenting a cross-section of the behavior on a project during any selected development phase. Describing how software development problems affect processes at different behavioral levels indicates how these problems ripple through a project.

The layered behavioral model encourages software process engineers to extend their evaluation of software engineering practices from individuals to teams and projects to determine whether the aggregate individual-level impacts scale up to an impact on programming in the large, and to allow them to explore multiproject and organizational impacts on projects.

Through our studies we learned much about process problems in practice. Most significantly we observed significant process variation and differences in the situations and subsequent performance in which software was being developed, thus prohibiting totally general, silver bullet[4] solutions to process improvement.

13.3 A DEFINITIONAL FRAMEWORK FOR SOFTWARE PROCESSES

This section presents a definitional framework for software processes corresponding to the layered behavioral model articulated in the preceding section. This framework is meant to answer the question of exactly what software processes do we need to be concerned about in continuous process improvement.

In the following paragraphs, we define the terms of our framework and illustrate the definitions by posing relevant process improvement concerns at that level.

Definitions

- Software process. The collection of related activities, events, mechanisms, tasks, and/or procedures seen as a coherent process involved in the production and evolution of a software system or set of systems that satisfies a given need.
- Software process model. A descriptive representation of a software process that supports explanation, reasoning, simulation, etc. A software process model should represent attributes or views of a range of particular software processes and should be sufficiently specific to allow reasoning about them.

Software process models are valuable for supporting effective process planning, enacting, predicting, monitoring, adapting, and correcting. They allow for the:

1. Enabling of effective coordination by facilitating the communication of a formalized process leading to a consensus understanding across the organization or project.
2. Enabling process reuse by facilitation of analytic selection of a process model from a base set of alternatives that include components and process abstractions. Reasoning about the alternatives is also enabled.
3. Support for process evolution, adaptation and correction due to the ability to define model-based process measurements, experience collection, and process rationale.

We now examine software process improvement concerns at the corporate, project, team, and individual levels in turn.

Corporate Process Strategies

Software companies face a spectrum of process choices. Three representative process strategies are discussed which depend upon where a company places itself in the spectrum of the software products marketplace, since it is the external marketplace pressures which determine the corporate incentives that tend to drive strategic process choices. These are: custom development of unique large systems, commercial package development and semi-custom systems development.

CUSTOM DEVELOPMENT OF UNIQUE LARGE SYSTEMS

For specific customers, companies (such as DOD aerospace contractors) of this type provide unprecedented, leading edge systems, fully customized for each application, such as a complex antiballistic missile control system. Customer requirements drive these unique systems, many of which may involve more research and invention than predictable engineering or production tasks. Companies in this market segment rely on highly skilled personnel theoretically capable of inventing new designs, as well as methods and tools, an needed by the application and as long as the customer is willing to pay and wait for the result. This fosters a job-shop approach, suited for such unique jobs. It seems to be adequate, only if a small group can build the system, if budgets, schedules, and long-term service requirements are not too stringent, and if there are adequate supplies of skilled personnel. In many cases such companies do not even realize that they have chosen such a strategy since they fall into this situation naturally as a consequence of "laissez-faire" management.

In a job shop environment, process improvement is typically done on a project-by-project basis although there exists a set of organizational processes (e.g., hiring) that need to be improved as well. Each project has an incremental cost, and therefore requires an associated return on investment. As more and more projects are completed, the associated dollar savings accumulate until a company's profit is affected. The goal of each process-improvement project is to eliminate waste and improve value. Products will be significantly improved by proper up-front process selection as well as by effective management of process-control methods. The application of process-control methods for predictable product outcomes is referred to as "project process management."

COMMERCIAL PACKAGE DEVELOPMENT

On the opposite side of the spectrum are the fully standardized program products or packages meant for widespread distribution and usage. Customers trade off the greater features and tailoring of a customized system for the lower price and immediate availability of such a package. Designing a good package might be costly and difficult, but the potential sales are huge for a best seller, such as a popular spreadsheet program (e.g., Excel or Lotus 1-2-3) for personal computers. Specific applications corresponding to the general needs of the mass market drive this type of product development. While there is no mass production there is electronic mass-replication of the system and its related documentations. This is a simple process and most of the real work is the research, design, and testing of the product. Companies in the package segment of the software industry create product-oriented projects and cultivate personnel highly familiar with both general application (such as word processing) and the common requirements of users. This approach works well as long as a few people can build a product, skilled people are available, and development costs are relatively unimportant compared to the potential sales of a popular product. This project-centered approach may not contribute in any way to an organization's ability to manage a series of projects effectively unless the product set constitutes a larger designed package (such as a family of related products).

ASSET BASED, SEMI-CUSTOM SYSTEMS DEVELOPMENT

A third type of software company, more recently emerging, exists in which the commonality of process and technology is exploited. In such a company the developers seek the efficiencies of scope across multiple projects in a bounded domain and offer products competing on the basis of a combination of price, performance, delivery, service, and reliability, among other characteristics. The Japanese software factory approach[8] is a well known example of this strategy at work. Software facilities operating like factories focus on a family of similar systems in a familiar domain (e.g., process control applications) and achieve high productivity through reusable components (and architectures), standardized processes, and technology to support teams of workers within those processes. More importantly they attempt to cultivate the necessary organizational and technical capabilities rather than hiring only skilled people. If a specific customer would want a unique custom system, a special project would be created or the work would be given to an expert subcontractor. The potential for real improvement is much greater in such a company which views its processes and previous developments as valuable assets to be managed, evolved, and applied as competitive weapons. In such a company, a project process is viewed in the context of a total business process. A software development project becomes an instance in the growth of a base of software assets.

Project Oriented Software Process Strategies

The primary focus of this section is to describe the concerns of software development processes from a product oriented project viewpoint. The *term software development* is taken to encompass the full range of software and system-related activities from problem statement through post delivery maintenance, modification, and evolution (i.e., cradle to grave, lifetime, or sometimes lifecycle).

Types of Project Process Models

Projects inherit constraints from the organizational process strategies chosen and create specific constraints of their own based on local circumstances. Simplistically, a large software project occurs within the context of an ongoing negotiation among what the user wants, what the customer can afford, and what the developer can build. This occurs within a management context that must deal with three principle factors: cost, schedule, and quality. Within that context there exists a range of possible strategies for defining an organized software development process on a large software project. This range is delineated by two extremes. On one end of the spectrum is the *job shop* philosophy in which each project requires a totally different process based upon specialized project criteria. On the other end of the spectrum is the *factory* philosophy in which a standardized process is designed in advance and is reused on each project. In the middle of the spectrum would be the *semi-factory* in which parts of the process are reused on each point within an adaptable framework addressing specific project needs. We expect that most large projects will continue to be in situations where initial selection and continued process adaptability is important and therefore presents the following set of high level process model types that are in use today on projects.

Four primary alternative project-level software process model types have been identified: 1. waterfall, 2. COTS adaptation and integration, 3. high-level specification transformation, and 4. exploratory/incremental. (See Table 13-1.) Each model is classified according to the situations in which it seems most applicable, and example applications are provided for clarification. How to determine, or select, an appropriate model, in the context of a given project, is also discussed. These models can also be used at the sub project level as well, and it is appropriate for more than one of these types to be used on a large project, leading to higher level models that contains these as sub process instances. The integration of sub projects using different process models is currently problematic. The ad hoc (i.e., undefined) process is beyond the scope of discussion in this section. It is not clear exactly how these model types fit as instances of any kind of process metamodel from which these inherit properties.

The waterfall model has been described in many publications; its applicability, however, has not. We see its primary usage in those situations in which the functionality, architecture, and technology are well understood. Examples of this might be inventory control and data reduction and reporting. The COTS adaptation and integration model is most applicable in situations in which the application

TABLE 13-1   Primary Alternative Software Project Process Model Types

Name	Situation Characteristics	Example Applications
1. Waterfall	Well-understood application, architecture, technology	Data reduction
2. COTS adaptation	Same as waterfall, but several commercial packages available	Inventory control
3. H/L specification transform	Ill-understood application, 4GL	MIS
4. Exploratory/incremental	Major application, and technology issues not understood, need for early subset demos	Military C3I
5. Ad-hoc/undefined	?	?

and technology is well understood, and where there are several commercial packages available that together achieve most of the functionality required. The added value becomes the adaptation and integration of those COTS systems. Example applications are financial management or document preparation. The high-level specification transformation model is most useful when the functionality required is not well understood but where 4GL technology is available for the creation of high-level "programs." Example applications include MIS or forms management. The exploratory/incremental model is most useful when the major application issues are not well understood (e.g., feasability, usage scenarios, functional features desired, etc.) and when a movement to more stable capabilities is desired. Major techniques to be used in the exploratory/incremental model are prototyping and risk management. We define these techniques as those that increase the probability of producing a useful, fieldable, and supportable system. Example applications include military C31, SDI, or real-time embedded avionics systems.

The major issue when choosing one of the model types is how to interpret the notion of well understood—that is, by whom is it well understood? We believe that this criterion must apply to all stakeholders in the process if the model is to be adapted effectively across the system's life.

There is obviously a relationship between these model types and external business constraints imposed by the customer both directly and indirectly through the corporate process strategies previously described. For example, in the context of military acquisition, aspects of the process (e.g., DOD-STD-2167A) may be pre-determined regardless of applicability.

The relationship of these project process models to the more technical design approaches, methods, techniques, and tools is such that the models are supported by these more specific items in specific situations by teams of professional software engineers.

Technical Team Process Approaches

In support of process-oriented process modeling, chosen approaches (and subsequently methods, techniques, and tools) help the team carry out the objectives of the project process and are mapped between each other for consistency. For example, the developmental project process approach in Cleanroom (see Chapter 18) describes the separation of requirements, development, and certification concerns inherited from the goals and objectives of the Cleanroom Lifecycle Process Model. Each of these concerns represents a different team using a different set of methods that are planned to be complementary.

- Approach to software development. A strategy for achieving the development of a software system in a way that conforms to some software process model. An approach can be expanded into a more detailed approach.

Software development methods and tools support the application of approaches to software development.

- Method. An explicit prescription for achieving an activity or set of activities required by an approach to software development.
- Technique. A systematic procedure by which a software engineering task is accomplished. Typically, a technique is considered to be supportive of and subordinate to a method.

In choosing a suitable method it is important to know with what approaches the specific method is consistent and how good the method is when it is compared with other methods consistent with the approach. To what extent or portion of the process does the method apply and to what extent can the method be supported by software tools. We have found the *Software Methodology Catalogue*[18] to be a useful reference when surveying methods for selection.

- Software tool. A program or collection of programs that can support the application of a method or technique.

Although this definition does not exclude general purpose tools, it does insist that tools can only be judged by the extent to which they support methods. For example, as in Cadre Teamwork's support for the DFD (dataflow design) method. While individual software tools are of undoubted value, coordinated collections of tools are attracting increasing attention. These are termed software development environments, or sometimes programming support environments, project support environments, software engineering environments, and integrated programming/project support environments.

- Software development environment. A coordinated collection of software tools organized to support some approach to software development or conform to some software process model. (sometimes called a Software Engineering Environment or SEE).

Individual Process Techniques

The extreme variation in the productivity of individual professional programmers has been reported to be as much as 26 to 1. Our studies showed that most programmers use idiosyncratic approaches to development based upon training and accumulated expertise based on applications done. They interact with others when information is perceived to be needed and use tools available to them to accomplish their jobs. Since we do not yet know enough about the cognitive processes of professionals, it seems inappropriate to attempt to model and control such activities at that level. However, in those situations when the individual interacts with team, project, and other organizational processes it makes sense to model that behavior. Process improvement at the individual level is accomplished primarily through planned education, training, and career development.

Having described the definitional framework of potential process concerns we turn our attention to establishing coherent programs for continuous process improvement with focused goals, objectives, and planned approaches.

13.4 THE GOALS OF
CONTINUOUS PROCESS IMPROVEMENT

This section discusses prototypical programs for a multiproject organization to facilitate continuous and sustained improvement focused on achieving strategic objectives as defined by a company. Such programs lay the infrastructure to enable the continuous improvement of an organization's software development process in order to achieve an end result of increased competitiveness by:

1. Increasing software product quality and customer satisfaction
2. Increasing software development productivity
3. Reducing the cost of software development
4. Reducing software schedule and technical risk
5. More accurately estimating costs, schedules etc.

While these goals represent the bottom line, they are sometimes difficult to measure because of the lack of an historical database within a company (or organization) as a baseline for comparison. Over time, after establishing an historical database, measurement of these fundamental objectives can and should be made. Collection and analysis of software metrics are the principal means of measuring progress.

Getting started on improvement is sometimes difficult to justify, yet we know from data reported from other ongoing software improvement initiatives Raytheon,[10] Hughes GSS,[12] and Lockheed,[17] that the potential return on investment (ROI) for implementing a continuous software process improvement program can be as much as 4:1 within the first 2 years—$4 saved for every $1 invested—thus providing significant motivation.

Two popular strategic improvement goal models are being used widely in the U.S. software industry today. These are:

1. The SEI Software Capability Maturity Model
2. The Malcolm Baldrige National Quality Award (MBNQA) criteria.

• The SEI Software Capability Maturity Model. The SEI has articulated a five-stage framework called the Capability Maturity Model (CMM) which organizes attention on certain management and engineering processes (e.g., CM, QA) as a prototypical large software organization would advance to become more effective over a set of related projects. This model is based on anecdotal data from IBM and on the principles of statistical process control applied to software engineering.[13] As an interim step to long term measured improvement, an indirect measurement of cost, schedule, and quality indicators can be made, using the SEI's model. Improvement objectives would then focus on achieving higher levels of maturity from a starting point established by an SEI assessment. Although not statistically validated due to the small number of sampled projects, limited data from a large aerospace contracting company has shown a possible correlation between increased SEI maturity levels and increased productivity. In that sample, level 1 projects reported an average productivity rate of 1 SLOC (Source Lines of Code) per hour, and level 3 projects reported an average productivity rate of 5 SLOC per hour.

Relatedly, a maturity model for software human resource development above the project level has been articulated by Curtis.[5] This model takes into consideration the high leverage organizational processes of: recruiting, selection, performance appraisal, training, compensation, career development, teamwork development, culture design, and organization design. The model examines each of these process areas as an organization might mature from totally unmanaged to optimized. Presumably, the Curtis model will eventually merge with the current SEI CMM.

- The MBNQA criteria. The Malcolm Baldrige National Quality Award (MBNQA) has generated significant interest in U.S. companies for initiating improvement programs based not only upon the guidelines and criteria espoused for higher quality, but also on the process by which companies apply and are evaluated against their competition. The evaluation looks at the approach, deployment, and results achieved toward a systematic prevention-based, measured improvement program in all business areas of the company. The examination results are heavily weighted towards achieving customer satisfaction and quality, but also looks at areas such as QA, human resources utilization, management leadership, information analysis, and strategic quality planning. In response to the MBNQA competition many software companies have used these criteria to initiate their continuous software process improvement program focused on achieving "best in class" results. Motorola's Six Sigma and Quality System Review (QSR) programs are examples of well structured initiatives in response to MBNQA criteria which is now being applied to software development.

Other less popular goal models are Crosby's Cost of Quality model in which the costs associated with various software techniques and technologies are broken up and tracked as the cost of performance (non varying), and the costs of conformance (to requirements) and non conformance. These costs can be tracked over time to show the benefit of implementing certain software engineering techniques on a set of projects. Other relative improvement models based on simple software metrics (e.g., productivity) have been less effective because they did not take a holistic view of the organization.

13.5 THE ASPIRE APPROACH

ASPIRE (which stands for A Software Process Improvement Realization Environment) is a meta model that is used to explain the programmatic approach to realizing the goals of a continuous process improvement effort. We have found it a useful contextual framework for explaining the interelationships of the various methods, techniques, and tools as they might be used in a structured approach to implementing continuous software process improvement in a given company or organization.

Regardless of the specific goal model used, a systematic and comprehensive approach for the realization of software process improvement is needed. In the following section the details of such an exemplary program are discussed. It is a recommended iterative approach (called ASPIRE) to continuous improvement that reinforces the more general goals previously mentioned. When carried out, such a program will establish the basis for and measure improvement progress in the areas of software development: cost, schedule, productivity, and quality while facilitating the necessary culture change. This is not the only approach but it is one that we found to help explain the principles as they work in practice. We offer it (ASPIRE) only as a convenient explanatory framework.

The following organizational strategies are pursued in ASPIRE: 1. to gain top-to-bottom organizational commitment, 2. to establish a focal point organization to catalyze this improvement initiative, and 3. establish widespread involvement and participation in continuous improvement activities.

TOP TO BOTTOM
ORGANIZATIONAL COMMITMENT

It is necessary to gain management and organizational acceptance of, and commitment to, a continuous software process improvement program and its objectives so that a software improvement culture can be established within an organization. Everyone in the organization (and not just software developers) must be committed to continuous software engineering improvement. This means that Software Process Improvement should be a regular topic of discussion on the agenda of every management meeting held at all levels of the organization. Specifically, process improvement metrics should be displayed just as budget and schedule status metrics are. The supportive policies and directives toward this end must be put in place. The business strategy must emphasize the importance of total customer satisfaction and software quality. Management must be aware of software issues and risks and must be encouraged to improve software capabilities. Policies and procedures must support a "software process first," systems engineering methodology. Finally, the resources must be allocated to make it all happen.

ESTABLISH A SOFTWARE
IMPROVEMENT FOCAL POINT

To catalyze the initiation of an improvement program we observe that it is necessary for any organization to get an unbiased, external view of their capabilities by a qualified expert (or team) that has had significant experience in helping organizations improve their software capabilities. An organizational capability must be put in place with the charter and duties of developing and maintaining software development policies, procedures, standards, and practices to cover project management, configuration management, quality assurance, technical development, etc. It also will develop criteria for software quality, the software engineering processes, and will evaluate and transfer technology to support improved development of new software assets, introduce rigor and new technology, and provide a means for technology transfer. Operational software engineering organizations will provide feedback to management on the progress of the improvement process and recommend changes in management policies and directives that will aid in achieving the software engineering improvement goals. It should be staffed with people fully responsible for achieving the initiative goals.

Additional leverage is gained from previous standards development efforts (internal and external) and appropriate advanced software technology R&D work. The establishment, evolution, and application of software policies and procedures to specific project situations and the capture of experiential knowledge is accomplished here. An historical database of key measures is created and managed.

WIDE SCALE PARTICIPATION, INVOLVEMENT AND EMPOWERMENT

Real improvement of software capabilities will require the involvement of many people to improve various aspects of the process which must continue and be sustained over many years. Improvements must be introduced on real-world programs in a phased, incremental and well scoped manner that is consistent with this goal. Incentives and rewards must exist for improving software capabilities. The effort must be continued until the methods and improvements become so ingrained in the culture that they are performed without apparent intellectual effort. It has been shown that organizations operating at low maturity levels have a tendency to abandon long-term improvement efforts when faced with short-term crises.

All processes can and should be continuously monitored and improved. Otherwise, they will become outdated by changes in technology, fall into a state of disorder, or become embedded in bureaucracy. All employees within a company should be concerned with and be on the lookout for effective ways of improving systems, organizations, and operations.

Current programs focus on principles of software process management, including: 1. productivity and quality through the use of quality control techniques, waste reduction, and institutionalized reuse; 2. process engineering activities of definition, monitoring, analysis, and improvements embodied in educational programs, standards, and planned technology insertion; 3. process efficiency through teamwork and communication including support by groupware for high performance teams; and 4. flexible organization evolution through coordinated policy, technology, and organizational structure centered around process management and improvement concerns. It is intended to have an overall consistent approach between recommended standards, appropriate software methodology, appropriate systems methodology, organizational policy/procedure, and computer infrastructure.

A Stepwise Approach to ASPIRE

Once a goal structure and general strategies for improvement are established ("yardstick" by which the progress of such an initiative will be measured over time) and strategies are outlined we can now turn to describing a possible iterative approach to be used in accomplishing strategic improvement objectives. This stepwise approach is intended to apply widely to all software related processes. Each process-improvement step involves a cycle of planning, implementing, checking, and evaluation.

The general steps to continuous process improvement that are part of the ASPIRE model are seen in Figure 13-4. The steps iteratively revolve around the strategies introduced in a previous section. These steps are:

1. Establishing an organizational commitment to continuous improvement
2. Perform an organizational assessment of overall software capabilities
3. Identify processes and associated criticality
4. Select processes for improvement, define ownership and user requirements
5. Organize an improvement team and develop an improvement plan
6. Review the current process
7. Establish measures of performance
8. Analyze, process, and identify improvements
9. Implement the process change(s)
10. Validate process-improvement effectiveness
11. Establish and maintain controls
12. Continuously improve (go to 1, 6, or 8).

We now describe and discuss each step in turn based on our experiences with such improvement programs.

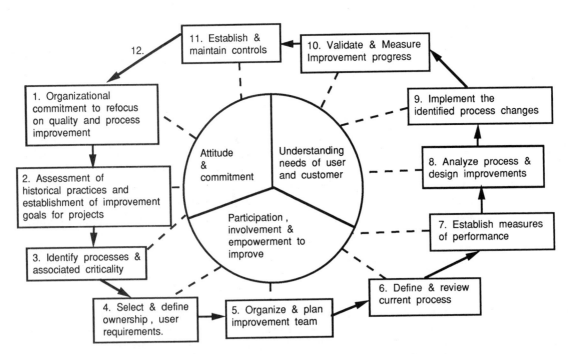

FIGURE 13-4. The ASPIRE approach to continuous software process improvement.

Step 1. Establishing the Need and Management Commitment for Continuous Software Process Improvement

Three years performing assessments, establishing and nurturing improvement initiatives in all the major departments of a large aerospace contractor company has shown that without the grass roots need to improve and the commitment and sponsorship to change, no initiative, no matter how well intentioned and well defined can succeed. The grass roots support can usually be related to a broad set of concerns about the company's competitiveness and an interest in knowing how they stack up to other similar organizations. The commitment of management to change is directly related to the underlying philosophy of continuous improvement, that is, that management owns the responsibility for process change (which most do not realize).

Building up the grass roots support requires selling the idea to the organization and involves significant effort in concept transfer and organizational education. Creating the catalyst for organizational change can mean identifying and cultivating high level sponsors, internal champions, risk takers, early adopters, change agents, and willing participants for pilot programs.

Sometimes commitment can be motivated by taking advantage of local concerns such as: 1. the need to prepare for externally imposed capability evaluations, 2. the need to provide a general capability for recommending improvements to ongoing projects and providing expertise and advice in process planning on new software projects, 3. providing training and certification of other evaluators for vendor certification, and 4. the need to establish a mechanism for ongoing collection of relevant project data so that software productivity and quality baselines are developed and tracked. Clear metrics of success in establishing the commitment are: number of briefings given, dollars allocated in plans, and testimonials to the importance.

Step 2. Performing an Organizational Assessment

An organizational process is the first step to appraisal of an organization's overall software process infrastructure, based on a review of the selected development projects and in-depth discussions with managers and practitioners. The criteria for selecting the projects to be sampled, the data collection instruments to be used, and the nature of the data collection and analysis process is designed in conjunction with the goals sought.

Typically, a small group consisting of a qualified and experienced team leader and selected internal members of the staff are commissioned, trained, and developed into an assessment team. They collect questionnaire and related process data from a representative set of current software projects. As a part of the typical ground rules, confidentiality provisions are put in place that allow only composite results to be reported. That is, the results are reported with no name attribution, and no group identification. This includes both horizontal (project to project) and vertical (line management chain) confidentiality. This helps to prevent the working of "hidden agendas." The results are the confidential property of the organization assessed. Assessment-specific data (recording forms, review tables, etc.) can be either destroyed or archived in a protected and sanitized statistical database.

The result of an organizational assessment is an identification of organizational strengths, opportunities for improvement, and expert recommendations on how to proceed. This constitutes what is called a road map for improvement and an identification of the strategies for implementing the recommended changes. What specific process areas that are focused on for improvement depends upon where the organization is in the maturation process. Improvement occurs from within the organization to be effective and, therefore, an action team to carry out the improvement implementation program is essential. This team will become the recipient of the assessment results and the active agents of internal change. They work within organizational structures and resource constraints to best leverage, coordinate, and optimize these efforts.

TOOLS FOR ASSESSMENT SUPPORT

New tools are emerging that enhances and support the process of assessing the maturity of an organization's software engineering capabilities. For example, SAIC's ASCENT was specifically designed to use the Software Engineering Institute's five-level software process maturity model and associated questionnaire. Such tools automate the most error-prone and tedious tasks associated with gathering and analyzing software process assessment data. Custom displays and reports—at the project specific and organizational levels—let the assessment team dynamically and quickly converge on the categories and findings most relevant to an organization. Such a toolset is composed of: 1. a highly interactive assessment questionnaire tool to collect the data, 2. a response analysis tool that facilitates the identification of cross-project anomalies and trends in the collected data through various graphical and non-graphical displays, and 3. other support tools, such as on-line help, a glossary, and questions browsers. Tools can be accessed directly or via hypertext-links embedded in each tool.

Assessment data capture tools allow the entering, viewing, and hyper navigation of: project information, questions, explanations to questions, responses to questions, identification of followup questions, and glossary terms as well as capabilities for the loading and saving of project data to databases or ASCII text files. For example, Figure 13-5 shows a typical user interface to such a data capture tool.

Assessment data analysis tools allow for the multiproject evaluation of previously collected project data as produced in the capture tool. Such a tool would allow: the loading of assessment data responses from generated text files or databases, selection of analysis categories from the overall SEI capabilities maturity model based upon relative positioning knowledge, the definition and selection of new categories, the profiling of organizational data (e.g., by maturity level, user selected categories, or statistical summaries), the visualization for anomaly detection and recording, customizable interview note capture, and the generation and the entering and viewing of additional analysis data for exploratory questions and requests for supporting materials. Automatic calculation of maturity levels and knowledge based report generation is enabled. An example user interface of such a tool is shown in Figure 13-6.

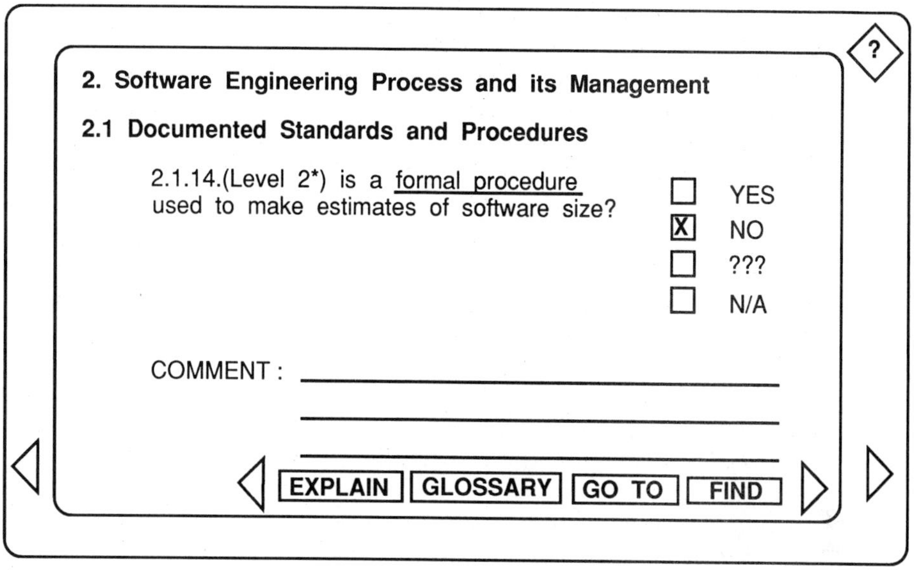

2. Software Engineering Process and its Management

2.1 Documented Standards and Procedures

2.1.14.(Level 2*) is a <u>formal procedure</u>
used to make estimates of software size?

☐ YES
☒ NO
☐ ???
☐ N/A

COMMENT : _____
          _____
          _____

?

◁ ◁ | EXPLAIN | GLOSSARY | GO TO | FIND | ▷ ▷

FIGURE 13-5. Assessment recording tool for viewing SEI assessment questions and entering responses.

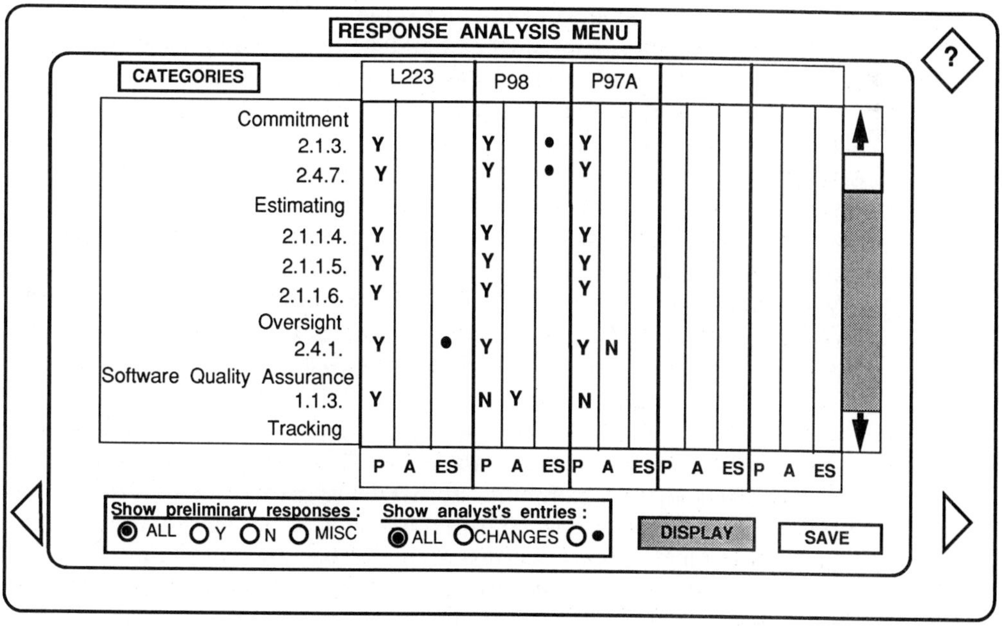

RESPONSE ANALYSIS MENU

CATEGORIES	L223			P98			P97A									
Commitment																
2.1.3.	Y			Y	●		Y									
2.4.7.	Y			Y	●		Y									
Estimating																
2.1.1.4.	Y			Y			Y									
2.1.1.5.	Y			Y			Y									
2.1.1.6.	Y			Y			Y									
Oversight																
2.4.1.	Y	●		Y			Y	N								
Software Quality Assurance																
1.1.3.	Y			N	Y		N									
Tracking																

P	A	ES	P	A	ES	P	A	ES	P	A	ES	P	A	ES

<u>Show preliminary responses</u> :   ⦿ ALL ○ Y ○ N ○ MISC

<u>Show analyst's entries</u> :   ⦿ ALL ○ CHANGES ○ ●

| DISPLAY | SAVE |

FIGURE 13-6. Data analysis tool for sets of projects.

Step 3. Identify Processes, Criticality and Selection

The goal of process identification is to determine which processes an organization owns and establish a prioritized list of processes for improvement. Trying to work on too many fronts simultaneously is not usually an effective use of resources. For an organization, the processes of interest are those directly associated with its mission and products. Cross functional processes of interest are those shared by more than one responsible organization. As part of process identification, it is important to determine who the customers are and which of the identified processes are important to them. The reason for determining the criticality of the identified processes is to select from those targeted for improvement a specific process that, if improved, will be the most beneficial. A ranking of the processes in the order of their criticality to the product and/or the customer is developed. One of the best ways of evaluating processes is from a cost standpoint using Pareto analysis.

Pareto analysis is a useful technique to help illustrate what processes are responsible for what costs. Data concerning process performance is organized to identify the cost of a given process and the most costly processes. The Pareto diagram is based on the assumption that 20% of processes are responsible for 80% of performance problems. By improving the 20% problematic processes, we will significantly improve the products and/or reduce costs. Typical processes targeted for improvement are often characterized by: poor cost performance, low capability, problem history, criticality to customer satisfaction, and acceptance, or by virtue of their effect on product life, reliability, and performance.

The one or ones that are most burdensome, or that have the greatest potential to provide value or will provide a significant return on investment are selected for improvement. At this point several simultaneous process improvement teams might be commissioned, each attacking a different process.

We proceed to discuss the situation in which a single process is selected. It is helpful at this point to set down the process (and problem) to be addressed, and the purpose of the improvement.

Step 4. Define Specific Process
Ownership and User Requirements

Once a specific process has been selected for improvement, a clear process owner must be established and the boundaries or scope of the process defined. Boundary definition includes location, number of employees involved within the process, suppliers, products affected, and customers.

When collecting or specifying process user requirements, it is important to keep in mind the needs of the customers of the product (output of the process) whether outside the company or in another department or organization within the company. Knowledge of customer requirements is necessary to understand the significance of a process to its users. An understanding of the customer's point of view will enable us to understand which process improvements will increase product quality.

In a large company it is sometimes unclear who owns a given process although it may be more clear who the process users are. Each process should have an identifiable ownership or its existence should be questioned. A process which touches multiple business functions has multiple ownership. Without a clearly identified owner, a process may receive insufficient attention and the efficiency of the process will degrade over time. This is a very common situation, and simply making people aware of the process and its lack of ownership solves the problem. For example, if formalized configuration management is necessary and there is no CM function.

A knowledgable process owner will understand the business impacts of the process, customer requirements, company policies, and change procedures, as well as the immediate and long-term consequences of process performance.

Properly scoping the process means analyzing it and documenting it as a "system" thus identifying the external interfaces, component parts, relationships, and implementing mechanisms.

Step 5. Organize a Focused Improvement Team

The next step in the improvement process is to commission and develop a team to work on the scoped improvement project. The team approach has the advantages of the power of working in groups, the ability to segment tasks and accomplish them in parallel, a larger skill base for improvement and participation, and buy in from a larger segment of the work force. These teams should include key process stakeholders, effective change agents, champions, cross functional representatives, and organizational change experts.

For example, a cross functional team may start a project to improve an engineering change and release process and would therefore include representatives from manufacturing, product assurance, materiel, and design engineering. A project to improve staff support might include secretaries and representatives from mail and distribution. Team building is important and the key is establishing effective coordination and communication. Staff planning considerations are important to get those people with the greatest chance of success assigned to the team. Good communication means assisting the individuals and organizations involved to understand their relationship to the improvement project. Users, customers, and suppliers should also be considered for team membership.

Process improvement teams work with the managers directly associated with the process, or the managers might be part of the team. Additional coordination and reporting may be made to a steering committee, quality improvement board, or process improvement task force. Team effectiveness depends upon management involvement and communication of team findings.

Step 6. Develop an Improvement Plan

Failing to plan is like planning to fail. The team develops a process-improvement plan to help keep the team on track. It should be appropriately scoped in relation to the size of the project. Such a plan includes: a clearly stated problem, the goals and objectives of the improvement project, a definition of the tasks and their interrelationships over time, estimated completion dates for key outputs, personnel requirements and cost estimates, plan change coordination procedure, and expected measures of effectiveness.

Although it may be unclear at this stage exactly how a process will be improved, having a plan enables the team to coordinate the improvement activities, time sequences, and expectations of the externally affected parties as well as to communicate with external groups. A plan is in some cases necessary prior to forming the entire team in which case Steps 5 and 6 are reversed.

Step 7. Detailed Analysis of the Current Process

Without a thorough understanding of the current operation of a given process, making effective improvements is not possible. A systematic and comprehensive evaluation of the operation of a process ("as is") is done. This will culminate in the definition of a detailed process model based upon: 1. review of documented policies, procedures, handbooks, methods, etc; 2. empirical observation of personnel performing process tasks to establish what is actually done (undocumented procedures); 3. examining and validating current measures of processes performance (e.g., customer satisfaction level); 4. further systematic definition of the process boundaries and interfaces; and 5. documentation of accept/reject criteria at major and minor check points.

Although simplistic tools such as dataflow diagrams have been primarily used in the past, a new more powerful tool to be used in this step is a process modeling system that allows the capture and examination of the meaningful dynamics in all the areas outlined above.

NEW TOOLS FOR PROCESS ANALYSIS AND DEFINITION

SPMS (Software Process Management System) is an example of an emerging tool set to support the software process engineer in the development, evolution, and support of organizational and project-specific software development process models. SPMS allows the process engineer to perform: experimentation in model development, process simulation, software quality measurement/analysis, and process improvement support. Part of achieving higher SEI level ratings is the ability to define the current software process (i.e., "as is" baseline) and the ideal process (i.e., "to be" goal) so that effective road maps to improvement may be developed and change may be managed and measured with process change indicators. An operational prototype SPMS (V0) was developed for the Defense Advanced Research Projects Agency's Software Technology for Adaptible Reliable Sytsems (DARPA/STARS) Program under contract to IBM and successfully demonstrated in July 1991. SPMS V0 is being used to help manage the SPMS development and is being installed for test usage in the SEI's Process Definition Project in September of 1991. We are currently involved in porting and strengthening the existing SPMS functionality from our prototyping environment (Mac II) to the IBM STARS SEE platform (IBM Risc System 6000) to be available in August of 1992 and then integrated into the IBM STARS SEE, and available for use by DOD demonstration projects in August of 1993. Advanced capabilities allow for: process model generation from reusable process components, integration with cost estimation system, process simulator graphical visualization, SEE interfaces, integration with process enaction and coordination technology, adaptability to additional process metrics, and definition tools and support for process rationale capture.

In many cases, evaluation of customer requirements and detailed assessment of the current process configuration will indicate possible methods of improvement. Although the process requirements may be understood the team may have no idea what is actually causing the problems in the processes involved. Causal analysis through problem solving techniques or the use of external experts in that process may be used at this point in the process improvement strategy.

Step 8. Establish Improved Measures of Performance

Clear, measurable definitions of targeted improvement objectives should be done. The criteria of specific levels of acceptable productivity, process capability or quality must be defined in "operational terms." For example, achieving "6-Sigma" software quality as at Motorola, improving the defect rates by 10% or moving to SEI level 3.

The following should be established: operational definitions for process and quality performance, a method of ensuring the consistency of operational definitions among employees, organizations, suppliers, and customers, and a process performance feedback mechanism for control and improvement if such mechanisms are nonexistent.

When establishing measures of improved performance the following issues need to be considered: what is required from the process, what level of performance is possible, what has the process performance historically been, what specifically can be done to make the process better, and what problems may be encountered along the way. Alternative strategies and contingency plans can be defined. The process model previously defined can then be modified and simulated to see if performance improvements are possible.

Step 9. Implementation, Improvement and Monitoring

A rich body of literature exists about organizational resistance to change[1] and how catalysts can effectively be used. It is no surprise that people generally resist change unless they see a clear benefit for themselves. Therefore improvements must be effectively introduced with the win-win benefit described and implemented on selected pilot projects to minimize the disruption to other ongoing projects. These can be scaled according to inherent risk, and serve as the seeds for wide scale transfer, if successful. In order to reduce the variability in implementing the new practices, communications and training is required so that everyone involved understands the new process in the same way. Otherwise, a situation is created in which multiple interpretations of the new process will lead to counterproductive practices.

Process change is accomplished by restructuring, streamlining, shortening, deleting nonvalue added steps, or otherwise changing the process so that it aligns with critical success factors established from the customer satisfaction viewpoint. It is necessary to establish new performance measurements, modify the existing process documentation, train and verify that employees understand and commit to the change, and coordinate as necessary with customers and suppliers.

Measurement and metrics are at the heart of a process improvement program. It is intended to measure both the cost and benefit of process improvements as the initiative progresses over the years using a "Process Improvement ROI" tool. This entails not only measuring the process, but also creating an environment that allows for process evolution and reformulation. Measurement makes it possible to establish a uniform quantitative quality policy.

Several alternative solutions may be articulated and each may appear to be attractive. Preliminary testing and validation of these alternatives will be helpful in determining the adequacy of the improvement. Methods for developing solutions include brainstorming, cause-and-effect diagramming, and nominal group technique. One source of information that is often not effectively utilized is the technical library. Many of the problems and potential solutions that are faced by the team have been addressed, documented, and previously published in trade journals, reports, and technical presentations.

Step 10. Validate Process-Improvement Effectiveness
Significant improvements can be verified against baseline performance measurements established before the process improvement implementation was begun. Real process improvement has occurred if customer satisfaction has increased, cost has been reduced, throughput has increased, processing time has been reduced, reliability has improved, the process has been centered on a customer target value, variability has been reduced, or rework has been reduced. Posting these improved measurements has been shown to reinforce continued efforts. Wide dissemination of lessons learned and rewarding of successful initiatives at the team level has long lasting positive effects.

Step 11. Establish and Maintain Controls
Process controls are subsequently established to keep process improvements from losing their effectiveness over time. The best process control strategy of all is to redesign the process so that the likelihood of error introduction is very low. Consider for example, the process of data entry into a computer database. In most systems the error rate for manual data entry is one permanent error in three hundred keystrokes. When a bar-code data entry system is used for the same operation, the error rate is one error in three million scans. An improved manual data entry system can never rival the performance and speed of a barcode data entry system, therefore proper technology can be critical to process performance.

A second major control strategy is timely quantitative feedback to the employees or systems associated with the process. Feedback considerations include frequency, real-time information availability, identification of primary process monitoring features, and integration of feedback directly into operating methods.

Typical process control techniques include the use of: basic statistical process control tools, audits, sampling techniques, process certification, customer surveys and interviews, quality function deployment data, and on line instrumentation feedback from an SPMS-like system.

Step 12. Iterate

Minor iterations occur by going back to Step 3 to select the next process from the prioritized list (of course this could occur in parallel as well) for improvement. Another minor iteration would occur if we went back to Step 9 to implement the same improvement on another pilot project.

Improvement teams go through a process of decommissioning in order to improve the meta improvement process by performing a post mortem, documenting lessons learned, and contributing to the corporate historical base of improvement data. At this point in the process, it may be important to release the team associated with the process improvement effort to work on other assignments. Project-by-project improvement teams need to be ad hoc in nature to avoid creating an additional burden on a company's organizational structure. Even though the ad hoc improvement team is disbanded, a natural team remains that surrounds the process. This team includes all personnel who work with the process: operators, engineers, supervisors, group leaders, and managers.

Continuous improvement is an ongoing part of each employee's work. Using the performance controls and feedback established previously, those involved with a process will continuously seek opportunities to improve it, thereby increasing customer satisfaction and the utility of the end products.

Iteration of the entire cycle can occur starting at Step 1. Re-assessments are performed periodically when significant progress is indicated or attention is necessary to stimulate the continuous improvement process. This approach has been shown in other companies to reinforce the accomplishment of improvement objectives that were set out in the initial improvement roadmap.[12]

13.6 NEW TECHNOLOGY FOR PROCESS IMPROVEMENT

Several related technologies are emerging to support the process driven software development environment of the future. Some of these are concurrent engineering, process management, intelligent groupware, AI-based design, prototyping, and evolutionary development, and incremental delivery techniques. When brought together with the goals and approaches of continuous process improvement this can lead us to a significantly enhanced paradigm for software engineering driven by living, adaptable, intelligent, active life cycle process models embedded in the heart of the work environment.

The Process Centered Software Engineering Environment

The purpose of this section is to discuss the emergence of SEEs in which models of software processes are defined and then "enacted." The word "enacting" has been used instead of alternatives such as "executing" or "interpreting" to preserve the concept that the mechanism for "running" process models is a symbiosis of human beings and computers, while delaying the allocation to either partner. "Executing" has strong connotations of machine execution; "interpreting" can denote activities in man and machine which are very different.

Enactability simply means the human beings involved in the software process receive computer guidance and assistance in what is an extremely complex activity. Put another way, models are just used "off-line," as a means of studying and defining processes, but also "on-line" while processes are being carried out, as a means of directing, controlling, monitoring, and instrumenting them.

Process enactments are written to define possible (allowable) patterns of behavior between nondeterministic human beings and systems constructed of computer programs. Modeling and programming the software process is an experimental testbed for introducing a new and potentially much more highly productive way of software system-building.

Process Automation Requirements for Next Generation SEEs

Although the technologies are still emerging, we see that active process support requirements for next generation SEEs are challenging. Support services will be needed for: products classes (inheritance, specialization), activity networks and their global "state" and variation possibilities, agents that perform activities (human or not), control flow, synchronization of activities and transfer of products between agents, dialogue and commitment, decisions, goals, long term process transactions, nondeterminism, multiple views or representations of process models, roles, rules, sharing and containment of complex document objects, hierarchy and decomposition of activities, and rich typing capabilities. In addition direct support for process engineering will be required with features for: process reuse and process change management. Organizations such as the European Computer Manufacturers Association (ECMA) are starting to examine standards for supporting process management.

PROCESS MODELING

New large scale software process models are emerging to meet the new emphases on iterative development.[3] Creating process models of the teamwork, cooperation, coordination, and communications aspects of large software projects is especially difficult because it is groundbreaking applied research. Attempts have been made to solve these types of problems in current technology by providing a passive, integrated project database. That is, it was assumed that by providing a shared information base in a software engineering environment that coordination would occur. This has been shown to be a false assumption. Languages which allow us to represent coordination activities in organizations are emerging from the computer sciences area of concurrent programming languages. However these languages are for systems of cooperating programs not for people. We will be exploring representation techniques for cooperative process modeling as well as integration with other process model aspects.

GROUPWARE FOR SOFTWARE
PROCESS COORDINATION

Current technology for process coordination in software development operates on the simple model of passive synchronization of programming level tasks through the check-in/check-out policies of centralized configuration management. Although workable for small, co-located teams where the real coordination is done "over the partitions," it is clearly not workable for large projects with several teams which may be geographically distributed. Current software engineering environment (SEE) technology prohibits certain types of close cooperation, such as cooperative authoring of a document or on-line team design reviews. General groupware technology is now emerging from the research labs.[16] Electronic mail is a primitive form of groupware without purpose. New varieties of groupware technology that might be applied directly to software engineering include: on line discussion groups, computer controlled video conferences, multimedia-context sensitive mail, intelligent routers and filters, WYSIWIS (What You See Is What I See) group interfaces, group decision support tools, strategic assumption surfacing tools, etc. For such technology to be most effective in software development environments, design groupware will have to capture and use critical coordination information not in today's SEEs. This might include: technical goals, issues (resolved and unresolved), action items, assumptions, commitments, and design rationale at various organization levels. This will enable the design environment to become an "active" coordination agent using the design groupware medium. We will be involved in an initiative to develop and evaluate a working prototype of a next generation groupware system for multiteam situations that overcome the limitations of current technology.

Intelligent Project Management Technology

Large software projects are currently organized and managed according to guidelines adapted from other fields. The goal of these guidelines is to hierarchically control the responsibilities, authority, and communications of a project team. Project management support systems are traditionally concerned with quantitative support, such as calculating costs, determining schedules, assessing risks, ensuring accurate accounting, and reporting variances. This quantitative support is primarily product oriented and focuses on what must be produced, when it will be produced, and how much it will cost, thereby attempting to reduce project management to a job-shop scheduling problem in which the product is produced mechanically by passing from one station to the next. From this point of view, the production process is prescribed and predetermined.

We are also actively involved in developing technology components that can provide managers with intelligent project management assistance. Using AI technology, these intelligent technologies help analyze project behavior, support managerial decision-making, provide real-time understanding of project status and problems, and assure complete and consistent project data from start to finish. By providing intelligent, automated support for successful management, software developers will be able to handle complex projects more effectively with reduced risk to budgets and schedules.

As pointed out above, the requirements for software engineering coordination technology include the storage of several new types of information, these include: responsibilities, commitments, skills/expertise, issues (open, resolved, dissolved), decisions, assumptions, goals and objectives, and shared models of product and process. These will require new technology to be developed to handle the different types of data (e.g., voice, video, pictorial) in an integrated fashion; a capability which does not widely exist at present.

13.7 CONCLUSION

Summary

This chapter on the subject of continuous software process improvement presented material that: 1. introduced and motivated the subject matter, 2. presented an empirical basis of software process phenomena, 3. described the definitional process framework, 4. presented the typical goal models for organizational software improvement programs, 5. introduced and described the ASPIRE model of iterative improvement realization, and 6. described the emerging technology base for process improvement.

In this chapter we have shown that improving software process quality involves focusing on the understanding and enhancement of the human processes underlying software development at all organizational levels. Once understood and properly focused improvement efforts can begin to provide methods and technologies to support these processes, and manage them effectively. Rigorous software process management techniques can be applied with the result that producing a well-designed deliverable product becomes the output of a well-managed set of human processes organized around focused objectives and supported properly by technology. Support for process modeling, simulation, enaction, and process evolution is needed in next generation process-oriented software engineering environments.

Acknowledgements

The empirical studies referred to in this chapter were performed while the author was at the MCC Software Technology Program. He gratefully acknowledges the other members of the empirical studies team who helped make that work possible, especially Bill Curtis. He also is thankful to the management of IBM FSD, DARPA STARS and Lockheed Research and Development Division for providing the support necessary for the research and development program in software process management. Thanks to Barb Smith for her assistance in preparing this manuscript and to my colleagues at SAIC STC for their encouragement, support, and helpful suggestions. Thanks to Bev Kitaoka of SAIC for the acronym ASPIRE. And mostly thanks to Judy, Billy, and Becky for their patience while I worked on this at night and on weekends.

References

1. Beer, M., Eisenstat, R., and Spector, B. 1990. "Why Change Programs Don't Produce Change," *Harvard Business Review,* Nov./Dec. 1990, pp. 158-166.
2. Boehm, B. W. 1981. *Software Engineering Economics,* Prentice Hall, Englewood Cliffs, NJ.
3. Boehm, B. W. 1988. "The Spiral Model of Software Development and Enhancement." *Computer* 21(5):61-72.
4. Brooks, F. P. 1987. "No Silver Bullet: Essence and Accidents of Software Engineering." *IEEE Computer,* 20(4), April 1987.
5. Curtis, B. 1990. "Managing the Real Leverage in Software Productivity and Quality." *American Programmer,* 3(7), Jul./Aug. 1990.
6. Curtis, B., Krasner, H., and Iscoe, N. 1988. "A Field Study of Large Software Projects." *Communications of the ACM,* 31(11), Nov. 1988.
7. Curtis, B., Krasner, H., Shen, V., and Iscoe, N. 1987. "On Building Software Process Models Under the Lamppost." *Proceedings of the Ninth International Conference on Software Engineering,* pp. 96-103.
8. Cusumano, M. 1991. *The Japanese Software Factories,* MIT Press, 1991.
9. DeMarco, T. and Lister, T. 1987. *Peopleware,* Dorset House, New York.
10. Dion, R. 1990. "Quantifying the Benefit of Software Process Improvement." Presentation at the SEI Software Process Improvement Workshop, Chantilly, VA 8-9 Nov. 1990.
11. Guindon, R., Krasner, H., and Curtis, B. 1987. "Cognitive Processes in Early, Upstream Design: Differences in Strategies Among Experienced Designers." *Proceedings of the 2nd Workshop on Empirical Studies of Programmers.* Norwood, NJ: Ablex Publishing.
12. Humphrey, W., Snyder, T., and Willis, R. 1991. "Software Process Improvement at Hughes Aircraft." *IEEE Software,* Jul. 1991.
13. Humphrey, W. 1989. *Managing the Software Process.* Addison Wesley, Reading, MA.
14. Imai, M. 1986. *Kaizen.* Random House, New York.
15. Krasner, H., Curtis, B., and Iscoe, N. 1987. "Communications Breakdowns and Boundary Spanning Activities on Large Programming Projects." *Proceedings of the Second Workshop on Empirical Studies of Programmers,* pp. 47-64. Norwood, NJ: Ablex Publishing.
16. Krasner, H. (Chair) 1986. *Proceedings of the Conference on Computer-Supported Cooperative Work.* Austin: MCC Software Technology Program.
17. Krasner, H. 1990. "The Costs and Benefits of SEI-style Software Process Improvement." Presentation at the SEI Software Process Improvement Workshop, Chantilly, VA 8-9 Nov. 1990.
18. Von Gerichten, L. et al. 1989. *Software Methodology Catalogue—Second Edition.* Teledyne Brown Engineering, U.S. Army CECOM Technical Report, C01-091JB-0001-01.

19. Walz, D., Elam, J., Krasner, H., and Curtis, B. 1987. "A Methodology for Studying Software Design Teams: An Investigation of Conflict Behaviors in the Requirements Definition Phase." *Proceedings of the Second Workshop on Empirical Studies of Programmers,* Norwood, NJ: Ablex Publishing.
20. Walz, D. 1989. A Longitudinal Study of Group Design of Computer Systems, Ph.D. Dissertation, University of Texas at Austin, December 1988.
21. Weinberg, G. M. 1971. *The Psychology of Computer Programming.* New York: Van Nostrand Reinhold.
22. Weinberg, G. M. 1988. *Understanding the Professional Programmer.* New York: Dorset House.

14

Statistical Methods
Applied To Software

D. A. Christenson
S. T. Huang
A. J. Lamperez
D. P. Smith

AT&T Bell Laboratories

14.1 INTRODUCTION

Statistical quality controls in hardware manufacturing have been well established for a long time.[5] The theory and application of control charts and acceptance sampling procedures for mass production manufacturing are well understood and practiced by quality professionals. However, only lately have statistical quality control techniques been attempted for software development.[9] Such techniques are harder to apply in software production because, as a rule, the task is not repetitive with the same short periodicity, the process variations are much larger, and the quality of inputs cannot be made uniform. Furthermore, there is not yet a coherent theoretical framework that prescribes systematic application of traditional quality control techniques to the software development process.

In this chapter, we will formulate a general quality control framework for a typical software development process and illustrate the use of several standard quality control techniques. The rest of this chapter is organized as follows:

- In Section 14.2, we discuss the foundations of statistical quality control and a range of management issues that relate to successful implementation of any statistical quality control program.
- In Section 14.3, we elaborate on the similarities and differences between the software development and the manufacturing process in order to get a better understanding of how statistical controls can be used in software development, and also what their limitations are.

- In Section 14.4, we illustrate the use of statistical quality controls in reviews of requirements and design documents. Such controls could also be extended to various other phases of software development.
- In Section 14.5, we illustrate the use of process modeling in the code inspection process, and how this might be used as a management tool.
- In Section 14.6, we illustrate the application of acceptance sampling in the software testing process.
- Finally, in Section 14.7, we summarize and draw some general conclusions about the use of statistical controls in the software development process.

14.2 MEASUREMENT AND MANAGEMENT

The foundations of statistical techniques in quality control rest on the ability to measure, repeatably and reliably. In the software development process, the fundamental units of measurement are not as well established as they are in hardware and manufacturing technology. Without a solid base of measurement, statistical control of software is meaningless and efforts to manage using it are doomed to failure. The fundamental units of statistical quality measurement required are those of production quantity, defect or fault, effort and cost.

Quantity Measurement in Software

The concept of "quantity" of software produced is important for a variety of statistical controls. At the same time, a universal definition of "quantity" is difficult to establish. The obvious candidate for software quantity measurement is the ubiquitous "line of code." Unfortunately, the appropriate definition of a line of code depends on the intended use of the measurement.[1, 2, 3, 4]

The quantity concept before the software product is coded is even more difficult to establish since the product at this stage of development typically consists of documents of English text and drawings of data/control flow information. Candidates are "function points," enumerated requirements, and pages of text. Each of these "production units" has pitfalls and virtues in various applications. The essential characteristic is to normalize project effort across meaningful design attributes.

Each project must decide what measure of quantity is appropriate at each phase. The major considerations should be:

1. Standards. Existing project standards may constrain the choice of the measure of quantity.
2. Consistency. Measurements should be made in the same manner for all software units in the project over time.
3. Variability. The variation in other related measures, such as productivity and fault density, should be reduced.

With regard to variability, an example will illustrate. It is very desirable to re-use code that has already been tested and has a very low fault level. Compared to newly developed code, re-used code involves much less development effort, and contains many fewer defects. Therefore, in determining the quantity of software developed, re-used code should not be counted. Although re-using code increases overall productivity, adding the amounts of re-used code and newly developed code to get a total quantity of code delivered increases the variability in "productivity" and "quality" measures. If there is a significant difference in the attributes of certain quantities, they should be treated separately. In this case, amounts of re-used code and newly developed code should be identified separately.

In any case, the concept of "quantity" is essential for meaningful statistical control—and a software project must meaningfully and unambiguously define the quantity variable at each stage of the software development process for effective control.

Fault Measurement in Software

The concept of a software "fault" is again difficult to practically establish in the software development process. The purpose of establishing rigorous definitions of "fault" in a software development process is to allow project level baselining of previous similar developments and establish meaningful standards for new development. The essential question to be answered is whether or not the product at this stage of development is good enough to continue to the next stage of development.

To be successful, the definition of a software fault must be objective and readily reproducible in the production process. It must not depend on differences of interpretation in the same logical task produced by different programmers. Ideally, the fault definition is automatically identified in the production process and fault statistics can be gathered periodically by running audit programs in the project library as production products are developed and modified.

For example, in the final stages of software development before customer delivery for one large software product, a "software fault" may be defined as a documented error condition which is corrected by a software change. Changes can occur in multiple software subsystems, however the "fault" is counted only once. This definition is reproducible and actionable for the project. Reported error conditions that do not result in a software change are not counted in the fault statistics (i.e., duplicates or "no problem").

The concept of software "fault" is more difficult to establish before the product exists in code. In the requirements and design phases, project standards and hence "faults" are more subjective and subject to the opinions of differing designers. Nevertheless, it is important to establish standards for reviews and document faults as they are understood and defined in the project. Statistical fault control obviously suffers from wider control limits at this phase of development, however meaningful standards can still be set and error limits defined.

Effort Measurement in Software

The cost of software development is fundamentally connected to the engineering effort required to produce it. Meaningful process improvement requires a management system that regularly collects effort and compares expected effort to actuals as process changes are identified and implemented.

The number and variety of systems in use to measure engineering effort on software are probably as diverse as the organizations that produce software. The essential attributes are the ability to measure effort in real time in categories meaningful to developers and managers, and some sense of continuity of definition between projects executed by similar engineering staff. The continuity allows comparison with previous efforts—and the real time feedback allows adjustment in progress.

Management Perspective

Instrinsically, software measurement is not as accurate and has lower precision when compared to measurement in other engineering disciplines. The process is also less "controllable." It is desirable to sharpen the technical capability of the measurement system and increase the accuracy of measurements. However, it is more important to look at measurement and statistical controls in the software environment as tools to accomplish management objectives; to effect the right behavioral changes. Having reasonable measures of, and guidelines for, quantity, quality, and effort is more important than having the "right" or technically correct measures.

14.3 CONTROL CHARTS FOR SOFTWARE METRICS

Control charts have been used in industry as a means of statistically evaluating and controlling the quality of various manufacturing processes. First the capability of a process and the normal statistical variations of the process are determined. From this characterization of the process, abnormal deviations of the process, and trends away from the norm can be detected and some corrective action taken.

The use of control charts in the software development process is necessarily different than their use in a manufacturing environment, but there are similarities. It might be useful to point out the similarities and differences in these two processes in order to get a better understanding of how statistical controls can be used in software development, and how they cannot be used.

Figure 14-1 shows a model of a manufacturing process. Typically the output stream of products issuing from the process is sampled, some measurement of attributes of the product are taken, and those measurements are compared with specifications. A control chart,* such as that shown in Figure 14-2, may then be

---

*A good treatment of control charts can be found in Reference 12.

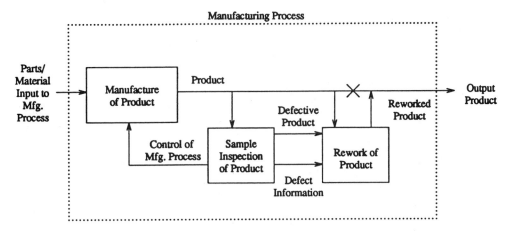

FIGURE 14-1. Model of a manufacturing process with inspection and feedback control.

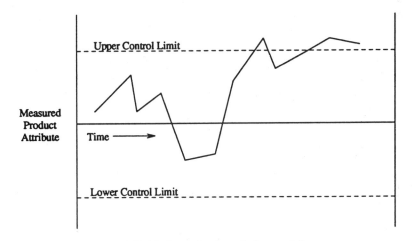

FIGURE 14-2. Example of a typical control chart.

used to determine if the attribute is within acceptable limits of the specification. Depending upon the attribute, different types of control charts would be used. For machined parts, the dimensions of the parts would be measured, and those measurements compared with specified tolerances on the control chart. If the dimensions of several parts in a succession were found to be out of tolerance, some control of the manufacturing process would be invoked.

First, the machine would be stopped, and any product that it produced might be sorted into acceptable and unacceptable units, and the unacceptable units would either be scrapped or reworked. Secondly, the machine would be adjusted to produce products within tolerance. If the machine was found to be incapable of producing products within tolerance, either the tolerances would have to be changed, or the machine would have to be replaced.

In the manufacturing environment, the quality of the incoming parts or material is usually well characterized. Previous quality control steps, such as the one described above, would have made this so. Also, the confidence in the ability of the machine to maintain tolerance for long periods of time, allows a periodic sampling technique to work.

A typical software development phase, on the other hand, would appear as in Figure 14-3. In a phase such as "design," one input to the process step would be a "requirements" document. The fact that people, and not machines, accomplish the production process, does not give us the same confidence in the resulting output as when a machine is used. Therefore, inspecting small samples of the output would not be effective. Instead, a 100% inspection would be more likely. Also, unlike manufacturing, the "specifications" for each software unit are different. The attributes of the product, and their measurement, are not precisely defined. "Measurement" of the attributes cannot be done objectively, but requires human judgement.

The "product" of the software design process is a design document. The "inspection" of this document would have to be accomplished by people with the expertise needed to judge the design against the specifications contained in the requirements document, and also against other criteria. Measurement of the quality of the output product of the phase, the completed design document, is difficult, if not impossible, to accomplish.

Table 14-1 summarizes the differences between a typical manufacturing process and software development. For the use of statistical methods of quality control in a software development environment, certain assumptions must be made. In the manufacturing case, it is assumed that the measurement of the appropriate attributes of the product can be done with the needed precision. Tools are available to do this. In the software development case, measurement of the attributes may involve tools also, but it relies more heavily upon the expertise of the people doing the measurement. During requirements, design, and coding

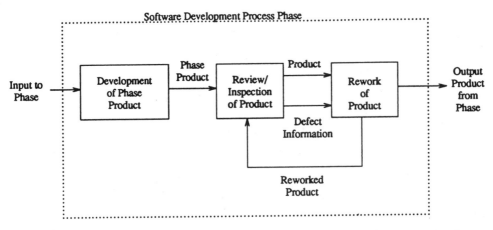

FIGURE 14-3. Example of a software development phase and use of "inspection" to control quality.

TABLE 14-1   Difference between Manufacturing and Software Development

	Manufacturing	Software Development
Input Quality	Uniform	Highly Variable
Input/Product Characteristics	Uniform	Unique; Different
Process Characteristic	Repetitive	Creative
Control Action	Well Defined	Ambiguous
Output Quality	Measurable	Not Measurable
Interplay of Measurement and Control	None	Significant

phases, inspection of the software products relies solely upon the expertise of the people doing the inspection. Human judgement alone determines how well the attributes of the software product meet the specifications. Later, during testing phases, tools are available to help the testing process, but human ingenuity is required for designing the tests that will be run, and human judgement is required in assessing the test results. We can assume that "measurement" will be done appropriately only if we have confidence in the people doing the "measurement," e.g., if they are experienced and well trained.

Finally, in the manufacturing case, some control is exercised over the manufacturing process, based on the results of inspection. This control will affect the quality of *future* product. The only control of the quality of the *current* product is to rework the product and correct any defects. In this sense, the software case is similar. Each software product is unique. We may be interested in the quality of future products, and may institute some controls to enhance that quality. But we are interested in the quality of the *current* product, and like in manufacturing, the only control that can be exercised is in reworking the product.

So there are two aspects of statistical quality control of software: 1. strategic control exercised over the development environment and overall process, and 2. tactical control over the quality of the *current* software product, exercised through some control over the *inspection and rework* of that product. It is important to consider both aspects of the scheme in developing management actions.

14.4 STATISTICAL CONTROLS APPLIED TO REVIEWS

Reviews and/or inspections of requirements and design documents, and inspection of code, should be an integral part of the software development process. Reviews and inspections are different processes, but for the purpose of statistical analysis, they can be treated in a similar way. In the following sections, we will talk about statistical analysis applied to reviews. However, everything said is equally applicable to inspections. For reviews of documents, size is referred to as "pages of documentation reviewed."* For inspection of code, this could be replaced by "lines of code inspected." Any discrepancies will be noted.

*If an entire document is not reviewed at a given review, just the pages reviewed should determine the size.

Some of the data obtained from reviews that are used to compute significant metrics, are the size of the document, the number of errors found, the number of hours spent and number of pages read by each of the participants preparing for the review, and the number of hours taken up in the review meeting. One key metric we will be discussing in this section is the error density, or number of errors found, divided by the number of pages reviewed.

Effectiveness Factors

Studies of review effectiveness have found that reviews which find the greatest density of errors:

* Involve documents with a small number of pages,
* Are prepared for well by the reviewers, and
* Have a low rate of review, in terms of document pages per meeting hour.

Other factors, of course, are of vital importance to the effectiveness of the review. The availability of reviewers with the appropriate expertise, for example.

Preparation rate is a metric defined as the average number of pages read by reviewers per hour, in preparation for the review. Figure 14-4 illustrates the rela-

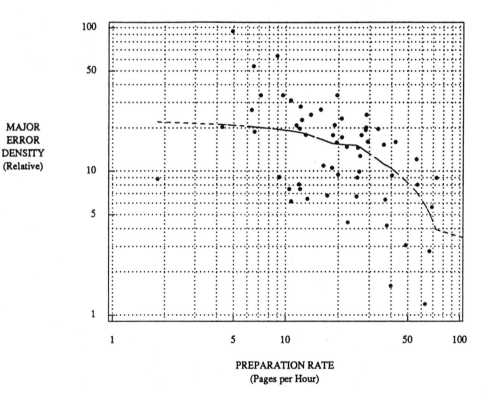

FIGURE 14-4. Variation of major error density with preparation rate.

tionship of preparation rate to the resulting density of major errors discovered in each document. Each point represents one review, and the line shows the average trend for reviews.

It is obvious that preparation rate has high correlation with the density of errors found. It is not clear which is cause and which is effect. One would think that slower preparation would yield a higher number of errors found, but it may also be that the presence of more errors necessitates greater preparation time.

Review rate will be defined as the number of pages reviewed in a document divided by the total duration of the review meeting(s). Figure 14-5 illustrates the relationship between the rate of document review and the resulting density of major errors discovered in the document. The density of major errors found is inversely related to the review rate. It is not surprising that the rate of reviewing a document at the review meeting is strongly correlated to the rate of preparation by the reviewers; this is shown in Figure 14-6. The higher the preparation rate, the higher the review rate.

Figure 14-7 shows the three most highly correlated review parameters as a function of the document size. The document size appears to be a major factor in determining the preparation rate and the review rate. For larger documents, the preparation rate and review rate are both increased. This in turn is at least partly

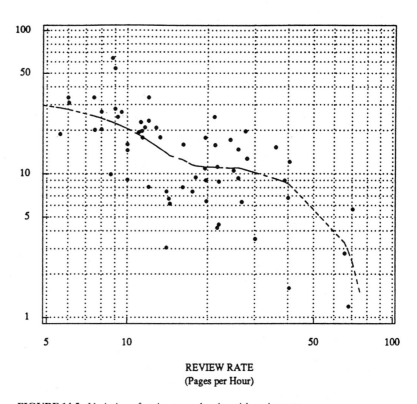

MAJOR ERROR DENSITY (Relative)

REVIEW RATE (Pages per Hour)

FIGURE 14-5. Variation of major error density with review rate.

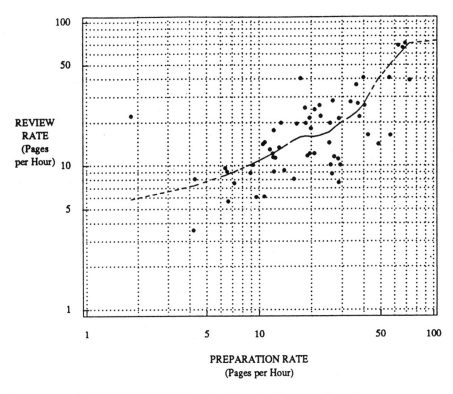

FIGURE 14-6. Variation of review rate with preparation rate.

responsible for the drop in error density with larger document sizes. Although the density of errors in larger documents may in fact be lower, we have no reason to believe so. And we will see shortly that this appears not to be the case.

The dashed lines are averages for the major error density, preparation rate, and review rate over the document size range. Proportional increases in the number of major errors found, in preparation time, and in meeting time would show as horizontal lines. The closer to horizontal the dashed lines are, the more is the tendency toward proportional changes over the size range.

Establishing Control Limits

From the relationships illustrated in the figures, it is clear that we should establish some objective criteria for making some judgement as to the effectiveness of a review. These criteria would include:

1. A preparation rate less than some maximum,
2. A review rate less than some maximum rate, and
3. An error density within some acceptable rance.

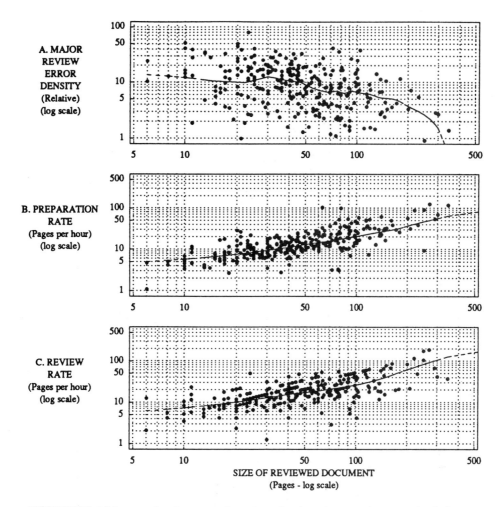

FIGURE 14-7. Major error density, preparation rate, and review rate versus document size for low level design reviews.

In order to do this, historical data collected from reviews must be available. Ideally, we would like to determine the levels of the above factors that resulted in reviews that were most effective. If the data is available on faults found during later testing than could have been found at the reviews, then the effectiveness of the reviews can be determined. It is more likely that such later testing data is not available, and some estimate must be made as to the most effective reviews.

We have seen in Figure 14-7 that smaller documents tend to have lower preparation rates and also tend to be reviewed more slowly. It would be reasonable to select reviews of documents, say those which are smaller than 50 pages, as having high probability of being the most effective.

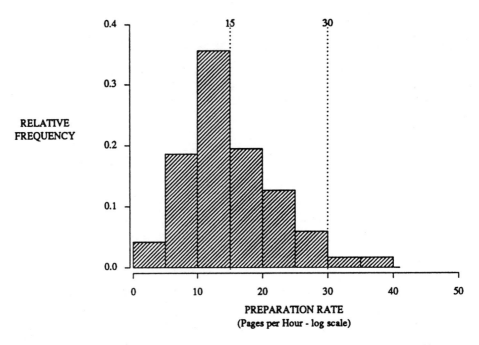

FIGURE 14-8. Distribution of preparation rate for low level design documents smaller than 50 pages.

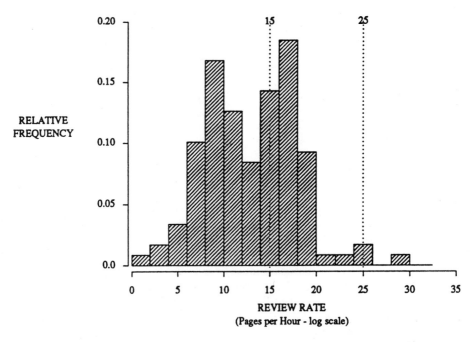

FIGURE 14-9. Distribution of review rate for low level design documents smaller than 50 pages.

TABLE 14-2   Typical Guidelines and Limits for Preparation Rate and Review Rate

	Document Type	Recommended	Maximum
Preparation Rate (Pages per Hour)	Requirements	5	15
	High Level Design	10	30
	Detailed Design	15	30
Review Rate (Pages per Hour)	Requirements	5	10
	High Level Design	10	25
	Detailed Design	15	25

Figure 14-8 shows the distribution of preparation rate for low-level design documents smaller than 50 pages. The mean is close to 15 pages per hour, and the 90th percentile of the distribution is about 30 pages per hour. So reasonable choices for a recommended and maximum level would be 15 and 30 respectively.

Figure 14-9 shows the distribution of review rate for low-level design documents smaller than 50 pages. The mean is close to 15 pages per hour and the 90th percentile of the distribution is close to 25 pages per hour. These would be the reasonable guidelines for low level design documents. Such guidelines may be found to be different for different types of documents. An example is shown in Table 14-2. We would like to establish an expected range for the density of major errors that might be found in the effective review of each type of document. This could be done by characterizing the distribution of the density of major errors found in the reviews of smaller documents. The overall average density of major errors for these reviews, as well as the variance of the major error density, can be determined. Now the distribution of error densities will not be uniform over all document sizes. This is so, because it is well known in statistics that the variance of a sample will be inversely proportional to the size of the sample. In the same way, the variance in the major error density in a document is inversely rated to the size of the document. If $\sigma(1)^2$ is the variance in the error density for a document of unit size, and p is the number of pages reviewed in a particular document, then the variance of the error density for that size document would be given by:

$$\sigma(p)^2 = \frac{\sigma(1)^2}{p} \tag{14.1}$$

To illustrate this, Figure 14-10 shows a plot of review error density versus the number of document pages reviewed. Superimposed on the plot are several curves showing approximate 1, 2, and 3 standard deviations from the mean, as a function of the number of reviewed pages. So it is clear that any limits on error density found at a review must depend on the number of pages reviewed.

Setting the error limits at one standard deviation from the mean would result in about 68% of all effective reviews having a major error density within the limits; two standard deviations, about 95%. If the upper limit on errors were chosen to be

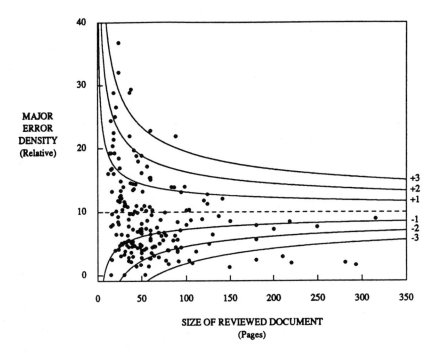

FIGURE 14-10. Major error density resulting from design reviews versus size of document.

2 standard deviations from the mean, the limit on errors found at a review, as a function of the number of pages reviewed, would be given by:

$$e_h(p) = \bar{e} + \frac{2\sigma(1)}{\sqrt{p}}$$ (14.2)

Where e_h is the upper limit, $\bar{e}$ is the historical average major error density for reviews of smaller documents, p is the number of document pages reviewed, and $\sigma(1)$ is the standard deviation at unit size. An expression giving an estimate for the variance, $\sigma(1)^2$, can be derived by rewriting Equation 14.1:

$$\sigma(1)^2 = p\sigma(p)^2$$ (14.3)

Given data from a number of reviews of smaller, similar type documents, $i = 1\ldots n$, e_i being the major error density found in each document with p_i pages reviewed, and $\bar{e}$ being the average major error density, the variance in the error density, $\sigma(p)_i^2$, for each review i is just the squared deviation from the mean:

$$\sigma(p)_i^2 = (e_i - \bar{e})^2$$ (14.4)

So an estimate of $\sigma(1)$ can be obtained by averaging the results of all these reviews:

$$\hat{\sigma}(1)^2 = \frac{1}{n}\sum_{i=1}^{n} p_i \sigma(p)_i^2 = \frac{1}{n}\sum_{i=1}^{n} p_i (e_i - \bar{e})^2 \tag{14.5}$$

Typically, the distribution of error densities is not normal, not uniform about the mean. The variance above the mean, σ_h^2, is usually higher than that below the mean, σ_l^2. We can deal with the upper and lower halves of the distribution separately. Two variances can be calculated using Equation 14.5 by separately averaging over the reviews having error densities *above* the mean, and those with error densities *below* the mean. The upper and lower density limits would then be calculated using:

$$e_h(p) = \bar{e} + \frac{2\sigma_h(1)}{\sqrt{p}} \qquad e_l(p) = \bar{e} - \frac{2\sigma_l(1)}{\sqrt{p}} \tag{14.6}$$

To avoid computations by the developers in trying to figure whether the number of major errors found at a particular review are within limits, a chart can be prepared, such as is shown in Table 14-3. A graphical form of this information is shown in Figure 14-13. Shown in the table are the range of errors that would be expected for a given number of pages reviewed. The acceptable range for the number of errors corresponding to a given page size p, is computed by multiplying the upper and lower error densities from Equations 14.6 by p. The acceptable range for error densities, will be a function of document type as well as the size. Different document types will probably have different mean error densities, and also different variances. Shown in the table are the ranges for two document types having different mean error densities (e.g., 100 and 25 errors per hundred pages). Actual values would, of course, depend on the historical information available.

Use of Control Charts

After having established guidelines and limits for the preparation rate and review rate, and also limits for the number of errors found as a function of document size, management attention is essential in affecting the effectiveness of the review process. Control charts are useful in tracking review parameters and displaying them for management attention.

Figure 14-11 shows control charts for preparation rate and review rate. As the preparation rate or review rate begins to show an increasing trend, management should determine what factors may be causing a higher rate(s). Is the schedule

TABLE 14-3   Examples of Acceptable Ranges of Major Errors for Number of Document Pages Reviewed

Pages	ACCEPTABLE ERROR RANGE For Mean Error Density (Errs/100 pgs) of: 100	25	Pages	ACCEPTABLE ERROR RANGE For Mean Error Density (Errs/100 pgs) of: 100	25
5	0-28	0-14	130	61-222	7-93
10	0-41	0-20	140	67-235	9-97
15	0-53	0-25	150	74-247	10-102
20	0-63	0-30	160	80-259	11-106
25	2-72	0-34	170	87-271	13-111
30	4-81	0-37	180	93-283	14-115
35	6-90	0-41	190	100-294	16-119
40	9-98	0-44	200	106-306	17-124
45	11-106	0-48	210	113-317	19-128
50	14-114	0-51	220	119-329	21-132
55	17-121	0-54	230	126-340	22-136
60	19-129	0-57	240	132-351	24-140
65	22-136	0-60	260	146-374	27-148
70	25-143	0-62	280	159-396	30-156
75	28-150	0-65	300	173-418	34-163
80	31-157	1-68	320	186-439	37-171
85	34-164	1-71	340	200-461	40-179
90	37-171	2-73	360	214-482	44-186
95	40-177	3-76	380	228-503	47-193
100	43-184	3-78	400	241-524	50-201
105	46-190	4-81	420	255-545	54-208
110	49-197	5-83	440	269-566	57-215
115	52-203	5-86	460	283-586	61-222
120	55-210	6-88	480	297-607	64-229
125	58-216	7-90	500	311-627	68-236

pressure on the project necessitating shortcuts? Is it lack of motivation on the part of the reviewers?

In addition to average preparation rate and average review rate, the changes in the average density of faults found during review can be tracked on a somewhat different type of chart, shown in Figure 14-12. Here, since the sizes of the documents are different, a new metric is being tracked, the relative deviation from the mean:

$$d_i = \frac{(e_i - \bar{e})}{\sigma(1)/\sqrt{p_i}} \tag{14.7}$$

Where d_i is the relative deviation from the mean, and the other variables are defined above for Equation 14.2 and Equation 14.4. This is the absolute deviation

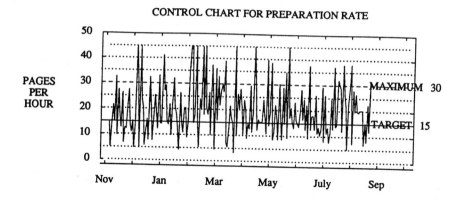

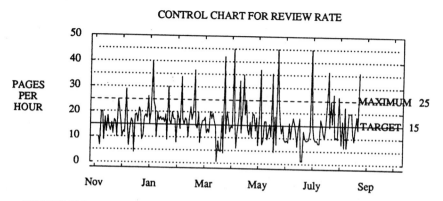

FIGURE 14-11. Control chart for the average preparation rate and review rate over time.

from the mean divided by the standard deviation *at the particular size of document.* Limits are set at ±2 for reference. If the average density of faults being found by reviews changes significantly, then a change in the average preparation rate and/or average review rate should also be looked for. If there is no significant change in either of these, the cause of the change in error density deviation should be investigated. Again management may be able to learn the cause and take some corrective action, if needed. Of course, if the error density is declining, this may be a good sign.

Figure 14-13 shows a different sort of chart for determining if the number of errors resulting from a document review was within limits for the document size. Here, the size of the document is plotted on the horizontal axis, and the number of errors found is plotted on the vertical axis. Upper and lower limit curves are shown corresponding to the ±2 standard deviations shown in Figure 14-10. This type of chart makes it easier to determine if the number of errors is within bounds when looking at individual reviews which will now be discussed.

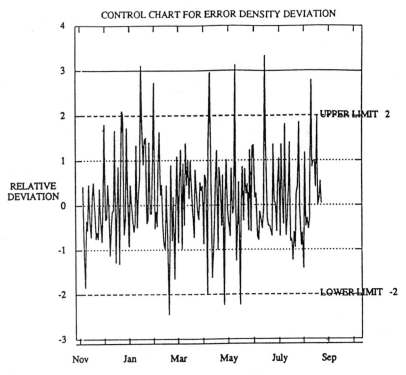

CONTROL CHART FOR ERROR DENSITY DEVIATION

FIGURE 14-12. Control chart for relative deviation of review error density from the mean.

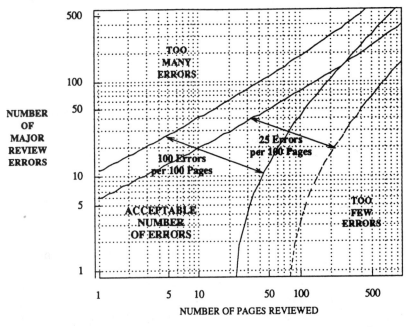

FIGURE 14-13. Example of a chart showing acceptable ranges of major review errors for two document types having mean error densities of 25 and 100 errors per hundred pages.

Judging Individual Reviews

Preparation rate, review rate, and error density are measurable indicators of possible review effectiveness. Other intangible factors, such as prior experience of reviewers must also be used.

Based on the limits derived above, we can base some judgement of the adequacy of review as follows. If all the following are true:

1. The preparation rate was no higher than the recommended rate,
2. The review rate was no higher than the recommended rate,
3. The error density was between the upper and lower limits,

then the document review should be considered successfully completed. If the preparation rate was below the maximum rate but not at the recommended rate, or the review rate was below the maximum rate but not at the recommended rate, the review may have been a good one, but may not have been as effective as it might have been. If the major error density is also lower than the lower limit, it is additional evidence that the review was less effective. Some judgment must be used in weighing all of the factors.

If the preparation rate was greater than the maximum, or the review rate greater than the maximum, there is a high probability that the review was not effective. The review issues should be resolved, and the document re-reviewed.

If the error density is above the upper limit, a re-review should be considered without regard for the preparation rate and review rate. Error densities in this range can be considered to be too high, whether the review was effective or not. In addition to a large number of possibly missed errors, there is a strong possibility that new errors would be introduced in correcting those found at the review.

The above recommendations are made with the assumption that other factors will enter into any decision to re-review. For example, a preliminary review of the document may have been conducted, in which case the error density discovered in the formal review may be justifiably low. The size of the document is also a significant factor. A small document, one of less than 5 pages, may not justify a second review. A large one, one of 100 pages or more, most likely would.

Results of Using Guidelines and Limits

When management is careful to establish review guidelines, budget the necessary time and resources, and track review results, the development organization should be expected to respond. Figure 14-14 shows data, taken from a set of reviews of low level design documents, in the same form as Figure 14-7. Comparing the two figures shows that the preparation rate for larger documents is lower and the review rates are generally lower with guidelines in place. Also, it is significant to note that the density of major review errors is also more uniform across the spectrum of document sizes.

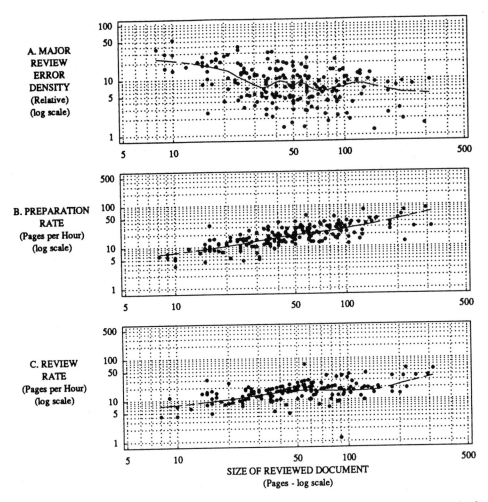

A. MAJOR REVIEW ERROR DENSITY (Relative) (log scale)

B. PREPARATION RATE (Pages per Hour) (log scale)

C. REVIEW RATE (Pages per Hour) (log scale)

SIZE OF REVIEWED DOCUMENT
(Pages - log scale)

FIGURE 14-14. Major error density, preparation rate, and review rate versus document size for low level design reviews after guidelines and limits in place.

14.5 STATISTICAL CONTROLS APPLIED TO CODE INSPECTIONS

Code inspections[6] have been used very effectively as part of the software development process. The inspection process can be enhanced by using statistical quality control techniques. As in the case of reviews, control charts can be used to track the metrics indicative of the effectiveness of code inspections, and have a beneficial effect. The exact form that these "control charts" take, depends upon the maturity of the inspection process within a software development organization, and the amount of historical data available.

The first approach is exactly the same as the approach taken for reviews. However, a second approach seeks to develop a model of the inspection process. A "model" relates the inspection parameters to the effectiveness of the inspection. Using a model of this type, some estimate can be made of the number of remaining errors in the code, or at least an estimate of the *probability* that more than an acceptable number of errors remain. As we will see, a chart can be devised which estimates the density of errors remaining after inspection, as a function of the model parameters. Parameters such as inspection effort and the density of errors found at the inspection meeting are significant.

Code Inspection Factors

Typical data reported on code inspection forms include the number of lines of code inspected, the total time spent by the inspectors preparing for the inspection meeting, the length of the meeting, and the number of errors found. Several factors[7, 8] in the inspections which correlated well with the density of errors discovered were: 1. the preparation effort intensity, or preparation divided by the code size. 2. the rate at which the code was inspected, and 3. the size of the unit of code.

- Preparation Effort Intensity. Prior to the actual code inspection meeting, the inspectors prepare for the inspection by studying the code and the design documents. Preparation effort intensity is defined as the total inspector preparation time divided by the number of source lines in the unit of code. Preparation effort intensity has been found to have high positive correlation with the density of errors found. Preparation Rate, another measure of preparation, was introduced in the earlier discussion of reviews. This is the average rate at which each inspector prepares for the inspection, and is equal to the number of source lines to be inspected divided by the average inspector preparation time. Preparation Rate is also equal to the number of inspectors divided by the Preparation Effort Intensity.
- Inspection Rate. During the actual inspection meeting, the inspectors read the code and look for errors. The inspection rate is defined as the number of lines of source code inspected divided by the total duration of the inspection meeting(s). The rate of inspection is not a completely independent variable. It partially depends upon the rate at which errors are being found, which in turn depends upon the amount of preparation and the density of errors present in the code. The density of discovered errors has been found to have an inverse relationship to the inspection rate. Figure 14-5 shows the typical relationship.
- Code Size. The size of the code being inspected has been found to be the major factor influencing the preparation effort intensity and the inspection rate. Larger units of code tend to receive proportionately less preparation and are inspected at a higher rate. This results in a lower density of discovered errors for larger units of code. The small to moderate sized units of code generally have high preparation effort intensity relative to the code size (low preparation rate), and also tend to have a low rate of inspection during the meeting. This results in a generally higher density of discovered errors for these units of code. Figure 14-14 shows the typical relationship of code size on

the other factors. As in the case with document reviews, there is a need to emphasize the importance of the critical inspection factors to the development community. A recommended preparation effort intensity level and a recommended inspection rate should be adopted by the project as goals. Also, a minimum preparation effort intensity level should be adopted as entry criteria for inspections. Likewise, a maximum inspection rate should be adopted as exit criteria from inspections. Upper and lower limits on the density of errors found should be selected, based on the error distribution from "effective" inspections. Use of an upper limit would point out code with a much greater than average error density. Using a lower limit would point out inspections that may not have been effective.

These control limits and recommendations should become an integral part of the code inspection process for a project. This can be facilitated by designing code inspection forms with accompanying instructions that contain the recommendations and limits. A code inspection Meeting Notice form, which identifies the inspectors and invites them to the inspection meeting, should be designed to emphasize scheduling sufficient time to inspect the piece of code of a given size. For large units of code, it should allow the inspection moderator to schedule a number of coordinated meetings. A Code Inspection Report form, which summarizes all the relevant parameters of the inspection, should be designed to highlight the preparation effort intensity, inspection rate, and total number of errors found relative to the code size. The form can also incorporate the control chart for errors on the reverse side for the convenience of the inspection moderator.

Project-wide averages for the critical inspection parameters should be reported with other project status information, and thus brought to the attention of the project managers. Control charts, such as those shown in Figures 14-11 through 14-13, should be used. These aspects of the total inspection process encourage each manager to be aware of the preparation time being taken by the inspectors, of the rate at which the code is being inspected, and how the resulting error density compared with the expected range for that code size. It also allows managers to exercise some judgement about the adequacy of the inspections, and decide on various courses of action based on the inspection results.

An Inspection Model

Although improvement can be made in the inspection process using the above methods, further improvement can be made. If the inspection process has matured in the organization, and sufficient data collected, a code inspection model can be developed. Having a model which would relate input parameters, such as the preparation effort intensity and inspection rate, to the resulting fraction of errors found in the code can be very useful. Using such a model, the effectiveness of inspections can be estimated. In fact, an estimate can be made of the density of coding errors remaining in the code after an inspection is completed. This estimate would be one of a number of factors used to estimate the quality of the software.

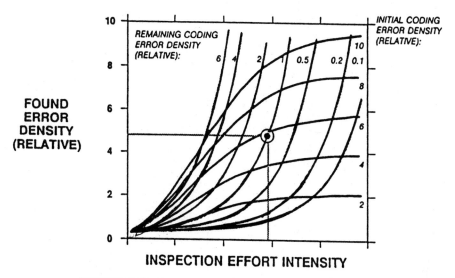

FIGURE 14-15. New prediction chart based on inspection model.

Using data obtained from several software releases, such a model was developed relating the fraction of initial errors found to the total hours of inspection effort per unit code size, or Inspection Effort Intensity.[10] From this model, a chart was devised as shown in Figure 14-15. Given the inspection effort intensity, and the density of coding errors found, an estimate for the remaining coding error density could be made from the chart. For example, the point shown in Figure 14-15 represents 5 errors per unit code size found by the inspection at a particular effort intensity. The horizontal sloped curves represent the initial coding error density, in this case the density was 6 errors per unit code size. The vertically sloped curves represent the *remaining* error density, in this case 1 error per unit code size. Based on the model estimate, and engineering judgement, one could decide whether the code should be re-inspected.

New Inspection Guidelines

One of the fundamental questions about inspections is: "How much inspection effort is worthwhile?" An inspection model provides the means to estimate this, given that some estimate of the average cost to find and fix an error in later phases of development is available. Below, is a simple equation for the total cost of coding errors in a software release, as a function of inspection effort intensity:

$$C_t(h) = C_h h + e_0 C_h wf(h) + e_0 A[1 - f(h)] \tag{14.8}$$

Where C_t is the total cost of coding errors in dollars per ncsl (non commented source line of code), C_h is the time cost of the people involved, h is the average code inspection effort intensity in person hours per ncsl, w is the average number of person hours per error needed to re-work inspection errors, e_0 is the initial

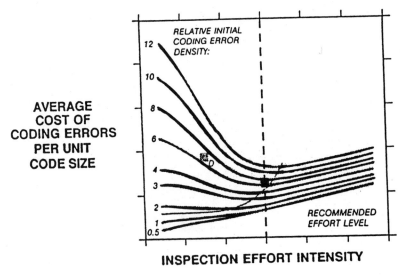

FIGURE 14-16. Cost of errors versus inspection effort intensity for various initial error densities.

coding error density, A is the average cost of an error missed by the inspection and found during later phases, and $f(h)$ is the model estimate of the fraction of errors found in the inspection, as a function of the person hours of inspection effort per unit code size. Figure 14-16 shows a plot of this equation for total cost of coding errors, versus inspection effort intensity, for several values of initial coding error density. Estimated cost parameters were used. This figure shows that there is a minimum total cost at some effort level, depending on the initial error density, and that more inspection effort is justified when there is a higher density of errors in the code. Conversely, if few errors are expected, little or no effort is justified. Point D in Figure 14-16 corresponds to the initial coding error density and inspection effort intensity of a particular software release. The model indicates that increased inspection effort would have reduced the overall cost of errors. As Equation 14.8 suggests, the actual point of minimum cost is highly dependent upon the average cost to find and fix an error later in the software life cycle. More inspection effort is justified if the later cost is high. The code inspection model can thus lead to identification of the appropriate effort level where the historical error density is known.

By selecting some target for density of errors remaining, a type of "control chart" can be produced as shown in Figure 14-17. Using the code inspection model, a curve of "constant remaining error density" can be plotted for the given target level. A point plotted on the chart at the density of errors found versus the effort intensity for a given inspection would show if the estimated density of errors remaining was above or below the target level. Inspections having a predicted density of remaining errors above this target would be candidates for re-inspection.

Conceptually, this is a big improvement. With a "control chart" based on historical data, like the one shown in Figure 14-13, a moderate amount of inspec-

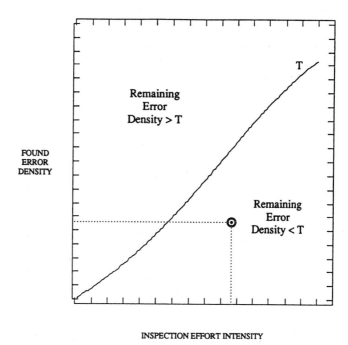

FOUND
ERROR
DENSITY

Remaining
Error
Density > T

T

Remaining
Error
Density < T

INSPECTION EFFORT INTENSITY

FIGURE 14-17. Code inspection control chart based on inspection model.

tion effort finding a moderate density of errors might be acceptable. However, the chart based on the inspection model may well predict a density of remaining errors higher than the target, suggesting a re-inspection of the code. Again, with the historical chart, a moderate effort finding a very low density of errors would imply that the code was not effectively inspected. With the new chart it might imply that the code was very clean to begin with and few errors remained. This new chart allows for *improvement* in the coding process, i.e., fewer errors being made by the developers, while the other type of chart is tied to the historical error density distribution. With this new chart, it is possible to have very clean code go through an inspection with moderate effort, and be fairly confident that the code will emerge from the inspection with high quality.

Figure 14-18 illustrates experience in tracking the gradual increase in both inspection effort intensity and found error density during a period when increasing effort intensity was being encouraged on a large software project. The point labeled "JAN" in the figure shows the average inspection effort intensity and found error density just prior to the establishment of the higher effort guidelines. The point labeled "APR" shows the average effort intensity and found error density three months after the guidelines went into effect. As the figure shows, the upward trend followed the model closely after the guidelines were established, and showed that the increased effort was fruitful. For comparison, the average effort intensity and found error density levels for four previous software releases are shown, points "A" through "D".

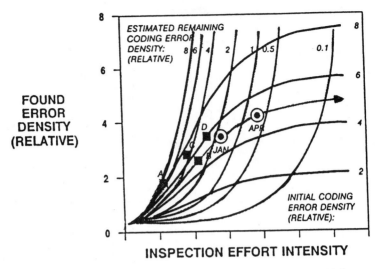

FIGURE 14-18. Improvement in inspection effectiveness after new guidelines.

Chart Refinement

Experience using a code inspection model shows that the model is relatively accurate where the average of a large number of inspections is involved, such as all the inspections comprising a large software release. However, predictions for individual inspections lack consistent accuracy when compared to results of re-inspections or results of unit testing the code. This can be disconcerting to project managers as well as to the development community.

Further analyses of the code inspection model's parameters and its corresponding predictions with re-inspection results and unit test data provided for the development of a revised chart. Instead of predicting that a unit of code had less than a given density of errors remaining, the revised chart is designed to estimate the *probability* that the code has less than a certain targeted density of remaining errors.

Using re-inspection data and unit test results, the actual effectiveness of inspections can be determined. One can then characterize the distribution of the ratio of the model's predicted remaining error density to the actual error density found by unit testing or re-inspection. The natural logarithm transformation of this ratio can be characterized by a probability distribution that is approximately normal, indicating that the ratio itself is roughly log-normal. This is depicted in Figure 14-19. Using the mean and standard deviations derived from this distribution, probability values can be easily assigned to the point estimates corresponding to the inspection model curves to yield the likelihood that a given inspection has a remaining error density (unit test error density) at or below a selected target. An example of this revised chart, which gives the probability that the density of remaining errors exceeds the selected target, is shown in Figure 14-20. The chart is

FREQUENCY

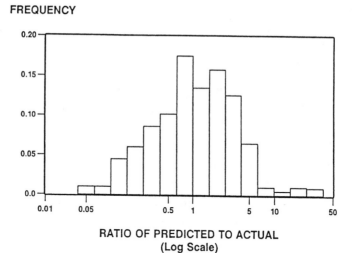

RATIO OF PREDICTED TO ACTUAL
(Log Scale)

FIGURE 14-19. Distribution of the ratio of predicted remaining errors to actual errors found in unit testing.

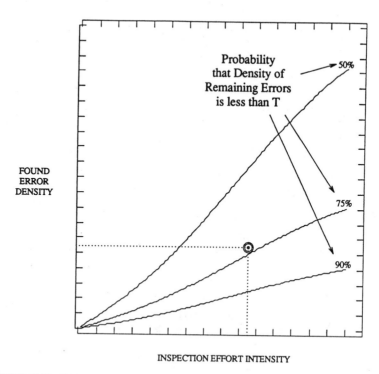

FIGURE 14-20. Revised inspection chart showing the probability of remaining error density exceeding a threshold.

used in the same way as that shown in Figure 14-17. A point is plotted on this revised chart, corresponding to the inspection effort intensity and found error density of a given inspection. The point falling close to the 75% line, as shown in the figure, would indicate that there was a 75% probability that the inspected code had less than the targeted density of errors remaining. Using this new chart, rather than estimating the exact density of remaining errors, software developers can assess the *risk* of having too many undetected errors.

14.6 SEQUENTIAL SAMPLING IN TESTING

When conducting testing to assess the quality of a software product, one would like to run a sufficient number of tests to provide confidence that either 1. the target level of quality has been attained, or 2. the present quality will not be tolerated by a customer. In other words, we wish to make a decision about releasing the software product to customers. The testing process could stop when evidence was provided for either case. The key question is how many tests are required before that decision can be made.

Sequential sampling is a method which seems ideally suited to address this question. Sequential procedures, in general, are characterized as test procedures for which the sample size required for decision-making is not known a priori, but rather is determined by the actual sampling results. The ultimate decision to accept or reject a "lot" of product, or a piece of software, can be made as soon as sufficient evidence is available. This is quite unlike standard fixed (single) sampling schemes for which information is evaluated only at the end of the entire process.[11] The particular advantage of sequential sampling is that the number of samples (tests) needed is from 80% to as little as 20% of the number required by fixed sampling.

How Sequential Sampling Works

Briefly, the process of sequential sample testing works as follows. We choose sample tests from the set of all possible tests and execute them, one at a time. We observe the number of tests that have been run, and the number of these that have failed. After obtaining the result of each test, we can decide to:

1. Stop testing because a sufficient number of the tests have been run without failing to give confidence that the software has an acceptable quality level, or
2. Stop testing because too many of the tests have failed already, indicating that the software has unacceptable quality, or
3. Continue testing because the testing results are not yet conclusive.

Thus, testing only needs to continue until a decision can be made.

A particular sequential sampling plan is characterized by the specific values of four parameters:

- p_1: The target quality level; generally denotes the fraction of defectives which is allowable (proportion of failed tests in this application),
- p_2: The absolutely unacceptable quality level; indicates the fraction of defectives which the customer will never accept,
- α: The maximum probability that the testing procedure rejects a product (or lot) of quality level p_1 or better,
- β: The maximum probability that the procedure accepts a product of quality level p_2 or worse.

The last two parameters are often referred to as producer's risk and consumer's risk, respectively. Together these parameters define boundaries of acceptance and rejection as shown in Figure 14-21. Testing ends when a point falls outside the

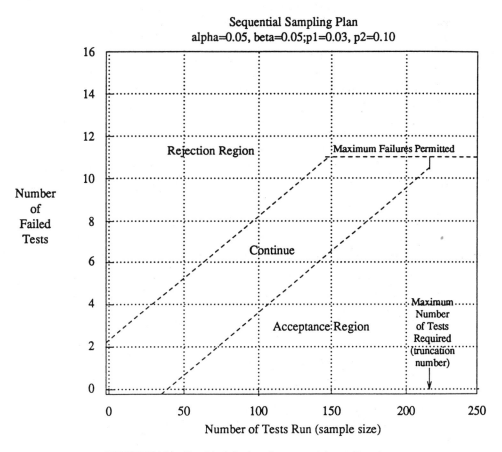

FIGURE 14-21. Graphical display of a sequential sampling plan.

"continue" region. If testing results fall in the "acceptance" region, the product has acceptable quality; if in the "rejection" region, the product has less than acceptable quality. Testing continues, as long as the results fall within the "continue" region, until some maximum required number of tests have been run, or a maximum permitted number of failures has occurred. At this stage, testing would conclude. The decision rule is to "reject" if the number of failures is greater than or equal to the maximum permitted number of failures for the particular sequential scheme, otherwise, "accept." Hence, we have run a sufficient number of tests to make a decision concerning the software product.

The equations of the boundary lines have the following form:

1. Acceptance line: $X_a = -h_1 + sN$
2. Rejection line: $X_r = h_2 + sN$

Where N is the number of tests run, X is the threshold number of failed test, and from Grant and Leavenworth[12] we have:

$$g_1 = \log \frac{p_2}{p_1}, g_2 = \log \frac{1 - p_1}{1 - p_2}, a = \log \frac{1 - \beta}{\alpha}, b = \log \frac{1 - \alpha}{\beta},$$

$$h_1 = \frac{b}{g_1 + g_2}, h_2 = \frac{a}{g_1 + g_2}, \text{ and } s = \frac{g_2}{g_1 + g_2}.$$

Target values can be chosen for p_1 and p_2 from customer expectations, industry standards, quality goals, or previous experience.

The maximum number of tests required is equal to a quantity known as the *truncation number*, which is developed in Reference 11. More will be said about this shortly. The maximum permitted number of failures is just the next whole number of failures above the point where the acceptance line boundary meets the truncation number of tests.

For the particular sequential sampling plan shown in Figure 14-21, $\alpha = 0.05$, $\beta = 0.05$, $p_1 = 0.03$, and $p_2 = 0.10$. Such a plan gives equations for the boundaries between the "Continue" and "Acceptance" and "Rejection" regions as follows:

1. Acceptance line: $X_a = -2.302 + 0.059n$
2. Rejection line: $X_r = 2.302 + 0.059n$

As derived from the above expressions, the maximum number of tests required is 210 tests, and the corresponding maximum number of failures is the next integer greater than $(-2.302 + 0.059 \times 210)$ or 11.

Selecting a Sampling Plan

Selection of the particular sampling plan to use must balance the desired accuracy and confidence with constraints on the number of tests one can reasonably run.

Some judgement must be exercised in finding this balance and selecting the appropriate set of parameters with corresponding sequential sampling scheme.

Figure 14-22 shows Operating Characteristic (OC) curves showing the probability of accepting a product for various values of p, where p would be the "true" percentage of failed tests if an infinite number of tests were run. The truncation scheme selected will have no real impact on the OC function. Of course, one would like high OC values for p near the target p_1 and low OC values for p near the threshold of unacceptability, p_2. Parameters for these curves are α and β, and the range of p is $p_1 \leq p \leq p_2$. For example, suppose we were to use the sequential testing plan from Figure 14-21. The target quality level is a failure rate $p_1 = 0.03$, and we want to be sure and reject software with a failure rate of $p_2 = 0.10$ or above. From Figure 14-22, the probability of accepting software with an actual $p = 0.05$ is about 70%. There would be a 30% chance of rejecting the software as unacceptable. With $\alpha = 0.01$, the probability of acceptance is raised to over 80%, but the number of tests required to give this higher confidence would be larger.

Next we consider the average number of test samples that would have to be taken until an accept/reject decision could be made. This number would be different for different sampling schemes, i.e, different values of the parameters. Figure 14-23 shows the Average Sample Number (ASN) needed for various values

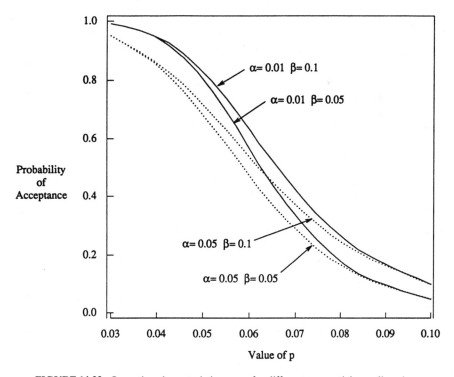

FIGURE 14-22. Operating characteristic curves for different sequential sampling plans.

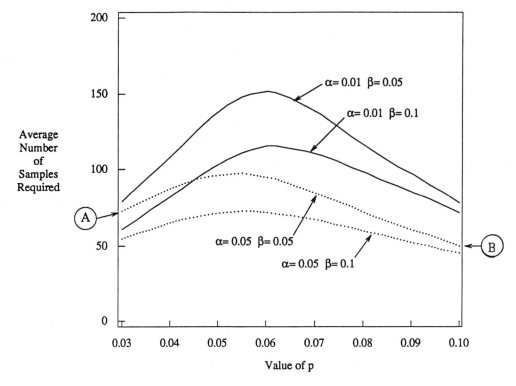

FIGURE 14-23. Average sample number curves for different sequential sampling plans.

of p, were p represents the underlying quality (failure rate) of the software. If we continue the example above with the software having an actual value of $p = 0.05$, the average number of tests that would have to be run for $\alpha = 0.05$ and $\beta = 0.05$ would be about 95. For $\alpha = 0.01$, the average number of tests would be increased to almost 140. As the figure shows, fewer tests are typically required to make a decision when the software has a p that is close to either the target, p_1, or the level of unacceptability, p_2. The average number of tests required is at a maximum when the quality of the software is midway between the two levels.

The maximum number of tests required to make a decision, called the truncation number, is equal to 3 times the greater of the two ASNs corresponding to the two parameters p_1 and p_2. Referring to Figure 14-23, for the sampling scheme above with $\alpha = 0.05$ and $\beta = 0.05$, the ASN corresponding to $p_1 = 0.03$ is about 70 (A), and that for $p_2 = 0.10$ is about 50 (B). The truncation number would be $3 \times 70 = 210$.

Figure 14-24 shows the potential savings in the number of tests run in a fixed sampling scheme versus a sequential sampling scheme with the same parameters. For this example, the sequential scheme provides a minimum 20% savings in sample size when the quality of the software product is close to the threshold level. When the actual quality of the software is significantly better or worse, a factor of 2 to 5 savings in sample size can be realized.

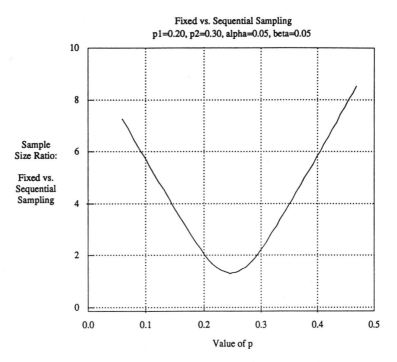

FIGURE 14-24. Ratio of sample sizes for a fixed versus a sequential sampling scheme with the same parameters.

A Practical Example

We will now illustrate how the use of sequential sampling would allow an earlier decision about the quality of a software product. Figure 14-25 shows simulated test data plotted on a sequential sampling chart. The sampling scheme used for this chart was:

Risk of rejecting good quality: $\alpha = 0.05$
Risk of accepting poor quality: $\beta = 0.05$
Target quality level (failure rate): $p_1 = 0.05$
Minimum acceptable failure rate: $p_2 = 0.15$

In this example, a total of 238 tests yielded 14 failures, giving a failure rate of 0.05, which is at the desired p_1 level. With this target failure rate, the software could have been accepted after running only 50 to 60 tests.

Concluding Remarks

The principles of sequential sampling seem ideally suited for the scenario commonly involved in software testing. With appropriate parameter choice, we can

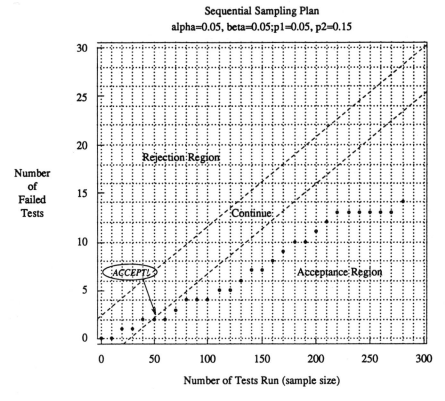

FIGURE 14-25. Example of simulated test data plotted on a sequential sampling chart showing earlier acceptance decision.

statistically determine the average number of tests that must be run before a decision can be made that:

- The software product is sufficiently near target quality, or
- It is significantly below the target quality level, and remedial action is warranted.

If the boundary into the "Acceptance Region" is crossed, the number of tests that were run to enter the region is an indication of how far above the target quality level the software might be. Fewer tests run would indicate better quality. If the boundary into the "Rejection Region" was crossed, fewer tests run would indicate poorer quality.

14.7 SUMMARY AND CONCLUSION

In this chapter, we have shown that, when viewed correctly, statistical controls can be used for software. Since software development has a great deal more variation than the typical manufacturing process, the statistical controls must be viewed differently.

For statistical control of software development, the focus must be on use as a management tool rather than on strictly technical considerations. Though technical considerations are important, use of statistical controls as management tools to motivate software developers and modify their behavior is far more important.

The keys to effective use of statistical controls in the software environment are *commitment* and *persistence*. Managers must be committed to allocating the necessary resources to allow their people to do what they are asked to do. And they must persist in the use of these controls for a long enough period of time to allow them to work.

References

1. Jones, T. Capers. *Programming Productivity,* New York: McGraw-Hill, 1986.
2. Yu, Weider D. "A Modeling Approach to Software Cost Estimation." *IEEE Journal on Selected Areas in Communications,* 8(2), Feb. 1990.
3. Yu, Weider D., Smith, D. Paul, and Huang, Steel T. "Software Productivity Measurements." *AT&T Technical Journal,* 69(3), May/Jun. 1990.
4. Humphrey, Watts S. *Managing the Software Process.* Reading, Mass.: Addison-Wesley Publishing Co., 1989.
5. AT&T. 1986. *AT&T Statistical Quality Control Handbook.* 2nd ed.
6. Fagan, Michael E. "Design and Code Inspections to Reduce Errors in Program Development." *IBM Systems Journal,* 15(3), 1976.
7. Buck, F. O. "Indicators of Quality Inspections." *IBM Technical Report TR21.802.* Systems Communications Division, Kingston, N.Y. 1981.
8. Ackerman, A. F., Fowler, P. J., and Ebenau, R. G. "Software Inspections and the Industrial Production of Software." *Software Validation.* H. L. Hausen (editor), Elsevier Science Publishers B.V. (North-Holland) 1984.
9. Christenson, D. A., and Huang, S. T. "Code Inspection Management Using Statistical Control Limits." *Proceedings of the National Communications Forum—1987,* 41(II), pp. 1095-1100.
10. Christenson, D. A., and Huang, S. T. "A Code Inspection Model for Software Quality Management and Prediction." *Proceedings of the IEEE Global Telecommunications Conference—1988.* Vol. 1, pp. 468-472.
11. McWilliams, T. P. "How to Use Sequential Statistical Methods." *ASQC Basic References in Quality Control: Statistical Technicals,* Vol. 13, 1989.
12. Grant, R. E. and Leavenworth, R. S. *Statistical Quality Control,* 6th ed. New York: McGraw-Hill, Inc., 1988, pp. 501-503.

General References

Fagan, Michael E. "Advances in Software Inspections." *IEEE Transactions on Software Engineering,* Vol. SE-12, No. 7, Jul. 1986.

Musa, J. D., Iannino, A., and Okumoto, K., *Software Reliability: Measurement, Prediction, Application,* New York: McGraw-Hill, 1987.

Snedecor, G. W. and Cochran, W. G. *Statistical Methods,* 8th ed. Iowa: Iowa State University Press, 1989.

PART IV

Achieving TQM in Software

15

Defect Prevention and
Total Quality Management

Robert G. Mays

IBM Networking Systems Laboratory

15.1 INTRODUCTION

Customers are now expecting higher levels of software product quality than ever before. In order to achieve ever higher levels of quality, the focus of software development must shift from defect detection to *defect prevention*. This shift represents a fundamental change in the philosophy of the development organization toward managing quality proactively, that is, toward correcting aspects of the development process that cause defects.

Activities that are aimed at detecting defects and correcting them, such as inspections and testing, are costly and do not add function or reduce development cycle time. They also tend to be limited in their effectiveness at achieving very low field defect rates. Defect prevention, on the other hand, focuses resources on correcting process flaws, thereby preventing the defects from being created in the first place, so that less effort is needed to detect and fix them later.

Prevention activities can be as simple as providing checklists and development guidelines, improving developer education and product documentation, and enhancing development tools. The overall investment in prevention can be as little as 1% of the development organization's resources, while reductions in product defect rates of 50% have been achieved. The cost of defect prevention activities are typically returned several times over in reduced testing and field support efforts.

In addition, defect prevention provides significant reinforcement of Total Quality Management principles within an organization. Defect prevention contributes to Total Quality Management by 1. improving product quality through preventing defects, 2. providing continuous improvement of development processes, methods and tools, and 3. increasing employee participation and buy-in in TQM activities.

Improved Product Quality

Defect prevention can result in significantly lowered field defect rates. A reduction of 50% in the defects that arise during development generally will result in a 50% reduction in the field defects as well. Moreover, the resources that were formerly spent correcting defects can be put toward developing additional function and reducing the overall development cycle time, both of which reflect higher product quality in the broader sense.

Continuous Process Improvement

Defect prevention provides a continuous focus on process improvement. "Process" is used here in the broad sense denoting all of the formal and informal stages and steps, methodologies, practices, techniques, and tools that are used to develop a product.

Defects occur because of flaws or difficulties inherent in the process or in its execution. For example, defects can result from failures to thoroughly prepare or educate developers, failures to communicate changes, or failures to provide adequate time or proper tools for checking design closure. Preventive actions on the other hand can address each one of these shortcomings by improving or fixing the process.

Defect prevention not only fine tunes an organization's current process and practices but also encourages identifying and implementing new processes, methods, and tools. For example, new design methods or tools might be introduced as the result of a suggested action. Once the new process or method is introduced, further preventive actions can help refine and fine tune that process.

Increased Employee Participation

Defect prevention activities encourage employee participation. The software development process ultimately operates at each individual developer's level. At this level, the detailed design and coding decisions are made, and this is where many of the defects occur. Defect prevention provides a vehicle for each developer to become directly involved in quality through analyzing the causes of defects, suggesting possible preventive actions, and then implementing them in their own work practices. Defect prevention activities become an on-going focus for each employee as part of TQM.

Defect prevention has been practiced in a number of software development projects mentioned in the literature.[1-7] Frequently the use of quality circles is cited. Invariably the activities of defect causal analysis and action implementation are used to achieve some or all of the following effects:

- Improve the process to prevent recurrence of future defects of the same kind
- Detect similar defects that may already exist in the product, and
- Improve defect detection methods (e.g., inspections and tests) to better detect similar defects in the future, to prevent their escape to the field.

This chapter will describe the principles of defect prevention in reference to a particular implementation within IBM Corporation known as the Defect Prevention Process.[1-4] The Defect Prevention Process provides a framework for achieving the objectives of preventing defects, continuously improving processes, and encouraging employee participation. The Defect Prevention Process has proven effective in improving product quality at a reasonable cost for implementation. It has been in use in some parts of IBM since 1983 and is currently becoming a standard practice in all of the major development laboratories in the company.

15.2 THE KEY ELEMENTS OF THE DEFECT PREVENTION PROCESS

There are four key elements of the Defect Prevention Process. In general, a successful implementation of the process incorporates all of these elements. However, an organization may develop variations or adaptations of these key elements, depending on its particular needs or its development process.

1. Causal analysis of defects and problems: perform regular analysis of defects and problems occurring in the process and suggest preventive actions. Causal analysis is done by the developers, that is, by the people who created the defects.
2. An action team to implement preventive actions: provide sufficient resources to implement the preventive actions in a timely way.
3. Periodic, timely feedback to developers: conduct regular reviews of the details of the process with developers and provide feedback on the process changes that have occurred from implemented actions. This periodic feedback is usually done in a kickoff meeting at the beginning of each development stage or step.
4. Tracking and analysis of data from the prevention process: provide a data base of the preventive actions for tracking and provide data about the defect prevention process itself for management control.

Also key to a successful implementation of the Defect Prevention Process is the integration of the prevention activities in the development process, so that they become part of everyone's job. In particular, the causal analysis and feedback activities must become part of the basic practices of the organization, much as inspections have been integrated in many development organizations. The prevention activities should not be a separate or isolated effort nor one that is conducted solely at the end of the development cycle, as with a post-mortem. Rather, it should have a continuous focus throughout the development cycle, involving all developers.

15.3 IMPLEMENTATION OF THE DEFECT PREVENTION PROCESS

The details of implementing the Defect Prevention Process are given in Reference 1. This section summarizes how the process can be implemented in a software development organization (Figure 15-1). In general the activities of the process are repeated for each major development stage or step, for example high-level design, low-level design, code, unit test, etc. If the development project is organized into teams of, say three to seven developers, the defect prevention activities are conducted at the team level.

Causal Analysis of Defects and Problems

During each development stage, defects are detected through inspections, reviews, or testing. When a number of defects have been collected, a causal analysis meeting is held by the team, usually for two hours. The team reviews the defects, determines their root causes and proposes actions to prevent similar defects in the future.

During the causal analysis meeting, the developers identify the causes of the defects that have occurred. Usually the developer who created the defect can best

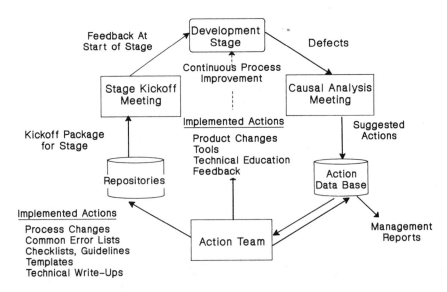

FIGURE 15-1. The defect prevention process.

TABLE 15-1   Causal Analysis Example

Defect Abstract	Cause Category	Cause Abstract	Stage Created	Suggested Actions
Referenced wrong control block for a response unit.	EDUC.	Didn't understand the router/sender build interface.	CODE	Create a user's guide for the router/ sender component.
Moved a control block field to an incorrect boundary.	COMM.	There was no documentation for the boundary requirement for that field.	CODE	Add control block boundary issues to common errors list. Create a technical write-up on control block boundaries.

identify its cause but many times a discussion involving the entire team will help clarify contributing causes. The team tries to propose actions that will eliminate the cause(s) and thus prevent recurrence of the defect. In addition, actions may be proposed that have no direct bearing on the specific causes or even on the defect in question, but which are good suggestions to be implemented for the organization.

In the last half hour of the meeting, the team also addresses broader problems that were experienced in the development stage just ending, or areas of process improvement that can be proposed, for example, project management issues that arose during the stage, or tool enhancement that are needed. Additional suggested actions are proposed.

In a typical causal analysis meeting, 10 to 15 defects are analyzed which result in 15 to 25 suggested actions. Suggested actions can address process improvements (e.g., process changes, additions to checklists, templates, guidelines, common error lists, etc.), tool improvements and enhancements, education offerings or improvements to existing education, improvements in communications procedures or project management practices, and changes to the product itself (e.g., component interface changes, improved product documentation, etc.). Suggested actions need to be described with specific details, not simply as vague suggestions for improvement, so that the action team can implement them readily.

Table 15-1 shows the results of the causal analysis of two typical defects from the coding stage. The defect is described briefly and a cause category is assigned (in this case, the defects had an education cause and a communications cause, respectively). The cause or causes are then described and the team makes suggestions for process improvement actions.

During the causal analysis meeting, the developers get direct feedback on the team's errors and their causes. This feedback in itself aids in preventing future defects by those developers.

Action Team to Implement Preventive Actions

Defect prevention must include a means of implementing the suggested actions that insures that they are implemented in a timely way. Timely action implementation requires that appropriate resources be allocated by management. The people who implement the actions should have the appropriate scope and authority within the organization to effect changes to the organization's processes and practices. And they should have the appropriate skills (e.g., product knowledge, process knowledge, tool development skills) to be able to implement the actions. In addition, the time that is devoted to action implementation should be protected from erosion by other development responsibilities the people may have.

The Defect Prevention Process calls for an action team (refer to Chapter 4) to be established to implement the preventive actions. The action team consists of developers from the area who work part-time to implement actions. The action team can serve the entire development organization (e.g., at a third or fourth-line management level) or can operate at a lower level (e.g., a second-line manager's organization). For a third or fourth-line organization of 150 to 250 people, an action team of 6 to 8 people might be needed. For an action team serving a second-line organization, 4 to 5 action team members might be needed.

In some organizations, a hierarchy of action teams may be most appropriate,[2] with "local" action teams to handle actions for each second-line organization and an "area" action team for the entire development organization.

Action team members are selected based on the skills needed. A software development organization typically needs action team members to handle process changes, educational offerings, and tool development and enhancement. The action team also needs representatives from the key technical areas in the organization, for example, design, development, test and service. Finally, a manager from the area is needed to handle suggestions for project management improvements and to assist in obtaining help for actions needing resources outside the action team. Table 15-2 shows typical action team roles and examples of actions each action team member would implement.

TABLE 15-2   Action Team Roles and Typical Actions

Action Team Member	Typical Actions Implemented
Process person	• Revise the change control process • Update checklists, common error lists • Develop a template for specification documents
Education coordinator	• Develop a new-hire education checklist • Arrange for an outside course offering • Coordinate weekly technical seminars
Tools developer	• Implement enhancements to tracking tool • Communicate tool requirements to other tool developers
Development representative	• Update the documentation of macros • Arrange for redesign/rewrite of a module • Coordinate getting write-ups of different technical areas of the product
Test representative	• Develop a template for test cases • Write up test execution guidelines
Manager	• Negotiate time for others in organization to work on actions • Implement project management improvements

Our experience is that a quality circle[8, 9] is generally not adequate to act as an action team for an organization. Quality circles typically operate at a department level and thus are limited in their scope and authority in the organization. In addition, the quality circle members may not have the skills needed to implement many of the suggested actions. Action teams, on the other hand, have the responsibility and scope of authority for the entire organization's process. Action team members are selected with the specific skills needed to implement actions.

Action team members generally work part-time on action implementation, spending perhaps 10 to 15% of their time on the task, and will serve on the action team for 1 to 2 years. The action team meets regularly (usually weekly or biweekly) to assign new suggested actions and review the status of open actions.

The action team serves as the focal point for process improvement in the organization. The team members become sensitive to what areas of the organization need improvement, and how to get the improvements adopted. Since the action team consists of developers from the organization, there is usually little resistance to adopting the implemented actions as part of the area's process.

Action teams generally have a backlog of actions needing to be implemented. Some teams use a method of prioritizing the actions based on estimates of their relative return on investment, in order to select which actions to address first. When an action is implemented, the action team communicates that fact to the organization in some way, for example, a notice in the area's newsletter or on-line bulletin board.

Periodic and Timely Feedback to Developers

Many actions result in information that is kept in on-line files which can be accessed by the developers. Such materials include, for example, process documentation, product technical information, checklists, common error lists, development guidelines and conventions, educational materials, project management guidelines, and tool documentation. The materials are typically placed in on-line repositories with appropriate indexes and search capabilities for easy access. Such repositories preserve the area's technical process and product knowledge.

Having on-line repositories, however, is not enough to ensure that the appropriate knowledge will be used by the developers during development. We have found that periodic reviews of this information are needed to remind developers of the process details that are critical to their work in a particular stage. It is necessary to provide feedback in a timely way, at the appropriate points in the development process.

The form that this periodic feedback takes is the stage kickoff meeting. Stage kickoffs are generally held by the team at the beginning of each development stage and are conducted by the team's technical leader. They usually last one to two hours. The team leader reviews the development process for that stage, focusing on areas that have been weak in the past, emphasizing new practices, and reviewing other enhancements to the organization's process, methods, and tools.

It is important that stage kickoff meetings be integrated into the development process, at the beginning of each development stage, and that the developers be directly involved. We have found that simply holding stage kickoffs can achieve significant reductions in defects for that stage. Kickoffs thus provide an immediate payback.

Tracking and Analysis of Data from the Prevention Process

Data are collected from the Defect Prevention Process to provide both the tracking of action status by the action team and the measurement of the process as a whole for management. The forms of data collection and tracking include:

1. A means of tracking actions as they are implemented, to ensure that the actions are implemented in a timely manner and are implemented correctly. The action team maintains a data base containing each action and uses reports from it to review and handle newly created actions, open actions being implemented, and recently closed actions. Among the data that are kept for each action are its priority, target date, estimated cost, and estimated effectiveness.
2. A means of measuring the Defective Prevention Process to ensure that the required activities are being done and that the level of investment in prevention intended by management is being achieved. Management uses these data to maintain its focus on the process. The action data base can be used to produce monthly management reports on (a) the level of investment in the process, that is, the time spent in prevention-related meetings, for action implementation and on education on the process, and (b) the work flow in the process, that is, the number of actions open at the beginning of the time period, actions created and closed during the period, and actions remaining at the end of the period. Management can use these data to monitor the organization's adherence to the process and to manage the backlog of unimplemented actions. Table 15-3 shows a typical status report for a six-month period for an action team serving a 250 person organization. In addition, adherence to the Defect Prevention Process activities can be encouraged by reporting the status of stage kickoff and causal analysis meetings in project status meetings.
3. A means of validating the effectiveness of the improvements once they are implemented. Certain types of defects that occur frequently (e.g., failure to free storage) can be tracked to see whether they recur after preventive actions have been implemented. To accomplish this, the action team can monitor selected types of defects. If the defects recur, further preventive steps can be taken. For example, the level of education related defects can be checked 6 and 12 months after an education program has been instituted; register destroyed defects can be checked before and after a register usage tool is introduced.

TABLE 15-3   Defect Prevention Process Status Report

Defect Prevention Process Summary for 07/01/90 through 12/31/90:

Activity	Number	Person Months
Actions closed	64	11.23
Causal analysis sessions	16	2.16
Kickoff meetings	3	0.22
Action team meetings	9	0.69
Classes on defect prevention	3	4.61
Total		18.91 person months
		or 1.57 person years

Action Team Work Flow:

Actions open at the beginning of period:	266
+ Actions created during the period:	82
− Actions closed during the period:	(64)
Actions open at the end of the period:	284

The Defect Prevention Process can have a profound effect on an organization. Ordinarily an organization's processes change very slowly. The developers, working within the process, typically do not consider that there are any means of improving the process and managers usually do not recognize the need for process specific process improvements. Even when the need for improvement is recognized, there has typically been no established way to effect process change. The Defect Prevention Process, on the other hand, provides a built-in mechanism for identifying needed process improvements and getting them implemented. Defect prevention in a sense "enlivens" the process by providing a means for constant focus on it in stage kickoff meetings, during causal analysis, and through the constant efforts of the action team.

In particular, we have found with the Defect Prevention Process that the development process becomes self-correcting. Wherever problems or defects occur in the process, causal analysis can address them and they can be corrected through preventive actions. If the process improvement does not eliminate the problem, the problems or defects will recur and will again be reviewed in subsequent causal analysis. Thus, the process is constantly fine-tuned.

The pace of process change is also accelerated. With the ongoing focus of causal analysis, process deficiencies are identified, and corrections are implemented by the action team. Those process deficiencies causing the most problems receive the most focus by the action team. In addition, process documentation becomes up-to-date and is actively used by the organization. The process is repeatedly reviewed in the stage kickoff meetings. As the process changes, the changes are reviewed with developers in subsequent kickoff meetings.

Ultimately the Defect Prevention Process results in a cultural change in the organization. The developers begin to take an active role in improving the processes they follow. The attitude of seeking constant improvement and prevention becomes the norm. The developers come to realize that they can influence their processes, their working environment, their tools and educational opportunities, and even the way they are managed. The developers become empowered through the Defect Prevention Process with the ability to change any aspect of their process.

15.4 APPLICATIONS OF THE DEFECT PREVENTION PROCESS

So far we have described the Defect Prevention Process in reference to the software development organization itself. Defect prevention can also be applied to other organizations involved in the development and support of a software product.[1,3] For example, the Defect Prevention Process can be used by: a systems test organization, information development (which develops product manuals and related documentation), software service (which handles diagnosing and fixing field problems), human factors (which analyzes, tests, and improves product usability), and product planners (who specify product requirements and formulate development plans).

In all cases, the organization adapts the four key elements of the Defect Prevention Process to their particular process and integrates the defect prevention activities into day-to-day work activities. For example, a systems test organization conducts causal analysis on test-case errors, build errors, test-execution errors, and defects that have escaped the test, to determine how to improve their processes and how to increase the effectiveness of the test. The test organization uses an action team, stage kickoff meetings, and an action data base, just like a development organization.

For a software service organization, the Defect Prevention Process would be adapted to the specific needs of their process. For example, a service organization handling customer calls answers a large number of calls every day. Numerous problems with the call process such as failures to call back within the prescribed time may occur each day. Because of the volume of potential defects, causal analysis generally needs to be preceded by initial data analysis, possibly using statistical methods, to determine the nature of a problem and its causes. A detailed investigation of the problem may be needed to pinpoint and verify the problem's causes prior to conducting the causal analysis meeting where preventive actions would be proposed.

The Defect Prevention Process would also need to be adapted to the organization that develops fixes for field defects (sometimes called the change team). These developers have a process that can differ significantly from the normal development process. In particular, there are no time-delineated development stages that are followed in designing, implementing, and testing a fix. Thus, stage kickoff meetings are not oriented to specific stages but consist of periodic process reviews which are held every two to three months.

15.5 BENEFITS AND COSTS OF
THE DEFECT PREVENTION PROCESS

In the practice of defect prevention, we have reported an initial reduction in the defect rates (defects per thousand lines of code detected during development) of about 54% in one product, compared with historical data for eight prior releases.[1] Table 15-4 summarizes these results. The quality improvement observed also applies to the product's field defect rates. To date, we have observed similar defect reductions in two other large program products, a major part of which can be attributed to following the Defect Prevention Process.

We also have indications from two of these three products that quality continues to improve after the initial decrease in the defect rates, although not as dramatically. For the first product, the continued reductions bring the overall reduction to approximately a 60% improvement over history. The reductions appear to be sustained but there are not yet enough data to demonstrate that the continued improvements are statistically significant. On the other hand, we have observed the problem in some development organizations that a loss of focus by management adhering to the process can result in erosion of the quality improvements. Failure to follow the process of causal analysis meetings, stage kickoffs and action implementation can result in increased defect rates, although not to the levels observed before using defect prevention. This effect applies more broadly to other elements of the process such as inspections and design practices, as well. Thus, high quality levels are critically dependent on management's constancy of purpose in supporting adherence to the process.

We have reported that the costs of implementing the Defect Prevention Process have been less than a person year per year or 0.5% of the development organization's resource.[1] These costs come from conducting the causal analysis, kickoff and action team meetings, and from action implementation. We have seen recently that the level of investment in some organizations has grown to slightly more than 1% of the organization's resources. The expectation is that an increased investment will result in greater quality improvements which are realized sooner.

TABLE 15-4   Defect Rates, History and the Defect Prevention Process

Development Stage	History (8 prior releases)	With Defect Prevention Process
Component level design	7.9	3.7
Module level design	18.6	6.9
Code	20.8	11.4
Unit test/Functional verification test	17.4	8.7
Product verification/System verification tests	3.3	1.8
TOTALS	68.0	32.5

Note: all defect rates are expressed in terms of defects per thousand lines of new and changed source instructions.

The example given in Table 15-3 shows, for an organization of approximately 250 people, an investment of 1.57 person years or about 1.3% of the area's resources over a six-month period. This includes the costs of action implementation (60%), defect prevention meetings (16%) and education classes on the Defect Prevention Process (24%).

As defects are prevented, less effort is taken up by the organization to fix defects during testing and from the field. An analysis we did of the typical costs of fixing defects uncovered during testing and by customers in the field shows that an investment of about 1% of an area's resources in the Defect Prevention Process will return somewhere between six and eight times the cost as savings to the organization. A typical organization of 200 people, which spends about 1.8 person years per year in defect prevention activities and achieves a 55% reduction in defects, will realize a savings of between 11 and 15 person years per year.

The most significant benefit of the Defect Prevention Process is higher product quality in the field. Our experience shows that defect reductions seen in development continue in the field at the same level or better. Fewer field defects result in fewer customer problems, fewer customer calls, and fewer fixes to be developed, tested, and distributed. Fewer defects ultimately result in lower impact to the customer which translates into higher customer satisfaction.

15.6 AREAS FOR FURTHER DEVELOPMENT

Further work is needed to refine the Defect Prevention Process to identify more accurate and effective preventive actions. In particular, better methods need to be developed to identify the chronic, recurring defects, and problem areas in the development process. Statistical Process Control methods can probably be employed in these analyses.

Methods of defect classification can also be developed to assist in isolating areas for specific focus for prevention. While defect classification will help identify areas for investigation, detailed causal analysis of a sampling of the defects will still be needed to identify the specific actions needed for prevention. The hope is that analysis of a set of similar defects, rather than individual, isolated defects, will result in broader, more effective suggested actions.

15.7 DEFECT PREVENTION AS PART OF TQM

The Defect Prevention Process can serve as a focus for Total Quality Management because of its broad applicability to all aspects of software development and its ability to involve employees directly in continuous process improvement. Defect prevention touches every element of TQM:

1. Management participation and leadership: Defect prevention requires the commitment and on-going support of management for initial implementation of the process and continued adherence. A manager serves on the action team. Actions for improvement frequently involve management practices in

the areas of project management and process control. In addition, managers can do causal analysis on their own defects and problems to improve the way projects are planned and managed. An application of the Defect Prevention Process by managers is currently being piloted in one development laboratory at IBM.

2. Goals and measurable objectives: Any implementation of defect prevention must include measurements and goals to be successful. Measurements can include the level of investment[10] in the process and the work flow of the action team (see Table 15-3). These measurements permit monitoring by management to ensure adherence to the process. The effectiveness of preventive actions can also be measured to demonstrate the contribution the actions have had on improving product quality.

3. Education: Classes in the Defect Prevention Process present the concepts of the process and prepare developers to lead causal analysis meetings and serve on an action team. We have found that education is critical to getting employee buy-in in the process. Defect prevention education should be one of the required employee courses for TQM.

4. Employee involvement and action teams: Active participation by all employees is key to the success of TQM. The Defect Prevention Process provides a way to involve employees directly in quality improvements as part of their day-to-day work. In a successful implementation of defect prevention, employees feel free to suggest improvements whenever an idea occurs to them, without waiting for a causal analysis meeting. Such miscellaneous suggestions from developers are a good indication of an established implementation of the process.

5. Customer emphasis: The Defect Prevention Process can be applied to all quality aspects that the customer perceives: product defects, usability problems, missed or incorrect requirements, performance or installation problems, and so on. It can also be applied to the company's interactions with customers, for example in understanding the causes of customer complaints, customer requests for assistance, or customer user errors, and in preventing them in the future.

For example, a method of causal analysis of customer user errors (problems customers have had using the product) has been developed and used by several organizations to identify product usability improvements. Instances of customer user errors are categorized by the major task and subtask the user was trying to perform. A Pareto analysis of the results is used to select areas for more detailed causal analysis by a product team. Examples of individual user errors from the selected areas are studied to determine how the product can be improved to prevent this class of errors. The suggested product improvements are then candidates for follow-on product releases.

6. Supplier certification and training: Suppliers can be encouraged to apply the Defect Prevention Process to their operations. The development organization can assist them in obtaining the needed education. Once implemented, defect prevention can assist in resolving problems that arise between the two

organizations. Problems arising from communication failures with the supplier can be worked on by both the development and supplier action teams.

7. Recognition: The Defect Prevention Process encourages every employee to contribute. The action team can recommend recognition for employees who have contributed significant preventive ideas or who have made special efforts to implement preventive actions. One organization established semi-annual recognition for contributions to defect prevention. Recognition in turn fosters an increased focus on defect prevention and quality in everyone's work.

15.8 SUMMARY

Total Quality Management calls for a cultural change. Both managers and employees need to change old modes of operation and look for areas of improvement. The Defect Prevention Process provides a key tool to achieving the cultural change. It is a process that systematically and continuously identifies areas for improvement, then implements those improvements, and provides continuous feedback to the organization.

Our experience is that developers become excited with the Defect Prevention Process because they see that they now have the ability to influence their processes, tools, work environment, educational opportunities, and even the way they are managed. The Defect Prevention Process provides them true empowerment. They are empowered by the system with the ability to improve it.

References

1. Mays, R. G., Jones, C. L., Holloway, G. J., and Studinski, D. P. "Experiences with Defect Prevention," *IBM Systems Journal,* 29(1):4-32.
2. Gale, J. L., Tirso, J. R., and Burchfield, C. A. "Implementing the Defect Prevention Process in the MVS Interactive Programming Organization," *IBM Systems Journal,* 29(1):33-43.
3. Mays, R. G. "Applications of Defect Prevention in Software Development," *IEEE Journal on Selected Areas in Communications,* 8(2):164-168.
4. Jones, C. L. "A Process-Integrated Approach to Defect Prevention," *IBM Systems Journal,* 24(2):150-167.
5. White, A. M. "Modern Practical Methods of Producing High Quality Software," *Quality Assurance,* 14(3):96-102.
6. Kolkhorst, B. G. and Macina, Anthony J. "Developing Error-Free Software," *IEEE Aerosp. Electron. Syst. Mag.,* 3(11):25-31.
7. Nakajo, T., Sasabuchi, K., and Akiyama, T. "A Structured Approach to Software Defect Analysis," *Hewlett-Packaged Journal,* 40(2):50-56.
8. Ishikawa, K. *What is Total Quality Control? The Japanese Way,* translated by D. J. Lu, Englewood Cliffs: Prentice-Hall, Inc.
9. Lee, B. K. "Implementing a Quality Circle Programme for Computer Professionals," *Comput. Syst. Sci. Eng.,* 1(1):65-67.
10. Dobbins, James H. and Buck, Robert D. "The Cost of Software Quality," in Schulmeyer, G. Gordon and James I. McManus, ed., *Handbook of Software Quality Assurance.* New York: Van Nostrand Reinhold, 1987 (first ed.), 1992 (second ed.).

16

Zero Defect Software Development

G. Gordon Schulmeyer, CDP

Westinghouse Electronic Systems Group

16.1 INTRODUCTION

The Total Quality Management (TQM) movement has seven recurring elements:

1. Management participation and leadership development
2. Goals and measurable objectives
3. Education and training
4. Employee involvement and action teams
5. Customer emphasis
6. Supplier certification and training
7. Recognition and incentivizing.[1]

These elements, except for supplier certification and training which do not apply, are encompassed in the zero defect software development method. The TQM elements that apply to the different facets of the zero defect software methodology are highlighted in this chapter, where appropriate.

The steps and concept behind zero defect software development which are covered here are based upon the detailed exposition in *Zero Defect Software.*[2]

First, the zero defects programs which have been used in industry are discussed before their application to software development. A number of models and issues concerning the software process are next investigated by highlighting inspection points.

The synergism of the important concepts in Shigeo Shingo's book, *Zero Quality Control: Source Inspections and the Poka-yoke System* (pronounced POH-kah YOH-kay) and the procedure charting of value analysis leads to a guide toward the achievement of zero defect software.

With the outline provided by the software development process chart (see the appendix to this chapter), the key issues of importance to its successful implementation are discussed. The customer is discussed in terms of the next person in line in the development process.

Errors are human and will always be made. The secret to successful zero defect software is to isolate the errors humans made along the way and remove them. Here, a software defect is any software failure delivered to the ultimate customer. Source inspections and successive inspections isolate errors manually, and poka-yoke techniques help prevent errors with an automated device, so no software defects get delivered.

The responsibilities of the individuals (workers) and the managers in the software development process are next examined, because it is only through people that the achievement of the zero defect software goal may be obtained.

16.2 ZERO DEFECTS PROGRAMS

In his book, *Quality is Free,*[3] Philip B. Crosby discussed quality through defect prevention, and the idea of a zero defects program. He states the underlying reasons for the zero defects program, as follows.

People are conditioned to believe that error is inevitable. We not only accept error, we anticipate it. We figure on making errors in typing a letter, programming a computer, etc., and management plans for errors that will occur. We feel that human beings have a "built-in" error factor. However, as individuals, we do not have the same standard of error acceptance. We do not go home to the wrong house periodically or drink salt water for lemon juice. We have a double standard—one for ourselves and one for the company.

The family creates a higher performance standard for us than the company. The company allows 20% of sales for scrap, rework, warranty, service, test, and inspection. Errors by people cause this waste. We must concentrate on preventing the defects and errors that plague us to eliminate this waste. The defect that is prevented does not need repair, examination, or explanation. All personnel must adopt an attitude of zero defects in the company.[3]

In some things, people are willing to accept imperfection; in others, the defects must be absent. Mistakes are caused by lack of knowledge and lack of attention. Knowledge can be measured and deficiencies corrected. Lack of attention must be corrected by the person himself or herself. Lack of attention is an attitude problem that may be corrected if there is a personal commitment to watch each detail and carefully avoid error. This leads to zero defects in all things.

When management and employees were committed to zero defects, people communicated an error-cause removal system. Errors dropped 40% almost immediately.

Zero defects is a management performance standard, not a "motivation" program. In 1980, in Tokyo, there was a party for Philip Crosby to celebrate 16 years of use of the zero defects programs in Japan. The United States, particularly the defense industry, went zero defects-happy for two years. Then the "motivation" wore off because American quality professionals never took time to understand the concept of zero defects.[4]

There are conflicting schools of thought about quality. One accepts only zero defects. The other says set an acceptable quality level (AQL) because the cost and effort to achieve zero defects are not worthwhile. Figure 16-1 shows an AQL chart under conditions where producing above AQL quality is out of control, but producing below AQL is too expensive to be practical.

Burrill and Ellsworth in *Quality Data Processing*[5] point out that Figure 16-1 does not adequately represent the cost of software system (critical product) failure. Their malfunction can generate costs that are extremely large compared with the cost of system development. This means that the cost of failure rises steeply as the percent of defectives increase.

Consider the cost of prevention plus appraisal. The traditional view is that this cost must become almost infinite to achieve zero defects. But this is not true for software systems. Examples of no defect software in the first year of operation show that zero defects can be achieved at a cost of prevention plus appraisal that is finite and reasonable. Also, the increase in this cost is not excessive as the percent of defects trends to zero.

For failure costs and prevention plus appraisal costs as shown in Figure 16-2, the total cost of failure decreases steadily as the percent defective trends to zero. So the minimum total cost of failure is at the point of zero defects. For these curves, the AQL is zero defects.[6]

Goals and measurable objectives constitute element two of the TQM movement. Taking the management commitment of zero defects and applying it to software

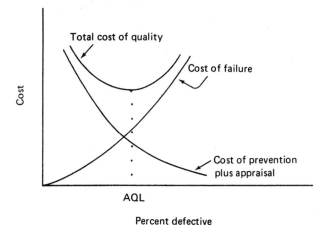

FIGURE 16-1. Traditional view of costs versus percent defective.[5]

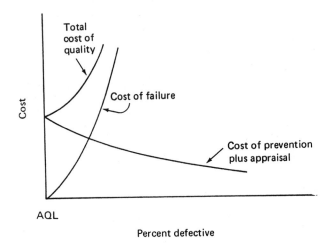

FIGURE 16-2. Cost versus percent defective for software systems.[7]

for zero defect software is obtainable and measurable while moving to fewer and fewer defects.

16.3 THE PROCESS

"A process may be described as a set of operations occurring in a definite sequence that operates on a given input and converts it to some desired output."[8] For software development, explicit requirement statements are required as input. The series of processing operations that act on this input must be placed in the correct sequence with one another, the output of each operation satisfying the input needs of the next operation. The output of the final operation is the explicitly required output in the form of a verified program. Thus, the objective of each processing operation is to receive a defined input and to produce a definite output that satisfies a specific set of exit criteria. A well-formed process can be thought of as a continuum of processing during which sequential sets of exit criteria are satisfied, the last set in the entire series requiring a well-defined end product.[8]

Would you calculate every week the results that go on your listing: i.e., correct the listing every week (Figure 16-3).[9] No one is so ignorant that they would not correct the program once, instead of continually correcting the results.

Figure 16-4 shows the same situation with some labels changed. It shows a staff repeatedly correcting defective products of a system rather than correcting the system that produced those defective products. Billions of dollars are spent correcting system defects without realizing that the wrong system is being corrected. The system for building systems should be corrected.

When a software developer says, "This is the problem," while pointing to listings, he or she is really only pointing out the symptom, not the problem. The real problem is a defective development procedure that allows defective code to be

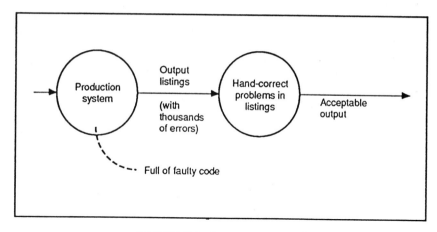

FIGURE 16-3. Correct the program.[9]

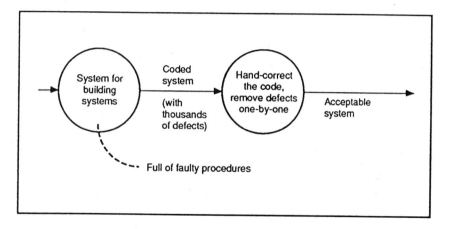

FIGURE 16-4. Correct the system.[10]

put there. We do not remove defects from the system for building systems, because we never go looking for them. It is better to correct the system for building systems so that it does not insert defects in the first place.[11]

Michael Fagan's landmark work[8] on the software development process using inspections to improve quality provided several charts showing that fewer errors resulted when the inspection was held closer to the work. Figure 16-5 shows an example of how design inspections, I_1, code inspections, I_2, and test inspections, I_3, resulted in 38% fewer errors per thousand lines of code (KLOC). Figure 16-6 compared the old approach with the one Michael Fagan proposed. It shows a reduction in overall schedule using requirements inspections, I_0, I_1, and I_2 embedded in the process.

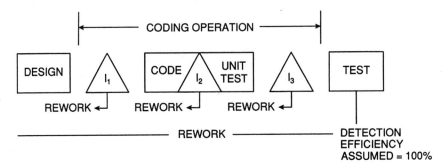

NET CODING PRODUCTIVITY

$I_1 + I_2 = \text{✕} - 123\%$ SAMPLE SHOWED 23% NET INCREASE
$I_1 + \text{✕} = \text{✕} - 112\%$
$\text{✕} + \text{✕} = \text{✕} - 100\%$

NET SAVING (PROGRAMMER HOURS/KLOC) DUE TO:
$I_1 = 94, I_2 = 51, I_3 = -20$

REWORK (PROGRAMMER HOURS/KLOC) FROM:
$I_1 = 78, I_2 = 36, -$

QUALITY
38% Fewer Errors/KLOC

FIGURE 16-5. Inspection model with statistics from sample problems.[12]

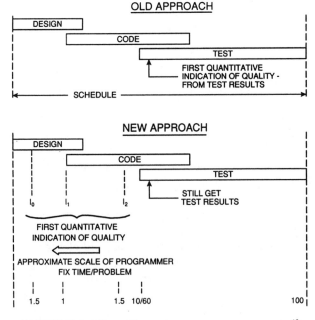

FIGURE 16-6. Effect of inspection on process management.[13]

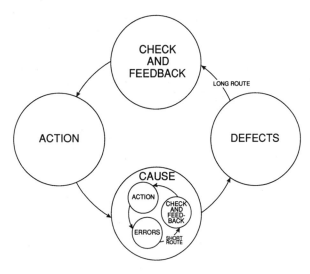

FIGURE 16-7. Cycle for managing errors and defects.

Shigeo Shingo[14] has devised a process cycle for the managing of errors and defects (Figure 16-7). The check and feedback portion is analogous to inspections I_0, I_1, I_2, and I_3 shown in Figures 16-5 and 16-6. Note that the short route, similar to Fagan's approach, gets closer to the workers. Getting the workers involved in the process of quality improvement of their own process is one of the driving forces behind the software development process chart which is discussed next.

16.4 SOFTWARE DEVELOPMENT PROCESS CHART

Shigeo Shingo's book, *Zero Quality Control: Source Inspections and the Poka-yoke System* convinced the author that Shingo's fundamental manufacturing ideas to achieve zero defects could be applied to software development. Shingo's approach, combined with concepts of value analysis, facilitated the generation of the Software Development Process Chart (see the appendix to this chapter).

The Software Development Process Chart starts with a modified collection of symbols usually used in value analysis to show paper flow in a company. With the use of this type of flow analysis, methods can be found to improve a process.

The appendix to this chapter displays the entire software development chart which is based upon the value analysis symbols produced by the author. It highlights how to improve the process. It is derived primarily from software development methods as outlined in DOD-STD-2167A, *Defense System Software Development.*

Every product, whether it be a document or a piece of software, has an informal review to check its integrity, when the self-check is performed by the worker who produced it. Such an examination also takes place whenever a work product is updated. This happens frequently during software development, and is called a self-check inspection. Such matters will be discussed in more detail later.

If this work product is to be handed on to an internal customer, this is the place to get the receiver involved in the process. The receiver has a vested interest in what he or she is going to have to work with, and so will have a vested interest in making sure that this is a good product. This is called a successive check inspection system, and will be discussed later.

After the generation or update of each work product, a quality review of the work product takes place. Of course, this is after the worker has reviewed his or her own work. The quality review requires independence of judgment to best achieve its results.

Every formal customer review, such as a critical design review (CDR), has an internal practice run to ensure readiness for the real thing. This dry run ensures that the customer sees only the correct results, not intermediate errors that previously occurred. This work has already been through multiple reviews. Poka-yoke techniques do not show up in this portion of the chart. This does not imply that they should not be used here. A discussion of the usage and how they might be used in the process is in Section 16.6, Isolating the Errors.

16.5 THE CUSTOMER

"Make the customer come alive for all employees. It is one thing to produce a quality product for an abstraction called the customer and a very different thing to do the job for the customers who are people, too.

The customer should be made to come alive for all employees, especially those who do not normally come into contact with the customers. Some methods are: distribute stories about how customers use the products, allow customers to directly address employees telling what it is like to do business with them, and have employees visit customer sites on field trips to see the product being used.

Where direct contact does not exist with the customer, explicitly identify and strengthen all customer connections for the employees. Specifically show how the employee's job has an effect on the customer, or if no effect exists, where the job might be eliminated.

The quality professionals in an organization have the know-how to preach the quality gospel. The employees must truly get into the church to hear it and respond to it. The focus of the sermon is one simple question: 'What can I do to deliver more value to our customers?' "[17] (Reprinted by permission of publisher from *Trainer's Workshop,* June 1987, copyright © 1987, American Management Association, New York. All rights reserved.)

Customer satisfaction must be considered from two viewpoints. First is the ultimate customer who is paying for the product or service. The second customer consideration relates to the next person in the chain of operations within an organization. Both must be satisfied for successful quality improvement.

Three major points to improve employee involvement with the ultimate customer are that every contact should be a quality interface, responsiveness to the customer is important, and involving customers in activities (for example, design reviews) related to their work helps to build a team approach that results in openness and trust.

The concepts applied to the ultimate customer are applicable to the internal customer. Meeting the internal customer's requirements completely and in a timely manner usually contributes to the ultimate customer's satisfaction. Infrequently there is a conflict and, when that occurs, the ultimate customer must come first.

Everyone has customers, and success comes from satisfying those customers. This is achieved by meeting customer expectations, which, of course, means meeting requirements. Customer satisfaction is an integral part of any quality improvement process. Goals, objectives, and action plans for internal and ultimate customer satisfaction must be established, measured, and managed.[18]

Successful companies are customer oriented. They work to please customers because *only customers can define quality.* Most companies in the United States are share-price oriented, they work to please the equity market, not the customers.

In order to be truly customer-oriented, every worker must find out what the next person in line needs to do a good job and the worker must provide it. In a well-managed business, each employee considers the next person in line as the customer and works to help that person to do a better job.[19] This is a vital concept in the software development process chart that can lead to zero defect software. This concept also is element 4 of the TQM movement, to have employee involvement and action teams. The employees become very involved when they are the internal customer. Employees should form action teams to discuss systemic errors that are being passed on to the internal customer, and more importantly, how to correct them.

Customer satisfaction is at the core of the revolution in total quality. Every person on a production line is the customer of the preceeding operation (called the internal customer above), so each worker's goal is to make sure that the quality of his or her work meets the requirement of the next person. When that happens throughout the organization, the satisfaction of the ultimate customer should be assured. This concept was revolutionary to some workers who realized that they have a customer.[20]

Element 5 of the TQM movement is customer emphasis and it has been made abundantly clear that the customer, both internal and external, is the key ingredient to the zero defect software development method.

16.6 ISOLATING THE ERROR

Since defects are generated during the process, you only discover those defects by inspecting goods at the end of the process. Adding inspection workers is pointless because you will not reduce defects without using processing methods that prevent defects from occurring in the first place.

It is an unalterable fact that processing produces defects and all that inspections can do is find those defects. So approaching the problem only at the final inspection stage is meaningless. Defects will not be reduced merely by making improvements at the final inspection stage, although such improvements may eliminate defects in delivered goods.

The most fundamental concept is to recognize that defects are generated by work and all final inspections—judgmental inspections—do is to discover those defects. Zero defects can never be achieved if this concept is forgotten.[21]

In terms of its effect on defect density, software testing borders on the irrelevant. In the United States, the range of defects per thousand lines of executable code is from 0.016 to 60, a factor of nearly 4,000. The way to make a drastic improvement in the quality of code that comes out of the testing process is to make a drastic improvement in the quality of code that goes into the testing process.[22] One way is to use computer-based systems to analyze product quality while the design details are merely images and symbols on a computer screen. Do this because 80% of all product defects get "designed in."[23]

There are three major inspection methods: (1) judgment inspections that discover defects, (2) informative inspections that reduce defects, and (3) source inspections that eliminate defects. Judgment inspections were just discussed above.

In an informative inspection, information about the occurrence of a defect is fed back to the specific work process, which then corrects the process. Consequently, adopting informative inspections regularly should gradually reduce production defect rates. There are three categories of informative inspections:

1. Statistical Quality Control Systems (SQCS),
2. Successive Check Systems (SuCS), and
3. Self-Check Systems (SeCS).

Statistical Quality Control Systems (SQCS) include the notion of informative inspections and use statistically based control charts. SQC systems use statistics to set control limits that distinguish between normal and abnormal situations. The essential condition identifying a method of inspection as an SQC method is the use of statistical principles.[24]

SQC systems suffer from two shortcomings:

1. Sampling is used. Would not it be better to use 100% inspections to find all abnormalities. One-hundred percent inspections, however, are expensive and time consuming. If low-cost, 100% inspections could be devised, would they not be preferable? This leads to poka-yoke devices.
2. SQC methods are too slow to be fully effective when considering feedback and corrective action.

The best way to speed up feedback and corrective action would be to have the worker who finds any abnormality carry out 100% inspections and immediately take corrective action. But objectivity is essential to the performance of inspections, and that is why inspections have been carried out by independent inspectors. An inspection can be carried out by any worker other than the one who did the processing. If this task is given to the nearest person, then one could have a successive check system of the following sort:

1. When A completes processing, A passes it on to B for the next process.
2. B first inspects the item processed by A and then carries out the processing assigned to B. Then B passes the item on to C.
3. C first inspects the item processed by B and then carries out the processing assigned to C. Then C passes the item on to D.
4. Similarly, each successive worker inspects items from the previous process.
5. If a defect is discovered in an item from the previous process, the defective item is immediately passed back to the earlier process. There, the item is verified and the error corrected. Action is taken to prevent the occurrence of subsequent errors.

Successive check systems represent an advance over control chart systems because it makes it possible to conduct 100% inspections, performed by people other than the workers involved in the processing.[25] This does not imply a look at the entire output data population for software, but a look at the computer programs and associated documentation.

The nature of informative inspections remains such that rapid feedback and swift action are desirable, and it would be ideal to have the actual worker involved conduct 100% inspection to check for defects. However, there are two flaws to be considered: workers are liable to make compromises when inspecting items that they themselves have worked on, and they occasionally forget to perform checks on their own.

If these flaws could be overcome, then a self-check system would be superior to a successive check system. In cases where physical, rather than sensory, inspections are possible, poka-yoke devices can be installed within the process boundaries, so that when abnormalities occur, the information is immediately fed back to the worker involved. Because abnormalities are discovered within the processes where they occur rather than at subsequent processes, instant corrective action is possible. So, a self-check system is a higher order approach that the successive check system to cut defects even further.[26]

Source inspections are inspection methods that are based on discovering errors in conditions that *give rise to defects* and performing feedback and action at the error stage so as to keep those errors from turning into defects, rather than stimulating feedback and action in response to defects.

Many people maintain that it is impossible to eliminate defects from tasks performed by humans. This stems from the failure to make a clear separation between errors and effect. Defects (delivered to the customer) arise because errors are made; the two have a cause-and-effect relationship.

It is impossible to prevent all errors from occurring in any task performed by humans. Inadvertent errors from occurring in any task performed by humans. Inadvertent errors are possible and inevitable. However, if feedback and corrective action are optimized, errors will not turn into defects. The principle feature of source inspections eliminates defects by distinguishing between errors and defects; i.e., between causes and effects.[27]

Bakayoke is Japanese for "foolproofing." A foolproofing device to prevent seat parts from being spot-welded backwards was installed in an Arakawa auto body plant around 1963. A worker asked hysterically if she was a "fool" who could mix up left- and right-hand parts. She was told she was not a "fool," but the device was inserted because anyone could make an inadvertent mistake.

When Shigeo Shingo was told that story, he sought a suitable term. He used poka-yoke (mistake-proofing) for the devices because they serve to prevent (or "yoke" in Japanese, "proof") the sort of inadvertent mistake (poke in Japanese) that anyone could make. Since the word poka-yoke has been used untranslated in English, French, Swedish, and Italian books, it is now current throughout the world.[28]

For software an example is the Software Life-Cycle Support Environment (SLCSE). Rather than supporting a single development methodology, SLCSE uses a modifiable tool-based approach in which an almost unlimited number of tools can be integrated to support various methodologies. Off-the-shelf or custom tools may be used so that changes in the modes or the development paradigm may be supported. Table 16-1 shows initial tool categories and representative generic tool

TABLE 16-1   Example Software Tool Types and Categories (Copyright © 1987 IEEE)[29]

General Support:
- Text editor
- Document formatter
- Command-language editor
- Electronic mail

Requirements analysis:
- Requirements generator
- Requirements documentor
- Consistency analyzer

Design:
- Design generator
- Design documenter
- Consistency checker

Coding:
- Language-sensitive editor
- Assembler
- Compiler
- Linker
- Debugger
- Assertion translator

Testing:
- Instrumeter
- Postexecution analyer
- Test-summary reporter
- Test manager
- Simulator

Prototyping:
- Window prototyper

Verification:
- Data tracer
- Code auditor
- Static analyzer
- Dataflow analyzer
- Interface checker
- Quality analyzer

Configuration Management:
- Software manager
- Documentation manager
- Test-data/results manager
- Change-effect manager

Project Management:
- Project planner
- Project tracker/reporter
- Problem-report processor
- Change-request

Environment Management:
- Method script editor
- Menu editor
- Keypad editor
- Command-procedure editor
- Global-command setup
- Tool installer/deleter

types for each category that will be supported by SLCSE. The tool categories reflect life-cycle phases or activities that span the entire cycle.[29] These tools are the equivalent of poka-yoke techniques for the software development process.

A poka-yoke system is a means and not an end. Poka-yoke systems can be combined with successive checks or self-checks and can fulfill the needs of those techniques by providing 100% inspections and prompt feedback and action. Successive checks and self-checks function only as information inspections in which feedback and action take place after a defect has occurred. In cases where repairs can be made, it looks as though no defects occurred, but these methods are inherently unable to attain zero defects.

Source inspections and poka-yoke measures must be combined to eliminate defects. The combination of source inspections and poka-yoke devices make zero quality control systems possible. This same combination applies to the software development process as outlined in the chart in the appendix. Again one must never forget that the poka-yoke system refers to a means, not an end.[30]

16.7 RESPONSIBILITY FOR ZERO DEFECT SOFTWARE

Success in quality—conformance to requirements—is a management issue. Management must recognize the weaknesses of the organization and see that quality concepts applied correctly will eliminate these weaknesses. Management establishes the organizational purpose, makes measurable objectives, and takes action required to meet the objectives. Management sets the tone for the people in the organization to look to. If people perceive management indifference to quality, indifference will permeate the organization. On the other hand, when management is perceived to have a quality commitment, quality will permeate the organization.[31]

Management must organize for quality. Simplicity with clear reporting enhances the ability to achieve quality. A clean, well-defined organizational structure and operation philosophy go together with process simplification. Process simplification such as proposed in the software development process chart leads to quality performance.

Many managers think they are committed to quality, while their subordinates perceive that they are not committed. This is cause for failure of many quality improvement programs. If it is perceived that quality is not a high management priority, then it will not be a high priority with the people. People must see management leading the quality improvement process and making it work on a continuing basis.

To achieve this commitment, management must understand quality and be involved in the process with active participation (Figure 16-8). Each person in the organization must see participation by the level above.

Management shows its commitment to quality by establishing a quality policy. The policy should set the expectations for quality and should apply to all departments and individuals in the organization. The policy needs to be simple, direct,

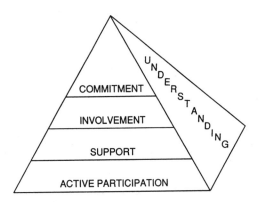

FIGURE 16-8. Management quality involvement.[32]

and concise. With proper management attention to establish the policy as the basis for quality performance, it becomes a rallying point for people to determine actions and priorities.

Management must show patience in its commitment to quality, because the quality improvement culture change is a long-term process. There is usually short-term improvement, but the big payoffs occur in future years. Management must show the tenacity necessary to leave no doubt as to their long-term quality commitment.

Management must eliminate all temptations to compromise conformance to requirements. It only takes one compromise to create doubt—forget that software unit test, ship that software design specification without software quality review. Once there is doubt, long-term consistent behavior on the part of (software) management is the only way to diffuse the doubt.

Management has the responsibility to continually educate, coach, and sell quality to the organization. Education provides the understanding, coaching defines the application, and selling establishes the desire. Element 3 of the TQM movement, i.e., education and training, is fulfilled when management takes its responsibilities for these functions seriously.

The greater challenge usually comes from those few people who do not believe in or resist getting involved in the quality process. They can be educated and they can be coached. The problem is usually getting them to participate in the quality process. Management may make them responsible for some important action or expose them to a "nonquality" situation (such as irate customers). Doing this is a way to sell them on the movement.[33]

The TQM movement element 1, management participation and leadership development, has been discussed above. Without software management buying into the zero defect software method it cannot succeed. Too often the cry has been heard "zero defect software is impossible," but management must provide the leadership to set the tone that zero defect software is possible or it will never be aimed for and achieved.

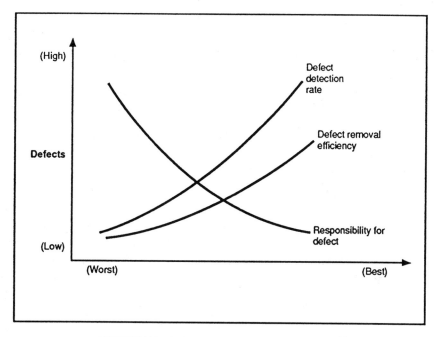

FIGURE 16-9. Individual differences among workers.[34]

Attention has been focused on management's responsibilities, it is also appropriate to focus some attention on worker's responsibilities. The differences among software workers as shown in Figure 16-9 is enormous. Expect variations on the order of 10 to 1 in performance in all but the smallest project team. These variations are not caused solely by the extreme cases; they apply across the entire spectrum of workers. Even if your workers are not at the extremes, you will see differences of three or four to one in your software project teams.

Poor performers are responsible for an order of magnitude more defects than the best performers; lower-average performers are responsible for twice as many as upper-average performers. There are people on almost all projects who insert spoilage that exceeds the value of the production. Taking a poor performer off your team can often be more productive than adding a good one. In a software project team of 10, there are probably 3 people who produce enough defects to make them net negative producers. The probability that there is not even 1 negative producer out of 10 is negligible. A high defect producing team (above 30 defects/thousand lines of executable code) may have fully half of its members in the negative production category.

There are two reasons why not much is done about negative producers: defect-prone people do not appear to be bad developers and the idea of measuring the individual is slightly repugnant to most people.

When we measure and allocate defects fairly and when we make the idea palatable to the people affected, we will find the worker who is defect prone. When we find defect-prone workers, it does not mean they should be fired, but only that they should not be allowed to write code. If A writes nearly defect-free products and B excels at defect detection and diagnosis, then assign them accordingly; let A write all the code and B do all the testing. It is unconscionable to ignore the differences between A and B. Assign them correctly and the differences in project results are quite significant.

Switching roles has been shown to improve quality by more than 75%. Making these changes illustrates the difference in cost between removing defects ($18,000) and abstaining from defects ($0). There were 36 more defects inserted when A and B were assigned without regards to B's defect production.

If you collect accurate defect rates and efficiencies without upsetting the people involved, note the results achieved. Not only has quality improved, but *each person's value to the project has been increased.* No one need be embarrassed to have been assigned tasks that make optimal use of their individual strengths. Even worker B, temporarily chastened to learn that all his or her testing and diagnostic skill barely made up for a high defect insertion rate, will know (once properly assigned) that his or her prior low value to the project was due to management failure, rather than to worker B failure. To get employees involved, as is required by element 4 of the TQM movement, these differences in the employee's value to a project often come from the team itself. In fact, it is better to have the team participate then to have management dictate.

A most important function of management is defaulted if the differences between people are ignored and they are assigned homogeneously. Measuring defect rates will prove that 25% or more of the staff should not be coding at all, and that some of the best coders should not be allowed to test.[35]

To close out this section on zero defect software responsibility it is important to emphasize that the people responsible get recognition and incentivization for small successes. Element 7 of the TQM movement is recognition and incentivizing that provides feedback for a job well done and in turn proves to be a motivating factor.[36] By incentivizing success toward fewer software defects the employees will be motivated toward the achievement of zero defect software.

16.8 CONCLUSION

As a software development manager and former software quality manager, I believe it is my duty to not only "preach" zero defects in software, but also to provide direction toward achieving it. I must also act on element 3 of the TQM movement of education and training to utilize TQM methods in software development. Using the software development process chart as a guide with source inspections and automated tools (poka-yoke), the direction is set. It has been successfully demonstrated in manufacturing by Shigeo Shingo. Now is the time for similar success in software development.

The payoff in software development is very high indeed. William Mandeville of the Carman Group, Inc. relates that 30 to 50% of product life cycle costs are wasted as the costs of poor quality. However, quality improvements of up to 75% of that loss are attainable.[37]

References

1. Moore, W. Savage. "Singing the Same 'Total Quality' Song," *National Defense* Mar. 1990, pp. 30-32.
2. Schulmeyer, G. Gordon. *Zero Defect Software,* New York: McGraw-Hill Book Co. 1990.
3. Crosby, Philip B. *Quality Is Free,* New York: New American Library, Inc. 1979, pp. 145, 146.
4. *Ibid.,* pp. 83, 84.
5. Burrill, Claude W. and Ellsworth, Leon W. *Quality Data Processing,* Tenafly: Burrill-Ellsworth Associates, Inc., 1982, p. 50.
6. *Ibid.,* pp. 49-51.
7. *Ibid.,* p. 52.
8. Fagan, Michael E. "Design and Code Inspections and Process Control in the Development of Program," IBM-TR-00.73, Jun. 1976, p. 125.
9. DeMarco, Tom, *Controlling Software Projects. Management, Measurement & Estimation,* copyright © 1982, Adapted by permission of Prentice Hall, (Englewood Cliffs: Prentice Hall Inc., 1982), p. 206.
10. *Ibid.,* p. 206.
11. *Ibid.,* pp. 205-207.
12. Fagan, Michael E. *op. cit.,* p. 127.
13. *Ibid.,* p. 144.
14. *Zero Quality Control: Source Inspection and the Poka-Yoke System,* by Shigeo Shingo, copyright © 1985 by the Japan Management Association, Tokyo; English translation copyright © 1986 by Productivity, Inc., PO Box 3007, Cambridge, MA. 02140. 1-(800) 274-9911. Reprinted by permission.
15. *Ibid.,* p. 53.
16. Graham, Jr., Ben S. "Procedure Charting," prepared for Ben S. Graham Conference, copyright © 1977.
17. Guaspari, John, "The Role of Human Resources in 'Selling' Quality Improvements to Employees," *Management Review,* Mar. 1987, pp. 20-24, Copyright © 1987 American Management Association, pp. 23, 24.
18. Cooper, Alan D. *The Journey Toward Managing Quality Improvement,* Orlando: Westinghouse Electric Corp. 1987, pp. 13-16.
19. Tribus, Myron, "The Quality Imperative," *The Bent of Tau Beta Pi,* (Spring 1987), pp. 24-27.
20. "The Push for Quality," *Business Week,* Jun. 8, 1987, pp. 130-143.
21. Shigeo Shingo, *op. cit.,* pp. 35-39.
22. DeMarco, Tom, *op. cit.,* pp. 216-218.
23. Kotelly, George V. "Competiveness = Quality," *Mini-Micro Systems,* 20(12):9, Dec. 1985, Cahners Publishing Co., Div. of Reed Publishing, Denver, CO.
24. Shigeo Shingo, *op. cit.,* pp. 58-59.

25. *Ibid.,* pp. 67-69.
26. *Ibid.,* pp. 77.
27. *Ibid.,* pp. 83-85.
28. *Ibid.,* pp. 45, 46.
29. Cavano, Joseph P. and LaMonica, Frank S. "Quality Assurance in Future Development Environments," *IEEE Software,* Sep. 1987, p. 29, copyright © 1987 IEEE.
30. Shigeo Shingo, *op. cit.,* pp. 92, 93.
31. Cooper, Alan D. *op. cit.,* p. 6.
32. *Ibid.,* p. 18.
33. *Ibid.,* pp. 17-20.
34. DeMarco, Tom, *op. cit.,* p. 208.
35. *Ibid.,* pp. 207-210.
36. Moore, W. Savage, *op. cit.,* p. 32.
37. Mandeville, William A. "Defects, and Software Quality Costs Measurements," *NSIA Fifth Annual National Joint Conference Proceedings* Feb. 1989, p. 6.

Appendix (Chapter 16)

Symbol Definitions

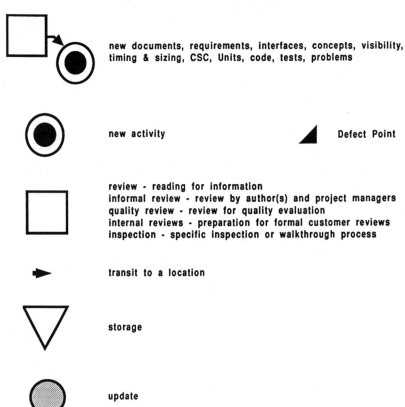

new documents, requirements, interfaces, concepts, visibility, timing & sizing, CSC, Units, code, tests, problems

new activity   Defect Point

review - reading for information
informal review - review by author(s) and project managers
quality review - review for quality evaluation
internal reviews - preparation for formal customer reviews
inspection - specific inspection or walkthrough process

transit to a location

storage

update

(collection of items

①   numbered return point

OK   acceptable to proceed

$\overline{OK}$ must be updated

D   long term delay (days to months)

△   researching or retrieving - time spent reading, obtaining information

Acronym List

CDR - Critical Design Review
CIDS - Critical Item Development Specification
CRISD - Computer Resources Integrated Support Document*
CSC - Computer Software Component
CSCI - Computer Software Configuration Item
CSOM - Computer System Operator's Manual*
CSU - Computer Software Unit
D.C. - Developmental Configuration
Doc. - Documentation
FCA - Functional Configuration Audit
FSM - Firmware Support Manual*
FQT - Formal Qualification Testing
Funct. - Functional
IDD - Interface Design Document
IRS - Interface Requirements Specification
Mgmt. - Management
PCA - Physical Configuration Audit
PDR - Preliminary Design Review
PIDS - Prime Item Development Specification
Prelim. - Preliminary
Qual. - Qualification
RFP - Request For Proposal
Rqmts. - Requirements
SCCB - Software Configuration Control Board
SDD - Software Design Document
SDF - Software Development File
SDP - Software Development Plan
SDR - System Design Review
SOW - Statement of Work
Spec. - Specification
SPM - Software Programmer's Manual*
SPR - Software Problem Report
SPS - Software Product Specification
SQPP - Software Quality Program Plan
SRR - System Requirements Review
SRS - Software Requirements Specification
SSDD - System/Segment Design Document
SSR - Software Specification Review
SSS - System/Segment Specification
STD - Software Test Description
STP - Software Test Plan
STR - Software Test Report
SUM - Software User's Manual*
TRR - Test Readiness Review
VDD - Version Description Document

*May be vendor supplied

Software Development
Process Chart

**System
Requirements
Analysis/Design**

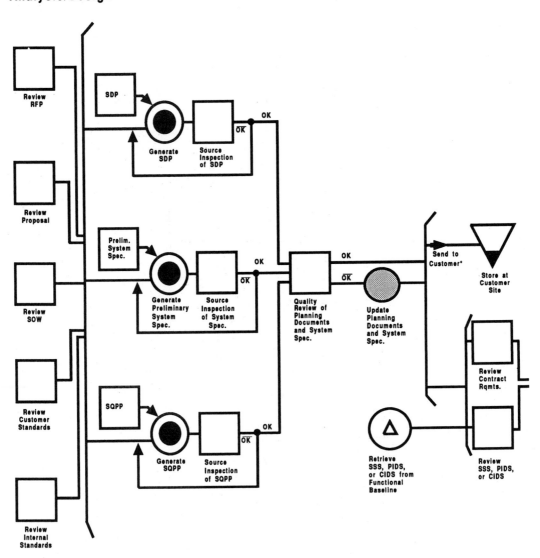

* Formal Delivery of SDP, SQPP

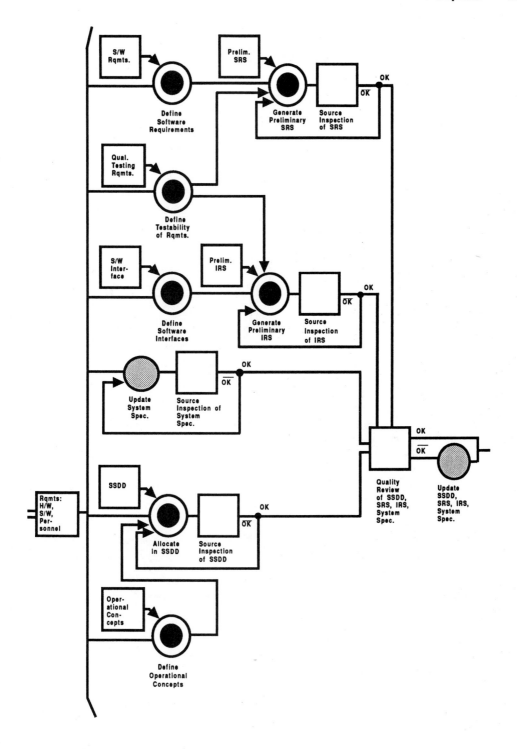

Software
Requirements
Analysis

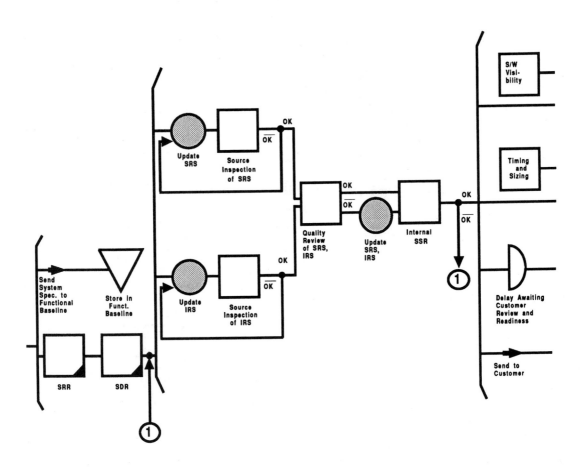

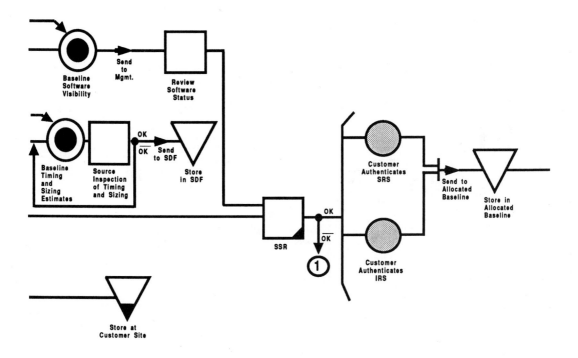

Preliminary
Design

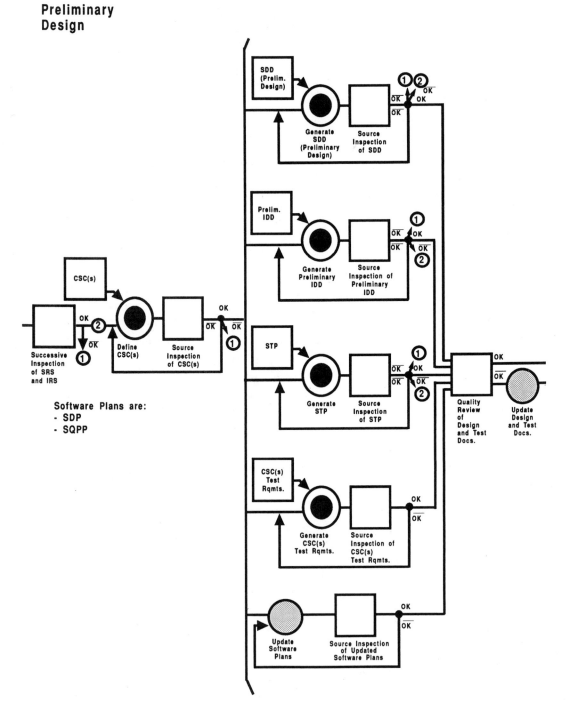

Software Plans are:
- SDP
- SQPP

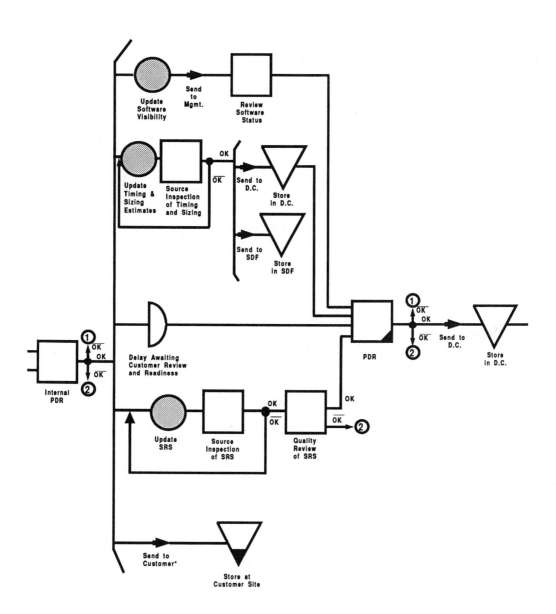

* Formal Delivery of STP and Preliminary SDD and IDD

Detailed Design

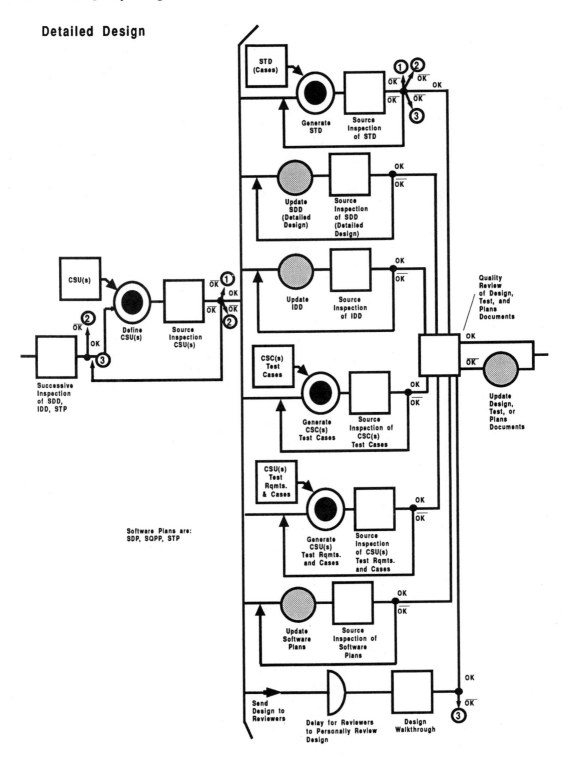

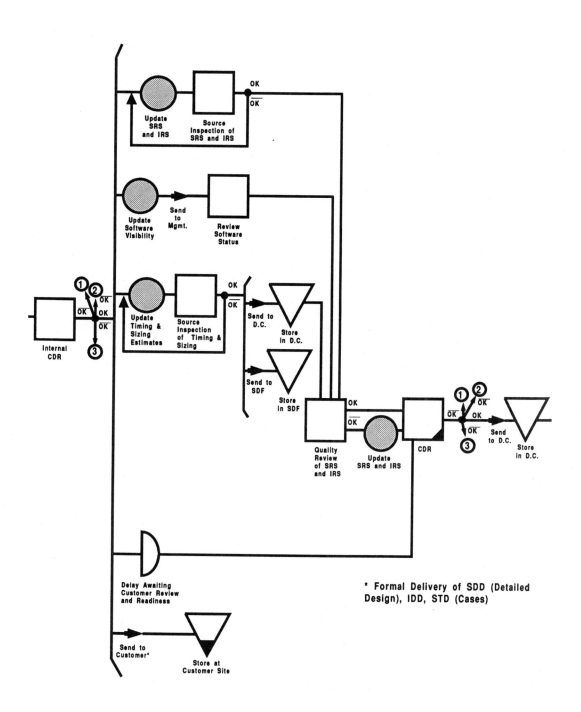

Update
SRS
and IRS

Source
Inspection of
SRS and IRS

OK

OK

Update
Software
Visibility

Send
to
Mgmt.

Review
Software
Status

Update
Timing &
Sizing
Estimates

Source
Inspection
of Timing &
Sizing

OK

OK

Send to
D.C.

Store
in D.C.

Send to
SDF

Store
in SDF

Internal
CDR

OK

OK

OK

OK

Quality
Review
of SRS
and IRS

OK

OK

Update
SRS and IRS

CDR

OK

OK

OK

OK

Send
to D.C.

Store
in D.C.

Delay Awaiting
Customer Review
and Readiness

Send to
Customer*

Store at
Customer Site

* Formal Delivery of SDD (Detailed
Design), IDD, STD (Cases)

Coding and CSU Testing

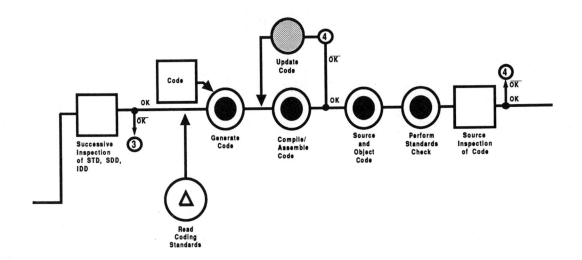

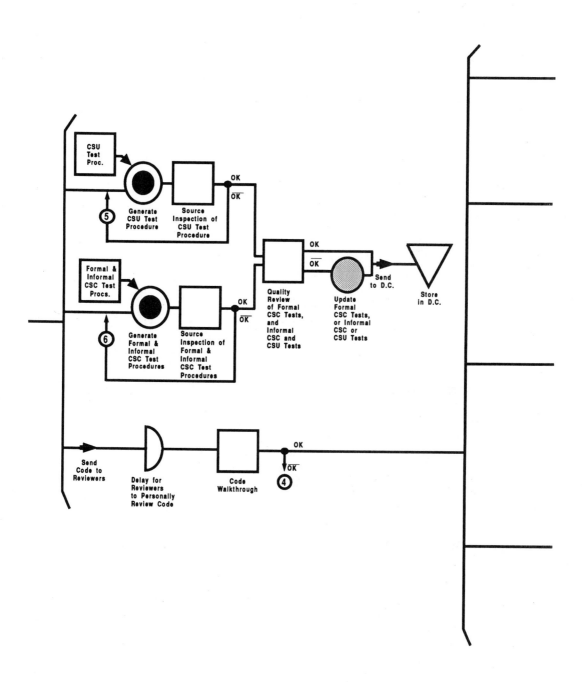

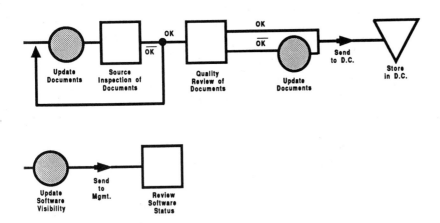

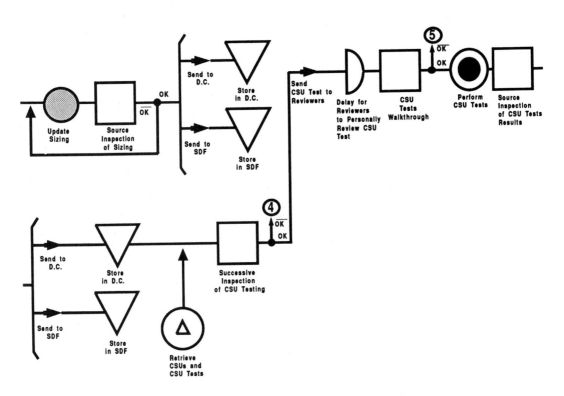

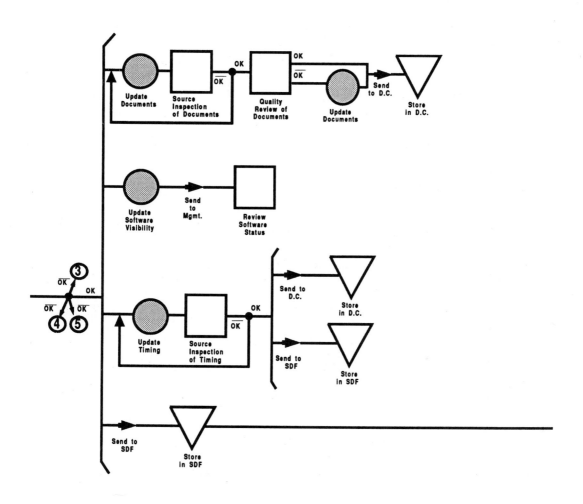

CSC Integration and Testing

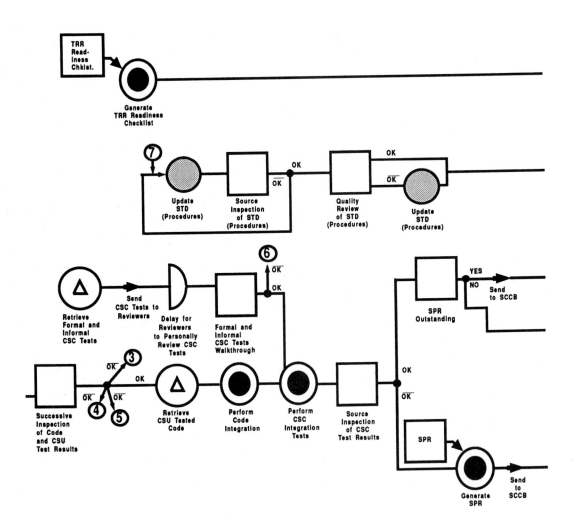

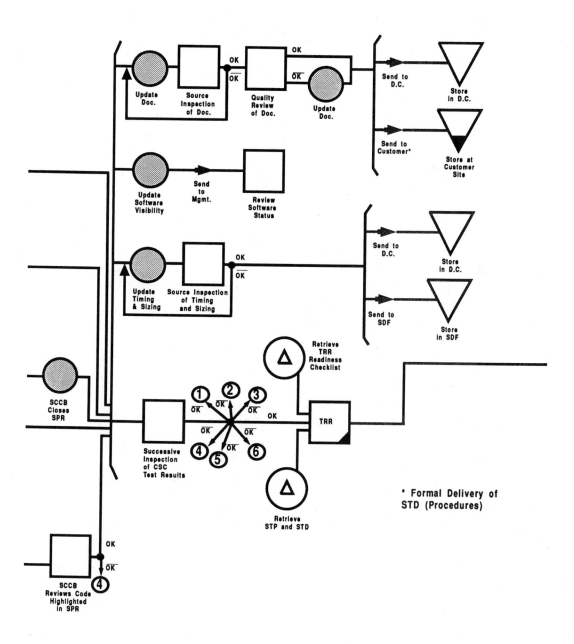

Update
Doc.

Source
Inspection
of Doc.

OK
OK

Quality
Review
of Doc.

OK
OK

Update
Doc.

Send to
D.C.

Store
in D.C.

Send to
Customer*

Store at
Customer
Site

Update
Software
Visibility

Send
to
Mgmt.

Review
Software
Status

Update
Timing
& Sizing

Source Inspection
of Timing
and Sizing

OK
OK

Send to
D.C.

Store
in D.C.

Send to
SDF

Store
in SDF

Retrieve
TRR
Readiness
Checklist

SCCB
Closes
SPR

① ② ③
OK OK OK

OK

TRR

Successive
Inspection
of CSC
Test Results

④ ⑤ ⑥
OK OK

Retrieve
STP and STD

* Formal Delivery of
STD (Procedures)

SCCB
Reviews Code
Highlighted
in SPR

OK
OK

④

CSCI Testing

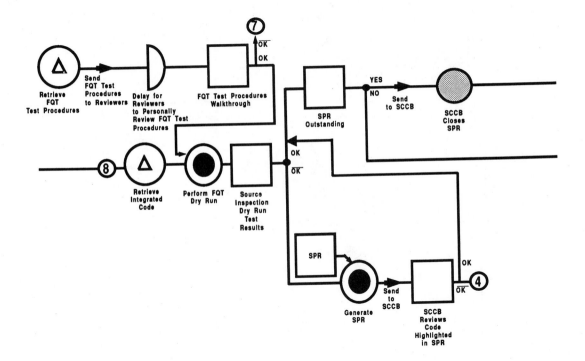

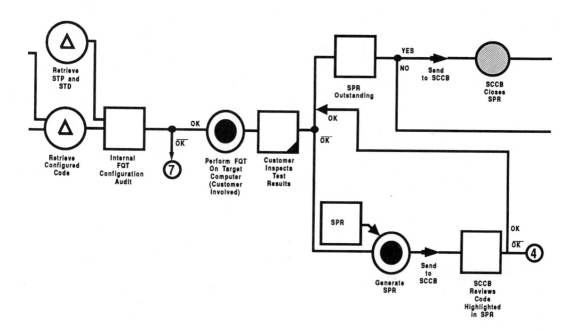

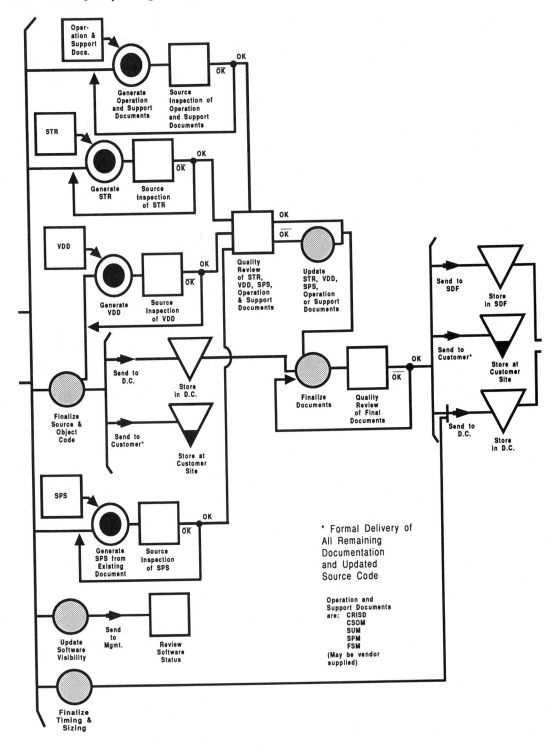

**System
Integration
and Testing**

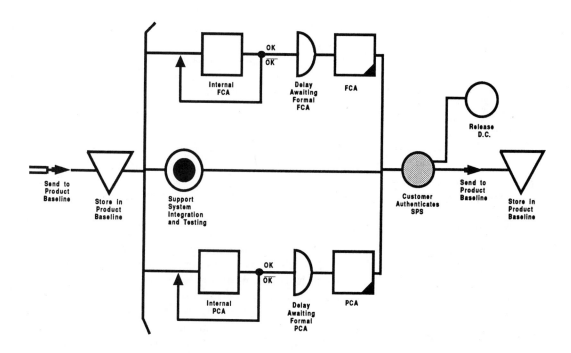

17

Statistical Process Control Applied to Software

Barba B. Affourtit
Interaction Research Institute

17.1 INTRODUCTION

Total Quality Management (TQM) involves participation of all members of an organization in the quest for continuous improvement. TQM represents a significant change from "business as usual" for most organizations—a transformation in the organizational culture. How can we achieve the cultural change needed for total quality? Organizational development studies have revealed that interventions like team building produce short term changes but sustain little long term effect.[1] The contrived exercises are completed and long forgotten once the team building session is over. The best way to create teamwork is to get people working in teams. Teamwork is maximized through common goals which members can work toward as a unified team and knowledge of the methods and tools that can be used to attain those goals.

Statistical Process Control (SPC) provides the methodology for beneficial change. SPC tools aid in process improvement by uncovering process dynamics. SPC tools also break down the barriers of defensiveness by displaying an objective assessment of what is occurring. When SPC is applied by teams, team members gain insight into each other as well as into the process. What is perceived as lack of care usually turns out to be lack of understanding. As these little mysteries are deciphered, the culture improves along with the process. Mutual efforts to understand and optimize organizational processes transform the culture through incremental improvement.

17.2 APPLICATIONS OF SPC

Basic Premises

Effective application of SPC requires unswerving belief in several basic premises:

- Pride in workmanship. Most people are intrinsically motivated to do a good job, but excellent quality is precluded by systems that do not enable people to do their best. Therefore, the primary job of management is to remove barriers and thereby create a system that allows people to enjoy their work and take pride in its outcome. A constant search for improvement opportunities is an integral element of effective process management.
- Theory of variation. If the same task is performed repeatedly by the same person, the outputs will not be identical. Variation is inherent in every process, whether the process is running the 100 meter dash, preparing an invoice, or writing code. However, the magnitude of variation exhibited in a process differs depending upon the conditions within which a process is performed. For example, a person preparing invoices in a quiet office would likely produce less variation than one who is constantly interrupted.

The challenge to anyone managing a process is to determine whether the variation exhibited is explained by chance or by exception. W. Edwards Deming[2] distinguishes two types of causes of variation.

- Special causes. Variation caused by special circumstances that can be pinpointed to a specific time or location.
- Common causes. Net effect of the numerous sources of variation inherent in the current system.

Determination of the type of cause is key to effective intervention, because the strategies for improvement are different. The type of cause also designates the responsibility for action. Correction of special causes requires action on the process (e.g., adjustment of machine settings) and can be accomplished by those executing the process. Common causes are inherent in the system and must be resolved by those who create the system within which operations are performed. Resolution involves a fundamental change in the system (e.g., improved operational instructions).

The most effective method for determining cause is the control chart, developed by Walter Shewhart in 1924.[3] Although the name is universally accepted, a control chart does not actually control anything. It is a decision support mechanism that provides a basis for action—the action controls the process. Control charts signal the existence of special causes when they appear and indicate the extent of variation resulting from common causes. Figure 17-1 displays a conceptual control chart.

Control limits serve as decision lines; i.e., limits derived from past experience which denote the range within which fluctuations are expected to fall. Special causes are denoted by points that fall outside of control limits or patterns in the

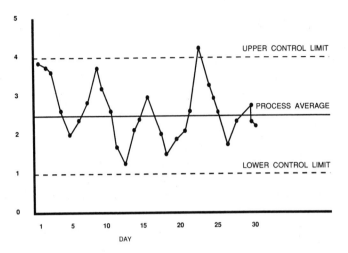

FIGURE 17-1. Conceptual control chart.

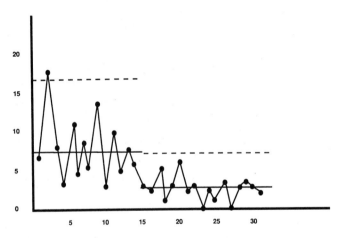

FIGURE 17-2. Control chart for defects per 1000 lines of code.

plotted points. A description of control chart signals is included in the *Statistical Quality Control Handbook* by Western Electric.[4]

It is important to note that the chart defines the system from which the data were collected. Changes in the system produce concomitant changes in performance. In software development, software engineering tools such as consistency checkers, syntax editors, and prototype design languages have markedly reduced coding defects. The chart in Figure 17-2 displays the number of defects per thousand source lines of code (KSLOC) before and after system improvements.

Figure 17-2 also displays two types of improvements—control and breakthrough. Control is secured by systematically removing special causes in response to control chart signals. A process in statistical control is preferable to an unstable process, since it enables prediction of future performance.

A process in statistical control is stable in the sense that its average and limits of variation are predictable. If a process stabilizes at an unacceptable performance level, a breakthrough is needed to attain further improvement. A breakthrough is achieved through a fundamental change in the process or system—new technology, standardization, training, etc. The control chart then displays the impact of the system change on process performance.

SPC can be applied to any process measurement. Since metrics provide the medium for informed decision making, selecting the appropriate measures to manage the process is key to effective application. Measures of customer satisfaction and performance outcomes pinpoint problems. Metrics that support process management disclose causes of problems. Actions taken to resolve problems improve the process, thereby improving the product and service delivered to customers.

Applications in Non-Manufacturing Environments

Examples of beneficial manufacturing applications abound, but administrative and service applications are just beginning to be developed. Many organizations which embarked on service applications in the 1980s discovered that although their manufacturing processes were well controlled, their non-manufacturing processes were ill-defined, uncontrolled, and error infested.

Organizations enjoying less than 1% manufacturing defect rates uncovered 15 to 20% rates for procurement and billing. The need was unequivocally demonstrated. Applications were explored, and benefits derived in areas that included data entry, billing, procurement, labor reporting, inventory control, planning and forecasting.

Advances in health care are offered as examples in response to claims that software development is too complex and influenced by too many variables for effective application of statistical process control. Clinical applications involve sources of variation that include the severity of the patient's condition as well as variation in practices of the many services performed during the patient's stay.

The critical path methodology was developed by New England Medical Center to standardize health care practices and thereby assure that each patient receives the proper care at the proper time. Critical paths are being developed for different services. Paths specify what needs to be accomplished during each day of the patient's stay to ensure that the patient recovers and can be discharged by the milestone date. The critical paths specify timeframes for tasks across all functions:

- Lab tests
- Physical therapy
- Diet (e.g., ability to tolerate solid foods)
- Patient education
- Medication
- Patient mobility
- Patient ability to administer self care (e.g., insulin shots, drainage of wounds)

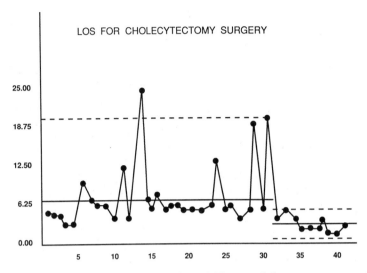

FIGURE 17-3. Length of stay (LOS) control chart.

Applying the critical path methodology in conjunction with SPC charts to monitor patient progress, Alliant Health System reduced the average length of time that patients required hospitalization. More importantly, the variation was reduced dramatically, as displayed in Figure 17-3.

Since explicit criteria must be met for the patients to be released, the reduced length of stay was not attained by pushing patients out the door before they were ready to be released. Patients recover more quickly when the necessary services are performed at the appropriate time.

The software development process parallels the medical example above in many ways. Effectiveness requires a concerted and coordinated effort across numerous diverse functions. The critical path method has long been utilized in software development to meet scheduled milestones. However software planning and control is typically conducted at a much higher level of detail. Software development could benefit from the standardization of practices and rigorous monitoring against those standards that has produced remarkable improvements in medical treatment.

Applications in Software Development and Support

SPC offers unlimited potential for contributing to the improvement of processes used to develop and support software. The common misconception that SPC cannot be applied to "one of a kind" operations has precluded exploitation.

SPC is applied to a process—not to a product. Although each software product is unique, the software life cycle attests to the fact that the processes through which products are created are repetitive.

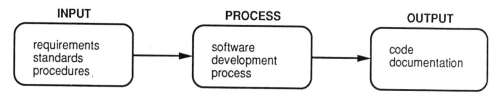

FIGURE 17-4. Software development process.

Viewing the software development process at the macro level, the customer is the user of the products and/or services (Figure 17-4). Explicit requirements, standards, and procedures are required as input. Software engineering tools facilitate the process. The ultimate output is the fully developed program/system along with supporting documentation.

Focusing in on a micro level perspective of each unit's contribution, the process is the work accomplished by the unit being diagrammed. The customer is the next person in the chain of operations and the supplier is in the preceding process. The concept of the internal customer has proven to be an effective countermeasure to suboptimization (e.g., optimizing one aspect of the process, possibly at the expense of the whole). Organizations like AT&T have expanded the internal customer concept into an operational procedure with entry and exit criteria for each process. Exit criteria are equivalent to entry criteria for the next process in the sequence of operations. Personnel from both processes conduct inspections to assure conformance to entry/exit criteria.

There are three categories of applications for software development:

1. Retrospective investigation of previous programs in order to improve the system that produced them.
2. Real time monitoring of present program in order to signal potential problems and institute appropriate countermeasures.
3. Historical assessment of human resources, schedule, and cost of previous projects in order to develop realistic estimates for future efforts.

Software metrics have been developed to provide management with a gauge to monitor the effectiveness of the software development process. Metrics signal when intervention is needed to rectify problems with cost, schedule, or reliability. Too often, the corrective action employed is inappropriate, due to the fact that the metric only indicates when and where a problem is surfacing but not why. For example, since delivery is of prime importance to most customers, metrics that monitor schedule adherence are instrumental in signaling deviations. The typical response is to allocate more human resources for the offending tasks rather than determining the cause. This often increases schedule slippage due to additional time consumed correcting errors introduced by personnel not yet up to speed. For more information on metrics see Chapter 6 and Reference 17.

The primary purpose of SPC methods is to facilitate process improvement by disclosing the causes of variation, as opposed to the common practice of managing the symptom. The level of detail of most metrics is insufficient to determine why. Therefore a systematic procedure is needed to determine the type of information required to meet an objective.

Process Management Cycle

The Process Management Cycle (PMC) is a systematic method for pursuing an investigation toward an improvement objective.[5] The PMC provides an operational procedure for applying statistical techniques. The PMC follows the same sequence as the scientific method that prevents overuse or misuse of statistical techniques by focusing the investigation on the type of information needed. The PMC is composed of four phases:

Phase 1. Identify . . . . . . Establish the objective
Phase 2. Analyze . . . . . . Locate the cause
Phase 3. Correct . . . . Modify the process
Phase 4. Evaluate . . . . . . Validate the solution

Identification. The identification phase discovers the condition that affords the greatest opportunity for improvement.

Analysis. The analysis phase searches for factors that influence the process being investigated and diagnoses their effect.

Correction. The correction phase establishes and implements a corrective action plan to address causes discovered during analysis.

Evaluation. The evaluation phase quantifies the impact of the action taken in order to determine whether the process modification should be institutionalized.

Process Management Tools

Techniques that are applied within the Process Management Cycle are listed in Table 17-1. Table 17-1 also includes the function and purpose of each technique, as well as applications of several key techniques.

It is critical to establish objectives that are aligned with the overall mission of the organization. Premature termination of quality improvement endeavors is usually linked to objectives that are not connected with organizational objectives or too ambiguous for efficient investigation. Quality Function Deployment (QFD) and Pareto diagrams are techniques that aid in relevant and viable quality improvement efforts.

Quality Function Deployment (discussed in Chapter 12) is a method that derives customer driven quality indicators. QFD identifies customer needs and translates them into measurable characteristics. For each characteristic that defines customer requirements, contributing processes are isolated and metrics that define quality for the internal processes are generated. This methodology links operational processes with organizational goals.

Pareto analysis targets improvement opportunities by revealing where the greatest proportion of problems are originating. The Pareto chart displayed in

TABLE 17-1   Process Management Cycle Techniques

Function	Technique	Purpose
Involvement Commitment	Quality Function Deployment....	Define requirements
	Nominal group...............	Locate opportunities
	Process flow Case and effect ··············	Define process
Innovation	Sequence effect brainstorming....	Organize causes
Categorize Contrast Highlight	Pareto diagram Bar graphs ··············	Narrow focus
	Matrix analysis..............	Discover cause type
Diagnose	Run chart...................	Reveal patterns
Monitor	Control chart................	Detect change
Evaluate	Scatter diagram..............	Quantify causal relationships
Display	Histogram...................	Observe distribution
Define	General statistics.............	Assess process
Specify	Process capability analysis.......	Compare process to objective

Figure 17-5 revealed that the majority of software defects were attributable to incorrect, incomplete, or ambiguous requirements. These findings led to allocation of a greater proportion of the development life cycle to requirements definition and analysis, resulting in improvements in meeting delivery schedules as well as in quality.

The matrix is an ideal technique for examining the interaction of two factors. The Entry Systems Division of IBM employed a matrix to conduct detailed analysis of usability for commercial systems. Usability was assessed via tests

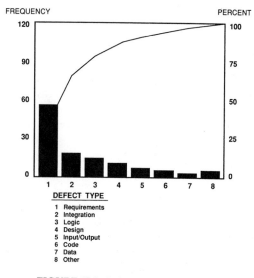

FIGURE 17-5. Software defects by type.

TABLE 17-2   Usability Matrix

Label	E1	E2	E3	E4	E5	E6	I1	I2	I3	I4	I5	I6	Total
1	1	0	1	1	1	0	0	0	1	0	1	0	6
2	1	1	1	1	1	1	1	1	1	1	1	1	12
3	1	1	0	1	1	0	0	0	1	0	0	0	5
4	1	1	0	1	1	1	1	0	1	0	1	0	8
5	1	0	1	1	1	1	1	0	1	1	0	1	9
6	1	1	0	1	1	0	1	1	1	1	1	1	10
7	1	1	1	1	1	1	0	0	0	0	0	0	6
8	0	0	1	0	1	1	0	0	1	0	1	0	5
9	1	0	1	1	1	0	1	1	1	1	1	1	10
10	1	1	1	1	1	1	1	0	1	1	1	1	11
11	1	0	1	1	1	1	0	1	1	0	1	1	9
12	1	0	1	0	1	1	0	0	0	0	0	1	5
13	1	0	1	1	1	1	0	1	1	0	1	0	8
14	1	1	0	1	1	1	1	0	0	0	1	0	7
15	1	0	1	1	1	1	1	0	1	1	0	1	9
16	1	1	0	1	1	0	1	1	1	1	1	1	10
17	0	0	0	0	0	0	0	0	0	0	0	0	0
18	1	0	1	0	1	0	0	0	1	0	0	0	4
19	0	0	1	1	1	0	0	1	1	1	1	0	7
20	1	1	1	1	1	1	1	0	1	0	1	1	10
Total	17	9	14	16	19	12	10	7	16	8	13	10	151

administered to randomly selected individuals from the potential user population. The tests measured unassisted completions of specified tasks. The matrix in Table 17-2 illustrates what the results of usability tests for a specific program might reveal.

The matrix shows performance on 20 tasks by six experienced (E1 to E6) and six inexperienced (I1 to I6) users. A 1 denotes successful completion of the task, a 0 failure to execute the task without assistance. Table 17-2 reveals that all users executed task 2, but all had trouble with task 17. Task 7 posed no problem for the experienced users but could not be completed by inexperienced users.

Data from the matrix can be further analyzed by a control chart for tasks completed. The control chart in Figure 17-6 shows that task 17 was significantly more difficult to execute than the other tasks.

The scatter diagram (Figure 17-7) for correlation and regression has four types of applications:

1. Comparison of measurement methods. Checks for agreement between two inspectors, tests, machines.
2. Cause and Effect Analysis. For cause and effect analysis, the x axis represents the cause, the y axis the effect, as displayed in the example in Figure 17-7 showing the relationship between the short transaction response time and coding productivity.

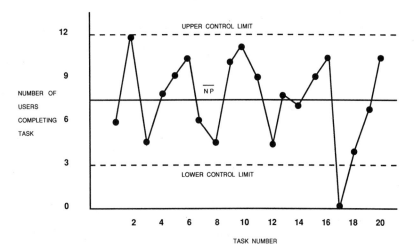

FIGURE 17-6. Usability test results.

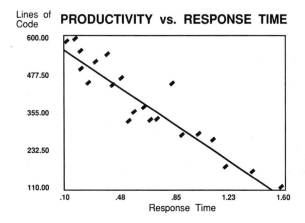

FIGURE 17-7. Scatter diagram for cause and effect analysis.

3. Trend analysis for planning and forecasting. This is a time series analysis with the *x* axis representing time, and the *y* axis denoting how the quality characteristic trends over time.
4. Plan versus actual. This application is similar to the comparison of measurement methods. The *x* axis represents the plan, the *y* axis the actual.

17.3 TYPES OF SOFTWARE APPLICATIONS

Project Planning

During the planning phase, estimates for resources, cost, and schedule are generated. Projection of the future based on the past carries the implicit assumption that

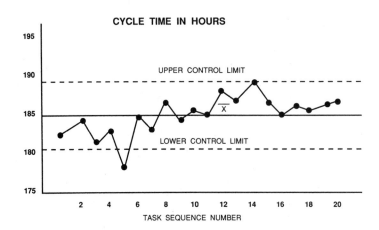

FIGURE 17-8. Individual measurements control chart.

conditions in the past will continue into the future. Therefore any quantitative solution must be ameliorated with qualitative knowledge of how this project may differ from previous ones.

Any projection process is inherently risky. However, Deming contends that estimation of the future based on the past is pure folly if the process is unstable.[2] Only a process that is stable has a definable capability. A process in statistical control provides the predictability needed for reliable estimation.

In addition to providing estimates that are reliable, SPC techniques aid in deriving estimates that are realistic. Even if the program is bound by a mandated delivery date, optimal apportionment of resources within the mandated time constraints can be accomplished with a reliable estimate of the human resource time needed to complete each task.

The work breakdown structure, developed during project planning, segments the development effort into tasks that are approximately equivalent with regard to human resource requirements. Historical data of cycle time at the task level provides an initial estimate of the person hours required to complete each task. Figure 17-8 displays an individual measurements control chart of cycle time over sequential tasks. Since all points are in control, the centerline provides a reliable estimate of average cycle time; the upper control limit is a worst case estimate. Given an expected delivery date, human resources required to complete the job within the time available can be easily determined. Cost is then derived by multiplying the human resource utilization by the prevailing labor rate.

Program Management

The software development industry has been plagued by schedule and cost overruns, to such an extent that overruns are practically a foregone conclusion. program management is an exercise in control. Resources, schedule, and cost are monitored against the plan. If deviations are excessive, corrective action is undertaken to align project execution with the plan. Since absolute adherence to the plan is impossible and impractical, a mechanism is needed to determine when deviations are large enough to warrant action. SPC techniques provide the decision support system to signal when intervention is needed and when it is not. Swift correction of pinpointed problems can circumvent the negative ramifications that many organizations are currently encountering.

Most organizations manage software development programs by monitoring some aspect of work accomplished versus resource utilization:

- Cycle time. Elapsed time to accomplish each task is compared against predicted time.
- Tasks completed. Number of tasks completed per milestone is compared to scheduled completions per milestone.
- Productivity. Work completed (e.g., lines of code) per segment of time (e.g., person month) compared against standards.

Since each project is unique, forecasts based on past performance may not be completely accurate. It is not unusual for worst case estimates to be exceeded. Adaptive forecasting utilizes continuous monitoring against the plan to determine when adjustments are needed. Whatever monitor is used, a comparison of plan versus actual signals potential problems. Figure 17-9 illustrates the use of a scatter diagram to compare plan versus actual. The 45 degree angle of the regression line denotes agreement. A trend below the regression line would indicate that actual is falling behind plan, alerting a schedule and cost overrun. Overruns occur because of underestimation of resource requirements during planning, or unforeseen (and perhaps avoidable) delays in execution.

"Seat of the pants" estimates are invariably grossly overoptimistic. A program manager for an environmental system devised a simple solution for modifying an overoptimistic plan. Recognizing that the development was behind schedule, he

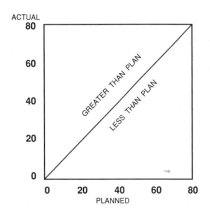

FIGURE 17-9. Planned versus actual unit test completions.

needed a means to determine when the effort would be completed. All tasks were enumerated on a spreadsheet. He determined the average amount of time to complete a task based on the number of tasks completed up to that point. Recording a 1 for each task completed and a 0 for each task remaining, the number of remaining tasks was determined. This result multiplied by the average time per task yielded an expected delivery date. The actual completion date was within days of the projection.

Reliability

Reliability represents the degree to which the software can be depended upon to perform its intended function. The formal definition is "the probability that the software will perform its intended function for a specific duration of time under given conditions." The time parameter may seem irrelevant for there are no hardware components to wear out. However, it takes a certain amount of time for the software to be subjected to all conditions.

Reliability is a user oriented measure. Therefore it follows that communication of user conditions is key to ensuring reliability. Since all possibilities are difficult to visualize by the specification writer, feedback of user conditions that resulted in failure is instrumental in improving current and future programs.

Software reliability is also improved by reducing the errors that lead to faults. Reduction is accomplished through a coordinated effort in detection and prevention. Errors discovered via inspection and test are removed to improve the reliability of the product. At the same time, errors are examined for cause to improve the quality of the process. Much of the effort is misdirected due to lack of distinction between special and common causes. There are three types of errors that can lead to faults:

1. Inadvertent. Inadvertent errors are random human errors. There is no particular reason for their occurrence. Occasional random errors are inevitable because of the inherent fallibility in human beings. Feedback of inadvertent errors to their originators is nonproductive, and can be counter-productive for there is no corrective action that the individual can pursue.

   The best countermeasure to inadvertent errors is poka-yoke (mistake proofing). Much of the quality improvement that has been achieved over the last decade is attributable to software engineering tools that have been developed to reduce the likelihood of human error (e.g., syntax checkers).

   Inadvertent errors discovered during inspection and test are candidates for poka-yoke (see Chapter 16). Each error can be examined by a team in order to develop foolproofing mechanisms to render it impossible, or at least improbable, for the error to occur again. Approximately 80% of process improvements devised by Japanese quality control circles were in the foolproofing arena.

TABLE 17-3   Error Breakdown Matrix

Error Type	Employee					
	A	B	C	D	E	Total
1	0	1	0	2	1	4
2	1	0	0	1	0	2
3	0	(7)	1	3	0	11
4	1	0	0	1	0	2
5	2	1	3	4	2	(12)
6	0	0	0	3	0	3
Total	4	9	4	(14)	3	34

2. Procedural or technique errors. This type of error is due to improper
   execution of a process due to misunderstanding, lack of skill, etc. These types
   of errors are exhibited as special causes.

   A breakdown of errors by originator is essential to disclose technique
   errors. Deming professes that the ultimate role of a supervisor is to help
   people do a better job. A matrix of errors by type and by individual like that
   exhibited in Table 17-3 aids the manager/supervisor in discovering and
   rectifying technique errors.

3. Structural errors. Structural errors are due to limitations in the system and/or
   process. Structural errors include screening and training procedures, tools to
   facilitate software development, formal and informal communication, or any
   other shortcomings in the system within which the work is performed.

   Variation attributable to common causes includes the inadvertent and the
   structural errors. It is impossible to separate the two, since one of the primary
   outcomes of systemic improvements to improve the structure is a reduction in
   inadvertent errors. Therefore, the optimal improvement strategy is to create a
   stable process by detecting and correcting technique errors denoted by
   signals of special causes, and then to concentrate on continuous improvement
   of the system, incrementally reducing variation to its absolute minimum.

Reducing Potential for Error

The previous section addressed quality improvement by systematically eliminating errors and their causes. The preventative approach reduces the potential for
errors to occur by controlling factors that are correlated with errors.

Standardization. Standardization is the most effective strategy for reducing
nonmanufacturing errors, since the main source of variation is people. When
operational methods are a function of individual idiosyncrasies, variation is the result. Even if all the methods are excellent, integration is difficult if they are different.

Ishikawa advocates standardization to enable the delegation of authority to subordinates.[7] The effect of standardization is a reduction in variation in the way the process is performed, with a concomitant reduction in errors and cycle time. The stabilized process attained through standardization provides a baseline from which creative process enhancements can be reliable measured.

Complexity. Intuitive logic indicates that complexity is positively correlated with errors. However, monitoring of actual practice in several organizations reveals that the reverse is true. In analysis of error rate by size, Dan Stout discovered that the smaller modules exhibited the higher error rates,[8] and other software quality professionals have expressed similar findings.

A likely explanation is that, recognizing the risk imposed by complex modules, risk mitigation techniques have been successfully practiced. The findings also indicate that the techniques should be utilized more extensively for less complex modules.

Changes. Changes impose a major threat to software quality. Every change creates a potential for introducing errors directly, or producing side effects that propagate errors. Configuration management contributes to quality by formalizing change requests and controlling the impact of change.

Quality of the current system is controlled by managing change; quality of future systems is improved by determining the reasons for change and reducing its occurrence. A control chart of engineering changes throughout the life cycle can be used to signal when an exceptional number of changes indicate a high level of risk. A Pareto breakdown of software engineering changes by cause reveals recurrent causes that can be resolved through system improvements.

Data quality. Assurance of data quality is a powerful countermeasure to software failures. The most common initiating event in software failure is related to the input data. Procedures to prevent poor data and to apprehend aberrations in the data and minimize their consequences should be designed into all software programs.

An example is the proper handling of out-of-range inputs without degrading the performance of functions not dependent on the input. When the condition occurs, a new input may be requested or a predefined default can be assigned, with a notification to the operator. This type of measure prevents abnormal terminations due to data errors.

Designing for data quality involves identifying all points in the process (manual as well as automated) where the data could lose its integrity using a data flow or process flow diagram. Once these control points in the process are identified, potential sources of variation in the data are examined using a cause and effect diagram. Feedback-control mechanisms are designed for each potential source of discrepancy.

Screening and Training

The variation among individuals involved in software development has been repeatedly demonstrated and documented. Research conducted by Tom DeMarco revealed that there are people on almost all projects who insert spoilage that exceeds the value of the production.[9] Further, taking a poor performer off a team can be more productive than adding a good one. DeMarco contends that it is unconscionable to ignore differences among people when assigning work. W. Edwards Deming advises that a leader be aware of differences among people in order to optimize everyone's abilities and inclinations.[2]

The challenge to management is to be able to distinguish differences in abilities and assign accordingly. SPC techniques provide a mechanism for detecting performance differences during screening and training. Figure 17-10 displays a typical learning curve; learning begins slowly, accelerates quickly, then levels off.

For defects, the trend is reversed but the pattern is the same. Figure 17-11 exhibits defects over time from initial employment to stabilization. Control charts can be used to monitor the journey through the learning curve and determine when training or apprenticeship has served its purpose.

Jim Dobbins found the same phenomena for entire projects.[10] After observing inspection results for a variety of projects and types of code, he found that defects per KSLOC stabilized after about 10,000 lines of code. This phenomena occurred on all new code development regardless of personnel, environments, and type of code.

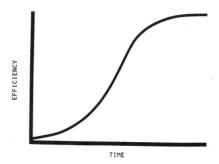

FIGURE 17-10. Learning curve.

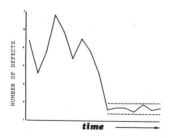

FIGURE 17-11. Defects trend.

17.4 APPLICATIONS WITHIN
LIFE CYCLE PHASES

Requirements

During the requirements analysis phase, customer needs are transformed into a concrete specification that becomes the foundation for development. The requirements specification is a translation of the voice of the customer that delineates what the software is to accomplish.

Roger Pressman describes the requirements analysis process as one of discovery and refinement.[11] Software is developed to fulfill a need. The analyst's job is to discover what the customer needs are and to translate those needs into functional and performance specifications. Since the customer needs are affected by what is possible and feasible, the process of generating requirements is an iterative process of communication. The ambiguity of the English language poses a challenge to any endeavor in which effectiveness is predicated upon successful communication.

Many organizations have devoted extensive effort to trying to evaluate their analysts. Since the ultimate measure of the quality of requirements is how well the program meets users needs, short term evaluation is impossible. Further, the pervasiveness of insufficient requirements indicates that a focus on the individuals doing the work is misdirected. Instead, we should abandon efforts to evaluate analysts and redirect those energies to improving the system through which requirements are generated.

The proportion of the life cycle costs incurred during the operations and maintenance phase (estimated at 40 to 60%) are a testimony to the fallibility of the requirements generation process. However, the modifications produced to correct shortcomings offer an improvement opportunity that has not been fully exploited. Current and future software development efforts could truly benefit from "lessons learned" from software in deployment. The Gulf War lessons learned repeatedly demonstrated that "user hostile" systems impede work proficiency. Many systems are being redesigned because they did not adequately support the fast paced decision-making environment for which they were developed.

The most useful information to improve the requirements analysis process is information about problems with systems currently in operations. Itemized descriptions of the specific aspect of the requirements that were insufficiently specified will disclose repetitive causes.

Less comprehensive but more timely assessment of the requirements generation process is through software engineering changes and design and code errors attributable to requirement discrepancies. Engineering changes provide an intermediate measure of the quality of the requirements, but a relatively small number of engineering changes does not equate to excellence. The requirements specification can be clear, concise, and complete, but completely miss the mark with respect to user's needs. However, feedback from engineering changes can be instrumental in discovering areas that require more probing to elicit customer needs.

The discussion thus far has concentrated on improving the requirements generation process through analysis of its shortcomings. The requirements generation process can also be improved through the use of SPC problem solving tools during requirements generation. The quality of requirements is predicated upon the successful acquisition of information regarding customer needs. Acquiring information from users can be facilitated by using techniques like the cause and effect diagram[12] to brainstorm sources of problems with the current system. Workshops of this type identify needs that the customer had not previously envisioned, much less specified.

Design

Requirements describe what the software will accomplish as perceived by the user community. Design specifies how the software will be developed. Like the requirements generation process, the design process is one of communication. Design translates the requirements specification into a methodology for execution. Spaghetti code is usually linked to an incomplete or unclear design. Tools like structure charts, data flow diagrams, and data dictionaries facilitate the design process.

Since efficiency is inversely related to the size of a project, good design practice is based on modularity—segmenting a large project into a set of smaller parts or modules that can function independently. Therefore continuous monitoring of size aids in optimizing productivity and also provides input for incremental adjustments to the project plan.

Since Michael Fagan's 1976 research paper[13] demonstrating that fewer errors occurred as the inspection was held closer to the worker, design and code inspections have become standardized procedures for detecting and correcting problems prior to testing. Design inspections examine the logic, efficiency, and clarity of the design as represented in the design documentation.

Pareto analysis of causes for design defects by McCabe and Schulmeyer[14] revealed that almost 60% of the defects are attributable to the design process itself. This finding substantiates the benefit of design inspections to provide detailed feedback on a relatively real time basis. This feedback enables the designer to realize improvement while working on the same project.

Since the impact of design inspections on the quality of the design is directly related to the quality of the inspection process, many organizations have found it fruitful to monitor characteristics of the inspection process. Both inspection time and preparation time have been found to be directly correlated with number of errors found, up to a point. The optimal time to allocate to inspection and preparation activities is the point where the defects found levels off.

The incremental functional verification of the pseudo code employed in Cleanroom development environments (see Chapter 18) provides the most timely feedback to designers. Further, Mills and Poore found that functional verification can be performed by the individuals who create the design, as opposed to design inspection that is only effective if conducted by an independent third party.[15] The extent to which functional verification succeeds or fails indicates whether the process is in control.

Other characteristics of the design that warrant monitoring are correctness, producibility, fault tolerance, testability, and maintainability. Correctness measures adherence of the design to the requirements specification. Monitoring correctness of the design documentation prior to onset of coding not only reveals insufficiencies in the design, but also isolates defects in the specification document. Jim Dobbins[16] recommends that specification defects are tracked as separate and distinct items on the inspection report for maximum benefit. Separate tabulations facilitate traceability of problems to their source and also enable assessment of the impact of specification defects.

Coding

Defects per 1000 lines of source code has withstood the test of time as a useful measure of the coding process. Measures of coding that compensate for complexity have more recently been derived (e.g., function points). Although such indices are useful for evaluative purposes, they mask causes with data that is massaged to produce a "fair" measure. A fair measure is one that compensates for variation. Since variation reveals improvement opportunities, indices that smooth the data are not sensitive enough for process control.

The effectiveness of the monitor is directly related to the timeliness of the feedback. Code inspection at the unit level is conducted immediately following clean compilation. The common assumption that the inspection must be performed by an objective third party is partially based upon a Theory X management perspective.[17] Typical justification is an assertion that coders will perform more diligent self checks when they know that inspection will immediately follow. This rationale presumes that the individuals will not do their best unless coerced by the threat of humiliation.

Process control in manufacturing has repeatedly demonstrated that process improvement is optimized through the immediate feedback afforded by self inspection. However, in labor intensive operations, an individual who makes an error is less likely to identify the error than an uninvolved third party. Therefore, self inspection must be augmented with an objective third party inspection.

Code inspection and test results reveal insufficiencies in all prior processes as well as the coding process itself. When defects are monitored over time, special causes signal problems attributable to fatigue, misunderstanding, ambiguous or incomplete specifications, complexity, or other unusual conditions.

SPC feedback during the code and unit test phase improves the process as well as the product. Correction of errors detected improves the product, investigation of cause improves the process.

Testing and Verification

The diagnosis and removal of faults has been estimated to consume more than half of software development costs (not including maintenance). Testing and verification are a critical phase in the life cycle, since this phase is completed when the product is deemed ready for deployment. SPC applications in testing and verification should concentrate on improving the development process as well as the testing process itself. There are three major types of applications in this phase:

1. Control and improve the testing and verification processes.
2. Improve quality of products being tested.
3. Improve processes through which products delivered to test are produced.

Control and Improve the Testing Process

Software quality professionals lament the ineffectiveness of testing in discovering and correcting all faults. Although detection of every fault is unachievable, the testing process can become more productive through meaningful feedback. Seeding errors into a program provides a standard for judging test effectiveness. Just as the accuracy of a laboratory test is validated by comparison of test results against standards with known values, seeding implants a specified number of errors into the code to determine the proportion of seeded errors discovered during testing. A tabulation of the proportion of faults detected indicates how well defect detection is proceeding.

Another important element in controlling the testing process itself is ascertaining testing progress. The number of test completions and problem reports that have been resolved are informative progress measures.

The purpose of testing is to find problems so that they can be rectified. A control chart of faults encountered per module identifies bug infested modules. Testing results have revealed that defects tend to occur in clusters, and a high incidence of defects detected indicates a large number of defects remaining. An exceptional error rate signals that perhaps the module should be rewritten, rather than expending additional resources in a futile effort to uncover and correct all errors.

SPC techniques can also be used to determine how much testing is enough. Predictors of the number of errors within a segment being tested can be derived through historical data on the number of errors in approximately equivalent segments. The historical data should be composed of the errors found during deployment as well as test.

When testing ceases to identify problems, does this mean that none are present, or that detection abilities have been exhausted? Insertion of new testers and monitoring for trend changes help answer that question.

The difficult decision to conclude testing is less soul wrenching if supported by meaningful information. Comparisons of test results against predictions of error concentrations provide a baseline. When there is a poor match, SPC techniques can be used to determine unique conditions and modify accordingly. The final decision is supported by attaining a balance between predicted and actual test results.

Maintenance

If the software is successful, maintenance will be the longest phase of the life cycle. The ultimate objective of maintenance is to ensure that customers are utilizing the software to its maximum benefit. Maintenance involves responding to customer problems and anticipating and meeting future needs with program enhancements.

SPC can be used to monitor the quality of the system being maintained as well as the effectiveness of the maintenance process. Useful monitors of the maintenance process include system availability, response time, interrupts, and field failures. Measures of the responsiveness of maintenance personnel include elapsed time to respond to and resolve user problems.

Measures of the quality of the system being maintained include hot line calls, problem reports, change requests, and system usage. Reliance on a single metric is inadvisable for evaluation of system effectiveness. A relatively small number of requests for changes could be indicative of nonuse, as opposed to user satisfaction with the current system.

Monitors of system usage are valuable customer satisfaction indicators. Initial usage considerably less than has been projected might be due to usability problems that need to be promptly addressed and rectified. A decline in usage in a mature system could indicate that enhancements have not kept pace with user needs.

Finally, maintenance findings regarding user problems and needs are useful for targeting improvement efforts into areas that will increase customer satisfaction.

Making it Happen

Most software developers maintain a healthy skepticism regarding the efficacy of SPC as a decision support tool. The concerns are legitimate. Since the primary source of variation is people, effective application is a formidable challenge. A catalyst is needed to capture the pioneering spirit of software developers to exploit the enormous potential offered by SPC methodology.

The most effective catalyst for SPC implementation is a demonstration of its benefits. Presentations of the benefits derived by organizations are useful, but a demonstration of improvements realized within the organization is much more compelling. Therefore, an incremental implementation strategy is ideal, beginning with a few high impact pilot projects. The initial endeavors develop expertise while creating the catalyst for expansion.

Training

Training in SPC methods is also best accomplished incrementally. Formal training in concepts and methodology is reinforced by "Just in Time" training in specific techniques. The formal training provides a "Gestalt" (i.e., concept of how all the pieces fit together to comprise the whole) and also helps create a vision of what can eventually be accomplished.

Learning theory shows that even the most conscientious students will retain only a small portion of the material unless application immediately follows training. To combat this universal tendency, Interaction Research Institute, Inc. (IRI) uses an "education and initiation" approach to concurrently train and implement a statistical process control methodology. Participants engage in developing a plan of investigation to pursue an objective that they identify and define during workshop sessions. The analytical plan is designed in sufficient detail to enable data collection and analysis immediately after the workshop session.

Since the most beneficial learning ensues through application, follow-up is critical to ensure the relevance and validity of the analytical approach. Development of in-house expertise is essential to afford accessibility of technical support and consultation when needed. A cadre of personnel who exhibit aptitude and interest in SPC methodology participate in initial training and facilitate initial projects. When quality improvement activities are expanded, the cadre have gained the experience and expertise to conduct training and consultation.

17.5 SUMMARY

Although measurement has been an integral element of the software development process for more than a decade, analysis of software metrics through SPC methodology is rare. This chapter illustrates some actual and potential applications. However, no two problems are alike. An approach that yields significant benefits in one organization may prove fruitless in another.

The purpose of data for SPC is diametrically opposed to current practices. The widespread use of data for evaluative purposes imposes a significant barrier to SPC implementation. The transition in focus from outcome to process is difficult when current practices are ingrained.

The key to effective application is to seek information to answer a question about the process. Benefit is a natural outcome when the tools are used as a medium to gain insight into process dynamics.

SPC is more than a set of tools to analyze data. It is a disciplined investigative approach that operationalizes the scientific method to search for causality. The logic supports all decision-making, whether or not data are used. By providing a medium for accurate assessment and appropriate response, SPC is an invaluable aid for effective process management.

References

1. Stodgill, R. M. *Handbook of Leadership,* New York: The Free Press, 1974.
2. Deming, W. Edwards, *Out of the Crisis,* Cambridge: MIT Center for Advanced Engineering Study, 1986.
3. Shewhart, Walter A. *Economic Control of Quality of Manufactured Product,* New York: D. Van Nostrand Company, Inc., 1931.
4. Western Electric Co., Inc. *Statistical Quality Control Handbook,* Charlotte, NC: Delmar Printing Company, 1956.

5. Affourtit, Thomas and Affourtit, Barba, *The Organizational Process Management Cycle Programmed Workbook,* Fairfax, VA: Interaction Research Institute, 1988.
6. Kelley, Kenneth H. "Methods Which Increase Quality and Productivity," *Proceedings of National Symposium on TQM for Software,* Washington, DC: The National Institute for Software Quality and Productivity, May 1-2, 1991.
7. Ishikawa, Kaoru, *Guide to Quality Control,* Tokyo: Asian Productivity Association, 1986.
8. Stott, Daniel R. "Managing Quality of Software: Road to Six Sigma," *Transactions—Annual Quality Congress 1991,* pp. 734-739.
9. DeMarco, Tom, *Controlling, Software Projects,* Englewood Cliffs, NJ: Prentice Hall Inc., 1982.
10. Dobbins, James H. "Inspections as an Up-Front Quality Technique," *Handbook of Software Quality Assurance,* New York: Van Nostrand Reinhold, (first ed., 1987), (second ed., 1992).
11. Pressman, Roger S. *Software Engineering: A Practitioner's Approach,* New York: McGraw Hill, 1987.
12. Ishikawa, Kaoru, *What is Total Quality Control? The Japanese Way,* Englewood Cliffs: Prentice-Hall, Inc., 1985.
13. Fagan, Michael E. "Design and Code Inspections to Reduce Errors in Program Development," *IBM Systems Journal* 15(3), 1976.
14. McCabe, Thomas J. and Schulmeyer, G. Gordon, "The Pareto Principle Applied to Software Quality Assurance," *Handbook of Software Quality Assurance,* New York: Van Nostrand Reinhold, 1992.
15. Mills, Harlan D. and Poore, J. H. "Bringing Software Under Statistical Quality Control," *Quality Progress,* Nov. 1988.
16. Dobbins, James H. *Software Quality Assurance and Evaluation,* Milwaukee: Quality Press, 1990.
17. Schulmeyer, G. Gordon and McManus, J. I. "Software Quality Assurance Metrics," *Handbook of Software Quality Assurance,* New York: Van Nostrand Reinhold, 1992.
18. McGregor, Douglas, *The Human Side of Enterprise,* New York: McGraw-Hill, 1960.

General References

Affourtit, Thomas, "Leadership and Management Training," *Human Resources Handbook,* Milwaukee: Quality Press, 1987.

Cave, William C. and Maymon, Gilbert W. *Software Life Cycle Management: The Incremental Method,* New York: Macmillan Publishing Company, 1984.

Deming Study Group of Greater Detroit, "Report of the Deming Study Group (II)," *Transactions—Annual Quality Congress 1991,* pp. 409-413.

Department of Defense, *Total Quality Management—A Guide for Implementation* (Draft) DOD 5000.51-G, 23 Mar. 1989.

Dunn, Robert H. *Software Quality Concepts and Plans,* Englewood Cliffs: Prentice Hall, 1990.

Gunther, Bert. "Process Capability Studies. Part 2: Rational Subgroups," *Quality Progress,* Apr. 1991.

Pall, Gabriel A. *Quality Process Management,* Englewood Cliffs: Prentice-Hall, 1987.

Smith, Robert K. "Why Good People Write Bad Code," *Transactions-Annual Quality Congress,* 1991.

Statland, Norman, *Controlling Software Development,* New York: John Wiley, 1986.

Ward, Michael, *Software That Works,* San Diego: Academic Press, 1990.

18

Cleanroom Engineering: Engineering Software Under Statistical Quality Control*

Harlan D. Mills, Ph.D.

Florida Institute of Technology
Software Engineering Technology, Inc.

18.1 WHAT IS CLEANROOM ENGINEERING?

Advanced companies in software technology and management can now create low or zero defect software products as part of company standards. Software development and maintenance is only a human generation old, and is thus extremely young and immature for managing and engineering software systems and products. This first generation has used heuristic, trial and error methods to cope with industrial demands for software. Errors have come to be considered necessary in software because of human fallibility. But errors are not necessary, and may be overcome by redefining the software development process as a legitimate engineering discipline based on sound mathematical foundations. The Cleanroom Engineering process provides such a discipline for companies to use in managing software while simultaneously ensuring the correctness of the product and increasing the productivity of the process.

The Cleanroom Engineering process develops software of certified correctness under statistical quality control in a pipeline of increments, with box structured design and functional verification but with no program debugging permitted before independent statistical usage testing of the increments. It provides rigorous methods for software specification, development, and certification which are capable of producing low or zero defect software of arbitrary size and complexity.

*Copyright © 1991 by Harlan D. Mills, All Rights Reserved

463

Box structured design is based on a Parnas usage hierarchy of modules. Such modules, also known as data abstractions or objects, are described by a set of operations that may define and access internally stored data. Functional verification is based on the fact that any program or program part is a rule for a mathematical function. It may not be the function desired, but it is a function.

The Cleanroom specification defines a sequence of nested increments which are to be executed exclusively by user commands as they accumulate into the entire system required. Each subsequence represents a subsystem complete in itself, even though not all the user function may be provided in it. As each specified increment is completed by the developers, it is delivered to the certifiers, who combine it with preceding increments, for testing based on usage statistics. For each subsystem, a certified correctness is defined from the usage testing and failures discovered and corrected, if any.

The Cleanroom process applies to all software, business or engineering systems, batch or real time. For example, the IBM COBOL Structuring Facility, a complex business and batch product of some 80,000 lines of PL/1 source code, was developed in the Cleanroom discipline, with box structured design and functional verification, but no debugging before usage testing and certification of its correctness. Two real time engineering systems include the US AF HH60 (helicopter) flight control program of some 33 KLOC (i.e., thousand lines of code) and the subsystem Coarse/Fine Attitude Determination System (CFADS) of the NASA Attitude Ground Support System (AGSS) of some 30 KLOC, both developed Cleanroom.

18.2 PART OF TOTAL QUALITY MANAGEMENT FOR SOFTWARE

Cleanroom Engineering plays a critical role in Total Quality Management for software. Total Quality Management has seven recurring elements which interact with Cleanroom Engineering as follows:

1. Management participation and leadership development. Management plays a necessary and critical role in Cleanroom Engineering. Software is only a generation old, without a long term set of standards, so management is frequently restricted to personnel and financial issues, leaving the technical work to people working in their own way without real management oversight. Cleanroom identifies the technical work for management leadership and control.

2. Establishing goals and measurable objectives. Cleanroom Engineering has goals of zero defect software and it measures progress in terms of certified correctness not only in the final product, but in all intermediate products used to create and manage the process. Cleanroom discipline is formally divided among specification, development, and certification of software, with no debugging permitted in development before statistical testing in certification.

3. Extensive education and training. Cleanroom Engineering requires extensive education and training in all three areas of specification, development, and

certification. Specification requires education in going from informal requirements for software to formal specifications that include function, performance,
and statistical usage. Development requires education for engineering design
of software to meet specifications and coding with no debugging permitted
before delivery to certification. Certification requires education for statistical
testing and evaluation of developed software that establishes mean time to
failures (MTTF) in normal statistical usage.

4. Employee involvement and action teams. Cleanroom Engineering requires
   deep employee involvement in using advanced techniques of software
   specification, development, and certification. The level of discipline in
   Cleanroom Engineering is much above current programming and software
   activities that depend on heuristic methods to produce software with
   expected errors that require substantial continuing corrections in distributed
   products. Cleanroom discipline expects to get software correct to begin with
   to a very high degree, and to remove practically all errors, if any, before
   release to users. Action teams are critical to understand user problems and to
   properly address them with software products.

5. Customer Emphasis. The entire focus of Cleanroom Engineering is to identify
   user problems properly in specifications, then to address them in development and certification. The software must meet customer needs in both
   function and performance. It must also be prepared for new customer needs
   as they arise in the future with sufficient documentation and well structured
   design to permit graceful change.

6. Supplier certification and training. Suppliers to software specification,
   development, and certification require certification of their capabilities and
   training to meet the high standards of Cleanroom Engineering. Specifications
   may be decomposed into separate efforts that are brought together, but need
   to be consistent in form and quality. Software development may be allocated
   to suppliers, but needs to be carried out in practically perfect form without
   debugging before delivery. Software certification may also be allocated to
   suppliers, but needs to be done with high confidence in the statistical work.

7. Recognition. Cleanroom Engineering responsibilities are sufficiently sharp
   that recognition of human performance is direct and focused. Rather than
   current difficulties in measuring human performance and responsibilities in
   software triumphs and disasters, Cleanroom activities divide and conquer software complexities. Software triumphs are common and expected in Cleanroom,
   and software disasters practically disappear. Cleanroom personnel require
   much higher education and training, where recognition of their potential
   appears first. Then, the entire performance in software engineering becomes
   visibly much higher than was believed possible.

18.3 BACKGROUND

In the heat of business and industrial operations it is hard to remember how very
young and immature software is, only a generation old. When accounting was only

a generation old it certainly did not have double entry bookkeeping. When civil engineering was a generation old it did not have the right triangle. While there has been an industrial explosion in the use of computers in all fields, scientific, engineering, manufacturing, marketing and commercial, ideas take time to develop and become known across the work force.

Tom Gilb has introduced an alternative concept of software process improvement through statistical quality control.[3] He described Fagan's Inspection Method which uses statistical data collection. While Gilb credits inspection for the near zero defect software on U.S. space shuttle missions, and inspection did indeed help, there were other critical factors which are discussed below. All programmers on the space shuttle missions satisfied a base curriculum of six pass/fail courses of the IBM Software Engineering Institute, beginning with basic sets and logic, understanding programs as rules for mathematical functions, and including functional verification of programs and modules[6] rather than axiomatic verification.

In this first generation of software development and maintenance, the primary methods of software specification and design have been heuristic and graphical, going from informal natural language to formal programming language by trial and error. Since humans are fallible, errors are entirely expected as programs are built. Unit testing is used without question and is regarded as a private activity for getting errors out of the small parts of programs before assembling and integrating them into larger parts. Then more errors are discovered in the larger parts as smaller parts are tied together. Finally, entire systems are frequently (almost always) delivered with more errors yet to be found. Users frequently find many more errors than the developers believed were there. As a result, many companies have learned to expose new software products to a select few customers for initial shakedown before distributing the products widely.

This first generation of methods and experiences seems to make sense, and advanced companies do better than others in using the best methods and management that can be found. And yet, even the advanced companies stub their software toes now and then. In fact, more systems and products than most casual observers might imagine are seriously delayed or even abandoned with the whole program written but with too many errors to be released. Hundreds of person years may be involved, but the software still cannot be made to work. Sometime ago, an airline reservation system could not be made to work and was not put into operation. The airline reservation systems that did not work made major differences in the business operations. For example, American Airlines currently makes more profits from its airlines reservation system than from its airline operations.

The first complete PL/1 compiler of a major computer company, which involved more than a hundred person years for its development, never saw the light of day. Although the private unit debugging was done, the entire compiler never could be made to work. In more recent times, several major personal computer upgraded products for word processing and financial analysis have been released more than a year after they were scheduled for release, at real cost to their producing companies.

One strange thing about most such software disasters is that the projects were not looked upon as dangerous undertakings at the start. Of course, any software effort is a bit risky because computer code is so detailed and programmers are a little unpredictable. But "nobody said it would be so hard at the outset." New and better heuristics, especially ones supported by CASE tools, are becoming available in object oriented methods. With object oriented methods, better approaches to high level designs and specifications seem possible. But the software rubber meets the road with the program code, and unit debugging is seldom questioned. Then larger parts and entire products are tested, often with good details kept on the coverage testing to ensure that every branch is exercised both ways, and all code is tested at least once. Yet in spite of the testing coverage, users often find unexpected levels of errors in operations, making the product marginal or unacceptable.

A History Lesson in Typewriting

These experiences are not surprising in this first human generation of software development. They just seem to be one of the problems facing people in the field. Or are they? A hundred years ago people faced another set of problems when using the new typewriter, which was invented late in the nineteenth century. How was one to type text and tabular material without errors at reasonable rates of speed? Typewriters were special machines for special purposes. Executives hand wrote their own letters by and large, as did assistants or secretaries. Typewriters were used to write reports and documents with relatively poor quality reprints compared to printing. They certainly did not replace assembling print for printing machines. Typewriting was error prone. One had to look at the keys, of course, while typing, so a reasonable way to accomplish the task was to memorize the text a sentence at a time. But in going back and forth between the text and the typewriter, small mistakes or lapses were very possible from time to time. Correcting a character, even a word, might not be so bad. Correcting a missed sentence at the beginning of a typed page was more easily fixed by starting the page over.

With this background for almost a generation of using typewriters, the new idea of touch typing, typing without looking at the keys, was a very strange one. "That's silly. Who could possibly do that?" In teaching typewriting, people who look at the keys can get useful work done in the very first day. In fact they learn practically all there is to know about a typewriter in the very first day, and just need to get more practice and skill by typewriting. In teaching touch typing, people get no useful work done in the first day or the first week. "Why would anyone spend time in such a useless activity?" Of course, we know that touch typing was to become an internationally useful method and one that put typewriters into business offices on a mass basis. Typewriter makers improved their products in many ways, but the reason typewriters were made in such quantities was because people learned how to use them well rather than because companies knew how to make them well.

There is a lesson in touch typing for software development. In software, teaching a programming language and how to compile and execute programs allows people to write programs immediately. Very likely, such programs will require considerable debugging, and many text books say just that. And with more and more experience in programming alone or in teams, errors and unit debugging are just an expected and integral part of programming. But people with the right education and training need not unit debug their software any more than people need to look at the keys when they type. Yet, just as in teaching touch typing, much less trial and error programming is done at the beginning in education, and many more formal methods in program design and verification are learned. When serious programming begins, only after formal methods are applied, very little debugging will be required, because of more explicit design and verification from specifications. But "why not let the computers find the errors, why make so much of a simple program?" For simple programs that may be a perfectly good question. But as programs get larger and more complex, computers do not find the errors, and much more time will be spent debugging than will be spent writing the code originally.

Zero Defect Software is Really Possible

In spite of the experiences of this first human generation in software development, zero defect software is really possible.[19] However, there is no fool proof logical way to know that software has zero defects. The proof is in the using of the software, without finding any failures. Mathematics is very helpful in creating software that executes with zero defects. But it is insufficient to guarantee it, in part because of human fallibility in using mathematics, in part because of mathematics own logical incompleteness. Statistics is also very helpful in creating software that executes with zero defects, but it too is insufficient. As noted, the proof is in the using.

Three illustrations of zero defect software follow.

First, the U.S. 1980 Census was carried out by a nationwide network system of 20 miniprocessors, controlled by a 25 KLOC program, which operated for its entire ten months in production with no failures observed. It was developed by Paul Friday, of the U.S. Census Bureau, using functional verification in Pascal. Mr. Friday was given the highest technical award of the U.S. Department of Commerce for the achievement.

Second, the IBM wheelwriter typewriter products released in 1984 are controlled by three microprocessors with a 65 KLOC program. It has had millions of users with no failures ever detected. The IBM team which created this software also used functional verification and extensive usage testing in a well managed environment to achieve this result.

Third, the U.S. space shuttle software of some 500 KLOC, while not completely zero defect, has been zero defect in flight. The IBM team which created this software also used functional verification, and extensive usage testing to achieve that result. The space shuttle software is such a large, complex, and visible product that there are real lessons to be learned from it. All programmers were required to complete a basic curriculum of six pass/fail courses in understanding programs as rules for mathematical functions, and functional verification of programs and modules.

18.4 BACKGROUND OF CLEANROOM SOFTWARE ENGINEERING

As noted in Section 18.1, the Cleanroom Engineering process develops software of certified correctness under statistical quality control in a pipeline of increments, with functional verification but no program debugging before independent statistical usage testing of the increments. It provides rigorous methods for three subteams in software specifications, development, and certification that are capable of producing low or zero defect software of arbitrary size and complexity. The Cleanroom Engineering process provides such discipline in simultaneously creating a correct product and increasing the productivity of the process.

The term Cleanroom is taken from the hardware industry to mean an emphasis on preventing errors to begin with, rather than removing them later (of course any errors introduced should be removed). Cleanroom Engineering involves rigorous methods that enable greater control over both product and process. The Cleanroom process not only produces software of certified correctness and high performance, but does so while yielding high productivity and schedule integrity. The intellectual control provided by the rigorous Cleanroom process allows both technical and management control.

Cleanroom Engineering achieves statistical quality control over software development by strictly separating the design process from the testing process in a pipeline of incremental software development. There are three major engineering activities in the process:[5, 11]

1. A specification team creates an incremental specification that defines a pipeline of software increments that accumulate into the final software product,[8] which specification includes the statistics of its use as well as its function and performance requirements.
2. A development team designs and codes increments specified using box structured design[9, 16] and functional verification of each increment, with delivery to certification with no debugging beforehand, and provides subsequent correction for any failures that may be uncovered during certification.
3. A certification team uses statistical testing and analysis for the certification of the software correctness to the usage specification, notification to developers of any failures discovered during certification, and subsequent recertification as failures are corrected.

As noted, there is an explicit feedback process between certification and development on any failures found in statistical usage testing. This feedback process provides an objective measure of the correctness of the software as it matures in the development pipeline. It does, indeed, provide a statistical quality control process for software development that has not been available in this first generation of trial and error programming.

Dealing with Human Fallibility

Humans are fallible, even when using sound mathematical processes in functional verification, so software failures are possible during the certification process. But there is a surprising power and synergism between functional verification and statistical usage testing.[11] First, as already noted, functional verification can be scaled up for high productivity and still leave no more errors than heuristic programming often leaves after unit and system testing combined. And second, it turns out that the mathematical errors left are much easier to find and fix during testing than are errors left behind in debugging, measured at a factor of five in practice.[11] Mathematical errors usually turn out to be simple blunders in the software, whereas errors left behind or introduced in debugging are usually deeper in logic or wider in system scope than those which have already been fixed. As a result, statistical usage testing not only provides a formal, objective basis for the certification of correctness under use, but it also uncovers the errors of mathematical fallibility with remarkable efficiency.

In Cleanroom Engineering a major discovery has been the ability of well educated and motivated people to create nearly defect free software before any execution or debugging, less than five defects per thousand lines of code. Such code is ready for usage testing and certification with no unit debugging by the designers. In this first human generation of software development it has been counter intuitive to expect software with so few defects at the outset. Typical heuristic programming creates fifty defects per thousand lines of code, then reduces that number to five or less by debugging.

The mathematical foundations for Cleanroom Engineering come from the deterministic nature of computers themselves. A computer program is no more and no less than a rule for a mathematical function.[6, 7] Such a function need not be numerical, or course, and most programs do not define numerical functions. But for every legal input, a program directs the computer to produce a unique output, whether correct as specified or not. And the set of all such input-output pairs is a mathematical function. A more usual way to view a program in this first generation is as a set of instructions for specific executions with specific input data. While correct, this view misses a point of reusing well known and tested mathematical ideas, regarding computer programming as a new and private art rather than as more mature and public engineering.

With these mathematical foundations, software development becomes a process of constructing rules for functions that meet required specifications, and thus the development need not be a trial and error programming process. The functional semantics of a structured programming language can be expressed in an algebra of functions with function operations corresponding to program sequence, alternation, and iteration.[6] The systematic top down development of programs is mirrored by describing function rules in terms of algebraic operations among simpler functions, and their rules in terms of still simpler functions until the rules of the programming language are reached. It is a new mental base for most programmers to consider the complete functions needed, top down, rather than computer executions for specific data.

Cleanroom Experiences

The IBM COBOL Structuring Facility (SF), a complex product of some 80,000 lines of source code, was developed in the Cleanroom discipline, with no debugging before usage testing and certification of its correctness. It converts an unstructured COBOL program into a structured one of identical function. It uses considerable artificial intelligence to transform a flat structured program into one with a deeper hierarchy that is much easier to understand and modify. The product line was prototyped with Cleanroom discipline at the outset, then individual products were generated in Cleanroom extensions. In this development, several challenging schedules were defined for competitive reasons, but every schedule was met.

The COBOL/SF products have high function per line of code. The prototype was estimated at 100 KLOC by an experienced language processing group, but the Cleanroom developed prototype was 20 KLOC. The software was designed not only in structured programming, but also in structured data access. No arrays or pointers were used in the design; instead, sets, queues, and stacks were used as primitive data structures.[12] Such data structured programs are more reliably verified and inspected, and also more readily optimized with respect to size or performance, as required.

COBOL/SF, Version 2, consisted of 80 KLOC, 28 KLOC reused from previous products, 52 KLOC new or changed, designed and tested in a pipeline of five increments,[5] the largest over 19 KLOC. A total of 179 corrections were required during certification, under 3.5 corrections per KLOC for code with no previous execution. The productivity of the development was 740 LOC per person month, including all specification, design, development, and management, in meeting a very short deadline.

The HH60 flight control program was developed on schedule. Programmers' morale went from quite low at the outset ("why us?") to very high on discovering their unexpected capability in accurate software design without debugging. The twelve programmers involved had all passed the pass/fail coursework in mathematical (functional) verification of the IBM Software Engineering Institute, but were provided a week's review as a team for the project. The testers had much more to learn about certification by objective statistics.[2]

The subsystem Coarse/Fine Attitude Determination System (CFADS) of the NASA Attitude Ground Support System (AGSS) of some 30 KLOC has been developed Cleanroom. Developed in Fortran, 62% of the subroutines, which averaged 258 source lines each, compiled correctly on first attempt, all but one of the rest compiled correctly on the second attempt. Compared with well measured related systems, the failure rate was down by a factor of 5 while the productivity was up by 70%.[4]

V. R. Basili and F. T. Baker, assisted by R. W. Selby, introduced Cleanroom ideas in an undergraduate software engineering course at the University of Maryland. As a result, a controlled experiment in a small software project was carried out over two academic years, using fifteen teams with both traditional and Cleanroom methods. The result, even on first exposure to Cleanroom, was positive in the production of reliable software, compared with traditional results.[20]

Cleanroom projects have been carried out at the University of Tennessee, under the leadership of J. H. Poore,[15] and at the University of Florida under H. D. Mills. At Florida, seven teams of undergraduates produced uniformly successful systems for a common structured specification of three increments. It is a surprise for undergraduates to consider software development as a serious engineering activity using mathematical verification instead of debugging, because software development is typically introduced primarily as a trial and error activity with no real technical standards.

18.5 BOX STRUCTURED SOFTWARE SYSTEM DESIGN

Box structured design is based on a Parnas usage hierarchy of modules.[16,17] Such modules, also known as data abstractions or objects, are described by a set of operations that may define and access internally stored data. In Ada, such modules are defined as packages, with operations defined by the calls of the procedures and functions of the packages, and internal data declared in the package.

Stacks, queues, and sequential or random access files provide simple examples of such modules or packages. Part of their discipline is that internally stored data cannot be accessed or altered in any way except through the explicit operations of the package. It is critical in box structured design to recognize that packages exist at every level from complete systems to individual program variables. It is also critical to recognize that a verifiable design must deal with a usage hierarchy rather than a parts hierarchy in its structure. A program that stores no data between invocations can be described in terms of a parts hierarchy of its smaller and smaller parts, because any use depends only on data supplied it on its call with no dependence on previous calls. But a specific realization of a package, say a queue, will depend not only on the present call and data supplied it, but also on previous calls and data supplied then.

The parts hierarchy of a structured program identifies every sequence, alternation, and iteration (say every begin-end, if-then-else, while-loop) at every level. It turns out that the usage hierarchy of a system of packages (say an object oriented design with all objects identified) also identifies every call (use) of every operation of every package. The semantics of the structured program is defined by a mathematical function for each sequence, alternation, and iteration in the parts hierarchy. That does not quite work for the operations of packages because of usage history dependencies. But there is a simple extension for packages that does work. It is to model the behavior of a package as a state machine, with its calls of its several operations as inputs to the common state machine. Then the semantics of such a package is defined by the transition function of its state machine (with an initial state). When the operations are defined by structured programs, the semantics of packages becomes a simple extension of the semantics of structured programs.

The Basis for Box Structured Design

While theoretically straightforward, the practical design of systems of Parnas modules[17, 18] (object oriented systems) in usage hierarchies can seem quite complex on first exposure. It seems much simpler to outline such designs in parts hierarchies and structures, for example in data flow diagrams, without distinguishing between separate usages of the same module. While that may seem simpler at the moment, such design outlines are incomplete and often lead to faulty completions at the detailed programming levels. In spite of their common use in this first generation of system design, data flow diagrams should only be used with rigorous design methods rather than by leaving critical requirements to details with incomplete specifications.

In order to create and control such designs based on usage hierarchies in more practical ways, their box structures provide standard, finer grained subdescriptions for any package of three forms, namely as black boxes, as state boxes, and as clear boxes, defined as follows.[10, 13, 14]

- Black box. External view of a Parnas package, describing its behavior as a mathematical function from historical sequences of stimuli to its next response.
- State box. Intermediate view of a Parnas package, describing its behavior by use of an internal state and internal black box with a mathematical function from historical sequences of stimuli and states to its next response and state, and an initial internal state.
- Clear box. Internal view of a Parnas package, describing the internal black box of its state box in a usage control structure of other Parnas packages; such a control structure may define sequential or concurrent use of the other packages.

Box structures enforce completeness and precision in design of software systems as usage hierarchies of Parnas packages. Such completeness and precision leads to pleasant surprises in human capabilities in software engineering and development. The surprises are in the ability to move from system specifications to design in programs without the need for unit/package testing and debugging before delivery to system usage testing. In this first generation of software development, it has been widely assumed that trial and error programming, unit testing and debugging were necessary. But well educated, well motivated software professionals are, indeed, capable of developing software systems of arbitrary size and complexity without program debugging before system usage testing.[5]

18.6 STEPWISE REFINEMENT AND FUNCTIONAL VERIFICATION OF SOFTWARE

Once the design is complete, the clear box at each level is expanded to code to fully implement the defined rule for the black box function at that level by stepwise refinement, as described by Wirth.[21] Following each expansion, functional verification is used to help structure a proof that the expansion correctly implements the specification. The nature of the proof revolves around the fact that a program is a rule for a function and the specification for the program is a relation or function. What must be shown in the proof is that the rule (the program) correctly implements the relation or function (the specification) for the full range of the specification and no more. Linger, Mills and Witt[5] have developed a correctness theorem which defines what must be shown to prove that a program is equivalent to its specification for each of the structured programming language constructs. The proof strategy is subdivided into small parts which easily accumulate into a proof for a large program. Experience indicates that people are able to master these ideas and construct proof arguments for very large software systems.

The development team expands each clear box in the usage hierarchy into the selected target code using stepwise refinement and functional verification. As the development team designs and implements the software, it is held collectively responsible for the quality of the software.

In describing the activities of software development, no mention is made of testing or even of compilation. The Cleanroom development team does not test or even compile. They use mathematical proof (functional verification) to demonstrate the correctness of programming units. Testing and measuring failures by program execution is the responsibility of the certification team.

The Basis for Functional Verification

Any program or program part is a rule for a mathematical function. It may not be the function desired, but it is a function. In structured programs, the rules are direct in form, building program rules out of just two function building operations, first, function composition which corresponds to sequential execution of program parts, and second, disjoint function union which corresponds to alternative execution of one program part or another, say in IF or CASE statements. Program iteration uses no more than these two operations together, and function recursion provides a useful view of an iteration process.

As noted, any program part or total program defines a single, possibly complex function. The function is seldom a numerical function in classical terms. Even numerical programs must deal with finite sets of numbers in which overflow and roundoffs depart from classical number systems. Given the text or name of a program or program part in whatever language, say a program in Ada

```
Alpha = with text_io;
            procedure Beta
            is
            . . .
            begin
            . . .
            end Beta;
```

the program function will be denoted by brackets [   ] around the name or text, as

```
[Alpha] = [with text_io;
               procedure Beta
               is
               . . .
               begin
               . . .
               end Beta;]
```

In this case [Alpha] is a set of ordered pairs

[Alpha] = {<X, Y>| Given initial state X, Alpha will produce final state Y}

The functional [Alpha] is determined by Ada text, but is independent of the language Ada. The same function can be defined in Fortran text, COBOL text, etc.

18.7 SOFTWARE ENGINEERING UNDER STATISTICAL QUALITY CONTROL

The statistical foundations for Cleanroom Engineering come from adding usage statistics to software specifications, along with function and performance requirements.[2, 11] Such usage statistics provide a basis for measuring the correctness of the software during its development, and thereby measuring the quality of the design in meeting functional and performance requirements. A more usual way to view development in this first generation is as a difficult to predict art form. Software with no known errors at delivery frequently experiences many failures in actual usage.

Statistical Certification

Cleanroom statistical certification of software involves the specification of usage statistics in addition to function and performance specifications. Such usage statistics provide a basis for assessing the correctness of the software being tested under expected use. An efficient estimation process has been developed for projecting mean time to failures (MTTF) of software under test while also under correction for previously discovered failures.[2]

As each specified increment is completed by the developers, it is delivered to the certifiers, who combine it with preceding increments, for testing based on usage statistics. As noted, the Cleanroom architecture must define a sequence of nested increments which are to be executed exclusively by user commands as they accumulate into the entire system required. Each subsequence represents a subsystem complete in itself, even though not all the user function may be provided in it. For each subsystem, a certified correctness is defined from the usage testing and failures discovered, if any.

It is characteristic that each increment goes through a maturation during the testing, becoming more reliable from corrections required for failures found, serving thereby as a stable base as later increments are delivered and added to the developing system. For example, the HH60 flight control program had three increments[2] of over 10 KLOC each. Increment 1 required 27 corrections for failures discovered in its first appearance in increment 1 testing, but then only 1 correction during increment 1/2 testing, and 2 corrections during increment 1/2/3 testing. Increment 2 required 20 corrections during its first appearance in increment 1/2 testing, and only 5 corrections during increment 1/2/3 testing. Increment 3 required 21 corrections on its first appearance in increment 1/2/3 testing. In this case 76 corrections were required in a system of over 30 KLOC, under 2.5 corrections per KLOC for verified and inspected code, with no previous execution or debugging.

In the certification process, it is not only important to observe failures in execution, but it is also important to observe the times between such failures in execution of usage representative statistically generated inputs. Such test data must be developed to represent the sequential usage of the software by users, which, of course, will account for previous outputs seen by the users and what needs the users will have in various circumstances. The state of mind of a user and the current need can be represented by a stochastic process determined by a state machine whose present state is defined by previous inputs/outputs and a statistical model that provides the next input based on that present state.[11]

Certification Tasks

In parallel with the Cleanroom development team, the Cleanroom certification team prepares to certify the software up to and including the increment being developed by the development team. The certification team uses the usage profile and the portion of the specification that is applicable to the increments to be verified to prepare test cases including proper outputs to tests.

When the development team has completed an increment, the certification team creates one or more successive versions of the accumulated system up through this increment. For each version the certification team compiles the increment, combines it with previous increments, and certifies the accumulated system through this version. If failures are encountered in the certification of a version, they are returned to the development team for analysis and engineering changes to whatever increments are causing the failures. While failures are likely to be caused by the latest increment added, previous increments may be at fault and changed as well, as noted in HH60 experience. Each redelivery of changed increments defines a new version. If no failures are encountered in the certification of a version, no additional versions are required.

Certifying Software

Software is either correct or incorrect in design to a well defined specification, in contrast to hardware which is reliable to a certain level in performing to a design assumed to be correct. For small and regular software, it may be possible to exhaustively test the software to determine its correctness. Even then, failures can be overlooked from human fallibility. But software of any size or complexity can only be tested partially, and typically a very small fraction of possible inputs is actually tested. At first glance, the fractions are so small for systems of ordinary size that the task of testing looks impossible. But when combined with mathematical verification, getting correct software is indeed possible.

Certifying the correctness of such software requires two conditions, namely (1) statistical testing with inputs characteristic of actual usage, and (2) no failures in the testing. For interactive software, the statistical correlation of successive inputs must be treated, as well. If any failures arise in testing or subsequent usage, the software is incorrect, and the certification is invalid. If such failures are corrected, the certification process can be restarted, with no use of previous testing results. Such corrections may lead to additional failures, or may not. So certifying the correctness of software is an empirical process which is bound to succeed if the software is indeed correct and may succeed for some time if the software is incorrect.

While possibly frustrating at first glance, this is all that can be asserted about the correctness of software. In both verification and testing, human fallibility is present. But on second glance, the sequential history of certification efforts provides a basis for assessing the quality of the software and expectations for achieving future correctness.

Certification Process

Certification of software on a scientific basis requires a statistical usage specification as well as functional and performance specifications. The testing must be carried out by statistical selection of tests from these specifications. Tests selected directly are ad hoc, and give no basis for statistical inference on the correctness of the software. Some uses of the software may be much more important than other uses, and the statistical selections can be given in various levels of stratified sampling. Thus, not only basic statistical usage is to be defined, but also the relative importance of correctness for each usage is to be defined. This is new information which is often not known until the software is put to actual use, but it should be generated with functional and performance specifications beforehand.

Next, the actual statistical testing must be carried out when the software is available, possibly in stratified form. One extreme form of stratified form is an important case chosen with probability 1 in that stratus. Next, if a failure is found in testing, the software should be returned to the developers for correction before further testing. When the correction is made, a new start of testing is begun. The Time to Failure (TTF) is recorded for each failure discovered. The Time without Failure (TWF) is tracked when no failures have appeared. This TWF can be tracked after the software is distributed to users as part of the characterization of its correctness. If failures appear with users, the same rules of correction and restart of TWF should occur.

As already noted, there is a profound difference between the correctness of software and the reliability of hardware. When software has hundreds or thousands of errors, its behavior may seem to approximate hardware reliability. But when software has under five errors, or possibly none, the statistics of hardware failures are not valid. In this first generation, it has seemed impossible to create zero defect software, but it can be, and has been done, as discussed below. Part of the issue is discovering a new human possibility, with more engineering education and engineering management. Part of the issue is the economic feasibility. It requires less human effort to produce zero defect software with new methods than to produce error prone software with older methods. The human effort required is both engineering verification and statistical testing, and they complement each other in unexpected ways.

Usage Specifications

A user's specification for a substantial software system will identify various classes of user commands and data for various parts of the system. For example, bringing up an interactive system at the beginning of the day will require and accept certain kinds of user commands and data that the ordinary interactive users may not even be aware of. But bringing the system up is an integral part of the system for a certain class of users. During the day, several distinct classes of users may be interacting simultaneously and independently, such as users adding data to the system, or users making enquiries, or users monitoring the system use and performance. Within each such class, several or many users may be interacting simultaneously and independently, as well.

However, as simultaneously and concurrently as these various users seem to interact with the system, the individual computers in the system each operate strictly sequentially in real time, shifting from one user to another so rapidly that each user gets almost immediate response, even though ten, or a thousand, other users may have been serviced between the user's stimulus and the system's response. As a rule, users are separated from one another because they are operating in different, relatively protected, data spaces that represent the tasks they are doing. But users can interact, intentionally or not, as their tasks become more intertwined.

For example, in an airline reservation system, a ticket agent may inquire about availability of seats on a given flight and get the response that seats are available. Then when the seats are requested a moment later, the response is that no seats are available. Other users have interacted in picking up the seats in the previous moment. Such system behavior is designed. It would be conceivable to design an airline reservation system such that seats could be held from inquiry to request, but it would require entirely different levels of data storage and processing. In this way, it is clear that user independence is relative, with economic and technical issues involved with multiple users in systems.

This understanding that significant software systems have different kinds of uses applies whether there are single or multiple users. A single user may be using a system in different ways at different times, even within a single session. The design of the software will typically reflect such different uses by packaging similar operations in common modules. For example, various kinds of data searching may be handled in a search module, but data retrievals may be handled in a different retrieval module. It also makes similar sense to identify similar stimuli response operations in specifications, entirely from the user point of view and state of mind. In particular, complex specifications need to be designed as carefully as programs to reflect the natural structure of the problem being solved and to find effective specification structures that reflect user activities and understandings.

Software Usage as a Markov Process

As noted, software specifications deal with functional behavior and performance. Functional behavior is ordinarily decomposed into various subfunctions in ways understandable by users, and is often obtained from users as requirements. Performance will usually affect design in fundamental ways. But expected usage of the software will have critical impacts on performance issues. For example, a data base system with very much more querying than data addition or deletion, may call for a design with high performance queries at the expense of data addition and deletion performance. And such a design can be entirely unsatisfactory with different usage. Thus expected usage statistics can play a key role in software system design.

However there is another critical use for usage statistics as part of software specifications. It is to permit the certification of software. Software behavior depends not only on how correct the software is, but also on how it is used. For every possible state of internally stored data, any command and input data is handled either correctly or incorrectly, and is denoted as a failure in the latter case at some level of seriousness.

Now, with a statistical usage specification for each possible internal state, the probability of each selection of commands and input data in such a state will be known. Next, the functional specification will define what the new internal state will become, as well as the response to the user. These two facts define a Markov process, namely the set of all internal data states and the probability of getting from each member of the set to the next member. Of course, some members may be terminal when the process terminates.

18.8 THE POWER OF USAGE
TESTING OVER COVERAGE TESTING

The insights and data of Adams[1] in the analysis of software testing, and the differences between software errors and failures, give an entirely new outlook to software testing. Since Adams has discovered an amazingly wide spectrum in failure rates for software errors, it is no longer sensible to treat errors as homogeneous objects to find and fix. Finding and fixing errors with high failure rates produces much more reliable software than finding and fixing just any errors, which may have average or low failure rates.

The major surprise in Adams' data is the relative power of finding and fixing errors in usage testing over coverage testing, a factor of 30 in increasing MTTF. That factor of 30 seems incredible until the facts are worked out from Adams' data. But it explains many anecdotes about experiences in testing. In one such experience, an operating systems development group used coverage testing systematically in a major revision and for weeks found mean time to abends (abnormal endings) in seconds. It reluctantly allowed user tapes in one weekend, but on fixing those errors, found the mean time to abends jumped literally from seconds to minutes.

The Adams data is given in Table 18-1.[1] It describes distributions of failure rates for errors in nine major IBM products, including the major operating systems, language compilers, and data base systems. The uniformity of the failure rate distributions among these very different products is truly amazing. But even more amazing is a spread in failure rates of over 4 orders of magnitude, from 19 months to 5000 years (60 K months) calendar time in MTTF, with about a third of the errors having an MTTF of 5000 years, and 1% having an MTTF of 19 months. With such a range in failure rates, it is easy to see that coverage testing will find the very low failure rate errors a third of the time with practically no effect on the MTTF by the fix, whereas usage testing will find many more of the high failure rate errors with much greater effect. Table 18-2 develops the data from Table 18-1, showing the relative effectiveness of fixes in usage testing and coverage testing, in terms of increased MTTF. Table 18-2 develops the change in failure rates for each MTTF

TABLE 18-1   Distributions of Errors (in %) Among Mean Time to Failure (MTTF) Classes

Product	MTTF in K Months							
	60	19	6	1.9	.6	.19	.06	.019
1	34.2	28.8	17.8	10.3	5.0	2.1	1.2	.7
2	34.2	28.0	18.2	9.7	4.5	3.2	1.5	.7
3	33.7	28.5	18.0	8.7	6.5	2.8	1.4	.4
4	34.2	28.5	18.7	11.9	4.4	2.0	.3	.1
5	34.2	28.5	18.4	9.4	4.4	2.9	1.4	.7
6	32.0	28.2	20.1	11.5	5.0	2.1	.8	.3
7	34.0	28.5	18.5	9.9	4.5	2.7	1.4	.6
8	31.9	27.1	18.4	11.1	6.5	2.7	1.4	1.1
9	31.2	27.6	20.4	12.8	5.6	1.9	.5	.0

TABLE 18-2   Error Densities and Failure Densities in the MTTF Classes of Table 18-1.

Property								
M	60	19	6	1.9	.6	.19	.06	.019
ED	33.2	28.2	18.7	10.6	5.2	2.5	1.1	.5
ED/M	.6	1.5	3.1	5.6	8.7	13.2	18.3	26.3
FD	.8	2.0	3.9	7.3	11.1	17.1	23.6	34.2
FD/M	0	0	1	4	18	90	393	1800

class of Table 18-1, because it is the failure rates of the MTTF classes that add up to the failure rate of the product.

First, in Table 18-2, line 1, denoted M (MTTF), is repeated directly from Table 18-1, namely the mean time between failures of the MTTF class. Next, line 2, denoted ED (Error Density), is the average of the error densities of the 9 products of Table 18-1, column by column, which represents a typical software product. Line 3, denoted ED/M, is the contribution of each class, on the average, in reducing the failure rate by fixing the next error found by coverage testing (1/M is the failure rate of the class, ED the probability a member of this class will be found next in coverage testing, so their product, ED/M, is the expected reduction in the total failure rate from that class). Now ED/M is also proportional to the usage failure rate in each class, since failures of that rate will be distributed by just that amount. Therefore, this line 3 is normalized to add to 100% in line 4, denoted by FD (Failure Density). It is interesting to note that Error Density (ED) and Failure Density (FD) are almost reverse distributions, Error Density about a third at the high end of MTTFs and Failure Density about a third at the low end of MTTFs. Finally, line 5, denoted FD/M, is the contribution of each class, on the average, in reducing the failure rate by fixing the next error found by usage testing. The sums of the two lines ED/M and FD/M turn out to be proportional to the decrease in failure rate from the respective fixes of errors found by coverage testing and usage testing, respectively. Their sums are 77.3 and 2306, with a ratio of about 30 between them. That is the basis for the statement of their relative worth in increasing MTTF. It seems incredible at first glance, but that is the number!

18.9 SUMMARY

Cleanroom Engineering develops software of certified correctness under statistical quality control in a pipeline of increments that accumulate into the specified software. In the Cleanroom process no program debugging is permitted before independent statistical usage testing of the increments as they accumulate into the final product. The Cleanroom process provides rigorous methods of software specification, development, and certification, through which disciplined software engineering teams are capable of producing low or zero defect software of arbitrary size and complexity. Such engineering discipline is not only capable of producing correct software, but also the certification of the correctness of the software as specified.

Of course, human beings are fallible, even when using sound mathematical processes for functional verification, so software failures are possible during certification in the Cleanroom process. But there is a surprising power and synergism between functional verification and statistical usage testing. First, as already noted, functional verification can be scaled up for high productivity and still leave no more errors than heuristic programming often leaves after unit and system testing combined. And second, it turns out that the mathematical errors left are much easier to find and fix during certification testing than are the errors left behind in debugging, measured at a factor of five in practice.

ACKNOWLEDGEMENTS

The author is indebted to many people, many of whom appear in the references below, who have been important in the discovery and development of the idea of Cleanroom Software Engineering. For this paper, the author notes special thanks to R. H. Cobb, R. C. Linger, J. McManus, J. H. Poore, and G. G. Schulmeyer for comments and suggestions.

References

1. Adams, E. N. "Optimizing Preventive Service of Software Products," *IBM Journal of Research and Development,* Jan. 1984.
2. Currit, P. A., Dyer, M., and Mills, H. D. "Certifying the Reliability of Software," *IEEE Trans on Software Engineering,* Vol. SE-12, No. 1, pp. 3-11, Jan. 1986.
3. Gilb, T. *Principles of Software Engineering Management,* Reading, MA: Addison Wesley, 1989.
4. Kouchakarian, A. and Basili, V. R. "The Cleanroom Case Study in the Software Engineering Laboratory: An Experiment in Formal Methods," SEL, University of Maryland, 1989.
5. Linger, R. C. and Mills, H. D. "A Case Study in Cleanroom Software Engineering: The IBM COBOL Structuring Facility," *Proceedings of COMPSAC'88,* IEEE 1988.
6. Linger, R. C., Mills, H. D., and Witt, B. I. *Structured Programming: Theory and Practice,* Reading, MA: Addison Wesley 1979.
7. Mills, H. D. "The New Math of Computer Programming," *Comm of the ACM,* 18(1), 1975.
8. Mills, H. D. *Software Productivity,* Boston: Little, Brown and Company, 1983.
9. Mills, H. D. "Structured Programming: Retrospect and Prospect," *IEEE Software,* Nov. 1986, pp. 58-66.
10. Mills, H. D. "Stepwise Refinement and Verification in Box-structured Systems," *IEEE Computer,* Jun. 1988, pp. 23-36.
11. Mills, H. D., Dyer, M., and Linger, R. C. "Cleanroom Software Engineering," *IEEE Software,* Sep. 1987, pp. 19-24.
12. Mills, H. D. and Linger, R. C. "Data Structured Programming: Program Design without Arrays and Pointers," *IEEE Trans on Software Engineering,* Vol. SE-12, No. 2, Feb. 1986, pp. 192-197.
13. Mills, H. D., Linger, R. C., and Hevner, A. R. *Principles of Information Systems Analysis and Design,* New York: Academic Press, 1986.

14. Mills, H. D., Linger, R. C., and Hevner, A. R. "Box Structured Information Systems," *IBM Systems Journal,* 26(4):395-413, 1987.
15. Mills, H. D. and Poore, J. H. "Bringing Software under Statistical Quality Control," *Quality Progress,* Nov. 1988, pp. 52-55.
16. Parnas, D. L. "A Technique for Software Module Specification with Examples," *CACM 15,* No. 5, May 1972, pp. 330-336.
17. Parnas, D. L. "Designing Software for Ease of Extension and Contraction," *IEEE Trans on Software Engineering,* Vol. SE-5, No. 3, Mar. 1979, pp. 128-138.
18. Parnas, D. L. and Wang, Y. "The Trace Assertion Method of Module-interface Specification," *Tech Rep.* pp. 89-261, Queen's University, TRIO, Oct. 1989.
19. Schulmeyer, G. G. *Zero Defect Software,* New York: McGraw-Hill, 1990.
20. Selby, R. W., Basili, V. R., and Baker, F. T. "Cleanroom Software Development: An Empirical Evaluation," *IEEE Trans on Software Engineering,* Vol. SE-13, No. 9, Sep. 1987.
21. Wirth, N. "Program Development by Stepwise Refinement," *CACM 14,* No. 4, Apr. 1971, pp. 221-227.

Appendix A

GLOSSARY OF ACRONYMS

4GL. Fourth generation language

7M. Seven management

ABEND. Abnormal ending

AF. Air Force

AGSS. Attitude ground support system

AHP. Analytic hierarchy process

AIAA. American Institute of Aeronautics and Astronautics

AI/NNWG. Artificial intelligence/neural networks working group

AQL. Acceptable quality level

ASCII. American Standard Code for Information Interchange

ASN. Average sample number

ASPIRE. A Software Process Improvement Realization Environment

ASW. Anti-submarine warfare

AT&T. American Telephone and Telegraph

ATF. Advanced tactical fighter

AVG. Average

C^2. Command and control

C^3I. Command, control, communications and intelligence

CASE. Computer aided software engineering

CAT. Corrective action team

c chart. Control chart—number of defects

CCPDS-R. Command center processing and display system—replacement

CD. Customer deployment
CDP. Certified data processor
CDR. Critical design review
CD/SD. Cost deployment/schedule deployment
CE. Concurrent engineering
CEO. Chief executive officer
CFADS. Coarse/fine attitude determination system
CM. Configuration management
CMM. Capability maturity model
CMU. Carnegie Mellon University
COBOL. Common Business Oriented Language
COCOMO. Constructive cost model
COMM. Communication
COQ. Cost of quality
COSMIC. Computer Software and Management Information Center
COTS. Commercial off the shelf
CPI. Continuous process improvement
CPU. Central processing unit
CQAP. Contractor quality assurance program
CQE. Certified quality engineer
CQFD. Comprehensive quality function deployment
CRWG. Computer resources working group
CSC. Computer software component
CSCI. Computer software configuration item
C/SCS. Cost/schedule control system
CSF. Critical success factors
CSU. Computer software unit
CWBS. Contract work breakdown structure
DAB. Defense acquisition board
DACS. Data and analysis center for software
DARPA. Defense advanced research projects agency
DB. Data base
DFD. Data flow diagram or data flow design
DID. Data item description
DLA. Defense Logistics Agency
DLAM. Defense Logistics Agency manual
DOD. Department of Defense
DODD. Department of Defense directive
DODI. Department of Defense instruction
DOE. Design of experiments
DPRO. Defense Plant Representative Office
DSMC. Defense Systems Management College
ECMA. European Computer Manufacturers Association
ED. Error density
EDUC. Education
EDWG. Education working group
ESC. Executive steering committee
ESG. Electronic systems group
EnvWG. Environment working group

FCA. Function configuration audit
FD. Function deployment or failure density
FQR. Formal qualification review
FQT. Formal qualification test
FQTR. Formal qualification test review
FSD. Full scale development or Federal Systems Division
GFE. Government furnished equipment
GFI. Government furnished information
GFP. Government furnished property
GQM. Goal, question, metric
GSS. Ground support system
H/L. High level
HOL. High order language
HP. Hoshin strategic planning
I_0. High level inspection
I_1. Low level inspection
I_2. Code inspection
I_3. Test inspection
ID. Identification or information deployment
IEEE. Institute of Electrical and Electronics Engineers, Inc.
I/O. Input/output
IOC. Initial operational capability
IQUE. In-plant quality evaluation
IRI. Interaction Research Institute, Inc.
IRS. Internal Revenue Service
IRS. Interface requirements specification
IS. Information systems
ISO. International organization for standards
ISTO. Information science and technology office
I&T. Integration and test
IV&V. Independent verification and validation
JIAWG. Joint integrated avionics working group
JLC. Joint Logistics Command
JUSE. Japanese Union of Scientists and Engineers
KLOC. Thousand lines of code
KSLOC. Thousand source lines of code
LCL. Lower control limit
LL. Lower level
LOC. Lines of code
LOS. Length of stay
MBNQA. Malcolm Baldrige National Quality Award
MCC. Microelectronics and Computer Technology Corporation
MIL. Military
MIS. Management information system
MITI. Ministry for International Trade and Industry
MP. Management and planning
MTTF. Mean time to failure
NASA. National Aeronautics and Space Administration
NCSL. Noncommented source line of code

NSIA. National Security Industries Association
OC. Operating characteristic
OHD. Objective-hierarchy diagram
OOA. Object oriented analysis
OOD. Object oriented design
OT&E. Operational test and evaluation
PAT. Process action team
PC. Personal computer
PCA. Philip Crosby Associates
p chart. Control chart-fraction defective = (units defective)/(number of units)
PDCA. Plan, do, check, act
PDL. Program design language
PDR. Preliminary design review
PDSS. Post deployment (delivery) support software
PGS. Productivity gain sharing
PM. Program/project manager, Person month
PMC. Process management cycle
POC. Price of conformance
PONC. Price of nonconformance
P^3I. Preplanned product improvements
PQIT. Process quality improvement team
PQT. Production qualification test
Q7. Quality seven
QA. Quality assurance
QAR. Quality assurance representative
QC. Quality circle or Quality control or Quality cost
QD. Quality deployment
QFD. Quality function deployment
QIT. Quality improvement team
QMB. Quality management board
QMC. Quality management council
QSR. Quality system review
R&D. Research and development
R&M. Reliability and maintainability
RAASP. Reusable Ada Avionics Support Package
RADC. Rome Air Development Center
RFP. Request for proposal
RISC. Reduced instruction set computer
ROA. Return on assets
ROI. Return on investment
RSO. Reusable software object
RTCA. Radio Technical Commission for Aeronautics
RWG. Reuse working group
SAIC. Science Applications International Corporation
SATRR. System acceptance test readiness review
SDCA. Standardize, do, check, act
SDD. Software design document
SDF. Software development file or facility
SDI. Strategic defense initiative

SDIP. Software development integrity program
SDP. Software development plan
SDR. Software or systems design review
SEE. Software engineering environment
SeCS. Self check system
SEI. Software Engineering Institute
SEPG. Software engineering process group
SEPO. Software engineering process organization
SF. Structuring facility
SLCSE. Software life cycle support environment
SLOC. Source lines of code
SMM. Software management manual
SMSC. Software management steering committee
SOW. Statement of work
SPA. Software process assessment
SPC. Statistical process control or Software Productivity Consortium
SPI. Software process improvement
SPMS. Software process management system
SPR. Software problem report
SQA. Software quality assurance
SQC. Statistical quality control or software quality control
SQCS. Statistical quality control system
SQD. Software quality deployment
SRR. Software or systems requirements review
SRS. Software requirements specification
SSR. Software specification review
SSS. System/segment specification or standard software schedule
SSWBS. Standard software work breakdown structure
SSWG. Systems software working group
STARS. Software technology for adaptable and reliable systems
STC. Software Technology Center
STD. Software test description or standard
STEC. Software tools evaluation committee
S/TQM. Software total quality management
STQWG. Software total quality working group
SuCS. Successive check system
TBD. To be determined
TD. Task deployment or technology deployment
TEI. Total employee involvement
TeX. Software typesetting system
TG. Technology group
T&E. Test and evaluation
T&I. Test and integration
TQ. Total quality
TQL. Total quality leadership
TQM. Total quality management
TRR. Test readiness review
TTF. Time to failure
TWF. Time without failure

u chart. Control chart-defects per unit
UCL. Upper control limit
VDD. Version description document
WBS. Work breakdown structure
WG. Working group
WGT. Working group team
WYSIWIS. What you see is what I see
ZDS. Zero defect software

Name Index

Subject Index